Lecture Notes in Computer Science 10926

Commenced Publication in 1973
Founding and Former Series Editors:
Gerhard Goos, Juris Hartmanis, and Jan van Leeuwen

More information about this series at http://www.springer.com/series/7409

Jia Zhou · Gavriel Salvendy (Eds.)

Human Aspects of IT for the Aged Population

Acceptance, Communication and Participation

4th International Conference, ITAP 2018
Held as Part of HCI International 2018
Las Vegas, NV, USA, July 15–20, 2018
Proceedings, Part I

 Springer

Editors
Jia Zhou
Chongqing University
Chongqing
China

Gavriel Salvendy
Purdue University
West Lafayette, IN
USA

and

Tsinghua University
Beijing
P.R. China

and

University of Central Florida
Orlando
USA

ISSN 0302-9743   ISSN 1611-3349   (electronic)
Lecture Notes in Computer Science
ISBN 978-3-319-92033-7   ISBN 978-3-319-92034-4   (eBook)
https://doi.org/10.1007/978-3-319-92034-4

Library of Congress Control Number: 2018944374

LNCS Sublibrary: SL3 – Information Systems and Applications, incl. Internet/Web, and HCI

Printed on acid-free paper

This Springer imprint is published by the registered company Springer International Publishing AG
part of Springer Nature
The registered company address is: Gewerbestrasse 11, 6330 Cham, Switzerland

Foreword

The 20th International Conference on Human-Computer Interaction, HCI International 2018, was held in Las Vegas, NV, USA, during July 15–20, 2018. The event incorporated the 14 conferences/thematic areas listed on the following page.

A total of 4,373 individuals from academia, research institutes, industry, and governmental agencies from 76 countries submitted contributions, and 1,170 papers and 195 posters have been included in the proceedings. These contributions address the latest research and development efforts and highlight the human aspects of design and use of computing systems. The contributions thoroughly cover the entire field of human-computer interaction, addressing major advances in knowledge and effective use of computers in a variety of application areas. The volumes constituting the full set of the conference proceedings are listed in the following pages.

I would like to thank the program board chairs and the members of the program boards of all thematic areas and affiliated conferences for their contribution to the highest scientific quality and the overall success of the HCI International 2018 conference.

This conference would not have been possible without the continuous and unwavering support and advice of the founder, Conference General Chair Emeritus and Conference Scientific Advisor Prof. Gavriel Salvendy. For his outstanding efforts, I would like to express my appreciation to the communications chair and editor of *HCI International News*, Dr. Abbas Moallem.

July 2018   Constantine Stephanidis

HCI International 2018 Thematic Areas and Affiliated Conferences

Thematic areas:

- Human-Computer Interaction (HCI 2018)
- Human Interface and the Management of Information (HIMI 2018)

Affiliated conferences:

- 15th International Conference on Engineering Psychology and Cognitive Ergonomics (EPCE 2018)
- 12th International Conference on Universal Access in Human-Computer Interaction (UAHCI 2018)
- 10th International Conference on Virtual, Augmented, and Mixed Reality (VAMR 2018)
- 10th International Conference on Cross-Cultural Design (CCD 2018)
- 10th International Conference on Social Computing and Social Media (SCSM 2018)
- 12th International Conference on Augmented Cognition (AC 2018)
- 9th International Conference on Digital Human Modeling and Applications in Health, Safety, Ergonomics, and Risk Management (DHM 2018)
- 7th International Conference on Design, User Experience, and Usability (DUXU 2018)
- 6th International Conference on Distributed, Ambient, and Pervasive Interactions (DAPI 2018)
- 5th International Conference on HCI in Business, Government, and Organizations (HCIBGO)
- 5th International Conference on Learning and Collaboration Technologies (LCT 2018)
- 4th International Conference on Human Aspects of IT for the Aged Population (ITAP 2018)

Conference Proceedings Volumes Full List

1. LNCS 10901, Human-Computer Interaction: Theories, Methods, and Human Issues (Part I), edited by Masaaki Kurosu
2. LNCS 10902, Human-Computer Interaction: Interaction in Context (Part II), edited by Masaaki Kurosu
3. LNCS 10903, Human-Computer Interaction: Interaction Technologies (Part III), edited by Masaaki Kurosu
4. LNCS 10904, Human Interface and the Management of Information: Interaction, Visualization, and Analytics (Part I), edited by Sakae Yamamoto and Hirohiko Mori
5. LNCS 10905, Human Interface and the Management of Information: Information in Applications and Services (Part II), edited by Sakae Yamamoto and Hirohiko Mori
6. LNAI 10906, Engineering Psychology and Cognitive Ergonomics, edited by Don Harris
7. LNCS 10907, Universal Access in Human-Computer Interaction: Methods, Technologies, and Users (Part I), edited by Margherita Antona and Constantine Stephanidis
8. LNCS 10908, Universal Access in Human-Computer Interaction: Virtual, Augmented, and Intelligent Environments (Part II), edited by Margherita Antona and Constantine Stephanidis
9. LNCS 10909, Virtual, Augmented and Mixed Reality: Interaction, Navigation, Visualization, Embodiment, and Simulation (Part I), edited by Jessie Y. C. Chen and Gino Fragomeni
10. LNCS 10910, Virtual, Augmented and Mixed Reality: Applications in Health, Cultural Heritage, and Industry (Part II), edited by Jessie Y. C. Chen and Gino Fragomeni
11. LNCS 10911, Cross-Cultural Design: Methods, Tools, and Users (Part I), edited by Pei-Luen Patrick Rau
12. LNCS 10912, Cross-Cultural Design: Applications in Cultural Heritage, Creativity, and Social Development (Part II), edited by Pei-Luen Patrick Rau
13. LNCS 10913, Social Computing and Social Media: User Experience and Behavior (Part I), edited by Gabriele Meiselwitz
14. LNCS 10914, Social Computing and Social Media: Technologies and Analytics (Part II), edited by Gabriele Meiselwitz
15. LNAI 10915, Augmented Cognition: Intelligent Technologies (Part I), edited by Dylan D. Schmorrow and Cali M. Fidopiastis
16. LNAI 10916, Augmented Cognition: Users and Contexts (Part II), edited by Dylan D. Schmorrow and Cali M. Fidopiastis
17. LNCS 10917, Digital Human Modeling and Applications in Health, Safety, Ergonomics, and Risk Management, edited by Vincent G. Duffy
18. LNCS 10918, Design, User Experience, and Usability: Theory and Practice (Part I), edited by Aaron Marcus and Wentao Wang

http://2018.hci.international/proceedings

4th International Conference
on Human Aspects of IT for the Aged Population

Program Board Chair(s): **Gavriel Salvendy, *USA
and P.R. China*, and Jia Zhou, *P.R. China***

The full list with the Program Board Chairs and the members of the Program Boards of all thematic areas and affiliated conferences is available online at:

http://www.hci.international/board-members-2018.php

HCI International 2019

The 21st International Conference on Human-Computer Interaction, HCI International 2019, will be held jointly with the affiliated conferences in Orlando, FL, USA, at Walt Disney World Swan and Dolphin Resort, July 26–31, 2019. It will cover a broad spectrum of themes related to Human-Computer Interaction, including theoretical issues, methods, tools, processes, and case studies in HCI design, as well as novel interaction techniques, interfaces, and applications. The proceedings will be published by Springer. More information will be available on the conference website: http://2019.hci.international/.

General Chair
Prof. Constantine Stephanidis
University of Crete and ICS-FORTH
Heraklion, Crete, Greece
E-mail: general_chair@hcii2019.org

http://2019.hci.international/

Contents–Part I

Aging and Interaction

Intergenerational Communication and Social Participation

Contents–Part II

Intelligent Environments for Aging

Games and Entertainment for the Elderly

Aging and Technology Acceptance

Desktop PC, Tablet PC, or Smartphone? An Analysis of Use Preferences in Daily Activities for Different Technology Generations of a Worldwide Sample

Christina Bröhl[✉], Peter Rasche, Janina Jablonski, Sabine Theis, Matthias Wille, and Alexander Mertens

Institute of Industrial Engineering and Ergonomics,
RWTH Aachen University, Aachen, Germany
c.broehl@iaw.rwth-aachen.de

Abstract. Our daily life is characterized by increasing digitalization. As a result digital technologies are becoming an integrated part of everyday activities. The most used devices are desktop PCs or laptops, tablet PCs, and smartphones, which mainly differ with regard to the screen size and the method of data entry. Given the growing diffusion of technological devices, the increasing ownership of multiple devices, and the resulting different usage patterns between devices, it is essential to gain insights into which devices are used for which activities. The aim of this analysis was to examine a total of 21 activities people engage in on a day-to-day basis with regard to desktop PC or laptop, tablet PC, and smartphone usage. When considering user characteristics with regard to technology, one of the most influential factors is the user's age. Therefore, the sample ($N = 1923$) was analyzed with regard to four different technology generations. Results show that there are significant differences in device usage between the activities under study and between the four analyzed technology generations.

Keywords: Human-system interaction · Ergonomic design · Handheld devices Usability · Ageing

1 Introduction

The proliferation of smartphones and tablet PCs is now increasing the time people spend engaging with digital content and the range of places in which they do so. In 2017 the market share of smartphones was 50.9%, desktop PCs[1] 44.8%, and tablet PCs 4.3% [1], whereas in 2015 the market share was highest for desktop PCs with 62.4%, followed by smartphones with 31.1% and tablet PCs with 6.5% [2]. These numbers show that the market share of smartphones increased and even got ahead of desktop PCs in recent years.

---

[1] Desktop PCs and laptops can be used interchangeably through the use of external screens and input equipment. Furthermore, desktop PCs and laptops are less usable – or not usable at all – in mobile situations than smartphones and tablet PCs. Therefore, desktop PCs and laptops are regarded as belonging to the same category and therefore are termed desktop PCs throughout this paper.

© Springer International Publishing AG, part of Springer Nature 2018
J. Zhou and G. Salvendy (Eds.): ITAP 2018, LNCS 10926, pp. 3–20, 2018.
https://doi.org/10.1007/978-3-319-92034-4_1

Although the boundaries between desktop PCs, tablet PCs, and smartphones are sometimes fuzzy, Lugtig and Toepoel [3] proposed that all devices can be classified along two dimensions: (1) method of data entry and (2) screen size. In order to use a desktop PC, information input is carried out by a combination of hand movements with a mouse and character entry is administered through a keyboard. Tablet PCs and smartphones on the other hand use touchscreens that are operated by finger contact with the screen while text entry is carried out via an on-screen keyboard. Another important difference between desktop PC, tablet PC, and smartphone is the size of the screen. Desktop PCs usually have a screen size of 17 inches or larger, while smartphones at the other extreme are endowed with a screen that is about 5 in. The size of tablet PCs can be ranked in between the sizes of smartphones and desktop PCs but the screen sizes of tablet PCs varies widely between 7 in. on the low end and 18.4 in. on Samsung's Galaxy View tablet PC as an example. Regarding the difference in screen size, variations may lead to differences in the visual presentation of information, which in turn might influence a user's perception of the information. Bruijne and Wijnant [4] studied the speed of the interaction comparing desktop PCs, tablet PCs, and smartphones and found that there was no difference between desktop PC and tablet PC usage, while smartphone users were slower than desktop PC and tablet PC users. The authors proposed the difference in screen size as a possible reason for their results, while variations in the Internet connection could not fully be ruled out. Overall, finger navigation is less precise than mouse navigation, which might lead to a decrease in interaction speed depending on the size of the device. Determined by the design of the software or the app, the necessity to scroll might also have an influence on speed and might cause smartphone usage to be slower.

Given the growing adoption of smartphones, the increasing ownership of multiple devices, and the resulting different usage patterns between desktop PC, tablet PC, and smartphone, it is essential to gain insights into which devices are used for which activities. Knowledge of the activities users pursue with which device might promote the design of relevant content in the form of, for example, user interfaces that are suited for interactions in mobile situations. In addition, knowledge of activities that are not pursued with a specific device up to now might give insights into possible problems and hurdles for the interaction. Knowledge about the non-use of a specific device may enable researchers and practitioners to consider ways to improve the interaction.

1.1   Previous Findings

So far, multiple studies have investigated different activities in relation to device usage. Jokela et al. [5] for example studied smartphone usage by means of a diary study and found that smartphones are used for a wide range of different tasks like e-mailing, text messaging, making phone calls, web browsing, social media, listening to music, and calculating. Commonly, the usage of smartphones also includes taking pictures, and for some subjects of the study the phone is in fact their primary camera. However, Jokela et al. [5] also found that smartphones are not regarded as suitable for handling large amounts of information or complex tasks. For complex tasks, which might include writing long texts, administering detailed work, and handling large amounts of content, the desktop PC or laptop is still the preferred device and has not yet been replaced by other devices in the way it has for entertainment-oriented tasks. Computers are also considered as reliable devices that participants fall back to when their other devices fail at a task.

In research carried out with a young age group Galley et al. [6] found that the main functions of tablet PCs are the spontaneous retrieval of information and in the entertainment sector. The advantages of easy interaction because of their small and handy sizes and better start-up times compared to desktop PCs and laptops are striking. Another major advantage is the handwriting recognition capability [7–9], but the lack of 3G support for tablet PCs was an often reported disadvantage [6], and moreover they are acknowledged to be unsuitable for the typing of long texts [5, 10]. With technological developments over the past decade having resolved the issue of 3G support for a variety of devices, including the tablet [11], the only remaining issue is the difficulty of administering complex or detailed work.

To summarize the tablet PC's position in comparison to other devices, it can be said that in spite of good prerequisites, a tablet is an "intermediate thing" [6] due to various restrictions compared to other devices such as laptops, smartphones, or analog tools. So it seems to find its purpose where the small smartphone reaches its limits and the large, feature-rich desktop PC is not practical enough [6]. However, some statistics suggest that the tablet hype is over because of stagnating sales figures while sales numbers of smartphones continue to increase [12]. The main cause for this development may lie in the fact that people are not changing or upgrading their tablet PCs as often as other devices, in addition to a lack of use in their everyday lives [13].

Age-Differentiated Analyses. In order to further study the importance of age in the use of computational devices, age-related analyses have been carried out (e.g. [14–17]). With regard to the general usage of technological devices, different distributions of ownership by age are noticeable. While ownership of smartphones in 2017 is more or less comparable between the age groups of 14–29 (95%), 30–49 (97%), and 50–64 years of age (88%), only 41% of persons who are older than 64 years own a smartphone [18]. Tablet PC ownership even drops to 3.4% in this age group. Tablet PC ownership is highest in the group aged up to 19 years (29.8%), while the respondents aged 20–29 (21.5%) and 30–39 years of age (23.6%) achieve similar rates. In the middle-aged group (40–59 years of age) tablet PC ownership varies between 6.9% and 14.8% [19]. With regard to desktop PC usage the younger groups showed similar penetration rates as in smartphone ownership (10–15: 97%; 16–24: 98%; 25–44: 97%) and reaches values of almost 100%. The group aged 45–64 years is behind the younger age groups with a penetration rate of 88%. As was the case in smartphone and tablet PC ownership, the oldest age group older than 65 only has a comparatively small share proportion of computer users (48%) [20].

There is also a gap between subjects of different ages with regard to activities in the entertainment sector. As a study on the use of social networks in relation to age in the USA in 2017 shows, mostly people between the ages of 18 and 29 are the ones who use social networks such as Facebook (86%) to connect with people, Instagram (58%) for sharing photos, and YouTube (71%) to watch videos [21]. On the other hand, people over 60 years of age have the largest proportion of those who do not use these services at all (27%). In addition, entertainment activities like listening to Internet radio and watching videos or TV programs online with a smartphone or tablet PC are significantly more common among younger age groups [22]. With regard to gaming, as an activity which is also included in the entertainment sector, age-related differences are also noticeable. Younger subjects are most likely to engage in gaming activities. Among subjects aged 16–24, 57% engage in gaming activities, followed by 39% of subjects aged 25–34. In contrast, users over 45 years of age are less likely to engage in gaming (16% of 45–54 s, 10% of 55–64 s, 4% of 65–74 s and 2% of over-75s). Regarding the device that is used for gaming activities it was found that users prefer smartphones and gaming consoles [23].

There is also a growing interest in online shopping, as was documented by Kuoppamäki et al. [22]. Surprisingly, the use of mobile input devices for online shopping does not differ between young and old consumers. Another service that is gaining increasing popularity and can not only be administered through personal contact but also through the use of desktop PCs or mobile devices is Internet banking [24]. Here, the most important variable that predicts the adoption of Internet banking services is age [25]. According to data from 2016, the usage of Internet banking differs between younger users, who most often use Internet banking for making cash withdrawals abroad or carrying out transfers, and older age groups, who prefer face-to-face service in bank branches [26]. No data are available about which device is preferred for Internet banking, but as banking is an activity that depends greatly on trust and is a rather complex activity, it can be expected that the desktop PC is the device that is used most often for banking activities.

Other activities that are often administered with smartphones and tablet PCs are navigation and buying tickets. Traditionally, maps that were either bought as large hardcopy versions or printed by using desktop PCs were used for navigation. Nowadays, navigation can easily be administered by mobile devices that use satellite information. But unlike younger users aged 18–29 years, who are likely to use their smartphones for turn-by-turn navigation (80%), the percentage of users who are 50+ and use their smartphone for navigation drops to 44.5% [27]. Young consumers, primarily aged between 16 and 24 years of age, are furthermore the most likely users to utilize the smartphone at least weekly as a ticket or boarding pass or to gain entry to an event [23]. The advantage of mobile ticketing lies in its general efficiency through the use of mobile technology, as access is possible independent of time and space. Furthermore, queues are reduced and activities like printing a ticket are made redundant [28].

Instant messaging has become a popular form of communication. In addition to the basic chatting feature, most instant messaging services provide additional features such as file transfer or video calling [29]. While the number of users of messaging apps worldwide in 2016 was 1.56 billion, the number by 2019 is expected to reach up to 2.18 billion and by 2021 2.48 billion, as forecasted by Statista in January 2018 [30]. According to a ranking of the most popular social networks and messengers, the Facebook Messenger and WhatsApp share the fourth place in January 2018 behind YouTube, and Facebook [31]. In Germany WhatsApp is one of the leading short message services [32]. According to a survey from the Social Media Atlas 2016/17, 55% of social media users in Germany actively use this instant messaging service [33]. Hameed and Kamran [34] reported that younger-aged participants may send and receive more than 100 text messages a day. In comparison, in 2011 adults aged over 55 sent or received on average a maximum of nine text messages a day [35], although Keränen et al. [36] pointed out that these numbers are increasing.

1.2 Technology Generations

Understanding user requirements is one essential part of studying human-computer interaction. Taking chronological age into account, however, is often not productive as aging processes are highly individual, resulting in ambiguous measurements. Therefore, considering the subject's age in combination with period and cohort effects seems promising. Age, period, and cohort effects must be considered as being interrelated, as it is impossible to deal with one without also dealing with the others. Age effects are the result of getting older and deal with specific effects in different age groups. Period effects are the consequences of influences that vary through time and are associated with all age groups simultaneously. Cohort effects are the consequences of being born at different times and are associated with variations in successive age groups in successive time periods (e.g. long-term habits or long-term exposures), so different generations are exposed to different factors. Estimating the effects of either one of those is not easy because the effects may be confounded with the others [37].

Building on existing theories regarding age-period-cohort models, the concept of technology generations was introduced by German sociologists in the early 1990s [38]. These researchers defined a technology generation as "groups of birth cohorts whose conjunctive experience with technology is differentiated by social change" (p. 493). The authors state further that technological change, and especially changes in basic technologies, enhances inter-cohort differences, thereby raising the likelihood of a conscious perception and description of differences as generational differences. The concept of technology generations includes technologically-related cohort effects and refers to cohort variations with regard to changes in the social and cultural environment.

A range of birth cohorts that show behavioral similarities or shared norms and values based on common sociological environments and predominant developments during the formative period (the period of time between adolescence and young adulthood, operationalized between 10 and 25 years) is called a generation. Studies about age cohorts have shown that after young adulthood, individuals are less likely to change their attitudes, norms and values. During the formative period, subjects undergo a number of crucial transitions, like from school to university or from parental home to independent living. Researchers found out that acquired norms, skills and values during that period tend to be constant and influence behavior later in life [39]. Sackmann and Weymann [38] point out that individuals experiencing the availability of the same types of products during the formative period display similar product usage many years later. Thus, different technology generations appear to behave differently with respect to technology, which is the result of differences in their experience gained in their formative years. Going further, Docampo Rama et al. [40], whose approach consisted of distinguishing technology generations by interface usage, infer that generation-specific technology experience could induce differences in the usage behavior of current consumer products. Older people may be at a disadvantage in using present complex user interfaces, as they did not acquire that skill in their formative period earlier in life.

The question then arises where the boundary between different birth cohorts occurred. Following earlier investigators [41, 42], Docampo Rama et al. [40] define changes in basic technology causing generational differentiation as the point in time where 20% diffusion within the population has been reached. At that point, it is regarded as likely that persons who do not have such technologies themselves have experienced them in their social surroundings (e.g. in their families, with their friends or at work). In order to get information about the degree of diffusion of a technology, Sackmann and Weymann [38] used qualitative interviews, group discussions, surveys, and secondary data analysis to develop and test their concept of technology generations. As a result of this, Sackmann and Weymann [38] distinguished generations from birth cohorts that currently are displaying similar behavior with regard to technology based on technological achievements in their formative periods. Hence, four different technology generations were initially identified:

- the mechanical generation (born before 1939)
- the generation of the household revolution (born between 1939 and 1948)
- the generation of technology spread (born between 1949 and 1963), and
- the computer generation (born between 1964 and 1979).

In 2013, a new generation was added by the authors to this typology of technology generations:

- the internet generation (born in 1980 and later)

In summary, generation-specific experience with technology might influence the usage of currently available technologies, as older people did not encounter the complex interaction patterns that are necessary to handle modern technologies in their formative period. Therefore, age differences in this study are analyzed with regard to different technology generations.

1.3   The Present Study

While previous work provides some approaches of analyzing different activities with regard to device usage, none of them takes a large group of users and a comparison between different devices into account. Furthermore, some numbers are quite obsolete, so that by now it can be expected that the numbers changed and need to be updated. Thus, the research that was conducted aimed to analyze the range of devices that are used for a total of 21 activities people engage in on a day to day basis. The activities were selected and reviewed in workshops with associates and scientists in the domains of psychology, computer science and engineering. To obtain a large sample size, the study was administered via an online questionnaire. Participants were assigned to four age groups according to the four youngest of the five technology generations proposed by Sackmann and Weymann [38]. The following research questions were addressed:

RQ1: Are there differences in the use of devices between different activities?
RQ2: Are there differences in the use of devices between different technology generations?

2 Method

2.1 Procedure

The questionnaire started with a short introduction of the study and demographic questions. After that, subjects were asked to specify with which device they administer different activities. The activities under study are depicted in Table 1. Subjects could specify whether they engage in those activities via desktop PC/laptop, via tablet PC, or via smartphone. Other answer options were "I engage in this activity via personal contact" or "I do not do". In addition, five activities (17–21) were added where the answer option "I engage in this activity via personal contact" is not possible and was therefore deleted.

Table 1. Activities that were analyzed and corresponding answering options

Activities	Answering options
(1) Internet banking, (2) acquire timetable information, (3) buying tickets, (4) navigating, (5) gaming, (6) writing letters, (7) shopping, (8) watching videos, (9) passing on confidential information, (10) watching television, (11) watching/reading news, (12) seeking information of everyday life, (13) taking notes, (14) using calendar function, (15) writing e-mails, (16) reading e-mails, (17) using short messaging services, (18) using video telephony, (19) sharing photos, (20) using social networks, (21) using voicemail	I engage in this activity via desktop PC/laptop, I engage in this activity via smartphone, I engage in this activity via tablet, I engage in this activity differently e.g. through personal contact, (only for activities 1–16) I do not do

2.2 Subjects

A total of 1923 subjects aged 19–77 took part in the online questionnaire. Their mean age was M = 49.67 years (SD = 14.96). The age structure was not equally distributed (Fig. 1). For the analysis, subjects were classified according to four age groups in accordance with the technology generations proposed by Sackmann and Winkler [43]. Due to a lack of subjects, the fifth group could not be studied. The resulting age groups are characterized as follows:

- The first group, called "the Internet Generation" and aged 19–36, consisted of $N = 461$ persons ($M = 30.6$, $SD = 4.24$).
- The second group, called "the Computer Generation" and aged 37–52, consisted of $N = 661$ persons ($M = 44.59$, $SD = 4.45$).
- The third group, called "the Generation of Technology Spread" and aged 53–67, consisted of $N = 514$ persons ($M = 60.51$, $SD = 4.4$).
- The fourth group, called "the Generation of the Household Revolution" and aged 68–77, consisted of $N = 287$ persons ($M = 72.6$, $SD = 3.05$).

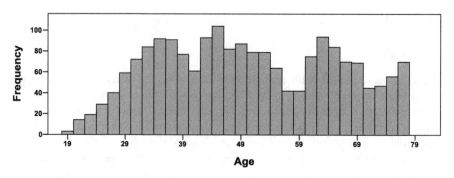

Fig. 1. Age distribution of participants

3 Results

In order to analyze differences between the four age groups, chi-square tests were analyzed for the different activities, as the measurement was at the nominal level. The level of significance was set to $\alpha = .05$. Effect sizes are depicted by Cramer's V and can be classified into low ($r \leq .10$), medium ($r \leq .30$) and large ($r \geq .50$) Field [44]. An overview of the results is shown in Table 2. Overall, significant differences were found between the tasks with regard to the activities and the four different age groups ($p < 001$). The detailed analysis of the specific results for each age group separately as well as a comparison between the age groups is added descriptively.

3.1 The Internet Generation

The Internet Generation as the youngest age group that was studied uses a smartphone for several of the activities that were analyzed and it was found that the smartphone is the most popular device in this age group. Figure 2 shows the rates of different activities according to device. Overall, the proportion of smartphone use never drops below 20%. This shows that the smartphone is a common device for all kinds of activities in the daily lives of young people. As such, the smartphone holds a leading position for sending short messages (78.6%), using voicemail (72.8%), sharing photos (67.6%) and using social networks (70.2%), appointment scheduling (67.6%), navigation (66%), and doing bank transactions (55.6%). The activity that the smartphone is used the least for is passing on confidential information (21.6%), and the proportion of young smartphone users who use their smartphone for watching TV is also low (23.7%) in comparison to the other activities. With regard to sharing confidential information, there was a high proportion of subjects who do not even carry out this activity (45%).

The tablet PC is more prominent regarding activities of the entertainment sector such as watching videos (23.5%), watching TV (20.8%), and gaming (22.1%). Desktop PCs are preferred when writing letters (38.5%) and writing e-mails (41.4%). But surprisingly, the smartphone has already replaced the desktop PC for writing e-mails (47.5%) and also for reading e-mails (smartphone: 54.2%, desktop PC: 29.5%).

Table 2. Results of significant chi-square tests ($p < 001$) for overall differences between technology generations

Activity	N	df	Pearson chi-square	Cramér's V
Internet Banking	1836	12	569.06	.32
Timetable Information	1708	12	340.50	.26
Buying Tickets	1810	12	436.73	.28
Navigation	1776	12	334.40	.25
Gaming	1783	12	436.72	.29
Writing Letters	1830	12	242.24	.21
Shopping	1764	12	502.88	.31
Watching Videos	1764	12	651.88	.35
Passing Confid. Information	1814	12	226.34	.20
Watching Television	1822	12	377.36	.26
Watching/Reading News	1667	12	328.69	.26
Seeking Information	1687	12	456.82	.30
Taking Notes	1774	12	233.74	.21
Calender	1754	12	317.09	.25
Writing E-Mails	1703	9	355.25	.26
Reading E-Mails	1649	9	451.48	.30
Short Messaging Service	1850	9	262.17	.22
Video Telephony	1827	9	427.74	.28
Sharing Photos	1801	9	451.22	.29
Social Networks	1784	9	603.475	.34
Voicemail	1843	9	296.83	.23

Comparison to Other Technology Generations. The proportion of subjects in the youngest age group that engages in the surveyed activities is at least 78%. In comparison, an average of 48.7% of the "Generation of the Household Revolution" does not carry out the surveyed activities. As a consequence, the results of the Internet Generation have a higher explanatory power than the results of the Generation of the Household Revolution. With regard to the activity "passing on confidential information" it is noticeable that the proportion of subjects engaging in this activity via a smartphone is low in all generations that were studied. Despite the low overall numbers using the smartphone in order to pass on confidential information, the proportion of subjects engaging in this activity in the Internet Generation is relatively high. It seems as if young people have more trust in technological devices and therefore share their confidential information via their smartphones.

Using the smartphone for watching TV does not seem very common, with 23.7% in the Internet Generation doing so. However, the other technology generations show even smaller numbers (the Computer Generation: 7.8%, the Generation of the Technology Spread: 2.5%, the Generation of the Household Revolution: 1.2%). It might be the case that using the smartphone to watch television is only on the rise and will spread among the other generations as well. Alternatively, older subjects might find the screen size not big enough for watching TV.

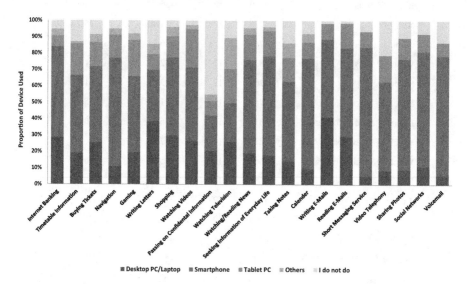

Fig. 2. Bar graphs for the different activities and the distribution of answers in percent for the Internet Generation

With regard to tablet PC usage it was noticed that the Internet Generation uses the tablet PC more often than any other generation. However, with an average usage of 13.8%, tablet PC usage is ranked in the lower segment.

3.2   The Computer Generation

Overall, the most popular device in the Computer Generation is the smartphone (on average 32.4%) followed by the desktop PC or laptop (on average 31.0%), as can be derived from Fig. 3, which shows bar graphs of the study results indicated in the percentages of device usage. For example, members of the Computer Generation more often use the desktop PC for shopping (48.7%) instead of the smartphone (23.1%). Smartphones are mainly used to send short messages (63.9%), for navigation (52.7%), and organizing appointments (51.60%). Surprisingly, this generation has a relatively balanced proportion of subjects that engage in specific activities and subjects that do not engage in those activities. For example, 33.8% use a smartphone for video telephony, while 47.1% do not, just as 37.9% use the smartphone to share photos, whereas 38.6% do not share their photos. Equally ambivalent is the use of social networks (smartphone: 41.8%, I do not do: 26.5%) and voicemails (smartphone: 47.9%, I do not do: 41.7%). Tablet PCs are used on average with a proportion of 8.23% in the specified activities, while gaming (15.7%) and watching videos (16.5%) still stand out with the highest percentages.

Comparison to Other Technology Generations. Compared to the Internet Generation, the preference for the desktop PC in competition with the smartphone shows an opposite order of precedence (Computer Generation: smartphone: 34%, desktop PC: 55.1%; Internet Generation: smartphone: 54.2%, desktop PC: 29.5%) and writing e-mails (Computer Generation: smartphone: 28.2%, desktop PC: 61.3%; Internet Generation: smartphone: 47.5%, desktop PC: 41.4%). The same pattern is seen in activities related to bank transactions (Computer Generation: smartphone: 25.4%, desktop PC: 47%; Internet Generation: smartphone: 55.6%, desktop PC: 28.6%) and watching videos (Computer Generation: smartphone: 23.1%, desktop PC: 48.7%; Internet Generation: smartphone: 44.7%, desktop PC: 26.7%). In comparison to device usage in the Internet Generation, where the smartphone is ahead of the desktop PC by over 30% points, the Computer Generation shows results that are similar, as smartphone and desktop PC usage only differ by roughly 1.5% points.

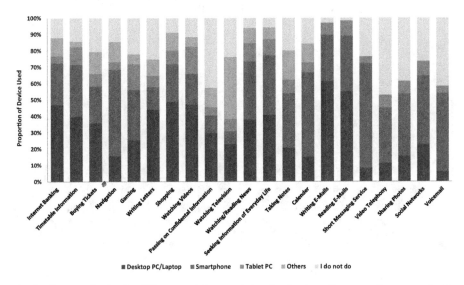

Fig. 3. Bar graphs for the different activities and the distribution of answers in percent for the Computer Generation

3.3 The Generation of the Technology Spread

The Generation of the Technology Spread is characterized by a high percentage of answers that state that the activity in question is not carried out (on average 32.6%), as is depicted by bar graphs in Fig. 4. It is particularly noticeable that this generation does not engage in activities that have emerged in recent years. Examples include video calling (72%), sharing photos (61.9%), social networking (52.9%), using voicemail (52.6%), gaming (47.3%), and watching TV (43.1%).

The device that most activities are carried out with is the desktop PC or laptop. The use of the PC is particularly evident in collecting timetable information (43.5%) and shopping (48.9%). Also, the gap between the proportions of smartphone and PC users in relation to reading (smartphone: 16.8%, desktop PC: 67.5%) and writing e-mails (smartphone: 13.4%, desktop PC: 73%), as well as writing letters (smartphone: 3.8%, desktop PC: 63.5%), is striking. The smartphone is used in particular for writing short messages (56.1%), sending voicemails (39.2%), acquiring calendar information (37.2%), and navigation (37.5%). Particularly notable is the low proportion of smartphone users in this category with regard to shopping (7.3%), watching videos (6.6%), writing letters (3.8%), and buying tickets (5.2%).

Comparison to Other Technology Generations. Noteworthy is also the fact that tablet PC usage is very limited in the Generation of the Technology Spread. The highest level of tablet PC usage was found in the category watching/reading news (15.2%). In comparison, the Computer Generation showed the highest proportion in tablet PC usage for the activities gaming and watching videos. Regarding smartphone usage the biggest difference was found between this group and the Internet Generation. Smartphone usage in the Internet Generation only rarely drops below 30%, whereas in this group smartphone usage is generally below 30%.

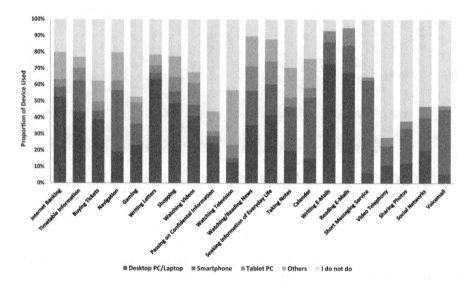

Fig. 4. Bar graphs for the different activities and the distribution of answers in percent for the Generation of Technology Spread

3.4   The Generation of Household Revolution

The most striking finding regarding the Generation of the Household Revolution is that most of the subjects under study stated that they are not engaging in the surveyed activities (on average 48.73%), as is depicted by bar graphs in Fig. 5. In exact percentages, this means that 33.1% of respondents do not use electronic devices to undertake bank transactions, 30.2% do not use them to collect timetable information, and 41.5% do not use them to buy tickets. In addition, 39.9% do not use a device for navigation, 42.2% of respondents do not watch TV on computer devices, 44.4% do not write notes on such devices, and 40.7% do not schedule their appointments with the help of an electronic calendar. Even more striking is the proportion of people who do not play computer games (67.4%), do not watch videos on a computer (66.9%), do not send short electronic messages (56.7%) or send voicemails (73.7%), do not make any video calls (83.1%), and do not share their photos electronically (78.1%). The activity that the most people in this age group do not engage in, however, is social networking, with a proportion of 86.9%. It might be possible that spouses or close relatives engage in those activities for the subjects in this group, which would explain the high levels of non-engagement in the surveyed activities. The fact that many things are generally not done electronically is also reflected in the levels of smartphone and tablet usage. It was found that only a small proportion of subjects in this generation use a smartphone, with the average proportion of smartphone users below 10% in this group. The only activity that stands out is using a smartphone in order to send short messages (38.7%). Compared to the smartphone, the tablet is even less used by this generation, so that the average proportion of tablet users is below 5%. Nonetheless, almost one in ten uses them to read news or to seek information on everyday life.

Comparison to Other Technology Generations. The electronic device that is most used by this age group is the desktop PC or laptop. A particularly high use of the PC is evident in the writing of letters (62.6%) as well as in writing e-mails (63.5%) and the reading of e-mails (59, 9%). These proportions of users are almost as high as in the Generation of the Technology Spread. Since there is a high proportion of subjects that do not engage in the surveyed activities, the explanatory power of device usage is less strong in this group than in the three younger technology generations.

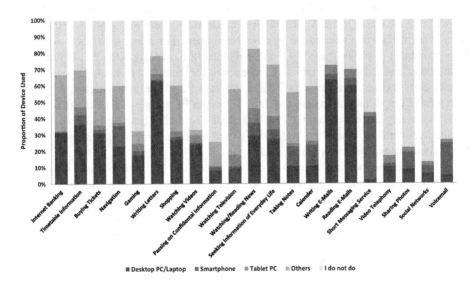

Fig. 5. Bar graphs for the different activities and the distribution of answers in percent for the Generation of Household Revolution

4   Discussion

Developing ergonomic user interfaces requires an understanding of which activities users carry out with their devices. The analysis presented in this paper provides up-to-date numbers of which activities are carried out by users, which devices are used for those activities, and which activities are not carried out with electronic devices but rather through personal contact. To understand how different age groups interact with electronic devices, the results were analyzed for four different technology generations.

First of all, it was noticeable that the proportion of subjects that stated that they are not engaging in the surveyed activities is steadily increasing the older the subjects get. It might be the case that the types of tasks subjects engage in are changing depending on age. As a result, for further analysis more tasks that are typically performed by older people should be added to the questionnaire, for example monitoring vital parameters.

Furthermore, results showed that the older subjects get, the more likely they are to use a desktop PC or laptop instead of a smartphone and/or a tablet PC. This trend might be caused by the fact that smartphones as well as tablet PCs were developed later than desktop PCs and laptops and therefore the diffusion is less progressed. Another explanation for not using smartphones and tablet PCs as often as desktop PCs and laptops might be their smaller screen sizes. Smaller screen sizes might be a problem for the elderly as aging is frequently associated with visual impairments as well as impairments in the fine motor skills required to input information when the screen is small.

Another interesting outcome was found in the statistical analysis. Effect sizes that were calculated for the chi-square tests that tested the differences between activities and age groups showed significant effects that can generally be classified as moderate according to the guidelines by Field [44]. The smallest effect sizes and the fewest differences between the age groups were found for the activities writing letters, taking notes, writing short messages, and passing on confidential information.

Comparing the results of the analyses presented in this paper to previous findings showed that the use of technological devices in the older group was a lot lower than the rates of ownership that were found by other researchers. For example, it has previously been found that of subjects aged 64 years and older 48% own a desktop PC, 41% own a smartphone, and 3.4% own a tablet PC. The result for the oldest technology generation of this study showed an average of 24% for desktop PC usage, an average of 7.2% for smartphone usage, and an average of 3.9% for tablet PC usage. Maybe the reason for this discrepancy lies in the sample. Previous studies tended to base their sample mainly on single cultural groups, whereas this study used a sample composed of subjects from the United States, Germany, China, and Japan.

With regard to the classification of the sample of the study there is one limitation that is worth noting. The participants were grouped into four different technology generations based on their age. As was already mentioned, age processes are highly individual and this makes the arrangement of participants in groups according to chronological age difficult. Furthermore, there are aging processes which might account for the differences in the studied activities, such as impairments in fine motor skills. To derive a complete picture, these factors need to be included in future research.

Table 3. Overall device preferences

Desktop PC: Writing letters
Writing e-mails
Passing on confidential

Smartphone: Taking notes
Using calendar function
Navigating
Using short messaging services
Using video telephony
Sharing photos
Using social networks
Using voicemail

4.1   Conclusion

Generally, the device that is used the most for the analyzed activities and taking all technology generations together is the smartphone, followed by desktop PC and tablet PC. With regard to the activities it was found that participants primarily use their smartphone for short message services, the tablet PC is primarily used for watching videos, the desktop PC is primarily used to write e-mails, while the answer option "other" was most commonly stated for watching TV.

Overall, the results of the questionnaire study show significant differences in the way technology generations carry out daily activities. This supports the structure of those age groups while highlighting the importance of studying age effects in human–computer interaction. It places particular challenges on computational design approaches that postulate accessibility and equal opportunities for all age groups. According to ISO/DIS 9241-11 [45] accessibility is defined as "usability of a product, service, environment or facility by people with the widest range of capabilities." It is noted that the concept of accessibility considers the whole range of user capabilities and is not restricted to users with disabilities. Bearing this approach in mind, the results of this study should be interpreted with regard to commonalities between the age groups in terms of device usage. As a result ten activities were extracted that are characterized by agreement in device preference for at least three of the four analyzed technology generations. The technology generation that showed a preference for another device was taken into account only as long as the deviation from the overall preference was less than ten percentage points. The resulting ten activities that are eligible for "design for all" approaches are depicted in Table 3. As a main result of this study was that a large proportion of older subjects do not engage in the activities that were surveyed, a next step would be to analyze why the elderly do not engage in those activities and how engaging in those activities can be supported.

Acknowledgements. This publication is part of the research project "TECH4AGE", which is funded by the German Federal Ministry of Education and Research (BMBF, Grant No. 16SV7111) supervised by the VDI/VDE Innovation + Technik GmbH.

References

1. StatCounter Global Stats: Desktop vs Mobile vs Tablet Market Share Worldwide December 2016–December 2017: Statcounter (2017). http://gs.statcounter.com/platform-market-share/desktop-mobile-tablet/worldwide/#monthly-201612-201712. Accessed 23 Jan 2018
2. StatCounter Global Stats: Desktop vs Mobile vs Tablet Market Share Worldwide January–December 2015: Statcounter (2015). http://gs.statcounter.com/platform-market-share/desktop-mobile-tablet/worldwide/2015. Accessed 23 Jan 2018
3. Lugtig, P., Toepoel, V.: The use of PCs, smartphones, and tablets in a probability-based panel survey. Soc. Sci. Comput. Rev. **34**(1), 78 (2015). https://doi.org/10.1177/0894439315574248
4. de Bruijne, M., Wijnant, A.: Comparing survey results obtained via mobile devices and computers. Soc. Sci. Comput. Rev. **31**(4), 482 (2013). https://doi.org/10.1177/0894439313483976
5. Jokela, T., Ojala, J., Olsson, T.: A diary study on combining multiple information devices in everyday activities and tasks. In: Begole, B., Kim, J., Inkpen, K., Woo, W., (eds.) The 33rd Annual ACM Conference, pp. 3903–3912 (2015)
6. Galley, K., Adler, F., Mayrberger, K.: Der längerfristige Einfluss von Tablets auf das Studium und die persönliche Lernumgebung Studierender. In: Rummler, K. (ed.) Lernräume gestalten - Bildungskontexte vielfältig denken, Münster, pp. 114–124 (2014)
7. Microsoft Corp: Physicians improve quality of care, save valuable time, and increase reimbursements through EMR System (2003). http://www.providersedge.com/ehdocs/ehr_articles/Physicians_Improve_Quality_of_Care–Save_Valuable_Time-Increase_Reimbursements_thru_EMR.pdf. Accessed 9 Jan 2018
8. Microsoft Corp: The toast of Las Vegas, Tablet PC transforms wine sales and promotions (2004)
9. Walker, G.: A detailed look at Microsoft's proposed Tablet PC. Pen Comput. Mag. (2001)
10. McClard, A., Somers, P.: Unleashed. In: Turner, T., Szwillus, G. (eds.) The SIGCHI Conference, pp. 1–8
11. Choi, Y., Ji, H., Park, J., Kim, H., Silvester, J.: A 3W network strategy for mobile data traffic offloading. IEEE Commun. Mag. **49**(10), 118 (2011). https://doi.org/10.1109/MCOM.2011.6035825
12. IDC: Worldwide mobile device sales forecast (2014). https://www.statista.com/chart/2829/worldwide-mobile-device-sales-forecast/. Accessed 10 Jan 2018
13. Brandt, M.: Tablets: the hype is over (2014). https://www.statista.com/chart/2829/worldwide-mobile-device-sales-forecast/. Accessed 10 Jan 2018
14. van Deursen, A.J., Helsper, E.J.: A nuanced understanding of internet use and non-use among the elderly. Eur. J. Commun. **30**(2), 171 (2015). https://doi.org/10.1177/0267323115578059
15. Eynon, R., Helsper, E.: Family dynamics and internet use in Britain, what role do children play in adults' engagement with the internet? Inf. Commun. Soc. **18**(2), 156 (2014). https://doi.org/10.1080/1369118X.2014.942344
16. Haddon, L.: The contribution of domestication research to in-home computing and media consumption. Inf. Soc. **22**(4), 195 (2006). https://doi.org/10.1080/01972240600791325
17. Frohlich, D.M.: Ageing and the digital life course. Popul. Age. **9**(4), 385 (2016). https://doi.org/10.1007/s12062-016-9150-6. Prendergast, D., Garattini, C. (eds.)
18. Bitkom: Share of smartphone users in Germany in 2017, by age group: Statista - The Statistics Portal (2018). https://www.statista.com/statistics/469969/share-of-smartphone-users-in-germany-by-age-group/. Accessed 16 Jan 2018

19. Tomorrow Focus Media: Age distribution of tablet PC users in Germany in 2015: Statista - The Statistics Portal (2015). https://www.statista.com/statistics/494534/tablet-age-distribution-of-users-germany/. Accessed 16 Jan 2018

20. Statistisches Bundesamt: Share of computer users in Germany from 2008 to 2015, by age group: Statista - The Statistics Portal. n.d. https://www.statista.com/statistics/489975/computer-usage-by-age-group-germany/. Accessed 23 Jan 2018

21. Statista Survey: Reach of selected social networks in the United States as of February 2017, by age group (2017). https://www.statista.com/statistics/305245/us-social-network-penetration-age-group/. Accessed 10 Jan 2018

22. Kuoppamäki, S., Taipale, S., Wilska, T.: The use of mobile technology for online shopping and entertainment among older adults in Finland. Telematics Inform. **34**(4), 110 (2017). https://doi.org/10.1016/j.tele.2017.01.005

23. Ofcom: Adults' media use and attitudes: report 2017: Ofcom. Accessed 14 June 2017

24. Gupta, S., Yadav, A.: The impact of electronic banking and information technology on the employees of banking sector. Manage. Labour Stud. **42**(4), 379 (2017). https://doi.org/10.1177/2393957517736457

25. Ho, D., Head, M., Hassanein, K.: Developing and validating a scale for perceived usefulness for the mobile wallet. In: Rocha, Á., Correia, A.M., Wilson, T., Stroetmann, K.A. (eds.) Advances in Information Systems and Technologies, Advances in Intelligent Systems and Computing, vol. 206, pp. 469–476. Springer, Heidelberg (2013). ISBN: 978-3-642-36980-3

26. Statista Survey: Customer-friendliness of certain banking services in the United States in 2016, by age (2016). https://www.statista.com/statistics/639679/customer-friendliness-of-certain-banking-services-usa-by-age/. Accessed 16 Jan 2018

27. Berenguer, A., Goncalves, J., Hosio, S., Ferreira, D., Anagnostopoulos, T., Kostakos, V.: Are smartphones ubiquitous? An in-depth survey of smartphone adoption by seniors. IEEE Consum. Electron. Mag. **6**(1), 104 (2017). https://doi.org/10.1109/MCE.2016.2614524

28. Mallat, N., Rossi, M., Tuunainen, V.K., Öörni, A.: The impact of use context on mobile services acceptance, the case of mobile ticketing. Inf. Manag. **46**(3), 190 (2009). https://doi.org/10.1016/j.im.2008.11.008

29. Statista: Statistiken zu Instant Messaging: Statista - The Statistics Portal. n.d. https://de.statista.com/themen/1973/instant-messenger/

30. eMarketer: Number of mobile phone messaging app users worldwide from 2016 to 2021 (in billions): Statista - The Statistics Portal. n.d. https://www.statista.com/statistics/483255/number-of-mobile-messaging-users-worldwide/. Accessed 23 Jan 2018

31. We Are Social: Ranking der größten sozialen Netzwerke und Messenger nach der Anzahl der monatlich aktiven Nutzer (MAU) im August 2017 (in Millionen): Statista - Das Statistik-Portal (2017). https://de.statista.com/statistik/daten/studie/181086/umfrage/die-weltweit-groessten-social-networks-nach-anzahl-der-user/. Accessed 23 Jan 2018

32. Statista: Statistiken zu WhatsApp: Statista - Das Statistik-Portal. n.d. https://de.statista.com/themen/1995/whatsapp/. Accessed 23 Jan 2018

33. Faktenkontor, IMWF, Toluna: Inwiefern nutzen Sie folgende Social Media Angebote in Ihrer Freizeit? Statista - Das Statistik-Portal (2016). https://de.statista.com/statistik/daten/studie/245427/umfrage/regelmaessige-nutzung-sozialer-netzwerke-in-deutschland/. Accessed 23 Jan 2018

34. Hameed, M.F., Kamran, S.: Problematic mobile phone consumption among young consumers: policy and research implications. Pak. Adm. Rev. **1**(1), 32–41 (2017)

35. Smith, A.: Americans and Text Messaging, How Americans Use Text Messaging: The Pew Research Center. Accessed 19 Sept 2011

36. Keränen, N.S., Kangas, M., Immonen, M., Similä, H., Enwald, H., Korpelainen, R., Jämsä, T.: Use of information and communication technologies among older people with and without frailty: a population-based survey. J. Med. Internet Res. **19**(2), e29 (2017). https://doi.org/10.2196/jmir.5507

37. Robertson, C., Gandini, S., Boyle, P.: Age-period-cohort models: a comparative study of available methodologies. J. Clin. Epidemiol. **52**(6), 569 (1999). https://doi.org/10.1016/S0895-4356(99)00033-5

38. Sackmann, R., Weymann, A., Hüttner, B.: Die Technisierung des Alltags, Generationen und technische Innovationen. Frankfurt/Main: Campus-Verl (1994). ISBN: 3593351773. http://www.soziologie.uni-halle.de/sackmann/docs/die-technisierung-des-alltags.pdf

39. Sroufe, L.A., Cooper, R.G., DeHart, G.B., Marshall, M.E., Bronfenbrenner, U.: Child Development: Its Nature and Course, 2nd edn. Mcgraw-Hill Book Company, Boston (1992)

40. Docampo Rama, M., Ridder, H.D., Bouma, H.: Technology generation and age in using layered user interfaces. Gerontechnology **1**(1), 25 (2001). https://doi.org/10.4017/gt.2001.01.01.003.00

41. Rogers, E.M.: Diffusion of innovations. Free Press of Glencoe, New York (1962). http://worldcatlibraries.org/wcpa/oclc/254636

42. Ryder, N.B.: The cohort as a concept in the study of social change. In: Mason, W.M., Fienberg, S.E. (eds.) Cohort Analysis in Social Research. Springer, New York (1985). https://doi.org/10.1007/978-1-4613-8536-3_2

43. Sackmann, R., Winkler, O.: Technology generations revisited: the internet generation. Gerontechnology **11**(4), 493 (2013). https://doi.org/10.4017/gt.2013.11.4.002.00

44. Field, A.: Discovering Statistics Using IBM SPSS Statistics, and Sex and Drugs and Rock 'n' Roll, 4th edn. Sage, Los Angeles, London, New Delhi (2013). 915 p. (MobileStudy). ISBN: 9781446249178

45. Ergonomics of human-system interaction – Part 11: Usability: Definitions and concepts: Beuth Verlag GmbH (9241-11) (2016). Accessed 1 Dec 2017

Assistive Technology and Emotions of Older People – Adopting a Positive and Integrated Design Approach

Ke Chen[✉]

School of Design, Hunan University, Changsha, China
kechen@hnu.edu.cn

Abstract. With ageing, older people's need for assistive technology is increasing. Older people's emotional responses towards assistive technology is not fully understood. The present study is aiming to understand older Hong Kong people's emotions elicited by using assistive technology. A qualitative research method was adopted in the current study. Face-to-face interviews and focused groups were conducted with 50 community-dwelling older adults in Elderly Services Centers in Hong Kong. Results indicate that the assistive technology experienced by older people include mobile phones, walking aids, hearing aids, emergency alarm services and computers. Older people have both positive and negative emotional responses in regards to assistive technology. Assistive technology has the potential to provide safety and secure and reduce risks for older people. However, it may also elicit negative emotions such as anxiety, frustrating, prejudice and discrimination. To increase an optimal user experience, we need to pay more attention to older users' emotional and psychological needs besides usability, and to adopt a positive and integrated design approach during assistive technology development. Several design suggestions were provided based on the results.

Keywords: Assistive technology · Ageing · Stigma · Emotional design

1 Introduction

Population ageing is prevalent and impacting every aspect of life. Ageing is associated with increase in non-communicable diseases and functional impairment in hearing and vision perception, mobility and cognitive abilities. Assistive Technology (AT) could be used to partially compensate for functional declines and improve independence of older people. For instance, mobility aids such as walking stick, wheelchair, and handrails could enhance mobility of older people with movement difficulty [1]. E-home monitoring system could detect emergency situations at home, thus increased safety and independent living [2, 3]. Older people with hearing defect may gain benefits from hearing aids [4].

Successful implementation of this technology into older people's daily lives is depending on their acceptance and continued usage. However, assistive technology might elicit negative feelings or emotions, which may result in abandon the product. Older people

© Springer International Publishing AG, part of Springer Nature 2018
J. Zhou and G. Salvendy (Eds.): ITAP 2018, LNCS 10926, pp. 21–29, 2018.
https://doi.org/10.1007/978-3-319-92034-4_2

expressed the concern of feeling of stigmatization and perceived visibility or attention received when using contactless monitoring devices in public settings [2, 5]. They were unwilling to use ATs that would make them feel undignified and embarrassed, or signify the users as loss of function or frail [1, 5].

The human centered approach emphasizes understanding and satisfying the needs, requirements and capabilities of users. Current research and practice in development of AT is aiming primarily at usefulness and usability, i.e., effectiveness, efficiency and satisfaction, by adopting human factors engineering and ergonomics approach. Moreover, theories in understanding technology acceptance, such as Technology Acceptance Model [6], the Technology Acceptance Model 2 (TAM2) [7], and the Unified Theory of Acceptance and Use of Technology (UTAUT) [8] were mainly focused on the technique matters such as usefulness and ease of use. The desirability and emotional responses from users during the course from product acquisition to usage is overlooked [9, 10].

Usability might determine whether a product could be used while emotions determines whether people are willing to use. Product emotions result from appraise of the product and could be attributed to product function, aesthetics, and associated meanings [11]. The emotions elicited from product include surprise, amazement, disappointment, satisfaction, disgust, attracted to, indignation, admiration, boredom, and fascination, etc. Norman has classified the product emotions into three levels: the visceral level is relating to the appealing and physical features of the product; the behavioral level is relevant to interaction and usability with the product; and the reflective emotion is connected to social image, meaning, culture, and long-term user experience [12]. To increase the acceptance and usage rate as well as an optimal user experience, there is a definite need for AT designers to go beyond traditional focuses on usefulness and ease of use to further explore emotion, motivation and meaning associated with using assistive technology. The emotional and psychological responses that occur before, during and after assistive technology usage should be given more consideration.

The present paper intents to make a contribution to a better understanding older people's emotions elicited from using assistive technology in Hong Kong. Assistive technologies (AT) here refers to products, environments and/or services in order to maintain or enhance functional health, security, safety and quality of life. The results of the study could benefit AT designers and developers.

2   Methods

2.1   Research Design

A qualitative research method was adopted in the current study. Face-to-face interviews and focused groups were conducted with 50 community-dwelling older adults in Elderly Services Centers in Hong Kong. Focus groups were adopted to capture a broad and diverse range of individual attitudes and thoughts concerning assistive technology, and reasons for using or not using assistive technology, as well as barriers and facilitators influencing older people's acceptance of assistive technology. Individual interviews were based on the tentatively theoretical constructs identified by focus groups so as to further explore personal usage experiences at a detail level. Invitation letters introducing the researcher as well as explaining the purpose of the study and the use of data were sent to local elderly centres which had participated in the phase I study. The centres were responsible for recruited members to participant in either individual interviews or focus group discussions. The sample size here was determined by theoretical saturation of data, which refers to the method where sampling continues until no new information or concepts are generated.

2.2 Participants

The mean age of participants were 67.47 years old, and 44 out of 50 of them were female. A number of 24 of the older adults participated in four focus groups, and 26 respondents participated in individual interviews. Most participants had obtained primary education and above (64%), lived with family members (84%), and were of middle economic status (86%). Many of them were married (38%); the rest reported marital status as widowed (32%) or divorced/separated (30%). Fifty percent of the participants self-reported fair health conditions; 44% reported their health conditions to be excellent or good; only 6% reported poor or very poor health conditions.

2.3 Procedure

An interview guide was used by the interviewer to ensure that all principal questions were addressed in focused group and individual interviews. The principle questions were *"What assistive technologies do you know or currently in use in your daily life?"*, *"What do you think of the idea of using assistive technology?" "What do you like and dislike about assistive technology?"*, *"What are the main reasons for using those technology?"*, *"What are the main reasons for not using assistive technology?"*, *"What are the difficulties/barriers when you are using assistive technology?"*.

The qualitative data were transcribed and coded using NVivo 10 software package. The frequently mentioned words or any meaningful units were marked and extracted, and then labeled with codes. Through constant comparison between transcripts, similar codes were combined into analytic concepts. Concepts were then grouped by similarity at a more abstract and theoretical level, whereby themes were finally identified.

3 Results

Thematic analysis was employed to generate insights into older people's feelings and emotions elicit from actual or anticipated use of assistive technology. The assistive technologies mentioned by older adults include mobile phones, walking aids, blood pressure monitor and blood glucose monitor hearing aids, emergency alarm services and computers.

Two themes were extracted from the emotional responses of older people towards various kinds of assistive technology (shown in Table 1). The positive emotions refer to perceived or experienced emotional benefits of using AT; while the negative emotions refer to the psychological and or social costs of using AT.

Table 1. Emotions associated with using assistive technology

Themes	Definition	Examples
Positive emotions		
Safety and security	The extent that technology is perceived to be safe and secure	*"Mobility aids can make me feel safe when I need to go out"* *"Digital locating devices are good for older people with dementia, because they won't be lost when they walk out alone"*
Useful and helpful	The AT is useful and would provide assistance for people in need	*"I have diabetes and hypertension; thus, I use blood pressure monitor and blood glucose monitor every morning"* *"Mobile phone is so useful, because we can easily find our children if there is any emergency"*
Negative emotions		
Anxiety	An individual's apprehension when he or she is faced with the possibility of using AT	*"I feel apprehensive about using electronic things"* *"My mom did not want to use a mobile phone because she does not know how to charge the battery, and she is afraid of making a mess"*
Confusing and frustrating	The experience of using AT is unpleasant and frustrating	*"Computers and smartphones are too complicated for me, and I always make mistakes and need my children to help me figure out"* *"My experience with my mobile personal emergency phone was unpleasant, because I do not know how to use it"*
Denying necessity	Deny the need for using ATs	*"I do not use walking stick, but occasionally I will use umbrella for the same purpose"* *"I am in good health currently, when I became older I would consider the assistance technologies"*
Prejudice and discrimination	Concern that using AT is associated with discrimination and negative reactions	*"I would not use emergency alarm service because I am not as weak as that"* *"I am not that old to use those stuff"* *"I would only use the mobility stick when I really can't be able to walk"*

Older people expressed some positive and favorable emotions with actual use of assistive technology. Older people were feeling more secure and safe with the usage of AT. Some of the participants mentioned that using a walking stick would "*make me feel more secure*" because it reduces the risk of falls or accidents. Moreover, not only the older adults themselves, with AT their caregivers and family members would also feel more secure ("*my daughter brought me this mobile phone with personal emergency services, without the phone, she is worried about me when I am out alone...*").

The positive emotional response from older adults is also attributed to the perceived instrumental benefits of actual use of AT, which helped users to achieve independence and valued outcomes. For example, older people with high blood pressure and diabetes found biochemical parameter monitor useful for self-monitoring. Mobile phones could help them to communicate with family members and friends whenever and wherever. Those instrumental benefits match older people's concern of independence and would lead to feeling of satisfaction.

Participants also expressed negative feelings in regards to AT. Anxious reactions were mentioned by the interviewees when interacting with new and digital technologies, like mobile phones and computer-related technology ("*I feel apprehensive about using electronic things*"). It seems that the user interface and operational process of electric technologies are too complicated for older participants, they were afraid of making mistakes and had frustrating experience ("*Computers and smartphones are too complicated for me, and I always make mistakes and need my children to help me figure out*").

Negative emotions associated with AT were also associated with deformed social image of the users. The assistive nature of AT is always associated with declined ability and defeat. It was found that there was generally a negative prejudice or some discrimination attached to the use of assistive technology like emergency alarm services and walking sticks; and when asked why participants did not want to use such technologies, they responded "*I am not that old to use*" and "*I do not need stuff like that.*" Some participants would deny the need of AT despite the benefit and would use other everyday common product to replace AT ("*I do not need a walking stick, I could use my umbrella instead*").

4   Discussion

The study investigated older people's emotional responses towards assistive technology. The results are in accordance with previous studies that older people have both positive and negative attitudes towards AT [2, 5, 13]. The study shows that the assistive technologies that older people had currently experienced were mainly focused on physical capacity compensation, in particular in the domains of mobility, safety, hearing and communication. It is found that the AT has the potential to enhance functional benefits via increasing independence and reducing risks for older people. Those instrumental benefits elicit positive emotional reactions like safety and secure. These positive emotions were also reported in previous studies relating AT usage among older people [2, 14]. Older people are preferring to ageing in place, that is to stay at home for as long as possible, whereby AT has the potential to maintain independence and help achieve the aim.

Negative emotions elicited by AT include anxiety, frustration and unpleasant, deny of need, and prejudice and discrimination. Although AT has physical and functional benefits, the assistive nature of AT might conflict with older people's psychological and social needs whereby the assistive technology might signify fragile, disability and reinforce ageism and isolation feelings. In our study, one participant voice out that he preferred to use umbrella or shopping trolley as mobility aids instead of walking stick or crane. This result is in accordance with the study of Claes et al. [2], which shows that although majority of the older people perceived the usefulness of home monitoring devices, they would only consider to actual use in later life or when their health has deteriorated. In the studies of Kelly et al. [4] and Parette and Scherer [15], older people also expressed cosmetic concern of using AT. To avoid to be seen as weak and to maintain social image and self-esteem, older people would deny their needs for AT, reduce the frequency or reject AT usage, although AT would provide benefits [15].

Moreover, older people had frustrating and unpleasant experience with digital technology due to complexity. Ageing is associated with declining in working memory and focusing of attention, therefore, older people may need more time and hand-on practice in learning new knowledge and skills [16]. Digital technology with complicated human-interface may confuse older users and result in cognitive overloading and anxious. The over-complexity of technology for older people was also reported from previous studies [1, 17, 18]. Without enough technical and human support for learning and usage, older people always had frustrating and unpleasant feelings with interacting with modern digital technology [13].

Product emotions are related to individuals concern [11, 19]. If the concern and the product features were matched, pleasant emotions will occur; otherwise, mismatch will result in unpleasant emotions. The results of study demonstrate that current Assistive Technology practice adopted a problem-driven approach whereby reducing risks and compensating for declined physical capacity was the main focus. However, social and psychological well-being of older adults were undervalued. Although current AT provides functional benefits for older adults but it also elicits negative prejudice and ageist stereotype, which may result in social exclusion and deceased self-esteem. It seems that by making use of AT, older adults' functional needs were met at the expense of compromising social and psychological benefits. Promoting a better quality of life in older adults, their feelings, motivations, and values have to be addressed [10]. Therefore, in order to maximize the benefits of AT usage and improve the well-being of older people, there is a need to turn the everyday assistive technology into desired, pleasant, and appealing objects by adopting a positive and integrated design approach into assistive technology development.

5   Positive and Integrated Design Approach

Positive and integrated design approach is aiming at increase people's well-being and enables human flourishing, through experiencing positive affect and pursuing personal goals [20]. The idea of positive design approach emphasizes design for happiness, including pleasure, personal significance and virtue of individuals [20]. This approach is different from current AT practice which is problem-driven aiming to eliminate or reduce physical and functional deficiencies, because eliminating deficiencies is not enough in the pursuit of quality of life and well-being of older people. Therefore, positive and integrated approach is advocated in AT development.

Based on the emotional themes evoked by using AT in older adults, some design guidelines were suggested here to align with the needs of older adults.

5.1   Aesthetic Features

According to Norman, the physical features of the product would initiate people's immediate emotional reacts [12]. Older people also care about the image they presented to others. The appearance of AT should avoid looking at traditional medical devices and minimize the perception of the assistive nature.

Desmet had adopted an emotional-driven approach in a children's wheelchair design [19], whereby wheelchair was interpreted as a playful outdoor transportation facilitator which encourage go out and explore instead of rehabilitation. Wheelchair users – the children and their parents – were participated in the design process and their emotional demands were assessed.

Given that assistive nature of product might elicit negative stereotype and signify fragile and weakness, the aesthetic features of AT should be free from stigma and be perceived by as neutral, pleasant and attracted. In the current study, older people used umbrella or shopping trolley as walking aids, which gives designers a direction that the appearance of AT could look as everyday normal objects to avoid deviance.

5.2   Usability

The AT should be easy to use. Ease of use impact on the technology acceptance and usage directly and indirectly through perceived usefulness [21]. Many older people have unpleasant interacting experience with digital technology because these devices were too complicated to operate and consume too much cognitive efforts. Whereas, informational and emotional supports were not provided.

The interface designers need to make allowances for cognitive capacities of ageing audiences. For example, physical changes in vision, hearing, and finger dexterity may lead to preferences for devices with larger fonts, sounds within certain frequency ranges, and layouts that require less precise finger movement [22]. Cognitive changes, such as reduced working memory capacity, declines in information processing speed, and ability to disregard unwanted information, create a need for technological interfaces that have fewer distractions, provide memory cues, and are simple to learn and understand.

5.3   Well-Being Promoting

The application domain of AT should go beyond compensation for physical defeat and activities of daily living. Social and psychological well-being of older people also need the intervention of AT. Social isolation is more pronounced among older people accompanied by a decline in health or increased impairment [23]. The key defense against social isolation is to improve communication and to develop a network of social support. Social robots and internet-based communication technology has been developed for older adults addressing social needs [24, 25]. AT which is fun, entertaining, joyful, educational and could boost happiness and well-being would be a new direction for development. There is also a consensus that using technology alone is insufficient to meet the needs of older people. Other supports, like information, training and supports should be also provided and integrated into technology usage cycle [2, 13]. The use of

AT should increase comfort, productivity and vitality. The interaction between AT should be empowering and help older people obtain sense of control and enhance self-esteem and self-confidence.

6 Conclusion

The present paper aimed to get a better understanding older people's emotions elicited from using assistive technology through a qualitative method, and tried to incorporate the positive and integrated design approach into assistive technology development to address emotional requirements. It is highlighted that in addition to functionality and usefulness, the emotional dimensions of AT usage should be considered during design process.

There are several limitations of the current study. Firstly, the health conditions and functional capacities were diverse among older people. The participants of the current study were recruited from community with good and/or fair self-reported heath conditions, and many of them did not have the actual experience with AT usage. The emotional reactions to AT they voiced out might be different from older people who were more physically dependent. In future studies, a sample with diverse heath conditions could be recruited. For example, older people living in elderly centres and whose who cannot independently complete daily activities of living could be recruited. Moreover, the emotions and needs from main care givers of older people could be investigated as well. Because study also reveals that the negative stereotype of using AT also impact family members [19]. Secondly, subjective and objective instruments could be used to measure emotions elicited by a specific AT produce or a design prototype of AT. For instance, the Product Emotion Measurement (PrEmo) is a questionnaire measured 14 emotions towards a specific product [19]. Other objective indicators like electrical signals produced by muscles, eye movement, and/or electroencephalography, could be used jointly with subjective responses in assessing human emotions.

References

1. Yusif, S., Soar, J., Hafeez-Baig, A.: Older people, assistive technologies, and the barriers to adoption: a systematic review. Int. J. Med. Inf. **94**(Supplement C), 112–116 (2016). https://doi.org/10.1016/j.ijmedinf.2016.07.004
2. Claes, V., Devriendt, E., Tournoy, J., Milisen, K.: Attitudes and perceptions of adults of 60 years and older towards in-home monitoring of the activities of daily living with contactless sensors: an explorative study. Int. J. Nurs. Stud. **52**(1), 134–148 (2015). https://doi.org/10.1016/j.ijnurstu.2014.05.010
3. Free, C., Phillips, G., Watson, L., Galli, L., Felix, L.M., Edwards, P., Patel, V., Haines, A.: The effectiveness of mobile-health technologies to improve health care service delivery processes: a systematic review and meta-analysis. PLOS Med. **10**(1) (2013). https://doi.org/10.1371/journal.pmed.1001363
4. Kelly, T.B., Tolson, D., Day, T., Mccolgan, G., Kroll, T., Maclaren, W.: Older people's views on what they need to successfully adjust to life with a hearing aid. Health Soc. Care Commun. **21**(3), 293–302 (2013)

5. Bright, A.K., Coventry, L.M.: Assistive technology for older adults: psychological and socio-emotional design requirements. In: Pervasive Technologies Related to Assistive Environments, p. 9 (2013)
6. Davis, F.D.: Perceived usefulness, perceived ease of use, and user acceptance of information technology. MIS Q. Manage. Inf. Syst. **13**(3), 319–339 (1989)
7. Venkatesh, V., Davis, F.D.: Theoretical extension of the technology acceptance model: four longitudinal field studies. Manage. Sci. **46**(2), 186–204 (2000)
8. Venkatesh, V., Morris, M.G., Davis, G.B., Davis, F.D.: User acceptance of information technology: toward a unified view. MIS Q. Manage. Inf. Syst. **27**(3), 425–478 (2003)
9. Mallin, S.S.V., Carvalho, H.G.D.: Assistive technology and user-centered design: emotion as element for innovation. Proc. Manuf. **3**(Supplement C), 5570–5578 (2015). https://doi.org/10.1016/j.promfg.2015.07.738
10. Xu, W.: Enhanced ergonomics approaches for product design: a user experience ecosystem perspective and case studies. Ergonomics **57**(1), 34–51 (2014). https://doi.org/10.1080/00140139.2013.861023
11. Desmet, P.: A multilayered model of product emotions. Des. J. **6**(2), 4–13 (2003). https://doi.org/10.2752/146069203789355480
12. Donald, A.N.: Emotional design: why we love or hate everyday things (2004)
13. Chen, K., Chan, A.H.: Use or non-use of gerontechnology–a qualitative study. Int. J. Environ. Res. Public Health **10**(10), 4645–4666 (2013). https://doi.org/10.3390/ijerph10104645
14. Pressler, K.A., Ferraro, K.F.: Assistive device use as a dynamic acquisition process in later life. Gerontologist **50**(3), 371–381 (2010)
15. Parette, P., Scherer, M.: Assistive technology use and stigma. Educ. Train. Dev. Disabil. **39**(3), 217–226 (2004)
16. Erber, J.T.: Aging and Older Adulthood, vol. 2. Wiley-Blackwell, Chichester (2010)
17. Heinz, M., Martin, P., Margrett, J.A., Yearns, M., Franke, W.D., Yang, H.I., Wong, J., Chang, C.K.: Perceptions of technology among older adults. J. Gerontol. Nurs. **39**(1), 42–51 (2013)
18. Chen, K., Chan, A.H.S.: Gerontechnology acceptance by elderly Hong Kong Chinese: a senior technology acceptance model (STAM). Ergonomics, 1–18 (2014). https://doi.org/10.1080/00140139.2014.895855
19. Desmet, P.M.A., Dijkhuis, E.: A wheelchair can be fun: a case of emotion-driven design. In: Designing Pleasurable Products and Interfaces, pp. 22–27 (2003)
20. Desmet, P.M.A., Pohlmeyer, A.E.: Positive design: an introduction to design for subjective well-being. Int. J. Des. **7**(3) (2013)
21. Chen, K., Chan, A.H.S.: Predictors of gerontechnology acceptance by older Hong Kong Chinese. Technovation **34**(2), 126–135 (2014). https://doi.org/10.1016/j.technovation.2013.09.010
22. Farage, M.A., Miller, K.W., Ajayi, F., Hutchins, D.: Design principles to accommodate older adults. Glob. J. Health Sci. **4**(2), 2–25 (2012)
23. McConatha, D.: Aging online: toward a theory of e-quality. In: Morrell, R.W. (ed.) Older adults, health information, and the World Wide Web, pp. 21–41. Lawrence Erlbaum Associates, Mahwah (2002)
24. Klamer, T., Allouch, S.B.: Acceptance and use of a social robot by elderly users in a domestic environment. In: 4th International Conference on-NO PERMISSIONS Pervasive Computing Technologies for Healthcare (PervasiveHealth) (2010)
25. Näsi, M., Räsänen, P., Sarpila, O.: ICT activity in later life: internet use and leisure activities amongst senior citizens in Finland. Eur. J. Ageing **9**(2), 169–176 (2012)

The Perception of Aging and Use of Robots

Yvonne Eriksson[✉]

Mälardalen University, Box 325, 631 05 Eskilstuna, Västerås, Sweden
yvonne.eriksson@mdh.se

Abstract. The implications of robots' design for their acceptance in nursing settings, particularly for elderly people and those involved in their care, have not been thoroughly considered from an information design perspective. This research gap is addressed here, as such a perspective enables consideration of several important socio-cultural aspects of robots, including potentially significant elements of visual culture. Since all these aspects influence views of robots as aids for elderly people, there is a need to understand how robots' design (in terms of appearance) and perceptions of aging influence intended elderly users, their relatives, caregivers and decision-makers. Robots materialize digital technology, both metaphorically and literally. AI and embedded systems enable robots to act, but the shape and materials selected to make them influence our interactions with them. Thus, as shown in this paper, application of an information design perspective can provide deeper insights about the influences of current and historical culture and media on both the perceptions and experiences of aging, and relations of these perceptions and experiences to the acceptance (or lack of acceptance) of robots as tools for nursing old people.

Keywords: Robots · Aging · Culture

1 Introduction

We are facing several major demographic and socio-economic challenges related to the nursing of elderly people. Costs of their care are rising because the population of elderly people is growing, while shortages of nursing staff and caregivers are envisaged due to the resulting demographic imbalance [1]. Potential solutions are offered by rapid developments in health technology, including robots designed to provide support in healthcare, nursing environments and domestic applications. Robots have been made and used for several decades, and portrayed in cultural media for almost a century, but they are minor and not entirely positive elements of elderly people's cultural heritage. Partly for this reason, elderly people have relatively little knowledge of, interest in, and acceptance of, digital technology generally and robots specifically [2]. The resulting resistance to the intrusion of digital technology into their lives is multi-dimensional, and some aspects have been addressed to varying degrees (as outlined in following sections). However, previous studies on robotics and culture have either generally ignored cultural heritage or focused solely on national differences and neglected other potentially relevant cultural factors. More specifically, the implications of robots' design for their acceptance in nursing settings, particularly for elderly people and those involved in their care, have

© Springer International Publishing AG, part of Springer Nature 2018
J. Zhou and G. Salvendy (Eds.): ITAP 2018, LNCS 10926, pp. 30–39, 2018.
https://doi.org/10.1007/978-3-319-92034-4_3

not been thoroughly considered from an information design perspective. This research gap is addressed here, as such a perspective enables consideration of several important socio-cultural aspects of robots, including potentially significant elements of visual culture. Since all these aspects influence views of robots as aids for elderly people, there is a need to understand how robots' design (in terms of appearance) and perceptions of aging influence intended elderly users, their relatives, caregivers and decision-makers.

Here, I argue that the perception of robots has been strongly influenced by the portrayals of robots in popular culture (which have frequently been scary and threatening), thereby extending previous studies on human responses to robots [3–6]. An early example was the destructive *Maschinenmensch* created by a deranged scientist called Rotwang to resurrect the women he had loved in Fritz Lang's movie *Metropolis* (released in 1927) and the novel with the same title by Thea von Harbou [19]. Since then, robots have played key roles, ranging from intensely malevolent to deeply altruistic, in numerous literary works and movies.

The discussion about technology and old people needs to be contextualized with respect to the perception of robots and how aging is perceived and understood in western culture. This paper discusses the relation between the experience of ageing and the perception of robots intended to play roles in the nursing or healthcare of elderly people from an information design perspective.

Moreover, cultural contexts must be considered to acquire deeper insights into elderly people's views and experience, the wider public's perceptions of elderly people, human responses to robots generally, and robots' potential roles in nursing the elderly specifically. For example, how much does the representation of aging and robots in culture and various media influence views regarding potential roles of robots in nursing old people? The aim of this paper is to contribute insights into how culture and media, current and historic, influence both the perception and experience of aging, and relations of these perceptions and experiences to the acceptance (or lack of acceptance) of robots as tools for nursing old people.

2   Background

According to the EU [7] and Swedish Digitalization Committee [8] we are facing changes that will pervade every part of society. The changes are expected to result in a flexible society where the citizens must be prepared for 'lifelong learning', including the acquisition of digital skills, to enhance both their personal lives and professional prospects [8]. The literality of the term 'lifelong' in this context is debatable, but it does encompass old age (especially the personal elements of lifelong learning). Thus, researchers in both information design and humanities disciplines have considered some relevant aspects of digitalization, but they have largely ignored others, including robots. To address the neglected issues, an information design perspective may be helpful for acquiring nuanced understanding of general perceptions of robots and effects of cultural factors on acceptance of or resistance to them. Moreover, combination of such a perspective with consideration of visual elements of cultural heritages should contribute to understanding of human-computer interaction (HCI) generally, and particularly the complex relations between the elderly, wider public, technology, cultural factors, and roles of robots in elderly care.

Interest in the influence of cultural factors on the design of robotic systems and use of robots has increased with the globalization of robotics, science and technology [4]. However, in robotic science a simple approach to culture has been generally adopted, involving grouping people by nationality, age and/or sex [4, 9–11], focusing particularly on differences in traditions between Oriental and Occidental cultures. Notably, people in the West are supposedly discomforted by social and humanoid robots and potential interactions with them due to human exceptionalism [4], while Japanese and Korean people are reportedly more comfortable with robots due to animist beliefs [9–11]. However, more nuanced analysis that does not rely on supposed national or ethnic characteristics (often based on crude historical categorizations) is required [12].

Culture can be defined as the ideas, customs and social behavior of a society, but it is rarely (if ever) perfectly homogenous and generally groups of people within societies have distinguishable subcultures. Buildings, artefacts, ethnicity and language are also parts of a culture, some but not all of which will be shared by all associated subcultures. Everything that is visible and created by people of today or in the past is an element of visual culture. Moreover, visual expressions in technology, design and art are clearly influenced by each other. Cultures can be partly delimited by geographical and political boundaries, but many aspects are cross-national as groups of people distributed over the globe can share common interests and through them create cultures with distinct symbols, vocabularies, lifestyles and dress codes [13]. Thus, a more nuanced definition of the culture of a group of people is needed, which encompasses (*inter alia*) class, lifestyle, gender and sexuality.

Elements of both 'high' and popular culture influence our understanding of phenomena generally [13], collectively providing a lens through which we perceive new and unknown things, and thus our perceptions of aging, old people and robots. However, studies on HCI and the elderly have paid little attention to the influence of cultural expressions such as visual art, movies, theatrical works and literature on our understanding of technology and aging. Many previous sociological studies of aging and culture have ignored the ways cultural texts, literature and movies construct multiple narratives of aging that to some extent conflict with social theories of aging [14]. In recent decades several Swedish novels about the experience of aging have been published, and visual artists have portrayed themselves and friends in the process of aging. However, effects of the representation of aging in literature and visual art on our perceptions of aging have been largely ignored by researchers.

Moreover, there is no coherent definition of old or elderly people [15]. Researchers often divide elderly people into two age-based groups: 65–80 years old and 80 to ca. 90 years old, implicitly defining the elderly as those who have reached standard Western retirement ages and (thus) are no longer contributing productively to the economic development of their societies. However, digital literacy is increasingly required throughout the population to meet numerous challenges [8], so age-related barriers to use of digital technology, especially in the nursing and healthcare of elderly people, must be addressed. To do so it is crucial to understand the development of robots, the aging population, cultural attachments to the past, the resistance to robots and digital technology associated with aging, and the complex interactions involved.

3 The Perception of Aging

Perceived associations between age and both knowledge and wisdom have profoundly changed recently. Since we admire and desire youth we do not value life experience as much as previous generations. Today people are active in old age compare to previous generations, people turning 65 years old are a target group for travel agencies and various kinds of consumptions. However, people are more active in old age than in previous generations, for example people in their late 60s are a major target group for travel agencies and retailers of various consumer goods.

People who do not yet fit into the categories (however defined) have a very vague idea of what it means to be elderly or old, inferred from paintings, photographs, books, movies and of course relatives and people in the neighborhood. However, both old people's perceptions of themselves and other people's perceptions of them change over time. Moreover, the clothes, norms and activities of elderly people affect both their behavior and the way they are perceived. As we age ourselves, our view of elderly people and our distinctions between the elderly and old change. Notably, people rarely identify themselves as old. This is because age can be regarded as a cultural construction that is symbolically located in a biological metaphor [16], but it is also a process and not a stage [14]. The experience of age is partly individual, but influenced by culture, gender, class, ethnicity and sexuality. However, age is not only something that we experience, it also affects how people are treated. This could partly be explained by age-associated roles that people tend to play. Teenagers and young adults often obviously play various roles, but we rarely recognize the role play among elderly to the same extent, although self-narration is important not only for description of the self, but also for the emergence and reality of identity [17]. The concept of age as an indicator of social status has been criticized [18], but it is still a basis for social discrimination and our expectations of elderly people, particularly in relation to technology.

Aging can also be regarded partly as a negotiation between the inside and outside, the experience of being the same as before but looking different. Simone de Beauvoir suggests that old age is an internalization of the difference between the subject and what she or he represents for the outside world [14]. "Within me it is the Other – that is to say the person I am for the outsider – who is old: and the Other is myself" [14]. Visible effects of aging differ among individuals, early signs may include loss of hair and/or gray hair.

Although we know our chronological age, the aging is abstract and so is recognition of the losses of capacities; it takes a while for people to realize that their eyesight, hearing, strength and stamina are not as good as they were.

This is not the only highly relevant aspect of the embodiment of human experience, i.e. the inextricable linkage between the human body and mind. We need a body in order to be human, and face to face interactions involving gestures play important roles in both communication and emotional relations [20]. Thus, communication is thereby embodied. Disembodiment occurs when a person's identity becomes separated from their physical presence, as in virtual reality. But the body doesn't really disembody. It simply floats into another space. The essence of it merges in with the other understandings of the body. One's consciousness extends to the edges of one's online identity. The second self becomes as much as the primary self, and one acts through it" [21]. These concepts raise intriguing questions about requirements for "face to face" communication with a robot, and our experience of (and responses to) non-human bodies. We can become emotionally involved with inanimate things, such as objects that remind us of certain times, places or people, and even mundane objects with no such resonance (such as an ordinary cup, lamp, chair or dress) although we receive no responses from them. Familiar objects are often highly valued and old people want to take them if they move to an old people's home, and now or in the very near future those valued things will almost certainly include smart phones, computers and other digital devices.

4   The Perception of Robots

Robots and robotic systems are associated with many apprehensions. It has been suggested robots are related to monsters [22, 23], because both monsters and robots are post-human, they are "the Other" [3]. Monsters are representations of peoples' fear and the world's perceptions. They make us re-evaluate cultural assumptions regarding ethnicity, gender and sexuality, the perception of differences and tolerance in relation to deviations [24].

However, resistance to robots also has deeply rational foundations, in fears that people may be replaced by robots in future labor markets or that robotic systems with Artificial Intelligence (AI) may attack or supplant humans, as in *Terminator* movies released in the 1980s and postulated by thinkers who cannot be easily dismissed such as Stephen Hawking [29]. One of the discussions related to AI concerns whether or not operators in manufacturing industries will serve the robots or vice versa. In increasing applications in these industries humans and robots work close to each other, and share working space. However, humans and robots very rarely handle the same components simultaneously.

Anxieties related to elderly care and robots include fears that inhuman care by robots will replace the human care provided by caregivers and that this will result in losses of caregivers' employment or devaluation of their work. The ambivalence regarding robots generally and as aids for the elderly in daily life is clearly relevant to robots' acceptance, and may be at least partly related to technical capacity being prioritized more than users' needs or responses during robots' developments. In efforts to address this issue, both nursing and healthcare scholars have considered what we can learn from monsters in popular culture [3]. Notably, researchers involved in the *Caring Monster* project found that monsters do not always have "monstrous" characters. Monsters' nature, meaning and position as "the Other" in relation to humans can change over time [3]. The philosopher Mark Coeckelburgh has raised a related discussion regarding what he calls doom scenarios [25] in relation to robots in elderly care. He argues that robots and other information technologies will inevitably become accepted parts of old people's lives, that it may not even be possible to discuss the elderly's capabilities independently of technology, and that technology must be defined [26].

However, many people's ideas about humans' relations with robots are imaginary, since most people have little or no personal experience of real robots. Thus, their ideas about robots emanate mostly from movies, TV programs, exhibitions or visits to manufacturing companies with various levels of automation. An interesting factor is that robots' appearances depend on their purposes, and we do not even recognize some (such as automatic lawn movers and vacuum cleaners) as robots. When customers visit some shops of the Japanese clothes manufacturing and retailing company Uniqlo they may meet a robot, called Wakamaru, designed by Toshiyuki Kita and made by Mitsubishi. Wakamura is a commercial product intended to increase the company's profits, but it is interesting from a perception perspective. Originally designed to assist the elderly or disabled, these robots are supposed to have abilities not only to pick out the right pants for you, but also to make eye contact and participate in a simple conversation. The harmless-looking little figure interacts and communicates with customers by using its AI to "look at them" through eye-like sensors and following their movements (Uniqlo.com). The interaction based on "eye contact" creates an emotional relation that is one-way but seems two-way because the robot apparently "looks at us" when we look into its "eyes" [5]. A two-armed robot called YuMi, produced by ABB Corporate Research, is also interesting in this respect. It was originally intended to participate in automated assembly processes, but when it was introduced it was displayed together with a painting by the robot in a department store window in Stockholm. The reason for showing the robot in that context was unclear since it was in an interior design setting, but it was probably at least partly intended to play down the presence of a robot, to create acceptance. When YuMi was first demonstrated by ABB the company emphasized its ability to interact with users by following their motion patterns, which created a feeling of communication between the humans and robot.

5   Robots' Appearance

Robots materialize digital technology, both metaphorically and literally. AI and embedded systems enable them to act, but the shape and materials selected to make them influence our interactions with them. Robots that are designed as humans are often experienced as uncanny as they are humanlike but not human.

There could be several reasons for this. One is the metaphoric link between robotic nature and lack of emotionality or empathy with other people. Another is the cognitive dissonance associated with encountering something that cannot be readily defined, understood and categorized as (for instance) a species, animal or human. Thus, it conflicts with our organization of knowledge, thinking and understanding of the environment, raising uncertainties about suitable responses.

Representations of bodies in cultural artefacts may also be important. From early Christianity the body was covered in visual representations, and naked bodies were not portrayed in Western art until the Renaissance. From then until modernism the naked female body was the most frequent motif in art. It was not until early 20th century when the male body became interestingly for the artist. Artists also portrayed the male body, to a lesser extent, particularly strong muscular bodies of working class or peasant men in the early 20th century [27]. Nevertheless, despite interest in the body's appearance there has been general acceptance of the Cartesian concept that the body is separate from the mind, which controls intellectual activities and the body (but not in the modern sense of body control in terms of self-monitoring, maintaining fitness etc.). Today we accept that our bodies are part of our identities and not separated from our minds. However, the Cartesian separation of mind and body might invoke a perception that robots' bodies are similar to ours, but not sufficiently familiar, and their intelligence may be out of control and alien.

Thus, robots' visual designs influence our perceptions of them, and we may even apply gender stereotypes to them, as people tend to think that robots with "male" and "female" torsos are respectively suitable for traditionally male and female tasks [28]. In addition, research indicates that people respond to single communication modalities (face, head, body, voice, locomotion) but this is not necessarily related to a higher degree of anthropomorphism [5]. These response patterns will probably influence the acceptance of robots in various contexts, and an intriguing question is whether robots will cement traditional stereotypical gender roles and codes or loosen them. The relationship between bodies' representations and gendered expectations of robots has been apparent at least since Rotwang made a female robot that met traditional ideals of beautiful women in *Metropolis*.

6   Living with Robots

Living with robots will not necessarily lead to replacement of humans. It could provide people with support that will increase their ability to meet friends and relatives, thereby strengthening their social life. In many cases robots may re-embody people who have lost full physical capacities. An example of a successful robot is the telepresence robot Giraff, which enables elderly people to remain in their homes for longer and retain connections with friends and family members who are elsewhere in the most personal manner possible. The robot can be moved around and display images of remote friends, family, doctors or nurses on its screen, almost as if they were in the same room.

Moreover, combination of the Giraff's telepresence capabilities and the Giraff Plus solution can help elderly people avoid needs to visit the hospital or a doctor (which can be very trying, especially if they have pain, movement problems or bad eyesight). The latter involves placement of sensors around a user's home to collect environmental and physiological data. The environmental sensors can detect motion, pressure, use of household appliances and the status of other fittings. For example, if a door or window is open a signal can be sent through the system to a caretaker, while the physiological sensors can measure blood-pressure, -oxygen and -sugar levels and send the information to the healthcare provider.

The Giraffe is already on the market but there is still no robotic guide dog. This is problematic for old people with bad eyesight, which could hinder them from taking walks by themselves, especially if they live in a large city with many people on the streets and heavy traffic. If young people lose their eyesight, they get mobility training and learn to walk with a stick and a guide dog. For an elderly person, this is probably too demanding, and it takes a while for the dog and its owner to get to know each other and learn how to communicate.

However, there would be numerous advantages if a user's stick and guide dog could be replaced by a robotic dog that could guide the user smoothly and safely along pedestrian paths and across streets through the ability to recognize traffic and people. Such a robot could also recognize routes and can tell the user where he or she is. The user could take walks whenever he or she wanted and be totally independent of a human assistant. In addition, the robotic dog could carry groceries from the store back home. For an old person of today this may seem like science fiction, but probably not for an old person in the near future. Today, many children and young adults are familiar with robots as toys, cleaning appliances and gardening devices. Robots are already parts of their daily lives, some of which they will have emotional attachments to and probably take with them as important souvenirs if and when they move to a home for the elderly in the future.

7 Conclusion

Age is not a condition, but there is a tendency in society and research to group people by age and to define users from specific age groups. The paper has discussed aging as a process and not a stage. Moreover, elderly and old people are concepts that are often used without any further problematization, but they are ambiguous. For example, they may be based on peoples' self-images or other people's perceptions of them. However, both self-images and other people's perceptions of elderly and old people are colored by culture and media.

However, increases in age of Western populations and advances in healthcare are leading to increasing expectations of lifelong health, rather than increasing afflictions by illness and weakness with age. Indeed, much of the loss of sensory capacities is already compensated by technological devices such as hearing aids and speech synthesizers.

When robots are introduced as alternatives for human caregivers, people are generally resistant. This is probably at least partly due to robots' portrayals, especially in popular culture. Thus, by applying an information design perspective we can gain deeper insights into the influences of historical and current culture and media on both the perceptions and experiences of aging, and relations of these perceptions and experiences to the acceptance (or lack of acceptance) of robots as aids for nursing old people. Robots could provide additional support for people who need help in their daily life. More relevant and important issues regarding robotic aids for elderly people may be the socioeconomic differences, particularly the gaps between those who can and cannot afford such aids.

A change in expectations regarding the requirements of elderly and old people is needed. Notably, to enable lifelong learning and help them to maintain independence it will be essential to develop educational practices that enable people who lack digital literacy to participate in and benefit from the digitalized society. Moreover, in order to develop well-designed robots that people of *all* ages can use, it will be essential to include users in the design process

Attitudes regarding robots and how they can support elderly and old people are changing, but there is still a fear that robots will replace humans. However, elderly people could potentially find that living with a robot was more secure and comfortable than encountering new human faces every day or week.

References

1. Puch, A., Pears, D.L. (eds.): Europe's Population and Laour Market Beyond 2000, Country Case Studies, vol. 2. Council for Europe Publishing (2000)
2. Nikou, S.: Mobile technology and forgotten consumers: the young-elderly. Int. J. Consum. Stud. **39**(14), 294–304 (2015)
3. Erikson, H., Salzmann-Erikson, M.: Future challenges of robotics and artificial intelligence in nursing: what can we learn from monsters in popular culture? Perm. J. Summer **20**(3) (2016). https://doi.org/10.7812/tpp14-243
4. Sabanovic, S., Bennett, C., Lee, H.R.: Towards culturally robust robots: a critical perspective on robotics and culture. In: Proceedings of the AMC/IEEE Conference on Human-Robot Interaction (HRI) Workshop on Culture-Aware Robotics (CARS), Bielefeld, Germany (2014)
5. Tsiourti, C.H., Weiss, A., Wac, K., Vince, M.: Designing emotionally expressive robots: a comparative study on the perception of communication modalities. In: HAI 2017, 17–20 October, Bieldfeld, Germany (2017)
6. Jung, E.H., Sundar, S.S., Waddell, F.T.: Feminizing robots: user responses to gender cues an robot body and screen. In: CHI 2016, 07–12 May, San Jose, CA (2016)
7. Eurostat. https://ec.europa.eu/digital-single-market/en/news/desi-2016-methodological-note
8. Digitalisering i tiden. SOU 2016:89
9. Geraci, R.M.: Spiritual robots: religion and our scientific view of the natural world. Theol. Sci. **4**(3), 229–246 (2006)
10. Kaplan, F.: Who is afraid of the humanoid? Investigating the cultural differences in the acceptance of robots. Int. J. Humanoid Rob. **1**(3), 465–480 (2004)
11. Kitano, N.: "Rinri" an incitement towards the existence of robots in Japanese society. Ethics Rob. **6**, 78 (2006)
12. Eriksson, Y.: Aspects of, cartography as a scientific and artistic practice. Image in Art and Sciences, Göteborg. Royal Society of Art and Science (2007)
13. Eriksson, Y.: Bildens tysta budskap. Interaktion mellan bild och text, (The silent message of pictures. The interaction between pictures and text). Studentlitteratur, Lund (2017)
14. DeFalco, A.: Uncanny Subjects. The Ohio State University Press (2009)
15. Eriksson, Y.: Technology mature but with limited capabilities. In: International Conference on Human Computer Interaction, Toronto (2016)
16. Spencer, P.: Anthropology and Riddle of the Sphinx: Paradoxes of Change in Life Cycle, ASA Monograph 28. Routledge, London (1990)
17. Kerby, A.P.: Narrative and the Self. Indiana University Press, Bloomington and Indianapolis (1991)
18. Longhurst, B., et al.: Introducing Cultural Studies. Routledge, London (2017)
19. Huyssen, A.: After the Great Divide: Modernism, Mass Culture, Postmodernism, Virose.pt, pp. 65–81 (1986)
20. Tversky, B.: Visual thoughts. Top. Cogn. Sci. **13**(3), 499–535 (2011)

21. Turkle, S.: Life on Screen. Identity in the Age of Internet, Simon & Schuster (2011)
22. Bennett, E.: Deus ex machina: AI apocalypticism in terminator: the sarah connor chronicles. J. Popul. Telev. **2**(1), 3–19 (2014)
23. Vinge, V.: The coming technological singularity: how to survive in the post-human era. In: Proceeding of Vision-21: Interdisciplinary Science and Engineering in the Era of Cyberspace, 30–31 March, Westlake, Cleveland (1993)
24. Cohen, J.J. (ed.): Monster Culture (seven thesis). Monster Theory: Reading Culture. University of Minnesota Press, Minneapolis (1996)
25. Coeckelburgh, M.: The moral standing of machines: towards a relational and non-cartesian moral hermeneutics. Philos. Technol. **27**(1), 61–77 (2014)
26. Coeckelburgh, M.: Using Words and Things. Language and Philosophy of Technology. Routledge, London (2017)
27. Garb, T.: Bodies of Modernity, Figure and Flesh in Fin De Siècle France. Thames & Hudson, London (1998)
28. Bernotat, J., Eyssel, F., Sachse, J.: Shape It – The Influence of Robot Body Shape on Gender Perception in Robots (2017)
29. www.newsweek.com/stephen-hawking-artificial-intelligence-warning-destroy-civilization-703630

Gendering Old Age: The Role of Mobile Phones in the Experience of Aging for Women

Carla Ganito[✉]

Research Centre for Communication and Culture, Human Sciences Faculty,
Catholic University of Portugal, Lisbon, Portugal
carla.ganito@ucp.pt

Abstract. Although the mobile phone is currently one of the most pervasive communication technologies, little discussion of it has been framed within a gender perspective and fewer of those discussions from an aging perspective. The study focuses on older women as a meaningful group; one that is constantly underrepresented in academic and commercial studies of the mobile phone. The focus of the research is on the use of the mobile phone by older Portuguese women using a Life Course approach. The key findings are that the mobile phone has different roles and affordances depending on women's life stages. If it is true that young women show a higher pre-disposition to a more diversified and intense use of the mobile phone, older women do not always correspond to the stereotype of lack of interest or skills, on the contrary the mobile phone seems to play a very important role in many of these older women's lives.

Keywords: Older women · Mobile phones · Gendering · Life course

1 Introduction

The paper aims to provide a better understanding of the relationship between women and technology through an inquiry into the significance of mobile phones in the lives of Portuguese women, focusing on older women. The results stem from a wider study of the mobile phone as a site where the nuances of women's experiences with technology becomes visible, through a life-course approach [1].

It is a feminist claim that our relation to technology is a gendered relation and that "technology itself cannot be fully understood without reference to gender" [2, p. 32]. If the mobile phone is an expression of our identity, then it also gendered. How does this gendering occur? The option for using the verb "gendering" is rooted in the understanding that gender is socially constructed. The aim is to study gender as a process [3].

If society is co-produced with technology, the gender effect cannot be ignored in the design, development, innovation and communication of technological products: "Technology, then, can tell us something we need to know about gender identity. Gender identity can tell us something we need to know about technology" [2, p. 42]. The emergent "technofeminism" theory proposes a relation in which technology is, at the same time, cause and consequence of gender relations [4, p. 107]. Technofeminism allows us to consider women's agency and offer a more complex account of the gendering process,

J. Zhou and G. Salvendy (Eds.): ITAP 2018, LNCS 10926, pp. 40–51, 2018.
https://doi.org/10.1007/978-3-319-92034-4_4

one that incorporates contradiction. The research took up Wajcman's challenge to provide a study of how different groups of Portuguese women responded and assimilated the mobile phone in their daily lives.

One of the first motivations for conducting this research is the empirical observation of how women feel so comfortable using the mobile phone. Younger or older they all carry one in their bags and treat it as a mundane object. This observation was followed by the statistical evidence that women, contrary to other technologies, were adopting mobile phones at the same rhythm as men [5]. The following step was to question this apparent equality in numbers [6]. In fact, much of the previous research on gender and mobile phone use was conducted in comparative terms, women versus men [7]. In this type of research, we end up finding no meaningful differences, such as …, between men and women. In addition, that lack of differences is left with no explanation. This work wanted to fill this gap and contribute to an explanation; thus, the research is not centered on differences between men and women, but rather on women's specific experiences, leaving space for the contradictory effects and meanings for different groups of women. Therefore, it is not about differences between men and women but about the different meaning of mobile phones and their trajectory in women's lives.

The research methodology aligns with the taking of a cultural perspective of mobile communications. Albeit blending quantitative and qualitative methods in an interpretative research strategy, the work clearly opts for a qualitative dominant mixed method designed to answer the question of what the meaning of the mobile phone for different groups of Portuguese women, at different life stages in their life trajectories, is. We argue that the role women play in their lives, either a spouse, a mother, a working woman, a caretaker, is determinant in their use of the mobile phone. Moreover, this role is determined by their position in the life course and not by their position in the cohort.

The key findings are that, contrary to a theory of a dominant use for a technology, an *Apparatgeist*, as proposed by Katz [8] the mobile phone has different roles and affordances depending on women's life stages. As embodied objects, mobile phones are part of very complex power relationships and if it is true that women have conquered mobility in many ways, they are still constrained in their achievements by an unbalanced gendering of time, space and expectations about their role in society.

For Katz and Aakhus [9] the logic that drives personal communication technologies, such as the mobile phone, is one of "perpetual contact". This has been a controversial theory with authors such as Mimi Ito strongly disagreeing with a theory of *Apparatgeist*. For Ito technologies are "both constructive and constructed by historical, social and cultural contexts" [10]. Our understanding is also that knowledge is always contingent, grounded on the theory "situated knowledges" [11], on the need to specify contexts. The research also rooted in the believe that the study of everyday use of technology, and new media, provides a significant contribution to the understanding of how these technologies unfold, of how they are domesticated [12].

Portugal has certain characteristics that make for an interesting case study for the study of the gendering of the mobile phone. Besides having a high mobile phone penetration rate it also has one of the highest employment rates for women. However, Portuguese society is also full of contradictions in what concerns gender equality: motherhood does not seem to hinder women's commitment to working outside the home but that does not translate into a more equal gender division of labor. Portuguese women end up being burden by the pressures of a double shift. They are also the main caregivers for children and the elderly and thus time constrains are amongst their main hurdles.

To analyze women's practices towards the mobile phone the research resorted to qualitative data to provide a more nuanced interpretation and understanding of the use of mobile phones by Portuguese women. Going through the numbers [13], we found that ownership seems to be especially determined by income level, age and education with the lowest percentages being for women that are older, retired, with no formal education, a low-income level, and the highest percentages for women that are younger, student or active workers with secondary education and a high income. It was also clear that the use of the mobile phone is mostly private with family members concentrating most of contacts. Friends are important for young women or for those women that are students. However, in the interviews, it was possible to identify that mature independent women also had a similar behavior to that of young women and students. Mature independent women, either because they do not have a stable relationship, are divorced or widows, have the need to reach out outside the family, resort to friends as their support network, and thus have similar practices to those of younger people.

The mobile phone is always the most private and personal technology for them, the one thing they are more physical close to; the one thing they always carry along. Albeit this proximity, there is a low level of personal choice. Women's phone choices suffer from the "wife-phone" and "job-phone" effect meaning that they either get them from their husbands, sometimes much like a used car, or they have a mobile that belongs to the company they work for. These effects sometimes lead to low levels of personalization. However, lack of personalization does not mean that they do not value the mobile phone. Women value the mobile phone not for the device itself but for the role it plays in their life, and they show a high degree of dependency across all life-stages although underlying reasons vary: for mature independent it is accessibility, and for empty nests a blend of autonomy and safety.

The research showed that mobile phones have different roles depending on women's turning point location, so it is all about the role women play and not about socioeconomics. Thus, contrary to the image projected in statistics, interviews provide a life trajectory for the mobile that does not present a linear trajectory across the life course of women's lives as shown by mature independent women and empty nesters.

The paper focuses on older women as a meaningful group; one that has been constantly underrepresented in academic and commercial studies of the mobile phone [14–16]. The field of mobile phone studies, as much of new media research, is centered on young people's practices and neglects adult women as an interesting and powerful group. The paper seeks to contribute to gain knowledge about the relationship between women and mobile phones and to critically investigate if and why mobile phones increase technological intimacy for women, and what is the trajectory of the mobile phone in women's lives? How do mobile phones enter women's lives, how do mobile phones evolve by means of use? The paper will give voice to older women to trace this trajectory and to investigate when do women come closer and distant to the mobile phone. How does the mobile phone affects women's experience of mobility? Two of the most important human perceptions are space and time. We define ourselves as human beings in a certain time and space context. These dimensions are being transformed as our experience is mediated by mobile technologies. But how is this transformation occurring in older women's lives? Are women conquering new spaces that were traditionally hostile to them? Do mobile phones affect the power regulation and negotiation of a woman's place? Are women allowed a larger scope in the management of their time?

2 Research Design

The qualitative data was drawn from 37 in-depth, semi-structured interviews, interviews to Portuguese women, from which one older mature independent, and seven empty-nesters, which are the two life-stages focused in this paper:

Mature Independent
- Ana, 56-year-old, assistant, single.

Empty Nesters:
- Deolinda, 51-year-old, hairdresser business owner, widow, now living in a new relationship;
- Fátima 2, 56-year-old, retired insurance professional, married, and grandmother of one;
- Fernanda F., 52-year-old, computer manager, married;
- Fernanda R., 65-year-old, retired topographer, married, grandmother of two. She was taking care of one of her grandchildren;
- Manuela, 56-year-old, pre-retired saleswoman, divorced in a new relationship;
- Maria, 60-year-old, retired teacher, married, grandmother of three;
- Paula, 59-year-old, retired administrative, married, grandmother of two. She takes care of one of her grandsons.

These women were aggregated into seven groups corresponding to a life course approach.

As a concept, the life course refers to the age-graded, socially embedded sequence of roles that connect the phases of life. As a paradigm, the life course refers to an imaginative framework comprised of a set of interrelated presuppositions, concepts, and methods that are used to study these age-graded, socially embedded roles [17, 18].

Some previous research on gender and technology seemed to argue that gender differences were less marked in the younger population [19] but other authors argue that gender differences in behavior are shaped as much by socialization as by generation [20]. In the scope of this latter view, gender roles would depend on the stage of life women and men are, and thus gender differences will not disappear in the future: "the behavior of adults who currently find themselves at these life stages would in this case be a better predictor of what future adult online behavior will look like than young people's current behavior" [21, p. 353]. Also, generations should not be regarded as homogenous groups, but rather as complex constructs [22].

To define the seven groups or seven life-stages we used a modified version of the market research study[1] of Portuguese consumers [23]. The study used five variables (marital status, age, occupation, number of people in the household and children and teenagers in the household) to reach the life cycle of the Portuguese consumer constituted by eleven distinctive groups: single dependent; young independent; nesting; married with children aged 0–6 years old; married with children aged 7–12 years old; married with children aged 13–17 years old; married with teenagers aged 18–24 years-old; other married coupled; sole caregivers; empty nests; independent over 35 years-old.

In our research, we have aggregated women into seven life stages: single dependent; young independent; nesting; mothers; single mothers; mature independent and empty nests. Women in the single dependent life stage are above 18 years old but still depend on their families financially and still live with them. In the next life stage young women have gained their financial independence, although they may still live with family they are able to control purchase decisions. The nesting life stage is determined by the beginning of a co-habitation relationship that might or not be formally constituted as marriage. The next life stage is that of motherhood; contrary to the Marktest study we have aggregated women with children at different ages but we acknowledge some differences in the use of the mobile phone according to the age of the kids and if they are old enough to have a mobile phone of their own. We then have single mothers either because they have become widows, because they have divorced or separated their partners. We were particularly interested in analyzing the effects of the absence of the masculine part of the couple in the relationship of women to technology. Women in the mature independent life-stage are those that are around the age of 35, have no children and either have never been involved in a co-habitation relationship or have divorced or separated their partners. Finally, empty nesters are women whose children have left home and who have retired or whose job has reached a stagnant level. This last stage has also become more complex to define, and thus presents much variability.

As for the selection of women for the seven groups we constructed a convenience sample. This is a non-probability sample that uses criteria that are useful to the research. This type of sample was chosen because it was the one that best fitted the "ideal types" strategy of analysis. However, although individuals are representative of a certain type and the interviews provide heterogeneity this is not a probabilistic sample and thus has to ambition to be statistically representative. Women interviewed were also identified by "snow-ball" from a pool of urban heterosexual women.

As an analytical strategy we used "ideal types". Max Weber used the notion of "ideal types" in association with the construction of pure cases to illustrate a conceptual category. In the scope of Max Weber's work, ideal types are fictions, but in this research, following a similar strategy by Turkle to study computer cultures [24], we have isolated real cases that serve the same function – to highlight particular aspects of the gendering of the mobile phone.

The ideal type analysis was conducted under the method used by Soulet [25] following the methodological proposal for an interactive approach to qualitative research design by Maxwell [26]. The method is structured into two levels of analysis.

---

[1] A sample of 10.093 interviews of the Portuguese population.

In the first level of local interpretation we look at each interview and how each life story helps us answer our research questions. At this first level the researcher starts by writing a synopsis, which is a synthesis of the discourse. This is the first level of abstraction and conceptualization. The following step is to write the inner history of the interview providing a chronological reading from the point of view of the interviewee in relation to the problem being analyzed. To complete the first level, the researcher draws a message that we can define as what each person wanted to tell us. These three steps are conducted for every single interview and then the researcher proceeds to the second level of global interpretation - a transversal interpretation of the individual stories, then of the aggregated ideal types, which in the scope of this research are the seven life-stages and finally the all stories as a whole.

To conduct this analysis, we did not wait for the categories to emerge from the analysis, rather our analysis was already informed by some major categories: identity, dependency, affectivity, norms and social fears, safety and control. Our goal in analyzing this category was: to provide an account of older women's daily lives (technology uses, media diets, routines), and determine its impact in their technological intimacy; to analyze the mobile phone use, the affordances it allowed to older women, such as identity construction, affectivity, safety and control; and how these affordances were translated into uses as those of personalization, micro-coordination, creativity, and entertainment.

3   Results

The stories of older women that we present here illustrate the multiplicity of facets of their emerging relationship with mobile phones, and how their life stories intersect with different specific uses of technology, and the mobile phone. This paper gives voice to their subjective experience of the mobile phone as a gendered technology, as a tool for "gender work" and "gendered work" [27]. For each life stage, we have chosen the stories of several individual women so that we can provide a deeper understanding of these women's lives as a whole.

Ana is an example of the challenges mature independent women face when they find themselves back or still in the game for a romantic relationship. Living alone these women use the mobile phone as a social networking tool and in that sense approach it in much the same manner than young dependent or teenagers. It is also a safety tool providing them freedom of movements even when alone. Finally, Fátima and Maria show how empty nests are not so empty after all. Even after retirement as is the case of Maria, many women find themselves having to take care of their grandchildren or return to work to provide extra money for their families. Fátima and Maria also represent opposite poles in terms of media ecology, which has provided very useful insights to how different media ecologies are determinant in the uses of the mobile phone.

3.1   Mature Independent: Ana D., Still in the Game

What we call mature independent women are those women that live solo, never married or are now single, through divorce, separation or because they have become widows and have no children. Ana is a 56-year-old woman that has was never married nor had a long stable cohabiting relationship. We could not find national statistics to support the evidence but international data points in the direction of a greater interest of single women for technology. According to the "Targeting the Single Female Consumer" report[2] single women were much more likely to say they would like to buy a home computer than married women and they were also more prone to innovation. The mobile phone caters to their solo lifestyles by providing a social networking tool and safety to sustain their independence and freedom of movements.

Ana D. a 56-year-old woman that lives alone with her cat. Ana is a very hard-working woman that keeps two jobs to uphold her independent lifestyle: "I would like to have a person to share my life with, but I don't sacrifice myself for that". She has a high media use that ranges from the TV to the daily use of the computer, reading books and going to the cinema. Because of her workload, she finds herself pressed for time: "I wanted to be able to give up my second job as a translator to be able to go to the beach more, spend more time with friends, go to concerts and museums". She also plays games on the computer and she does not like to share neither the computer nor the mobile phone, "I have too many private messages there".

Safety was the trigger for getting a mobile phone: "Once I got stuck on the high-way and I could not reach a person. I felt I had to get something to talk with my dad. Before that I felt that no one needed to know my whereabouts, but we can also lie with the mobile phone". Today she has two, a job-phone and a personal one. The personal one she chose because it took good pictures and because it was a clamshell model, "I am very distracted, and I kept making calls by mistake". She uses the camera to take pictures of the cat, but the main purpose of the mobile is to keep her company and an emotional reassurance tool: "I keep all my messages and notes in there". If she could choose she would have an iPhone because she confesses to enjoy technology and would value having Internet and e-mail access.

For Ana it would be hard to go without her mobile, "without noticing we pour our memory into it" and she feels calmer with she has it. Emotional reassurance and freedom of movements are for her the main benefits. These are also important benefits for empty nesters.

3.2   Empty Nesters: Fátima and Maria, Nests Not So Empty After All

Empty nesters are finding out that their nests are not so empty after all and that they are so time constrained as they were before, when they had a job. For them the mobile phone means safety and a connection with the outside world. They show high usage and leisure uses when combined with low Internet usage or lack of Internet skills.

As we could see form the quantitative analysis, ownership and use drops for older womenwomen, but we must understand that this is a nuanced reality. We are going to tell the story of two friends, Fátima and Maria, to illustrate the importance of inter-preting the use of the mobile phone in articulation with the user's media ecology. Fátima, with low Internet skills, is strongly dependent on her mobile phone: "I feel

---

[2] Source: Business Insights.

naked without it (…) it is always in my pocket and goes with me everywhere (…). It is how I keep in touch and it is safety, now even more", but Maria says she rather use the computer. Companies often underestimate the interest of older women on mobile technology [28]. however, our interviews have shown that they are keen to understand, enthusiastic to learn, and use some advanced features of mobile phones such as MMS (multimedia messaging services).

Maria is a 60-year-old retired school teacher that was obliged to take full time care of two of her three grandchildren, a nine-year-old-boy and a three-year-old girl. She also looks after another granddaughter. Because of that, she says that she "wakes up running and sleeps running against time. Now that I am retired it is even worse that when I was working, and my husband only helps with the car pools because I don't drive which is actually my main regret". The daily routine of taking care of three children leaves little space for leisure activities like the radio or the TV. However, she does use the Internet daily for everything from paying the bills to searching health topics related to the kids.

Time constrains also inhibit a closer relationship with friends which she describes as having the same issues. To keep in touch, she rather uses the landline phone because from her point of view it is cheaper than the mobile. She has one over eight years, but she says she did not want one and still does not use it much. But with the increasingly complex school schedules she now started to value the mobile phone: "I went to pick up the kids from school, but it started to rain, and I had no way to call my husband. I am starting to recognize that it comes in hand."

Although she considers herself very proficient in the use of the computer, on the mobile phone she only uses voice and read text messages and neglects all other features including personalization. Her friend Fátima is on the opposite pole.

Fátima is a 56-year-old retired insurance professional that also takes care of one grandson, she does embroidery as a hobby, and made a small business out of it. During the week, her life revolves around the television, which is always on, "I have five TV sets, one for each room and I go around the house I always have one turn on and sometimes they are all turn on". However, Fátima never used the computer or the Internet; and her husband performs all online activities. However, it is completely different with the mobile phone, she has one over many years and she uses voice and text messages to keep in touch with friends and family and to coordinate the daily activities. She even uses it for her small handicraft business: "it keeps me company and it is also a way to feel safer. I once had a flat tire in the middle of nowhere and I truly regretted not having a mobile phone". Fátima also valued having a camera feature and took pictures of her grandchild to send or show his mother and keep as a souvenir.

Fátima never turns her mobile phone off and she carries it everywhere, in fact, she was one of the fewest women that kept her mobile phone on the table during the whole interview. Fátima is a good example that the mobile phone provides a communication channel for those women that have no Internet skills; it is their way of keeping in touch by sending text messages and conducting their casual conversation.

4 Conclusion, Discussion and Limitations

The paper's main aim was to better understand the trajectory of the mobile phone in older women's lives. A striking finding in our research was that the trajectory of the mobile phone across life-stages does not have an expected adoption curve as older women do not always correspond to the stereotype of lack of interest or skills, on the contrary the mobile phone seems to play a very important role in many of these older women's lives. Because this research was qualitative and restricted to Portugal and to an urban sample, it would be interesting to provide an extensive analysis through a cross-country quantitative survey based on a life-stage approach. It would also be interesting to compare older men and older women's life-stages and life courses and understand the differences in touch-points with technology and the difference in affordances at each life stage. This could serve as a basis for the definition of better gender politics in schools, companies and society at large.

In the stage of mature independent the irregular trajectory of the mobile phone becomes very clear. These women, some even above the age of 50, use the mobile phone in much the same way a young independent would use it; the mobile phone becomes again a social networking tool. For the empty nesters, the mobile phone brings a diversified set of affordances: safety, connection with the outside world, entertainment. These women even show a high usage rate and leisure practices when combined with low or lack of Internet skills. Fátima is one of the best examples of the deep connection that empty nesters can have with the mobile phone: "I feel naked without it (…). It is always in my pocket and goes with me everywhere (…). It is how I kept in touch and it is safety, now even more". We could not help but notice the resemblance between Fátima's discourse and that of the young dependent women interviewed. For the empty nesters, their fragility originates mainly on their own biological aging process that sometimes also leads to isolation. For them the mobile phone means safety and a lifeline to the outside world as well expressed in the words of Fátima: "I feel naked without it (…) it is always in my pocket and goes with me everywhere (…). It is how I keep in touch and it is safety, now even more". It is also a source of entertainment and leisure when combined with low Internet usage or lack of Internet skills.

What is transversal to all these women is that the mobile phone is always the most private and personal technology they use or own. They also show a high degree of dependency across life stages although, as we have seen, the underlying reasons for that dependency may vary.

Although many of the studies are centered on teenager's personalization practices, in the interviews the group of women that was more enthusiastic about personalization were the empty nesters, which might reinforce the job-phone effect theory. Empty nesters are retired and thus have only personal phones and have more freedom for personalization as explained by Manuela (56-year-old, pre-retired saleswoman, divorced in a new relationship, empty nester), an empty nester: "I have three mobile phones, one for each provider. I like to play games, take pictures and use the text-messages. I use the pictures that I take to personalize it and I have a ring-back tone service in two of them. I don't have it in all three because it becomes too expensive bit I like to know that when people are calling they are going to hear a music that I chose".

The paper gave voice to older women so that they could explain how the mobile phone affected their experience of mobility. The mobile phone enables women to keep in touch despite their space constrains. It becomes an especially useful tool when they see their mobility reduced in certain stages of their lives such as when they become older: "At this stage in my life is when I value it the most to be available and to be in touch with people and to do my things with grandchildren. I don't drive so I am always dependent on my husband to pick me up and the mobile is helpful to coordinate things". (Maria, 60-year-old, married empty nester). It allows them to extend to outer spaces a function that they valued so much in the landline telephone – keeping in touch with those that are emotionally important, it is what Klára Sándor calls "mental safety in your pocket" [29]: "It would be extremely complicated to be without the mobile phone. I would be a nervous rack. If I forget my mobile phone it seems that I am lost and that I need exactly all that I have on my mobile phone. I did not feel this before but now it seems that the mobile phone is part of us. I rarely forget it at home because the first thing I do in the morning is placing it in my handbag. I feel much more reassured when I have it and I now it is turned on, so I do not switch it off when I go to bed. Someone might need my help". (Fernanda F., 52-year-old, married, computer manager, empty nester)

In Portugal, a country that registers one of the highest employment rates for women, women's time constrains are high. According to the national survey on the uses of time [30] the combined professional work, household and family care average duration is 6.96 h for the employed male population and 8.67 h for women with the great discrepancy being that household chores only account for 20 min in the male population and 3 h in the female population. Leisure time is also reduced for women with the average being 2.30 for the male population and 1.42 for the female population. These numbers even show a bigger gap in the unemployed population where men only devote 2.08 h to household chores and family care versus 5.58 h for women and in the retired population where numbers are very similar 2.08 for men and 5.19 for women. These time differences are absorbed by leisure time to which retired men devote 5.26 h versus 3.24 h for women So, even in advanced life stages the constrains on women's tine are not reduced. This portrait of time constrains for retired women is well described by one of the empty nesters women interviewed: "I wake up in a hurry and I sleep in a hurry. Now that I am retired it is even worse than when I was working. In the morning must dress two kids, get them ready and take them to school. I come back to pick up my other granddaughter. Then I make lunch for her and my husband and I clean up the house. I give lunch to my granddaughter and at half past three I must pick the kids from school. We get home and it is time for bath e get my smallest granddaughter ready for her mother to pick her up and lately my daughter is doing her master's degree so many times she ends up sleeping over and instead of two grandchildren at my care I end up with three. It is time to get them asleep and go to sleep in a hurry so that the show can start all over again the next morning. My husband who is also retired only helps with the car pools. He sometimes only makes everything worse because he likes to see everything tide up but he only does something when it is strictly necessary or I ask him to do it. With all this I end up having little or no time for television or a book. I never had so little time as now. When I worked, I had more time. At the weekends it is time for heavy duty cleaning and sometimes we go down to our house in the country where I also end up doing the cleaning". (Maria, 60-year-old, retired teacher, married, grandmother of three, empty nester)

Time is indeed the best example of how women have moved so much and at the same time, stand so still. Women live "in the fast lane" [31] and the accounts of daily routines of the women we interviewed are a vivid example of competing priorities, of juggling spheres, due to women's professional commitments. However, women's time is constrained by gendered domestic division of labor where women are still perceived to have the sole or main responsibility for household work and family care giving and management. This trait especially burdens mothers in dual earning households but is also extended into later life stages such as empty nesters with grandchildren to take care off. Women's time is also not theirs, their rhythms are dictated by others, by others' needs. In this context of "temporal crisis" many address the mobile phone as a tool of acceleration that would increase pressure on an already stressful environment. Nevertheless, what our interviews have shown once again is that the nature of a technology or an artefact can only be understood in the co-construction with user and context. Women have shown a clear agency in the use of the mobile phone. Experiences vary across life stages in accordance with different time needs but what they have in common is that the mobile phone was incorporated into their lives as a tool for the management of their interactions with family and friends and for the micro-coordination of their everyday lives.

Throughout their life stages, women face different challenges and needs that are expressed in different relationships with technology. It is not a linear progression but instead is related to their "situated knowledges" and specific locations. Each woman tells a different story, has a different voice. The question is if someone is listening.

Acknowledgment. This paper was supported by "Papers @USA Grants" 2018 from the *"Fundação Luso-Americana para o Desenvolvimento"*.

References

1. Ganito, C.: Women Speak. Gendering the Mobile Phone. Universidade Católica Editora, Lisbon (2016)
2. Cockburn, C.: The circuit of technology: gender, identity and power. In: Silverstone, R., Hirsch, E. (eds.) Consuming Technologies: Media and Information in Domestic Spaces, pp. 32–48. Sage, London and New York (1992)
3. Pilcher, J., Whelehan, I.: 50 Key Concepts in Gender Studies. Sage, London (2004)
4. Wajcman, J.: Technofeminism. Polity Press, Cambridge (2004)
5. Ganito, C.: As Mulheres E Os Telemóveis: Uma Relação Por Explorar. Comunicação Cultura 3, 41–58 (2007)
6. Ganito, C.: Moving acts: transforming gender. In: 6th International Workshop on Phenomenology, Organisation and Technology (2008)
7. Fortunati, L.: Gender and the mobile phone. In: Goggin, G., Hjorth, L. (eds.) Mobile Technologies. From Telecommunications to Media, pp. 23–34. Routledge, New York (2009)
8. Katz, J.: Magic Is in the Air. Mobile Communication and the Transformation of Social Life. Transaction Publishers, London (2006)
9. Katz, J., Aakhus, M.: Perpetual Contact: Mobile Communication, Private Talk, Public Performance. Cambridge University Press, Cambridge (2002)

10. Ito, M., Okabe, D., Matsuda, M. (eds.): Personal, Portable, Pedestrian. Mobile Phones in Japanese Life. MIT Press, Cambridge and London (2005)
11. Haraway, D.: Situated knowledges: the science question in feminism and the privilege of partial perspective. Feminist Stud. **14**(3), 575–599 (1988)
12. Loos, E.F., Mante-Meijer, E., Haddon, L.: The Social Dynamics of Information and Communication Technology. Ashgate, Aldershot (2008)
13. Araújo, V., Cardoso, G., Espanha, R.: A Sociedade Em Rede Em Portugal 2008. Apropriação Do Telemóvel Na Sociedade Em Rede [Network Society in Portugal. Mobile Phone Appropriation in the Network Society]. Obercom, Lisbon (2009)
14. Ratzenböck, B.: Everyday life interactions of women 60+ with ICTs: creations of meaning and negotiations of identity. In: Zhou, J., Salvendy, G. (eds.) ITAP 2017. LNCS, vol. 10297, pp. 25–37. Springer, Cham (2017). https://doi.org/10.1007/978-3-319-58530-7_3
15. Ratzenböck, B.: "Let's take a look together": walking interviews in domestic spaces as a means to examine ICT experiences of women 60+. J. Commun. Public Relat. **18**(1(37)), 49–64 (2016)
16. Rosales, A., Fernández-Ardèvol, M.: Beyond WhatsApp: older people and smartphones. Rom. J. Commun. Public Relat. **18**(1(37)), 27–47 (2016)
17. Mortimer, J.T., Shanahan, M.J. (eds.): Handbook of the Life Course. Springer, New York (2004)
18. Kriebernegg, U., Maierhofer, R., Ratzenböck, B. (eds.): Alive and Kicking at All Ages: Cultural Constructions of Health and Life Course Identity, vol. 5. Transcript Verlag (2014)
19. Ling, R.: Adolescent Girls and Young Adult Men: Two Sub-Cultures of the Mobile Telephone). Telenor Research and Development, Kjeller (2001)
20. Grint, K., Gill, R. (eds.): The Gender-Technology Relation. Contemporary Theory and Research. Taylor & Francis, London and Bristol (1995)
21. Helsper, E.J.: Gendered internet use across generations and life stages. Commun. Res. **37**(3), 352–374 (2010)
22. Loos, E.F., Haddon, H., Mante-Meijer, E. (eds.): Generational Use of New Media. Ashgate, Farnham (2012)
23. Marktest.: O Perfil Do Consumidor Português [The Profile of the Portuguese Consumer]. Marktest, Lisbon (2006)
24. Turkle, S.: The Second Self: Computers and the Human Spirit. Granada, London (1984)
25. Soulet, M.-H.: Gérer Sa Consommation. Drogues Dures Et Enjeu De Conventionnalité. Éditions Universitaires Fribourg Suisse, Fribourg (2002)
26. Maxwell, J.A.: La Modélisation De La Recherche Qualitative: Une Approche Interactive. Editions Universitaires, Paris (1999)
27. Rakow, L.: Gender on the Line. University of Illinois Press, Urbana and Chicago (1992)
28. Kurniawan, S.: An exploratory study of how older women use mobile phones. In: Dourish, P., Friday, A. (eds.) UbiComp 2006. LNCS, vol. 4206, pp. 105–122. Springer, Heidelberg (2006). https://doi.org/10.1007/11853565_7
29. Sándor, K.: Mental safety in your pocket. In: Nyíri, K. (ed.) A Sense of Place: The Global and the Local in Mobile Communication, pp. 179–190. Passagen Verlag, Vienna (2005)
30. Perista, H. (ed.): Os Usos Do Tempo E O Valor Do Trabalho: Uma Questão De Género [The Uses of Time and the Value of Work: A Matter of Gender], vol. 15. Ministério do Trabalho e da Solidariedade, Lisbon (1999)
31. Wajcman, J., Bittman, M., Brown, J.: Intimate connections: the impact of the mobile phone on work/life boundaries. In: Goggin, G., Hjorth, L. (eds.) Mobile Technologies: From Telecommunications to Media, pp. 9–22. Routledge, New York and London (2008)

A Change Is Gonna Come
The Effect of User Factors on the Acceptance of Ambient Assisted Living

Patrick Halbach, Simon Himmel[✉], Julia Offermann-van Heek,
and Martina Ziefle

Human-Computer Interaction Center, RWTH Aachen University,
Campus-Boulevard 57, 52074 Aachen, Germany
{halbach,himmel,vanheek,ziefle}@comm.rwth-aachen.de
http://www.comm.rwth-achen.de

Abstract. In the course of demographic change, an increasing proportion of older people in need of care pose enormous burdens for the care sectors of today's society, which could dramatically aggravate in the next decades. Developing Ambient Assisted Living (AAL) technologies is one approach to support older people and people in need of care to live as long as possible independently at their own home. Besides technical opportunities and functions, future users' acceptance is decisive for the success and long-term usage of innovative technologies. Thus, for AAL technologies it has to be explored which factors are crucial for acceptance and to what extent those factors differ with regard to diverse user groups. Referring to existing technology acceptance models (in particular the UTAUT2-model), it is questionable whether such models can be adapted and are appropriately usable for the context of AAL technologies. In this paper, we therefore investigate potential users' attitudes towards AAL systems as well as the importance and relationships of technology-related and user-specific characteristics in a scenario-based online questionnaire study using an adapted and extended version of the UTAUT2-model. The undertaken adaption led to a better understanding of influencing factors for AAL acceptance: privacy concerns need to be addressed as an additional predictor. Regarding user factors, age, Attitude Towards Technology (ATT), and caregiving experience were revealed as influencing factors, whereas gender and health status did not show any effects on AAL acceptance.

Keywords: Ambient Assisted Living · Technology acceptance
UTAUT2 model · User diversity · Aging

1 Introduction

An aging population and rising care needs in the course of demographic change represent enormous strains for today's societies and in particular for the care sectors [1]. An increasing number of older people in need of care due to chronic

© Springer International Publishing AG, part of Springer Nature 2018
J. Zhou and G. Salvendy (Eds.): ITAP 2018, LNCS 10926, pp. 52–69, 2018.
https://doi.org/10.1007/978-3-319-92034-4_5

diseases or disabilities is confronted with a lack of care specialists especially in geriatric and nursing care institutions [2,3]. One approach to address this growing gap refers to the development of ICT and AAL technologies in order to enable a safer and facilitated life for older people within their individual home environments. Those very diverse technical approaches can be used to detect falls [4,5], to monitor vital parameters, to facilitate life by smart automation, or to serve as a daily reminder, e.g., for drugs or (medical) appointments [6,7]. Although the technical possibilities and functions are promising, those systems have rarely been used in real life so far [8]. This is exactly the area technology acceptance research focuses on, aiming for an understanding and weighting of factors that influence the acceptance and adoption of technologies [9]. In light of demographic change and rising challenges, user diversity in terms of age, gender, and health status has to be integrated in technology acceptance models to examine if different factors are decisive for e.g., younger vs. older or healthy vs. diseased people's perception of supporting technologies. In this study, we therefore adapted the UTAUT2 model to the context of a holistic AAL system in order to examine acceptance-relevant factors, especially focusing on differences regarding user diversity (i.e. age, gender, attitude towards technology, health status, caregiving experience).

2   Perception of AAL Technologies

This section presents Ambient Assisted Living (AAL) technologies and systems as a possible solution to the challenges of demographic change, and raises the questions of user acceptance and the impact of user diversity factors.

2.1   Acceptance of Assisting Technologies

As introduced, present and future western societies face great challenges dealing with the effects of demographic change [1]. Besides political and societal processes [10], technical inventions can play a crucial role providing solutions to these challenges. With the development of 'ubiquitous computing' [11] and continuous improvements in information and communication technologies (ICT) [12], the widespread and everyday use of smart home [13] and AAL technologies, from the technological point of view, could be state of the art. There are several research projects and prototypes for single as well as ubiquitous home integrated assistive technologies [14,15]. However, AAL technologies, as one sort of smart home solutions, still do not play a key role in assisting everyday life. Besides challenges of market entrance barriers for new technologies [8], there is one key player for the use of AAL-technologies: the user's acceptance.

Considering technology acceptance research there are several approaches in modeling the understanding, measuring, and prediction of usage intention of technologies. Starting with the Theory of Planned Behavior (TBP) [16] and the Technology Acceptance Model (TAM) [17], which both have their advantages and disadvantages [18] and the integration of several other models [19], these models were continuously improved, extended, and also led to a Unified Theory of Acceptance (UTAUT) [20]. This unified model was extended as the UTAUT2 model [21] and is used in this research paper. Although the unified models tempt to be used as they come for all technologies, the adjustments for the specific type of technology is still necessary (here AAL technologies, see Sect. 3.2.2). In order to apply new attributes to existing models, an exploratory and qualitative pre-study leads to new insights for new technologies in addition to a validating quantitative model-based user study.

2.2   Effects of User Diversity on AAL Acceptance

Regarding technology usage and the factors influencing acceptance as well as usage intention, the greatest empirical variance is caused not by one technology or technology attributes but by the user itself [22,23]. To understand acceptance it is crucial to know and understand the user, as diverse as she or he is. Concerning the definition of AAL-technologies, the user addressed is an older or needing adult, whose condition could be improved or could stay better by applying to these technologies [14]. Therefore, three influencing user factors play an important role when analyzing AAL acceptance: age, gender, and health status. As there are several studies on the impact of theses factors on medical and assisting technologies with different outcomes (from positive and negative to no significant influence) [24–26] and there are also interacting effects [22], we will not state three different hypotheses, but examine their individual impact on our adapted UTAUT model.

In addition, the general attitude towards technology (ATT) [27] often influences technology acceptance [28], although recent studies also showed different effects on acceptance of AAL technologies and the intercorrelation with gender and age [22,25]. However, the effect of ATT on factors influencing the usage intention will be examined in our adapted UTAUT model.

Recent research shows another factor influencing AAL acceptance concerning the private [29] and professional [30] caregiving point of view. Caregiving experience as a user factor will be a fifth factor influencing UTAUT predictors in this research study (see Fig. 1).

3   Empirical Approach

This section describes the qualitative preceding study presenting the basis for our quantitative approach, the online questionnaire design, our applied statistical procedures as well as the study's sample.

3.1   Qualitative Prestudy (in AAL Research Context)

Preliminary to the development of the questionnaire, two focus group studies were performed. The two groups differed in age: the younger group with 5 participants had a mean age of 24.4, whereas the 7 participants in the older group were on average 60.7 years old. For obtaining comparable results, a joint focus group guide was used in both groups. The group discussions were recorded and later on transcribed, so that a code system based on an inductive approach could be created to group and compare the contributions of the participants.

Both group discussions were started with a brief introduction in aims and capabilities of Ambient Assisted Living, followed by detailed video presentations of four concrete AAL systems. The participants were asked to discuss their initial impressions of the systems and to form and rank general requirements and conditions for using an AAL system. At the end of the group sessions, new living concepts as for example multi-generational houses were discussed as an alternative to AAL.

The evaluation revealed several conformities and also differences between the younger and older group. For the presented systems, the younger group tended to choose their role as an involved relative over emphasizing their own situation as older adults. Thereby, they rated the usability of the devices for the current elderly generation. Regarding privacy concerns and evaluating the usefulness, the age difference seemed to be not decisively. The groups chose the same favorite out of the four systems and also had similar concerns using a camera-based system for fall detection.

In consensus, it was stated as a general requirement, that the privacy in no case should be fully devoted to a complete security. Also, the alarms generated by the system should not be handled by relatives but special emergency centers. The younger group added, that the system should act unobtrusively and only step in if the user needs help. The older adults claimed that they want to choose the recipients of the collected data.

The permanent recording and processing of audio and video signals through sensors was rejected by both groups. Only the infrared sensor (which technically also works like a video camera) seemed to be an acceptable trade-off between privacy protection and system detection precision.

Several social factors also emerged in the discussions. The older participants mentioned, that the use of such a system also depends on the social integration of elderly people. If there is a large family which lives nearby, they rated the use as rather superfluous and preferred the care of a relative over a system. But for living alone seniors they valued AAL as notable improvement and saw it as a possible way of connecting to far off living relatives.

With those findings, a further quantitative study seemed quite interesting to have a closer look on the similarities and differences of different age groups in behalf of AAL use intention, requirements and conditions and also for detecting further user factors which influence those properties.

3.2   Questionnaire Study

The questionnaire consisted of three parts who were used for (1) obtaining demographic information, (2) presenting an AAL scenario and (3) evaluating the scenario through UTAUT items. The design was motivated by the findings of two focus group interviews with each 5 and 7 people carried out prior this study.

3.2.1 SF-12 and Health Scale for AAL

The SF-12 delivers a physical and psychological component summary for the classification of the current health state of an individual [31]. The greatest advantage of this measurement lies in its low item count as it uses only a third of the 36 questions originally used in SF-36 which it was derived from for determining the two values. For this study, only the physical component summary was considered, because our study was limited to systems that treat physical health impairments.

To obtain a greater focus on the AAL context, we used a further scale which asks for different medical needs and chronic diseases [27]. The scale value indicates, if one of the four used items was answered with yes and therefore a participant has some kind of health impairment (value = 1 for health impairment, 2 for no impairment for uniformity with SF-12). The strong correlation with the physical component summary of the SF-12 shows its validity and suitability for evaluating the physical health state in AAL context ($r(147) = 0.413$; $p < 0.01$).

3.2.2 Adjusting UTAUT to AAL Contexts

The UTAUT model was initially created by Venkatesh et al. in 2003 and received a revision in 2012 to extend the original model with HM, PV and HT as additional constructs to the existing PE, EE, SI and FC [20,21]. It provides age, gender and experience as influencing user diversity factors. The optimization in 2012 were validated through a user study concerning the use of mobile Internet technology.

For using UTAUT2 with our user study, we had to fit the items to AAL contexts and the scenario which was used in our questionnaire design (see Sect. 3.2.3). The existing constructs already cover interesting influence areas such as the Expectancy to which degree effort is accepted to derive benefit from an AAL system (EE). Also the relevance of Social Influence (SI) mirrors in AAL contexts and possibly clarifies the role of relatives in decision making to buy or not to buy such a system. The construct Price Value (PV) seemed questionable as the scenario in our study was based on an exemplary system.

The qualitative prestudy showed privacy as an important component of the discussed requirements and conditions for system use. Therefore, we designed the construct Privacy Concerns, which deals with fears in terms of privacy and data security and also includes conditions for the involvement of relatives and doctors. Other research indicated, that also the design of the system components and their integration into the user's home could play a role for acceptance [32]. The second added construct Design and Integration covers the perception of the system in visual aspects.

3.2.3   Questionnaire Design

The first part of the questionnaire contained general demographic items (age, gender, education level). For a deeper insight on possible factors for AAL acceptance, user factors like health status (measured through SF-12 and own scale, see Sect. 3.2.1), social situation and attitude towards technology (ATT, Cronbach's Alpha $\alpha = 0.844$) were measured. The analysis of the social situations contained the living situation (alone/in community), the availability and distance to caregiving relatives, and prior knowledge of caregiving (if he/she gives active care or if a family member needs care).

The questionnaire's second part started with an introduction into a scenario. It was used to familiarize the participants with possibilities to use an AAL system in everyday life and pointed out security functions (fall detection, reminder for medicine intake) as well as comfort functions (automatic light switch, fitness tracker). The scenario narrated a full regular day living with the system, beginning with waking up in the morning till going to bed at the end of the day. It also involved communication with a doctor and family members.

Subsequent to the scenario, the UTAUT items were surveyed. They were randomized for each participant and comprised 36 items spread over the dimensions Performance Expectancy (PE), Effort Expectancy (EE), Social Influence (SI), Facilitating Conditions (FC), Hedonic Motivation (HM), Price Value (PV), Experience and Habit (EH), Behavioral Intention (BI) who were derived from the UTAUT2 model of Venkatesh et al. (2012) and Privacy Concerns (PC) and Design and Integration (DI) who were added due to the experiences of the prior focus group studies. Each dimension contained 2 to 5 items. Completing the full questionnaire took about 25 min. All items were set as mandatory, so that only complete datasets were used for further analysis. Data was collected in Germany in summer 2016 by using an online survey tool and in addition a paper-and-pencil questionnaire to both enable younger and older people's participation, because we wanted to collect a preferably broad age span for comparing differences through age in further analysis. Participation was voluntary and not gratified.

3.3   Statistical Methods

All items concerning the UTAUT model and ATT were evaluated through a 6-Point Likert scale (1 = totally disagree to 6 = totally agree). Data was analyzed using bi-variate correlations and independent-samples t-tests of model- and user-related factors,

3.4   Description of the Sample

In total, n = 177 people participated voluntarily in our study and filled in the online survey. In order to reach also older people who wouldn't have access to the online survey, also a printed paper-based version of the questionnaire was provided. Due to incomplete answers, 32 data sets were excluded so that 145 complete data sets remained for the further evaluation.

The mean age of the participants (n = 145) was 41.6 years (SD = 17.56; min = 19; max = 75) The sample comprised 53.1% females and 46.9% males. 43% of the total sample completed an university degree which shows an above average level of education in comparison to the German population, of which 16% hold an university degree [33].

The measurement of the participants' health state was conducted by inquiring the SF-12 and an own scale (compare Sect. 3.2.1), which correlated strongly and showed with a mean of 52.1 (SD = 7.34) for the SF-12 a slightly better average than the standardized value for the American population (Mean = 50, SD = 10). As measured by the own health scale, 38.1% of the sample had to deal with some kind of health impairment in their everyday life.

Furthermore, some questions aimed on analyzing the experience and contact with caregiving tasks of the participants through affected family members. 27.1% of them stated that at least one of their family members were in need of care. 8 participants (5.1%) took active care for a family member.

Concerning attitude towards technology, the sample had above average means compared to the German population (Mean = 4.9, SD = 0.87). The scale ATT consisted of five items and showed a high reliability (Cronbach's Alpha α = 0.844).

Describing our sample, the overall correlations between the examined user factors can be seen in Table 1. It shows that age and health correlated meaning older people had more health impairments, lower caregiving experience, and a slightly lower ATT as well as there were slightly more older men than women. Also women had a lower ATT than men. Participants with a better health status had a slightly higher ATT.

For further analyses, group segmentations referring to age and ATT as user diversity factors were carried out using a median split. Thereby, two age groups were differentiated: "young" ($\leq$40 years) and "old" (>40 years). Referring to ATT (min = 1; max = 6), a group with a comparably "lower ATT" score ($M \leq$ 5) and a group with a "higher ATT" score (M > 5) were considered.

Table 1. Inter-correlations of user factors (bottom), ATT = Attitude Towards Technology, Health = Physical Health Status (SF-12), CGEXP = Caregiving Experience). †= $p < .1$, * = $p < .05$, ** = $p < .01$.

	Age	Gender	Health	ATT	CGEXP
Age	—	.166*	−.368**	−.206*	−.219**
Gender		—		.307**	
Health			—	.177*	
ATT				—	
CGEXP					—

4   Results

This section presents the results of our quantitative questionnaire study starting with the results referring to the adapted UTAUT2-model (model-related dimensions) and followed by analyses regarding user diversity influences. Subsequently, the results of regression analyses are presented (a) for the whole sample and (b) for diverse user groups (participants with a low and a high ATT; participants with/without caregiving experience).

4.1   General UTAUT Results

The main approach of this study was to examine the suitability of the UTAUT model evolved by Venkatesh et al. and to modify it for AAL contexts, if necessary. As described in Sect. 3.2.3, we aimed to fit the existing UTAUT model to AAL contexts and therefore added the dimensions Privacy Concerns and Design and Integration.

Most of the classic dimensions gained high reliability scores (Cronbach's Alpha above $\alpha = 0.8$, see Table 2). SI an FC still showed values above $\alpha = 0.5$. Only the Price Value was unacceptable in its reliability with $\alpha = 0.451$ and was not considered for the further evaluation.

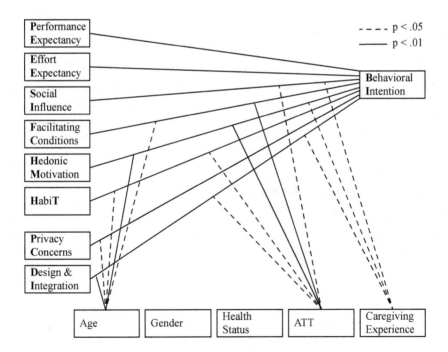

Fig. 1. General influence of UTAUT dimensions on Behavioral intention, $n_{total} = 145$.

Table 2. Correlations of user factors (bottom) and the AAL system's evaluation (upper) on the adapted UTAUT model's dimensions (PE = Performance Expectancy, HM = Hedonic Motivation, HT = Habit, EE = Effort Expectancy, SI = Social Influence, FC = Facilitating Conditions, BI = Behavioral Intention To Use, ATT = Attitude Towards Technology, HEALTH = Physical Health Status (SF-12), CGEXP = Care Giving Experience). $^{†} = p < .1$, $* = p < .05$, $** = p < .01$.

	PE	EE	SI	FC	HM	HT	PC	DI	BI
PE	—	.787**	.566**	.584**	.565**	.801**	−.652**	.193*	.787**
EE		—	.530**	.678**	.637**	.824**	−.591**	.275**	.779**
SI			—	.345**	.327**	.430**	−.380**		.463**
FC				—	.638**	.717**	−.426**	.335**	.708**
HM					—	.740**	−.483**	.392**	.723**
HT						—	−.639**	.314*	.851**
PC							—		−.689**
DI								—	.239**
BI									—
Age				−.166*	−.236**	−.170*	−.171*	−.481**	
Gender		−0.156†							
Health									
ATT		.138†	−.172*	.373**	.317**	.191*		.187*	.161†
CGEXP		.149†	.166*		.173*			.171*	

In terms of interrelatedness, DI and SI revealed the weakest correlations to the other UTAUT dimensions. PE, EE, FC, and HT were strongly correlated with BI and also among each other. PC showed consistently at least medium negative correlations with the UTAUT dimensions and also a strong correlation with BI ($r(147) = −0.689$, $p < 0.01$).

4.2   Influence of User Diversity

We included various factors regarding user diversity in our study to investigate their influences to the applied UTAUT model. Besides the classical factors for user diversity like age and gender, also the health state, the attitude towards technology, and the caregiving experience were examined to check their relevance for the AAL context.

1. **Age:** The age of the participants correlated with FC, HM, EH, PC, and DI as stated in Table 2. With raising age, the participant's evaluation of their ability to use the system, the fun, concerns with Privacy, and importance of design and integration decreased. The factors PE, EE, SI, and BI were not related to age for this sample. Especially the missing correlation to BI, which was used to evaluate the acceptance in the UTAUT model, showed an interesting result.

By investigating relations to the other user diversity factors, two significant correlations were obtained: with raising age, the attitude towards technology and the health state decreased.

2. **Gender:** T-Tests revealed that only the EE dimension of the UTAUT model was rated slightly different by women compared to men. Men were less willing to put effort in learning the system use (Mean = 4.2, SD = 1.16) than women (Mean = 4.5, SD = 1.05, t(145) = 1.9, p = 0.06).

3. **Health Status:** As mentioned in Sect. 3.2.1, the health scale was significantly related to the SF-12. Surprisingly, the current health state of the participants didn't show any impact on the UTAUT factors.

4. **ATT:** The ATT showed small correlations with the UTAUT dimensions SC and DI and medium correlations with FC and HM. In contrast to the other User diversity factors, the ATT indicated a relationship to the Behavioral Intention.

5. **Caregiving Experience:** The results revealed significant group differences for the Caregiving Experience with the factors EE, SI, HM, and DI (see Table 2).

4.3   Intention to Use Results

To analyze the predictors for the intention to use more precise relating to the emerging user diversity factors, a regression analysis was conducted. At first, the analysis of the whole sample indicated HT, PE, PC, and FC as predictors with 80.3% explained variation of variance (see Fig. 2). In addition, we conducted regression analyses to uncover user diversity influences. As gender and health status revealed almost no significant correlations with the model-related dimensions, those two factors were not investigated in more detail. Instead, the factors age, ATT, and caregiving experience were focused: "young" vs. "old" (see Fig. 3), comparably "lower" vs. "higher" scores ATT (see Fig. 4), and "having" vs. "having no caregiving experience" (see Fig. 5).

The regression analysis for the two age groups revealed two different models: for the young group, 76.6% variance of AAL acceptance was explained based on the model dimensions HT, PC, and PE; for the older group, the regression model explained 83.0% variance of AAL acceptance based on five model dimensions: HT, HM, PE, SI, and DI.

The regression analysis for two ATT groups revealed HT, PC, and FC as coincident predictors for the two groups. The model explained a higher variance of AAL acceptance for the low ATT group $(adj.r^2 = .810)$ compared to the high ATT group $(adj.r^2 = .769)$. The results showed differences for the relevance of HM, which was an additional predictor for the high ATT group and PE as a predictor for the low ATT group. HT was the most predictive factor for both groups, whereby this factor differentiated clearer from the other predictors for the high ATT group.

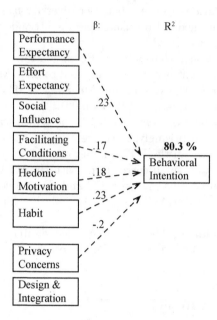

Fig. 2. General influence of UTAUT dimensions on Behavioral intention, $n_{total} = 145$.

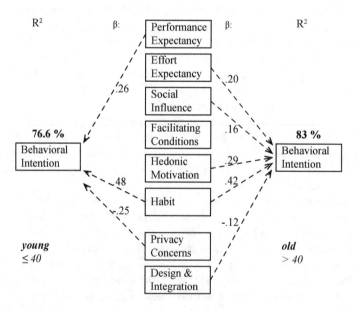

Fig. 3. Influence of UTAUT dimensions on Behavioral intention, comparing younger ($\leq$ 40) and older ($>$ 40) participants.

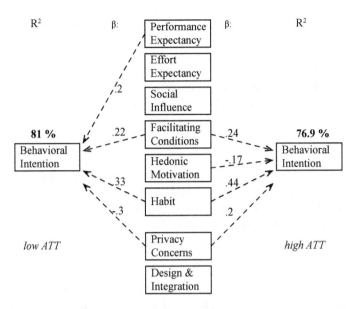

Fig. 4. Influence of UTAUT dimensions on Behavioral intention, comparing participants with lower and higher scores referring to their attitude towards technology.

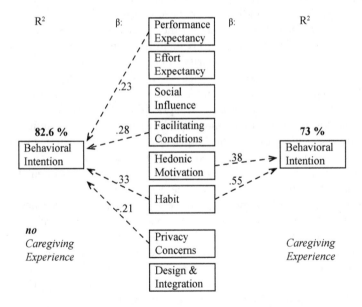

Fig. 5. influence of UTAUT dimensions on Behavioral intention, comparing participants with and without caregiving experiences.

The comparison of the regression analysis results for the caregiving experience groups showed very different models. The only similarity laid in the predictor HT, which explained the highest amount of variance variation for both models. For participants with caregiving experience, HM was the only further predictor and 73.0% of variance were explained. For participants without caregiving experience, the model reached an adjusted R square of 82.6% and was - in contrast - based on four predictors: HT, FC, PE, and PC.

5   Discussion

Within this section, the results are discussed starting with an assessment of using an adapted version of the UTAUT2-model for the evaluation of AAL technology acceptance. Further, user diversity influences are discussed, limitations of the presented study are considered, and recommendations for future research are given.

5.1   Using Acceptance Models for AAL

The previously reported results show, that the UTAUT2 model contains several constructs which are affecting the behavioral intention. The most influencing constructs were HT,PE, and EE which leads to the assumption that in particular the familiarization to everyday use, the effective advantage, and the required effort for using an AAL system matters for its acceptance. Therefore, it is important that such systems are easy to integrate into the user's everyday life offering clearly visible advantages, while the additional expense is preferably low. Further, privacy concerns are also a crucial factor for acceptance since the measured construct influences all other UTAUT factors negatively including the behavioral intention. AAL systems thus should provide high security of personal data and the user's privacy.

Those findings are also supported through previous research. Weegh et al. examined 16 papers to develop an Acceptance Model based on TAM2 by Venkatesh and Davis and the System Acceptability Model by Anderson. Besides additional acceptance criteria as financial ability & willingness, human replacement, awareness, and government/politics/legal aspects, their findings also include perceived usefulness, perceived ease of use, control and security, privacy versus independence/safety, user involvement, reputation/alignment to current lifestyle, and experience as relevant for the acceptance.

The study of Steele et al. focusing on a concrete wireless sensor based system showed that it is rather important for the user that the system is affordable and that he is able to interact with it and stays in control [34]. Most of the participants were unable to fully recognize the potentials of such a system and took the view that it should be used for emergencies only in the sector of elderly care. Interestingly, they also were at least concerned about the privacy of the collected health data because the fast availability of help was far more important for them than their privacy of medical data. Steele concluded, that a system with a simple interface and least amount of interaction are more likely to be accepted by elderly persons.

The results of Demiris also show that the user's perceptions of AAL technology focuses mostly on a reactive role (for detecting emergencies). For the participants of his study, privacy importance was depending on the level of need [32].

Regarding to medical technology in particular, Ziefle et al. saw the Importance of Privacy in terms of data protection as a strong universal claim which corresponds to the perception in our results. Hence, the importance and relevance of privacy as an acceptance criterion can be rated as very high and should be included by acceptance models for AAL technology.

Further research should also examine to include additional factors for measuring acceptance such as Steinke, who considered trust as further extension and found positive influence of trust at perceived ease of use and perceived reliability, though trust seemed not to be directly related to the intention to use [35].

Concluding, the application of our adapted UTAUT model pointed out, that it is feasible to measure the acceptance of AAL technologies with conventional acceptance models, but that a certain adaption to this context is mandatory and the proposed model is still not complete since it omits further possible barriers besides the privacy concerns.

5.2   Influence of User Diversity

The observed influences of user diversity indicate that gender and health status seem irrelevant for the behavioral intention. In contrast, age, the individual attitude towards technology (ATT), and caregiving experience influenced AAL acceptance.

Ziefle et al. analyzed the attitudes of users towards different types of AAL services and found that the evaluation of different usage settings of AAL is unrelated to age and gender interpreting that the precautious attitude towards AAL applications is a universal phenomenon [23].

The performed regression analysis in our study with grouping the participants into low or high ATT resulted in a closer understanding of its effect on the behavioral intention which also appeared slightly in bivariate correlations ($r(147) = 0,161$, $p = 0,051$). Previous research already demonstrated that the acceptance of AAL systems significantly depends on the participant's experience with information and communication technology and increases with higher experience [36].

In other studies, the influence of age and health status has a contrary influence at the intention to use. While Himmel et al. found, that the acceptance of AAL technologies rises for older and more ill persons [22], Steinke revealed that younger people with a better perceived health condition are more willing to use AAL [37]. This shows, that those two user diversity factors seem to be too unspecific for differentiating of user groups. A possible improvement in further studies would be to connect them to other factors like the living situation as made by Steinke in 2012 [38]. However, as shown in Fig. 3 the current results revealed age-specific influences on the UTAUT dimensions: while younger people focus more strongly on Performance Expectancy and Privacy Concerns, for older people Effort Expectancy, Social Influence, Hedonic Motivation, and Design and Integration are more important.

Caregiving experience appeared as an additional interesting factor for user diversity and showed several relations to UTAUT dimensions (EE, SI, HM, DI) although it was only surveyed with one item and the investigated participants were not chosen in regard of this factor. The regression analysis revealed that the existence of caregiving experience lowered the count of UTAUT constructs as predictors for Behavioral Intention. This could lead to the assumption that experience with care simplifies the look on AAL systems, because it strengthens the awareness of the problems which are tackled by those systems and supportive technology for caregivers is initially rated more valuably. The study of Siegel et al. shows already, that the perspective of care professionals differs from the perspective from the actual target group as they directly refer to cognitive or health impairments while evaluating such technology [39]. It would be interesting to combine these perspectives in future research.

Having the demographic change in mind it can also be estimated that the raising demand for care will require new approaches including caring relatives and new community concepts as stated by Hong et al. [40]. For this development it is indispensable to further investigate the acceptance criteria for AAL technologies depending on more facets of caregiving experience.

5.3   Limitations and Future Work

Our empirical approach provided valuable insights into a model-based evaluation of a holistic AAL system and the suitability of adapting the UTAUT2-model for the context of AAL technologies. Nevertheless, there are some limitations and suggestions for subsequent research in the field, that should be considered.

Referring to the applied methodology, the dimensions of the UTAUT2-model were successfully adapted and extended for the context of AAL technologies and systems. However, the model-based approach is restricted on a fixed number of dimensions. In a very sensible field like care, aging, and assisting technologies, more affective evaluations (beyond the model-based factors) are of importance to do justice to perceived benefits or concerns referring the usage of technologies. Thus, future studies should aim for a combination of model-based and affective evaluations. Another aspect refers to the fact that the results depend on the applied method: in the present study a scenario-based approach with a "fictive" and not a real AAL system was under study. As previous studies showed [41] evaluations of a fictional system might influence the results and could lead to an overestimation of perceived barriers and an underestimation of potential benefits for instance. Thus, it is of importance for future studies to aim for hands-on evaluations of AAL technologies and systems.

There are also some limitations with regard to the study's sample. First, the sample size was sufficient and the sample was balanced regarding gender and age. In contrast, there were significantly high proportions of people with high or very high levels of education and additionally also a very positive attitude towards technology (ATT). For future studies it would be useful to aim for a more diversified spectrum concerning education level and attitude towards technology in order to do also justice to people with low education levels and a more negative attitude towards technology.

As a last sample-related aspect, the study was conducted in Germany representing only a single, very country- and culture-specific perspective. As health care systems, their (financial) regulation, and policy circumstances are extremely country-specific, we assume that also the acceptance of AAL technologies and systems as well as the trade-offs between benefits, barriers, and use conditions differ depending on diverse countries and cultures. Therefore, it is of importance to aim for comparative studies in the future addressing direct culture- and country-comparisons of AAL technology acceptance.

Acknowledgments. The authors want to thank all participants for their openness to share opinions on a novel technology. This work was funded by the German Federal Ministry of Education and Research project Whistle (16SV7530).

References

1. Bloom, D., Canning, D.: Global Demographic Change: Dimensions and Economic Significance. Technical reprt w10817, National Bureau of Economic Research, Cambridge, MA, October 2004
2. Shaw, J., Sicree, R., Zimmet, P.: Global estimates of the prevalence of diabetes for 2010 and 2030. Diabetes Res. Clin. Pract. **87**, 4–14 (2010)
3. Siewert, U., Fendrich, K., Doblhammer-Reiter, G., Scholz, R.D., Schuff-Werner, P., Hoffmann, W.: Health care consequences of demographic changes in Mecklenburg-West Pomerania. Deutsches Ärzteblatt Int. **107**(18), 328–34 (2010)
4. Cheng, J., Chen, X., Shen, M.: A framework for daily activity monitoring and fall detection based on surface electromyography and accelerometer signals. IEEE J. Biomed. Health Inform. **17**, 38–45 (2013)
5. Droghini, D., Principi, E., Squartini, S., Olivetti, P., Piazza, F.: Human fall detection by using an innovative floor acoustic sensor. In: Esposito, A., Faudez-Zanuy, M., Morabito, F.C., Pasero, E. (eds.) Multidisciplinary Approaches to Neural Computing. SIST, vol. 69, pp. 97–107. Springer, Cham (2018). https://doi.org/10.1007/978-3-319-56904-8_10
6. Baig, M.M., Gholamhosseini, H.: Smart health monitoring systems: an overview of design and modeling. J. Med. Syst. **37**, 9898 (2013)
7. Lutze, R., Waldhör, K.: Integration of stationary and wearable support services for an actively assisted living of elderly people: capabilities, achievements, limitations, prospects—a case study. In: Wichert, R., Mand, B. (eds.) Ambient Assisted Living. ATSC, pp. 3–26. Springer, Cham (2017). https://doi.org/10.1007/978-3-319-52322-4_1
8. Wichert, R., Furfari, F., Kung, A., Tazari, M.R.: How to overcome the market entrance barrier and achieve the market breakthrough in AAL. In: Wichert, R., Eberhardt, B. (eds.) Ambient Assisted Living. ATSC, pp. 349–358. Springer, Heidelberg (2012). https://doi.org/10.1007/978-3-642-27491-6_25
9. Rogers, E.M.: Diffusion of Innovations, 5th edn. Free Press, New York (2003)
10. Inglehart, R.: Modernization and Postmodernization: Cultural, Economic, and Political Change in 43 Societies. Princeton University Press, Princeton (1997)

11. Abowd, G.D., Mynatt, E.D.: Charting past, present, and future research in ubiquitous computing. ACM Trans. Comput.-Hum. Interact. (TOCHI) **7**(1), 29–58 (2000)
12. Silverstone, R., Morley, D., Dahlberg, A., Livingstone, S.: Families, technologies and consumption: the household and information and communication technologies (1989)
13. Cook, D.J., Das, S.K.: How smart are our environments? An updated look at the state of the art. Pervasive Mob. Comput. **3**(2), 53–73 (2007)
14. Siciliano, P., Marletta, V., Marletta, V., Monteriu, A.: Ambient Assisted Living. Springer, Cham (2015). https://doi.org/10.1007/978-3-319-18374-9
15. Monekosso, D., Florez-Revuelta, F., Remagnino, P.: Ambient assisted living [Guest editors' introduction]. IEEE Intell. Syst. **30**(4), 2–6 (2015)
16. Ajzen, I.: The theory of planned behavior. Organ. Behav. Hum. Decis. Process. **50**(2), 179–211 (1991)
17. Venkatesh, V., Davis, F.D.: A theoretical extension of the technology acceptance model: four longitudinal field studies. Manage. Sci. **46**(2), 186–204 (2000)
18. Mathieson, K.: Predicting user intentions: comparing the technology acceptance model with the theory of planned behavior. Inf. Syst. Res. **2**(3), 173–191 (1991)
19. Williams, M.D., Rana, N.P., Dwivedi, Y.K., Lal, B.: Is UTAUT really used or just cited for the sake of it? A systematic review of citations of UTAUT's originating article. In: ECIS, p. 231 (2011)
20. Venkatesh, V., Morris, M.G., Davis, G.B., Davis, F.D.: User acceptance of information technology: toward a unified view. MIS Q. **27**(3), 425–478 (2003)
21. Venkatesh, V., Thong, J.Y., Xu, X.: Consumer acceptance and use of information technology: extending the unified theory of acceptance and use of technology. MIS Q. **36**(1), 157–178 (2012)
22. Himmel, S., Ziefle, M.: Smart home medical technologies: users' requirements for conditional acceptance. i-com **15**, 39–50 (2016)
23. Ziefle, M.Z., Röcker, C., Holzinger, A.: Perceived usefulness of assistive technologies and electronic services for ambient assisted Living. IEEE (2011)
24. Or, C.K., Karsh, B.-T.: A systematic review of patient acceptance of consumer health information technology. J. Am. Med. Inform. Assoc. **16**(4), 550–560 (2009)
25. Wilkowska, W., Gaul, S., Ziefle, M.: A small but significant difference – the role of gender on acceptance of medical assistive technologies. In: Leitner, G., Hitz, M., Holzinger, A. (eds.) USAB 2010. LNCS, vol. 6389, pp. 82–100. Springer, Heidelberg (2010). https://doi.org/10.1007/978-3-642-16607-5_6
26. Ziefle, M., Rocker, C., Holzinger, A.: medical technology in smart homes: exploring the user's perspective on privacy, intimacy and trust, pp. 410–415. IEEE, July 2011
27. Himmel, S., Zaunbrecher, B.S., Wilkowska, W., Ziefle, M.: The youth of today designing the smart city of tomorrow. In: Kurosu, M. (ed.) HCI 2014, Part III. LNCS, vol. 8512, pp. 389–400. Springer, Cham (2014). https://doi.org/10.1007/978-3-319-07227-2_37
28. Ajzen, I.: Perceived behavioral control, self-efficacy, locus of control, and the theory of planned behavior. J. Appl. Soc. Psychol. **32**(4), 665–683 (2002)
29. van Heek, J., Himmel, S., Ziefle, M.: Helpful but Spooky? Acceptance of AAL-systems contrasting user groups with focus on disabilities and care needs, pp. 78–90. SCITEPRESS - Science and Technology Publications (2017)
30. van Heek, J., Himmel, S., Ziefle, M.: Caregivers' Perspectives on Ambient Assisted Living Technologies in Professional Care Contexts. In: Proceedings of the International Conference on ICT for Aging well (ICT4AWE 2017), (Setúbal, Portugal). SCITEPRESS - Science and Technology Publications (2018)

31. Ware, J., Kosinski, M., Keller, S.D.: SF-12: How to score the SF-12 physical and mental health summary scales, 2nd edn. Health Institute, New England Medical Center, Boston (1995)

32. Demiris, G., Hensel, B.K., Skubic, M., Rantz, M.: Senior residents' perceived need of and preferences for "smart home" sensor technologies. Int. J. Technol. Assess. Health Care **24**, 120–124 (2008)

33. "Bildungsstand der Bevölkerung, Technical report, Statistisches Bundesamt, Wiesbaden, November 2015

34. Steele, R., Lo, A., Secombe, C., Wong, Y.K.: Elderly persons' perception and acceptance of using wireless sensor networks to assist healthcare. Int. J. Med. Inform. **78**, 788–801 (2009)

35. Steinke, F., Ingenhoff, A., Fritsch, T.: Personal remote assistance in ambient assisted living-experimental research of elderly people's trust and their intention to use. Int. J. Hum.-Comput. Interact. **30**, 560–574 (2014)

36. Gövercin, M., Meyer, S., Schellenbach, M., Steinhagen-Thiessen, E., Weiss, B., Haesner, M.: SmartSenior@home: acceptance of an integrated ambient assisted living system. Results of a clinical field trial in 35 households. Inform. Health Soc. Care **41**(4), 1–18 (2016)

37. Steinke, F., Bading, N., Fritsch, T., Simonsen, S.: Factors influencing trust in ambient assisted living technology: a scenario-based analysis. Gerontechnology **12**, 81–100 (2014)

38. Steinke, F., Fritsch, T., Brem, D., Simonsen, S.: Requirement of AAL systems: older persons' trust in sensors and characteristics of AAL technologies, p. 1. ACM Press (2012)

39. Siegel, C., Hochgatterer, A., Dorner, T.: Contributions of ambient assisted living for health and quality of life in the elderly and care services - a qualitative analysis from the experts' perspective of care service professionals. BMC Geriatr. **14**(1), 112 (2014)

40. Hong, S., Vincenzo, D.F., Ning, G., Chris, B.: The missing ones: Key ingredients towards effective ambient assisted living systems. J. Ambient Intell. Smart Environ. **2**, 109–120 (2010)

41. Wilkowska, W., Ziefle, M., Himmel, S.: Perceptions of personal privacy in smart home technologies: do user assessments vary depending on the research method? In: Tryfonas, T., Askoxylakis, I. (eds.) HAS 2015. LNCS, vol. 9190, pp. 592–603. Springer, Cham (2015). https://doi.org/10.1007/978-3-319-20376-8_53

Acceptance and Practical Use of Assistive Technologies for Frail Seniors and Caregivers: Interview Surveys on Nursing Homes

Akihiko Kamesawa[1([X])], Reina Yoshizaki[2], Shiho Hirose[3], Nana Shinozaki[4],
Ren Komatsu[2], Satomi Kitamura[4], Ou Fu[5], Ningjia Yang[2], Ayako Ishii[4],
Yuka Sumikawa[4], Taiyu Okatani[5], Kazuki Kaneko[2], Yoshiyuki Nakagawa[2],
Taichi Goto[4], Takahiro Miura[6], Taketoshi Mori[4], Tohru Ifukube[6],
and Junichiro Okata[2,6]

[1] Graduate School of Arts and Sciences, The University of Tokyo,
7-3-1 Hongo, Bunkyo-ku, Tokyo 113-8656, Japan
akky6126@yahoo.co.jp
[2] Graduate School of Engineering, The University of Tokyo,
7-3-1 Hongo, Bunkyo-ku, Tokyo 113-8656, Japan
[3] Graduate School of Frontier Sciences, The University of Tokyo,
7-3-1 Hongo, Bunkyo-ku, Tokyo 113-8656, Japan
[4] Graduate School of Medicine, The University of Tokyo,
7-3-1 Hongo, Bunkyo-ku, Tokyo 113-8656, Japan
[5] Graduate School of Information Science and Technology, The University of Tokyo,
7-3-1 Hongo, Bunkyo-ku, Tokyo 113-8656, Japan
[6] Institute of Gerontology, The University of Tokyo,
7-3-1 Hongo, Bunkyo-ku, Tokyo 113-8656, Japan

Abstract. Nowadays, with population aging, shortage of care workers is becoming a serious problem in Japan. Therefore, the introduction of assistive technologies at nursing care sites is a measure expected to reduce the work burden of caregivers. However, there is not much knowledge of assistive technologies required for a smooth introduction yet. Thus, especially regarding monitoring sensors, our study clarified the factors of technology acceptance and their influence on nursing care sites by interview surveys to the caregivers in nursing homes. In addition, based on the findings obtained from the survey, we presented several policies for future surveys about the introduction of assistive technologies in nursing care sites.

Keywords: Adaptation · Assistive technology · Monitoring system · Seniors
Caregivers

1 Introduction

Population aging is progressing globally. This demographic movement is an almost irreversible phenomenon, and each country needs to take appropriate measures, such as an increase in social security and medical expenses. In particular, the trend is remarkable

© Springer International Publishing AG, part of Springer Nature 2018
J. Zhou and G. Salvendy (Eds.): ITAP 2018, LNCS 10926, pp. 70–84, 2018.
https://doi.org/10.1007/978-3-319-92034-4_6

in Japan. It is estimated that the aging rate will exceed 30% in 2025, and the number of elderly people is estimated to increase by more than seven million people [7]. In addition to the aging rapidly proceeding in this way, the declining birthrate is also a factor that is spurring the population decline. The declining production-age population due to the declining birthrate is pressing the review of fundamental reforms of the conventional social security system that has supported the life of the elderly after retirement.

Along with the aging society, one of the areas where measures are most needed is the care field. Elderly people who need medical care and nursing care also are expected to continue to increase, but there is a decisive seriousness of lack of caregivers. The Japanese Ministry of Health, Labor, and Welfare (MHLW) calculates that nearly 400,000 caregivers will run short by 2025 [8]. In fact, among nursing care workers, dissatisfaction is raised not only in terms of work volume, wages, and working hours, but also, because of the physical and mental burden. A survey on long-term care work in Japan, conducted in 2016, reports that as for dissatisfaction concerning the burden of working conditions and work, 53.2% said that "labor is insufficient" and "wages are low for job content" at 41.5%, "paid vacation is difficult" at 34.9%, and "the physical burden is large" at 29.9% [6]. One common background to these reasons is that work productivity is poor. Care workers must provide suitable care for each elderly person. Therefore, it is difficult for them to work efficiently, and the working environment has not been improved at nursing care sites.

One of the effective breakthroughs in this situation is the introduction of assistive technologies at nursing care sites. It is expected that these technologies will help reduce or eliminate the workload of care workers and improve productivity by helping with or substituting for care. At the same time, even for elderly people, the burden on the mind and body is reduced by reducing unnecessary care and the possibility of achieving sustainable care. The Japanese Government actively encouraged the dissemination of medical devices, including assistive devices, by revising the law in 2014.

However, the introduction of assistive technologies is still stagnant at Japanese nursing care sites. Assistive technologies are not actively used by nursing care workers. According to a questionnaire survey conducted by the MHLW, about half of the subjects did not recognize the care robot [7]. However, about a 40% "expectation for reduction of nursing-care burden by introduction" was confirmed, and it is known that there is sufficient need for assistive technologies. Under such circumstances, MHLW notes that there is a mismatch between the nursing care site and the development side. There may be a lack of knowledge for advanced assistive technologies and some prejudice in the care field. Since nursing care has been done by the hands of people than before, care workers may feel resistance to lack of physical contact. Meanwhile, as to the development side of assistive technologies, it is pointed out that the practical needs of nursing care sites are not sufficiently drawn [7]. Certainly, unless it has enough usefulness to be used in care practice, it may rather cause some danger and productivity decline. In order to improve the situation, to revitalize their communication will be necessary for the nursing care workplace and the technology development side. However, there are not many studies focusing on needs research and technology acceptance in assistive technologies. We need to advance such a study from the aspect of both quantitative and qualitative researches.

Therefore, the purpose of our research is to clarify a part of technology acceptance and user evaluation of assistive technologies at nursing care sites. For this reason, we conducted interview surveys at a nursing home that introduced specific assistive devices (targeting monitoring systems in this research) and another that have not been introduced, and compared the results. We can define a monitoring system as a device intended to prevent or detect falling of an elderly in advance, such as when getting up from bed or walking in a living room. A monitoring system having such a function is expected not only to ensure the safety of the elderly but also to contribute to the reduction of the frequent patrol in a nursing home of nursing workers. However, its introduction is not progressing. For this reason, examining cases of introducing monitoring sensors will lead to improvement of the relationship between elderly people and nursing care workers.

The main questions explored in this study are as follows:

Q1. What are the factors that achieve the acceptance of a monitoring system?
Q2. By introducing a monitoring system, how has the nursing care changed?

2 Related Work

This chapter reviews previous studies related to this research. Section 1 introduces some well-established technology acceptance models as a model for analyzing factors for accepting technology. This section especially reviews a technology acceptance model for elderly people. Section 2 reviews several user studies related to assistive technologies for elderly people. These studies focus on the usefulness and impact of assistive technologies rather than individuals using assistive technologies. Taking into account both viewpoints, this study examines a monitoring system.

2.1 Technology Acceptance Models

The technology acceptance model (TAM) [1, 2] shown in Fig. 1 is one of the basic models for explaining and predicting the factors determining user attitude towards accepting new technology. Better measures explaining the factors that influence an individual's intention to technology can encourage technology acceptance by manipulating or changing the factors. Therefore, TAM proposes essentials among these factors and shows mutual relationship among the essential factors. TAM incorporates six factors listed as follows [20]:

- External variables (EV), such as demographic variables, the influence of perceived usefulness (PU), and perceived ease of use (PEU).
- Perceived usefulness (PU) is defined as 'the extent to which a person believes that using the system will enhance his or her job performance.'
- Perceived ease of use (PEU) is 'the extent to which a person believes that using the system will be free of effort'.

- Attitudes toward use (A) is defined as 'the user's desirability of his or her using the system'. Perceived usefulness (PU) and perceived ease of use (PEU) are the sole determinants of attitude toward the technology system.
- Behavioural intention (BI) is predicted by attitude toward use (A) combined with perceived usefulness (PU).
- Actual use (AU) is predicted by behavioural intention (BI).

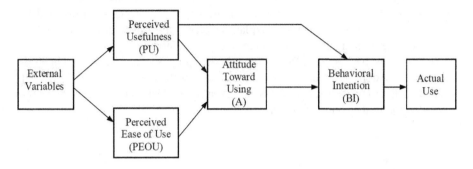

Fig. 1. Technology acceptance model (TAM) (Malhotra and Galletta 1999 [14])

It can be said that this diagram has served as a basic explanation model of technical acceptance [10, 26, 27], but some problems remain on the other hand. One of the aspects of the TAM of individuals that is not taken into consideration, is a lack of social factors in the model. Therefore, when considering such social aspects, Venkatesh et al. extended the TAM and proposed the Unified Theory of Acceptance and Use of Technology (UTAUT), which attempts to explain the behavioral intention to use technology and technology usage behavior [29].

Factors constituting the properties of UTAUT are divided into two types. The first type are the determining factors of the acceptance of technology, such as the expected performance, the expected lifespan, the social impact and the facilitating conditions. These factors directly affect the acceptance of technology and are the independent variables in the model. The second type are the individual factors, such as gender, age, experience and autonomy of use, which are the intermediary factors that affect technology acceptance. These variables are not presented as the direct factors of technology acceptance, but as the variables that indirectly influence technology acceptance through changing the former four factors as the medium. Using UTAUT that is configured in this way, Venkatesh et al. reported that it was able to explain 70% of the individual's intention to use information technology [29].

The fact that UTAUT not only included factors of social influence, but also personal factors, indicates that it is also effective in explaining the technology acceptance of specific users, who have been narrowed down in advance. This viewpoint gives the possibility of explaining the technology acceptance of seniors in particular. Various developmental models for technology acceptance by seniors have been proposed. The next section reviews such technology acceptance models for seniors.

Seniors are said to be different in personal and social aspects from others. Indeed, aging has been found to have a remarkable influence on the acceptance of technology.

For example, previous studies have reported that technology acceptance [17] and usage of new technologies [19] decrease with increasing age. While a decrease in technology interest has been reported, there are also studies reporting the importance of experience with technologies. Künemund and Tanschus report that experiences involving technology have a greater influence on technology interest than a simple age effect [12]. It has also been reported that the technical acceptance of seniors changes in each property characterizing seniors, such as physical aspects [4, 22, 24], cognitive aspects [4, 24], social aspects [13, 22], and psychological aspects [21, 32]. It has been clarified by previous studies that it is difficult to explain or predict the specificity of technology acceptance of seniors in general technology acceptance models.

Based on this background, Renaud and Biljon proposed the Senior Technology Acceptance & Adoption model for Mobile technology (STAM) shown in Fig. 2 [20]. STAM modeled the acceptance process as driven by the factors that influence mobile phone adoption in the context of elderly mobile phone users.

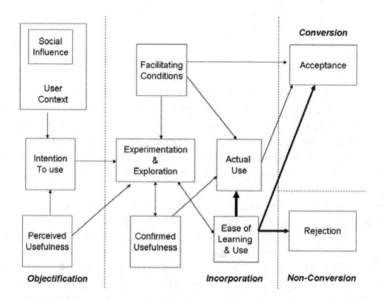

Fig. 2. Senior technology acceptance model (STAM) (Renaud and Biljon 2009) [20]

The model emphasizes the distinction between acceptance and adoption of technology. Acceptance is attitude to technology determined by various factors while adoption is a process starting with the technology and ending with the user embracing the technology and making full use of it. Based on the adoption process [13], they proposed a model that can analyze key factors that influence acceptance in each stage. In explaining technology acceptance, it is extremely important to capture adoption as another aspect. In technology engagement, people are involved whether they accept it or not in how they use it. Therefore, taking adoption into account seems to enable capturing even more practical use of technology.

For the adoption process, Renaud and Biljon rely on the technology adoption process proposed by Silverstone and Haddon [23]. Silverstone and Haddon argued that domestication is important for technology to be used in practice, and that the process leading to domestication can be analyzed in four stages. The four processes are appropriation, objectification, incorporation, and conversion, respectively, as shown in Table 1.

Table 1. Domestication adoption process dimension (Lee 2007) [13]

Dimension	Description	Examples of potential themes relevant in user experience research
Appropriation	Process of possession or ownership of the artifact	– Motivation to buy a product – Route to acquire information about a product – Experience when purchasing a product
Objectification	Process of determining roles product will play	– Meaning of a technology – What function will be used in users' life? – Where is it placed? How is it earned?
Incorporation	Process of interacting with a product	– Difficulties in using a product (usability problems) – Learning process (use of instructional manual)
Conversion	Process of converting technology to intended feature use or interaction	– Unintended use of product features – Unintended way of user interaction – Wish lists for future products

Based on this viewpoint, this study investigates acceptance and adoption of assistive technology for seniors in nursing care sites. The nursing care site is a practical site where people are in contact and interact every day. Therefore, as suggested by STAM, deepening consideration is important not only for acceptance but also for adoption at the same time.

2.2   User Study

Assistive technologies for seniors are technologies used to help the elderly with their daily problems [30]. For example, cognitive assistive equipment, the movement supporting equipment, communication robot, and so on, have been developed in addition to the monitoring system. Nelson and Dannefer reported that heterogeneity increases with age and the needs and capacity of elderly people for technology are diverse [18]. It is also known that aging causes changes in physiological and cognitive abilities and affects the ability of older people to use technology [4, 24]. These studies claim the need to appropriately know the characteristics of the relationship between the elderly and the technology.

For example, important findings have been obtained regarding communication robots. Wu et al. reported that barriers to the introduction of robots specialized in communication functions are unfamiliarity with computer technology and concern for lack of communication with people [33]. In addition, some studies have proposed concrete practical policies and development guidelines for communication robots. Wada has conducted experiments using the therapeutic robot and has developed the manual of the robot therapy for seniors [31]. Miura et al. explains the impression of the seniors' communication robot based on the difference in physical weakness through the scores on the systems' usability scale (SUS) and the interview survey [16].

In addition, equipment for seniors is also studied from the viewpoint of technology design. Kobayashi et al. show guidelines on design about the target size and the method of the initial setting of the user interface by conducting experiments on the seniors' use of touch panel devices [11].

On monitoring systems, there have been some previous research. Veer et al. revealed that adequate coaching and training are necessary for introducing technology by a questionnaire survey targeting nurses in the Netherlands [28]. Iio et al. clarified the relationship between the range of fall detection and feeling of security and the difference of intention to use between seniors living in nursing homes and other seniors from an interview survey on seniors and caregivers who actually use a fall detection monitoring system [9]. Dolničar et al. reported that monitoring sensors were accepted positively, particularly by caregivers while both the caregivers and the elderly showed a concern that the monitoring system would reduce the opportunities for visits through interview surveys conducted by actually introducing equipment in Slovenia [3].

3 Research Design

The findings of this study were obtained by comparing the results of two interview surveys. The first interview survey was conducted with the staff of Nursing Home 1 (NH1), which did not use a monitoring system, and the second interview was conducted with the staff of Nursing Home 2 (NH2), which actively used a monitoring system. The surveys for both nursing homes lasted several hours and were conducted between February and August 2017, respectively. Semi-structured interviews were adopted for the surveys.

3.1 Interview to NH1

The survey was conducted in NH1 by interviewing three caregivers. The main question of this survey was either why the monitoring sensors had not been installed in the facility, or why they had ceased to use the monitoring sensors once they had been introduced. Although there was a range of sensors, we chose to listen mainly to the functions that were common to each sensor.

NH1, which was the subject of the survey, was a relatively small facility, with almost 30 private rooms and 36 employees. Twenty-nine elderly people were present, and the average age was about 87 years old.

3.2 Interview to NH2

The survey was conducted in NH2, by interviewing one caregiver and two managers. The main question of this survey was the background of the introduction of the monitoring system, the opinion on the function of the monitoring system after introduction, and the change from the introduction to the present. The monitoring system introduced in the NH2 is a silhouette image sensor by an infrared camera that mainly aims at motion detection. The state of the care receiver is determined by a computer, which sends a silhouette image of the surroundings of the care receiver's bed at all times, from the image sensor through the wireless connection. When an action for alarm is detected from the determined state, the alarm is sent to the mobile device of the caregivers and the silhouette movie is saved before and after 10 s. The silhouette movie being taken constantly can be seen in real time from the mobile device of the caregiver.

NH2 had 120 private rooms and 45 employees, which was a relatively bigger facility than NH1. There were 41 elderly people who were present, and the average age was 87 years old.

The transition on use of the monitoring system in NH2 from the introduction was as follows. Through several adjustments, NH2 was able to fix the practical use of the monitoring system. Figure 3 shows the approach in chronological order.

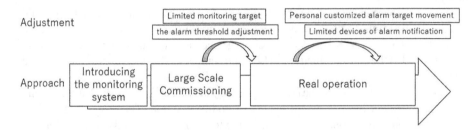

Fig. 3. The transition from the introduction of the monitoring system

4   Findings

In this chapter, we show the results of interview surveys to Nursing Home 1 (NH1), where monitoring systems have not been installed, and Nursing Home 2 (NH2), where monitoring systems have already been installed. Each interviewee had a lot of various answers, but we show the difference between NH1 and NH2 based on three major points: correspondence to alarm notification, difference in the concept of privacy, and visualization of life rhythm as an unexpected effect.

4.1   Settings of Alarm Notification

When a monitoring sensor detects the elderly person falling and getting up, the system will alarm the caregiver. The caregiver will receive the notification through the tablet at hand and can check the situation of the elderly person. The interview surveys found that notification through an alarm created difficulties common to both sides.

In the survey for NH1, we found some negative opinions about the monitoring system. One of their concerns was stress caused by the alarm. NH1 had installed a monitoring system before, but there were many false alarms due to slight body movements by the elderly. Thus, the NH1 staff had to go to the elderly's room every time the alarm sent notification. Such a situation increased the number of visits and their psychological stress. It confirmed the paradox that the technology that should originally have reduced the work of caregivers would rather increase it.

Such a situation was confirmed in NH2. NH2 also originally installed monitoring systems in order to reduce the number of patrols at night, but the staff said that the installation caused confusion due to too many alerts. In the case of NH2, however, they could successfully solve such problems by dealing with them. NH2 collaborated with the developer side and could successfully renovate the system.

One of their ideas was to limit the target. The necessity of assistive technologies changes greatly depending on the bodily abilities of the elderly. In other words, measures such as introducing them collectively for all rooms of the nursing home will not only increase the amount of work but also cause unnecessary expenses. Initially, NH2 introduced monitoring sensors for all rooms on a trial basis, but now, only the room for the elderly suffering from dementia is equipped with the sensors. This may reduce the risk of injury.

Furthermore, NH2 changed the detecting system based on each target. They could change the function of the monitoring system according to the elderly by limiting the target. It enabled the sensor to detect each stage such as when the elderly sit up in bed, sits at the end of the bed and stands up. This contrivance can decrease the staff's workload greatly.

These results suggest that the personal adaptation of technology is needed. In nursing care, each resident has a different degree of bodily function. Therefore, it should be needed to change functional settings according to each person. In this case, uniformity of functions may lead to increase the risk of injury and workload.

4.2 Privacy

As to the installation of the monitoring sensor, we should consider about the privacy [15, 34]. Its function of monitoring the target may hinder his/her privacy, so the elderly do not have a good impression on the system. Even in the field of nursing care, the behavior of residents is always detected by the camera and thus the elderly cannot escape from the camera as long as they are in the room. These ethical resistances to the system have been shared among people.

The same situation was also confirmed in NH1 where monitoring systems have not been installed. NH1 staff said they wanted to minimize the use of monitoring systems basically because they thought that the use of them was a deterrence to residents. They also suggested that installing monitoring sensors might indirectly narrow the possibility of residents' behavior. As Townsend, Knoefel, and Goubran report [25], they also have a concept of a trade-off between safety and privacy given by the monitoring sensor.

On the other hand, in NH2, we did not find such trade-off scheme at all. Surprisingly, NH2 staff said that the privacy of residents was reversely secured when they introduced monitoring sensors. Since they could control the monitoring system, NH2 staff successfully reduced the number of patrol. The staff said that this ingenuity increased the private time for residents. Nursing care leads to some mental diseases not only for caregivers, but also, for the elderly. The installation of the monitoring systems reduced caregiver's unnecessary assistance, so the elderly might have a sense of rest. This result is partially consistent with the survey conducted by Dolničarr et al. [3], but NH2 staff have no fear of decreasing the number of visits.

Considering the answers by NH2, the problem is not a trade-off between safety and privacy, but a trade-off between gaze and contact on privacy inhibition. The monitoring sensor might cause a hindrance of privacy, but at the same time, it contributes to reducing direct interpersonal contact. NH2 staff found positive aspects of monitoring sensors.

It seems that the way of thinking about privacy and the unexpected effect of the monitoring systems are found in the consistent use of them by NH2 staff. It should be noted that this fact was not found at the interview with NH1 staff. They did not notice the positive effect of monitoring sensors, which brought not only unnecessary work but also invasion of the elderly's privacy. NH2 staffs said that reducing staff's work volume is the result of securing residents' privacy. The function of the monitoring sensor is not only to detect dangerous behaviors of residents.

As we use certain technology constantly, sometimes, we can find it has some unexpected functions. Of course, we cannot find whether the function will have a positive or a negative effect, but these results suggest that it is important for technology acceptance in practical situations. Nursing care also has many practical and interactive scenes. Caregivers and the elderly keep in touch with each other on a daily basis; thus, assistive technologies that mediate between them might have an unexpected result. Considering this situation, we should take these side effects into consideration when we develop a new device.

4.3 Visualization of Life Rhythm

As another unexpected effect, one more thing can be mentioned. According to NH2 staff, they are currently using the image of the room recorded by the monitoring sensors to accurately grasp residents' lifestyles and ADL. The monitoring sensor introduced in NH2 has the function of recording for 10 s before and after a specific operation is detected. Initially, this function was incorporated in order to examine the cause of the fall afterward. However, in addition to that, the NH2 staff saw this video from another perspective and helped to objectively grasp the behaviors of residents. By virtue of the accurate understanding of the life rhythm and physical ability of the residents, which they could only know subjectively until now, it has become possible to provide more appropriate personal assistance.

NH2 staff pointed out that they were able to improve the excretion QOL of residents by carefully grasping their life rhythm. When the elderly excrete by themselves, they must do such movements as sitting up and rising, and the monitoring sensor detects the situation. As intended usage, it would have been within the extent that caregivers remotely confirm the appearance on the tablet. However, the NH2 staff became aware of the timing of the overall excretion of the day through the alarm and the appearance of an image. As a result, it became possible to go to the room when the residents were needing to excrete, and safe and efficient assistance became possible.

On the other hand, the motion pictures of the monitoring sensors also proved to contribute to the proper grasp of ADL or physical ability of the residents. The NH2 staff said that there are occasions when they assisted the elderly more than was necessary, and that it is difficult to assist them appropriately. Unnecessary nursing care interferes with the elderly exerting their own physical functions, and this may result in them becoming weaker. The monitoring system solved such dilemmas. By viewing the motion pictures of residents' movements, it became possible for caregivers to understand their appropriate need for assistance. NH2 staffs said that there were some residents who took an active action that they would not have expected at all. In other words, the monitoring system has the potential to lead to an improvement in the physical functions of the elderly.

The practice of daily care by caregivers included these potential functions. It may be difficult for technology developers to anticipate multiple functions that the monitoring system can have in the development stage. The interview survey conducted by this research suggests that technology should be developed in collaboration with caregivers and that technology acceptance will be completed when the communication is successful.

5   Discussion

In this chapter, we would like to add some implications in the context of technology acceptance from findings mentioned above. Due to the nature of the survey, this research was not carried out based on the series of TAMs mentioned in Sect. 2. It was found that the application of these models was not successful because of the specificity of the nursing care. These facts seem to lead to the improvement of TAMs and a contribution to user study.

5.1   Correlation Between Caregivers and Elderly People in Technology Acceptance

One of the factors of difficulty in applying TAMs is that in the nursing care field, technology acceptance is never done by one person but can be accomplished in the interaction between caregivers and elderly people. As assistive technologies are used by humans and for humans, uncertainty increases, and further flexibility is required of them. Even if they are accepted by caregivers, if incompatibilities arise due to the physical or mental attributes of the elderly people who are cared for, practical use does not go well. Sometimes it can also cause fatal danger. In nursing care sites where safety is required, assistive technologies must be designed for each elderly person. At the same time, assistive technologies must also contribute to the efficiency of the caregiver's work. Instead, even though it is optimized for the elderly, if it increases the workload of nursing care workers, problems such as shortage of personnel and job separation can be caused.

The problem concerning the setting of the alarm indicated by our research reflects such a correlation. Our study revealed that technology acceptance was achieved through personal adaptation of alarm detection and decrease of work volume. Even in previous studies, both aspects have been pointed out separately. The survey of the fall detection monitoring sensors for the elderly in the nursing home by Iio revealed the relationship between accuracy of the detection and safety in nursing care [9]. A survey of nurses who work at a medical and welfare center in the Netherlands conducted by Veer et al. [28] pointed out that proper coaching and training on the use of technology is necessary. Thus, these studies suggest that technology acceptance should be considered from both sides of the subject and object simultaneously.

The previous models, such as TAM, targeted individuals exclusively. Attributes of others who interact with him or her are merely considered as social aspects of him or her or factors on the usefulness of technology. However, at nursing care sites, the attributes of both caregivers and the elderly are equally important, and the usefulness of technology and technology acceptance are closely linked in the correlation. Therefore, to construct a model that predicts the introduction of assistive technologies at a nursing care site, it is necessary to think about schemes that put these two attributes and relationships in range.

5.2 Finding Potential Usages by Users

Second, the findings of our study suggest that continued practice may result in discovery of new functions of technology. The interview survey revealed that the monitoring system contributes to securing privacy in another way and that it is also helping to improve QOL and ADL by grasping appropriate life rhythm and physical abilities, which is the function and effect discovered in daily practical use by caregivers. This aspect has affinity with cases indicated by Forlizzi and DiSalvo [5]. They pointed out that practical use of the cleaning robot changed user and family behavior and emphasized the importance of grasping how human interaction with robot has changed. Our study makes the same conclusion. Particularly in nursing care sites, the relationship between caregivers and the elderly is so close that it seems that the long-term impact of assistive technologies on them cannot be missed.

These points are not related to technology acceptance, but technology adoption emphasized by Renaud and Biljon [20]. In proposing STAM, they presume stepwise changes in how to engage with technology. In the process of Objectification to Incorporation and (Non-)Conversion, a notion that technology acceptance is not only understood by mere attitude, but decided in the practical use of technology is assumed. As mentioned above, the interview survey conducted by our study also confirmed the gradual change of technology adoption.

However, the potential use of monitoring systems by caregivers revealed by our study cannot be described as Conversion. NH2 staff keep using the primary usage at the development stage while using another method at the same time. Such a fact can be said to be Diversification rather than Conversion. Diversification of usage shows that the Adoption Process is never a single track; it may be a multi-track structure. Based on these findings, the technology adoption process may need to be refreshed.

It seems that further research is necessary to determine if the suggestions described above only remain in the specificity of nursing care facilities subject to this interview survey. From now on, an investigation into such viewpoints will also be required in other areas.

6 Limitation

In our study, interviews were only conducted with caregivers, and not with the elderly. Although it is difficult to conduct interviews with the elderly, because of their physical or mental weakness, it is necessary to collect their direct opinions on assistive technologies. It is our intention to change the nature of the interviewees in our future research.

7 Conclusion

This study investigated the possibility of introducing assistive technologies in nursing homes. Through the interview surveys, we established what the barriers are to introduction of monitoring systems, as well as the actual practical effects of doing so. The main contribution of our research was to clarify the specificity of technology acceptance and technology adoption at the nursing care sites. The discovery of the correlation between the caregiver and the elderly in terms of technology acceptance may lead to the further improvement of TAM for assistive technologies. In addition, the potential usage found in nursing care sites explains the phase of conversion to the technology adoption process, in detail. The results suggest that the construction of more appropriate models is required in the future.

Acknowledgements. We are very grateful to the two nursing homes that cooperated with us in conducting our interview surveys. Also, this study is based on work supported by the JSPS Program for Leading Graduate Schools (Graduate Program in Gerontology, Global Leadership Initiative for an Age Friendly Society, The University of Tokyo).

References

1. Davis, F.D.: Perceived usefulness, perceived ease of use, and user acceptance of information technology. MIS Q. **13**(3), 319–340 (1989). http://www.jstor.org/stable/249008
2. Davis, F.D., Bagozzi, R.P., Warshaw, P.R.: User acceptance of computer technology: a comparison of two theoretical models. Manag. Sci. **35**(8), 982–1003 (1989). https://doi.org/10.1287/mnsc.35.8.982
3. Dolničar, V., Petrovčič, A., Šetinc, M., Košir, I., Kavčič, M.: Understanding acceptance factors for using e-care systems and devices: insights from a mixed-method intervention study in Slovenia. In: Zhou, J., Salvendy, G. (eds.) ITAP 2017. LNCS, vol. 10298, pp. 362–377. Springer, Cham (2017). https://doi.org/10.1007/978-3-319-58536-9_29
4. Farage, M.A., Miller, K.W.: Design principles to accommodate older adults. Glob. J. Health Sci. **4**(2), 2–25 (2012)
5. Forlizzi, J., DiSalvo, C.: Service robots in the domestic environment: a study of the roomba vacuum in the home. In: Proceedings of the 1st ACM SIGCHI/SIGART Conference on Human-Robot Interaction, HRI 2006, pp. 258–265. ACM, New York (2006) http://doi.acm.org/10.1145/1121241.1121286
6. Foundation, C.W.: Heisei 28 nend "kaigo roudou jittai chousa" no kekka (results of 2017's survey of nursing care labor survey) (4th Aug 2017), 18 February 2018. http://www.kaigo-center.or.jp/report/pdf/h28_chousa_kekka.pdf

7. The Japanese Ministry of Health, Labour and Welfare: Fukushi yougu kaigo robotto kaihatsu no tebiki (guideline for development of welfare equipment and nursing care robot) (2014)

8. The Japanese Ministry of Health, Labour and Welfare: 2025 nen ni muketa kaigo jinzai ni kakaru jukyuu suikei (kakutei chi) ni tsuite (on supply demand estimate (fixed value) for care workers for 2025) (24th June 2015), 18 February 2018. http://www.mhlw.go.jp/file/04-Houdouhappyou-12004000-Shakaiengokyoku-Shakai-Fukushikibanka/270624houdou.pdf _2.pdf

9. Iio, T., Shiomi, M., Kamei, K., Sharma, C., Hagita, N.: Social acceptance by senior citizens and caregivers of a fall detection system using range sensors in a nursing home. Adv. Robot. **30**(3), 190–205 (2016). https://doi.org/10.1080/01691864.2015.1120241

10. King, W.R., He, J.: A meta-analysis of the technology acceptance model. Inf. Manag. **43**(6), 740–755 (2006). http://www.sciencedirect.com/science/article/pii/S0378720606000528

11. Kobayashi, M., Hiyama, A., Miura, T., Asakawa, C., Hirose, M., Ifukube, T.: Elderly user evaluation of mobile touchscreen interactions. In: Campos, P., Graham, N., Jorge, J., Nunes, N., Palanque, P., Winckler, M. (eds.) INTERACT 2011. LNCS, vol. 6946, pp. 83–99. Springer, Heidelberg (2011). https://doi.org/10.1007/978-3-642-23774-4_9

12. Künemund, H., Tanschus, N.M.: The technology acceptance puzzle. Zeitschrift für Gerontologie und Geriatrie **47**(8), 641–647 (2014). https://doi.org/10.1007/s00391-014-0830-7

13. Lee, Y.S.: Older adults' user experience with mobile phones: identification of user clusters and user requirements. Ph.D. thesis, Virginia Polytechnic Institute and State University (2007)

14. Malhotra, Y., Galletta, D.F.: Extending the technology acceptance model to account for social influence: theoretical bases and empirical validation. In: 1999 Proceedings of the 32nd Annual Hawaii International Conference on Systems Sciences, HICSS-32. Abstracts and CD-ROM of Full Papers, vol. 1, 14 p., January 1999

15. Mittelstadt, B., Fairweather, N.B., Mcbride, N., Shaw, M.: Ethical issues of personal health monitoring: a literature review, pp. 313–321, January 2011

16. Miura, T., Goto, T., Kaneko, K., Sumikawa, Y., Ishii, A., Doke, M., Suzuki, K., Okatani, T., Kubota, A., Zhang, M., Kinoshita, Y., Yoshinaga, H., Tsuruta, M., Kominami, Y., Nihei, M., Inoue, T., Kamata, M., Okata, J.: Need and impressions of communication robots for seniors with slight physical and cognitive disabilities: evaluation using system usability scale. In: 2016 IEEE International Conference on Systems, Man, and Cybernetics (SMC), pp. 004088–004092, October 2016

17. Morris, M.G., Venkatesh, V.: Age differences in technology adoption decisions: implications for a changing work force. Pers. Psychol. **53**(2), 375–403 (2000). https://doi.org/10.1111/j.1744-6570.2000.tb00206.x

18. Nelson, E.A., Dannefer, D.: Aged heterogeneity: fact or fiction? The fate of diversity in gerontological research. Gerontologist **32**(1), 17–23 (1992). https://doi.org/10.1093/geront/32.1.17

19. Peacock, S.E., Künemund, H.: Senior citizens and internet technology. Eur. J. Ageing **4**(4), 191–200 (2007). https://doi.org/10.1007/s10433-007-0067-z

20. Renaud, K., van Biljon, J.: Predicting technology acceptance and adoption by the elderly: a qualitative study. In: Proceedings of the 2008 Annual Research Conference of the South African Institute of Computer Scientists and Information Technologists on IT Research in Developing Countries: Riding the Wave of Technology, SAICSIT 2008, pp. 210–219. ACM, New York (2008). http://doi.acm.org/10.1145/1456659.1456684

21. Ryu, M.H., Kim, S., Lee, E.: Understanding the factors affecting online elderly user's participation in video UCC services. Comput. Hum. Behav. **25**(3), 619–632 (2009). http://www.sciencedirect.com/science/article/pii/S0747563208001696, including the Special Issue: Enabling elderly users to create and share self authored multimedia content

22. Mallenius, S., Rossi, R., Tuunainen, V.K.: Factors affecting the adoption and use of mobile devices and services by elderly people-results from a pilot study. Ann. Glob. Mobility Roundtable **31**, 12 (2007)
23. Silverstone, R., Haddon, L.: Design and the domestication of information and communication technologies: technical change and everyday life. In: Communication by Design: The Politics of Information and Communication Technologies, pp. 44–74. Oxford University Press (1996)
24. Tenneti, R., Johnson, D., Goldenberg, L., Parker, R.A., Huppert, F.A.: Towards a capabilities database to inform inclusive design: Experimental investigation of effective survey-based predictors of human-product interaction. Appl. Ergon. **43**(4), 713–726 (2012). http://www.sciencedirect.com/science/article/pii/S0003687011001700
25. Townsend, D., Knoefel, F., Goubran, R.: Privacy versus autonomy: a tradeoff model for smart home monitoring technologies. In: 2011 Annual International Conference of the IEEE Engineering in Medicine and Biology Society, pp. 4749–4752, August 2011
26. Turner, M., Kitchenham, B., Brereton, P., Charters, S., Budgen, D.: Does the technology acceptance model predict actual use? A systematic literature review. Inf. Softw. Technol. **52**(5), 463–479 (2010). http://www.sciencedirect.com/science/article/pii/S095058490 9002055. TAIC-PART 2008
27. Šumak, B., Heričko, M., Pušnik, M.: A meta-analysis of e-learning technology acceptance: the role of user types and e-learning technology types. Comput. Hum. Behav. **27**(6), 2067–2077 (2011). http://www.sciencedirect.com/science/article/pii/S0747563211001609
28. de Veer, A.J., Fleuren, M.A., Bekkema, N., Francke, A.L.: Successful implementation of new technologies in nursing care: a questionnaire survey of nurse-users. BMC Med. Inf. Dec. Making **11**(1), 67 (2011). https://doi.org/10.1186/1472-6947-11-67
29. Venkatesh, V., Morris, M.G., Davis, G.B., Davis, F.D.: User acceptance of information technology: toward a unified view. MIS Q. **27**(3), 425–478 (2003). http://www.jstor.org/stable/30036540
30. Vichitvanichphong, S., Talaei-Khoei, A., Kerr, D., Ghapanchi, A.H.: Adoption of assistive technologies for aged care: a realist review of recent studies. In: 2014 47th Hawaii International Conference on System Sciences, pp. 2706–2715, January 2014
31. Wada, K., Ikeda, Y., Inoue, K., Uehara, R.: Development and preliminary evaluation of a caregiver's manual for robot therapy using the therapeutic seal robot Paro. In: 19th International Symposium in Robot and Human Interactive Communication, pp. 533–538, September 2010
32. Werner, J.M., Carlson, M., Jordan-Marsh, M., Clark, F.: Predictors of computer use in community-dwelling, ethnically diverse older adults. Hum. Factors **53**(5), 431–447 (2011). https://doi.org/10.1177/0018720811420840. PMID: 22046718
33. Wu, Y.H., Wrobel, J., Cornuet, M., Kerhervé, H., Damnée, S., Rigaud, A.S.: Acceptance of an assistive robot in older adults : a mixed-method study of human-robot interaction over a 1-month period in the Living Lab setting. Clin. Interv. Aging **9**, 801–811 (2014)
34. Yusif, S., Soar, J., Hafeez-Baig, A.: Older people, assistive technologies, and the barriers to adoption: a systematic review. Int. J. Med. Inf. **94**, 112–116 (2016). http://www.sciencedirect.com/science/article/pii/S1386505616301551

Older People and Technology Acceptance

Blanka Klimova[✉] and Petra Poulova

University of Hradec Kralove, Rokitanskeho 62, 500 03 Hradec Kralove 3, Czech Republic
{blanka.klimova,petra.poulova}@uhk.cz

Abstract. Currently, the number of people at the age of 65+ is rising at frenetic pace. For instance, in developed countries, the number of older adults forms 24% and this number should rise to 33% by 2050. Therefore, there is a need to prolong an active life of older people, who want to lead active, fulfilling and quality life in a sense of their inclusion, socialization and independence. This can be achieved not only by continuous support from their family members, but current trends show an important role of information and communication technologies (ICT) in this process. The purpose of this study is to explore technology acceptance models, as well as the factors influencing the acceptance of technologies by older people, such as the key demographic characteristics (i.e., age or education), which can accelerate or slow down their acceptance of ICT devices. The methods used in this study include a method of literature review of available sources exploring the acceptance of ICT devices by older people, a method of comparison and evaluation of the findings from the selected studies on this topic. The findings of the reviewed research studies indicate that the presented four theoretical models provide sound theoretical bases for potential empirical studies exploring the acceptance and use of technologies by older people. However, more attention should be paid to their support in the form of training, as well as meeting their unique personal needs. Future research should focus on the acceptance and use of mobile devices and their effectiveness on the improvement of quality of life of older generation groups.

Keywords: Older people · Technological devices · Acceptance · Models · Factors
Benefits · Limitations

1 Introduction

Ageing is becoming a big social issue nowadays. In 2000, the number of people at the age of 65+ in the world reached 12.4% and this number is expected to grow to 19% by 2030 [1]. In developed countries, this number of older adults forms 24% and it should rise to 33% by 2050 [2]. In Europe the population group aged 65+ represents 18% of the 503 million Europeans, which should almost double by 2060 [3]. Therefore, there is a need to prolong an active life of older people, who want to lead active, fulfilling and quality life in a sense of their inclusion, socialization and independence. This can be achieved not only by continuous support from their family members, but current trends show an important role of information and communication technologies (ICT) in this process. These ICT devices can promote autonomy of older people by facilitating the

© Springer International Publishing AG, part of Springer Nature 2018
J. Zhou and G. Salvendy (Eds.): ITAP 2018, LNCS 10926, pp. 85–94, 2018.
https://doi.org/10.1007/978-3-319-92034-4_7

execution of many routine activities, such as shopping or communication. Their use also offers cognitively and intellectually challenging activities that can empower older people. Thus, the use of ICT devices can maintain them independent, active and socially inclusive. In fact, there are certain prerequisites, which can trigger their use and acceptance by older people. These include a steady rise in the number of older people worldwide, ICT as a tool for providing older people with the promise of greater independence, and the fact that the generation of baby boomers approaching retirement is relatively comfortable using ICT [4].

As research shows, older people are nowadays more digitally literate, especially those parents of baby boomers, and 80% of them have access to the Internet [4–6]. Furthermore, there is an increasing number of those older individuals who own and use mobile devices, such as a mobile phone. For instance, 78% of older people at the age of 65+ own a mobile phone in the USA, as well as in the UK [7, 8]. In the Czech Republic, it is 91% [9]. In fact, currently mobile devices seems to be more exploited than the desktop computers [10].

The purpose of this study is to explore technology acceptance models, as well as the factors influencing the acceptance of technologies by older people, such as the key demographic characteristics (i.e., age or education), which can accelerate or slow down their acceptance of ICT devices. In addition, the authors aim at emphasizing the main benefits and limitations of technology acceptance by this group of people.

2   Methods

The methods used in this study include a method of literature review of available sources exploring the acceptance of ICT devices by older people, a method of comparison and evaluation of the findings from the selected studies on this topic, as well as the discussion of the findings from the authors' own empirical studies on this research topic. The literature search was conducted in the acknowledged databases Web of Science, Scopus, and ScienceDirect. Altogether over 36,000 articles were generated from all three databases where the key words *older people* AND *technology acceptance* were inserted. Nevertheless, only few related to the research topic.

For example, in the Web of Science 167 articles were found. The first one appeared already in 1996. However, most of the articles on the research issue started to be published after 2010 as Fig. 1 below illustrates. The topic of the majority of studies relates to health monitoring and assisted living technologies. This is not surprising since older people are mainly concerned at this age in maintaining their health conditions. The number of articles on the pure exploration of older people and their acceptance of technologies was relatively scarce.

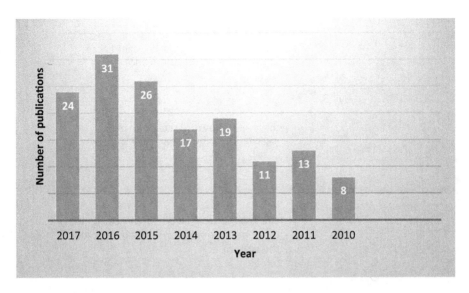

Fig. 1. An overview of the number of publications on the research topic in the Web of Science, authors' own processing based on the data from the Web of Science [11].

3   Findings and Discussion

The research on the acceptance of technologies by older people firstly concerns the exploration of the existing models describing successful acceptance of technological devices by older individuals. Overall, there are four models. The first, original one is the Technology Acceptance Model (TAM) developed by Davis in 1989 [12]. This model is based on two basic constructs: perceived usefulness (i.e., the level to which an individual reckons that exploiting a particular system would improve his or her job performance) and perceived ease of use (i.e., the level to which an individual reckons that exploiting a particular system would cause smaller effort). Thus, if the individual believes that the technological devices is useful and s/he can use it independently, s/he will develop a positive attitude and his/her behavior will lead to the adoption of such a technological device. On the contrary, if his/her personal needs are not satisfied, s/he will reject it.

The second model, which is based on TAM, is the so-called Unified Theory of Acceptance and Use of Technology (UTAUT) model, developed in 2003 by Venkantesh et al. [13]. This model consists of four basic constructs determining person's behavioral intention to exploit the system and his/her usage behavior (Fig. 2 below).

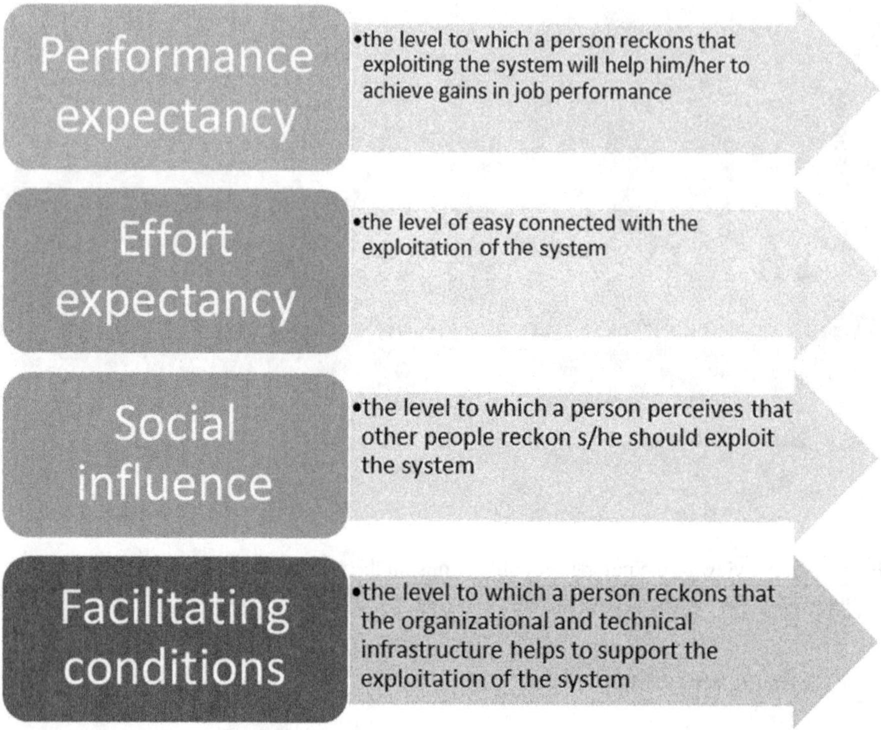

Fig. 2. Unified Theory of Acceptance and Use of Technology (UTAUT) model (authors' own processing).

The extent to which each key construct influences the user's intention to use the technological device is influenced by four factors, which are as follows: gender, age, experience, and voluntariness of use [14]. The functionality of this model in practice has been recently evidenced by Macedo [15], who applied this model with 278 Portuguese older adults. Especially behavioral intention appeared to be significantly effective on determining the actual use of technological devices.

The third model, based on TAM and UTAUT, is the Senior Technology Acceptance Model (STAM), aimed particularly at older generation groups [16, 17]. This model was developed by Renaud and Van Biljon in 2008 [16]. It consists of three stages: objectification (i.e., the intention to exploit the technological device, to see whether it is useful and easy to use or not); incorporation (i.e., further exploration and experimentation with the technological device); and conversion (i.e., either accept or reject the technology on the basis of real life experience).

The fourth model, developed by Kim et al. [14] in 2016, includes the key elements of all three prior models, but incorporates another four new components; one more stage - intention to learn, including three new factors: self-efficacy (i.e., the level to which a person thinks s/he is able to do the task), conversion readiness (i.e., ability to accept a new device), and peer support (i.e., people in his/her surrounding having experience with the new technology). Figure 3 below illustrates this model.

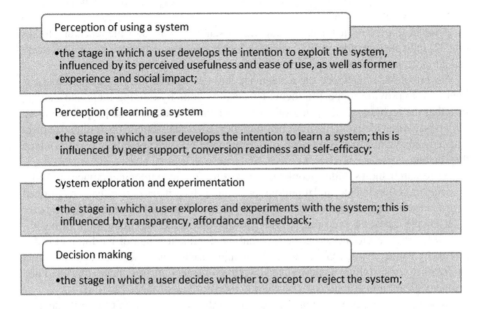

Fig. 3. Technology acceptance model for older adults (authors' own processing).

Thus, there are altogether four stages/phases leading to the acceptance or rejection of a technological device. As it has been already pointed out, there are also several factors determining and facilitating indirectly and directly the acceptance of technologies by older people. Peek et al. [18] group them into six categories:

1. concerns regarding technology (e.g., high costs or privacy implications and usability);
2. expected benefits of technology (e.g., improved safety and perceived usefulness);
3. need for technology (e.g., healthcare reasons);
4. alternatives to technology (i.e., family members can help and substitute the technology);
5. social impact (i.e., communication with friends or family members);
6. characteristics of older adults (i.e., they wish to age in their homes, in the environment where they feel comfortable and safe).

These categories/topics are also discussed by Chen and Chan in their study on gerontechnology acceptance by elderly in Honk Kong [19].

The most decisive factor for the technology acceptance by older people seems to be the age. According to this criterion, seniors can be divided into three age groups: 55–64 years, 65–74 years, and 75+ years. Seniors aged 55–64 years are usually parents of the baby boomers. They are well-educated older individuals with desire to socialize and a love for active lifestyles. Their income is also quite favorable. Even in their retirement they are eager to pursue education, either formally or informally [20]. The use of technological devices dramatically declines at the age of 75 years, when older people start to be affected by cognitive and physical impairments [20, 21]. This finding has been also confirmed by authors' study [9].

Another important factor is an educational status. Findings of the research studies [20, 22] indicate that older individuals with higher education are more willing to accept and adopt technological devices than those with lower education.

Nevertheless, to enhance the acceptance and use of technologies by seniors, it is important to provide support to them. This can be done by training them and making sure that the technological device suits their personal needs and age [23]. Righi et al. [24] expands that technologies designed for older individuals should be designed to meet situated and dynamic needs/interests of the communities (and not only of care) to which they belong.

As research shows, older people accept and use the technological devices in order to socialize, communicate, and monitor their health [9]. As it has been already mentioned in the part on Methods, research studies on the use of health-related technologies for older people are quite widespread. Older people are in fact the main users of health-related Internet services despite the fact that the dominant group of the Internet use is formed by young people [25]. They predominantly use technological devices, including the Internet, for searching health-related information, receiving reminders for scheduled visits, medication instructions, or consulting a doctor at a distance [26–28].

In addition, there is an increasing trend towards the exploitation of mobile devices by older generation [7, 29]. In fact, surveys, e.g., [9, 10] report that mobile and tablet internet usage exceeds desktop computers. Some of the seniors even use a smartphone, but the number of these people is still very low. The reasons include a number of constraints [22, 30–32]. Figure 4 below illustrates these barriers.

Therefore, the designers of technological devices aimed at older people should bear in mind the following principles:

- vision and hearing of the elderly people (e.g., suitable font size, usually bigger than 16 pixels, contrast ratios with text, or provision of subtitles when video or audio content is fundamental to the user experience);
- motor control (e.g., bigger buttons at least 9.6 mm or bigger screen device);
- device use (user-friendly);
- relationships (e.g., enable connection with a smaller, but a more important group of people such as their family members and friends);
- cognitive capacities of the elderly (e.g., provision of services such as reminders and alerts as cues for habitual actions) [33].

However, older people should be systematically made aware of the benefits of technological devices because they can provide them with a number of benefits such as reduction of travel costs (i.e., they do not inevitably have to see their doctor face-to-face if they need, for example, a prescription or some professional consultation); avoidance of social isolation (i.e., technological devices can enable them easier communication with their family members or friends and thus avoid their loneliness); decrease reduction of pressure on (family) caregivers; maintenance of their independence in executing tasks of daily life; or enhancement of feeling of safety [34–37]. On the contrary, of course, there are certain limitations and barriers preventing older people from accepting new technological devices (cf. [38]). Table 1 below summarizes the main benefits and limitations of the acceptance and use of technological devices by older people.

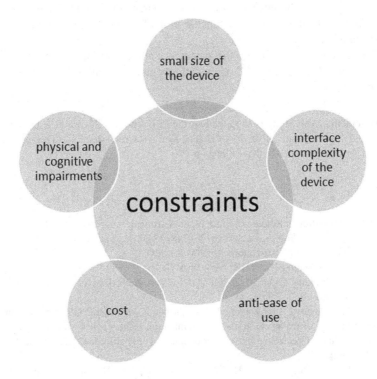

Fig. 4. Constraints of a technological device for older individuals (authors' own processing).

Table 1. Main benefits and limitations of the acceptance and use of technological devices by older people (authors' own processing).

Benefits	Limitations
• maintenance of independence and aging in place	• certain technological constraints of the devices
• reduction of economic and social burden	• physical and cognitive impairments of this group of people
• enhancement of feelings of safety	• cost of the device
• health-related services and control	• a lack of training
• reduction of social isolation	• a lack of the awareness of the benefits of the use of the device
	• stigma of using an assistive technological device
	• a lack of intention to learn
	• security and reliability concerns

4 Conclusion

The findings of the reviewed research studies indicate that the presented four theoretical models provide satisfying theoretical bases for potential empirical studies exploring the acceptance and use of technologies by older people, such as [15] or [17]. However, more attention should be paid to their support in the form of training, as well as meeting their unique personal needs.

Future research should focus on the acceptance and use of mobile devices, such as smartphones, and their effectiveness on the improvement of quality of life of these older generation groups.

Acknowledgements. This study is supported by the SPEV project 2018, run at the Faculty of Informatics and Management, University of Hradec Kralove, Czech Republic. The authors thank Josef Toman for his help with the data collection.

References

1. Vafa, K.: Census Bureau Releases Demographic Estimates and Projections for Countries of the World (2016). http://blogs.census.gov/2012/06/27/census-bureau-releases-demographic-estimates-and-projections-for-countries-of-the-world/
2. World Population Ageing 2013. UN, New York (2013)
3. Petterson, I.: Growing Older: Tourism and Leisure Behaviour of Older Adults. Cabi, Cambridge (2006)
4. Klimova, B., Simonova, I., Poulova, P., Truhlarova, Z., Kuca, K.: Older people and their attitude to the use of information and communication technologies – a review study with special focus on the Czech Republic (Older people and their attitude to ICT). Educ. Gerontol. **42**(5), 361–369 (2016)
5. Wu, Y.H., Damnee, S., Kerherve, H., Ware, C., Rigaud, A.S.: Bridging the digital divide in older adults: a study from an initiative to inform older adults about new technologies. Clin. Interv. Aging **10**, 193–201 (2015)
6. Heart, T., Kalderon, E.: Older adults: are they ready to adopt health-related ICT? Int. J. Med. Inform. **82**, e209–e231 (2013)
7. Pew Research Center: The Demographics of Device Ownership (2015). http://www.pewinternet.org/2015/10/29/the-demographics-of-device-ownership/
8. Adults' Media Use and Attitudes Report 2014 (2014). http://stakeholders.ofcom.org.uk/market-data-research/other/research-publications/adults/adults-media-lit-14/
9. Šimonová, I., Klímová, B., Poulová, P., Pražák, P.: The use of ICT devices by older people with a special focus on their type and respondents' age – a Czech case study. Educ. Gerontol. **43**(12), 641–649 (2017)
10. StatCounter: Mobile and Tablet Internet Usage Exceeds Desktop for First Time Worldwide (2016). http://gs.statcounter.com/press/mobile-and-tablet-internet-usage-exceeds-desktop-for-first-time-worldwide
11. Web of Science (2017). http://apps.webofknowledge.com/Search.do?product=WOS&SID=C2TMWq9F8rnnGhDVkIU&search_mode=GeneralSearch&prID=da7f67df-a1b9-4a62-b29d-93c351c42a43
12. Davis, F.D.: Perceived usefulness, perceived ease of use, and user acceptance of information technology. MIS Q. **13**, 319–340 (1989)

13. Venkatesh, V., Morris, M.G., Davis, G.B., Davis, F.D.: User acceptance of information technology: toward a unified view. MIS Q. **27**, 425–478 (2003)
14. Kim, S., Gajos, K.Z., Muller, M., Grosz, B.J.: Acceptance of mobile technology by older adults: a preliminary study. In: Proceedings of MobileHCI 2016, pp. 1–11. ACM, Florence (2016)
15. Macedo, I.M.: Predicting the acceptance and use of information and communication technology by older adults: an empirical examination of the revised UTAUT2. Comput. Hum. Behav. **75**, 935–948 (2017)
16. Renaud, K., Van Biljon, J.: Predicting technology acceptance and adoption by the elderly: a qualitative study. In: Proceedings of the 2008 Annual Research Conference of the South African Institute of Computer Scientists and Information Technologists on IT Research in Developing Countries: Riding the Wave of Technology, pp. 210–219. ACM (2008)
17. Shonhardt, C.: Older Adults and Technology: Adoption and Acceptance Comes from Relationships and Encouragement from Younger Generations (2017). https://scholarworks.bgsu.edu/cgi/viewcontent.cgi?article=1019&context=oagec
18. Peek, S.T.M., Wouters, E.J.M., van Hoof, J., Luijkx, K.G., Boeije, H.R., Vrijhoef, H.J.M.: Factors influencing acceptance of technology for aging in place: a systematic review. Int. J. Med. Inform. **83**(4), 235–348 (2014)
19. Chen, K., Chan, A.H.S.: Gerontechnology acceptance by elderly Hong Kong Chinese: a senior technology acceptance model (STAM). Ergonomics **57**(5), 635–652 (2014)
20. Sperazza, L.J., Dauenhauer, J., Banerjee, P.: Tomorrows seniors: technology and leisure programming. J. Commun. Inform. **8**(1) (2012)
21. Klimova, B., Valis, M., Kuca, K.: Dancing as an intervention tool for people with dementia: a mini-review. Curr. Alzheimer Res. **14**(12), 1264–1269 (2017)
22. Ma, Q., Chan, A.H.S., Chen, K.: Personal and other factors affecting acceptance of smartphone technology by older Chinese adults. Appl. Ergon. **54**, 62–71 (2016)
23. Steel, D.M., Gray, M.A.: Baby boomers' use and perception of recommended assistive technology: a systematic review. Disabil. Rehabil. Assist. Technol. **4**, 129–136 (2009)
24. Righi, V., Sayago, S., Blat, J.: When we talk about older people in HCI, who are we talking about? Towards a 'turn to community' in the design of technologies for a growing ageing population. Int. J. Hum. Comput. Stud. **108**, 15–31 (2017)
25. Bujnowska-Fedak, M.M.: Trends in the use of the Internet for health purposes in Poland. BMC **15**, 194 (2015)
26. Rockmann, R., Gewald, H.: Elderly people in eHealth: who are they? Proc. Comput. Sci. **63**, 505–510 (2015)
27. Siliquini, R., Ceruti, M., Lovato, E., Bert, F., Bruno, S., De Vito, E., et al.: Surfing the internet for health information: an Italian survey use and population choices. BMC Med. Inform. Decis. **11**, 21 (2011)
28. Kaiser Family Foundation: E-health and the Elderly: How Seniors use the Internet for Health Information. Key Findings from a National Survey of Older Americans (2013). https://kaiserfamilyfoundation.files.wordpress.com/2013/01/e-health-and-the-elderly-how-seniors-use-the-internet-for-health-information-key-findings-from-a-national-survey-of-older-americans-survey-report.pdf
29. Srb, L.: Senioři rádi využívají mobilní telefony, nové technologie jim však mnohdy brání. (Older People Like to Use Mobile Phones, New Technologies, However, Very Often Prevent them from it) (2012). http://mobilizujeme.cz/clanky/seniori-radi-vyuzivaji-mobilni-telefony-nove-technologie-jim-vsak-mnohdy-brani/
30. Hong, S.G., Trimi, S., Kim, D.: Smartphone use and internet literacy of senior citizens. J. Assist. Technol. **10**(1), 27–38 (2016)

31. Hwangbo, H., Yoon, S.H., Jin, B.S., Han, Y.S., Ji, Y.G.: A study of pointing performance of elderly users on smartphones. Int. J. Hum. Comput. Interac. **29**(9), 604–618 (2013)
32. Mohadis, H.M., Ali, N.M.: A study of smartphone usage and barriers among the elderly. In: Proceedings of the 3rd International Conference on User Science and Engineering: Experience. Engineer. Engage, pp. 109–114. Institute of Electrical and Electronics Engineers Inc. (2014)
33. Campbell, O.: Designing for the Elderly: Ways Older People use Digital Technology Differently (2015). http://www.smashingmagazine.com/2015/02/designing-digital-technology-for-the-elderly/
34. Beer, J.M., Takayama, L.: Mobile remote presence systems for older adults: acceptance, benefits, and concerns. In: Proceedings of the 6th ACM IEEE International Conference on Human-Robot Interactions (HKI 2011), pp. 19–26. ACM, Lausanne
35. Macedo, I.M., Pinho, J.C., Liao, M.N.: Investigating the impact of Internet usage and acceptance on active ageing among older adults. Confronting contemporary business challenges through management innovation, pp. 1448–1456, Cascais, Portugal
36. Mitzner, T.L., Boron, J.B., Fausset, C.B., Adams, A.E., Charness, N., Czaja, S.J.: Older adults talk technology: technology usage and attitudes. Comput. Hum. Behav. **26**(6), 1710–1721 (2010)
37. Hola, J., Pikhart, M.: The implementation of internal communication system as a way to company efficiency. E&M **17**(2), 161–169 (2014)
38. Yusif, S., Soar, J., Hafeez-Baig, A.: Older people, assistive technologies, and the barriers to adoption: a systematic review. Int. J. Med. Inform. **94**, 112–116 (2016)

Keeping in Touch: Mobile Apps Use by Older Adults

Dalit Levy[1]([✉]) and Elena Simonovsky[2]

[1] Zefat Academic College, Zefat, Israel
dalitl@zefat.ac.il
[2] Kibbutzim College of Education, Tel Aviv, Israel

Abstract. The presentation is based on a qualitative research that followed the process of adjustment to tablet computers by males and females aged 65+. The purpose of the study was to characterize the lifestyle of the population commonly called "the Third Age" regarding the use of touch-screen technology. From the analysis of the data accumulated through ethnographic observations in the homes of the participants and through in-depth interviews with them, a multilayered model emerged, including four dimensions relevant to living with a tablet at the third age: Activity, Learning, Independence, and Barriers. This led to proposing a new model of aging which combines extensive use of devices with integrated touch-screen technology, referred to as "Aging Model 2.0". The research suggests that the use of advanced technology may contribute to a new representation of older adults in society, which, in turn, may lead us to reevaluate our relationship with our parents and grandparents.

Keywords: Assistive technologies · Touch-screen technologies · Web 2.0

1 Introduction

The world of technology, communications, society, culture, and education is undergoing extensive transformations that deeply influence all of us. At the same time, we are witnessing a remarkable increase in longevity that has led to an aging population [1]. This presentation deals with the confluence of these two important sociocultural trends, focusing on the impact that innovative technology might have on older adults, hereby referred to as "the Third Age".

Tablets and smartphones, built on touch-screen technology, are thought of as an answer to some of the problems of third-agers who are challenged by traditional computers [2]. A touch-screen user is within touching distance of the potential services and treasures of the Internet, while accessibility of the interface symbols and icons lessens the frustration of the adult users and might help them to keep in touch with family, friends, and caregivers.

The use of tablet computers by members of the Third Age population group is a relatively new phenomenon, adding a new dimension to the existing theories regarding aging in the modern era. This phenomenon was examined in our study using an ethnographic approach that allows for a description of human and social situations through the individual subjective perspective of the participants. The presentation will discuss

© Springer International Publishing AG, part of Springer Nature 2018
J. Zhou and G. Salvendy (Eds.): ITAP 2018, LNCS 10926, pp. 95–107, 2018.
https://doi.org/10.1007/978-3-319-92034-4_8

the resulting emergent model of aging termed "Aging Model 2.0", to reflect the variety of web 2.0 tools [3] that our research participants have been using.

2   Theoretical Background

This section details the two sociocultural trends that meet at the intersection of this study, namely the gradual increase in number of the older population around the globe (in Sect. 2.1), and the digital revolution affecting every aspect of our lives (in Sect. 2.2). Section 2.3 ties both trends by discussing the fields of assistive technologies gerontechnology.

2.1   Current Aging Models

The Third Age population is very heterogenic and characterized by changes that impact on everyday functions in varying degrees [4]. The literature makes a distinction between normal aging and pathological aging. In addition, different aging models are described, distinct from one another mainly in the way they define the basic concepts and by using different research paradigms. However, a common feature in these models suggests that individuals from the Third Age group can break the boundaries, despite all of the stigmas regarding aging. One of the models suggested in the literature is referred to as "Successful Aging" [5]; Nimrod and Kleiber [6] propose a theory combining innovation with successful aging; other models refer to "Creative Aging", "Active Aging", and "Productive Aging". The concept of "Positive Aging" [7] combines all of these models and theories and presents us with a strategic policy for achieving the optimal conditions for the Third Age population, to encourage their positive involvement in social and economic life, as described in Fig. 1.

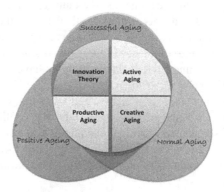

Fig. 1. Aging models

The global process of aging is occurring concurrently with huge advances in technology, commonly referred to as a digital revolution effecting every aspect of our lives, including the growing population of the third age. The next sections discuss these impacts.

2.2   The Internet and the Digital Revolution

Technology nowadays is more and more perceived as a tool for empowering citizens. Applications, such as Twitter, Facebook, YouTube, and instant messaging allows user communities to find answers, conduct research, communicate, share and create ideas. This situation presents society with challenges which are dealt with throughout the world using national plans for digital citizenship which include digital literacy and ethics; growing accessibility; educating for digital consumerism, digital law and order, and digital health; and cyber-security and protection of users' privacy [8]. Such empowerment-by-digital-technology plans are thought to impact all the parts of the society, including the elderly, and to assist in closing digital gaps. The section discusses these impacts through the lens of two terms: Web 2.0 [3] and World 2.0 [9].

The rise of the Internet is one of the driving forces for this digital revolution. The World Wide Web, initially created as a method for computers to communicate between themselves, has evolved during the first decade of the 21st century as a tool of communication between individuals using Web 2.0, for creating and sharing content. "Web 2.0 is a set of economic, social, and technology trends that collectively form the basis for the next generation of the Internet - a more mature, distinctive medium characterized by user participation, openness, and network effects" [10, p. 4].

The term "Web 2.0" describes applications with simple user interfaces, which receive data from a number of sources including the users themselves, while maintaining continuous automatic updating, updated by numerous users or simultaneously with them. The process creates a communal web, which provides a dynamic and richer user-experience that allows for both consumption and production of content, for creating interactive programs and applications, and for sharing. These tools are accessible on line and using them does not require installation on a personal computer.

Web 2.0 involves not only new cutting-edge technology, but also a new digital culture, which transcends the closed and conservative ways of social actions and interactions. This change was brought about by billions of people around the world with access to the Internet and is reflected in terms such as social media and new media. The actions and reactions of Web 2.0 users are often characterized as agile, interactive, creative, and willing to share [10].

During the years since the term Web 2.0 was proposed in 2006, the main principles for designing and programming Internet webpages have been continuously adjusted to the sociocultural trends such as agility, dynamicity, openness, and collaboration. At the same time, while the mobile revolution has joined forces with the Internet revolution, numerous types of Web 2.0 applications have been flooding the cyberspace. Among these are social networks like Facebook and Twitter where users share information and knowledge about everything, including issues of health and illness and plenty of other issues that are relevant for the Third age. For example, Twitter hosts a wide range of information and updates regarding common 65+ health issues and diseases, such as Alzheimer's and dementia. There is also sharing of tweets by experts through Twitter. Professional medical experts, health groups, and commercial companies use such new-media channels in order to trade information on medical and pharmaceutical research, Alzheimer and dementia risk factors, and ways to reduce risks [11].

The complex two-way relationship between mobile devices, computers, and humans has received a significant impetus in light of the Web 2.0, which foresaw the change in the relationship between Internet users and Internet content, as well as the change in the relationship among users themselves. As a result of the discussion revolving around the cultural changes in the digital age, the idea of life in the "World 2.0" space was introduced in 2009 [9]. World 2.0 is a digital ecological system: a hyper-linked space with its various parts, globally complex and full of human-computer interactions, non-human interactions and inter-human interactions. The potential embodied in this is already affecting society. Flexible working-time from in or out of the office requires the various organizations to be flexible through their connection to the Internet. Online purchases provide more than the item purchased, but also membership in the shoppers' community. The online gaming phenomenon is expanding throughout the world. Cloud technologies allow for easy and immediate access to information and communication from everywhere and through any mobile device. Collaboration and active participation with family and friends, colleagues and clients are possible from anywhere in the world any time. Web 2.0 tools provide the technological basis for all these as well as for a variety of digital citizenship projects which serve the purposes of reducing the digital gap. On the down side of World 2.0, the book "Alone, Together", discusses the increasing dependence of the people and the society on these advanced Web 2.0 technologies, tools, and applications [12]. The author, Sherry Turkle, claims that the digital revolution changes not only our behavior - it also influences our very essence and create a new type of personality. As the title of her book hints, Web 2.0 technologies are not truly connecting us to others – we are not together in the "old" sense of the word. Accordingly, we are more alone, when humanity shuts itself off from the world through communicating with the world.

A variety of tablet computers, along with smartphones, are the main method of assimilating the Web 2.0 applications in World 2.0. Structurally, the tablet computer is a screen, which reacts to the touch of a finger. Below the surface is a computer, which usually includes a processor, hard drive, memory, and wireless network connections. Although many believe that the first tablet computer was the iPad, introduced by Apple in 2010, the history of touch-screen devices goes back to the 1960s. Due to space limitations, this fascinating history cannot be detailed here. However, it is worth noting that the technological development of tablet computers with touch screens has both introduced a new computing paradigm and enabled the spreading of World 2.0. The devices in this new paradigm are small, personal, lightweight and affordable, connected by wireless and equipped with a range of simple multimedia and modular software for data-search, learning and games. As reflected by Steve Jobes' vision from 2005, the tablet computer comes with a touch screen and without an integrated keyboard or unnecessary buttons. Indeed, the iPad declared by Jobes in 2010 marked the rise of this new paradigm, sometimes referred to as the "post-PC age".

The tablets, built on touch-screen technology, are thought of as an answer to the problems of third-agers who are challenged by traditional computers. A touch-screen user is within touching distance of the potential services and treasures of the Internet, while accessibility of the interface symbols and icons lessens the frustration of the adult user. Research shows a proven psychomotor advantage of tablet computers versus the ordinary mouse and keyboard [2, 13]. The touch-screen reduces by 35% the time that the adult invests in movement on the screen compared with the mouse. There is also a decrease in the number of errors with an accompanying increase in efficiency. Although the advantages remain, it should be noted that touch-screen devices require motoric skills, which are difficult for people who suffer from arthritis, tremors and other problems [14].

To summarize this section, living in World 2.0 involves touch interfaces that are being employed everywhere. In ticket-vending machines for public transport, shows and the arts; in queue-number machines for clinics, banks and post offices; in information screens of interactive boards and electronic guides in many public places; and of course, for personal communication and multimedia: smart mobile phones, hand-held computers and various tablets. Elderly people living in the same world experience the nature of World 2.0 and participate in the interactions influenced by the digital revolution through extensive use of Web 2.0 tools in these tablet computers. Thus, the worlds of technology and real life interact in the digital ecological system of World 2.0 – a global, complex space that is full of human computer interactions, artificial interactions and interpersonal interactions. The Third Age population group is an integral part of this hyperlinked system, hence the importance of dealing with the impact of World 2.0 on them.

2.3 Assistive Technologies and Gerontology

Technology that used to be available in the past only to a selected few has now become much more accessible, more efficient and faster and used by many for a variety of purposes. Technologies that were initially developed for military uses are making their way into our civilian life and into everyday applications, similar to the Internet, which initially served the professional science community, and then made its way into everyone's daily routine. Technological gadgets which began as amusing toys, have found their way into education, medicine, nursing and rehabilitation, allowing people with various disabilities to be integrated into their natural habitat, while maintaining the highest degree of independence and an acceptable standard of living.

The developing sector of technology referred to as *assistive technologies* emphasizes technologies that help users to bypass their disabilities and lead a normal life [15]. In the past, assistive technological tools would assist disabled users with mainly physical and sensory disabilities. Today, in parallel to the digital revolution, the field is reaching additional special populations, such as the elderly and persons with cognitive disabilities. Moreover, it has merged with nursing technology and preventing certain medical problems, such as dementia and depression, socio-psychological problems, such as loneliness and dependence on others for everyday functions, and so on. In addition, communication applications of Web 2.0 type and new technologies help create an infrastructure for exchange of medical information, for supporting high risk patient groups, for treatment and prevention of injuries and disease, when elements such as time and distance are crucial for successful professional intervention [16].

Assistive technology not only modifies the home allowing an elderly person an independent life style, but also assists in mobility and tourism. New applications are constantly introduced which allow functioning at a level which was previously impossible, and the 65+ population is the fastest growing sector of Internet consumers. Creating an interpersonal interaction online opens a new window of opportunity for those people feeling distressed, when medical treatment and counseling is inaccessible due to excessive physical demands or language barriers, and mobility difficulties in emergencies, such as war, terrorist attack or natural disasters. The online connection is much faster and effective in traumatic and post-traumatic times in support groups for chronic diseases, depression and anxiety, than organizing and operating face-to-face groups. Access to general medical information and personal data allows health insurance policyholders to book doctor's appointments, receive test results and medical counseling in their homes, check health-related data regardless of time, seek and locate emotional support online [16].

Indeed, various studies indicate a connection between Internet usage and the level of a person's independence, and his or her cognitive and physical performances [8]. However, scientists do not consider the Internet as a "miracle drug" for coping with the changes of aging and studies conducted prior to the introduction of touch screen devices have not found conclusive evidence for the hypothesis which claims that using a computer at an older age is efficacious. Still, it has been suggested that computer-based communication has great potential for supporting people of advanced age [17].

Gerontechnology is defined as the utilization of technology to improve the welfare of adults and elderly people using tools available to us everywhere and at any time [18]. The aim of gerontology is to enhance the level of functioning and the quality of life of elderly persons who have experienced changes in their health, with physical and psychological limitations caused by their age. The emphasis is on safety issues for people requiring assistance by maintaining age-friendly environments that allows effective access to everyday services, such as automatic illumination of rooms and hallways at nighttime [15]. In addition to these mechanical accessories, a wide range of sensor-based applications has been developed. These include digital secretaries to remind us of the time for medication; video-conference applications that allow us to remain in constant touch with family members, doctors and patients; and the smart systems that can aid people in taking the right pill, in reading a brochure and providing additional information, converting sound and voice to text for the hearing-impaired or text to sound for the visually-impaired [18]. The relevance of these technologies has also been tested in the field of book reading for people with mobility limitations. In addition, sensor systems set up at elderly homes can collect different vital signs such as weight, blood pressure and other data; create an information database to aid prevention of health risks, such as falling, prevention of future asthma attacks, heart attacks, blood pressure spikes or diabetes by notifying relatives or caretaker, recording sleep, description of sleep quality and the time a person is awake and active. Using such systems allows the patient's physical activity to be monitored, increases the level of safety and creates a friendly living environment. However, these uses might constitute for the elderly population an invasion of privacy.

More and more sectors of the third-age population nowadays interact with various technologies in their day-to-day activities. It is highly desirable therefore that new technologies are adapted for use by all age groups, including those over 65. At the same time, new technology is still mostly inaccessible to those in the elderly population who lack additional income apart from their pensions, and the high cost of new technology usually prevents them from using it, while creating digital and inter-generational differences. Increasing the gap between young and old mostly excludes the latter from modern life, isolates, depresses and maybe even shortens their life span. One of the programs for reducing this gap is the 'Active Aging 2.0' [8] which operates on a Web 2.0 platform. This program promotes a wider use of social media and cooperative digital communication tools by members of the elderly community in order to transform them into active digital citizens in the virtual space of society.

The digital gap is not only a function of poverty and technology costs. Among the contributory causes of technology-exclusion is the low level of graphic design adaptation, for example, low contrasts of text on screens, which affects the interpretation of the text and increases the length of time it takes for elderly people to read the text. Researchers relate such design issues to a lack of awareness of the importance of the new technology and its positive effects on the aging process [18]. Technology experts, designers and engineers often neglect the elderly population, thereby increasing the gaps and preventing them from using the technologies. Among the barriers are myths relating to the interaction between a human being and a computer. Those myths are popular among engineers and programmers, and throughout society, even among elderly people themselves [19]. The most obvious myth is that people of the middle generation and certainly people of the young generation will use computers without a problem, once they approach the third age. This myth is accompanied by abstention and a lack of investment in the current elderly population regarding advanced technologies. Other myths are that old people are not interested in using computers, that they are unaware of the capabilities of computers because they perceive them as useless and unnecessary, that they are unable physically to use technology, and that they simply cannot understand the interactivity of computer technology.

The findings of the current study bring evidence against some of these myths in the case of third-agers using new technologies introduced by the first generation of tablets. In that way, our work seeks to raise awareness to the importance of interweaving new technologies and gerontology, as well as to the positive effects such use might have on the aging process.

3   Method

Three research questions directed the study: (1) How and for what purposes do third-agers use their tablets? (2) What are the advantages and disadvantages of using tablets, as seen and expressed by the participants? And (3) What changes to the current aging models are introduced through the use of tablets by third-agers?

In order to answer these questions, we used a combination of ethnographic observations and open interviews, a combination which allows cross-reference of data collected from multiple, and independent sources. The participants were nine males and females ages 65+ who have been using tablet computers for no more than two years, and one young IPad applications developer. The participants vary in terms of socio-economic level, health status, knowledge and pre-existing experience of this type of technology as well as place of residence. The data were obtained in the homes or places of employment of the participants. All of the participants received a general explanation regarding the general topic of the study and all of them expressed their agreement to be interviewed, while maintaining their confidentiality.

As is customary in an evolving study, the qualitative analysis phase [20] began simultaneously with the gathering of the data, occasionally affecting the order of data gathering and the composition of the participants. During the first analytic step, five categories of uses emerged from the inductive analysis of the data gathered from the participants, as is presented in Table 1.

Table 1. Mobile apps use by older adults

Emergent Category	Specific use
a. Active lifestyle	Sport activities, Shopping, Work duties, Individual interests, Reading, Driving, Excursions and Trips, Crafts, Photo taking, Music
b. Being a technophile	Advanced uses based on a rich technological biography, Combining the use of PCs and Tablets
c. Digital citizenship	Digital literacy, Digital Ethics, Digital communications, Accessibility, E-commerce and digital consumption, Digital Health
d. Lifelong learning and independence	Empowerment, Respect, Pleasure, Creativity, Need for recognition, Decision making, Control, Autonomy, Professional and self-development
e. Relationships with the children	Alerts, Reversal of roles in the family, Need for continuous keeping-in-touch, Advice in purchasing the tablet

Later in the analysis, the wide array of emergent categories was re-arranged in four dimensions: (1) Activity; (2) Learning; (3) Independence; and (4) Barriers. It has been apparent in all the four dimensions that the use of tablets by the third-age population changes various aspects of their daily lives. This led to suggesting the Aging Model 2.0, representing how the integration of advanced technologies at the Third Age may improve the daily function of that population. The emergent model is presented next.

4   Findings: Towards a New Aging Model

Overall, the participants in this study found use of the touch screen devices easy and intuitive, and used them for a variety of purposes that led to, among other things, the creation of personal, family, social and professional activities. As Table 1 above shows, the third agers used mobile apps on their tablets for a variety of personal, family, and social activities: in one case, the interviewee even regarded the tablet as a family member. They also used mobile apps for keeping up-to-date and learning for professional needs and found that the tablets contributed to their independence in decision-making and control of information and time-organization. In some cases, using the tablet was described as a way for mediating and reducing social gaps.

The inductive analysis of the participants' discourse regarding their use of mobile apps also raised a range of difficulties and barriers that exist between the elderly population and the innovations of technology [1]. Table 2 contains two categories in this regard: difficulties that were described by the participants, and issues related to age losses that were expressed by them.

Table 2. Difficulties and barriers

Difficulties in using touch screen technology	Barriers related to age losses
• Complexity of technology	• Memory decline and physical losses
• Time constrains	• Chronic diseases
• Software complications	• Diseases and death of relatives
• Issues of saving and locating saved files	• Economic dependence
• Difficulties with attention distribution between input/output devices	• Reducing circle of friends
• Fear of harming	
• Failure of digital skills acquisition	

Following the range of the uses (Table 1) as well as of the difficulties found in the first analytic step (Table 2), the analysis continued seeking for advantages and disadvantages of "keeping in touch", namely using touch-screen technologies, as these were expressed by our third age participants. As expected, our interviewees noted the price as a disadvantage, as well as the need for Wi-Fi installation at home. They also mentioned short battery life, insufficient memory and one-way camera as disadvantages. Ergonomically, they noted both issues of sharpness and clarity of graphics and text in some applications [19] and issues of placing the tablet when they wanted or were forced (for health reasons) to use it in bed. Another issue raised by our third-agers was the continuous need for advice and support.

As a possible solution to some of these disadvantages, guidelines are suggested [21] for three aspects of website design to accommodate the elderly population: (1) legible text design, (2) increase in memory, (3) easier navigation and accessibility to internet content. Although articulated in the pre-tablets era, applying these guidelines into tablets and applications design is supposed to result in more accessible websites and more access to online information for members of the elderly community, as well as increasing their enthusiasm towards technology. Recently, this point of view has been receiving growing public attention in defining a common cause to bridge the digital divide in this community. The way that third-age population see the advantages and the disadvantages of using tablets at their age might guide tablets designers, application programmers, supporters and helpers in creating more accessible and assistive technologies and services directed at this growing population.

The wide array of emergent categories described above was further re-arranged in four dimensions: (1) Activity; (2) Learning; (3) Independence; and (4) Barriers. One example, included in the third dimension of Independence, is expressed via the title of a previous account of this study [22]: "Meet Vasia, our new family member". The words of this title appear in an interview with one of the female participants, who told us about her husband's human attitude towards his tablet, including naming it with a traditional Russian name. She added: "*I was mad at him at first. We said, wait until he stops playing with it, until he has had enough, but he didn't stop, and we had to enlarge the family to include Vasia. We now welcome it, knowing for sure that my husband is more with Vasia than with us*" (interview on June 14, 2013).

Another example categorized under the same dimension of Independence is the fear of being dependent on younger family members. Shai told us in his interview about how he succeeded in directing both his children into the computing profession, and proudly described his daughter's career in an international information security company as well as his son's senior job in a major telecommunication firm. He added: "*I was once their advisor, now I use their advice. The roles in our family have been reversed. I just don't want it to become complete dependence*" (interview on July 31, 2013).

An interesting example from the first dimension - Activity – is taken from an interview with Willy, the husband who named his tablet Vasia. Willy is a retired medical doctor who still works in his profession. He connects computers and tablets directly to his ability to continue working at his age: "*I always need to be updated with all the news in my professional field. The computer is the ideal tool for that. As it turned out, I use my computer and tablet at least two hours a day. I read articles and medical news*" (interview on June 14, 2013).

The Activity dimension was widely mentioned by our participants not only with regard to professional needs, as in the aforementioned example, but also in a variety of other categories such as physical activity: running, walking, dancing, swimming, etc.; cognitive activity: reading, games, crosswords, etc.; social activity; touring and tourism; and new-media activity. Moreover, some participants described technology using specific verbs and expressions hinting at an active and dynamic perception, as is shown in the bulleted excerpts, where the verbs of activity are capitalized.

- "you can't GO with technology, you can only GO after it" (Dan, February 19, 2013)
- "…the technology RUNS …you don't even need to get out of bed – you touch, and you FLY …" (Dan – 2nd interview, July 1, 2013)
- "…now (with the tablet) I have no problem waiting – I am PLAYING. I have something to DO" (Rina, May 30, 2013)
- "In my age it is harder to RUN with technology…" (Sami, May 31, 2013)
- "You can't make it with the RATE of technology change" (Shai, July 31, 2013)

These examples draw a partial picture of the phenomena investigated, and the citations only briefly exemplify the rich data obtained through a vast description of the participants' use of tablets and their accompanying discourse. Even though, contrary to the persistent stereotype concerning conservatism among the elderly population, the inductive analysis shows active people who are open to technological change, despite the difficulty stated by some, mainly regarding the operation of regular computers.

From our analysis it is apparent that the use of tablets and mobile apps by the third-age population changes various aspects of their daily lives. We therefore suggest that the existing aging models, as these have been presented in the literature and summarized in Sect. 2.1 above, might also exhibit some transformation in the wake of World 2.0 [9], and propose to incorporate this emergent model into the preexisting aging models (see Fig. 2). Such integration could contribute to a new and different representation of the Third Age population in society, to encourage us all to re-evaluate our relationship with our parents and grandparents and allow the members of the Third Age population group to re-evaluate their abilities regarding modern technologies that are relevant to our coexisting lives.

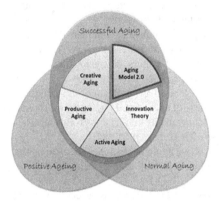

Fig. 2. Aging model 2.0 as the 5th element in the array of existing aging models [7].

5 Conclusions

The findings of this study describe people who are active, open to technological changes, and who incorporate the tablets and mobile apps into everyday life, enabling ease of searching for and reading information, promoting social, family and professional communication and assisting in time management and leisure. The data also introduce compensation for old-age losses [4, 13], reduction of social gaps, higher mobility and social involvement and ultimately happiness. These findings shatter the prejudices regarding old age and aging as a limitation [1, 19].

From an analysis of the data accumulated through ethnographic observations and through in-depth interviews with the participants, emerged a structure, Aging Model 2.0, as a conjunction of the aspects relevant to living with a tablet and to using mobile apps at the third age. The name "Aging 2.0" echoes the varied Web 2.0 tools which the participants used and the online world in which we – and they – live. Aging Model 2.0 also represents how the integration of advanced technologies at the Third Age may improve the daily function of that population.

It is our sincere hope that this study and the proposed model will contribute to raising social awareness of this issue and to a change in popular pre-existing misconceptions and prejudice in the public, and at the same time enable Third Agers and those who support them to successfully integrate and utilize touch screen technology into their everyday life.

References

1. Charness, N., Boot, W.R.: Aging and information technology use: potential and barriers. Current Dir. Psychol. Sci. **18**(5), 253–258 (2009)
2. Findlater, L., Froehlich, J.E., Fattal, K., Wobbrock, J.O., Dastyar, T.: Age-related differences in performance with touchscreens compared to traditional mouse input. In: Proceedings of the SIGCHI Conference on Human Factors in Computing Systems, pp. 343–346 (2013). http://www.cs.umd.edu/~jonf/publications/Findlater_AgeRelatedDifferencesInPerformance WithTouchscreensComparedToTraditionalMouseInput_CHI2013.pdf. Accessed 22 Feb 2018
3. O'Reilly, T.: What is Web 2.0: design patterns and business models for the next generation of software. Commun. Strategies **1**, 17 (2007)
4. Baltes, P.B.: On the incomplete architecture of human ontogeny. Selection, optimization, and compensation as foundation of developmental theory. Am. Psychol. **52**(4), 366–380 (1997)
5. Rowe, J.W., Kahn, R.L.: Successful aging. In: Dychtwald, K. (ed.) Healthy Aging: Challenges and Solutions, pp. 27–44. Aspen, Gaithersburg (1999)
6. Nimrod, G., Kleiber, D.: Reconsidering change and continuity in later life: toward an innovation theory of successful aging. Int. J. Aging Hum. Dev. **65**(1), 1–22 (2007)
7. Rudman, D.L.: Positive aging and its implications for occupational possibilities in later life. Canad. J. Occup. Therapy **73**(3), 188–192 (2006)
8. Consoli, D.: A model of active aging 2.0 to stimulate older adults in the use of virtual social networks. Intergenerational Solidarity and Older Adults' Education in Community, 296 (2012)
9. Karakas, F.: Welcome to world 2.0: the new digital ecosystem. J. Bus. Strategy **30**(4), 23–30 (2009)
10. O'Reilly, T., Musser, J.: Excerpts of Web 2.0 Principles and Best Practices. O'Reilly Media (2006). http://oreilly.com/catalog/web2report/chapter/web20_report_excerpt.pdf. Accessed 2 Dec 2013
11. Robillard, J.M., Johnson, T.W., Hennessey, C., Beattie, B.L., Illes, J.: Aging 2.0: health information about dementia on twitter. PLoS ONE **8**(7), e69861 (2013).
12. Turkle, S.: Alone Together: Why We Expect More From Technology and Less From Each Other. Basic Books, New York (2011)
13. Kaplan, A.: Preface to Paradise, Life in the Current Site of Old Age. Series for Sociology and Anthropology. Tel Aviv (Hebrew), Rasling (2013)
14. Caprani, N., O'Connor, N.E., Gurrin, C.: Touch screens for the older user. In: Cheein, A.F. (ed.) Assistive Technologies, pp. 95–118 (2012). http://cdn.intechopen.com/pdfs/31905/InTech-Touch_screens_for_the_older_user.pdf. Accessed 22 Feb 2018
15. Piattini, M.: The role of ICTs in ageing. LYCHNOS **8**, 60–64 (2012). http://www.fgcsic.es/lychnos/upload/publicacion.14.ficPDF_ingles.LYCHNOS_8_ING_web.pdf. Accessed 23 Aug 2012
16. Hall, A.K., Stellefson, M., Bernhardt, J.M.: Healthy aging 2.0: the potential of new media and technology. Preventing Chronic Disease **9**, E67 (2012)
17. Dickinson, A., Gregor, P.: Computer use has no demonstrated impact on the well-being of older adults. Int. J. Hum. Comput. Stud. **64**(8), 744–753 (2006). https://doi.org/10.1016/j.ijhcs.2006.03.001
18. Cohen-Mansfield, J., Biddison, J.: The scope and future trends of gerontechnology: consumers' opinions and literature survey. J. Technol. Hum. Serv. **25**(3), 1–19 (2007). https://doi.org/10.1300/J017v25n03_01

19. Wandke, H., Sengpiel, M., Sönksen, M.: Myths about older people's use of information and communication technology. Gerontology **58**(6), 564–570 (2012)
20. Guba, E.G., Lincoln, Y.S.: Fourth Generation Evaluation. Sage, London (1989)
21. Hart, T., Chaparro, B., Halcomb, C.: Evaluating websites for older adults: adherence to senior-friendly guidelines and end-user performance. Behav. Inf. Technol. **27**(3), 191–199 (2008). http://psychology.wichita.edu/surl/usabilitynews/61/older_adults.htm. Accessed 30 Aug 2013
22. Levy, D., Simonovsky, E.: "Meet Vasia, our new family member": tablets use by older adults. In: Shoniregun, C.A., Akmayeva, G. (eds.) Proceedings of the World Congress on Education (WCE-2015), pp. 132–136 (2015)

Study on the Current Situation of Urban Empty Nest Elderly of Community Home Care and Innovation Strategy

Ruiqi Li[✉], Ya-jun Li, and Xingxing Gao

Nanjing University of Science and Technology, Nanjing, People's Republic of China
305211092@qq.com

Abstract. The empty nest elderly family refers to a childless family or an elderly family who live apart from their children. In China the traditional mode of providing for the aged has always been based on the family support for the aged, that is, family members providing care for the elderly. However, with the deepening degree of population aging, especially the influence of the one-child policy, empty nest family will be one of the main forms of Chinese home. On the whole, the empty nest family in China is in the transition period from passive acceptance to active choice. Based on the survey of the current situation of the empty nest elderly in Gulou District of Nanjing. It is found that there is a contradiction between the lack of demand for the elderly and the coexistence of service. Through the analysis and research of the survey data, this paper puts forward the construction of the model of intelligent service system for the urban empty nest family and make the research of innovation strategy from the point of view of supply and demand matching, then gives some suggestions on the right and responsibility orientation of different subjects.

Keywords: Empty nest elderly · Community home care
Supply and demand matching · Innovation strategy

1 Introduction

With the deepening of population aging, the increase of population mobility, the number of empty nest family and even the elderly living along is increasing. The number of empty nest families in China increased by about 13.3% and 4.79% in 2010, respectively, compared with 1990 and 2000 [1]. As of 2014, the empty nests in our country have already accounted for half of the total number of elderly people [2]. China's report on the development of the aging industry (2014) shows that the proportion of the future empty nest elderly population is expected to break through 70% [3]. The changes in the population structure influenced by the one child policy have led to the challenge of the traditional family pension model. With the increase of empty nest families, family-care becomes more and more difficult. People begin to seek and accept social support methods such as community endowment, institution-care, and so on. Community home care shows a strong comprehensive advantage [4]. So it is important to study on the current situation of urban empty nest elderly of the community home care, to understand

© Springer International Publishing AG, part of Springer Nature 2018
J. Zhou and G. Salvendy (Eds.): ITAP 2018, LNCS 10926, pp. 108–117, 2018.
https://doi.org/10.1007/978-3-319-92034-4_9

the needs of the empty nest elderly, the supply of the aged service and the use of the supply service. This will be useful for improving the quality of life of the empty nest elderly and solving the worries of young people.

The theoretical basis of the empty nest family is the "family life cycle", the empty nest period is a stage of the family life cycle. Glick [5], the American social demographer, first proposed a relatively complete family life cycle theory in 1947. He divided the family life cycle into 6 stages: generation, development, stability, contraction, empty nest and disintegration, and thought that families had different contents and tasks in different life cycles. With the development of society, the order of traditional family events has changed (such as cohabitation before marriage, the increase of divorce rate, etc.). On the basis of this, American family sociologist Duvall [6] further divides the family life cycle into 8 stages. The theory of empty nest family based on "family life cycle" points out that the elderly in empty nest families should experience not only the transformation of life cycle from middle age to old age, but also the transformation of family cycle from core or main family to empty nest family. In the process of transformation. If the elderly do not adapt well, it is extremely easy to cause a variety of physical and mental problems, not only affects the quality of life of the elderly, but also bring influence to the family, which caused a series of social problems, such as empty nest elderly lack of living care, lack of medical care, lack of material security, lack of spiritual comfort, and so on.

The emergence of empty nest family is the result of external objective factors and individual choice and other factors, and the type of empty nest elderly is pluralistic. It has been found that there are significant differences in the urban and rural, age and the way of living for the different types of empty nest elderly. Costa [7] pointed out that urban empty nest elderly have more economic independence than rural empty nest elderly and less demand for their children's economic support. Sun [8] pointed out that the economic condition and daily life self-care ability of couples in empty nest families are better than those of other types of empty nest elderly. The living conditions of the elderly living alone are worrying, and their children's economic support and care support are more needed.

2 The Current Situation of Urban Empty Nest Elderly

2.1 Research Data Sources

The survey was conducted in Gulou District of Nanjing City, Jiangsu Province, China. The respondents were elderly people over 60 years old who lived alone or lived with their spouse. The sample selection was conducted by multistage random sampling, and the empty nest families were surveyed by household interview. A total of 160 samples were selected and 153 were successfully interviewed. Only one elderly person was selected in each family. Among the elderly people visited, 71 were males, 46.4%, and 82 were females, accounting for 53.6%. The content of the study includes information about the marital status, working conditions and number of children of the elderly people, and the investigation and analysis of the demand, supply and utilization of the service for the elderly. *The following* Table 1 *gives the basic situation of the subjects.*

Table 1. Basic situation of urban empty nest elderly (N = 153)

Variable	Classification standard	Number	Percentage (%)
Gender	Male	71	46.4
	Female	82	53.6
Age groups	60–69	74	48.4
	70–79	64	41.8
	80+	15	9.8
Physical condition	Healthy	58	37.9
	Moderate inability	83	54.3
	Severe inability	12	7.8
Source of income	Pension or social security	55	35.9
	Support for children or relatives	71	46.4
	Minimum living security	14	9.2
	Other ways	13	8.5
Degree of education	Illiterate, Primary school	80	52.3
	Junior school	40	26.1
	High school or above	33	21.6
Marital status	Live with a spouse	129	84.3
	Unmarried, Widowed, Divorce	24	15.7
Number of existing children	0–1	32	20.9
	2	55	35.9
	3+	66	43.2

2.2   The Reason of Empty Nest and Pension Mode Select

There are more than one reason for the empty nest of the elderly, and the empty nest family is the result of a variety of reasons, such as the individual, the family and the society. The results of the survey show that the different reasons for the empty nest are as follows. **Personal reasons:** ① The elderly want to live independently, and hope that later years have more freedom and autonomy, accounting for 22.2%. Most of them are younger elderly who are economic independence, rich in mental life and in good physical condition. ② 13.7% of the elderly chose to take the active empty nest because they do not want to leave the long - living environment. **Family reasons:** ① 32.7% of the elderly want to live together with their children, but because they are different from their children in life habits and values, they choose to live independently to avoid conflicts. ② 24.2% of the elderly who do not want to increase their children's burden and choose to live independently. ③ There are 5.9% of the elderly people who are unable to live with their children because of their children's material conditions. ④ In addition, 2 empty nest elderly have to be live alone because they are abandoned by their children, although their children have good material conditions. **Social reasons:** ① Due to the improvement of economic and housing conditions, many children are separated from the elderly after marriage, and this kind of empty nest family accounts for 61.4%. ② 38.3% of the empty nest families are caused by their children studying, working and living in a different place.

The results of the survey on the residence will of urban empty nest elderly is shown in Table 2. 74.5% of the elderly think that "Not living with children but in the same city" is their preferred way of living. The other 14.5% of the elderly think that living together with their children is a better way. It is shown that, the elderly people's attitude to empty nests is obviously not as reject as a dozen years ago. Even many elderly choose to be active nest in order to live an independent life. This change shows that the old-age mode in China is developing from the traditional family pension to the social endowment.

Table 2. The residence will of urban empty nest elderly (N = 153)

The residence will of urban empty nest elderly	Number	Percentage (%)
Not living with children but in the same city	114	74.5
Living with their children	22	14.5
Living in a pension institution	14	9.1
Do not care	3	1.9

2.3   The Demand, Supply and Utilization of the Service for the Elderly

General research holds the statement that "Empty nest elderly, as a relatively vulnerable group in the social population, are mainly characterized by economic fragility, physiological fragility and psychological fragility". But the survey results show that most of the urban empty nest elderly are economically independent and have some economic foundation, which is also one of the factors that they can live separately from their children. In addition, the results of the survey of empty nest elderly by ADL scale show that, most empty nest elderly can take care of themselves, but at the same time there are still some problems in their lives, such as cleaning, going to hospital and so on.

Alderfer [9] integrated Maslow's five levels of demand into three needs and became ERG theory, which he thought people have three core needs: existence, relatedness, growth. This study is combined with the ERG theory to investigate the situation of 20 old-age service projects in urban empty nest elderly. Table 3 is a part of the survey data.

Table 3. The service status (part) for the urban nest elderly (N = 153) (%)

Tapes of demand	Service Items	Service demand	Service supply	Service utilization
Existence	Food service	54.9	40.5	29.4
	Doing housework	43.1	34.0	12.4
	Help with personal hygiene	11.8	41.8	6.5
Relatedness	Accompanied for the medical	34.6	16.3	4.6
	Agency agent	23.5	12.4	9.8
	Accompany chat	13.7	53.6	7.2
Growth	Legal aid	9.8	49.7	5.9
	Recreational activities	21.6	38.6	16.3
	learning activities	15.0	20.3	9.2

At present, the empty nest elderly has the highest demand for meals, up to 54.9%. Followed by the needs of doing housework, 43.1%. And there's a lot more than 20% of the empty nest elderly people's needs for Relatedness and Growth. Service supply refers to the situation of service supply for the elderly. The supply rate of most services is more than 20% except the rate of Accompanied for the medical is 16.3% and 12.4% of the Agency agent. Comparison of service demand and service supply shows that the supply of Help with personal hygiene and Accompany chat is greater than the demand, but the supply of Food service and Doing housework is lower than the demand. In reality, though there are many services that are larger than demand, there are still large gaps between supply and demand due to the uneven distribution of pension services resources. Service utilization refers to the use of the service provided by the elderly at least once. The gap between service supply and utilization reflects the widespread problem of services excess in the present community home care service.

The survey results show that the current community home care service mode is obviously insufficient for the empty nest elderly to meet the needs of elderly services, and the utilization rate of empty nest elderly is low. This is because the community home care service focused more on the provision of "service for the aged", the government also pay more attention on the service resources and the supply capacity when carrying out the service process. Empty nest family will be one of the main forms for the elderly in the future. The care resources of the empty nest family are different from other elderly people, so when we supply services, we need not only to consider the service resources and the supply capacity, but also to consider the demand difference caused by the characteristics of the empty nest elderly.

3   Intelligent Pension for Urban Empty Nest Elderly

3.1   Starting Point and Principle

From the analysis of the previous article, we found that the supply and demand of the elderly service is not matched at present. Therefore, on the basis of meeting the needs of the elderly through integrating the existing pension service resources, we can form complementary advantages among different pension services. So as to achieve the goal of lower cost, more efficient, faster, higher quality, higher satisfaction and higher value increment of pension services. In order to ensure the rationality of the intelligent pension service system, we must follow the following five basic principles: The systematic principle, The right principle, The fairness principle, The selectivity principle and The gradualness principle.

The Systematic Principle.   The intelligent pension system is part of the whole elderly service system. The effectiveness of its functions depends on the coordination of the other components in the entire elderly service system. Only by ensuring the integrity and hierarchy of all the elements in the intelligent pension service system, and with the coordinated development of other components of the system, can we achieve the goal of health care for the elderly.

The Right Principle. The right to existence is a basic human right, and the basic conditions needed to maintain a citizen's normal life should not be affected by the increase of age and the decline of physical function. The elderly should not be regarded just as a disadvantaged group or service passive recipients, but they should be regarded as participants and beneficiaries of social development. We should design the elderly service system and ensure the accessibility of the service on the basis of the interests of the elderly.

The Fairness Principle. From the perspective of rights, every elderly should have equal pension services, but this does not mean that every elderly enjoys the same elderly services. We should follow the principle of relative fairness when constructing intelligent elderly service system, so that different categories of elderly can adopt their own pension service mode and avoid egalitarianism.

The Selectivity Principle. The selection body and beneficiaries of the intelligent pension system are all elderly people. And are influenced by many factors such as physical condition, living condition, family caregivers, economic status and education level, there are obvious differences in the choice of elderly people. On the basis of respecting the choice of the elderly, it is necessary to provide a multilevel and diversified service mode and content.

The Gradualness Principle. From the continuity of the model operation, we should not only ensure that the elderly can enjoy the economic and social development results, but also do not exceed the economic and social capacity of our country. For the elderly, sustainability also means the expansion of the service content to reduce the discomfort caused by changing the place of residence.

3.2 Supply and Demand Matching

The intelligent pension system breaks through the traditional elderly service mode with the concept of the core of the endowment resources, but the core of the service and service process. The focus of attention has been changed from "providing for the aged" to "service demand satisfaction", which needs to meet the needs of the elderly. Complex service needs determine the provision of services for aged should including life services, medical services, agency services, professional services (finance, law, etc.) and so on. In reality, elderly people may need a single service or a combination of services. At the same time, different services will also have different providers. This makes a higher requirement for the matching of demand and supply.

As shown in Fig. 1. The interaction between the elements of the intelligent pension system is nonlinear. Each service subject integrates places, pension facilities, information, knowledge and other resources into a service capability with a certain function and value, providing services in the form of different service subjects. In the service process, service positioning and matching are carried out according to the needs of the elderly, and service is invoked to meet the requirements. In the intelligent pension system, the subjects of demand and supply may not be at both ends of the value chain, but on the notes of the value network. A subject may have dual roles of demand and supply at the same time. For example, healthy elderly with service demand can also become a provider of pension services. The matching between demand and supply of elderly services is completed by a service mediator, which may be an entity, such as information platform, community pension service center, etc., or a functional node of each subject. The basic logic of the intelligent pension system is the service supply based on the needs of the elderly and the service ability matching.

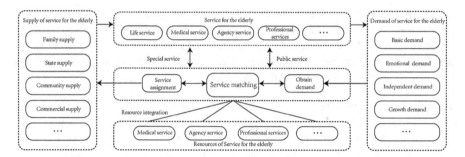

Fig. 1. The matching framework of supply and demand for the elderly service.

3.3 Innovation Strategy of Intelligent Pension System

The characteristics of the intelligent pension system require that its innovation strategy should cover the whole process of demand side, supply side and demand supply matching in the whole time and space dimensions. This requires innovation strategies, including not only the content and form innovation of facilities, products and services, but also the process innovation, management innovation and business mode innovation of services. This paper puts forward the innovation and optimization framework of the intelligent pension system (see Fig. 2).

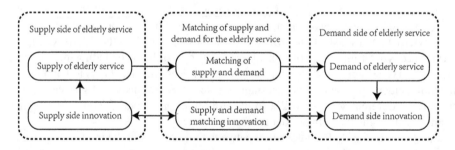

Fig. 2. Innovation strategy framework of intelligent pension system.

The basic logic of the whole framework is the matching of demand supply and the two path cycle. The matching of demand supply is corresponding to demand side innovation, supply side innovation and supply and demand matching innovation. The two path is the driving innovation of "demand - supply" and the promotion of "supply - demand", and the two paths circulate through the three parts.

Driving innovation path is an innovation mechanism from the demand side to the supply side. The service is driven by the requirements. The service is driven by the requirements. The characteristics of the service for elderly determine that this is an interactive process, and the people who need the service are also involved in the service process. Therefore, definite and express service demand more efficiently and accurately is a basic part of the demand side innovation. At the same time, the strategy such as booking services, special services, such as the peak equilibrium help transfer the pension needs, and contribute to the prediction and scheduling of the supply side. When service providers are assigned to service tasks, services are provided by integrating resources.

Promoting innovation path is an innovative mechanism from the supply side to the service side. Service providers expand their service abilities by expanding service resources, improving their quality of service. Through the strategy of service push, service marketing and so on, the service provider can excavate and create new needs for the elderly, then realize the innovation of the intelligent pension system.

3.4 The Mode of Intelligent Pension System

The service demand of the elderly has a variety of characteristics, and it often needs a number of service chains to co-ordinate the completion of the service for the elderly. The synergy between multiple service chains has become the Intelligent pension system. Each service chain represents the service chain that meets the different needs of the elderly, such as the catering service chain, the medical service chain, and so on. Figure 3 is the model of Intelligent pension system.

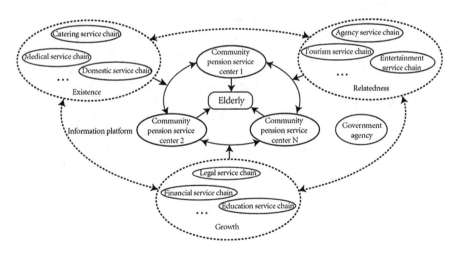

Fig. 3. The model of intelligent pension system.

Different service chains are classified according to ERG theory, and provide different services for the elderly through collaboration or independent action. The community pension service center is the core of the Intelligent pension system, and the different community pension service centers carry out the allocation of the service for the elderly according to their own circumstances. Information interaction between different service providers on information platform. In addition, government agencies are embedded in the whole service system, playing the role of policy guidance and supervision. Different service providers need a clear position of responsibility in the Intelligent pension system.

3.5   Orientation and Suggestion of Different Service Providers

In the Intelligent pension system, the function of the government is to provide a good policy and institutional environment for the formation and development of the whole system, and act as a referee to ensure the healthy development of the pension service market. ① Policy formulation. The government needs to strengthen the formulation and implementation of relevant policies. ② Perfect the law, such as the long-term care insurance law, the practice law of the nursing staff, etc.

In the system, the community pension service center should not only play the role of the main service provider, but also improve its platform role. ① Integration of resources. Integrate the existing public service resources, such as education, culture, sports and other service facilities for the use of the elderly. Integrate all kinds of social service resources, including business organizations and non-profit organizations providing services for the elderly together. ② Supervision. While strengthening the supervision and management of its own elderly service facilities, it is necessary to strengthen the supervision of third party service providers in order to safeguard the rights of the elderly. ③ Information interaction. Through the establishment of the information base of the elderly, including the old people's family, health, demand and other information, to achieve the efficient supply of services.

The third party service providers including business organizations and non-profit organizations. They raise the quality of life for the elderly by providing all kinds of support to the community pension service center and the elderly. ① Rich service content. Improve the content and professionalism of the service, and providing pertinent and rich service for the aged based on the individual differences of the elderly. ② Improve service quality. Ensure the level and quality of service by training the skills of the service staff, and setting strict standards for the service process. ③ Innovate service model. For example, through the integration of social, community, and institutional pension resources to make the pension institutions adapt to the community. This model is especially suitable for urban empty nest elderly, fully satisfied with their needs for professional pension services without leaving home.

4   Conclusion

With the deepening of population aging, the advancement of urbanization and the implementation of the one-child policy, the number of empty nest families will increase day by day, and will become one of the main housebound forms for the elderly in China. The family pension in the community is an important model to solve the problem of the elderly in the empty nest. Based on the survey of the current situation of the empty nest elderly in Gulou District of Nanjing. It is found that there is a contradiction between the lack of demand for the elderly and the coexistence of service. Through the analysis and research of the survey data, this paper puts forward the construction of the model of intelligent service system for the urban empty nest family. This is to help solve the problem of the elderly in the empty nest and improve their quality of life.

Acknowledgments. This work has been supported by the National Social Science Fund, Research on the service mode of home care for the elderly under the support of the community pension service center. Project number 16BSH127.

References

1. Jiang, X., Zheng, Y.: Analysis of the transformation of the living style of the elderly in China and analysis of its influence mechanism. J. Guangxi Univ. Nationalities Philos. Soc. Sc. Ed. **01** (2014)
2. Chang, W.: The state health planning committee reported that half of the elderly Chinese families "empty nest" living. Old Comrades **14,** 14 (2015)
3. Chen, Y.: Population aging brings a lot of industrial opportunities.[EB/OL]. China economic network (2014). http://www.ce.cn/xwzx/gnsz/gdxw/201409/23/t20140923_3584030.shtml. Accessed 10 June 2016
4. Tian, X.: A comparative study of the pension industry and the pension industry–taking Japan's pension industry and the pension industry as an example. J. Tianjin Univ. Soc. Sci. Ed. **1**, 29–35 (2010)
5. Glick, P.C.: The family cycle. Am. Sociol. Rev. **12**(1), 164–174 (1947)
6. Duvall, E.M.: Family development's first forty years. Fam. Relat. **37**(2), 127–134 (1988)
7. Costa, D.L.: Displacing the family: union army pensions and elderly living arrangements. J. Polit. Econ. **105**(6), 1269–1292 (1997)
8. Sun, J.: The status quo and the changing characteristics of the living style of the elderly in China – based on the analysis of the data of "six general" and "five general". Popul. Res. **6**(6), 35–42 (2013)
9. Alderfer, C.P.: An empirical test of a new theory of human needs. Organ. Behav. Hum. Perform. **4**(2), 142–175 (1969)

Overcoming the Vulnerability of Older Adults in Contemporary Media Ecosystem (International Policies and Bulgarian Survey)

Lilia Raycheva[1(✉)], Nadezhda Miteva[1], and Dobrinka Peicheva[2]

[1] Faculty of Journalism and Mass Communication, The St. Kliment Ochridsky Sofia University, Sofia, Bulgaria
lraycheva@yahoo.com, hopeace@abv.bg
[2] Faculty of Philosophy, The Neophite Rilski South-West University, Blagoevgrad, Bulgaria
peichevad@gmail.com

Abstract. Population ageing and the development of modern media digital environment are two interlinked processes in contemporary world. A new media ecosystem, combining the traditional and the online media, has been formed. The trend of population ageing determines the need for urgent prevention of digital generation divide, i.e. of the vulnerability and the social exclusion of older people from the modern information and communication environment. In order to deal with the challenges to population ageing, it is important to analyze how these issues are presented in the media, and to seek information on the current good practices and deficits regarding media and older adults. For this purpose, the proposed text is based on a selection of important general and specialized institutional documents of the United Nations, the Council of Europe and the European Union on age discrimination and media policies. Against this background the paper presents the results of a survey, conducted to measure the extent of vulnerability of older users of media content, compared to younger generations in the constantly changing media ecosystem.

Keywords: Older adults · Vulnerability · Policies on ageing usability
Media ecosystem

1 Introduction

The rapid development of information and communication technologies greatly influence the transformation of the media - from linear to non-linear services, and the audiences - from passive consumers to active prosumers (producers and consumers). And if the processes of politicization of the media and mediatization of politics are most closely associated with the traditional media (print, radio and television), the online media space (social networks, blogs, vlogs, etc.) makes the audiences active participants in the communication process. Thus, in the contemporary media ecosystem people can enter an unmediated, direct dialogue. While traditional media can rely on codes of ethics, self-regulation and co-regulation in compliance with professional principles, the content in the online environment can hardly be regulated and it is difficult to organize public

© Springer International Publishing AG, part of Springer Nature 2018
J. Zhou and G. Salvendy (Eds.): ITAP 2018, LNCS 10926, pp. 118–134, 2018.
https://doi.org/10.1007/978-3-319-92034-4_10

correction of the politics. It is not only via the traditional media that awareness of the shortcomings of the policies on ageing can be raised but it could be done via online communication as well.

No matter how positive the impact of ICT applications and media developments on progress in all areas of life might be, it is no less true that they pose challenges to the social stratification of society. In contemporary ICT and media realm it is important to focus on the problem of overcoming prejudices and negative stereotypes regarding generation differences as well as on the capacity of older people to take part in, and contribute to intercultural dialogue. Therefore, media and information literacy programs acquire additional importance in today's communication environment.

The trend of population ageing determines the need for urgent prevention of the social exclusion of older people from the modern information and communication environment.

This article is based on two interlinked research questions. The first one aims at studying a selection of important general and specialized institutional documents of the United Nations, the Council of Europe and the European Union on ICT and media policies with regard to ageing and age discrimination. Based on this background, the second research question aims at examining the vulnerability of older users of media content, compared to younger generations in constantly changing media ecosystem in Bulgaria.

2   Framework of ICT and Media Policies on Ageing

2.1   United Nations' and European Union's Age Anti-discrimination Policies

The population trends display the growing percentage of the aged population. Although it is expected that the overall population of the European Union will grow to 532 millions by 2060, the population in nearly half of the member states (Bulgaria, Croatia, Germany, Greece, Estonia, Hungary, Latvia, Poland, Portugal, Rumania, Slovakia, Slovenia, and Spain) will decrease. The prognoses show also that the ratio of people above 65 years to those between 15 and 64 will increase from 27.8% to 50.1% [1].

Despite these forecasts, the amount of attention devoted to older people is still not proportionate to the challenges they face in the modern world. For instance, in the United Nations *Universal Declaration of Human Rights (UDHR)*, adopted in 1948, as well as in the *International Covenant on Economic, Social and Cultural Rights* (1966) and the *International Covenant on Economic, Social and Cultural Rights*, which lay the basis of the *International Bill of Human Rights* (adopted in 1976), age discrimination is not explicitly referred to. Article 2 of the United Nations *Universal Declaration of Human Rights*, which sets out the basic principles of equality and non-discrimination in the enjoyment of human rights and fundamental freedoms, forbids the making of distinctions of any kind, including race, colour, sex, language, religion, political or other opinion, national or social origin, property, birth or other status, but it does not mention those related to age [2].

In the *European Convention on Human Rights (ECHR)* (formally entitled *Convention for the Protection of Human Rights and Fundamental Freedoms*), adopted in

1953 by the Council of Europe, there is likewise no specific text concerning age discrimination. For the 47 member states, Article 14 specifically prohibits discrimination based on sex, race, colour, language, religion, political or other opinion, national or social origin, national minority, property, birth or other status such as sexual orientation, but not discrimination based on age. Only in the provisions regarding the members of the European Court of Human Rights, there is a limitation regarding the terms of office and dismissal: the term of office of judges shall expire when they reach the age of 70 [3].

Thorough institutional attention for the ageing population began to appear as late as in the last decade of the 20th century. On December 16, 1991 the United Nations General Assembly adopted *Principles for Older Persons* (Resolution 46/91). The outlined 18 principles are grouped under five themes: independence, participation, care, self-fulfilment and dignity. In the section on dignity there is a text against age discrimination: "Older persons should be treated fairly regardless of age, gender, racial or ethnic background, disability or other status, and be valued independently of their economic contribution" [4].

The *Madrid International Plan of Action on Ageing* (MIPAA) and the *Political Declaration*, adopted by the *Second World Assembly on Ageing* in April 2002, are still among the global guiding documents that have a priority focus in the areas of the rights of older adults and their well-being in a supportive environment [5].

Certain provisions on the equal and respectful treatment of old people are present in the *Charter of Fundamental Rights of the European Union*, drafted in 2000, which entered into force after the *Treaty of Lisbon* on December 1, 2009. Thus Article 21: *Non-Discrimination* stipulates that "Any discrimination based on any ground such as sex, race, colour, ethnic or social origin, genetic features, language, religion or belief, political or any other opinion, membership of a national minority, property, birth, disability, age or sexual orientation, shall be prohibited". Special attention is paid to the rights of the elderly: according to Article 25, the Union recognizes and respects the rights of the elderly to lead a life of dignity and independence and to participate in social and cultural life [6].

Since the start of the second decade of the 21st century, there have been active efforts to promote the adoption of a special *Convention on the Rights of Older Persons* by the UN. Alas, with no success, so far. It is perfectly obvious that these rights cannot be thoroughly defined and protected without taking into consideration the modern information and communication environment. Although many institutional documents related to technology, business models and the editorial responsibility of the media have been adopted, the multi-faceted attitude at older people as objects of coverage and as subjects of the communication process have still not been treated properly and effectively. Nevertheless, the trend is that older adults are not only passive users of the traditional media (press, radio, and television), but they are also becoming prosumers, i.e. active participants and creators of content in the online space.

2.2 European Policies on ICT and Media with Regard to Ageing

Information and Communication Technologies

Contemporary information and communication technologies can help older adults to improve the quality of their well being, preserve their health, and live longer independently.

In connection with the commemoration of 2012 as the *European Year for Active Ageing and Solidarity between Generations* the Eurostat published a statistical portrait of the European Union. Its section on "Silver Surfers" is devoted to the better use of the potential of ICT for healthy and independent ageing. This includes: social inclusion, access to public services, lifelong learning, social and economic activeness. Statistical data show growing use of the Internet in the age groups 55–64 years and 65–74 years for electronic mail correspondence; for seeking information on goods, services and health; for reading newspapers online; for participating in education activities, etc. E-banking and e-shopping have become increasingly popular lately [7].

In the "Ageing Well in the Information Society" communication, published in 2007 and launched within the framework of *i2010 Initiative on e-Inclusion*, the European Commission presented an Action plan for enhanced application of ICT in dealing with the important economic and social challenges caused by ageing of the European population [8].

It is expected that in 2020 a quarter of Europe's population will be over 65, while expenditure on retirement and health care will have tripled by 2050. The Action plan is oriented to promote and coordinate the development of ICTs associated with services for older people in the European Union in order to enable them:

- at the workplace – to prolong their working life through development of electronic skills, while maintaining work-life balance;
- in society – to stay socially active and creative, through networking and access to public and commercial services, thus reducing the social isolation of older people, particularly in rural areas;
- at home – to encourage a higher quality of life and maintain higher degree of independence [9].

The aim of the plan is to both help older people to achieve a safer and more independent old age and to promote the products and services of ICTs for people with disabilities and for older adults. It also aims at giving political and industrial impetus for creating and enlarging instruments and ICT services accessible to old users and seeking solutions for the challenges of ageing. These tasks enhance social inclusion of the elderly and are further developed in the *H 2020 EU Research and Innovation program* [10].

The political debates about "the graying of Europe" are based on ageing prognoses, some of them outlined in the comprehensive Europe 2020 *Strategy for Smart, Sustainable and Inclusive Growth*. The Strategy envisages the development of technologies in a way that they would enable older adults to live ambient supported independent and healthy life and to take an active part in society. The program in the field of digital technologies for Europe (*A Digital Agenda for Europe*) is fundamental to the Strategy and aims to accelerate high-speed access to the Internet and to increase the benefit of the digital market for households [11].

Media

Providing high speed access to advanced public services and diverse multimedia content for work, training and entertainment has become the mainstay of the knowledge based society. Contemporary broadband connections have great impact on improving life quality, as well as on intensifying social cohesion, especially for the older adults. Therefore intensive improvement of ICT skills and digital literacy are critical to the effectiveness of any media strategy to further advancement from 'user-centered' to 'user-driven' developments for achieving the universality of the digital services.

The technical possibility of combining different media in modern mobile communication devices is facilitating the emergence of new hybrid forms. The options to choose different communication platforms and, consequently, the possibility of satisfying specific individual needs, also increase. To improve their quality of life, older adults today have larger choices to attain equity through inclusion, provided by the new communication technologies and hence, to attain individual and social satisfaction.

Despite the rapid development of ICT and online services, television continues to be the most preferred source of information and entertainment for most European households. The main internationally acknowledged instruments in the field of TV broadcasting continue to be the *European Convention on Transfrontier Television (ECTT)* of the Council of Europe, adopted in 1989 and the *Audiovisual Media Service Directive (AVMSD),* which has been introduced in 2007 by the European Commission. The *ECTT* and the amending Protocols on the one hand, and the *AVMSD* on the other, have similar objectives, although the intention of the *AVMS Directive* is to create a common market in broadcasting.

As a legally binding document, the aim of the *European Convention on Transfrontier Television* is to facilitate the transfrontier transmission and retransmission of television programme services. It also lays down a set of minimum rules concerning the responsibility of broadcasters with regard to European content of programming; advertising, teleshopping and sponsorship, the protection of certain individual rights, etc. [12].

The Audiovisual Media Service Directive (AVMSD) as a successor of the *Television without Frontiers Directive* 89/552/EEC (1989) offers a comprehensive legal framework that covers all linear (broadcasting) and non-linear (on-demand) audiovisual media services, and provides less detailed and more flexible regulation and modernized rules on TV advertising in order to better finance audiovisual content. The *AVMS Directive* also upholds the basic pillars of Europe's audiovisual media model. In particular, the *Directive* underlines the importance of promoting media literacy, development of which can help people to "exercise informed choices, understand the nature of content and services, and take advantage of the full range of opportunities offered by new communication technologies" [13].

Both instruments, the *ECTT* and the *AVMSD*, however, do not have a special focus on the production and dissemination of content aimed at the aged population.

The rapid changes of the audiovisual market require a thorough refining – under a broad consensus – of the existing norms in the *ECTT* and the *AVMSD*. The challenge is whether the regulatory changes should anticipate or follow media practices.

In times of intensive social, economic and technological transformations, the very paradigm of the media inevitably changes as well. The media are becoming convergent phenomena. Audiences also change: they are shifting from massive to individualized, from passive to active. A number of issues, important also for the older people, stay increasingly important, such as: freedom of expression and access to information; pluralism of opinions and variety of contents; professional standards and journalistic ethics; transparency of ownership and accountability to the audience; protection of underage and vulnerable social groups; cooperation between regulation, self-regulation and co-regulation; and the expansion of the social media.

In its volume "Global Population Ageing: Peril or Promise?" The World Economic Forum pays a special attention to the very important question as to whether the portrayal of ageing in media and advertisement influences society's views and responses to population ageing. And also, whether media messaging creates a distorted view of ageing [14].

Further on, the World Economic Forum in its White Paper on *Digital Transformation of Industries: Media, Entertainment and Information* points out the widespread recognition among different stakeholders that the role of digital technology is rapidly shifting from being a driver of marginal efficiency to an enabler of fundamental innovation and disruption [15].

Also, the demographic shifts may have a dramatic impact on consumers' expectations from media and communication industries, as well for their ICT literacy and skills while navigating the digital world. In this sense the habits of the millennials (the generation born between 1981 and 1997) differ from those of the older adults (55+). The demand for technology services that offer convenience, memorabilia and instant access to content anywhere and anytime by the younger population is often juxtaposed to the preferences of the older people for health and wellness, entertainment and education services designed especially for them.

In this new realm it is very important to analyze how the businesses and the audiences of the media and communication industries will gain more value than disruption. The future when artificial intelligence will rigorously impact the creative process in media and communication, thus replacing the multi-channel experiences, is not that distant. Measures should be foreseen to prevent consumers' vulnerability especially from the expanding information overload and the growing digital fatigue.

3   Surveys on Trust in Media in Bulgaria

3.1   Outline of the Focused Survey

Contemporary media ecosystem challenges elderly audiences in many ways. To name a few – these are the fast and growing technological developments, the diversification of information resources (especially in the Internet), the rise of nonprofessionals' generated content, the distribution of distorted or fabricated information, etc.

To measure the extent of vulnerability of older users of media content, compared to younger generations in constantly changing media ecosystem a focus group survey has been initiated by the Faculty of Journalism and Mass Communication of the St. Kliment Ohridsky Sofia University.

Apart from studying the elderly audiences' vulnerabilities, the focus of the survey is to identify behavioral differences among the Bulgarian generations as well as their defense capabilities when facing untrustworthy information in contemporary media and communication environment.

Another focus is rooted in the importance attributed to the fake news phenomenon in all its dimensions as well as to its negative impacts on society. This phenomenon is perceived as a form of hybrid threat for EU security and fighting it is in the focus of a number of activities of the European Commission, namely – the activities of the Commissioner for Digital economy Maria Gabriel, the European Parliament and the Council of the EU [16].

Having in mind the dire consequences for the society brought by devaluation of truth and the distribution of fake news, Pope Francis proposed to dedicate the 2018 World Day of Social Communications to these problems in order to support journalists in their mission to speak truth and to send a message to the world "The truth will set you free: Fake news and journalism for peace" [17].

The subject of the survey is the preferences of the different generations towards various types of media, their interests in different thematic areas, the degree of influence and the means of counteracting fake news.

The methods used are as follows:

– field questionaire and poll;
– data analysis;
– comparative analysis based on age;
– comparative analysis based on data from similar surveys;
– documents and statistics research.

The term *generations* is used in relation with the different age groups, differentiated by the degree of their labor activity. For the purposes of this research the traditional divide in four age groups has been applied: 18–30 (mostly students), 30–55 (actively working people), 56–63 (pre-retirement age, with dampening activity on the labor market), and 64+ (retired, non-working). Table 1 shows the respondents divide by age and by education.

Table 1. Level of education of generations

Education	Age 18–30	Age 31–55	Age 56–63	Age 64+
Primary (%)	0	0	0	11
Secondary (%)	72	42	64	79
Higher (%)	28	58	36	11

The term *vulnerable* is used for groups who can not fully participate as users of the media ecosystem due to lack of knack or competences to use contemporary technical means of communication and are not capable to counter harmful or untrustworthy content. Also these are people who are threatened by social isolation.

The term *fake/false* refers to falsified news content, disguised as legitimate news produced in order to attract users and to increase profit or to pursue political goals [18–21].

The survey is part of a broader field survey, conducted in September and October 2017 among 77 respondents (aged 18–64+). It is not representative. The questionnaire is composed of ten questions, seven - closed and three - semi-open. A control question is included, the purpose of which is to establish the level of understanding of the questions and/or the bona fide attitude of the respondents to the problems, subject to research.

4   Results

The research found out drastic differences regarding the type of preferred media among the different generation groups. While young users devote their time mostly to online media, older users aged 64+ give their preferences to the press and the television. Since people encounter only the direct impression of the media they use, it is logical to conclude that they run upon untrustworthy content in the same type of media (Fig. 1).

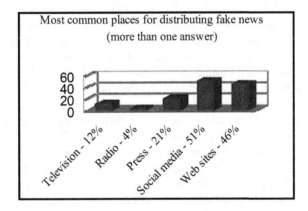

Fig. 1. Most common places for distributing fake news

The assumption that the young devote much of their media time mainly to Internet activities, including social networks and social media, is confirmed. However, the data show that this statement also applies to their parents. In fact, people in active working age (35–44 and 45–55) are the largest groups of users of two of the most popular networks in Bulgaria and Europe - Facebook and Twitter [22]. The demographic profile of the Bulgarian users of social media and social networks builds on preferences by all age groups, including people in the 64+ range, albeit less than others. These preferences explain why social networks and social media are recognized by all respondents, including retirees, as mainstream fraudulent content generators (51% of all respondents point to them as a preferred distribution environment, and 68% - as a primary source of fake news. Political actors collect 29% of the responses and media comes third with 25%) (Fig. 2).

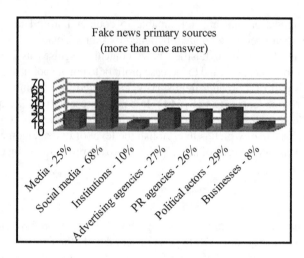

Fig. 2. Fake news primary sources

As the age of social networking and using of social media grows, the segment of social media and social networks is gradually diminishing as a source of fake content, but it does not disappear completely. Only the oldest respondents give the political class an advantage over this indicator. This is easy to understand given the fact that people of retirement age are keenly interested in politics and government news as their well-being (the size and increase of their earnings, health insurance, social benefits - personal assistant, heating support, etc.) and sometimes - and their survival - depend to a large extent on the decisions of the public authorities.

All this determines the interest of the older audience in topics related to domestic politics, security and public order, economy and finance. These are topics that are directly related to the lives, health and safety of the elderly and their families. For this reason, they are most sensitive to the spreading of false and distorted facts precisely on this subject. 79% of the people in pre-retirement age and 63% of the retired people claim that fake information most often refers to issues of domestic policy, economy, crime, and security. For young people under 30, politics is a distant abstraction without a clear framework. For them free time, not professional development, has been a cult. Their interests are related to sports, lifestyle of public figures and celebrities, and for this reason the majority of them (78%) claim that the media most often speculate about the facts of the celebrities' lives. The middle age generation tries to stick to the pattern of being informed on a wider range of issues. The opinion of the respondents aged 30–55 is that untrue information is distributed in a balanced way between domestic politics, economy, crime and public order, and the lifestyle of celebrities (Fig. 3).

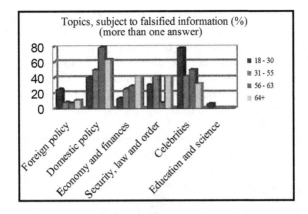

Fig. 3. Topics, subject to falsified information

A large number of respondents (57%) encounter unreliable information each day, and over a quarter say they fall into fake news every week. Less than 3% insist that they have never encountered media fiction. These percentages portray the Bulgarian audience as being conscious and, to a large extent, literate enough to recognize untrue information.

The highest (67%) is the percentage of recognition of fake news in the younger part of the audience (18–30 years old), and the lowest - in people at pre-retirement and retirement age (56–64+) - 42% and 47%. The explanation is not so much in the higher media literacy of young people, as in the way media is consumed by them and even in their lifestyle (Fig. 4).

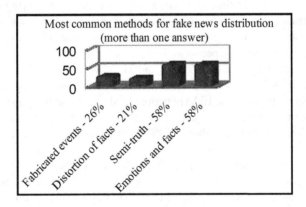

Fig. 4. Most common methods for fake news distribution

The main source of information about the younger generations is online media and chatting with friends (direct or computer-mediated). Not to trust institutions and author-itative personalities is a matter of principle, although groundless. The elderly consump-tion pattern is distinguished by higher level of trust in linear electronic media.

Over half of the elderly categorically recognize false news as mixing real facts with fiction (half-truth), on the same footing as the circumstances that influence the audience's emotions and beliefs in order to ignore objective facts.

The older audiences are aware of the nuances and the various forms of "fake news". They have the confidence to recognize them and counteract them. As the age of the respondents grows up, their confidence that they will not be affected by the harmful effects of untrustworthy information increases (Fig. 5).

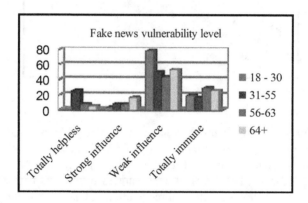

Fig. 5. Fake news vulnerability level

For younger users, high self esteem is likely to be tied to the fact that they are very well familiar with the technological environment in which fake content is prioritized. As they devote much of their time to it, they have the means of identifying and blocking technology (software, mobile applications) on unreliable sites and enjoy the support of their online community. Young people are hardly under the influence of traditional media (radio, television and the press) as they rarely (or at all) do not use those [23]. In addition, the audiences aged 18–30 (65.5%) and 31–55 years (33.33%) tend to carry out their own research on the reliability of information, including – the usage of specialized software or mobile applications. Elderly people tend to rely on the good faith of journalists and content authors (63%), and most of all, on their own life experiences of distinguishing the truth from falsehood (50% of 56-63-year-olds and 32% of the aged 64+).

At first glance, this puts the older users in the position of the most vulnerable part of the media audience. But not if the modern view is taken that the public is sustainable, including significant attempts at manipulation, triggering various emotional, value and cognitive barriers, and when it prefers to get social referrals from close people instead of media. At the same time, these audiences are susceptible to messages that are timely, interesting, personally oriented and which meet their expectations, understanding and experience, messages that help decrease their feelings of being socially insecure as well as reduce their psychological and cognitive discomfort [24]. On the other hand, especially this segment of the audiences seem to be the subject of personalized media messages, and is underestimated in the development of policy and marketing strategies (Fig. 6).

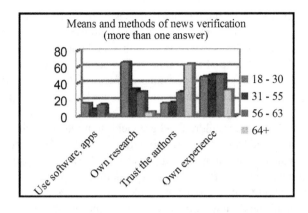

Fig. 6. Means and methods of news verification

The fact is that with age, the percentage of people willing to use technical means to denounce unreliable content is decreasing. However, to consider that insufficient technical and media literacy are inherent characteristics of people of retirement age is wrong. Their technical skills and abilities must be seen in the historical context of the time they have been acquired and developed.

During the EU Online Media Summit, organized by the European Broadcasting Union on 22 October 2015 in Dublin, Ireland [25], it was pointed out that young retirees in Western Europe are an underestimated (market and not just market) niche. The clarification that this is valid for Western Europe societies is by no means casual. Experts stated that "young retirees", i.e. people aged about 60, can be productive (both "lucrative" and still active in the economy). These are people with still strong social activity and social contacts. They have free financial resources (pensions) that they would like to spend. Moreover, despite the perception that information technology and new media are "on and off" for the young people, in fact, for the "young retirees in the West" the digital world is no strange at all. In fact, today's "young retirees" are the people who created the Internet and laid the foundations for satellite technologies, mobile communications and everything that is now taken for granted and is easy to use. On the other hand, this is the generation that grew up with punk, with the music of Sex Pistols, and it can hardly be called "congested" (conservative). In short, young retirees are a niche that is actively present in the digital society and is waiting to be recognized in the digital services market.

In Bulgaria, the technological revolution is not as backward in comparison with the Western world. In the 20s of the 20th century the Bulgarians listened to their own national Radio. The Bulgarian National Television, which began broadcasting in the late 1950s, was the first in the Balkans. The 70s and the 80s were marked by the rise of electronics. At that time Bulgaria produced its own brands of computers, computing machines, processors, magnetic heads, compact discs, radio and television sets, telephones, radio navigation equipment, etc. Bulgarian scientists and engineers participated in space programs and projects. 1975–1990 were the golden years of Bulgarian electronics. With total exports of the country in 1989 of 13.5 billion BGN, machine-building and electronics - the two most intellectual branches of industry, accounted for nearly 60%. They employed about 600,000 people (a large number of them - well-educated engineers, scientists and business executives), with a total country population of nearly 8 million people. The backbone of these industry branches are the generations born in the 1950s and the 1960s [26] - today's "young retirees" of Bulgaria aged between 60 and 70, as well as people on the border of active working age and pre-retirement, perceived as the "the technological generation" (the baby boomers), unlike the "internet generation" (X and Y) of their children and grandchildren today. Their contribution to the Bulgarian economy and society is strongly felt today. After the political changes of 1989, part of this valuable resource has drained abroad. However, those who stayed in the country are among the people who set the foundations of private initiative in high-tech manufacturing and services. These are people who are able to get their professional chance and for whom the digital world is not alien. That is why the "generation" of people around 50–67 has to be separated in a special group when discussing financial security, handling modern technical devices, making decisions, forming and main-taining an opinion.

Communication technical literacy, as far as it is fundamental to the functioning of consumers in the modern information ecosystem, has one more specific feature among the elderly in Bulgaria. Like "young retirees" who do not have technical education and have not worked in technology sectors, older people are also interested in developing skills to work with online information sources, smartphones and social networks, call and messaging applications such as Skype, Messenger, WhatsApp, etc. [27, 28] This literacy is often the only chance for communication between older people and their descendants, scattered, mostly on economic downturns, at different points in the global-ized world [29]. On the other hand, it enables pensioners to establish contacts and thus overcome social exclusion.

Respondents of the survey are most likely to have the greatest importance in terms of age (78%), education (50.64%) and residence (27%) as factors determining the extent of unreliable consumer impact. The most vulnerable are the adolescents aged 15–18 (28.33%), as well as the elderly aged 64+ (28.33%), those with the primary education (38%), and residents in small settlements in the countryside (18%).

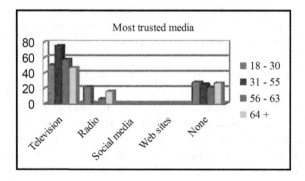

Fig. 7. Most trusted media

According to the survey, television continues to enjoy the trust of over half of the respondents, and remains the most preferred among people in active and retirement age.

Every sixth of the respondents relies for trustworthy information on the radio, while social networks and the social media as well as websites are completely discredited. Almost 33% of the users state that there is no such media which can be trusted (Fig. 7).

The results of the survey confirm the sustained trust in television as a medium in Bulgaria, registered in the last two years by the Open Society Institute within the framework of the Report on Public Attitudes to Democracy, the Rule of Law and Fundamental Rights. According to the report, television is the main source of information for 74% of Bulgarians in 2016 [30]. The Alpha Research Agency in its National Representative Survey indicates television as the main source of information, especially on domestic and international issues for 90% of the Bulgarians [31]. Compared to other EU countries, Bulgarians watch more television, read less newspapers and listen less to radio programmes [32]. This resilience to the interest in television in Bulgaria is against the backdrop of a worldwide decline in traditional media consumption, as recorded in 2016 [33].

5   Discussion

When assessing the media vulnerability of older people in Bulgaria, it should be borne in mind that they are not a homogeneous group of people. Apart from the traditional division of people at pre-retirement and retirement age, there is another intermediate demographic group, whose characteristics are sharply different from the traditional perception of older adults in Bulgaria. The "technological" generation (today's Bulgarians at the age of 50–67), which ensured the boom of the high-tech industry in Bulgaria in two socio-economic systems, has a high social status, a good financial position and opportunities for coping in the modern ICT environment. Media and political PR specialists should view them as a group with significant, underestimated potential, rather than as people with disruptive functions in society.

Enhancing the communication and media literacy of the elderly should be encouraged by the governmental and the NGO sector as it satisfies several needs simultaneously: communicating with relatives who have emigrated abroad, overcoming social exclusion by establishing contacts with people with similar interests, diversifying the channels for obtaining a variety of information, providing an opportunity to check its credibility, etc.

6   Conclusion

Population ageing and the developments of modern media ecosystem are two interlinked processes in contemporary world. The trend of population ageing determines the need for urgent prevention of the vulnerability and the social exclusion of older people from the modern information and communication environment.

In answering the first research question the undertaken analysis on policies of UN, CoE and EU with regard to ageing and age discrimination, as well as on corresponding ICT and media policies indicates some significant tendencies:

- legally: there is a general insufficiency of internationally binding legal instruments to provide reliable regulatory mechanisms against age discrimination as well as for a more balanced and adequate media coverage of older people;
- technologically: the dynamic progress of ICTs is challenging the very concept of the traditional media. Digital technologies, broadband and web casting increase the number of channels, thereby providing users with multiple choices of linear and non-linear programming. As positive as these opportunities may be, they also pose significant challenges to media consumption by the older population;
- socially: the contemporary ICT based environment has an ambivalent impact on media consumption. Older people are both consumers and creators of content, and moreover, they mutually socialize with one another. However, the merge of essential characteristics of journalism, PR and advertising and the loose professional standards increase the vulnerability of the audiences from the distributed content.

Answering the second research question, based on the results of the presented surveys, it can be noted that the teenagers and the oldest, poorly educated, mostly living in the countryside users of media content can be considered as truly vulnerable participants in the contemporary media ecosystem. Communication skills tend to converge rather than distinguish young people from older generations. But while for adolescents it is due to their immaturity, for the elderly it is a stable part of their value system. Namely this group of older adults has no other means of protection against unreliable and manipulative information, apart from the credibility and professionalism of journalists and of its own long life experience. Elderly people can withstand media impact when it is contrary to their established beliefs, knowledge and patterns of behavior. However they can not counteract the personified, reliant on their feelings and highest values, influence.

Prejudices and negative stereotypes are among the major current challenges relative to the life of the ageing population in the modern information and communication environment. Identifying the ways in which these prejudices may be effectively overcome will help to prevent vulnerability and to neutralize the rise of barriers to the full participation of older people in socio-cultural processes.

Acknowledgements. The text has been developed within the framework of two COST Actions of the European Commission: IS1402: *Ageism - A Multi-National, Interdisciplinary Perspective* and IS1404: *Evolution of Reading in the Age of Digitization*. The research has been supported by the National Scientific Fund of Bulgaria: projects DCOST 01/10-04.08.2017; DCOST 01/11-04.08.2017; DCOST 01.13/04.08.2017; DCOST 01.25/20.12.2017, and DN 05/11-14.12.2016. Some of the results have been presented at the International Conference "Consuming the Environment 2017 – Multidisciplinary Approaches to Urbanization and Vulnerability". University of Gävle, Gävle, Sweden (December, 3–5 2017).

References

1. European Commission: The 2015 Ageing Report. Economic and Budgetary Projections for the 28 EU Member States (2013-2060) (2015)
2. United Nations: The Universal Declaration of Human Rights. http://www.un.org/en/universal-declaration-human-rights/index.html
3. Council of Europe: European Convention on Human Rights. http://www.coe.int/en/web/human-rights-convention
4. United Nations: The United Nations Principles for Older Persons. http://www.olderpeoplewales.com/en/about/un-principles.aspx
5. United Nations ESCAP: Madrid International Plan of Action on Ageing. http://www.unescap.org/resources/madrid-international-plan-action-ageing
6. 6 European Union: Charter of Fundamental Rights of the European Union. http://eur-lex.europa.eu/legal-ontent/EN/TXT/HTML/?uri=CELEX:12012P/TXT&from=EN
7. EUROSTAT Statistical Books: Active Ageing and Solidarity between Generations. A Statistical Portrait of the European Union (2012). http://ec.europa.eu/eurostat/documents/3217494/5740649/KS-EP-11-001-EN.PDF/1f0b25f8-3c86-4f40-9376-c737b54c5fcf
8. Peicheva, D., Raycheva, L.: The Transformation of Reading among the Ageing Population in the Digital Age. In: Zhou, J., Salvendy, G. (eds.) ITAP 2016. LNCS, vol. 9754, pp. 216–225. Springer, Cham (2016). https://doi.org/10.1007/978-3-319-39943-0_21
9. European Commission Ageing Well in the Information Society: Action Plan on Information and Communication Technologies and Ageing. http://eur-lex.europa.eu/legal-content/BG/TXT/?uri=URISERV:l24292
10. European Commission H 2020: The EU Framework Program for Research and Innovation. https://ec.europa.eu/programmes/horizon2020/
11. European Commission. Europe 2020: A European Strategy for Smart, Sustainable, and Inclusive Growth. http://eur-lex.europa.eu/LexUriServ/LexUriServ.do?uri=COM:2010:2020:FIN:EN:PDF
12. Council of Europe: European Convention on Transfrontier Television. http://conventions.coe.int/Treaty/EN/Treaties/Html/132.htm
13. European Commission: Directive 2007/65/EC of the EP Parliament and of the Council Amending Council Directive 89/552/EEC on the Coordination of Certain Provisions Laid Down by Law, Regulation or Administrative Action in Member States Concerning the Pursuit of Television Broadcasting Activities. http://eur-lex.europa.eu/LexUriServ/LexUriServ.do?uri=CONSLEG:1989L0552:20071219:EN
14. Milner, C., Norman, K., Milner, J.: The Media's Portrayal of Ageing. In: Global Population Ageing: Peril or Promise? World Economic Forum. https://cdn1.sph.harvard.edu/wp-content/uploads/sites/1288/2013/10/PGDA_WP_89.pdf
15. World Economic Forum: White Paper on Digital Transformation of Industries: Media, Entertainment and Information. http://reports.weforum.org/digital-transformation/wp-content/blogs.dir/94/mp/files/pages/files/wef-dti-mediawhitepaper-final-january-2016.pdf
16. European Union: Joint Report to the European Parliament and the Council on the Implementation of the Joint Framework on Countering Hybrid Threats - A European Union Response. http://eur-lex.europa.eu/legal-content/EN/ALL/?uri=CELEX:52017JC0030
17. Harries, E.: Pope Zeroes-in on Fake News for Next Communications Day. https://www.catholicnewsagency.com/news/pope-zeros-in-on-fake-news-for-next-communications-day-94809
18. Wardle, C.: Fake News. It's Complicate. https://medium.com/1st-draft/fake-news-its-complicated-d0f773766c79

19. Weedon, J., Nuland, W., Stamos, A.: Information Operation and Facebook (2017). https://fbnewsroomus.files.wordpress.com/2017/04/facebook-and-information-operations-v1.pdf
20. Silverman, C.: Verification and Fact-Checking. http://verificationhandbook.com/additionalmaterial/
21. Nielsen, R. Graves, L.: News You Don't Believe: Audience Perspectives on Fake News. http://reutersinstitute.politics.ox.ac.uk/sites/default/files/2017-10/Nielsen%26Graves_factsheet_1710v3_FINAL_download.pdf
22. MarkBit Demography of the Users of Social Networks. http://markbit.net/trends/infographic/social_media_demographic/#lightbox/0/. (in Bulgarian)
23. Capital: Young People Do Not Trust Media. http://www.capital.bg/politika_i_ikonomika/bulgaria/2013/12/01/2194058_mladite_hora_ne_viarvat_na_mediite/. (in Bulgarian)
24. Petev, T.: The Communication Helix. Askoni-Izdat, Sofia (2010)
25. Eurovision: Online Media Summit. A Day for Inspiration and Sharing Ideas. https://www.ebu.ch/files/live/sites/ebu/files/Events/Media%20Online/Online_Plenary_and_Summit/OnlineSummit_Agenda_Final-1.pdf
26. InvestBulgaria Agency: Sectors (Machine Building. Electrical Engeneering and Electronics. Information Technology). http://www.investbg.government.bg/sectors/index/index/lang/bg
27. BNR: Grandparents Are Surfing the Net. http://bnr.bg/vidin/post/100562322/babi-i-dadovci-sarfirat-iz-mrejata. (in Bulgarian)
28. 24 Chassa: Lady Mayor Teaches in Bulgarian via Skype the Children of the People Making Their Living Abroad (2015). https://www.24chasa.bg/novini/article/4820322. (in Bulgarian)
29. Capital: Hi, Grandma! Blog Introduces Older People to New Technologies and Social Networks. http://www.capital.bg/light/lica/2017/06/09/2985550_hi_baba/. (in Bulgarian)
30. Open Society Institute: Democracy and Civic Participation. Public Attitudes to Democracy, the Rule of Law and Fundamental Rights in 2016. http://osi.bg/downloads/File/2017/Democracy%20Survey%202016%20BG.pdf
31. Alpha Research: Survey by Konrad Adenauer Foundation & Alpha Research: Media and Foreign policy - Opinions of the Bulgarians. http://alpharesearch.bg/bg/socialni_izsledvania/socialni_publikacii/izsledvane-na-fondaciya-konrad-adenauer-_amp-alfa-risarch_-medii-i-vanshna-politika-mneniya-na-balgarite.878
32. European Commission: Standard Eurobarometer 82. Media Use in the EU. http://ec.europa.eu/public_opinion/archives/eb/eb82/eb82_media_en.pdfStandardEurobarometer82
33. WARC: Traditional Media Time Declines. https://www.warc.com/NewsAndOpinion/News/36905

Long-Term Appropriation of Smartwatches Among a Group of Older People

Andrea Rosales[✉], Mireia Fernández-Ardèvol,
and Núria Ferran-Ferrer

Universitat Oberta de Catalunya, 08041 Barcelona, Spain
arosalescl@uoc.edu

Abstract. In this paper, we analyze long-term appropriation of smartwatches among a group of older people. For the purpose of the study, we provided five older individuals (aged 71 to 80; three women, two men) with Android smartwatches. We interviewed participants after 2 and 12 months of smartwatch usage and observed its usage in an informal gathering 12 months after the end of the study. Drawing on Morville's model of user experience (2004), we focus on how the smartwatch was (not) useful, usable, valuable, and desirable for each participant in each stage of the process. Results show the relevance of valuableness and desirability in the (non-)appropriation of smartwatches for those participants. Specifically, participants used the smartwatches to express their sporty, techie and fashion identities.

Keywords: Older people · Wearable · Smartwatch
Appropriation · UX

1 Introduction

Significant attention has been given to smartwatches in research into human-computer interaction in recent years. On the one hand, they offer access to basic smartphone information while leaving the hands free, supposedly allowing users to interact in a more natural way. On the other hand, they allow an intimate connection to be created with user's body, thus allowing certain body indicators to be obtained [1, 2]. Research into the topic is growing steadily. In part, this research is related to understanding smartwatch perceptions and usage, but it is also related to new possibilities for interaction. There is particular interest in how these watches could compensate for physical and cognitive decline often associated with older people [3, 4]. To further this understanding of how best to take advantage of this technology for older people, we present a case study analyzing long-term appropriation of smartwatches among a group of older individuals.

We provided five older individuals (aged 71 to 80; three women, two men) with Android smartwatches. The project was designed to follow their experiences over 12 months. Thus, we interviewed participants 2 and 12 months after the start of the study through informal interviews. In addition, 12 months after the end of the study, that is, 24 months after the study had started, when participants had no further commitments with the study, an informal gathering was held so that we could observe if participants

© Springer International Publishing AG, part of Springer Nature 2018
J. Zhou and G. Salvendy (Eds.): ITAP 2018, LNCS 10926, pp. 135–148, 2018.
https://doi.org/10.1007/978-3-319-92034-4_11

were using the smartwatches or not. We briefly chatted with each participant about their use. Our aim was to address the following research question: How do usefulness, usability, valuableness and desirability influence long-term appropriation of smart-watches among a group of older individuals?

In this paper, we present the evolution of participants' user experience (UX) to show how they did or did not become long-term users of the device. The results revealed different facets that influence smartwatch user experience. In general, smartwatches were useful and usable for most participants, but these were not the main reasons for (non-) appropriation. Otherwise, valuableness and desirability were key factors for (non-) appropriation of the smartwatches. Thus, engaged participants, those that kept using the smartwatch 24 months after the start of the study, found it valuable and used the device to express their sporty, techie and fashion identities or to obtain social recognition. The findings help to better understand the challenges facing the appropriation of smartwatches and other technological devices, especially among older people.

2 Related Work

In recent year, research has focused its attention on the perceptions of smartwatches and smartwatch usage. Both sides of the consumer process contribute to understanding the appropriation of a new technology [5]. Different studies have looked at smart-watches from the perspective of usefulness, usability, valuableness, and desirability, which will be further explained in Sect. 3. However, these aspects have been studied based on non-users or in short-term studies (less than 6 months) and with mostly young participants.

According to a survey of 226 potential users, where the average age was 21, "perceived usefulness and visibility (which is related to desirability) are important factors that drive adoption intention" [6] p. 276. According to another survey of 212 potential users (of whom 13.2% were 55+), relative advantages (usefulness), ease of use (**usability**), result demonstrability and enjoyment (valuableness) have a significant impact on users' attitude toward a smartwatch. In addition, attitude significantly influences smartwatch acceptance [7].

Some studies have explored how regularly people use smartwatches which is an indicator of their **usefulness**. Based on surveys with 90 Apple watch users, after 120 days of use (4 months), researchers identified that only 4.5% had stopped using the smartwatch [8]. A study based on data collected through activity trackers involving 50 students over 203 days (6 months approx.) concluded that the students wore the smartwatches an average of 10.9 h on weekdays and 8.4 during weekends [9]. Another study tracked the smartwatch activities of 307 anonymous users, with no demographics provided. According to the results, smartwatches are used more frequently throughout the day and for briefer periods of time than smartphones [10]. In addition, an analysis of the smart-watch logs of 27 participants from a university campus concluded that "smartwatch usage is more uniformly distributed compared to that of smartphones" [11].

According to previous studies, the main added value of smartwatches (or **valu-ableness**) is the possibility of reading notifications [12, 13]. In interviews with 10 smartwatch users, who had owned their smartwatches for at least three months confirmed that "Users see a large benefit in receiving notifications on their wrist" [14] p. 3557. One of the main reasons is "lack of impact of watch glances on conversation" [15] p. 3582, for example, among school teachers [16]. Personal interest and activities also shape smartwatch user experiences [17].

The influence of **desirability**, those aspects related with style and identity, on smartwatch appropriation has been discussed in different studies. Style is part of the smartwatch experience [13, 18]. "Individuals with a high level of vanity would consider using smartwatches to be more enjoyable (and) one's need for uniqueness was found to be a critical predictor of how much one would perceive smartwatches to be enjoyable and useful for expressing oneself" [19] p. 9. Croncretely,"display shape and standalone communication are more critical factors influencing respondents' smartwatch choices than brand and price" [20].

3 Methods

The empirical evidence presented here comes from a case study originally designed to analyze the processes of smartwatch adoption and appropriation by older people. We provided a Moto G 360 smartwatch to participants, all of whom had to have a compatible Android smartphone. Participants had to be 65 or older. They already needed to be active users of smartphones, be strongly committed to following the study, and not have a smartwatch. They could choose between the Moto G 360 1st generation (1.6″ screen) and the Moto G 360 Sports 2nd generation (1.37″ screen), models available on the market at the beginning of the project. Participants received monetary compensation for time spent in interviews and were able to keep the smartwatch after 12 months of participating in the project. This particular study is part of a wider project, where we tracked their smartwatch activities with an app, conducting another three interviews to get bimonthly reports, but such information was not used for the purposes of this paper. Following approved ethical protocols, participants could stop their collaboration with the project at their convenience. They could do whatever they wanted with the smartwatch during and after the study period, just as long as they committed to giving the bimonthly interviews and using the tracking system for one year to participate in the project.

We use a mixed methods approach, combining reported speech with observations in real-life settings [21]. For the purpose of this paper, we conducted two semi-structured interviews, the first interview after two months and the second interview after twelve months of having the smartwatch. Twenty-four months after the start of the study, we met with the participants in an informal gathering, where we observed if they were using the smartwatches and briefly chatted with them to ascertain if they were using them regularly or not. Thus, we have combined detailed qualitative information on their experiences at months 2 and 12 with concrete qualitative data for month 24.

The study involved 5 participants: 3 women and 2 men, aged 71 to 80. In this paper we will refer to them as: W1, W2 W3, M1, M2. They are participants from an adult education center. We had met them previously because one of the paper's authors often volunteers as an ICT teacher and other research projects had been conducted at the center.

We used 4 of the 7 facets proposed by Morville [22] to understand different aspects of user experience; specifically, how useful, usable, desirable and valuable a product is for a user in any given moment. The 4 facets allowed a holistic understanding of each individual user experience, and were useful as a strategy to spark discussion with participants about their user experiences. We did not use the other 3 facets described in Morville's framework, namely that a product be findable, credible and accessible, as they were not closely related with the smartwatch experience analyzed in this study.

We will explain the four concepts we did use as described by Morville and how they relate to this project.

- Useful. The user should find some utility. In this project, we specifically considered if people used the smartwatch regularly as an indicator of usefulness, and what for?
- Usable. The product should be easy to use. Thus, we considered if they had problems, questions or issues they would like to clear up and have not yet learned about.
- Valuable. The product must provide an added value to the user, in comparison to other products. Specifically, we considered what participants found to be most valuable about the smartwatch in their opinion.
- Desirable. It refers to the power and value of image, identity and other elements of emotional design. In this study, this is how participants associate it with their personal identity.

In the first interview, we included several questions related to the participants' user experience, and we extracted topics related with all 7 facets described by Morville. As the most common topics found in this interview had to do with usefulness, usability, valuableness, and desirability, we ignored Morville's other three facets. In the second interview, we focused in questions related to these 4 facets. In the results for both interviews we extracted the comments related with the four facets. We assessed if their comments were positive ↑, ambivalent ↑↓ or negative ↓. Finally, we compared the experiences they reported during the first and second interviews with the observations made at the informal gathering after 24 months.

4   Results

At month 12 of the study, the five users reported that the smartwatch was **useful**. They were able to include it in their everyday life and use it for a variety of purposes, depending on their interests. However, two of them (W1 & W3) stopped using the smartwatch after month 12 of the study, once their commitment to the project was over. In the month-12 interviews, they stated that, although it was usable and useful, it was not valuable or desirable enough. Contrarily, by month 12, the other 3 participants found it valuable and desirable. At month 24 they were still consistently using the smartwatch, even though their commitment to the project had ended.

Except for a few problems at the beginning of the study, each participant learned to use the smartwatch. However, each one only became an expert in the features that interested them the most. Except for one participant (W2), the rest found the smartwatch **usable**. Despite the difficulties encountered, W2 was one of the participants still engaged at month 24. For all three engaged users, the smartwatch was **valuable**, although for different reasons. The activity tracker was the most valuable for M2 while the notifications were what W2 most appreciated. M1 found it valuable for the notifications, the maps and the music control. For all three, **desirability** played a role in smartwatch appropriation. The smartwatch helped to express their identity, whether it be sporty, techie or fashion-related, or to obtain social recognition. In the following sections, we provide details of the evolution of each participant's user experience.

4.1   W1, The Disenchanted

At month 12, she wears it every day, all day, at home and outside. The reports from the first and the second interviews are consistent; she finds it useful and usable. However, the smartwatch does not seem valuable and desirable to her (See Tables 1 and 2). She considers it just a cool thing, and more interesting for young people. When she started using the smartwatch, she had expectations about how it could change people's lives. However, after 12 months of usage, these expectations have not been met, and she can find no reason to continue using the smartwatch. In fact, by the end of the project, she gave the smartwatch to her nephew.

Table 1. W1, Interview 1

↑	Useful	She uses it to check the time and notifications, which happens very often because she has a pretty active social life
↑	Usable	She finds it is easy to use, and, when asked, she gives this example: ... *during Christmas, he* [her nephew] *un-configured it* [...] *so I did the setup again* [...] *step by step*
↑↓	Valuable	She states *this is practical, because you wear it here (showing the wrist).* However, she expects to get more out of it, to learn more things about it
↓	Desirable	She likes its practical features, but she doesn't show any signal of emotional engagement with the device itself. She does not associate it with aspects of her identity, and she does not express any sign that the smartwatch clashes with her identity

Table 2. W1, Interview 2

↓	Useful	She wears it regularly and reports that she frequently uses it, only because she has a very intense social life: *I wear it. As I wear it, I use it. Look, not long ago I had a WhatsApp, now it comes another, that is, they are arriving.*
		However, she is clear about the fact that she won't keep using it: *I think that when we finish everything* [the project]*, I'll give it away. Because I have a nephew who is twelve years old, nearly thirteen, and he loves it*
↑	Usable	She has no usability issues but has not explored the smartwatch that much during this time. She doesn't know anything new about the smartwatch, since previous interview
↑↓	Valuable	She finds it practical: *If they call me on my cellphone and I do not hear it, it vibrates here. And this is great for me. For example, I am in a class, and I stop, and suddenly pa-pa-pa, in class. If I'm interested… I take it. If I'm not interested…. The whatsapps too. Yes, for this, it is very practical.* However, she could take it or leave it: *If I wear the other one* [classic watch]*, I have enough. If I have it* [smartwatch]*, I look at it*
↓	Desirable	She doesn't identify with the smartwatch, she refers to is as a generational issue: *What do you want me to tell you? It's more like a hobby. And it's such a cool thing, for example, for kids. But for us, I do not know… not sure if it's worth it*

4.2   W2, Proud User

She uses it all day, at home and outside. Although she still has some usability issues and does not make extensive use of the smartwatch, she is a proud user and wants to show it off whenever there is an opportunity (see Tables 3 and 4).

Table 3. W2, Interview 1

↑	Useful	She says she use it every, and all day, at home and outside. She mostly uses it to check the time
↓	Usable	She states that it has been easy to use. Although, at the same time, she only uses it to check the time, and she would like to do other things but has not figured out how to do them: *sometimes, I want to do something and it is difficult*
↓	Valuable	She does not report any use, beyond checking the time
↑	Desirable	The smartwatch gives her a positive image, and she tries to take advantage of this. She says that, when she meets up with somebody, she asks, *Did you notice, did you notice?* (pointing at the smartwatch). Then she has the opportunity to explain all the advantages of the smartwatch

Table 4. W2, Interview 2

↑↓	Useful	She wears it every day and all the time. Although she does not report frequent use, she adds: *this month I've been a little bit out of it... I haven't used the computer, either. Although the smartphone, yes!*
↓	Usable	She does not feel she has a good handle on using the smartwatch: *The steps themselves, mmm, this, if I were more confident, when I'm going to walk, yes, I would wear it, because it's comfortable [...] if I put it on right.* She adds: *When these things start to fail, mmmm, it is as if you have a Mercedes; has it failed me, or have I failed?*
↑	Valuable	She finds it valuable because: *I know when they call me. Mmm, if I do not hear the phone, the clock tells me that I have an email, that I have a message. If I'm waiting for those calls, then I go to the phone; otherwise, I don't bother*
↑	Desirable	She continues to be a proud user of her smartwatch: *I say, [...] come on, look what I've got! Look what I've got!*

4.3   W3, Communications

She uses it daily. It plays a role in her everyday communication, allowing her to keep an eye on the notifications on her smartwatch. However, it is not an essential device for her, and she is somewhat ashamed of it (see Tables 5 and 6).

Table 5. W3, Interview 1

↑	Useful	She uses it daily, although not at home or the gym, since she usually wears other watches. She finds it useful. She uses it to check the time, her steps and to manage notifications: *sometimes it turns on when I receive a message and, then, I see it.* She also changes the screen design depending on what she is wearing
↑	Usable	She does not have usability issues. She also does not have questions about other the smartwatch's other features
↓	Valuable	She does not find it valuable: *Well, if they give it to me, fine, but buy it, I think... I do not see it as useful*
↓↑	Desirable	She is not proud of it: *I usually have it covered. [...] But not because I don't like it and its spectacular, but because people our age say: "Well, what an ugly watch this woman is wearing", you know?* She does not like its design or the fact that it is a techie device: *No, it's not nice, not for me. Young people do say: "Oh!" They are more into these technologies... they want to have everything.* However, changing the smartwatch face every day to match her outfit makes her happy

Table 6. W3, Interview 2

↑↓	Useful	She uses it daily, basically to see notifications; she does not check how many steps she's taken any more. She does not change the watch face anymore
↑	Usable	She makes very basic use of it, mostly to check notifications. Although she has noticed that even with the same setup all the time she sometimes does not receive notifications (which was a common problem with the smartwatches they were using but was barely noticed by the other participants)
↓	Valuable	She reports that it is not valuable for her: *There is no big difference from wearing any other* [watch]
↓	Desirable	She said she is not proud of wearing the smartwatch

4.4   M1, The Techie

Although he was fairly skeptical at the beginning of the study, as an explorer, he has explored all the possibilities of the smartwatch. He makes extensive use of it, particularly regarding things that matter to him, such as notifications, music and maps. Moreover, the smartwatch lets him express his techie identity (see Tables 7 and 8).

Table 7. M1, Interview 1

↓	Useful	He wears it every day. Although, he says he does not know if the smartwatch is useful. He doesn't want it to consume him like the smartphone: *When you receive a WhatsApp, there are people that feel the need to check who sent it. I don't*
↓	Usable	Apparently, discovering its features has not been easy, because at this point he still states: *I do not know which features it has*
↓	Valuable	At this point he is not clear if the smartwatch is in fact valuable, but he still has high expectations not yet met by it: *I would like it to behave like a smartphone, except that I can't talk. [...] I think, this has just arrived, I don't know have far it can go, but, in the news they say we'll be able to pay with the smartwatch*
↑	Desirable	The smartwatch is in line with his techie identity. He identifies himself as a person who is willing to use technologies, and that is where his interest in the smartwatch lies: *We should take into account that there are people, the same age as me, and older, [...] let's say, that don't want to know about the Internet and computers at all.* Specifically, he says the smartwatch is a *technology that may be a bridge that will lead to more... more interesting milestones, [...] otherwise we would still be stuck in the Stone Age*

Table 8. M1, Interview 2

↑	Useful	He finds it useful, not only because he uses it every day, but also for its many features: *I use it every day. Every day. I mean, I use the clock every day because I've gotten used to it.* In addition, he would buy it: *Now that I have used it, and they are less expensive, probably not this one, but another, yes, for sure, I would buy [another]*
↑	Usable	He does not report any usability issues. On the contrary, he has explored many of the smartwatch's features, which he learned how to use on his own
↑	Valuable	*I use mainly the features that are related with my interest, for notifications, for the maps and the music; those are the three more relevant uses*
↑	Desirable	The smartwatch enhances his techie identity. He volunteers as a smartphone teacher for older people, and having a smartwatch gives him extra authority on the subject. According to him, *I have to be up-to-date*

4.5   M2, The Sportsman

He uses it every day, all day, and even during the night. He is highly proficient in using the activity tracker. He has great interest in showing his walking achievements on the smartwatch and places great value on using it for walking. The smartwatch contributes to his sporty identity, as you can see in the following tables (Tables 9 and 10).

Table 9. M2, Interview 1

↑	Useful	He wears it every day and, according to him: *what I do most is [check] the heart rate and walking ... [check] the steps [...] and also, it notifies you when there is a call*
↑↓	Usable	He shows great proficiency in managing the pedometer. However, he is not receiving WhatsApp or email notifications, and he does not know why
↑	Valuable	It is valuable for him, as he walks every day, and he enjoys having a record of his activity, and he also checks how fast he goes while walking
↑	Desirable	He uses it to express his sporty identity, by sharing his sports milestones with others. For example, he reported that while he was buying sneakers, and another client asked him if they were durable, and he answered, showing the smartwatch: *Look at how many steps I've taken*

Table 10. M2, Interview 2

↑	Useful	He uses it every day; he says that he will keep using it in the same way. He uses it to manage notifications and to keep track of his sports activities
↑	Usable	He does not have problems using the smartwatch. He emphasises that he has no problems with the features he uses the most, and he is interested in more but has not explored the watch further
↑	Valuable	He likes watches and states that: *if it gives me more data... better*
↑	Desirable	The smartwatch reinforces his techie and sporty identity. He keeps sharing his sports achievements with his acquaintances through the smartwatch

5 Discussion

According to previous studies, usefulness, usability, valuableness and desirability all influence to a greater or less extent smartwatch appropriation [6, 7].

One study had shown that, after 4 months of usage, a minority of smartwatch owners (4.5%) cease to use them [8]. Although the two studies are not comparable, the abandonment of the smartwatch was not so minor in our study. Two participants out of five stopped using the smartwatch, once their commitment to the project was over. The fact that the study was long-term and that participants were highly committed to it both had an influence on this. On the one hand, participants were under no obligation to use the smartwatch during the first 12 months; they just had to commit to giving the interviews and handing over the logs on their smartwatch activities. However, they most likely felt that they should use it, thus affecting usage. On the other hand, during the month-12 interviews, it was clear that the actions and reports of the two participants who eventually abandoned the smartwatch were not consistent. It was clear that they were not engaged completely with the device, thus we expected them to stop using the watches. Moreover, the fact that one of the researchers had engaged previously with the community, lending to a more ethnographic approach [23], allowed us to meet participants informally at events beyond the project itself. While, the project was designed to last 12 months, we decided to take advantage of this relationship to understand appropriation beyond the project, which is something very uncommon in research, despite its relevance [24, 25].

Interestingly, the two to stop use were two of the three women in the group, while the two men were still engaged with their smartwatches after 24 months of use. In other studies analyzed, most participants were men [8, 9]. Which is something that would require further analysis.

The other three participants were still using the smartwatches at month 24. Many smartwatch routines follow the habits acquired in regular wristwatch routines [26], and this should have helped participants to appropriate the smartwatch. In fact, the three engaged users were all fans of watches and were used to wearing watches. However, the two participants who stopped using the smartwatches also were used to wearing watches every day. The effort-benefit ratio of smartwatches differs from that of standard watches, and thus it was not only a matter of inherited routines for the two who decided not to continue use.

In previous studies, users have questioned the limited features of smartwatches [27], particularly compared to smartphones [13], and users' interest in replacing their smartphone with a smartwatch has been analyzed [28]. This was also an issue in the first interviews in our study, but after 12 months of smartwatch use it ceased to be one. With usage, they came to understand how the device was meaningful or not in their everyday lives based on its own features or significance.

Lundell (2016) classified smartwatch users among communicators and techies. Communicators use the smartwatch mainly to manage notifications, and techies feel they can identify with the techie values communicated through the use of the smartwatch. However, for the participants in this study, having the watch merely as a tool for managing notifications was not reason enough to continue using it. The two participants who ceased use were very active users of the notifications, as both of them have very active social lives, but they did not find it valuable enough and were not able to identify themselves with the smartwatch. Thus, similar to activity trackers, both image (desirable) and hedonic motivation (valuable) play an important role in intention to use [29].

According to previous studies, the most used/valuable/reported feature is checking notifications [12, 13]. This was indeed the single usage that was common to all participants in the study. However, it was not the most valuable feature for all of them, nor was it the reason for using the smartwatch daily. The sporty guy in this study used the notifications like everyone else, but his main reason for using the smartwatch was to keep track of his sports achievements and share them easily from his wrist, thus reinforcing his sporty identity.

The analysis shows the relevance of a smartwatch's **desirability** in is appropriation (or not) for all participants. Style-based choices constitute a relevant part of the smartwatch experience [13, 18]. However, this not only refers to size, shape or color, but to the features provided and the cultural meaning of the smartwatches. The values socially attributed to the object should be in consonance with user identity, so the object is used it to express personal identity. Since artifacts are ascribed with cultural meaning, both in their production and consumption [30], participants used the smartwatch to express their sporty, techie or fashion identities. Sportsmen mainly use the smartwatch to follow their sports activities and socially share their sporting achievements. Similar to what Lundell and Bates describe [8], techies explore all the possibilities that smartwatches have to offer, know how to use many of those features – not only the ones they use most often – and advertise them. Fashion lovers use smartwatches to obtain social recognition, following the techno-optimistic idea that early adopters are respected by peers [31] thus using it as a desirable product.

6 Conclusion and Limitations

We studied smartwatch appropriation among a group of 5 older individuals aged 71 to 80 over the course of 24 months. Specifically, we analyzed how usefulness, usability, valuableness and desirability influenced smartwatch appropriation. For most of the participants, the smartwatch was useful and usable, but these were not the main reasons for adoption. It was valuableness and desirability that played a key role in smartwatch appropriation. Thus, smartwatches, and probably other technological devices, play a key role in expressing user identity. In this study, we observed how participants used the smartwatches to express their sporty, techie and fashion identities. Thus, identities or the cultural meaning of the devices should be taken into account when designing technologies that are meant to play a significant role in the lives of older people. Although, the sample of the study is very short, we choose such approach in order to get a deep understanding of the user experience, in a longitudinal perspective. We know that the reports from participants should be influenced by their interest to participate in a research project, and receive a smartwatch for doing so. We compensate such bias, by collecting the experiences of participants once their commitment with the project was over.

Acknowledgments. We are indebted to all the participants of our study for having allowed us to become members and feel part of their communities at Àgora. This research project has been partially funded by the Spanish Ministry of Economy and Competitiveness (FJCI-2015-24120) and the Social Sciences and Humanities Research Council of Canada through the Ageing + Communication + Technologies project (895-2013-1018).

References

1. Motti, V.G., Caine, K.: Smart wearables or dumb wearables? In: Proceedings of the 34th ACM International Conference on the Design of Communication - SIGDOC 2016, pp. 1–10. ACM Press, New York (2016). https://doi.org/10.1145/2987592.2987606
2. Rosales, A., Sayago, S., Blat, J.: Beeping socks and chirping arm bands: wearables that foster free play. IEEE Comput. **48**(6), 41–48 (2015). https://doi.org/10.1109/MC.2015.168
3. Ehrler, F., Lovis, C.: Supporting elderly homecare with smartwatches: advantages and drawbacks. Stud. Health Technol. Inform. **205**, 667–671 (2014)
4. Casilari, E., Oviedo-Jiménez, M.A.: Automatic fall detection system based on the combined use of a smartphone and a smartwatch. PLoS ONE **10**(11), 1–11 (2015). https://doi.org/10.1371/journal.pone.0140929
5. Silverstone, R., Haddon, L.: Design and the domestication of ICTs: technical change and everyday life. In: Silverstone, R., Mansell R. (eds.) Communication by Design. The Politics of Information and Communication Technologies, p. 74. Oxford University Press, Oxford (1996)
6. Chuah, S.H.-W., Rauschnabel, P.A., Krey, N., Nguyen, B., Ramayah, T., Lade, S.: Wearable technologies: the role of usefulness and visibility in smartwatch adoption. Comput. Hum. Behav. **65**, 276–284 (2016). https://doi.org/10.1016/j.chb.2016.07.047
7. Wu, L.H., Wu, L.C., Chang, S.C.: Exploring consumers' intention to accept smartwatch. Comput. Hum. Behav. **64**, 383–392 (2016). https://doi.org/10.1016/j.chb.2016.07.005
8. Lundell, J., Bates, C.: Understanding user experience journeys for a smart watch device. In: Nah, F.H., Tan, C.H. (eds.) HCIBGO 2016. LNCS, vol. 9752, pp. 424–433. Springer, Cham (2016). https://doi.org/10.1007/978-3-319-39399-5_40
9. Jeong, H., Kim, H., Kim, R., Lee, U., Jeong, Y.: Smartwatch wearing behavior analysis. In: Proceedings of Conference on Interactive, Mobile, Wearable Ubiquitous Technology, vol. 1, pp. 1–31 (2017). https://doi.org/10.1145/3131892
10. Visuri, A., Sarsenbayeva, Z., van Berkel, N., Goncalves, J., Rawassizadeh, R., Kostakos, V., Ferreira, D.: Quantifying sources and types of smartwatch usage sessions. In: Proceedings of the Conference on Human Factors in Computing Systems - CHI 2017, pp. 3569–3581. ACM Press, New York (2017). https://doi.org/10.1145/3025453.3025817
11. Liu, X., Chen, T., Qian, F., Guo, Z., Lin, F.X., Wang, X., Chen, K.: Characterizing smartwatch usage in the wild. In: Proceedings of Conference on Mobile System Application and Services (MobiSys 2017), pp. 385–398 (2017). https://doi.org/10.1145/3081333.3081351
12. Min, C., Kang, S., Yoo, C., Cha, J., Choi, S., Oh, Y., Song, J.: Exploring current practices for battery use and management of smartwatches. In: Proceedings of the International Symposium on Wearable Computers - ISWC 2015, pp. 11–18. ACM Press, New York (2015). https://doi.org/10.1145/2802083.2802085

13. Schirra, S., Bentley, F.R.: It's kind of like an extra screen for my phone. In: Proceedings of the Conference on Human Factors in Computing Systems - CHI EA 2015. pp. 2151–2156. ACM Press, New York (2015). https://doi.org/10.1145/2702613.2732931
14. Cecchinato, M.E., Cox, A.L., Bird, J.: Always on(line)? In: Proceedings of the Conference on Human Factors in Computing Systems - CHI 2017. pp. 3557–3568. ACM Press, New York (2017). https://doi.org/10.1145/3025453.3025538
15. McMillan, D., Brown, B., Lampinen, A., McGregor, M., Hoggan, E., Pizza, S.: Situating wearables. In: Proceedings of the Conference on Human Factors in Computing Systems - CHI 2017, pp. 3582–3594. ACM Press, New York (2017). https://doi.org/10.1145/3025453.3025993
16. Quintana, R., Quintana, C., Madeira, C., Slotta, J.D.: Keeping watch. In: Proceedings of the Conference on Human Factors in Computing Systems - CHI EA 2016, pp. 2272–2278. ACM Press, New York (2016). https://doi.org/10.1145/2851581.2892493
17. Fernández-Ardèvol, M., Rosales, A.: My interests, my activities: learning from an intergenerational comparison of smartwatch use. In: Zhou, J., Salvendy, G. (eds.) ITAP 2017. LNCS,vol. 10298, pp. 114–129. Springer, Cham (2017). https://doi.org/10.1007/978-3-319-58536-9_10
18. Cecchinato, M.E., Cox, A.L., Bird, J.: Smartwatches. In: Proceedings of the 33rd Annual ACM Conference Extended Abstracts on Human Factors in Computing Systems - CHI EA 2015, pp. 2133–2138. ACM Press, New York (2015). https://doi.org/10.1145/2702613.2732837
19. Choi, J., Kim, S.: Is the smartwatch an IT product or a fashion product? A study on factors affecting the intention to use smartwatches. Comput. Hum. Behav. **63**, 777–786 (2016). https://doi.org/10.1016/j.chb.2016.06.007
20. Jung, Y., Kim, S., Choi, B.: Consumer valuation of the wearables: the case of smartwatches. Comput. Hum. Behav. **63**, 899–905 (2016). https://doi.org/10.1016/j.chb.2016.06.040
21. Creswell, J.W.: Research Design: Qualitative, Quantitative, and Mixed Method Approaches. SAGE Publications, Thousand Oaks (2003)
22. Morville, P.: User Experience Design. http://semanticstudios.com/user_experience_design/
23. Blomberg, J., Burrell, M.: An ethnographic approach to design. In: Jacko, J.A., Sears, A. (eds.) The Human Computer Interaction Handbook: Fundamentals, Evolving Technologies, and Emerging Applications, pp. 965–988. Lawrence Erlbaum Associates, Mahwah, (2003)
24. Bossen, C., Dindler, C., Iversen, O.S.: User gains and PD aims. In: Proceedings of the Biennial Participatory Design Conference on - PDC 2010, p. 141. ACM Press, New York (2010). https://doi.org/10.1145/1900441.1900461
25. Righi, V., Sayago, S., Ferreira, S., Rosales, A., Blat, J.: Co-designing with a community of older learners for over 10 years by moving user-driven participation from the margin to the centre. CoDes. Int. J. CoCreation (2018). https://doi.org/10.1080/15710882.2018.1424206
26. Lyons, K.: What can a dumb watch teach a smartwatch? In: Proceedings of the International Symposium on Wearable Computers - ISWC 2015, pp. 3–10. ACM Press, New York (2015). https://doi.org/10.1145/2802083.2802084
27. Kim, D., Lee, Y., Rho, S., Lim, Y.: Design opportunities in three stages of relationship development between users and self-tracking devices. In: Proceedings of Conference on Human Factors Computing System - CHI 2016, 699–703 (2016). https://doi.org/10.1145/2858036.2858148

28. Pizza, S., Brown, B., McMillan, D., Lampinen, A.: Smartwatch in vivo. In: Proceedings of the Conference on Human Factors in Computing Systems - CHI 2016, pp. 5456–5469. ACM Press, New York (2016). https://doi.org/10.1145/2858036.2858522
29. Sol, R., Baras, K.: Assessment of activity trackers. In: Proceedings of the International Joint Conference on Pervasive and Ubiquitous Computing Adjunct - UbiComp 2016, pp. 570–575. ACM Press, New York (2016). https://doi.org/10.1145/2968219.2968323
30. du Gay, P., Hall, S., Janes, L., Madsen, H., Mackay, H., Negus, K.: Doing Cultural Studies: The Story of the Sony Walkman. Sage Publications Inc., London (2013)
31. Rogers, E.M.: Diffusion of innovations (1995)

Attitudes Towards Aging and the Acceptance of ICT for Aging in Place

Eva-Maria Schomakers[(⊠)], Julia Offermann-van Heek,
and Martina Ziefle

Human-Computer Interaction Center, RWTH Aachen University,
Campus-Boulevard 57, 52074 Aachen, Germany
{schomakers,vanheek,ziefle}@comm.rwth-aachen.de

Abstract. Facing the demographic developments in the Western world, Information and Communication Technologies (ICT) designed to support older people can represent a promising approach for the overloaded health care systems. Most older adults prefer to age in place in their home environment. Assistive ICT can support older adults in staying independent, connected, and healthy and provide help in emergency situations. However, older adults represent a special group regarding the use of ICT: they are still often less experienced and cautious in adapting new technologies. Correspondingly, acceptance poses the greatest barrier for the success of assistive ICT. Older adults are not a homogeneous group, they differ in their experience with technologies, attitudes towards aging, and ideas for quality of life. In a questionnaire approach, N = 166 participants' attitudes towards aging and evaluation of two examples of ICT are assessed. The analysis shows, that technology generations differ in their opinions about aging as well as their assessment of assistive ICT. Attitude towards aging, gender, education, health status, and other attitudes form a multifaceted picture of influences on the acceptance.

Keywords: Technology acceptance · Aging · Attitudes towards aging
Information and communication technologies · Assistive technologies

1 Introduction

The demographic developments in Western countries pose tremendous social, political, and economic challenges. Germany is one of the countries where the demographic change has advanced the most. In 2014, one fifth (21%) of the population was aged 65 or older, 11% were older than 75 years old [1]. At the same time, birth rates have been inflating for decades so that less people can pay and care for the increasing number of older people. Most people enjoy a long life and stay fit for a long time, but the growing number of older people combined with more very old people leads to an increase of long-term care patients [1]. 64% of people aged 90 or older are in need of long-term care; chronic diseases, and multi-morbidity lead to high care needs (ibid.). But most older people desire to stay home as long as possible [2]. In the last decades, many technologies have been developed to assist aging in place with support of daily life, help in emergency situations as well as medical support. These can become solutions in

© Springer International Publishing AG, part of Springer Nature 2018
J. Zhou and G. Salvendy (Eds.): ITAP 2018, LNCS 10926, pp. 149–169, 2018.
https://doi.org/10.1007/978-3-319-92034-4_12

addressing the rising costs and resource problems in the health care sector as well as the elderly's desire to age in place.

2   ICT to Support Aging in Place

Current developments around ambient intelligence and smart homes provide more and more possibilities to assist old and (chronically) diseased persons in their daily chores and medical treatment, enabling independent living, and improving quality of life. The term Ambient Assisted Living (AAL) is often used to describe these technologies [3]. AAL includes the use of ICT devices, services as well as holistic systems that are integrated in the home environment [4].

One of the prominent use cases of AAL are personal safety and fall detection systems, as falls and fall-related injuries represent a significant threat to the health, independence, and even life of older people [5]. Having experienced a fall often results in fear of falling which can lead to decreased mobility and reduced participation in activities [6]. Additionally, family and caregivers are impacted by the concerns about unexpected falls. After a fall has occurred, it is critical to get help fast and avoid involuntarily remaining on the ground for longer time, which substantially increases the physiological and psychological risks [3]. Personal Emergency Response Systems enable seniors to either contact an emergency center themselves via a wearable button, or are designed to automatically detect falls, e.g., camera-systems. Thus, they prevent "long lies" and provide a feeling of security for patients and their relatives [6].

Supporting health management is another promising area of AAL. For example, poor medication management is a frequent problem and can impose a serious risk especially for older people as they use more medication and more of those with a high potential for medication misuse than other age groups. Forgetting to take prescribed medication, taking the incorrect amount, or incorrect medication can lead to numerous health consequences and does not only happen to older people with cognitive or memory impairments [5]. Medication management tools and reminders can help seniors to take the correct amount of medication at proper time [7].

Despite the promising potential and increasing number of available AAL devices and systems, they are not yet widely used.

2.1   Technology Acceptance, User Diversity, and Age

Technology Acceptance by potential users is critical for the success of AAL technologies (e.g., [8]). To explain the relationship between attitudes, intentions, and use behavior and to identify the factors that influence the technology acceptance by users, several technology acceptance models have been proposed and refined in the last half century. As one of the first, the *Theory of Reasoned Action* (TRA) proposes that behavioral intentions are the central element determining actual behavior, and that these are a function of attitudes towards behavior and subjective norms [9]. As an adaptation of the TRA, the *Technology Acceptance Model* (TAM, by [10]) targets user acceptance of ICT and focused on the two key components *perceived ease of use* and *perceived usefulness* as antecedents of the intention to use a technology. The *Unified Theory of Acceptance and Use of Technology* (UTAUT, by [11]) extends the *TAM* and is the first to include user characteristics (age, gender, and experience) as influencing factors.

Research in technology acceptance by older adults has shown, that attitudes, experiences, and self-efficacy in interacting with ICT are critical factors for the acceptance and adoption [12]. For example, experiences with technologies vary very much in older adults and also other individual differences can shape attitudes, e.g., gender, education, and social background. For example, women usually report lower levels of technical self-efficacy [13], or age and gender show interaction effects regarding the acceptance of medical assistive technologies [2].

On the other hand, age itself influences technology adoption. In general, older adults' willingness to use assistive technology is high, but older adults are known to adopt new technologies slower than younger people [12]. Aging brings changes in perceptual, cognitive, and psychomotor skills that can result in difficulties with handling devices or in the acquisition of the necessary skills [14]. Differences in physiological and psychological abilities are also large as aging is an individual process and these differences can be still enhanced by diseases and chronic conditions [15], contributing to even stronger heterogeneity of technology use behavior within the group of older adults.

Additionally, experiences and social and cultural environment play a crucial role and age can be a "carrier variable" for these. Different generations experienced different technologies and interfaces during their upbringing and education years, the so-called formative period. These generation-specific experiences with technology have an effect on the usage behavior and attitudes towards technology during their whole life span [16]. For the German population, five generations were distinguished [17] according to the product types predominant during their formative period: the *mechanical generation* (born before 1939), the *generation of household revolution* (born 1939-1948), the *generation of technology spread* (born 1949–1963), the *computer generation* (born 1964–1978), and the *internet generation* (born after 1977).

Besides the individual, age-related, and generational influences, the type of technology [18, 19] and application context [20] can impact acceptance patterns. Theories of technology acceptance have mainly focused on the two key components perceived usefulness and perceived ease of use, so far. But studies have shown, that additional motives and barriers play a crucial role in the context of assistive technologies for older adults (e.g., [21, 22]). AAL technologies are designed to operate in our homes and close to our bodies, are associated with negative aspects of aging, illness, and even with surveillance. Thus, barriers regarding stigmatization, privacy, and usability are predominant. Studies show, that users acknowledge the potential of AAL technologies, but are also concerned because of barriers. Thus, trade-offs between perceived benefits and barriers are crucial for the acceptance of AAL technologies [23].

The perception of benefits and the perceived necessity is tied to the desires and needs of the potential users. Regarding AAL technologies, aging concepts could determine the perception of benefits and barriers of AAL technologies and research [15] showed, that the understanding of age and aging has been changing. Aging is - on the one hand - associated with health issues, loneliness, and limitation of autonomy and mobility, but more and more seniors live an active lifestyle and feel old at a later point in live. Good health, social relationships, and independence are important constituents of quality of life in older age [24] and AAL technologies have the potential to improve one or more of these areas.

2.2   Focus and Aim of the Study

Many variables have been identified in research that may influence the acceptance and adoption of ICT for aging in place by older adults. To improve the understanding of technology acceptance of assistive ICT, this study analyses individual characteristics and attitudes for their influence on the acceptance of two exemplary AAL technologies and the evaluation of benefits and barriers. The main focus is directed on differences in the evaluation by different technology generations in order to comprehend attitudes in the special groups of today's and tomorrow's older adults as potential users of AAL technologies. Additionally, the effects of gender, health status, and education as well as technical self-efficacy are explored. As wishes and ideas of life in older age may differ, also the influence of attitudes towards aging on the acceptance and evaluation of barriers and benefits are studied. The evaluation of motives and barriers of the presented technologies' adoption is presented in detail to deeper understand the reasons for differences in technology acceptance. For this explorative approach, a user-centered study was chosen. In a questionnaire study, users of different technology generations were asked about their attitudes towards ageing and evaluated two examples of AAL technologies. The detailed methodological approach is presented within the next part.

3   Methodological Approach

Within the following section, the design of the questionnaire, applied statistical procedures, and the study's participants are described. For the present study, an online questionnaire was conceptualized based on a preceding qualitative study [25] in order to reach a larger sample focusing on older people, their wishes and needs concerning life quality in older age, their attitudes towards aging as well as their perceptions and acceptance of AAL and ICT technologies in different application contexts.

3.1   Questionnaire Design

In the first part of the questionnaire, the participants were asked for demographic characteristics such as gender, age, and educational level as well as their perceived age. The participants assessed nine items referring to quality of life in older age (based on [2]). Further, the participants assessed four items belonging to a positive attitude and six items referring to a negative attitude towards aging. Addressing attitudinal characteristics, the participants evaluated their technical self-efficacy in interacting with technology (using four items; based on [26]), their disposition to privacy (using three items; based on [27]), and their disposition to trust (using three items; based on [28]).

To be able to characterize the participants, they further indicated (yes/no) if they suffer from a chronical disease, if they have to do medical check-ups regularly, and if they have to rely on medical aids (e.g., blood glucose meter, heart pacemaker). Additionally, the participants evaluated their subjectively perceived health status.

In a next step, two randomized application contexts and respective medical technologies were introduced to the participants: the first one referred to a medical emergency scenario and focused on diverse technologies that could be used for fall detection (e.g., emergency buttons, camera systems, motion detectors, and smart watches). The second application context referred to facilitating everyday life for people in older age who become forgetful or suffer from dementia by using technical reminders for drugs or appointments (e.g., smartphones, laptops, audio assistant, smart TV, or smart watches).

Following each application context, the participants were asked to evaluate the acceptance of fall detection (Cronbach's α = .840) and medical reminders (Cronbach's α = .766) by using each three items, perceived motives and barriers by using each nine items. To evaluate these items, the participants were asked to put themselves in a scenario of a 71-year old, who lives alone, is faced with minor health problems and a general frailness. The items and scenario are based on a preceding qualitative study [25]. Further, all items were evaluated on six-point Likert scales (1 = min: "I strongly disagree"; 6 = max: "I strongly agree").

3.2 Sample Description

A total of n = 166 participants filled out the online questionnaire completely. The participants were on average 51.42 years old (SD = 16.10, min = 15, max = 88) and 60.8% were female (39.2% male). As highest educational level, most of the participants (66.9%) reported to hold a university degree. 19.3% hold a university entrance diploma, 9.0% a completed apprenticeship and 4.8% a secondary school certificate. Asked for their perceived age, the participants indicated on average to feel younger than their real age (M = 43.77, SD = 13.98, min = 10, max = 76). In more detail, the majority (74.3%) indicated to feel younger, 22.3% to feel just as old as they are, and only 3.4% to feel older (1 to 5 years) than their real age. Regarding their subjectively perceived health status (min = 1, max = 6), the participants reported to feel very well on average (M = 4.91, SD = 0.78) and none of the participants indicated to need care. The subjective health status declined moderately with aging (r = −.215, p = .005). Considering attitudinal characteristics (min = 1; max = 6), the participants reported a moderate technical self-efficacy (M = 4.21, SD = 1.16), a moderate trust in other people (M = 4.15, SD = 0.78), and rather neutral needs for privacy (M = 3.71, SD = 0.98). Technical self-efficacy differed strongly between men (M = 4.67, SD = 1.18) and women (M = 3.91, SD = 1.04) ($F(1,164)$ = 19, $p < .001$).

3.3 Data Analysis

Prior to detailed statistical analyses, item analyses were calculated to ensure measurement quality and a Cronbach's alpha >0.7 indicated a satisfying internal consistency of the scales. Afterwards, data was analyzed by correlation and MANOVA analyses. The level of significance was set at 5%. Post-hoc analysis procedures were based on Gabriel's procedure as the group sizes were unequal. For analyzing effects of age as influencing user factor, the following four technology generations were distinguished based on [17]: the first generation *Internet* referred to people aged between 14 and 36 ($n = 33$, 19.9%); the second *Computer generation* included people aged between 37 and 53 years ($n = 49$, 29.5%); the third generation - *Technology Spread* - referred to people aged between 54 and 68 years and was the largest group ($n = 65$, 39.2%); finally, the last group *Household Revolution* referred to $n = 19$ participants (11.4%) aged 69 years and older.

4   Results

In the following results section, we will first look at the factors for *Quality of Life in Older Age* and *Attitudes towards Aging*, before the general acceptance as well as motives and barriers of using fall detection and medical reminders are discussed. For each topic, first we will present the general evaluation and the differences between technology generations, before we take a short, explorative look at the influences of other user factors: age, health status, education level, and attitudinal variables such as technical self-efficacy, need for privacy, and attitude towards aging.

4.1   Quality of Life in Older Age

The respondents rated how relevant they considered different aspects for quality of life in older age. Factors regarding social life, autonomy, and health care were included. Overall, the participants showed agreement to all items related to quality of life (cf. Fig. 1). On average, *to be independent in older age* was evaluated as the most important factor ($M = 5.51$, $SD = 0.68$). Second most important was *to have a stable social network* ($M = 5.49$, $SD = 0.74$). The lowest but also still positive evaluations referred to the aspects *not to be a burden for others* ($M = 4.60$; $SD = 1.31$) and *regular monitoring of one's health status* ($M = 4.29$, $SD = 1.16$). As all factors were evaluated to be important, the dimensions social life, autonomy, and health care all contribute to quality of life in older age.

Generational Differences: There are some significant differences in the evaluation of Quality of Life related factors between the technology generations ($F(27,468) = 1.66$, $p = .021$) (see Fig. 1). For the household revolution generation, *competent medical care* contributed less to quality of life in older age ($M = 4.74$, $SD = 1.15$) than it did for the internet generation ($M = 5.48$, $SD = 0.71$). Similarly, the oldest group deemed a *stable social network* significantly less relevant ($M = 5.00$, $SD = 1.15$) than the 54–68 year olds ($M = 5.58$, $SD = 0.56$) and the 37–53 years olds ($M = 5.63$, $SD = 0.68$), for whom this was the most important factor. *Competent medical care* and a stable *social network* were not as important to the technology spread generation as to the others, but to them it was more important *not to be a burden to others* in older age. The group of 54–68 years olds saw greater relevance in *access to information* ($M = 5.15$, $SD = 0.87$) than the other groups.

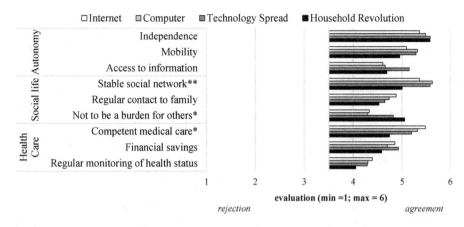

Fig. 1. "Quality of Life in Older Age" items differing between four technology generations ($*$ = $p < .05$, $**$ = $p < .01$).

Other User Factors: As illustrated before, the group of the elderly is heterogeneous. Thus, in the following paragraph, gender, education level, and health status were analyzed for their influence on the evaluation of "Quality of Life in Older Age" factors. No significant effect of gender on all aspects of quality of life was observed. The results showed a tendency, that women deemed the *social network* more important than men (M_w = 5.60, SD = 0.71; M_m = 5.21, SD = 0.77) and men showed a tendency to evaluate all aspects less important than women, except for the *monitoring of health status* and *independence*. Education levels did also not influence the importance of the factors in our sample. A better subjective health status was slightly related to *independence* being perceived as more important (r = .192, p = .013).

4.2   Attitudes Towards Aging

On average, the participants had a positive attitude towards aging (M = 4.39, SD = 0.65, min = 1, max = 6). *To be able to stay in contact with friends and family* was a part of aging that was the most agreed to on average (M = 5.28, SD = 0.93). The participants also agreed with other positive aspects of aging such as *making plans* (M = 4.69, SD = 1.01), *being more relaxed* (M = 4.72, SD = 1.11), and *keep on learning* (M = 4.69, SD = 0.96). Concerns related to aging like *decreasing health* (M = 3.92, SD = 1.08) and *being less fit and lively* (M = 3.90, SD = 1.10) were slightly endorsed. In contrast, other negative aspects such as *being dependent* (M = 3.16, SD = 1.24), *being a burden to others* (M = 2.97, SD = 1.08), and *loneliness* (M = 2.89, SD = 1.19) were slightly rejected by the participants. The negative aspect to expect *less enjoyment* (M = 2.28, SD = 1.16) in older age was most rejected by all participants.

Generational Differences: Referring to the overall attitude towards aging, the group of 54 to 68 year olds (technology spread) showed the most positive attitude (M = 4.60, SD = 0.59) that significantly differed from the two younger generations (F(12,

483) = 5.47, p = .001). The internet generation showed the comparatively least positive attitude (M = 4.08, SD = 0.56). Positive and negative aspects of aging are examined independently, as a factors analysis showed these to be quite distinct. In a multivariate analysis of variance on the four positive aspects of aging, differences between generations are obvious (F(12, 483) = 2.35, p = .006). The generation of technology spread saw all positive factors more prevalent than the other generations. That one becomes *more relaxed* was not as much part of the picture of aging that young people have, as it was in other groups. Only for *keep on learning* no differences between the generations were prevalent. The technology generations (see Fig. 2) evaluated negative aspects of aging differently (F(18, 477) = 1.91, p = .014). Especially the youngest generation (internet generation) pictured aging going along with *becoming less fit and lively*, and sees aging more tied with *being a burden* and *being less dependent* than the other generations. The oldest generation (household revolution) rejected more than others that aging leads *to being lonely* and does not approve as much as the other generations that it comes along with *decreasing health* and *being less fit and lively*. Altogether they rejected the negative aspects of life in older age the most. The computer generation's opinion was mostly average, but for *dependence*, which they perceive as a part of aging, more than the older generations.

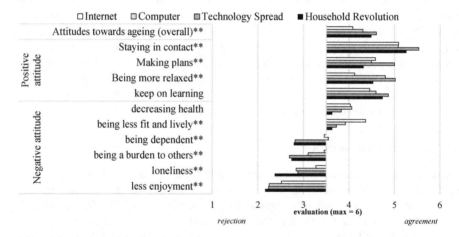

Fig. 2. "Attitude towards Aging"-related factors differing between four technology generations (* = p < .05; ** = p < .01).

Other User Factors: No effects of gender or education level were detected for either positive or negative factors. The perception of old age going along with *still making plans* was higher with a better health status (r = .155, p = .46). Healthier participants also tied *decreasing health* more to aging (r = .171, p = .028).

4.3   Technology Acceptance of Fall Detection and Medical Reminders

As shown in Fig. 3, the acceptance of fall detection and medical reminder technologies was generally high (M_{fall} = 4.96, SD_{fall} = 1.02; M_{rem} = 5.03, SD_{rem} = 0.05).

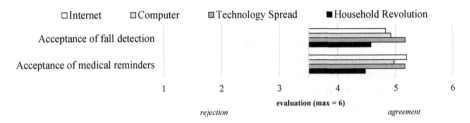

Fig. 3. Acceptance of medical reminders and fall detection differing between four technology generations.

Generational Differences: The oldest generation showed significantly less acceptance of medical reminders (M = 4.48, SD = 1.08) than the internet generation (M = 5.19, SD = 1.00) and the generation of technology spread (M = 5.16, SD = 0.81; F (3, 162) = 3.03, p = .031). A similar tendency that did not reach significance could be observed in the case of fall detection (F(3, 162) = 2.055, p = .108, n.s.): the oldest generation showed again the lowest acceptance (M = 4.58, SD = 1.23), while internet (M = 4.83, SD = 1.04), computer (M = 4.92, SD = 1.08), and in particular the technology spread generation (M = 5.17, SD = 0.85) showed higher acceptance evaluations.

Other User Factors: Technology acceptance was also influenced by other user factors (see Table 1). Women accept medical reminders less than men (M_w = 4.92, SD_w = 104, M_m = 5.21, SD_m = 0.76, F(1,161) = 4.13, p = .044). Additionally, the confidence in one's abilities in interacting with technology (technical self-efficacy) was related with the acceptance of medical reminders (r = .209, p = .007) and fall detection (r = 1.66, p = .032). Further, the acceptance of fall detection showed relationships to one's need for privacy (r = .184, p = .018) and to a positive attitude towards aging

Table 1. Correlation and inference statistical analyses of user factor influences on acceptance (n.s. = not significant (p > .05), * = p < .05, ** = p < .01, *** = p < .001

	Acceptance of medical reminders	Technical self-efficacy	Need for privacy	Attitudes towards aging	Gender
Acceptance of fall detection	.371**	.166*	.184*	.169*	M_w = 4.94, SD = 1.13, M_m = 4.99, SD = 0.82 n.s.
Acceptance of medical reminders		.209**		.	M_w = 4.92, SD = 1.04, M_m = 5.21, SD = 0.76 p < .05

($r = .169$, $p = .03$). As expected, the acceptance of medical reminders was positively related to the acceptance of fall detection ($r = .371$, $p = .0001$), but only on a moderate level. These results and differing influences of user factors show, that technology acceptance differs between technologies even if the context (ICT for aging in place) stays the same.

4.4   Motives to Use Fall Detection

Additional to asking for general acceptance of the technologies, motives and barriers for using the respective technologies were assessed. Overall, a moderately high agreement to all motives was observed ($M = 4.80$, $SD = 0.96$). *To get help in a case of emergency* was the most important motive for using technology in this case ($M = 5.40$, $SD = 1.08$), followed by *staying independent* ($M = 5.05$, $SD = 1.18$). *Facilitation in everyday life* ($M = 4.44$, $SD = 1.41$) and *comfort* ($M = 4.07$, $SD = 1.37$) were the least important motives.

Generational Differences: Many differences within the evaluation between the generations could be observed ($F(27,462) = 1.67$, $p = .020$) (see Fig. 4). Taking the average of all motives, the generation of technology spread agreed most to the benefits ($M = 5.07$, $SD = 0.79$) and the generation of household revolution agreed the least ($M = 4.38$, $SD = 1.36$) ($F(3,162) = 3.91$, $p = .010$). This pattern was prevalent with all benefits, and significant differences were found for *facilitation of everyday life* (F $(3,161) = 2.77$, $p = .044$), *independence* ($F(3,161) = 3.86$, $p = .011$), *staying home* (F $(2,162) = 4.54$, $p = .004$), and *comfort* ($F(3,162) = 46.825$, $p = .000$).

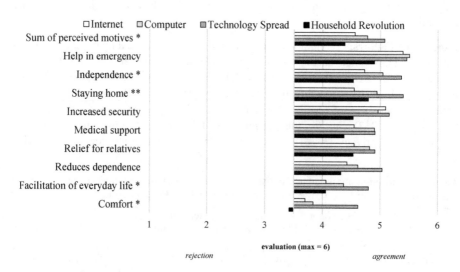

Fig. 4. Motives to use fall detection differing between technology generations (* = $p < .05$; ** = $p < .01$).

Other User Factors: The results revealed no significant effects of technical self-efficacy, gender, or health status on the evaluation of the motives to use fall detection. However, a positive image of aging was related to a positive perception of many motives (for details see Table 2). Also, a higher need for privacy was related putting more importance on *medical support, staying home,* and *comfort.* A higher education level was related to perceiving *help in emergency* ($r = -.170$, $p = .028$) and *medical support* ($r = -.205$, $p = .008$) as less important for the use of fall detection technology.

Table 2. Correlation analysis results of motives to use fall detection and user factors ($* = p < .05$; $** = p < .01$).

Motives for using fall detection	Positive attitude towards Aging	Need for privacy	Education level
Facilitation of everyday life	.245**		
Increased security			
Independence	.248**		
Reduced dependence	.159*		
Help in emergency		.178*	−.170*
Medical support		.230**	−.205**
Staying home	.208**		
Comfort	.164*	.191*	
Relief of relatives			

4.5 Barriers of Using Fall Detection

The barriers of using technology for fall detection were partly rejected and partly accepted, resulting in an average acceptance close to the midpoint of the scale ($M = 3.44$, $SD = 0.95$). The barriers concerning *data security* ($M = 3.93$, $SD = 1.40$), *privacy* ($M = 3.94$, $SD = 1.44$), *feeling of surveillance* ($M = 3.95$, $SD = 1.49$), and *not enough human contact* ($M = 3.84$, $SD = 1.37$) were rather agreed to by all generations, except of the oldest. Factors regarding technology in general were mostly rejected: *missing trust into technology* ($M = 2.80$, $SD = 1.24$), *too much technology* ($M = 3.01$, $SD = 1.39$), *dependence on technology* ($M = 3.05$, $SD = 1.40$), and *complex interaction with technology* ($M = 3.10$, $SD = 1.42$).

Generational Differences: In a multivariate analysis of variance on all barriers, no differences between the technology generations were observed. Because of the rather small group sizes, tendencies are still reported (see Fig. 5). The generation of household revolution agreed the least on the benefits of fall detection as it was described above, but this group also rejected the barriers the most. Especially barriers regarding *privacy, feeling of surveillance,* and *data security* were rejected which are agreed upon by the other generations. Interestingly, this generation who is described as least experienced with technologies, rejected *complexity of interaction with technology* as a barrier more than the other generations.

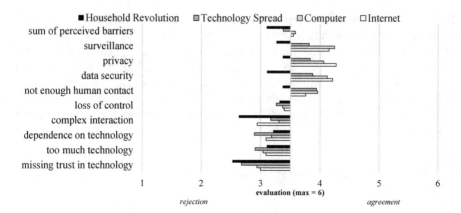

Fig. 5. Barriers of fall detection usage differing between technology generations.

Other User Factors: No significant effects of gender and education level were detected. A positive attitude towards aging did not show any relationship with the perception of the barriers, but a higher need for privacy was related with barriers regarding privacy, data security, and dependence on technology which were perceived more important. At the same time, technical self-efficacy was related to not perceiving the barriers as that much important that relate to technology itself being the problem (*not enough human contact, missing trust in technology, too much technology, and complex interaction*). Subjective health status was related to *dependence on technology* ($r = -.157$, $p = .044$) and *complex interaction* ($r = -.167$, $p = .032$), so that a better subjective health status leads to these two barriers being perceived as less important barriers (Table 3).

Table 3. Correlation analysis results of barriers of using fall detection and user factors ($* = p < .05$; $** = p < .01$).

Barriers of using fall detection	Technical self-efficacy	Need for privacy	Subjective health status
Surveillance		.224**	
Dependence on technology		.186*	−.157*
Loss of control		.227**	
Violation of privacy		.306**	
Not enough human contact	−.164*		
Missing trust in technology	−.228**		
Data security		.386**	
Too much technology	−.210**		
Complex interaction	−.269**	.155*	−.167*

4.6   Motives to Use Medical Reminders

Again, an overall moderately high agreement was observed (M = 4.80, SD = 0.97). In this case, differences in relevance between the motives were very small. The most important motive to use medical reminders was now *autonomy* (M = 5.07, SD = 1.1), closely followed by *facilitation of everyday life* (M = 4.98, SD = 1.07), *staying home* (M = 4.95, SD = 1.34), and *medical support* (M = 4.95, SD = 1.09). *Comfort* was again the least important motive (M = 4.58, SD = 1.36).

Generational Differences: The technology generations differed in their perception of the motives of medical reminders ($F(27, 465)$ = 1.94, p = .004) in a similar pattern as in the case of fall detection (cf. Fig. 6): Averaging all motives, the generation of technology spread again agreed most to all motives (M = 5.06, SD = 0.84) and the generation of household revolution the least (M = 4.5, SD = 1.34). The generation of technology spread perceived especially the following motives as more important than the other generations: *reduced dependence* (M = 5.11, SD = 1.01), *help in emergency situations* (M = 5.34, SD = 1.13), *staying home* (M = 5.28, SD = .086), and *comfort* (M = 4.66, SD = 1.16). *Comfort* was not a relevant motive for the oldest generation to use medical reminders (M = 3.58, SD = 1.17).

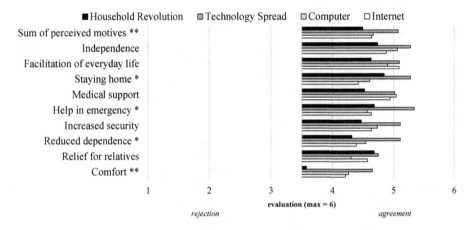

Fig. 6. Motives to use medical reminders differing between technology generations.

Other User Factors: Like the evaluation of fall detection, the results revealed relationships between a positive attitude towards aging, technical self-efficacy, and need for privacy and the motives to use medical reminders (see Table 4): a positive attitude towards aging showed a positive relationship to *independence* (r = .189, p = .015), *reduced dependence* (r = .217, p = .005), *staying home* (r = .283, p = .000), and *relief for relatives* (r = .169, p = .031). Need for privacy was positively related to *facilitation of everyday life* (r = .161, p = .04), *help in emergency* (r = .179, p = .022), as well as *comfort* (r = .166, p = .034). No relationship of the evaluation of the motives with education level and subjective health status as well as no differences between women and men were detected.

Table 4. Correlation analysis results for motives to use medical reminders and user factors ($*= p < .05$; $** = p < .01$).

Motives to use medical reminders	Attitudes towards aging	Need for privacy
Facilitation of everyday life		.161*
Increased security		
Independence	.189*	
Reduced dependence	.217**	
Help in emergency		.179*
Medical support		
Staying home	.283**	
Comfort		.166*
Relief for relatives	.169*	

4.7   Barriers of Using Medical Reminders

Overall, the relevance of the barriers was slightly less pronounced ($M = 3.19$, $SD = 1.06$) as in the case of fall detection ($M = 3.44$, $SD = 0.95$). The most important barrier was *data security* ($M = 3.69$, $SD = 1.55$), the least important barriers was *missing trust in technology* ($M = 2.67$, $SD = 1.24$).

Generational Differences: The results revealed no significant difference between the technology generations in the perception of barriers. Still, the tendency was observed (see Fig. 7), that the oldest generation rejected the barriers more than the other generations ($F(27, 468) = 1.44$, $p = .073$) as it was also the case for fall detection.

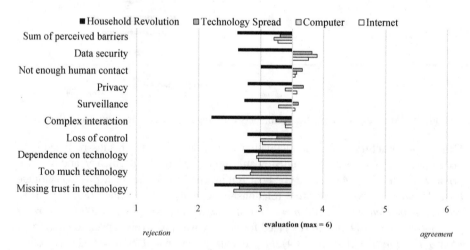

Fig. 7. Barriers of medical reminders differing between technology generations.

Other User Factors: Again, the results showed no significant effects of gender. Similar to the case of fall detection, a higher need for privacy correlated with perceiving barriers regarding *privacy*, *data security*, and also *too much technology* as more important (see Table 5). Further, higher technical self-efficacy again related to *missing trust in technology* ($r = -.206$, $p = .008$), *too much technology* ($r = -.279$, $p = .000$), *complex interaction* ($r = -.254$, $p = .001$) being all perceived as less important. Level of education correlated negatively with the perception of the barriers *not enough human contact* ($r = -.207$, $p = .008$) and *missing trust in technology* ($r = -.159*$, $p = .042$). Also, a better subjective health status correlated negatively with the agreement to the barrier *not enough human contact* ($r = -.227$, $p = .003$). Thus, the healthier participants were, the lesser was their requirement for human contact.

Table 5. Correlation analysis results of barriers of using medical reminders and user factors ($* = p < .05$; $** = p < .01$).

Barriers of using medical reminders	Technical self-efficacy	Need for privacy	Education level	Subjective health status
Surveillance		.308**		
Dependence on technology		.19*		
Loss of control		.313**		
Violation of privacy		.366**		
Not enough human contact		.222**	−.207**	−.227**
Missing trust in technology	−.206**		−.159*	
Data security		.412**		
Too much technology	−.279**	.168*		
Complex interaction	−.254**			

5   Discussion

The present study revealed insights into attitudes towards aging and the acceptance of AAL technologies and user diversity. Differences in evaluation between technology generations of aspects of aging and the assessment of AAL technologies, as well as of the user factors gender, education, health status, technical self-efficacy, and attitudes on trust and privacy were analyzed.

5.1   Perceptions Concerning Aging and Quality of Life

Our analysis showed, that technology generations indeed differed in their perception of aspects of quality of life in older age and attitudes towards aging. The oldest generation (household revolution) attached more importance to not being a burden rather than social contacts and medical support for quality of life in older age, and rejected all negative aspects of aging very much. These participants are already in retirement age.

From these different attitudes, especially compared to the generation of technology spread, one could hypothesize that being in this age relativized wishes and concepts of aging and of how quality of life can be achieved. On the other hand, these differences could be generational, as norms and experiences with other people aging may differ to the younger generations. The generation of technology spread, that reaches retirement soon, had a very positive attitude towards aging and rejects all negative aspects but for health problems. For Quality of Life they deem a stable social network and access to information as very important. In comparison, the youngest generation, showed the least positive attitude towards aging and associated especially decreasing health and dependence on others with aging.

In this study, other user factors were analyzed for their influence on the given constructs. Gender and education level did not influence the evaluation. Subjective health status correlated weakly with the relevance of independence for quality of life and decreasing health as well as making plans as associations with aging. As subjective health status declines with age, it can be a moderator of the effects of age. On the other hand, health status itself can relativize the importance of life aspects. Those with worse health status report not to put that much emphasize on competent medical care, maybe because they have learned to live with their illness.

5.2   User-Specific Perceptions of AAL and ICT Technologies

Our results showed, that the technology generations differ in the evaluation of medical technology, especially in the perception of motives to use ICT for aging in place. The oldest generation, that of household revolution shows again attitudes most different from the other generations. The general acceptance of fall detection and medical reminders was lower in this generation. These results are in line with previous research showing that older adults are slower in adapting new technologies (e.g., [12]) and accentuates again the importance of technology acceptance as a barrier against the widespread use of AAL technologies. Considering the evaluation of benefits and barriers, motives were mostly perceived as less pronounced, but barriers were rejected more rigorously than by younger generations. Especially privacy and data security related barriers were rejected stronger, showing that this is not the key barrier for the oldest generation. Thus, the elderly do simply not perceive these technologies as that helpful.

Surprisingly, complex interaction as a barrier against adoption is also more rejected than by other generations. In this study, the oldest generation is the generation of household revolution, that has already experienced many technical devices in their formative period and during their working life. In older studies, the older adults belonged to the mechanical generation, that were less experienced. Claßen [29] found, that the household generation perceives interaction with technical devices easier than the mechanical generation. Moreover, no differences in technical self-efficacy between the generations could be detected in this study. The results could be an indicator, that the gap between the now older adults and younger generations is narrowing, at least regarding usability issues as barriers. On the other hand, the questionnaire was distributed online, reaching only internet users. Hence, it could be that our sample of older adults is more technically affine than the average of their generation, explaining these results.

The technology spread generation showed the highest general acceptance of the presented technologies and the highest agreement to all motives to use them. Additionally to their positive image towards aging, this generation has much more experience with technology and uses many electronic devices and the internet in their everyday live compared to the older generation (e.g., 77% of the Germans aged 45 to 64 used mobile internet in 2016 [30]). But the internet generation - also often called the *Digital Natives* because they were surrounded and have been using electronic devices since their early childhood [31] - agreed to the motives to use technology almost as little as the oldest generation did. This shows, that experiences and habits to use technologies are not the only variables influencing the technology assessment. One could speculate that these young adults are very far away from aging and as they also show a more negative attitude towards aging, they do not see the added value of the evaluated AAL technologies.

Further, gender did only influence the acceptance of medical reminders. Women report a lower level of acceptance. At the same time, confirming previous research, e.g., [32], women indicated to be less confident in interacting with technical devices. This technical self-efficacy played a role for the acceptance of both technologies, with a higher self-efficacy relating to higher acceptance. The sample size of this study does not suffice to analyze interaction effects, but we can hypothesize that the gender effects on acceptance are mediated by technical self-efficacy.

Technical self-efficacy did not show any relation to the perception of motives, but a higher self-efficacy and a lower importance of those barriers regarding technology itself (e.g., too much technology, complex interaction, missing trust) were moderately related in both technology examples. Despite the fact, that in this study no significant relationship between age and technical self-efficacy was found, it could be one main moderating variable explaining the differences of the technology generations.

Education level was related to the perception of some motives to use fall detection and some barriers to use medical reminders, but always as just a small effect. A few barriers to use fall detection and medical reminders also showed a weak correlation with subjective health status. These results only show that there are influences, but are too weak and, in the case of health status, also too much interdependent on the other analyzed variables, e.g., age, to provide further insights into the effects.

Attitudes towards aging showed weak relationships with the acceptance of fall detection as a more positive attitude was related to higher acceptance. At the same time, a more positive attitude led to higher agreement to many motives to use fall detection and medical reminders. The results indicate that with a more positive attitude towards aging the support technology can offer is perceived as more useful. The construct is promising to explain differences in acceptance pattern and should thus be further elaborated and studied for effects on technology acceptance.

The individual need for privacy in general correlated weakly with the acceptance of fall detection. A higher need for privacy was associated with a higher acceptance. As the presented technologies for fall detection also included privacy-invasive technologies like camera or microphone systems, these results seem contradictory on a first sight. On the base of the current data, however, we cannot explain this finding. We can only speculate whether participants with a higher need for privacy rather wanted to be monitored by electronic cameras than by human nurses or focused on more privacy-maintaining technologies like wearable buttons when evaluating fall detection technologies. Need for privacy also related to some motives to use fall detection and medical reminders and showed moderate relationships with the perception of many barriers to use these technologies. As expected, especially barriers regarding privacy and data security were more important to those with a higher need for privacy. Many AAL technologies raise privacy concerns as important barriers against adoption (e.g., [19, 30]). Thus, it is important to include personal dispositions to privacy into the analysis of technology acceptance to better understand different user perspectives.

5.3   Limitations and Future Research

Our empirical research showed that technology generations and other user factors form a multi-faceted picture that influences the acceptance of ICT for aging in place and the perception of motives and barriers to adoption. But limitations should be taken into account regarding some methodological aspects and sample. For the analysis of single effects, the sample size was adequate, but no interaction effects could be examined. From a statistical point of view, most observed effects are small and, as the user factors itself are partly correlated, weak effects can be questioned or be attributed to mediating variables. Future research therefore should collect a larger sample to replicate the findings.

In this questionnaire approach, personal scenarios and pictures of the technologies were used to help the participants to empathize as much as possible with the hypothetical situation of being aged and using AAL technologies. But this cannot be compared to being in this situation as well as to have the opportunity to use technologies and get to know their different advantages and drawbacks in person. The technology examples used in this approach were simple descriptions of the function, e.g., a camera system or wearable button, simple enough to be understood by every participant. For further research, it would be helpful to study technology acceptance of specific systems. As the development of AAL technologies has come forward, research into the acceptance of specific system characteristics could help developing more accepted technologies.

The concept of attitude towards aging has emerged from this study as promising to better understand acceptance patterns of older adults. Rather than only monitoring age as a carrier variable, attitudes of aging and aging concepts reflect the "product" of individual experiences, biographies as well as societal frames which might be more insightful to understand the impact of aging. Further research extending this explorative approach is needed to develop and refine this construct, and to identify its influences on technology acceptance of different technologies for older adults.

Mirroring previous research, concerns regarding privacy and data security have emerged as most important barriers against the adoption of both exemplary AAL technologies. Additionally, it could be shown that the individual disposition to privacy influences the evaluation of these barriers. More research should be conducted to better understand privacy concerns in detail and the individual differences of potential users. The trade-offs between privacy concerns and perceived benefits seem to be crucial to the acceptance of assistive ICT and need to be studied further.

Finally, in this study differences between German technology generations were assessed. On the one hand, the perspective of Germans in the specific German culture and health care system is only one of many and could differ to other countries. On the other hand, we saw indicators that the oldest analyzed generation, that of the household revolution (aged 69 years or older), does not perceive usability barriers as relevant as seniors in older studies, that belonged mostly to the mechanical generation. Longitudinal approach to distinguish effects of age and generation are needed in order to understand technology acceptance not only of today's but also of tomorrow's older adults.

Acknowledgements. The authors thank all participants for their openness in sharing their opinions. Furthermore, the authors want to thank Nils Plettenberg for research assistance. This work was funded by the German Federal Ministry of Education and Research (in parts: projects Whistle 16SV7530 and MyneData (KIS1DSD045)).

References

1. Haustein, T., Mischke, J., Schönfeld, F., Willand, I., Theis, K.: Older People in Germany and the EU (2016)
2. Wilkowska, W., Ziefle, M.: User diversity as a challenge for the integration of medical technology into future smart home environments. In: Ziefle, M., Röcker, C. (eds.) Human-Centered Design of E-Health Technologies: Concepts, Methods and Applications, pp. 95–126. Medical Information Science Reference, New York (2011)
3. Cardinaux, F., Deepayan, B., Charith, A., Hawley, M.S., Mark, S., Bhowmik, D., Abhayaratne, C.: Video based technology for ambient assisted living: a review of the literature. J. Ambient Intell. Smart Environ. **1364**, 253–269 (2011)
4. Blackman, S., Matlo, C., Bobrovitskiy, C., Waldoch, A., Fang, M.L., Jackson, P., Mihailidis, A., Nygård, L., Astell, A., Sixsmith, A.: Ambient assisted living technologies for aging well: a scoping review. J. Intell. Syst. **25**, 55–69 (2016)
5. Yared, R., Abdulrazak, B.: Ambient technology to assist elderly people in indoor risks. Computers **5**, 22 (2016)
6. Chaudhuri, S., Thompson, H., Demiris, G.: Fall detection devices and their use with older adults: a systematic review. J. Geriatr. Phys. Tehr. **37**, 178–196 (2014)
7. Rashidi, P., Mihailidis, A.: A survey on ambient-assisted living tools for older adults. IEEE J. Biomed. Heal. Informatics. **17**, 579–590 (2013)
8. Merkel, S.: Technische Unterstützung für mehr Gesundheit und Lebensqualität im Alter: Herausforderungen und Chancen [Technical support for more Health and Quality of Life in Older Age: Challgendes and Opportunities]. Forsch. Aktuell, Inst. für Arbeit und Tech. (IAT), Westfälische Hochschule, University Applied Science (2016)
9. Ajzen, I., Fishbein, M.: Understanding Attitudes and Predicting Social Behavior. Prentice-Hall, Englewood Cliffs (1980)
10. Davis, F.D.: Perceived usefulness, perceived ease of use, and user acceptance of information technology. MIS Q. **13**, 319–340 (1989)
11. Venkatesh, V., Zhang, X.: Culture and technology adoption: theory and empirical test of the unified theory of acceptance and use of technology (UTAUT) in the us vs china. J. Chem. Inf. Model. **53**, 1689–1699 (2013)

12. Czaja, S.J., Charness, N., Fisk, A.D., Hertzog, C., Nair, S.N., Rogers, W.A., Sharit, J.: Factors predicting the use of technology: findings from the center for research and education on aging and technology enhancement (CREATE). Psyhol. Aging. **21**, 333–352 (2006)
13. Ziefle, M., Schaar, A.K.: Gender differences in acceptance and attitudes towards an invasive medical stent. Electron. J. Heal. Inf. **6** (2011). www.eJHI.net
14. Chen, K., Chan, A.H.S.: Review a review of technology acceptance by older adults. Gerontechnology **10**, 1–12 (2011)
15. Jakobs, E.: Alter und Technik (2008)
16. van de Goor, A.G., Becker, H.A.: Technology generations in the Netherlands: a sociological analysis. Shaker Pub, Maastricht (2000)
17. Sackmann, R., Winkler, O.: Technology generations revisited: the internet generation. Gerontechnology **11**, 493–503 (2013)
18. van Heek, J., Himmel, S., Ziefle, M.: Caregivers' perspectives on ambient assisted living technologies in professional care contexts. In: 4th International Conference on Information and Communication Technologies for Ageing Well and e-Health (ICT4AWE 2018). SCITEPRESS (2018)
19. Himmel, S., Ziefle, M.: Smart home medical technologies: users' requirements for conditional acceptance. I-Com. J. Interact. Media. **15**, 39–50 (2016)
20. van Heek, J., Arning, K., Ziefle, M.: Where, wherefore, and how? Contrasting two surveillance contexts according to acceptance. In: 6th International Conference on Smart Cities and Green ICT Systems (Smartgreens 2017), pp. 87–98. SCITEPRESS (2017)
21. Jaschinski, C., Allouch, S.B.: An extended view on benefits and barriers of ambient assisted living solutions. Int. J. Adv. Life Sci. **7**, 40–53 (2015)
22. Peek, S.T.M., Wouters, E.J.M., van Hoof, J., Luijkx, K.G., Boeije, H.R., Vrijhoef, H.J.M.: Factors influencing acceptance of technology for aging in place: a systematic review (2014)
23. van Heek, J., Himmel, S., Ziefle, M.: Helpful but spooky ? Acceptance of AAL-systems contrasting user groups with focus on disabilities and care needs. In: Proceedings of the 3rd International Conference on Information and Communication Technologies for Ageing Well and e-Health (ICT4AWE 2017), pp. 78–90 (2017)
24. Bowling, A., Gabriel, Z., Dykes, J., Dowding, L.M., Evans, O., Fleissig, A., Banister, D., Sutton, S.: Let's ask them: a national survey of definitions of quality of life and its enhancement among people aged 65 and over. Int. J. Aging Hum. Dev. **56**, 269–306 (2003)
25. Schomakers, E.-M., van Heek, J., Ziefle, M.: A game of wants and needs. The Playful, user-centered assessment of AAL technology acceptance. In: ICT4AgeingWell 2018. SCITEPRESS (2018)
26. Beier, G.: Kontrollüberzeugungen im Umgang mit Technik [Technical Self-Efficacy]. Rep. Psychol., 684–693 (1999)
27. Xu, H., Dinev, T., Smith, H.J., Hart, P.: Examining the formation of individual's privacy concerns: toward an integrative view. In: International Conference on Information Systems (2008)
28. McKnight, D.H., Choudhury, V., Kacmar, C.: Developing and validating trust measures for e-commerce: an integrative typology. Inf. Syst. Res. **13**, 334–359 (2002)
29. Claßen, K.: Zur Psychologie von Technikakzeptanz im höheren Lebensalter: Die Rolle von Technikgenerationen [Psychology of Technology Acceptance in older age: the role of technology generations]. Dissertation (2012)
30. Statistisches Bundesamt Destatis: Private Haushalte in der Informationsgesellschaft - Nutzung von Informations- und Kommunikationstechnologien [Private Household in the Information Society - Use of Information and Communication Technologies] (2017)

31. Prensky, M.: Digital natives. Digit. Immigrants. Horiz. **9**, 1–6 (2001)
32. Wilkowska, W., Gaul, S., Ziefle, M.: A small but significant difference - the role of gender on acceptance of medical assistive technologies. In: Leitner, G., Hitz, M., Holzinger, A. (eds.) USAB 2010, LNCS 6389, pp. 82–100. Springer, Heidelberg (2010)

A Qualitative Investigation on Chinese Middle-Aged People's ICT Adoption and Use

Shijie Song[1(✉)], Jianjun Sun[1], Bin Geng[1], and Yuxiang Zhao[2]

[1] Nanjing University, Nanjing, China
ssong@smail.nju.edu.cn
[2] Nanjing University of Science and Technology, Nanjing, China

Abstract. Information and communication technologies show many advantages in addressing the challengers resulted from population ageing. However, there is a 'intergenerational gap' of ICT adoption and use between older adults and young people and divided by middle-aged generation. This study aims at exploring middle-aged people's ICT adoption and use to better understand the 'generational gap'. The semi-structure interview is employed in the study. The qualitative data is analyzed from four themes, including the access to ICTs, access to ICT support, influencing factors on ICT adoption and use, and the attitudes on ICT adoption and use in the future. Based on the analyses, the theoretical and practical implications are discussed respectively.

Keywords: Digital divide · ICT adoption · Middle-aged population
Qualitative method

1 Introduction

During the past couple of decades, world's middle-aged and older adults population are increasing dramatically due to the continuous decline in fertility and general increase in the average life span [1]. The population aging trend leads to the increase of health expenditure [2], and becomes one of the greatest challenges globally.

Information and communication technologies (ICTs) show a huge potential to improve the ageing population's life quality [3], and reduce the social expenditures [4, 5]. However, there is a 'intergenerational gap' of ICT adoption and use between older adults and young people. According to the China Internet Network Information Centre (CNNIC) [6], as the age increase, the proportion of Internet users to the nation population decreases from the middle-aged generation, as shown in Fig. 1.

Illustrated by Fig. 1, the 'intergenerational gap' of ICT adoption and use is separated by the middle-aged group. Moreover, as the middle-aged people will eventually step into the aged life stage, we propose to choose the standing point of middle age to understand the ICT adoption and use, for bridging the 'intergenerational gap'.

Data source: China Internet Network Information Centre [6]; National Bureau of Statistics of China [7];

© Springer International Publishing AG, part of Springer Nature 2018
J. Zhou and G. Salvendy (Eds.): ITAP 2018, LNCS 10926, pp. 170–178, 2018.
https://doi.org/10.1007/978-3-319-92034-4_13

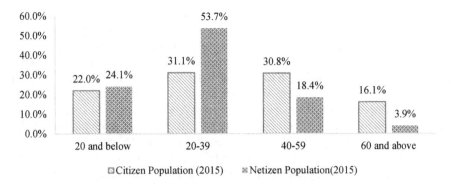

☐ Citizen Population (2015)   ⊠ Netizen Population(2015)

Fig. 1. Age structure comparison

2 Literature Review

In the early investigation on general ICT adoption and use, age is not an extensively explored factor. Although the theory of planned behavior (TPB) [8] and the unified theory of acceptance and use of technology (UTAUT) [9] both include the age as a moderator, the original forms of other adoption models such as technology acceptance model (TAM) [10] or the theory of reasoned action (TRA) [11] do not specifically exam the role of age in ICT adoption and use.

However, more and more studies suggest that the age indeed matters in ICT adoption and use. The failure of traditional adoption models in predicating older adult's ICT adoption can be regarded as an indirect evidence to indicate that age matters. For example, Heart and Kalderon [12] report that TPB is only partially supported in older adult's health-related ICT adoption; Braun [13] reports the similar findings that TAM can only partially explain the older adults' SNS adoption behaviours; Magsamen-Conrad, Upadhyaya, Joa and Dowd [14] suggest that only two determinants out of four in UTAUT have good explanatory power in predicting people's tablet adoption when the sample group ranged from 19 to 99 year old. Additionally, some inter group studies provide some direct evidences. Czaja and Sharit [15] report that the middle-aged and the older adults perceived less comfort, efficacy and control over ICT than the younger generation. Morris and Venkatesh [16] find various influencing factors between older and younger workers in workplace condition, and report that older people are more likely influenced by subjective norm and perceived behavioral control while the younger ones are more strongly influenced by attitude in ICT adoption and use.

Based on such age awareness, order adult's ICT adoption draws much attention and becomes a hot research topic. Qualitative methods (e.g., in-depth interview [17, 18], focus group [18–20], grounded theory [21], literature survey [22], and case study [23], etc.) are commonly adopted in this research area to understand the older adult's ICT adoption and use. These studies indicate that attitudes and abilities are two main predictors when exploring the older adult's technology use [3]. However, it seems that the relationship, namely positive attitude vs. negative attitude, or use vs. non-use, is not one coin's two sides. As reported by the prior works, positive attitudes are affected by the weighing between perceived benefit against cost [19, 20]; while the negative attitudes frequently associated with limited relevance of new technologies [17, 24], health risks, and social problems arising from using technologies (e.g., social isolation and addiction) [21]. Despite some common conclusions, such as the important role of external supporting and training in support the older adults' ICT use [18, 23], the more ambivalent points remain unclear. As what Lee and Coughlin [22] suggest, a holistic view is much needed in understanding older adults' acceptance and use of emerging new technologies (which are not limited to web-based internet technologies, but with a wider coverage of smartphones and sensor-based Internet of Things).

Despite the growing attention on older adult's ICT adoption, the prior literatures rarely touched the middle-aged population which may step into the aged group sooner or later. Thus, our study aims at focusing on the middle-aged people's ICT adoption and use to bridge the research gaps.

3 Research Questions

This study is built on the basis of two theoretical assumptions: (1) The middle-aged population shares many similarities with the older generation in ICT adoption and use, as the two generations both can be viewed as 'digital immigrants' [25]. 'Digital immigrants' and 'digital natives' are a pair of terms created by Marc Prensky [26], the former referring to those who learnt to use IT devices at some stage during their adult lives, while the latter referring to those who have born in a digital world with ubiquitous ICT applications. This assumption enables us to re-examine the older adult's ICT adoption and use in middle-aged generation settings. (2) We further assume that the middle-age people yet have unique characteristics compared with older adults, as the former group has more exposure to ICT environment.

To compare with the older adult's ICT adoption research of Selwyn [17], Heart and Kalderon [12], we raise the following research questions:

- How do middle-aged people access to ICTs?
- What access do middle-aged people have to ICT support?
- What factors are associated with middle-aged people's access to ICT?
- What attitudes do middle-aged people have on ICT use in the future?

4 Research Design

4.1 Research Method

This study employs semi-structured interview as the research method, and follows a general interview approach [27]. The adoption of semi-structured interview is based on two reasons. First, prior studies suggest that the traditional quantitative models do not show a good explanatory power in predicting people's ICT adoption and use when the sample group includes middle-aged and older adults as stated previously [14, 28]. Second, semi-structured interview is wildly acknowledged as an effective approach of probing attitudes. It gives interviewer multiple choices in the wordings, helps respondent recall the memory, and enables the respondent to clarify the interested and relevant issues [29].

4.2 Interviewees and Interview Process

The participants of this study are recruited from a local community at Nanjing, China. The paper-based recruitment notices were posted at the main traffic entrances of the community; at the same time, the electronic notices were distributed via the community's households online chatting groups. After two week's recruiting, a total of 19 volunteers responded. Since the 'middle age' is a loosely defined term, commonly involving one of the three occasions, 40−59, 40−65, or 45−65 years old, this study uses the 40−59 years old occasion. After identifying the age, eventually 12 participants were recruited from whole volunteers.

The interviews take 7 days to complete. At the first two days, 2 people were invited randomly to the first-round pilot interviews. The interview questions and wordings were revised in the pilot study. The rest 10 formal interviews were scheduled to take 20 to 40 min at the common activity space in the community. Each participant was offered a small gift valued around 5 dollars after the interview. The demographic summary is shown in Table 1.

Table 1. Demographic Summary

Age	Gender	Smartphone use experience (Years)	Education	Professionals
49	F	3.5	Junior college degree	Hospitality sector
50	M	2	Bachelor	Educational sector
50	M	3	Bachelor	Manufacturing sector
46	F	4	Bachelor	Public sector
58	F	2.5	High school	Retired
55	M	1.5	Senior secondary school	Self-employed
48	M	3	Senior secondary school	Retailing sector
49	F	5	Master	Public sector
49	F	4	Bachelor	Manufacturing sector
52	F	3.5	Bachelor	Educational sector
54	M	1	Junior secondary school	Self-employed
55	F	3	Senior secondary school	Retired

5   Results

The interview results are compared under four key themes that guided the interviews: access to ICTs, access to ICT support, influencing factors on ICT adoption and use, and the attitudes on ICT adoption and use in the future.

5.1   Access to ICTs

First, the results show that the transition of socio-technical infrastructure is the pre-condition for middle-aged people's ICT adoption. The interviewees from this study all report that their uses of new ICTs are tightly accompanied with their use of smart phones. The phenomenon indicates that the adoption of ICT is embedded in the development of socio-technical systems. On the one hand, the low price and avail-ability of smart phones, together with the ambient affordable wireless connection, pull the user to the information age; on the other hand, the upgrade of technical systems which makes the outdated tools be no longer accessible, is a push factor for users to adopt the new technology.

When do you begin to use the mobile apps such as WeChat?

Previously, my phone is not the smart one. It can only make the calls and send the text messages... it's nearly impossible to find such phones in the stores nowadays... As soon as I transferred to this smart phone 4 years ago, I began to use the apps...

Additionally, the transition of socio-technical infrastructure also leads to cultural changes about the ICT use. Being exposed to such cultural environment in which the use of ICT becomes a social wave, the actors will get access to more hints, reasons, and opportunities of knowing the ICT, which may further result in the actual adoption behaviors.

Why do you begin to use the mobile apps?

I think most people around me own smartphone now. It's obvious, no matter on bus station or in supermarket, people are always watching at their phones ... I heard a new word to call them, 'phubber'? (laughing) But it's so normal today.

5.2   Access to ICT Support: Intergenerational Learning

This study reveals that the intergenerational learning plays a notable role in supporting middle-aged people's ICT use at different stages. At the initial-adoption phase, younger generation usually plays a dominant role in helping older generation accept the ICTs. At the post-adoption phase, the younger generation acts as the recommender and facilitator in older generation's ICT continuous use.

How do you know the apps?

This phone was brought by my daughter. She taught me how to use the touch-screen mobile phone. She helped me do the default settings and install the initial apps... My daughter recommended this app to me (interviewee show a cloud-music app on her phone screen). I like it very much ...

How do you solve the problems in smartphone app using?

My method is to keep learning. First, I'll have a glance at the version update logs of 'what's new' then I'll try to use it by myself. If I'm still not clear, I'll ask. When I'm at office, I'll ask my young colleagues; when I'm at home, I'll enquiry my son ... Occasionally if these ways all don't work, I'll ask my young colleagues to teach me hand by hand, so I can mimic them to use ...

5.3 Influencing Factors on ICT Use

First, this study finds that the socio-technical infrastructure development can result in the non-institutional changes on the ways of regulating how the information can be shared or exchanged, which can further influence the actors' subjective norms.

What kinds of information do you get and share via WeChat?

From nowhere we [people in the office] have many various chat groups in WeChat. We [colleagues] share many things from routine conversations to job-related topics... in practice even some formal notices are distributed via it...I cannot say someone will necessarily miss the important information if he or she doesn't use WeChat, given we have other channels to distribute the notices simultaneously. Nevertheless, if the majority are using it to communicate, I think it's better to follow.

Second, the results show that the perceived value is one of the most significant motivation for interviewees to adopt ICTs, which is in accordance with the findings revealed by many prior studies [30]. However, besides the similar findings, we also identify that the perceived value may come from different sources. For example, the satisfying user experience can increase the intrinsic motivation of users; the monetary incentives can influence the extrinsic motivation of users; and the peer influence can affect both the intrinsic and extrinsic motivations.

What factors encourage you to use the apps in your smartphone?

The [offline] stores also usually encourage me to pay the bills by mobile payment apps, and some discount I will get then. It's not a big number, usually from several dimes to a couple of Yuan, but better than nothing.

I feel that the apps indeed make my life be easier from many ways... so I persist in using them ...sometimes [the hints] are got from the others, when I see someone else use the [certain] app and [the app] looks good, I will also try it...

Third, the interviewee's long-term crisis awareness on technology development is another important factor for predicting middle-aged people's ICT adoption and use. Unlike the technostress of technology, the long-term crisis awareness is individual's positive response to technology development with potential actionable coping strategies.

The technology is developing so fast. If we don't follow the steps [of technology's development] from now on, we won't catch and be accustomed to the age when we get older.

5.4 Attitude on ICT Use in the Future

It is commonly believed that older people perceive less comfort, efficacy, and control over ICT use than the younger generation. In this study, however, the middle-aged participants mostly show very positive attitudes on ICT use for the situation at present and the situation in the future. The possible explanation is that the experience of ICT use can modify the negative effects and lead to more positive attitudes [15].

Additionally, the interviews indicate the middle-aged people also hold the expectations on ageing-related customized design in the future.

Do you feel anxious about the high speed of technology development? Are you afraid of losing your control when confronted with the ever-changing societies in the future?

Not at all … Indeed, the technology changes our life a lot, but it also truly improved our life… I don't worry about the technology in the future when I get older … I believe in that technology will always let our life be more convenient …

No anxiety from me. Even if the technology grows faster in the future, I can learn anyway, as what I did before. But not sure whether it applies to others if someone is illiterate … I believe the [system] designers will take care of older adults' needs such as to make the fonts bigger [which is good for the older adults] …

6 Discussion

Based on the analysis, we found that the middle-aged people's access to ICT depends on socio-technical infrastructure development, which includes the access to the hard-wire devices and the exposure to the ICT-related cultural environment. The intergenerational learning plays a fundamental role in supporting middle-aged people's ICT adoption and use. The younger generation, or called 'digital natives', can effectively help the middle-aged generation complete the transition as 'digital immigrants' and master the ICT use. Additionally, we found that middle-aged people's ICT uses are significantly influenced by subjective norms, perceived value, and long-term crisis awareness. Furthermore, the middle-aged people report positive attitudes towards ICT use in the future, which suggests they are ready to be stepped into the ICT-facilitated ageing society in the future.

Some practical implications can be drawn from the major findings. First, the system designers can leverage the effectiveness of intergenerational learning by providing the collaborative task affordance, such as family games, to encourage the 'digital natives' and 'digital immigrants' to work together. Second, it is important to make the older users to perceive the value. Word-of-mouth marketing strategies and monetary incentives are possible ways. Third, the system designers should take care the age-related cognitive and physical changes when doing the system development.

7 Limitation and Future Study

As a piece of exploratory research, this study contains a couple of limits. First, the qualitative research approach with the local sampling will scarify the external validity. Considering the ICT adoption and use is heavily influenced by socio-technical infrastructure, the findings discovered in Chinese context may not be generalized to different technical and cultural settings in western countries. Besides, some possible association effects (e.g. effects of information literacy on ICT use, gender effects on ICT use, etc.) were not examined in this study due to the constraint of sample size. Moreover, this study only revealed a part of the positive influencing factors on middle-aged people's ICT adoption and use, while the more negative obstacles on middle-aged people's ICT use remain untouched, which may be addressed in the future studies.

References

1. Centers for Disease Control and Prevention: Trends in aging–United States and worldwide. MMWR. Morb. Mortal. Wkly Rep. **52**, 101 (2003)
2. Bloom, D.E., Chatterji, S., Kowal, P., Lloyd-Sherlock, P., McKee, M., Rechel, B., Rosenberg, L., Smith, J.P.: Macroeconomic implications of population ageing and selected policy responses. Lancet **385**, 649–657 (2015)
3. Charness, N., Boot, W.R.: Aging and information technology use: potential and barriers. Curr. Dir. Psychol. Sci. **18**, 253–258 (2009)
4. Anderson, G.F., Frogner, B.K., Johns, R.A., Reinhardt, U.E.: Health care spending and use of information technology in OECD countries. Health Aff. **25**, 819–831 (2006)
5. Chaudhry, B., Wang, J., Wu, S., Maglione, M., Mojica, W., Roth, E., Morton, S.C., Shekelle, P.G.: Systematic review: impact of health information technology on quality, efficiency, and costs of medical care. Ann. Intern. Med. **144**, 742–752 (2006)
6. China Internet Network Information Centre: 39th Report (2017). https://cnnic.com.cn/IDR/ReportDownloads/
7. National Bureau of Statistics of China: Annual Data. (2017) http://www.stats.gov.cn/english/Statisticaldata/AnnualData/
8. Venkatesh, V., Morris, M.G.: Why don't men ever stop to ask for directions? gender, social influence, and their role in technology acceptance and usage behavior. MIS Quart. **24**, 115–139 (2000)
9. Venkatesh, V., Morris, M.G., Davis, G.B., Davis, F.D.: User Acceptance of Information Technology: toward a unified view. MIS Quart. **27**, 425–478 (2003)
10. Venkatesh, V., Davis, F.D.: A theoretical extension of the technology acceptance model: four longitudinal field studies. Manage. Sci. **46**, 186–204 (2000)
11. Fishbein, M., Ajzen, I.: Belief, Attitude, Intention and Behavior: an Introduction to Theory and Research (1975)
12. Heart, T., Kalderon, E.: Older adults: are they ready to adopt health-related ICT? Int. J. Med. Inf. **82**, e209–e231 (2013)
13. Braun, M.T.: Obstacles to social networking website use among older adults. Comput. Hum. Behav. **29**, 673–680 (2013)
14. Magsamen-Conrad, K., Upadhyaya, S., Joa, C.Y., Dowd, J.: Bridging the divide: Using UTAUT to predict multigenerational tablet adoption practices. Comput. Hum. Behav. **50**, 186–196 (2015)
15. Czaja, S.J., Sharit, J.: Age differences in attitudes toward computers. J. Gerontol. Ser. B : Psychol. Sci. Soc. Sci. **53**, P329–P340 (1998)
16. Morris, M.G., Venkatesh, V.: Age differences in technology adoption decisions: implications for a changing work force. Pers. Psychol. **53**, 375–403 (2000)
17. Selwyn, N.: The information aged: a qualitative study of older adults' use of information and communications technology. J. Aging Stud. **18**, 369–384 (2004)
18. Chiu, C.-J., Hu, Y.-H., Lin, D.-C., Chang, F.-Y., Chang, C.-S., Lai, C.-F.: The attitudes, impact, and learning needs of older adults using apps on touchscreen mobile devices: results from a pilot study. Comput. Hum. Behav. **63**, 189–197 (2016)

19. Melenhorst, A.S., Rogers, W.A., Caylor, E.C.: The use of communication technologies by older adults: exploring the benefits from the user's perspective. In: Proceedings of the Human Factors and Ergonomics Society Annual Meeting, pp. 221–225. SAGE Publications Sage CA, Los Angeles

20. Mitzner, T.L., Boron, J.B., Fausset, C.B., Adams, A.E., Charness, N., Czaja, S.J., Dijkstra, K., Fisk, A.D., Rogers, W.A., Sharit, J.: Older adults talk technology: technology usage and attitudes. Comput. Hum. Behav. **26**, 1710–1721 (2010)

21. Chen, K., Chan, A.H.S.: Use or non-use of gerontechnology—a qualitative study. Int. J. Environ. Res. Public Health **10**, 4645–4666 (2013)

22. Lee, C., Coughlin, J.F.: Perspective: older adults' adoption of technology: an integrated approach to identifying determinants and barriers. J. Prod. Innov. Manage **32**, 747–759 (2015)

23. Barnard, Y., Bradley, M.D., Hodgson, F., Lloyd, A.D.: Learning to use new technologies by older adults: perceived difficulties, experimentation behaviour and usability. Comput. Hum. Behav. **29**, 1715–1724 (2013)

24. Selwyn, N., Gorard, S., Furlong, J., Madden, L.: Older adults' use of information and communications technology in everyday life. Ageing Soc. **23**, 561–582 (2003)

25. Chris Zhao, Y., Xu, X., Sun, X., Zhu, Q.: An integrated framework of online generative capability: interview from digital immigrants. Aslib J. Inf. Manage. **66**, 219–239 (2014)

26. Prensky, M.: Digital natives, digital immigrants part 1. Horizon **9**, 1–6 (2001)

27. Myers, M.D., Newman, M.: The qualitative interview in IS research: examining the craft. Inform. Organ. **17**, 2–26 (2007)

28. Deng, Z., Mo, X., Liu, S.: Comparison of the middle-aged and older users' adoption of mobile health services in China. Int. J. Med. Inform. **83**, 210–224 (2014)

29. Louise Barriball, K., While, A.: Collecting data using a semi-structured interview: a discussion paper. J. Adv. Nurs. **19**, 328–335 (1994)

30. Melenhorst, A.-S., Rogers, W.A., Bouwhuis, D.G.: Older adults' motivated choice for technological innovation: evidence for benefit-driven selectivity. Psychol. Aging **21**, 190 (2006)

Senior Citizens Usage Towards and Perception of Modern Technology in India

J. Antony William[(✉)] and Ramaswami Murugesh

Department of Computer Application,
Madurai Kamaraj University, Madurai, India
antony.william@gmail.com, mrswami123@gmail.com

Abstract. India is the second largest populated country and one the fast growing developing countries in the world. As we grow up and getting older, problems associated with aging is increasing rapidly – medical, biological, psychological, economic, and social etc. Population ageing and growing number of elderly population demands for healthcare and technology enabled-services. Factors associated with ageing population are essential for to ensure progress in development and sustainability. In response to the rapid population growth, the industry and market for older adults is growing with the introduction of new technology-enabled products and services. The advancement of technology and technology-enabled services are proliferating. However, their rate of adaption is very low. As the society is progressively moving towards digital, there is an increasing risk of excluding users with particular access needs. Among those at risk of digital exclusion are many older people and other differently-abled people for whom the technology is difficult to access. We foresee a great challenge in identifying factors affecting older people adopting new technologies and provide support to aging. To assess senior citizens usage towards and perception of modern technology in India, a survey was conducted with a random sample of 25 participants over 60 years of age using smart phone and living in Bengaluru city. The survey was carried out individually face to face followed by semi-structured interviews. The participants expressed that they are not scared and hesitant to use technology. They are also aware of the value of new technologies and show their willingness to adopt, if it improves their quality of life with security. The implications of the results are discussed in this paper.

Keywords: Senior citizen · Population aging · Technology adoption
Technology usage · Assistive technology · Technology perception

1 Introduction

Population aging is the most significant global phenomenon today. The 20th century has witnessed the increased proportion of aging population in all the countries. In the coming millennium, it is expected to increase further due to the improvement in life expectancy all over the world, particularly public health and medical advancements. Population aging has become the most important social transformation of the 21st century.

© Springer International Publishing AG, part of Springer Nature 2018
J. Zhou and G. Salvendy (Eds.): ITAP 2018, LNCS 10926, pp. 179–193, 2018.
https://doi.org/10.1007/978-3-319-92034-4_14

By 2050, the elderly population of Asia over 60 years will double by the mid-century reaching to 1.3 billion (United Nations 2015a, b). On the other side steadily declining birth rate and fertility trends, lead to increase in the share of aged in total population of the world and this has brought enormous challenges to many aspects of life.

In India, the proportion of the population aged 60 years and above was 7% (88 million) in 2009 and was projected to increase to 20% (315 million) by the year 2050 (Subaiya and Bansod 2011). The demographics of population aging in India shows that the proportion of population aged 15–59 and 60 years and above are projected to increase while 0–14 years are projected to decline rapidly (Subaiya and Bansod 2011) (see Fig. 1). The United Nations Population Division projects that after the year 2050 the elderly population will outnumber children (United Nations 2010).

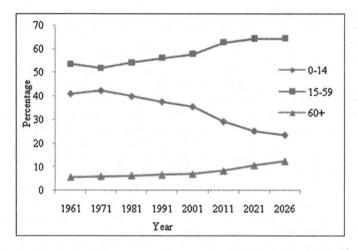

Fig. 1. Population by broad age groups in India, 1961–2026.

The population aging process began in the last century with developed countries and currently encompassing developing countries as well (United Nations 2015a, b). India is not an exception to this aging phenomena. The structure of the population has changed over the years and will further and the proportion of older persons in the population will increase. As we age, problems associated with aging is increasing rapidly – medical, biological, economic, social etc. In the scenario of large elderly population, the country needs more technology-enabled health care services, facilities and resources.

In response to the rapid population growth, the industry and market for older adults is growing with the introduction of new technology-enabled products and services. However, their rate of adaption is very low. As the society is progressively moving towards digital, there is an increasing risk of excluding users with particular access needs (Milne et al. 2005). Among those at risk of digital exclusion are many older people and other differently-abled people for whom the technology is difficult to access. We foresee a great challenge in identifying factors affecting older people adopting new technologies and provide support to aging.

Elderly users are progressively limited in their ability to use and access information due to multiplicative effects might come with increasing age factor. Many older people are having difficulties in using modern smart devices due to increased complexity in accessing information both in terms of functionality and interface design. Research shows that older people have more difficulty in using touch interfaces in comparison to the younger population (Page 2014). The world demography shows that due to various developments a proportional increase of older people engaged in effective use of technology to lead independent life. Population ageing and growing number of elderly population demands for care and technology enabled-services. Factors associated with ageing population are essential for to ensure progress in development and sustainability.

In this context, an important fact which needs to greater attention is that in the developing countries like India, older persons are increasingly living independently due disintegration of the joint family and the rise of nuclear and extended family systems (Chadda and Deb 2013). Technology has been shown to be beneficial to older people and question is one has to access how the technology/technology enabled-services going to improve the quality of elderly people. This paper reviews the senior citizens usage towards and perception of modern digital technologies in an Indian context.

2 Technology Usage and Adoption

We are living in a fast changing technological period and modern technologies have become part of our everyday life. Smart modern devices connected to the internet, have changed the way we communicate, work and live our life. We use on a daily basis from computers, cell phones, tablets, laptops and entertainment systems to refrigerators and kitchen applications. As people age, technology and technology enabled services have a great potential to improve the quality of life. Technology adaptation is a great concern today. It is all around us and if we have not adapted to that may feel we are not in control of ourselves. Its significance has not been overlooked by the business world, which daily introduces hundreds of smart technology-enabled services to the public. Over the period technologies designed for a mass market are not adequately sensitive to the needs of older people. Sara J. Czaja and Joseph Sharit in their study on the aging of population said, "In general, today's elderly are healthier, more diverse and better educated than previous generations". So, the potential future of the technology is to help older people to improve physical and emotion well-being.

Many shortcomings are faced by senior citizens regarding usage of modern smart devices due to increased complexity in accessing information both in terms of functionality and interface design. The capabilities of older people are very diverse in their capabilities and ageing factor increases the learning curve to acquire new knowledge. As the Information Society is moving more towards digital, it is becoming clear that several already disadvantaged groups are being excluded. Literature review shows that not enough attention is paid to the interaction design that would actually accommodate individual needs and preferences of elderly users in an Indian context.

3 Research Methodology

Demographic and technology prior-experience questionnaires were conducted with a selective sample of respondents over 60 years of age using smart phone (android) and living in Bengaluru. A survey was conducted with structured questionnaires followed by a semi-structured interview. The data collection technique used is self-administered questionnaires where participants were presented with the questionnaires in persons. The aim and objective of the study was explained and the participant was allowed to complete set of questionnaires after which the semi-structured interview was conducted. The intension of semi-structured interview was to know more about the role of technology in their life, aspiration and expectation from the modern technology and technology-enabled services. The number of participants was 25 and the language used was English. All participants were approached in their residence with prior appointment and the study was carried out individually face to face. In total 25 participants were selected for the study and all were healthy aged 60–75 years old. The majority of the participants were lived with their spouse and some alone with broad span of socioeconomic status.

We have chosen Bengaluru city for our research study because of its multi-cultural nature and home to large number of people migrated from other Indian states because of better standard of living, climatic condition, well infrastructure and better employability. Current population of Bengaluru is estimated to 10 million and by 2031 the population is projected 20.3 million (Bangalore Metropolitan Region Development Authority 2017). Average literacy rate of Bengaluru is 87.67% (Census 2011). The city is ranked number three in terms of most populous city in India after Mumbai and Delhi and has modern face of developed economy. It has emerged as the IT capital of India which attracted people from across India and abroad. In Bengaluru, numbers of senior citizens are ever increasing due to increasing nuclear families with few children in the society and other social conditions and this is going continue as population ages. There is a growing challenge in terms of elderly care and assisted living.

Inclusion criteria to identify the subjects for research study was senior citizens aged 60 above, using smart phone (android) and living in Bengaluru City. Exclusion criteria used for this research study are below 60 years old, non-android phone users and rural population. The reason for these criteria is to review the current Senior citizens usage towards and perception of modern technology.

4 Result

A total of 25 participants were involved in this study. During the study, it was observed that 92% of the participants were male and 8% of the participants were female. 48% of the participants were graduates, 24% of the participants were post-graduates, 12% of the participants were diploma holders, 12% of the participants were completed pre-university college (PUC) and 4% of the participants were completed high school as shown in the Table 1.

Table 1. Participant information.

Qualifications	Senior citizens
Graduates	48%
Post-graduate	24%
Diploma	12%
Pre-university college	12%
High school	4%

The results of the study and discussion are centered on frequency of technology usage, android phone usage, commonly used android phone apps, awareness and familiarity with commonly used control buttons of android phone, awareness and familiarity with commonly used control buttons of Microsoft Office applications, awareness and familiarity with commonly used control buttons of internet browser, awareness and familiarity with commonly used control buttons of digital camera and awareness and familiarity with commonly used control buttons of home entertainment system.

4.1 Frequency of Technology Usage

To investigate frequency of technology usage among senior citizens, we have looked into the digital products and services that are matching the interests and functional needs of the senior citizens. We have chosen 8 products for this study and the percentage of frequency of the technology usage by senior citizens given in the Table 2.

Table 2. Percentage of frequency of technology usage by senior citizens.

Digital products/applications	Use it everyday	Use it few times a week	Use it once a month	Used in the past	Never used
Android phone	100%	0%	0%	0%	0%
Google search	72%	8%	0%	0%	20%
Internet browser	56%	12%	4%	8%	20%
YouTube	48%	16%	12%	4%	20%
Windows application	44%	16%	0%	12%	28%
Digital camera	40%	0%	12%	24%	24%
Printer	32%	12%	16%	8%	32%
Tablet	28%	4%	0%	4%	64%

The study shows that the senior citizens are actively engaged with digital products and services. The Table 2 shows that 100% use android phone, 72% use google search, 56% use internet browser, 48% use YouTube, 44% use Windows applications, 40% use digital camera, 32% use printer and 28% use tablet on every day basis. Here, the most used are android phone, google search, internet browser and You Tube which are very much internet dependent. The tablet is the product least used by the senior citizens. Significant usage of internet-based technologies reveals that these technologies support their daily activities.

A significant percentage of participants used these digital products in the past due to their professional experience which is directly linked with their education. The overall percentage of frequency of usage goes from android phone to tablet as listed in the Table 2, where applications like Google Search, Internet Browser, You Tube, and Windows Applications are part of the android phone. This explains the relative advantage of internet-based activities in achieving their overall goals and diverse interactive applications to assist them.

4.2   Android Phone Usage

Mobile phone is no longer just a communication tool rather it has become a personal computer with advanced features and they have become virtual assistances. In this context we have carried out the study to investigate the android usage among senior citizens by selecting 9 apps which are relevant to the study (see Fig. 2). The chart shows that 100% use for making phone calls, 100% for sending and reading SMS (short message service), 80% for checking time, 76% for calculating, 68% for setting alarm, 64% for reading and sending emails, 64% for social media, 48% for surfing internet and 36% for making video calls.

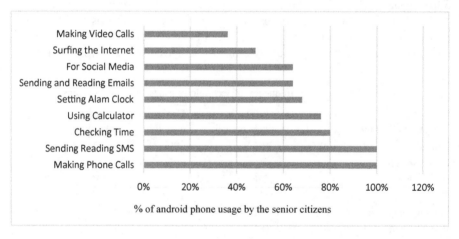

Fig. 2. Percentage of android phone usage by the senior citizens.

The above figure implies three categories of android phone usage by the senior citizens. Firstly, the phone is used for basic mobile services to allow users to make calls and send text messages. Secondly, the phone is used as clock and calculator. The participants feel that the mobile provides functionality to set alarms, add timers and keep track of time around the world using world clock. The calculator app provides simple and advanced mathematical function and they feel that it really helps them to do daily tasks. Thirdly, the phone is used for email, social media, internet surfing and for making video calls. Many senior citizens perceive additional usefulness of new technologies in comparison to traditional communication mediums. The Table 3 gives detailed information about commonly used apps by the senior citizens.

Table 3. Percentage commonly used mobile apps by senior citizens.

Commonly used apps	% of usage
Phone	100%
Contact	96%
Messaging	92%
WhatsApp	84%
Camera	84%
Calculator	84%
Email	84%
Calendar	72%
Google	64%
Maps	60%
Music	60%
YouTube	60%
Flashlight	48%
Skype	40%
Weather	36%
Sound recording	32%
Radio FM	28%
FlipKart	24%
Twitter	24%
Play games	20%
Voice search	20%
Play music	20%
Do it later	20%
Hangouts	8%
Drive	8%
Amazon kindle	8%
Health manager	8%
Health tracker	8%
Newsstand	4%
BP watch	4%
iCare	4%

The Table 3 clearly illustrates how each and every app is been used by the senior citizens to fulfill their needs for information, communication and entertainment. It is also self-evident that these apps assist them in daily life situations. The senior citizens reported that they use wide variety of applications and also it indicates that they are very much engaged larger part of social network and in one device they are able to fulfill many of their needs. Due to the demand and availability of the developer tools made rapid expansion into every single requirement. The usage of mobile apps is remarkably increasing among senior citizens.

4.3 Awareness and Familiarity with Commonly Used Control Icons of Android Phone

Navigation is an important aspect of any device/application to meet the goal and the control icons of mobile are guiding principles to create interaction system that naturally align with the user's mental models. To investigate how well the senior citizens are aware and familiar with control icons of android phone, we have selected icons which are commonly used in phone as well as in most of the applications (see Fig. 3).

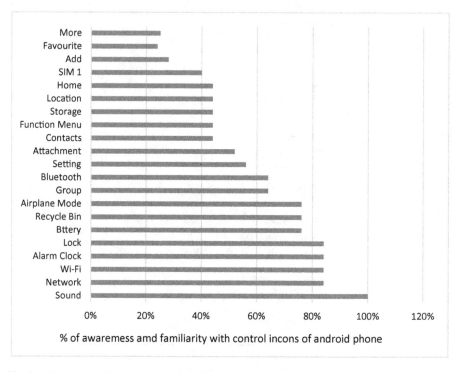

Fig. 3. Percentage of awareness and familiarity with commonly used control icons of android phone by the senior citizens.

The study shows awareness and familiarity of control icons by the senior citizens with 100% sound, 84% network, 84% Wi-Fi, 84% alarm clock, 84% lock, 76% battery, 76% recycle bin, 76% airplane mode, 64% group, 64% Bluetooth, 56% setting, 52% attachment, 44% contacts, 44% function menu, 44% storage, 44% location, 44% home, 44% SIM1, 28% add, 25% more and 24% favorite. The result tells that significant number of senior citizens are acquainted with the control icons mobile as well as various applications. This is very clear coming out when we look at the result of mobile usage and commonly used mobile apps in the Sect. 4.2. Moreover, it correlates with the kind of activities they perform to support their daily life.

4.4 Awareness and Familiarity with Commonly Used Control Icons of Microsoft Office Applications

Microsoft Office icons are essential communicative elements that clearly identify the action the user is taking when they use as a command. To investigate how well the senior citizens clearly identify meaning and function, we have selected commonly used Microsoft Office icons for the study (see Fig. 4). The result shows that 64% undo, 64% redo, 56% spell check, 52% search, 40% save and 40% new file control icons aware and familiar with selected control icons. The study indicates that the senior citizens have knowledge of working and managing Microsoft Office documents.

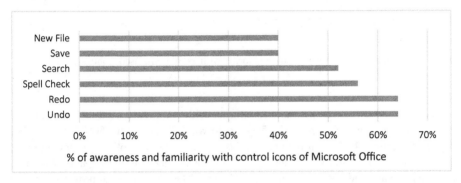

Fig. 4. Percentage of awareness and familiarity with commonly used control icons of Microsoft Office applications by the senior citizens.

All the senior citizens studied in this research study are retired persons and it proves that they were using Microsoft Office applications before retirement. They were all exposed to computing technologies in one way or another and this has brought confidence in them to use various applications in android phone.

4.5 Awareness and Familiarity with Commonly Used Control Icons of Web Browsers

The web browser control has several functions found among common web browsers to access and view websites. The internet and our lives have changed over the past few decades due to proliferating and multifaceted web information connecting every user worldwide regardless of time and space. Internet browsers are the gateway to access and we information and in this context it is essential to investigate awareness and familiarity with control icons of internet browser. We have selected commonly used control icons from Microsoft Internet Explorer, Mozilla Firefox and Google Chrome for the research study (see Fig. 5).

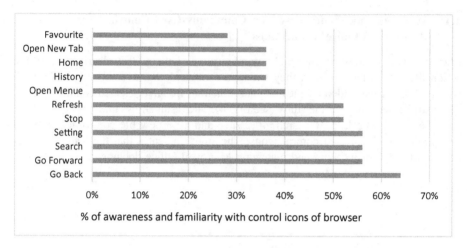

Fig. 5. Percentage of awareness and familiarity with commonly used control icons of web browsers.

The graph shows awareness and familiarity with commonly used control icons of internet browsers are 64% go back, 56% go forward, 56% search, 56% setting, 52% stop, 52% refresh, 40% open menu, 36% history, 36% home, 36% open new tab and 28% favourite. The study indicates a significant number of participants who use computer and android phone are familiar and aware of control icons of browsers. It also correlates with the activities of social networking and email applications. The participants said that the internet has created an opportunity to interact with family, friends and gain new knowledge from their home.

4.6   Awareness and Familiarity with Commonly Used Control Buttons of Digital Camera

Digital camera has become part of everyday life and its usage from taking selfies to family photos to documenting everyday life. Also it has lots of other uses than just holiday snaps and has become most used device of this age. The value of digital camera has increased manifold after the inception of internet. People share their lives openly n social media platform. In this context, we have selected the commonly used digital camera buttons to understand their awareness and familiarity (see Fig. 6).

The study shows that the participants are aware and familiar 60% delete, 56% play, 56% zoom in, 56% zoom out, 52% flash, 40% video, 40% setting, 40% voice recording, 40% landscape, 40% auto, 28% power, 24% sports, 25% night portrait, 25% close up and 16% portrait buttons. This indicates that the senior citizens are exposed to digital camera and they are active in using the camera in different modes of setting to fulfill their needs.

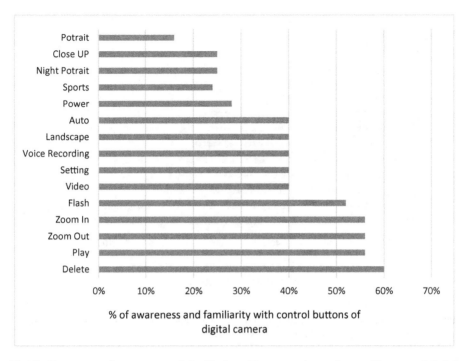

Fig. 6. Percentage of awareness and familiarity with commonly used control buttons of digital camera by the senior citizens.

4.7 Awareness and Familiarity with Commonly Used Control Buttons of Entertainment System

Today, the electronic industry is providing numerous products and services to the consumer. For senior citizens, it is big challenge to engage themselves during the day. Spending time with entertainment system like television and home theater music systems are very prominent today. To investigate the awareness and familiarity we have selected commonly used control buttons of entertainment system remote control (see Fig. 7).

The study shows that the senior citizens are aware and familiar with 100% volume, 100% channel, 88% mute, 76% play, 72% rewind, 68% power, 64% pause, 64% fast forward, 44% favourite, 44% return, 36% stop, 32% source and 32% open/close control buttons of entertainment system remote control.

This study indicates that the senior citizens are very much engaged with television during the day because television and music system make them cognitively engaged and assure companionship to them. The television provides not only entertainment programs but also knowledge, technology, science, sports, well-being etc. The television has become another family member with whom they can interact socially at any point of time.

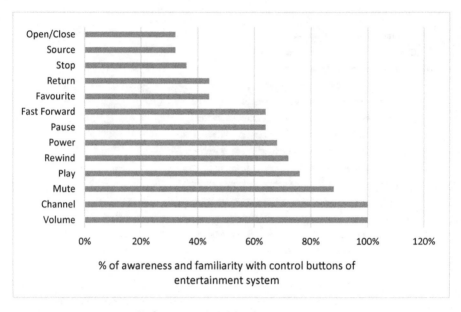

Fig. 7. Percentage of awareness and familiarity with commonly used control buttons of entertainment system remote control by the senior citizens.

5 Conclusion

Population ageing and growing number of elderly population is significant over decades. Smart technologies and services are proliferating. However the rate of adaption is very low due to various socioeconomic, physical and psychological factors. There is an increasing risk of excluding senior citizens with particular access needs. As the society is moving towards digital, the senior citizens do not want to exclude themselves rather they want to keep up with the current technological trend. They accept that they have to progress and learn to use technology and this becomes need of the hour. Smart technologies show great benefits among senior citizens and for successful acceptance their needs, perception, concerns, awareness and usage must be carefully evaluated. A survey was conducted with structured questionnaires followed by a semi-structured interview in Bengaluru city with a selected sample size of 25 senior citizens using smart phone technology.

All the participants said that technology is good and they are open to new technology. The reason given by elderly people for saying technology is good are "it improves life if used properly, helpful for day-to-day activities, to be part of change, when judiciously used, very good, younger use bad things, all the technology has brought us easy accessibility, learn lot of things, always good - should not have choice, enhance better quality of life, it helps so many new things every day, the world is going fast with technology and we can learn everything, improves your knowledge and takes you to the current technology, all feature is one service, to update present trend, good for new generation, it makes life easier and simpler, common man benefited by technology, it simplifies everything, it speeds up the process and when used properly".

Senior citizens frequently use 100% android phone on a daily basis and the applications like google search and You Tube are also significantly used. This shows that they are able to perceive additional values other than the traditional communication. Senior citizens perceive the benefits of technology use and are actively engaged in terms of services it offers to them. The percentage of android phone usage illustrates that how categorically senior citizens engaged larger part of social network and in one device they are able to fulfill many of their needs. The percentage of awareness and familiarity with control icons of mobile, Microsoft Office, Internet browser, digital camera and entertainment systems are giving insight that the senior citizens are able to perform tasks in day-to-day life and fulfill their need. Although their fluency may differ from individual to individual.

Our analysis demonstrated that income, education level and social support appear to affect technology usage, perception and adoption. In general, we found that senior citizens use variety of modern technologies and technology-enabled services. We also noticed that the higher education levels directly related to overall perception, attitude and usage of technologies. The presence of family and friends also increases broader usage of modern technologies because of their assistance in teaching and learning. Senior citizens perceive the additional usefulness of modern technologies and they are not scared to use modern technologies.

The factors affect their usage and perception are user friendliness and accessibility issues. The factors enhance their usage are technology supported activities, suitability and contained useful applications. Understanding current usage and perception of modern technology in Indian context is complex but it is very essential to understand their concerns. The contemporary senior citizens are looking for value added services that can make their everyday life and tasks easier and provide added security.

Acknowledgement. The authors are grateful to the Department of Computer Application, Madurai Kamaraj University and National Institute of Design for providing an opportunity and guidance. We express our sincere thanks to all the senior citizens who participated in the research for their patience, cooperation and support.

References

Cerella, J.: Information processing rates in the elderly, Psychol. Bull. **98**(1), 67–83 (1985)

Venkatesh, V., Morris, M.G., Davis, G.B., Davis, F.D.: User acceptance of information technology: toward a unified view. MIS Q. **27**(3), 425–478 (2003)

Milne, S., Dickinson, A., Carmichael, A., Sloan, D., Eisma, R., Gregor, P.: Are guidelines enough? An introduction to designing web sites accessible to older people. IBM Syst. J. **44**(3), 557–571 (2005)

Page, T.: Touchscreen mobile devices and older adults: a usability study. Int. J. Hum. Factors Ergon. **3**(1), 65–85 (2014)

Chadda, R.K., Deb, K.S.: Indian family systems, collectivistic society and psychotherapy. Indian J. Psychother. **55**(6), 299–309 (2013)

Pavel, M., Jimison, H., Hayes, T., Kaye, J.: Technology in support of successful aging. Bridge–Linking Eng. Soc. **39**(1), 5–12 (2009)

Mitzner, T.L., Boron, J.B., Fausset, C.B., Adams, A.E., Charness, N., Czaja, S.J., Dijkstra, K., Fisk, A.D., Rogers, W.A., Sharit, J.: Older adults talk technology: technology usage and attitudes. Comput. Hum. Behav. **26**(6), 1710–1721 (2010)

Fleck, R.: Rating reflection on experience: a case study of teachers and tutors reflection around images. Interact. Comput. **24**(6), 439–498 (2012)

Elsevier, B.V.: Moving towards inclusive design guidelines for socially and ethically aware HCI. Interact. Comput. **17**(5), 485–505 (2005)

Demiris, G., Rantz, M.J., Aud, M.A., Marek, K.D., Tyrer, H.W., Skubic, M., Hussam, A.A.: Older adults' attitudes towards and perceptions of 'smart home' technologies: a pilot study. Med. Inform. Internet Med. **29**(2), 87–94 (2009)

Stray, C., Peschl, M.F.: Representation still matters: cognitive science and user interface design. Behav. Inform. Technol. **17**(6), 338–360 (1998)

Peek, S.T.M., Wouters, E.J.M., van Hoof, J., Luijkx, K.G., Boeije, H.R., Vrijhoef, H.J.M.: Factors influencing acceptance of technology for aging in place: a systematic review. Int. J. Med. Inform. **83**, 235–248 (2014)

Birren, J.E., Fisher, L.M.: Aging and speed of behaviour: possible consequences for psychological functioning. Annu. Rev. Psychol. **46**, 329–353 (1995)

Czaja, S.J.: The impact of aging on access to technology. Accessibility Comput. **83**, 7–11 (2005)

Plazaa, I., Martína, L., Martinb, S., Medranoa, C.: Mobile applications in an aging society: status and trends. J. Syst. Softw. **84**, 1977–1988 (2011)

Birren, J.E., Morrison, D.F.: Analysis of the WAIS subtests in relation to age and educational. J. Gerontol. **16**, 363–368 (1961)

Barnarda, Y., Bradleyb, M.D., Hodgsona, F., Lloydc, A.D.: Learning to use new technologies by older adults: perceived difficulties, experimentation band usability. Comput. Hum. Behav. **29**, 1715–1724 (2013)

Baltes, P.B., Lindenberger, U.: Emergence of a powerful connection between sensory and cognitive functions across the adult life span: a new window to the study of cognitive ageing. Psychol. Ageing **12**, 12–21 (1997)

Arab, F., Malik, Y., Abdulrazak, B.: Evaluation of phon age: an adapted smartphone interface for elderly people. Interact **2013**, 547–554 (2013)

Hofer, S.M., Alwin, D.F.: Handbook of Cognitive Aging: Interdisciplinary Perspectives. Sage Publications, California (2008)

Subaiya, L., Dhananjay, W.: Demographics of Population Ageing in India. Institute for Social and Economic Change, Bangalore, United Nations Population Fund, New Delhi, Institute of Economic Growth, Delhi (2011)

O'Brien, M.A., Olson, K.E., Charness, N., Czaja, S.J., Fisk, A.D., Rogers, W.A., Sharit, J.: Understanding technology usage in older adults. In: Proceedings of the 6th International Society for Gerontechnology, Italy (2008)

Culén, A.L., Bratteteig, T.: Touch-screens and elderly users: a perfect match? In: ACHI 2013 The Sixth International Conference on Advances in Computer-Human Interactions, France (2013)

Chernbumroong, S., Atkins, A.S., Yu, H.: Perception of smart home technologies to assist elderly people. In: The 4th International Conference on Software, Knowledge, Information Management and Applications (SKIMA 2010), Bhutan (2010)

Borah, H., Shukla, P., Jain, K., Kumar, S.P., Prakash, S., Gajrana, K.R.: Elderly in India. Ministry of Statistics & Programme Implementation, Government of India, New Delhi (2011)

Department of Economic and Social Affairs, World Population Prospects. United Nations, New York (2015a)

Department of Economic and Social Affairs, World Population Ageing. United Nations, New York (2015b)

Bangalore Metropolitan Region Authority, Bangalore Metropolitan Region Revised Structure Plan-2031, Bengaluru (2017)

UN World Population Prospects 2017. https://esa.un.org/unpd/wpp/Graphs/Demographic Profiles. Accessed 15 Jan 2018

Infogram. https://infogram.com/percentage-distribution-of-population-by-broad-age-groups-1g0 gmjw34yj8p1q. Accessed 30 Jan 2018

Population Reference Bureau. http://www.prb.org/Publications/Reports/2012/india-older-popula tion.aspx. Accessed 30 Jan 2018

Population Census 2011. https://www.census2011.co.in. Accessed 30 Jan 2018

A Study on the Behavior of Using Intelligent Television Among the Elderly in New Urban Areas

Cuiping Wu and Xiaoping Hu[(✉)]

School of Design, SCUT, Guangzhou, China
Cuiping.Wu@springernature.com, hxp523@163.com

Abstract. Objective: This paper centers on the behavior of using intelligent television among the elderly in new urban areas. The purposes of this study are: 1, finding if there is potential tendency of them to use intelligent television. 2, if there are significant differences in the aspect of physiological and psychological characteristics among the elderly who live in new urban areas, in small cities and in big cities. 3, finding out existing problems and their real needs and their wishes when using intelligent televisions. 4, providing meaningful references and theoretical foundations for entrepreneurs, markets and relevant departments in this field.

Background: Nowadays, the world is at a stage of rapid development, on the one hand, more and more people from the countryside flocking into the city, at the same time, many rural areas are developing themselves, which results in the accelerating process of urbanization and rapid rise of new cities. On the other hand, the aging of population situation becoming increasingly severe, older people experiencing problems with seeing or hearing (which afflict at least 20% of people over 65) find television easier to deal with, since it provides both verbal and visual information together [1]. Thus watching TV is the first choice for the elderly on home entertainment. However, more and more old people haven't prepared fully both physically and mentally to adapt to this kinds of changes, which leads to a series of social phenomena about how new urban senior citizens fit into the society. For example, masses of high-tech equipment and intelligent products have been brought about by the rapid development of information and intelligence, it tends to lead to confusion and frustration to the elderly in the course of using them. When it comes to old people who living in new urban areas, it is difficult for them to use a such thing. And it cannot be defined as a good intelligent product to meet their own entertainment needs and spiritual and cultural needs.

Methods: In this study, through the application 5W2H design method (who-the elderly; what-behavior of using intelligent television; when-when they use intelligent television; where-their own house; why-current products and relevant services are not good enough to satisfy their needs; how-analyze and figure out their true needs and propose practical suggestions; how much-make sure they can use intelligent televisions easily and enhance their sense of happiness), questionnaire survey (150 questionnaires were distributed equally in three groups) and in-depth research (5 senior representatives were observed and asked thoroughly in the process of using intelligent television). The study was conducted from May 2017 to January 2018 in 3 cities (Guangzhou, Wuhu, Maanshan) in China.

© Springer International Publishing AG, part of Springer Nature 2018
J. Zhou and G. Salvendy (Eds.): ITAP 2018, LNCS 10926, pp. 194–205, 2018.
https://doi.org/10.1007/978-3-319-92034-4_15

Results: The combining researches roughly demonstrated that there are several problems for most of the respondents in using intelligent television: 1, many treat intelligent television as normal television and refuse to learn how to maximize the usability of smart devices. 2, there are some differences among the elderly in new urban areas, in small cities and in big cities, but there are major differences between individuals. 3, the existing problems lies in: (a) hard to find which button on the remote control determines which function on the television screen along with too many buttons, messy function layout, unreasonable operation system, etc., (b) high error rate when using intelligent television; (c) lower subjective satisfaction during the due entertainment activity. 4, a large proportion of current standards for intelligent television are not very suitable for them in terms of: (a) too many buttons in one remote control, and sometimes there are even more than one remote control. (b) too many information on the screen. (c) lack of teaching video about how to use intelligent television.

Contribution: The value of this study lies in: 1, building a basic framework of '3E'Model (Easy and Efficient for the Elderly). 2, providing some references for the improvement of designing intelligent televisions and related devices. 3, enhancing the old people's quality of recreational life and sense of fulfillment by reducing anxiety and better understanding during using intelligent televisions. 4, proposing the concept of intelligent television in the future. The prospect of personalized information services and interfaces, which can intelligently adapt to our changing circumstances and contexts, has the potential to dramatically change the way that we interact with a wide range of online services [2].

Keywords: The elderly · New urban areas · Intelligent television Usability · '3E'Model

1 Background

1.1 Social Background: Ageing and Urbanization

1.1.1 Ageing

According to statistics, when the global population reached 7 billion in 2012,562 million (or 8.0%) were aged 65 and over. In 2015, 3 years later, the older population rose by 55 million and the proportion of the older population reached 8.5% of the total population [3]. Ageing is a global challenge we face together. Asia stands out as the population giant. Take China as an example, the population aged 60 and above reached 222 million in 2015, accounting for 16.15% of the total population. By 2020, the elderly population is expected to reach 248 million, with an aging population of 17.17% [4]. These findings indicate the importance of developing the pension industry and designing relevant products and services.

1.1.2 Urbanization

China's urbanization is fast, from 1979 to 1992, the urbanization rate increased from 18.96% to 27.46%. From 1993 to 1992, the figure increased from 27.9% to 39.09%. In 2015, the total population of China (mainland) is 1374.62 million. Among them, the permanent urban resident population is 771.6 million (or 56.10%) [5]. In all types of cities, it can be roughly divided into three categories: big cities, small cities and new urban areas. The birth of new urban areas dates back to The Garden City Theory (Howard, 1898) and The Satellite City Theory (Ewen, 1922), is the result of the expansion of big cities, refers to those small new cities that has just developed along with relatively complete public infrastructure along with modern lifestyle. However, the speed and quality of urbanization in China is lack of coordination. The speed of urbanization lags behind the demand of rural residents to integrate into modern urban civilization [6]. As more and more people become residents of new urban areas, among which old people become a big part of it. And in this case, it is a huge challenge for modern industry and social development.

1.2   Seniors and Intelligent Products

1.2.1   Physiological Features of Seniors

The elderly were slow in movement and learning, and their operating ability and reaction speed were reduced, combined with impaired memory and loss of cognitive function, their self-care ability of daily living gradual declines. Dimming eyesight and failing hearing can reduce physical, functional, emotional, and social well-being. Visual and hearing impairments decrease independence in performing the activities of daily living, getting from place to place, or communicating with others [7]. Besides, memory loss plays an important part in the process of ageing. Luckily, the memory decline of the elderly is not a total recession, but a partial decline, mainly in the long term memory, mechanical memory and reappearance of memory decline faster. What's more, some old people have poor coordination in motor coordination, which has made it difficult for them to operate sophisticated products. Therefore, in the product design for the elderly, the function partition should be obvious, and the size of the button should be larger, so as to reduce the probability of misoperation.

1.2.2   Psychological Features of Seniors

Loneliness and dependence are the two main characteristics of senior citizens. Loneliness means that the elderly cannot consciously adapt to the surrounding environment, lacking or unable to carry out meaningful thoughts and emotional exchanges. Loneliness can be easily turned to depression and anxiety. Dependence refers to the elderly's lack of confidence, passive obedience, emotional vulnerability, hesitancy, shrinking, etc., they tend to rely on others to do everything, including making their own decisions. Long-term dependence on the mind can lead to emotional instability and sensory degeneration. Luckily, research found that emotional support between the elderly and their children is an important factor in the mental health study of the elderly, which is more likely to inhibit the growth of depression in the elderly than economic support and household chores [8].

1.2.3   The Penetration of Intelligent Televisions

With the development of information and technology, lots of intellectualized and interactive products continue to emerge. However, people who used to live in countryside cannot fit the modern products very well in a short time, especially among old people. This is embodied in their daily life, such as usage of intelligent products, experience of modern services and so on. A significant number of senior citizens worldwide watch televisions for daily entertainment. There are around 423 million TV users in China, among which, the penetration rate of intelligent TV users is close to 60%, mainly distributed in the urban areas and towns covered by network [9]. Old people are loyal users of watching television, however, older people who live in new urban areas are more or less trapped in the use of intelligent television. Most of the intelligent televisions on the market do not meet the ergonomic requirements, especially for the most target group–the elderly. The buttons are numerous and the interface layers are nested. It is difficult for ordinary people to use them, not to mention old people. Thus this subject is worthy to be studied carefully.

2 Methods

2.1 Aim

In this project, based on the combination of '5W2H analysis' and 'participatory design', in the form of 'questionnaire survey' and 'in-depth survey', developed a rough '3E'(Easy and Efficient for the Elderly) Model for the elderly (≥ 60 years) in new urban areas, in order to help them (better) interact with intelligent television. The model was also designed to support television business and manufacturing in preparing their products with elderly patients. An overarching aim of the project was to develop '3E' model in a participatory way to increase usability and satisfaction. This paper describes the basic framework and usage process of this model, how to apply this method into the product designing and interface optimizing and the lessons learned during this process.

To be specific, the application '5W2H analysis' involve 7 aspects (who-the elderly who live in new urban areas, in small cities and in big cities; what-behavior of using intelligent television, such as the use habit of remote control and understanding of the various functions of TV screens; when-when they use intelligent television; where-their own house; why-current products and relevant services are not good enough to satisfy their needs; how-analyze and figure out their true needs and propose practical suggestions; how much-make sure they can use intelligent televisions easily and enhance their sense of happiness), '5W2H analysis' was invented by the U.S. Army Ordnance Repair Division in World War II, it is simple and convenient to use, easy to understand, and full of rich enlightenment, now been widely used in enterprise management, technical activities and decision-making. In this study, it was used not only to complete investigation and analysis, but to make up for the consideration of design activities. Secondly, the concept of 'participatory design' originated in the Nordic countries in the 1960s. Nowadays, it refers to, at the different stages of the innovation process, all interested parties are invited to work with designers, researchers, developers, to define problems, products, solutions, and the positioning of the assessment [10]. In this study, 5 specific interviewees from three different cities were asked to be observed and interviewed thoroughly in the process of using intelligent television. In addition to the accurate, in-depth investigation, extensive questionnaire survey also provided data support for the establishment of the model.

2.2   Participants and Requirement

In this project, 150 questionnaires were distributed equally in three groups, old people (≥ 60 years) who live in new urban areas (e.g. partial areas in Maanshan), in small cities (e.g. Wuhu) and in big cities (e.g. Guangzhou). 5 specific interviewees were from 3 different areas, 3 in Maanshan, 1 in Wuhu and 1in Guangzhou. Maanshan is a typical case of urbanization development, many places have experienced a shift from rural to urban areas. In these new urban areas, many older people just have intelligent television in their homes. Wuhu, as a third-tier city with less population, is a small city for investigate. The penetration rate of smart TV is general. While Guangzhou, is a typical big city, its intelligent television penetration rate ranked first with 97.3% [11]. These 5 specific interviewees in three different cities were deeply analyzed in the aspect of usage behavior characteristics and specific needs.

3   Case Study

3.1   Basic Questionnaire Survey Description

150 questionnaires were distributed equally in three groups, the recovered valid questionnaire was 117 copies, effectiveness is 78.00%. The results of behavior of personal information and watching TV are shown in the Tables 1 and 2 below.

Table 1. Personal information among the three groups.

All (117)	Percent of living with spouses	Percent of living with children	Mental health degree (five-point scale)	Physical health degree (five-point scale)
Guangzhou (42)	69.05%	34.88%	4.55	3.79
Wuhu (37)	78.38%	62.16%	4.57	3.97
Maanshan (38)	81.58%	57.89%	4.53	3.92
Average	76.07%	51.28%	4.55	3.89

Table 2. Behavior of personal information and watching TV among the three groups.

All (117)	Percent of willingness to use intelligent TV	Average number of intelligent TVs	Average time on TV viewing	Percent of using intelligent function	Percent of using other smart devices (e.g. smart phone)
Guangzhou (42)	92.86%	2.72	1.67	92.86%	97.62%
Wuhu (37)	91.89%	2.14	3.16	86.49%	78.38%
Maanshan (38)	94.74%	2.16	3.84	73.68%	63.16%
Average	93.16%	2.38	2.85	84.62%	80.34%

The result shows that: (1) There are little differences among the elderly in new urban areas, in small cities and in big cities both physically and mentally. (2) There is an obvious tendency of the elderly to use intelligent televisions. (3) There is no obvious regional difference among all the groups, they are all willing to use intelligent TV. (4) A positive correlation exists between using smart devices like smart phone and using of intelligent function of TV. (5) Watching TV longer does not increase the frequency of using intelligent functions of TV.

If the questionnaire was used independently to test the user satisfaction, the results may not be comprehensive enough, and there may be large or small errors. Thus five examples are selected for deeper investigation, in this part, '5W2H analysis' was introduced to the comprehensive description of the whole process of watching intelligent television (Table 3).

Table 3. Basic personal information about 5 specific interviewees.

Interviewee	Area	Age	Number of intelligent TVs	TV viewing average time	Whether or not to use intelligent function
A	Guangzhou	61	3	0–1	Yes
B	Wuhu	60	1	2.5	Yes
C	Maanshan	65	2	4–5	Yes
D	Maanshan	62	1	3	Yes
E	Maanshan	73	1	3–4	No

3.2 Existing Problem Analysis

As the most important home entertainment equipment of the past, television's position is being threatened by the Internet gradually. But as an important part of domestic life, television will not disappear, at least not soon. In this field, there are some phenomena worth exploring.

Despite the rapid development of intelligent television, due to the lack of unified intelligent television standards and different TV interfaces [12], it is hard to get old people to learn and use them well. If a unified and universal operation system was adopted, the learning time and difficulty of intelligent television will be reduced.

In the use of intelligent television, there is one particular phenomenon need to pay attention to. In China, many families are lived in the type of young people and old people, young people accept the new knowledge and learn new things quickly. Almost everyone is equipped with a mobile phone, some even have two or three mobile phones. It's easy for them to use intelligent television, however, they tend to watch TV shows on mobile phones or on the Internet, so they seldom watch TV. On the other hand, some old people tend to have strong desires to use intelligent television, but due to their own and external factors, TVs intelligence function are not being used properly and thoroughly.

By digging deeper, it is not difficult to find television users have been used to their own habits for years. It takes time to adapt to the transition from ordinary TV to intelligent TV. The use of intelligent TV can be very tricky than ordinary TV sets. For example, there are several key issues affecting the user experience such as shifting delay and playing buffer. These are caused by the defects of existing technical levels.

Table 4. The '5W2H analysis' about 5 specific interviewees.

Who	A	B	C	D	E
What (behavior)	Basically use smart features without obstacles. But seldom use. Prefer to use a computer	Basically use smart features without obstacles	Basically use smart features without obstacles. Own two TVs	Some obstacles exist. Watch TV series & films	Never use intelligence function
When (frequency and time)	Guests visit (once a week)	After supper (Fixed TV programs)	After work (Eat with one TV, then with another one until sleep)	Working clearance	After the afternoon's walk. (often watch health programs and news)
Where	Living room & two bedrooms	Bedroom	Living room & bedroom	Living room	Bedroom
Why (current usage status)	Work involves computers So tends to watch programs and news on computers	Just retired, keep the old fixed living habit	To busy work during the day to do other leisure activities	Just started using smart phone	Keep the old living habit, the intelligent TV was bought by his daughter
How (current use problems)	Less customized Unneeded functions	Too many buttons Has to use both remote controls	Too many buttons The interface is too complicated	Too many buttons The interface is too complicated	Too many buttons that never been used. Hard to remember
How much (desired effect)	More customized Find favorite options quickly	Easier and faster to operate	Two TV programs can be synchronized	Intelligent functional partitions can be easier to understand and operate	Unneeded functionality can be removed

However, we can reduce the user's dissatisfaction by other means. Borrow another example from a high-tech restaurant in Ginza, Japan, an animation of AR synthesis is played in the process of waiting. The anxiety of waiting has been greatly reduced, and it completely changed the traditional restaurant business model.

Back to the current situation of intelligent TV usage in China, an awkward situation can be concluded, that is, 'Young people don't watch intelligent TV, old people can't watch intelligent TV'. To find out what exactly hinder older people from using intelligent television, '5W2H analysis' was used to depict existing situations and problems (Table 4).

3.3 Design Points Analysis

Through the above investigation and research, the whole process of watching intelligent television is generally described. It helped to find out design problems existing in contemporary intelligent televisions and consumers' expectations of them. It can be demonstrated by the following design points list, so that the foundation for the later models can be laid (Table 5).

Table 5. Design problems and consumers' expectations of intelligent television.

Remote control	Television screen	User behavior	Other points
Buttons are too small Not easy to operate	The color is too loud	Need to learn how to use intelligent TV	Fewer repetitive ads. At least not dull
Too many buttons Many are extremely low in frequency	Less customized	Too many related accessories compared to ordinary TV	Insufficient memory. Many APP installed can cause jam
Unreasonable layout Can cause pressure	The logical process is chaotic	Some functions do not want	Rely on the network excessively
Words printed on it are easy to wear out and hard to recognize	Too many partitions. some functions cannot be found easily	Easy to generate electrostatic precipitation	Voice recognition is not accurate and effective
Uncomfortable to hold and use	Hurt eyes	Too many steps to find a program	Lack of unified standard

4   '3E'Model

4.1   Build Model

4.1.1   First Iteration

'3E', known as Easy and Efficient for the Elderly, is a model built to better study the behavior of using intelligent television among the elderly. It aims at not only providing practical advice on improving user's satisfaction but constructing a theoretical framework for iterative innovation design method. In the first place, the model was based on the social background of aging and intelligence, along with physiological features and psychological features of seniors, behavior of using intelligent television. Then select the appropriate model for reference on this project. A theoretical model of special product design for the elderly has great reference value in the development of '3E'Model. The model includes the 'Influencing affecting factors—design theory induction—inspection & evaluation' mode, which shows inducing process and key content of theory of special product design for the elderly [13]. In this article, more attention was paid to the actual users' experience and enterprises' production reference, so that it can carry out more succinctly and efficiently. First, the model was built in the form of 'Affecting factors—Design theories—Evaluation'.

The first part is background analysis, which has been divided into social background, industry background and user's personal background. They can provide strategic support and motivation for the development of products and industries.

The second part is theoretical part, as for the elderly product design and intelligent product design, a lot of design methods and principles can be found, and the design processes are varied. It is difficult to design a theory that can take all the details that need to be considered at the same time. But building a basic framework that has more flexible space to adapt the change of different situations is feasible.

The third and final part is the evaluation section, including design methods and design realization.

According to the research information from charts before, the first version of '3E'Model was been established (Fig. 1).

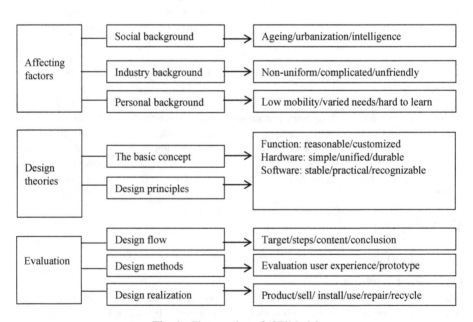

Fig. 1. First version of '3E'Model

The first version of '3E' Model basically expounds three aspects of product design for the elderly, but for this article, it needs to make appropriate adjustment, in the hope of giving more theoretical guidance meaning and providing more suggestions on practical usage and manufacture.

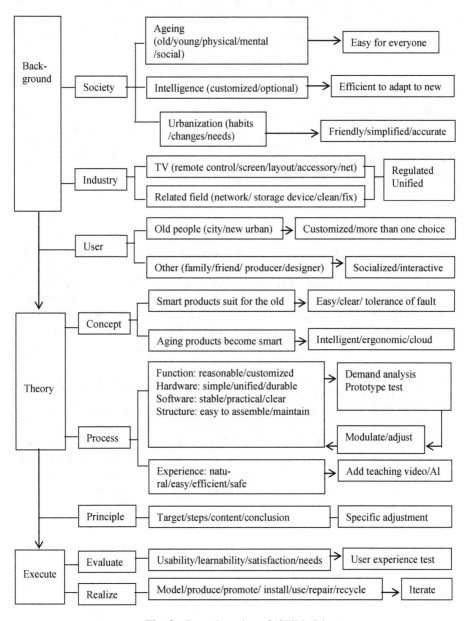

Fig. 2. Second version of '3E' Model

4.1.2   Second Iteration

After the collision of various design propositions and absorb the experts' opinions in this field. Combined with the target group's real needs, more specific details were raised. The idea to involve their users into this iterative designing process, can also provide a new perspective for design thinking among the elderly and saving the awkward situation of current behavior of using TV.

In addition, when it comes to the related design of intelligent product design, this model further refined the framework, and implanted the requirement points concluded of the previous paper, in order to form a more substantial and more effective framework (Fig. 2).

4.2   Discussion

The '3E'Model now includes the 'Background—Theory—Execute' mode, combining with the methods of participatory research, it is not just a matter of principle-making framework, it is more of a question-inspirational guidebook. Along with the actual demand points proposed in the case study part, a more objective and perfect description of the behavior of the elderly using intelligent television.

5   Conclusion

Based on social ground of ageing, intelligence and urbanization, this paper researched the behavior of using intelligent television among the elderly in new urban areas, in small cities and in big cities. Through the application 5W2H design method and in-depth research, combined with participatory design, a rough model –'3E Model' was built. It can help find out existing problems and users' real needs and their wishes when using intelligent televisions. Also, it aims at providing meaningful references and theoretical foundations for entrepreneurs, markets and relevant departments in this field.

However, the defect is still evident, more research need to be done. For example, differences among the elderly in new urban areas, in small cities and in big cities are easily can be seen through the chart, differences among the elderly who live alone, who live with their spouses and who live with their children should be analyzed too. While in the building process of '3E Model', more details and practical tests could be added.

From a perspective of business, this study provides an open framework to meet the requirements of product design and industry development. While from a perspective of academic, it built a theoretic foundation to tackle the challenge of intelligent product design among elderly users.

References

1. Studies Analyze Elderly Use of Television. http://www.medialit.org/reading-room/studies-analyze-elderly-use-television
2. Smyth, B., Cotter, P.: A personalized TV listings service for the digital TV age (2000)

3. US Census Bureau, An ageing world: 2015 (2016)
4. Analysis and investment strategy research report of China's pension industry (2016)
5. Bei, G.: Analysis on the influence of residential arrangement on mental health of rural elderly (2011)
6. Big data analysis of population urbanization in China (2017). www.askci.com
7. Peisan, W.: Discussion on the development urbanization speed in China (2011)
8. Rovner, B.W., Gaudli, M.: Depression and disability associated with impaired vision: the MoVIES Project. (1998)
9. Big data report of digital TV industry, ICIBD (2017)
10. User experience entry-50. Participatory Design. https://zhuanlan.zhihu.com/p/25993931
11. Radio & TV Broadcast Engineering (2000)
12. Series specification on intelligent television, China electronic video industry association (2014)
13. Gangqiang Z., Teng, D., Yuwei, D.: Theoretical Model of Special Product Design for the Elderly (2016)

Aging and Interaction

Evaluation and Analysis of the Features and Applications of 3D Model Platforms

Chia-Ling Chang[(⊠)] and Siou-Wen Wang

Department of Education Industry and Digital Media,
National Taitung University, Taitung, Taiwan, ROC
idit007@gmail.com, taberu9@gmail.com

Abstract. As the 3D printer technology has been enhanced, 3D printers are more affordable and popularized. With the concepts of crowdsourcing, open source and sharing, 3D model platforms have become the highlight of the next wave of 3D printing industry. There are numerous articles on 3D printing technology, hardware and equipment, and materials. However, few articles deal with the topic of 3D model platforms for in-depth investigation. In this study, contents of those models that are available on 7 well-known 3D model platforms and their website functions are evaluated. The evaluation includes 4 primary dimensions which include website description, model file information, website function, and social interaction. These four dimensions are further classified into 22 items for the cross-verification of 3D model platforms. The application features of each 3D model platforms are identified. In addition, the three challenges for the future development of 3D model platforms are concluded as follows. (1) Insufficient format information of the file for download. (2) Unclear intellectual property (IP) licensing status of model files. (3) Security vulnerability of file information.

Keywords: 3D model platforms · 3D printing · Maker

1 Introduction

With the development of open source code, hardware, and community sharing, the maker movement sprang up everywhere. Product manufacturing can be realized not only in factories but also in houses or personal studios. The influence of digital software resources and smart machines on the manufacturing industry has created a new wave of social and technological revolutions [1]. The Internet allows makers to show their own design information and manufacturing knowledge to the world in an easier way. They are able to share design and manufacturing knowledge so that the original barrier between different societies or cultures has disappeared. During this wave of revolution, the most important thing is the creation of digital fabrication tools. These digital fabrication tools are more affordable and their popularization has changed the current working model of our society. Common digital fabrication tools include 3D printer, 3D scanners, laser cutters, digital milling machines, digital guillotines, numerical control (NC) machines, computerized numerical control (CNC) machines, and computer aided manufacturing (CAM) machines. Among them, the development in the 3D Printing technology is fastest and it has a wide range of applications.

© Springer International Publishing AG, part of Springer Nature 2018
J. Zhou and G. Salvendy (Eds.): ITAP 2018, LNCS 10926, pp. 209–222, 2018.
https://doi.org/10.1007/978-3-319-92034-4_16

The 3D printing technology originated from the patented 3DPTM process that was invented by the Massachusetts Institute of Technology. Various types of computer aided design (CAD) software can be used to build model files. By utilizing the additive manufacturing approach, a three-dimensional structure is created by the superposition of layers of materials. The inception of the 3D printing technology began in the 1980s. In recent years with the open source trend of the maker movement and some important patented technologies, the fast innovations in the 3D printing technology lead to an era with the embodiment of digital data.

In 2007, the first desktop 3D printer RepRap which adopted the open source code was born. This is an important milestone for the maker movement. After that, affordable 3D printer MakerBot sprang up and it allows makers to realize their creations in an unconstrained style. It means a lot to makers and the effects are just like the personal computer that appeared 30 years ago. It has changed the production and operation model of the manufacturing industry. Common people are able to assess the printing quality, speed, range of printable size, output stability, and price of each model that is available. By selecting a machine that meets personal requirements, everyone can realize his/her dream of fabricating any object freely by 3D printing [2]. The growth in the sales volume of consumer 3D printers below USD 5,000 is huge. The target customers include makers, enterprises, schools, laboratories, and personal studios. The upstream and downstream industries that are related to 3D printing have developed into a big market with a business scale of billions of US dollars around the world and the market keeps growing.

With the advance in technology, the equipment, materials, and software that are used on 3D printers have gradually become mature. The development in makerspace is also rising and flourishing. However, it can be found from the current situation that, most of the users are still confined by the capability of the modeling software when fabricating their creations. Even if they can build a model, they might still encounter problems with the analysis of slicer software, calculation of support material parameters, and the adjustment of printing details. For most of the users, this has become a common bottleneck for beginners who still lack of technical capability (Fig. 1). Moreover, the open source and sharing, crowdsourcing concepts encourage makers to share their own creations. As a result, in addition to the original business of hardware developments, some 3D printing hardware manufacturers also started to build their own database of 3D model files (hereinafter referred to as 3D model platform) in order to assist users in printing their 3D artworks. In addition, 3D modeling software companies and various government organizations also allocate resources in constructing 3D model platforms and related services. In the future, the biggest source of revenue for 3D printing business comes from the 3D model platform, instead of equipment or consumables [3].

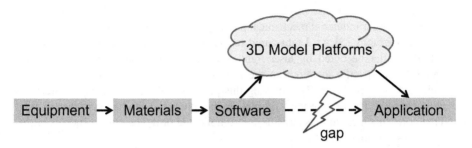

Fig. 1. Emerging 3D model platforms

2   Investigation of 3D Printing Technology

As compared to conventional manufacturing approaches, the advantages of 3D printing technology are as follows. (1) A higher degree of freedom for the structural design: The 3D printing technology can realize the direct printing of complicated structures without considering the problems of cutting or mole release. Therefore, a higher degree of freedom is allowed for designs that use 3D printing technology. (2) A lower cost for small-scale manufacturing: 3D printing technology can save the development cost of tooling/mold and reduce the problem of material wastes during small-scale manufacturing. (3) Rapid forming of custom products: When making a product by 3D printing, the configured precision and the sample size affect the required time for manufacturing. A product can be complete within several hours to a couple of days based on the current technology. The precision of the finished product that is obtained from the additive manufacturing approach is determined by the thickness of the layers for superposition. At the moment, the precision of 3D printed products is generally within the range of 100–200 um. The precision of some 3D printers can be below 10 um [4]. The investigation of 3D printing is generally carried out from four aspects which are respectively technology and equipment, material, software, and printing applications as follows.

2.1   Technology and Equipment

There are more than a dozen of 3D printing technologies depending on their forming techniques. The technologies have been improving and they cover a wide range from basic designs to the production of custom products with high difficulty. Five of the most common forming techniques are summarized as follows [4–7].

1. Fused deposition modeling (FDM): This is the most common technique. The working theory is to heat the raw material to its semi-molten state and squeeze the material to the printing base plate. The material restores to the solid state after it cools down. Repeat this deposition process so that the three-dimensional object will be formed. Since it is required to wait for each layer of material to cool down during printing, this approach could lead to minor misalignments during the deposition of the lower layer of material. Moreover, the raw material could deform a bit during the process of cooling down. However, the material cost of FDM is lower and the required time for producing larger

objects is shorter. The final product is sturdier and it is suitable for models with simple styles and larger industrial mechanical parts.

2. Stereolithography (SLA): Light-cured resins are used as the raw material which is solidified after be cured by laser light. During printing, the laser light irradiates precisely on specific locations in the raw material pool so that the raw material solidified layer by layer. By repeating this process, a three-dimensional object can be stacked up. The final product presents higher precision and better surface quality. Therefore, this technique is suitable for complicated or delicate parts such as crafts, necklaces, or hollow parts.

3. Selective Laser Melting (SLM/DMLS): This forming technique is similar to selective laser sintering (SLS). However, it required a higher laser power since the materials are mainly metal based. Virtually any metal material that can be prepared as small powders can be used as the raw material for the SLM technique.

4. Selective Laser Sintering (SLS): This technique is to utilize the energy from infrared laser beams to sinter metal powders including steel and titanium or thermoplastic macromolecular materials such as nylon or ceramic powders. On the processing platform, a computer is responsible for analysing the coordinate data including points, lines, and surfaces of the 3D model file layer by layer until a complete model file for sintering is acquired. The maintenance cost of such equipment and its consumables are relatively higher as compared to other techniques.

2.2   Printing Materials

Printing materials can be classified into three categories by their characteristics. These three categories include metal materials, non-metal and non-biomaterials, and biomaterials which can be further classified into several sub-categories for different types of printing technologies. Metal materials include various types of metal powders. Non-metal and non-biomaterials include thermoplastic materials such as ABS or PLA, light-cured resins, ceramic powders, gypsum powders, and wax. Common materials that are used by consumer 3D printers include ABS and PLA [8].

2.3   Software

Although the approach used by each 3D forming technique might be different from others, the first step is usually to build the 3D model by CAD software. The 3D model is then sliced in the slicer software so that each slice can depict the inner and outer profile of each section of the 3D model. After that, the profile of each of these slices needs to be converted into G-code parameters in order to configure the printing parameters for the 3D printer. G-code is a set of instructions that are used by numerical control (NC) machines. It can be viewed as the language for an operator to communicate with his/her NC machines. The NC control codes can be manually entered or automatically generated by computer software so that the cutting tools of a NC machine will move in a configured way [6]. The final step is to check the model file for any broken surface or insufficient support structure so that the model won't collapse during printing.

Modeling Software. As 3D printing is getting more popular, a diversity of modeling software packages has appeared. The modeling software can be classified into five categories which include basic stack-up, parts design, model animation design, sculpture modeling, and architecture modeling. According to our own experience and the discussions on 3D printing communities, the features of different 3D modeling software packages that are commonly used by makers, schools, and the industry are described as follows.

1. TinkerCAD: TinkerCAD is a free on-line 3D modeling software package that allows users to build models by drag and drop parts. It takes 2D files as the input and can generate 3D files accordingly. Therefore, it is very suitable for beginners. The TinkerCAD interface allows its users to freely adjust, save, and share on-line 3D files. It can also generate 3D files directly in the .STL format for 3D printing.
2. 123D Design: As compared to TinkerCAD, the 123D Design software is more advanced and intuitive. A beginner can easily start from scratch to build a model. A great amount of basic models are already stored in the software so that any user can edit the basic models and generate resulting 3D files in the .STL format.
3. SketchUp: It features a free and easy-to-use interface, which contains design tools and plug-ins for its user to create complicated 3D objects. This modeling system is composed of only lines and curves and this makes it suitable for architecture and engineering industry. However, this software doesn't allow the direct output in . STL format but an additional .STL output module is required to be installed.
4. FreeCAD: FreeCAD is a fully open source parametric engineering CAD software package. It is very suitable for the design of basic parts. Parametric modeling allows users to adjust parameters instead of meshes. The target users include engineers and product designers who need a professional way of modeling. This open source software runs on Windows, Mac, and Linux operating systems.
5. Rhinoceros (Rhino3D): This is a 3D modeling software based on non-uniform rational b-splines (NURBS). It has been very popular due to its functions and the diversity of its applications. It is easy to learn and it takes a wide variety of document formats. It is often used by industrial designers, architects, jewel designers, and artists to carry out rapid prototyping.
6. Solidworks: It is generally accepted as the mainstream 3D design software for commercial products and mechanical engineering. In addition to 3D modeling, SolidWorks also provides a variety of simulation, kinetics, design verification tools, and the reverse engineering capability. Solidworks is a powerful software package which is suitable for industrial components/parts design.
7. Cinema 4D: It is a general-purpose 3D modeling software package which is most used in designs, animations, and rendering applications. The highlight of this software is on 3D graphics and 3D model fabrication. The Maxon computation software includes several design options such as procedural/polygonal modeling, animations, lighting, textures, and rendering.

8. Autodesk 3D: It is mostly used in architectural, civilian, and mechanical engineering and has been a well-established CAD software for modeling since 1982. It is widely used in 2D drawings, architectural drawings, computer chipset designs, and basic 3D designs. It is one of the favourite drawing tools for designers and makers around the world. It features a 3DPRINT program that allows its users to directly send 3D models to 3D printing service providers.
9. Maya: It features an intuitive design interface that is suitable for creating characters, roles, and geographic scenes. It is one of the favorable 3D modeling tools among designers. The main applications include 3D animations and visual designs since it allows its user to change the proxy mesh based on the original mesh.
10. ZBrush: ZBrush is a new emerging modeling software package, which is suitable for creating different role types of characters. The appearance of ZBrush indicates a revolution of 3D modeling. This 3D printing software integrates 3D and 2.5D modeling with textures and painting. It allows a designer to create 3D models with amazing details such as different styles, textures, convex and concave features, and materials.

Slicer Software. In addition to a good printing tool, slicer software plays a very important role in 3D printing for a finished product with good printing quality. The configuration of parameters including the fill density, base, and support structure and a designer's own experience are the factors that are critical to the printing quality and the yield rate. A 3D model needs to be saved in the format of .STL or .OBJ files so that the model can be further sliced into layers by the slicer software. The instructions and parameters of the printing process are saved as G-code files so that a 3D printer can decode and carry out the printing process. There are more than a dozen open source slicer software packages available at the moment. Four of them are commonly used in the industry. They include three free software packages such as Cura, Kisslicer, and Slic3r and the paid version of Simplify3D. The features of these software packages are described as follows for the reference of a designer to choose the one that fits his/her requirements the best.

1. Cura: It is developed by Ultimaker and is one of the most commonly used software packages on open source 3D printers. It performs very fast at the slicer analysis and the printing and slicing functions can be used at the same time. Its main advantage is its interface which is very easy to learn. It is suitable for the beginners in the 3D printing territory. It also takes.jpg files as the input to print photos out.
2. Slic3r: It is the most popular slicer software for 3D printing on the market. Its main function is to carry out the slicer analysis of the .STL model files and convert the data into 3D printing instruction codes (G-Code). It is especially suitable for round objects with a shell such as a spiral vase.
3. Simply3D: It is gradually gaining popularity since it provides powerful functions for the slicer process. It features the most adjustable parameters and it has the highest yield rate and the best printing effect for delicate parts. It can be connected using a USB cable and it costs at only USD 150.

4. Kisslicer: This slicer software can print the most delicate surfaces. The surface of the finished part is the most delicate. However, the user interface is more complicated and it is more difficult to use for a beginner.

3   Evaluation and Analysis of the Features and Applications of 3D Model Platforms

3D model platforms form a critical part of the supply chain of the 3D printing industry. During the earlier stage of its development, it provided original equipment manufacturer (OEM) printing services such as making prototypes for customers. Nowadays, 3D model platforms provide a variety of diversified 3D model files for users to download. In addition, these platforms also allow professional users to upload their design works to the platform in order to facilitate the development of the 3D printing industry. There are more than ten 3D model platforms with a high level of user activities. The studies by vMaker (2015) [9] and Yusuf (2018) [10] proposed some good 3D model platforms. The platforms that are recommended by several makers based on their own experiences are also included in the investigation in this study. A total of seven 3D model platforms are analyzed and as follows.

1. Thingiverse: This platform is supported by the 3D printer manufacturer MakerBot. It is the largest platform in the world and has been operating for the longest time. It is the best introductory platform for beginners with a diversified collection of different types of model files. Its main collection includes household applications, action figures and toys, and engineering parts. Its interface is easy to use and it provides a search bar for a quick search in addition to the existing classifications. It also allows a user to preview the results. More than 1 million 3D models are collected in this platform and the total number of downloads exceeds 200,000,000. They often organize featured contests to encourage more people to exploit the potential of 3D printers.
2. MyMiniFactory: The total number of their files is less than the others. However, there are less duplicated objects and the yield rate and quality of model files are higher since their model files are always examined before being uploaded to the platform. The interface is available in six languages. Among all categories, the Scan the World category is the popular one since it features the 3D files of renowned artworks from various museums around the globe such as the Michelangelo's David at the British Museum and the Venus de Milo at the Louvre Museum.
3. Yobi3D: Yobi3D is a website that is developed by a Taiwanese design team. It features a search engine which operates in a way similar to Google for 3D model files. It collects more than 1 million 3D models. A quick search for models is available by keywords. Real-time previews are also available on-line so that a user can carry out the analysis of printing difficulty in order to determine the printer model that is suitable for a specific model file. Moreover, this platform also allows a user to configure the definition of his/her own printer in order to reduce the failure rate. The available model types include common action figures, engineering parts, home utilities, flowers and plants, and animals. It supports multiple languages.

4. Pinshape: This platform is supported by the Canadian 3D printer manufacturer Formlabs. The models that are collected on this platform are very delicate. It allows its users to determine whether to pay for a file that is downloaded. However, 90% of their files are free to download. It features the support of streaming by 3DPrinterOS. A user can edit, slice, and print any of their files on-line without downloading the file. It not only allows a designer to share his/her designs, but also can protect the original files. It also offers on-line custom services to designers at a price.

5. CGTrader: This platform is created by the 3D modeling vendor Marius Kalytis. The original target customers include 3D animations and the gaming market until it started to provide its users with the service of downloading 3D models recently. CGTrader features textures for most of its 3D models and therefore only 3D color printers can support this feature. It allows designers to upload their own files and profit from selling these files. A higher price tag is set for a model that is more delicate. The models can also be used for 3D animations. The platform also has a section specific for free files. By the end of June 2017, a total of 500,000 model files are collected and the total number of registered users reached 1 million.

6. Cults: This platform is the largest 3D model platform in France. It supplies 3D printing models of high quality for both free and paid downloads. A user needs to register a user account before he/she can download files. The 3D models that are collected on this platform are mostly provided by professional designers. A user is allowed to designate a designer to create designs for him/her. This platform has 40,000 model files which are provided by 8000 designers. A reminder on the website notifies its users not to sell the model files to other websites.

7. YouMagine: This platform is supported by 3D equipment vendor Ultimaker. The models that are collected on this platform are full of textures and many professional model files are already with colors. Therefore, the model files are more suitable for advanced users. YouMagine is different from others that it is devoted to protecting its 3D designers. In 2015, it announced 3DPL which permits the open source code that is specifically to 3D printing target users.

3.1   Descriptions of Dimensions for Analysis

The observation in this study indicated that the above-mentioned 3D model platforms offer a wide variety of model files even though they might just operate for a relatively short period. Each of these platforms has its own distinguishing features. The analysis in this study includes 4 primary dimensions which are respectively the website description, model file information, website function, and social interaction. The dimensions can be further classified into 22 items for analysis as shown in Table 1. These 22 items provide a helpful way to determine the application features of each 3D model platform.

Table 1. Dimensions for the analysis of 3D model platforms

Website description	Model information	Website function	Social interaction
Organization	Description of model file	Browsing function	Collection function
Date of issue	Model quality	Search function	Download counts
Country	Photo of finished part	Membership	User feedbacks
Model attributes	3D preview	Membership fee	Ways of sharing
APP support or not	Download format	Language	
	Descriptions of printer settings	Tag functions	
	Creative Commons		

According to the items in Table 1, a total of 10 makers who frequently use 3D model platforms are invited for the investigation. From the communities that are maker-relevant, the discussion threads on the above-mentioned 3D model platforms are available and can serve as a good reference for the analysis of these 3D model platforms. The results of the analysis are summarized in Table 2 as follows.

4 Discussions

Based on Table 2, the discussions on these 3D model platforms are as follows.

1. 3D model platforms emerged since the past decade and developed rapidly for the last five years. Most of the 3D platforms are built up and supported by hardware/equipment manufacturers. The intention is to twofold. First, the platforms can assist users in printing their 3D artworks. Second, 3D printer lovers are gathered on the platform so that enterprises are able to interact with their users. Among these platforms, Cults was built up with the assistance from the government. Various 3D equipment vendors and governmental agencies also allocated resources in 3D model platforms and services. It is clear that the biggest source of revenue no longer comes from the equipment or consumables but from the database of 3D model files [3]. These platforms also created a more direct and closer relationship with users.
2. Although there is a wide variety of models that are collected on these platforms, a majority of these files are action figures, household applications, and engineering parts, followed by ornamental accessories, animals and plants, and educational models. Cultural models or artworks are still of minority.
3. At the moment, only Thingiverse and MyMiniFactory provide their support to apps. A user can use their apps to browse through and search for models and interact with other users. However, none of the apps allows its users to download models (Table 3).

Table 2. Analysis of 3D model platforms (1/2)

website		Thingiverse	MyMiniFactory	Yobi3D	Pinshape	CGTrader	Cults	Youmagine
Website description	Organization	MakerBot	MyMiniFactory	n/a	Formlabs	CGTrader	Cults3D, France Post	Ultimaker
	year	2008	2013	2014	2013	2011	2013(FB)	
	Country	USA	Britain	Taiwan	USA, Canada	Lithuania	France	Netherlands
	Attributes	Household applications, Figurine and toy, Engineering parts, Accessories, 3D printer parts et. al.	Household applications, Figurine and toy, Engineering parts, Accessories, Museum collections Assistive products et. al.	Household applications, Figurine and toy, Engineering parts, Plant and animals et. al.	Household applications, Figurine and toy, Engineering parts, et. al.	Household applications, Figurine and toy, Engineering parts, Plant and animals Food medicine et. al.	Household applications, Figurine and toy, Engineering parts, Accessories, Plant and animals et. al.	Household applications, Figurine and toy, Engineering parts, Food et. al.
Model information	APP support		•					
	Description	•	•	•	•	•	•	•
	Quality	Good	Excellent	Good	Good	Good	Excellent	Good
	Photo of work	•	•	•	•	•	•	•
	3D preview	•	•					
	Download format	.stl,obj, .es .xml	.stl obj	.obj, .stl, .fbx, .max .3ds,.ma,.mb, blen, .3dm,.da, .dwg .dxf, .lwo, .ply, .skp	.stl,.ob, .zip	.obj,.stl, .fbx .max, .3ds, .skp	.stl	.stl
	Descriptions of settings	•	•		•	•		
	Creative Commons	(CC icons)	(CC icons)	Not marked	(CC icon)	Not marked	(CC icons)	(CC icons)

Table 3. Analysis of 3D model platforms (2/2)

website		Thingiverse	MyMiniFactory	Yobi3D	Pinshape	CGTrader	Cults	Youmagine
Website function	Browsing function	•	•	•	•	•	•	•
	Search function	•	•	•	•	•	•	•
	Membership	•	•	•	•	•	•	
	Membership fee				▲	▲	▲	
	Language	English	English, French Spanish, German, Chinese, Italian, et. al.	English, French Spanish German Chinese. et. al.	English	English	English, French, Spanish	English
	Tag functions	•	•		•	•	•	•
Social interaction	Collection function	•	•		•	•	•	•
	Download counts	•	•		•	•	•	•
	User feedbacks	•	•		•	▲	•	•
	Ways of sharing							

4. From the aspect of model file information, all of these platforms provide descriptions of their model files so that a user can understand what the model is, what it is for, and what does it feature. The models from MyMiniFactory and Cults have better printing quality. Most of these platforms provide photos of finished parts after being printing out. The Yobi3D platform doesn't provide such photos since it operates as a search engine with a collection of 3D model files. From the aspect of 3D preview, Thingiverse, MyMiniFactory, Yobi3D, Cults, and Youmagine allow their users to view a model in 360° by dragging the model with a mouse. For model downloads, the formats of .STL and .OBJ are the most common file types.

5. For printer settings, only Thingiverse, MyMiniFactory, and CGTrader provide their users with the information of printer settings. The information include the actual dimensions, available formats, suitable printing technology, time required for printing, number of surfaces, file size, and any plug-in used. From the aspect of copyrights, most of the platforms clearly marked the privilege of Creative Commons (CC) except for Yobi3D and CGTrader. Therefore, most of the users can understand the applicable range of a model file under the Creative Commons license.

6. For the functions that are available on their interfaces, common functions such as browsing and searching are available on these platform. Memberships are provided by these platforms although it is not required to register as a member in order to download files. The membership deals with the interactive functions such as storing a model file or sharing a model file with others.

7. These platforms offer free downloads of model files. Among them, Pinshape, CGTrader, and Cults allows their users to pay for upgraded versions of a model file of high quality. Except for Yobi3D as a search engine, all the other six platforms provide their users with a tag function so that an uploaded file is tagged with several keywords. This function makes users easier to find and classify a model file.

8. In addition to social interactions, these platforms also provide their users with the Collect function for all of their model files. After registering as a member, a user can collect their favorable model files. Except for Yobi3D, the other six platforms mark the download counts for each model file. It is easier for a user to know how popular a model file is. On the other hand, the platform administrator can plan further cooperation with potential designers with a higher level of popularity. From the aspect of user feedback, except for Yobi3D, the other five platforms including Thingiverse, MyMiniFactory, Pinshape, Cults, and Youmagine allow their users to give feedback to their model files. Users are also allowed to upload photos of the printed part of a model part so that other users have a better idea of how the model file looks like after being printed. However, CGTrader users can only provide their feedbacks in texts since it doesn't allow its users to upload photos as their feedbacks.

9. Providing different ways of sharing a model file means a lot to a designer to make his/her model file public. Each of these platforms provides 3–8 different ways of sharing a file including Facebook, Twitter, Pinterest, Google+, Tumblr, Reddit, Stumbleupon, Linkedin, and Email. It is a faster way for a user to share his/her model files to others and this function also greatly enhance the visibility of a model file.

5 Conclusions and Challenges

With the advance in 3D printer technology, 3D printers are more affordable and popularized. There have been numerous studies of 3D printing technology, hardware/equipment, and materials. With the trend of crowdsourcing, open source and sharing, it is obvious that one of the critical parts of the future 3D industry lies in the 3D model platforms. However, few studies have carried out extensive investigation and comparison of 3D model platforms. In this study, seven 3D model platforms that are commonly used by maker communities are reviewed and analyzed from four dimensions which include website description, model file information, website function, and social interaction. It is known from the analysis that, Thingiverse and MyMiniFactory are the top two 3D model platforms that perform better on these four dimensions. A 3D modeling beginner is advised to use Thingiverse as the first step of his/her exploration. For advanced users or other users within special territories such as arts or assistive devices, MyMiniFactory should be able to meet their requirements. A designer can build his/her own brand by uploading models. After that, he/she can charge his/her customers for custom services such as 3D design, modeling, and printing. In general, the above-mentioned 3D model platforms have provided sufficient functions. However, they still need to overcome the challenges ahead as follows.

1. Insufficient format information of the file for download: Most of the current 3D model platforms provide files in .STL format for download. This file format is simple and it is easy for output so that it can be applied to virtually all 3D printers. However, the .STL format handles only the profile of a model without any information of color, material, or texture. Therefore, the printed parts have no color, texture, or detailed features. In an effort to enhance the printing technology, the American Society for Testing and Materials (ASTM) has been promoting new file formats including AMF and 3MF as the future download formats in an attempt to resolve the printed parts' problems of color, material, and texture.

2. Unclear intellectual property (IP) licensing status of model files: Most of the model files that are available on these 3D model platforms are licensed under the Creative Commons. This approach can acknowledge users of the file's licensing status when they download a model file for use. However, these platforms lack a mechanism of examining whether a model file that is uploaded by one user might infringe the other's copyright. In the future, 3D model platforms need to stipulate their regulation on examining any copyright infringement issue of the model files being uploaded.

3. Security vulnerability of file information: All of the platform administrators are encouraging their users to upload model files. However, they do not monitor or control the quality of the files being uploaded. They cannot guarantee the security of a model file which might contain a virus. This poses a potential risk to the platform itself and the security of user information. Therefore, these platforms are advised to implement risk management on their model files. In order to guarantee information security, a file is required to pass the secure authentication mechanism before it can be uploaded to the platform.

Acknowledgements. This study received partly financial support from the Ministry of Science and Technology, under Grant No. MOST 106-2221-E-143-004.

References

1. Lipson, H., Kurman, M.: Fabricated: The New World of 3D Printing. Wiley, New Jersey (2013)
2. Tanaka, H.: FabLife–デジタルファブリケーションから生まれる「つくりかたの未来. O'Reilly Japan, Inc., Tokyo (2012)
3. Ting, Y.S.: Self-made era: 3D printing faces security issues, Makerpro.cc. https://makerpro.cc/2014/11/3d-printing-has-to-face-safety-issue/. Accessed 16 Nov 2017
4. Wong, K.V., Hernandez, A.: A review of additive manufacturing. ISRN Mech. Eng. **2012**, 1–10 (2012)
5. Chang, J.L.: 3D Printer and Makers Business Model. Tunghai University, TaiChung (2014)
6. Lin, D.S.: 3D printing development. Sci. Develop. **503**, 32–37 (2014)
7. OpenTech Co. Ltd., 3D Printer - Beginner's Guide v.1 (eBook), pp. 31–38 (2015)
8. Huang, Y.P.: Extending 3D printing to Direct Digital Manufacturing - The case of XYZprinting, Inc. National Taiwan University of Science and Technology, Taipei (2017)
9. vMaker, Do you know these 8 practical 3D model websites? https://vmaker.tw/archives/4818. Accessed 12 Jan 2018
10. Yusuf, B.: Free STL Files & 3D Printer Models – 34 Best Sites. https://all3dp.com/1/free-stl-files-3d-printer-models-3d-print-files-stl-download/#grabcad. Accessed 05 Jan 2018

It Still Matters: Preference in Visual Appearance of Stimuli Among People in the Late Stages of Dementia

Wei-Ying Chou[1](✉) (iD), P. John Clarkson[2] (iD), and Christine Waszynski[3]

[1] Arm Ltd., CPC1 Capital Park, Cambridge CB21 5XE, UK
wei.y.chou@gmail.com
[2] Engineering Design Centre, University of Cambridge, Cambridge CB2 1PZ, UK
[3] Geriatrics Program, Hartford Hospital, 80 Seymour St, Hartford, CT 06102, USA

Abstract. Introduction: This study aims to examine the emotional response towards visual stimuli in people with an advanced stage of dementia. **Methods:** One-to-one interview sessions were conducted with nineteen (17 females and two males) nursing home residents to investigate their response toward different visual stimuli. Fifteen positive images selected from the International Affective Picture System (IAPS) were used as visual stimuli. Participants' attitude and attention toward each stimulus was rated using the Observational Measurement of Engagement Tool (OME); their difficulty in recognising each stimulus was rated via a 3-point scale. **Results:** Stimuli contained children's faces received significantly higher attitude and attention scores than all the other stimuli ($p < 0.05$). Stimuli containing animals received the 2nd highest attitude and attention scores. Stimuli contained human faces or animals appeared to be more recognisable, especially the ones include children' faces. A strong, positive correlation between the attitude and recognisable ranking was identified, which was statistically significant ($p = 0.000$). The similar results have been found between the attention and recognisable ranking ($p = 0.002$). **Discussion:** The results of this study reveal that the people with moderate or severe stages of dementia still respond strongly to Kindchenschema (baby-schema). It provides designers with better insights into how to develop products/interventions for people with dementia, in particular for those in the advanced stage.

Keywords: Emotion design · Product appearance · Dementia care

1 Introduction

The rapid speed of global aging and the increasing prevalence of dementia have highlighted the importance of long-term care. Currently, around 46.8 million people worldwide are living with dementia. This number will almost triple by 2050 [1]. Improving the quality of and strategies for dementia care should be a central goal for researchers and clinical practitioners.

© Springer International Publishing AG, part of Springer Nature 2018
J. Zhou and G. Salvendy (Eds.): ITAP 2018, LNCS 10926, pp. 223–234, 2018.
https://doi.org/10.1007/978-3-319-92034-4_17

Empirical evidence shows that positive emotions are related to physical health, mental health and general well-being [2]. Higher ratios of positive to negative affect have been found in those who were mentally flourishing [3]. In response to the move of emotionally orientated and person-centered dementia care [4, 5], several design studies have been done to explore the design of personalized artifacts for people with dementia, in order to improve subjective well-being and maintain personhood. This form of personalized design project focuses on creating artifacts with a reminiscence function. It often starts with case studies and interviews to understand the life story of a person with dementia and creates personal items based on the life story [6, 7]. Although the results of this approach are positive, the effort required to create personalized artifacts limits its accessibility. It takes great effort to create personalized products for people with dementia. In one design project, for example, it required 30 volunteers, including designers, artists, caregivers, scientists, and therapists, to work a full day together to make three personalized dementia aprons [6]. This does not include the time that the research group spent on collecting life stories and preferences from the people with dementia.

So far, less attention has been paid to non-personalized products design in the dementia product design area. The effect of reminiscence approaches, such as using personal images/video and familiar music to improve mood and well-being people with dementia, has been well documented by many studies [8, 9] and therefore become predominate. The effect of non-personalized items in mood change is less addressed. It is unfortunate as non-personalized products can be produced on a large scale with less personal research work required.

According to Norman's model of emotion design, an individual's emotion experience toward products is affected by three design aspects: visceral, behavioral, and reflective [10]. Personalized items provide socio-pleasure and ideo-pleasure to people with dementia, and thus elicit positive emotion in respect of reflective design. Non-personalized products, on the other hand, are more likely to elicit positive emotion through visceral and behavioral aspects. Investigating the emotional response toward different product appearance can guide designers to create non-personalized products that people with dementia will likely prefer and engage with. This study, therefore, aims to examine the emotional response towards visual stimuli in people with an advanced stage of dementia.

2 Methods

2.1 Procedure and Measurements

One-to-one interview sessions were conducted with nineteen (17 females and two males) participants to investigate their response toward different visual stimuli. All the participants were nursing home residents with a moderate to advanced stage of dementia (CDR2-CDR3), all are white. The average ages of them is 90.7 ± 8.3 years old. Fifteen positive images selected from the International Affective Picture System (IAPS) [11] were used as visual stimuli. Those images were grouped in four groups, which are: (1) Portraits; (2) Landscapes; (3) Animals; (4) Food. Apart from these IAPS images, one neutral image was used as the control stimulus.

The participants' attitude and attention toward each stimulus was measured using the Observational Measurement of Engagement Tool (OME), a tool which was developed to record the response of individuals with dementia to the stimuli. The OME has shown a high degree of validity, inter–rater agreement (84%), and intra-class correlation (0.78) [12]. Residents' attention towards an image group was noted on a 4-point scale: *(1) not attentive, (2) somewhat attentive, (3) attentive*, and *(4) very attentive*. Residents' attitude towards an image group was noted in a 7-point Likert scale: *(1) very negative, (2) negative, (3) somewhat negative, (4) neutral, (5) somewhat positive, (6) positive,* and *(7) very positive* [13].

The residents' difficulty in recognizing the subject of the images was recorded based on a 3-point scale: *(0) Not difficult, (1) Somewhat difficult*, and *(2) Difficult/No response*. *Not difficult* means the resident recognized the main subject of the image quickly (in 5 s) without showing any difficulty. *Somewhat difficult* means the resident appeared to have some difficulty in response to the image but could recognize the main subject with the researchers' instruction. *Difficult/No response* means the resident showed no response or could not recognize the image even with the researcher's help.

The response was rated by a researcher during the interviews and two coders after the interviews (by listening audio recordings). These two coders had received the instruction of how to rate the events before they started. The researcher accompanied the coders while they were rating and played the audio files for them. Each audio file was only played once, to simulate the on-site rating situation.

2.2 Image Selection and Classification

This study used in 15 IAPS images and one control image (Table 1). These IAPS images are selected based on their emotion rating data provided in the manual [11]. IAPS provide ratings of three emotional dimensions for each image: pleasure, arousal, and dominance. The first two dimensions, pleasure and arousal, are known as core affect described in the circumplex model of emotion [14, 15], and therefore be chosen to be used in this study for image selection. Pleasure refers to the pleasure/misery of an emotion; arousal refers to the level of arousal/sleep induced by an emotion. All data was rated on a 9-point scale, with 9 referring to the highest rating and 1 referring to the lowest rating.

As the goal of this study is to elicit positive emotion, only images with high pleasure ratings were selected. These images were then classified into three groups based on their arousal level: (A) High levels of arousal; (B) Moderate levels of arousal; and (C) Low levels of arousal. The reprehensive emotion of these three groups, based on the circumplex model of emotion, are *excitement, pleasure*, and *relaxation*, respectively. Four subject groups were identified, based on the main subject of these images. The four groups are: *(1) Portraits*; *(2) Landscapes*; *(3) Animals*; and *(4) Food*. Group (1) contains six images and can be divided into two subgroups: *(1a) Images without children*; *(1b) Images including children*. Group (2) contains six images and can be divided into two subgroups: *(2a) Images without people*; *(2b) Images including people* (Fig. 1).

Table 1. The details of images used in this study

Image description (IAPS No.)	Arousal (SD)	Valence (SD)	Emotional groups	Subject groups
Hang glider (5626)	6.10 (2.19)	6.71 (2.06)	(A)	2b
Hiker (5629)	6.55 (2.11)	7.03 (1.55)	(A)	2b
Sailboat (8173)	6.12 (2.30)	7.63 (1.34)	(A)	2a
Skier (8190)	6.28 (2.57)	8.1 (1.39)	(A)	2b
Water skier (8200)	6.35 (1.98)	7.54 (1.37)	(A)	1a
Baby (2071)	5.00 (2.34)	7.86 (1.32)	(B)	1b
Family (2340)	4.9 (2.20)	8.03 (1.26)	(B)	1b
Romance (4601)	5.08 (2.01)	6.82 (1.22)	(B)	1a
Mountains (5660)	5.07 (2.62)	7.27 (1.59)	(B)	2a
Ice cream (7330)	5.14 (2.58)	7.69 (1.84)	(B)	4
Cow (1670)	3.05 (1.91)	6.81 (1.76)	(C)	3
Bunnies (1750)	4.10 (2.31)	8.28 (1.07)	(C)	3
Couple (4700)	4.05 (1.90)	6.91 (1.94)	(C)	1a
Sky (5594)	4.15 (2.76)	7.39 (1.45)	(C)	2a
Winner (8330)	4.06 (2.28)	6.65 (1.52)	(C)	1a
Control (-)	-	-	-	-

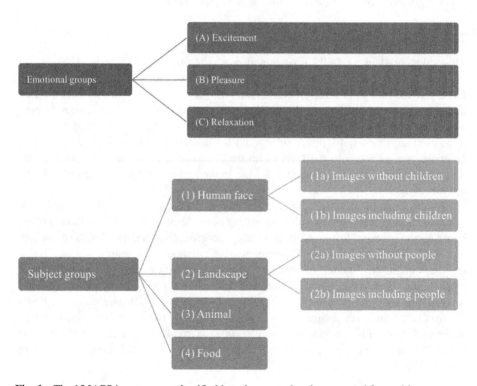

Fig. 1. The 15 IAPS images were classified into three emotional groups and four subject groups.

2.3 Data Analysis

All statistical analyses were performed by using IBM SPSS Statistics version 20. The OME were treated as interval data, in the assumption that the distances between each of the scale elements are equal. The results of recognizing ratings were analyzed as ordinal data. The ranks of OME and recognizing have been made to clarify which stimuli have better results. Friedman's test was used to examine the difference of OME scores between the image groups. Wilcoxon signed rank test was used as the post hoc test. To clarify whether the residents' emotional response to an image was affected by their ability to recognize it, the Spearman's rank-order correlation was run to determine the relationship between these variables. Inter-rater reliability of the researcher and the two coders was assessed using a two-way mixed, consistency, average-measures Intraclass Correlation (ICC) [16, 17].

3 Results

Among these 19 residents, four of them were excluded as they responded with indifference to the images. With the 15 residents, only one resident could recognize all the images without any difficulty. In the worst case, a resident could only recognize two images without any difficulty. Table 2 lists the reconcilability ranking of the 16 images. Generally, images in the emotional group (B) and (C), and those that contained human faces or animals (subject group (1) and (3)) appeared to be more recognizable, especially the ones include children' faces. The landscape pictures seemed to be less recognizable.

Images containing children's faces (group 1b) received significantly higher attitude and attention scores than all the other groups (Tables 3 and 4). Images containing animals (group 3) received the 2nd highest attitude and attention scores, although there are still significant differences between these and group (1b). No significant difference was found between group 1 and group 3. Those results indicate that compared with the images of landscapes and objects, images of human faces and animals are the better materials to elicit positive emotions in people with dementia, with the images containing children' faces producing the best results. The image of object (group 4) appear to have the lowest attitude score, compared with other IAPS images.

To clarify whether the residents' emotional response to an image was affected by their ability to recognize it, the Spearman's rank-order correlation was run to determine the relationship between these variables. A strong, positive correlation between the attitude and recognizable ranking was identified, which was statistically significant (rs (16) = 0.902, p = 0.000). Similar results were found between the attention and recognizable ranking (rs (16) = 0.705, p = 0.002). Table 5 presents the ranking of the three variables measured in this study: attitude, attention, and recognizing. It appears that the images containing children's faces had the highest ranking in all the three aspects. Images with human faces were more easily recognized by the residents and had higher ranking of attitude and attention. Landscape images were generally less favorable. Stimuli contained human faces or animals appeared to be more recognizable, especially the ones include children' faces. A strong, positive correlation between the

Table 2. The recognisable ranking of the 16 images.

Image (IAPS no.)	Emotional groups	Subject groups	Difficult in recognizing (%)*	Somewhat difficult in recognizing (%)*	No Difficult in Recognizing (%)*	Recognizable ranking
Baby (2071)	(B) Moderate	(1b) Human face, including children	0.0	0.0	100.0	1
Family (2340)	(B) Moderate	(1b) Human face, including children	0.0	0.0	100.0	1
Romance (4601)	(B) Moderate	(1a) Human face, without children	15.6	0.0	84.4	3
Couple (4700)	(C) Low	(1a) Human face, without children	13.3	4.4	82.2	4
Winner (8330)	(C) Low	(1a) Human face, without children	2.2	17.8	80.0	5
Cow (1670)	(C) Low	(3) Animal	8.9	11.1	80.0	6
Bunnies (1750)	(C) Low	(3) Animal	11.1	11.1	77.8	7
Skier (8190)	(A) High	(2b) Landscape, including people	4.4	28.9	66.7	8
Water skier (8200)	(A) High	(1a) Human face, without children	2.2	33.3	64.4	9
Mountains (5660)	(B) Moderate	(2a) Landscape, without people	22.2	33.3	44.4	10
Sailboat (8173)	(A) High	(2a) Landscape, without people	17.8	40.0	42.2	11
Hiker (5629)	(A) High	(2a) Landscape, including people	6.7	60.0	33.3	12
Control image	–	–	24.4	46.7	28.9	13
Hang glider (5626)	(A) High	(2b) Landscape, including people	6.7	71.1	22.2	14
Ice cream (7330)	(B) Moderate	(4) Food	44.4	33.3	22.2	15
Sky (5594)	(C) Low	(2a) Landscape, without people	35.6	44.4	20.0	16

*Coders voted how much difficulty (difficult, somewhat difficult, no difficult) a resident showed in recognizing an image. The results were divided by 45 (the total votes of each image) to get the percentage.

attitude and recognizable ranking was identified, which was statistically significant ($p = 0.000$). The similar results have been found between the attention and recognizable ranking ($p = 0.002$).

Table 3. The post hoc results of the attitude scores

p value	(1) Human face			(2) Landscape			(3) Animal	(4) Food	(5) Control
	(1) Total	(1a) Without children	(1b) Including children	(2) Total	(2a) Without people	(2b) Including people			
(1) Human face	(1) Total	0.001*	0.001*	0.001*	0.001*	0.003*	0.932	0.002*	0.001*
	(1a) Without children		0.001*	0.009*	0.011*	0.061	0.088	0.014*	0.001*
	(1b) Including children			0.001*	0.001*	0.001*	0.001*	0.001*	0.001*
(2) Landscape	(2) Total				0.798	0.776	0.005*	0.088	0.012*
	(2a) Without people					0.798	0.005*	0.201	0.013*
	(2b) Including people						0.010*	0.059	0.041*
(3) Animal								0.002*	0.001*
(4) Food									0.656

Table 4. The post hoc results of the attention scores

p value	(1) Human face			(2) Landscape			(3) Animal	(4) Food	(5) Control
	(1) Total	(1a) Without children	(1b) Including children	(2) Total	(2a) Without people	(2b) Including people			
(1) Human face	(1) Total	0.001*	0.001*	0.001*	0.001*	0.001*	0.95	0.073	0.001*
	(1a) Without children		0.001*	0.084	0.069	0.272	0.051	0.972	0.006*
	(1b) Including children			0.001*	0.001*	0.001*	0.002*	0.001*	0.001*
(2) Landscape	(2) Total				0.421	0.363	0.002*	0.379	0.022*
	(2a) Without people					0.382	0.002*	0.221	0.123
	(2b) Including people						0.004*	0.382	0.020*
(3) Animal								0.033*	0.001*
(4) Food									0.024*

Table 5. Overall responsiveness to 16 picture stimuli: Ranking of different aspects of variables. Ordered by attitude ratings.

	Emotional groups	Subject groups	Ranking: Attitude	Ranking: Attention	Ranking: Recognizing
Baby (2071)	(B) Moderate	(1b) Human face, including children	1	1	1
Family (2340)	(B) Moderate	(1b) Human face, including children	2	2	1
Bunnies (1750)	(B) Low	(3) Animals	3	3	6
Cow (1670)	(C) Low	(3) Animals	4	4	5
Winner (8330)	(C) Low	(1a) Human face, without children	5	10	4
Romance (4601)	(B) Moderate	(1a) Human face, without children	6	11	2
Couple (4700)	(C) Low	(1a) Human face, without children	7	5	3
Water skier (8200)	(A) High	(1a) Human face, without children	8	6	8
Sailboat (8173)	(A) High	(2a) Landscape, without people	9	9	10
Skier (8190)	(A) High	(2b) Landscape, including people	10	8	7
Mountains (5660)	(B) Moderate	(2a) Landscape, without people	11	12	9
Hang glider (5626)	(A) High	(2b) Landscape, including people	12	13	13
Hiker (5629)	(A) High	(2b) Landscape, including people	13	14	11
Sky (5594)	(C) Low	(2a) Landscape, without people	14	16	15
Ice cream (7330)	(B) Moderate	(4) Food	15	7	14
Control image	–	–	16	15	12

The averaged ICC = 0.82 (range 0.62–1) for the three rating variables (attention, attitude, and difficulty in recognizing), suggests an excellent agreement between the three coders. The averaged ICC for each variable was reported as follows: attitude: 0.85 (range 0.67–0.93); attention: 0.74 (range 0.63–0.89); difficulty in recognizing: 0.88 (range 0.62–1).

4 Discussion

The visual appearance of products plays a vital role in how people respond to them [18]. The results of this study revealed that this phenomenon can still be found in people in the late stages of dementia. Compared to images of animals, landscape, and food, the research participates tend to have less difficulty in recognizing portraits. A clear preference of images of children and animals has also been identified. In addition, the results suggested a positive correlation between the attitude and reconcilability rankings, which means images that were easily recognized tend to receive better responses from people with dementia.

As the dementia progresses, many people experience difficulties in recognizing familiar objects or surroundings. People in the advanced dementia often lose their ability to interact with stimuli but still reserve some ability to response to human interaction. This phenomenon was reflected by this study. Most of the research participates, even those in the late stages of dementia, were able to appreciate portrait images. In fact, while some participants experienced difficulties in understanding the three adult portraits, none of them showed difficulties in appreciating the images of baby and small children. This result suggests that portrait images are the better choice to provide visual stimulation for people in the late stages of dementia. Lack of spatial awareness is often found in people with dementia. Pictures taken from a view of a long shot (for example, "hiker (5629)") or a detail shot (for example, "ice cream (7330)") might make it difficult for the people with dementia to recognize them, which could limit their enjoyment of these images. The results of this study also suggest a positive correlation between the attitude and recognizably ranking. It once again emphasizes the importance of "product appearance." As a stimulus evokes people's emotional response though its aesthetic impression, semantic interpretation, and symbolic association [18], it is predicable that limitations to interpreting a stimulus affect the individual's emotional response toward it. It is not unusual, however, to see long shot and detail shot images are displayed on nursing homes walls. These images could serve a role to entertain the staffs and visitors, but less likely to be effective visual stimuli for people in the late stages of dementia.

According to the ethologist Konrad Lorenz [19], baby-schema, such as a round face, large eyes, a small nose, a high forehead (see Fig. 2), evoke positive emotions and motivate caretaking behavior in human beings. This theory has been confirmed by several behavioral studies, which indicated that faces with high baby-schema were found to be more attractive and elicited stronger motivation of caretaking [20, 21]. In real life practice, some kindergartens arrange children to visit nursing homes, suggesting it encourages social engagement and promote physical activity of nursing home residents [22]; Pet therapy is adopted by many nursing homes as a regular activity, with positive effects demonstrated by many research papers [23]. In addition, given the benefits of interacting with little children and pets, baby dolls and robotic animals have been developed for people with dementia for therapeutic purpose. Although the evidence is still weak (no large-scale study have been conducted so far), some studies suggested doll therapy and robot therapy might improve communication and reduce behavioral symptoms [24–27]. Besides, although they are not real babies and animals, it has been found that products with a physical appearance of baby-schema can elicit caretaking behavior in people with dementia. For example, in one case study, a research participate with dementia apologized to Paro, the baby harp seal robot with clear baby-schema appearance (Fig. 3), before he had to leave [27].

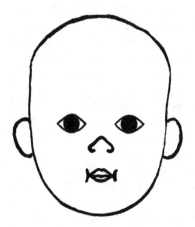

Fig. 2. The ideal face that contains all the features of baby-schema. Source: [21]

Fig. 3. Paro, the baby harp seal robot comes with a round face, large eyes, and a small nose. Source: [27]

Despite doll therapy and robotic therapy being adopted by more and more nursing homes, they are still seen as controversial interventions. Some family members were upset to see their loved ones being "treated as child" [28]. Besides, it raises ethical concerns of not telling people with dementia that what they are holding in arms are not real creatures but dolls and robotics [29].

The integration of baby-schema into daily products without having the products mimic the behaviors of babies and animals might be a more preferable approach. In fact, baby-schema has been applied in everyday products as an approach of emotional design. For example, it has been found that people had a more positive response toward cars with baby-schema features, and no habituation has been found after repeated exposures [30]. Our study has shown that the research participates manifested a more positive response towards the images of little children and animals. It could be explained that these types of images are simply more preferable, as they all contain the characteristics of baby-schema. Further research might work on how to effectively integrate baby-schema into product design and investigate its effect of eliciting positive emotions in people with dementia.

References

1. Prince, M.A., Bryce, R.A., Albanese, E.A.B., Wimo, A.C.D., Ribeiro, W.A.E., Ferri, C.P.A. E.: The global prevalence of dementia: a systematic review and metaanalysis. Alzheimer's Dementia **9**(1), 63–75 (2013)
2. Steptoe, A., Wardle, J., Marmot, M.: Positive affect and health-related neuroendocrine, cardiovascular, and inflammatory processes. Proc. Natl. Acad. Sci. U.S.A. **102**(18), 6508–6512 (2005)
3. Fredrickson, B.L., Losada, M.F.: Positive Affect and the Complex Dynamics of Human Flourishing. Am. Psychol. **60**(7), 678–686 (2005)
4. Kitwood, T.M.: Dementia Reconsidered: The Person Comes First. Open University Press, Buckingham (1997)
5. McCormack, B.: Person-centredness in gerontological nursing: an overview of the literature. J. Clin. Nurs. **13**(3A), 31–38 (2004)
6. Treadaway, C., Kenning, G.: Designing sensory e-Textiles for dementia. In: Amaresh, C., Toshiharu, T., Yukari, N. (eds.) Proceedings of the 3rd International Conference on Design Creativity, pp. 235–242. The Design Society, Glasgow (2015)
7. Wallace, J., Wright, P.C., McCarthy, J., Green, D.P., Thomas, J., Olivier, P.: A design-led inquiry into personhood in dementia. In: Brewster, S., Bødker, S. (eds.) Proceedings of the SIGCHI Conference on Human Factors in Computing Systems, pp. 2617–2626. ACM, New York (2013)
8. Woods, B., O'Philbin, L., Farrell, E.M., Spector, A.E., Orrell, M.: Reminiscence therapy for dementia. Cochrane Database Syst. Rev. (3) (2018). Art. No.: CD001120
9. Götell, E., Brown, S., Ekman, S.L.: The influence of caregiver singing and background music on vocally expressed emotions and moods in dementia care. Int. J. Nurs. Stud. **46**(4), 422–430 (2009)
10. Norman, D.A.: Emotional Design: Why We Love (or Hate) Everyday Things. Basic Books, New York (2004)
11. Lang, P.J., Bradley, M.M., Cuthbert, B.N.: International affective picture system (IAPS): affective ratings of pictures and instruction manual. Technical report A-8. University of Florida, Gainesville (2008)
12. Cohen-Mansfield, J., Dakheel-Ali, M., Marx, M.S.: Engagement in persons with dementia: The concept and its measurement. Am. J. Geriatr. Psychiatry **17**(4), 299–307 (2009)
13. Cohen-Mansfield, J., Marx, M.S., Dakheel-Ali, M., Regier, N.G., Thein, K.: Can Persons with Dementia be engaged with stimuli? Am. J. Geriatric Psychiatry **18**(4), 351–362 (2008)
14. Russell, J.A.: A circumplex model of affect. J. Pers. Soc. Psychol. **39**(6), 1161–1178 (1980)
15. Russell, J.A., Barrett, L.F.: Core affect, prototypical emotional episodes, and other things called emotion: dissecting the elephant. J. Pers. Soc. Psychol. **76**(5), 805–819 (1999)
16. Hallgren, K.A.: Computing inter-rater reliability for observational data: an overview and tutorial. Tutorials Quant. Methods Psychol. **8**(1), 23–34 (2012)
17. McGraw, K.O., Wong, S.P.: Forming inferences about some intraclass correlation coefficients. Psychol. Methods **1**(1), 30–46 (1996)
18. Crilly, N., Moultrie, J., Clarkson, P.J.: Seeing things: consumer response to the visual domain in product design. Des. Stud. **25**(6), 547–577 (2004)
19. Lorenz, K.: Die angeborenen formen möglicher erfahrung. Zeitschrift Für Tierpsychologie **5**(2), 235–409 (1943)
20. Glocker, M.L., Langleben, D.D., Ruparel, K., Loughead, J.W., Gur, R.C., Sachser, N.: Baby schema in infant faces induces cuteness perception and motivation for caretaking in adults. Ethology **115**(3), 257–263 (2009)

21. Sternglanz, S.H., Gray, J.L., Murakami, M.: Adult preferences for infantile facial features: an ethological approach. Animal Behav. **25**(PART 1), 108–115 (1977)
22. Dean J.: Play dates foster friendships between Melbourne kindergarten kids and nursing home residents. http://www.abc.net.au/news/2016-11-28/play-dates-strong-friendships-kids-nursing-home-residents/8064636. Accessed 01 Mar 2018
23. Filan, S., Llewellyn-Jones, R.: Animal-assisted therapy for dementia: A review of the literature. Int. Psychogeriatr. **18**(4), 597–611 (2006)
24. Alander, H., Prescott, T., James, I.A.: Older adults' views and experiences of doll therapy in residential care homes. Dementia **14**(5), 574–588 (2015)
25. Bisiani, L., Angus, J.: Doll therapy: a therapeutic means to meet past attachment needs and diminish behaviours of concern in a person living with dementia - a case study approach. Dementia **12**(4), 447–462 (2013)
26. Braden, B.A., Gaspar, P.M.: Implementation of a baby doll therapy protocol for people with dementia: innovative practice. Dementia **14**(5), 696–706 (2015)
27. Marti, P., Bacigalupo, M., Giusti, L., Mennecozzi, C., Shibata, T.: Socially assistive robotics in the treatment of behavioural and psychological symptoms of dementia. In: The First IEEE/RAS-EMBS International Conference on Biomedical Robotics and Biomechatronics, pp. 483–488 (2006)
28. Mitchell, G., Templeton, M.: Ethical considerations of doll therapy for people with dementia. Nurs. Ethics **21**(6), 720–730 (2014)
29. Johnston, A.: Robotic seals comfort dementia patients but raise ethical concerns. http://kalw.org/post/robotic-seals-comfort-dementia-patients-raise-ethical-concerns#stream/0. Accessed 01 Mar 2018
30. Miesler, L., Leder, H., Herrmann, A.: Isn't it cute: an evolutionary perspective of baby-schema effects in visual product designs. Int. J. Des. **5**(3), 17–30 (2011)

An Evaluation of User Experience of Web Main Menu on Different Mobile Devices

Kuo-Liang Huang[1](✉), Hsuan Lin[2], and Chia-Chen Lu[3]

[1] Department of Visual Arts and Design, Nanhua University,
Chiayi, Taiwan (R.O.C.)
shashi@nhu.edu.tw
[2] Department of Product Design, Tainan University of Technology,
Tainan, Taiwan (R.O.C.)
te0038@mail.tut.edu.tw
[3] Department of Industrial Design, Tunghai University,
Taichung, Taiwan (R.O.C.)
cclu@thu.edu.tw

Abstract. These days, we live in a multi-screen world with various devices for personal use. Designing a website that can provide the best user experience and increasing customer retention rates for more websites are both crucial. This study aims to explore which RWD main menu design can provide the best user experience (UX). By taking different website samples, this study analyzes the relevance between "website main menu design factors" and "different user experience dimensions" using an experimental method. Our results indicate the criteria for the best design parameters for RWD main menus for laptops, tablet PCs, and smartphones in order to create the best web experience for the user.

Keywords: User experience · Responsive Web Design (RWD)
Interaction interface · Menu

1 Introduction

Ericsson, one of the biggest and most famous technology companies, pointed out in the Ericsson Mobility Report that the number of portable device users in the world surpassed 7.6 billion in the first quarter of 2017 and continues to grow by 1 million new users every day (Ericsson 2017a). This type of development means that every person is getting more and more mobile devices. With the most obvious devices being smartphones, tablet PCs, and laptops, we are entering a multi-screen world, and the greatest distinction among these various devices is that every screen has a different size and aspect ratio. Based on previous findings, the top three activities that people use these mobile devices for are social networking, video streaming, and web browsing (Ericsson 2017b). For designers, how to create digital content whose layout can function on screens with different sizes and aspect ratios is a very difficult and challenging issue. If each edition has to be separately developed for each web browsing vehicle, the development costs will significantly increase, and the maintenance of the function and content will become more difficult (Gardner 2011). Therefore, Ethan Marcotte

© Springer International Publishing AG, part of Springer Nature 2018
J. Zhou and G. Salvendy (Eds.): ITAP 2018, LNCS 10926, pp. 235–251, 2018.
https://doi.org/10.1007/978-3-319-92034-4_18

developed the concept of responsive web design (RWD) in 2010, pointing out that RWD is the technology used for web design. Through the inspection mechanism, the layout and navigation can be automatically adjusted for the screens of different devices in order to maintain the standard of the content, reduce the time spent on zooming, moving, and scrolling while browsing the content, and provide a better user experience for the users (Marcotte and Eyrolles 2017).

The term "user experience" refers to the user's response and feeling after using the product, information system, or other service. User experience contains the user's recognition, emotion, preference, and awareness and can affect the user with regard to making a distinctive judgment between a company and its competitor based on impression, thus determining the customer retention rate of a company or a website (Gardner 2011). Interface is the outermost level of user experience; therefore, a better user experience can be provided to the user if the quality of the design is better. The information specialists Morville and Rosenfeld (2006) proposed that the menu that is responsible for the web navigation plays a crucial role in linking the web information interface and is a very important area with significant function. Most researchers wonder how a website's main menu in a multi-screen world with different sizes and aspect ratios can be properly designed to provide the best user experience and increase the customer retention rates for more websites. Therefore, this study aims to explore the following questions: (a) In different mobile devices, which kind of RWD design parameter group in the main menu is better? (b) In different mobile devices, what is the difference between various RWD design parameters and different user experience dimensions?

2 Literature Review

2.1 Responsive Web Design

In recent years, situations like multiple browsers on devices and different sizes and aspect ratios of different screens have created some problems to the layout of web content, as well as have seriously impacted the web browsing experience. To obtain better browsing efficiency, different web versions were traditionally designed for different devices; however, doing so can have a bad effect on web maintenance. Therefore, Ethan Marcotte became the first to publish an article, "Responsive Web Design, RWD," on the webzine, A List Apart (alistapart.com). He argues that a web edition should not be developed and created for just one device and its resolution but should be developed and created to be used with all web browsing devices (Marcotte 2011). Such technology lets the user read and navigate on different browsers with less time spent zooming, moving, and scrolling and provides the user the best web browsing experience. In summary, RWD has several main purposes (Doyle 2011): (a) to adjust the display style of the interface to fit any size and resolution of a screen; (b) to adjust the size and location of the main menu to fit the resolution of the screen; (c) to prepare images with a smaller file size for mobile devices; (d) to simplify page elements for mobile devices; and (e) to provide a larger link or button that is easy to touch and use on devices with small resolution. Therefore, Peterson (2014) suggests that RWD is not only the visual performance of a website but also includes technology and the user experience (Fig. 1).

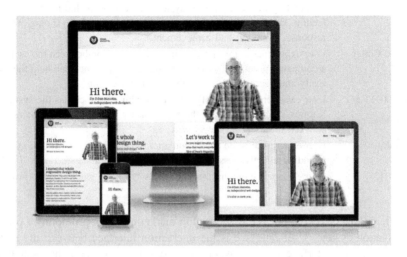

Fig. 1. Ethan Marcotte across four different breakpoints Source: https://responsivedesign.is/examples/ethan-marcotte/

The information specialists Morville and Rosenfeld (2006) in *Information Architecture for the World Wide Web* explain that a website's main menu is a "site-wide navigation system" responsible for connecting web information and is also a very important area with the crucial role of linking the interface of web information. Likewise, Garrets (2010) in *The Elements of User Experience: User-Centered Design for the Web* argues that the main menu is an information structure that decides three ways of interaction between the user and the web: information design, interface design, and navigation design.

2.2   Human–Computer Interaction and User Experience

Currently in the design of human-computer interaction (HCI), the main focus has changed from usability-oriented interaction to user experience (UX) (Huang and Chen 2013; Huang et al. 2014a; Partala and Kallinen 2011). It also emphasizes the need to consider behavior models, needs, attitudes, and other possible problems from the user's perspective for the design, as well as lets the user experience become a part of the design thought process (Huang et al. 2014b; Kincl and Štrach 2012; Kotamraju and van der Geest 2012). User experience is still a new concept; therefore, many scholars have defined it differently ideas, and we have organized their concepts and definitions in Table 1 below:

Table 1. Concepts and definitions of user experience

Scholar	Concept and definition
ISO (2009)	User experience is the user's thought and response when using or anticipating to use a product, system, or service, including the user's feeling, belief, preference, recognition, physical and psychological response, behavior, and achievement
Goto and Cotler (2004)	User experience is the entire feeing and interaction between the user and a company, product, or service. Good user experience can help the user easily and successfully finish the task requirements
Roto (2007)	User experience is not only for the user but also includes the system features and the quality of the experience with regard to the interaction between the user and the system
Kuniavsky (2010)	User experience is the perception after the user interacts with the system, including effectiveness, efficiency, and emotional satisfaction
Kraft (2012)	User experience emphasizes the user's "feeling" when using a product

The term "user experience" is mostly used in marketing when promoting a product or information system. User interface is the interaction interface between the system and the user. The interface is used by the user to help understand the system and properly use it; the interface helps the system deliver information. A good user interface (UI) design can provide easier and more effective service to improve the system and enhance the frequency of use and satisfaction (ISO 2009; Lasseter 1987).

In summary, the role that user experience plays is becoming more and more important for the user in the design of HCI (Partala and Kallinen 2011). For users, the experience is continuous, and the feeling can be established by the interaction between the user and the product, information system, or interactive process of the service. Therefore, all the thoughts, feelings, and recognitions that the user has during the interactive process create the user experience. Said user experience from the interaction between the user and the system is a crucial factor that decides whether a website is successful or not. User experience has developed into a significant issue of human-machine interaction and interface design (Hassenzahl and Tractinsky 2006), and the behavior analysis theory of the user can be considered an important reference for improving such designs (Butler and Jacob 1997).

2.3 Measuring User Experience

Different measurement tools have been created as user experience has grown as a primary consideration. Hartson and Pyla (2012), in The UX Book: Process and Guidelines for Ensuring a Quality User Experience, indicate that a scale is the main tool for collecting users' subjective data among all methods for measuring user experience. It can not only be used as a standalone measurement method but can also be regarded as a supplementary tool for the data of an experimental method. Moreover, in Measuring the User Experience: Collecting, Analyzing, and Presenting Usability Metrics, Albert and Tullis (2013) claim that a scale can help provide such important information as user perception and interaction. Currently, many different scales for user experience have been developed and widely used, and the most popular ones are briefly described below:

(a) ASQ (after-scenario questionnaire)

This questionnaire was developed by Lewis (1991). The scale, which has three items per set, is used for every question, and three basic dimensions are involved in every question: effectiveness, efficiency, and satisfaction. The web interface of Gary Perlman can be evaluated using a subjective method.

(b) SUS (system usability scale)

This subjective perception scale, which was developed by Lewis and Sauro (2009), is frequently used for analyzing the usability of a product. Taking cross-examination as a method, the purpose is to help businesses understand the usability of a product and compare it with the previous product or a competitor's product. Meanwhile, data collection and analysis can be easily accomplished; therefore, only a small workforce and few expenses are required to easily satisfy the business's needs.

(c) QUIS (questionnaire for user interaction satisfaction)

This questionnaire was created by Brooke (1996) to measure the subjective feeling of the user in a multidimensional way after operating a system. This questionnaire has five parts: (i) system total response; (ii) screen display; (iii) interface words and information display; (iv) learning; and (v) software function.

(d) UEQ (user experience questionnaire)

This questionnaire was created by Laugwitz et al. (2008), who collected and verified the data of more than 9,000 people in different systems, such as commercial software, web, online shopping, and social media for many years. Currently, the version has been translated into 16 languages, which can be found on the UEQ-Online website of user experience scale (http://www.ueq-online.org) established by Hinderks, Schrepp, and Thomaschewski. Six dimensions and 26 items are included in the scale, as shown in Table 2.

Table 2. UEQ dimension and item description

Dimension	Item	Concept and definition
Attractiveness	annoying-enjoyable	According to the impression of this system, does the user like it?
	good-bad	
	unlikable-pleasing	
	unpleasant-pleasant	
	attractive- unattractive	
	friendly-unfriendly	
Efficiency	fast-slow	Is the user able to use this system quickly and efficiently, and can the user interface look more organized?
	inefficient-efficient	
	impractical-practical	
	organized-cluttered	

(*continued*)

Table 2. (*continued*)

Dimension	Item	Concept and definition
Perspicuity	not understandable-understandable	Is the user able to easily understand how to easily operate and use it as quickly as possible?
	easy to learn-difficult to learn	
	complicated-easy	
	clear-confusing	
Dependability	unpredictable-predictable	Is the interaction between the user and the system in control? Can the user predict the security of the system in the interactive process?
	obstructive-supportive	
	secure-not secure	
	meets-does not meet expectations	
Stimulation	valuable-inferior	Is the process of using the system interesting? And does the user have the motivation for further use?
	boring-exciting	
	not interesting-interesting	
	motivating-demotivating	
Novelty	creative-dull	Is the system design more creative or innovative? Can it attract the attention of the user?
	inventive-conventional	
	usual-leading edge	
	conservative-innovative	

Compared with other scales that measure user experience, UEQ provides a better and more complete user experience dimension, while its feature of having less items and using adjectives with opposite meanings can shorten the time needed for the memory to work, thus quickly obtaining the user's real response and feelings. Therefore, we adopted UEQ as the measurement tool in this study.

2.4 Technology Acceptance Model

To explore how much the user can accept the information system, Davis (1989) developed a technology acceptance model (TAM) that is generally considered the theoretical foundation for predicting and explaining a user's behavior regarding new technology (Huang et al. 2014b; López-Nicolás et al. 2008; Venkatesh et al. 2003). The reason is that TAM can provide effective and accurate prediction of usefulness and ease of use of an information system (Kim 2008; Schepers and Wetzels 2007; Taylor and Todd 1995). In TAM, the user's actual usage is determined by the following process. First of all, the user's perceived usefulness (PU) and perceived ease of use (PEOU) in the system will mutually affect the user's attitude (ATUT), and ATUT and PU will determine whether behavior intention (BI) can be accepted (Davis et al. 1989; Huang et al. 2014a). Furthermore, PU, which means that the user's performance of the work can be achieved by using the system, will not only affect the positive correlation of ATUT and BT but will also be affected by the positive correlation of PEOU. PEOU, which refers to how the user feels about the ease of use of an information system, will affect the positive correlation of PU and ATUT. ATUT, which refers to the user's feelings about and response to the system, will be affected by the positive correlation of PU and PEOU. Finally, BI, which refers to how much behavior intention the user has, will be affected by the positive correlation of PU and ATUT (Fig. 2).

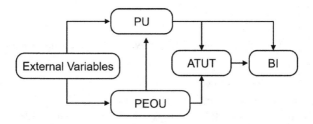

Fig. 2. Technology acceptance model framework (Davis et al. 1989)

3 Method

Regarding the purpose and question, this study uses Davis's TAM Model as the theoretical foundation to understand what effects the different "outer variables" of a RWD main menu have on user experience for the user's PU, PEOU, and ATUT, as well as to predict and explain which design parameter group of the main menu can provide the best user experience (Fig. 3).

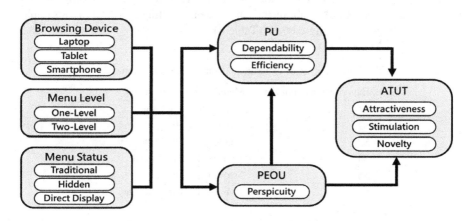

Fig. 3. The study framework and variable level

3.1 Typical RWD Main Menu Extraction and Production

With regard to RWD outer variables, many relevant RWD design forms can be chosen in order to obtain a different but significant form for the main menu. First, we obtained the "Top 100 websites" front pages selected from a popular evaluating website, "Awwwards," and printed them on A4 paper. Next, we invited four professional web design specialists to carry out morphological analysis on the layout parameter of the most frequent RWD main menus and "Top 100 websites" by means of focus groups to obtain the typical different items and categories. Moreover, we performed a representative analysis on the size and resolution of different web browsing devices, the results of which are shown in Table 3.

Table 3. The analytic results of responsive web design main menu forms

Item	Category
Menu level	(a) one-level, (b) two-level
Menu status	(a) traditional, (b) hidden, (c) direct display
Browsing device	(a) Laptop (14", 1920*1080 px), (b) Tablet PC (10.1", 1280 × 800 px), (c) Smartphone (5.7", 1440*720 px)

"Menu level" refers to the levels of the menu information framework. One-level means only one level is on the menu, and two-level means a classified menu. "menu status" has three typical categories: (a) Traditional – it is at the top of a webpage and is regularly displayed; (b) Hidden – it is closed when entering a webpage and can be displayed after clicking on the zoomed screen of the main menu; and (c) Direct display – it is shown in the center of the screen with a large size when entering the webpage and can be automatically closed by clicking an item. Laptops, tablets, and smartphones are the most frequent "browsing devices," and the typical device size can be decided according to the screen size and resolution of different devices. Six (2X3) different experimental samples of the main menu can be seen, resulting in a total of 18 samples for the three typical browsing devices (Table 4).

Table 4. The list of experimental sample design parameters

Experimental sample no.	Menu level	Menu status
S1	One-level	Traditional
S2	One-level	Hidden
S3	One-level	Direct display
S4	Two-level	Traditional
S5	Two-level	Hidden
S6	Two-level	Direct display

We used Bootstrap 4 to produce the webpage experimental samples, including jquery.js standard library, the CSS style sheet of bootstrap framework, JavaScript runtime library, and self-written CSS style sheet. Considering that the user may be affected by other factors of the main menu in the sampling, the color, word size, and web elements of the samples will be properly controlled. Furthermore, considering the user's situational simulation, the carousel banners that are frequently used on the web will be added to help respondents easily fit into the situation (Fig. 4).

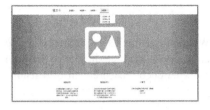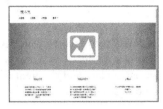

Fig. 4. Extracted experimental sample: Laptop, Tablet PC, and Smartphone, from left to right

3.2 The Experimental Design and Process

Research participants are qualified if they meet the following conditions: (a) having the online experience of using the three devices of laptop, tablet PC, and smartphone; (b) do not have significant visual or hearing impairment after correction; and (c) have the stability of body and mind and an age range between $18 \sim 60$. Furthermore, for the experiment design, we used the within-subjects design so that all participants can experience every situation of the experiment. In order to properly control irrelevant variables and obtain the causal relationship, the laboratory experiment is chosen to use. UEQ is considered the measurement scale, and the semantic differential scale with seven intervals from the Chinese Version of the official website is used. The original order and reverse questions will be kept. Instruments and materials include: (a) Devices: Laptop (14", 1920*1080 px), Tablet PC (10.1", 1280 $\times$ 800 px), and Smartphone (5.7", 1440*720 px);(b) A projector. The experimental process can be seen in Table 5.

Table 5. The experimental process

Step	Description	Duration
1. Situation setting	Only the respondent and the researcher remain in a confined space without disturbance, and the temperature is maintained between 24–26 °C	2 min
2. Warm up and introduction	The researcher uses a PPT file to describe the purpose of the study, the process, the scale, and the operation of the devices	8 min
3. Experiment	Browse six different experimental samples in sequence. Start with the laptop to browse experimental sample 1 and fill in the UEQ scale. Then do it again with the tablet PC and the smartphone. After that, change to sample 2 and complete all 18 samples to evaluate the causal relationship between stimulus and response. The tablet PC and the smartphone can be browsed either vertically or horizontally to resemble the real situation	40 min
4. Data confirmation	Collect the data and ensure all information has been completely filled out	

4 Results

The purpose of this study is to explore which RWD main menu design parameter group can create the best user experience. We also want to understand the difference between main menu design parameters and different user experience measurement dimensions in different mobile devices.

4.1 Basic Outline of the Experimental Samples

In the experiment, the effective sample size was 46, including 20 women (43%) and 26 men (57%). The age range was between 20–53 years ($M = 27.84$, $SD = 12.44$). With 26 items in the UEQ scale, the information of the six dimensions of attractiveness, perspicuity, efficiency, dependability, stimulation, and novelty was collected using a semantic differential scale with seven intervals. First, we reversed the score of the reverse questions and changed the original seven scales of $1 \sim 7$ to $-3 \sim +3$. When the value is positive, it means the positive value is in fact the negative value. Next, we added all scores of each dimension and averaged them to obtain the stimulus of the participants in every experimental sample and evaluate the average result based on different user experience dimensions. Therefore, the evaluation and preference of user experience can be seen by the scores shown in Table 6.

Table 6. The evaluation results of UEQ dimension means in different experimental samples

Sample		S1	S2	S3	S4	S5	S6
Laptop	Attractiveness	1.85	−2.83	0.83	1.2	−0.2	1.16
	Perspicuity	2.1	−0.45	1.69	3.78	1.46	1.02
	Efficiency	1.52	−1.2	0.25	3.27	−1.3	1.2
	Dependability	2.25	−1.27	1.21	2.74	−0.99	1.25
	Stimulation	0.09	−0.05	1	0.48	0.01	0.96
	Novelty	−2.18	1.19	1.49	−2.21	1.23	1.5
	Score	5.63	−4.62	6.48	9.25	0.21	7.08
Tablet PC	Attractiveness	1.83	−0.16	1	1.21	−0.16	1.33
	Perspicuity	1.89	0.25	2	2.82	0.2	1.93
	Efficiency	2.01	−0.98	0.26	2.82	−0.96	1.49
	Dependability	2.16	−0.73	1.49	2.8	−0.75	1.72
	Stimulation	0.01	1	1.73	0.74	−0.01	1.25
	Novelty	−2.15	0.26	1.24	−2.2	0.99	1.23
	Score	5.75	−0.36	7.71	8.2	−0.69	8.95
Smartphone	Attractiveness	−2.37	1.77	1.93	−2.31	1.82	1.97
	Perspicuity	0.75	1.7	2.21	0.74	1.98	2.4
	Efficiency	−0.91	1.39	1.47	−1	1.75	2.4
	Dependability	−0.9	1.9	3.18	−0.7	2.25	2.2
	Stimulation	−1.94	1.22	1.48	−0.41	1.23	1.52
	Novelty	−0.74	−0.38	−0.2	−1.58	−0.23	−0.01
	Score	−6.11	7.6	10.07	−5.27	8.81	10.47

From the previous table, we can see that S4 has the best evaluation, and S2 has the lowest evaluation for the laptop. For the tablet PC, S4 and S6 have the best evaluations, and S2 and S5 have the lowest evaluations. For the smartphone, S3 and S6 have the best evaluations, and S1 and S4 have the lowest evaluations. All of the above results can be considered the basic evaluation results, but further analysis is required to understand the relevance between different user experience dimensions and design factors.

4.2 The Construction of Relevance Between Different User Experience Dimensions and Design Factors

Quantification I, a qualitative multiple regression analysis, is a categorical multiple regression analysis method that is used to measure how intensely a description variable (qualitative item) can affect a purpose variable (Chen 2011). In order to get function relations between the variable (purpose variable) and other "qualitative" items (0 or 1 dummy variable can be taken), multiple regression analysis is used to measure how intensely a description variable (qualitative item) affects the purpose variable. Every description variable (qualitative item) consists of many categories. If all samples are selected in every item and only one of them can be selected, the regression model can be established to predict the variability of information and event. The description variable is qualitative (nominal scale); and the purpose variable is quantitative (metric ordinal scale) (Chen 2011).

When the respondents were in the process of the experiment, the results were evaluated by entire experimental samples. The entire RWD included different design forms; therefore, we could not neglect the potential effect of design factor forms on the respondents' user experience while the respondents were evaluating the samples. Furthermore, the relevance of design factors on the entire RWD must also be calculated. This study used experimental samples to obtain the stimulus of the respondents and then the subjective evaluation by means of UEQ and main menu design parameters to obtain the quantitative relationship between "the categories of design factor forms" and "user experience dimensions." Quantification I is a qualitative multiple regression analysis that can establish the relationship between user experience dimensions and design factor categories. Therefore, this study adopted the analytic technology of quantification I to determine relevance.

The Construction of Relevance Between Laptop and User Experience

We took the eight experimental webpage samples for the laptop as description variables and the averages of the six user experience dimensions as the purpose variables to analyze the relevance between "the six dimensions of user experience" and "web design factors," as shown in Table 7.

According to the theory of quantification I, we can see that if the value of item partial correction (IPC) and categories score (CS) is greater, then the effect of the item or the category on user experience dimensions is also greater. IPC is used to express a user experience dimension that has a preference for an item (design factor). CS is used to express how intense the relationship between the categories of design factor and a user experience dimension may be. A positive value means positive relevance, and a

Table 7. The Quantification I analytic results of the Laptop

Item	Category	Attractiveness		Perspicuity		Efficiency		Dependability		Stimulation		Novelty	
		CS	IPC	CS	IPC	CS	IPC	CS	IPC	CS	IPC	CS	IPC
Menu Level	One-Level	-0.38	0.49	-0.49	0.64	-0.43	0.75	-0.13	0.82	0.07	0.23	0.00	0.20
	Two-Level	0.38		0.49		0.43		0.13		-0.07		0.00	
Menu Status	Traditional	1.19	0.89	1.34	0.87	1.77	0.97	1.63	1	-2.12	0.98	-2.37	1
	Hidden	-1.85		-1.10		-1.87		-1.99		0.75		1.04	
	Direct Display	0.66		-0.24		0.10		0.37		1.37		1.33	
Constant Term		0.34		1.60		0.62		0.87		0.41		0.17	
		R= 0.89		R= 0.88		R= 0.97		R= 0.99		R= 0.98		R= 0.99	
		R^2= 0.80		R^2=0.78		R^2= 0.94		R^2= 0.98		R^2=0.96		R^2=0.99	

negative value means negative relevance. The coefficient of determination (R2) refers to the reliability of the entire prediction model. When closer to 1, the reliability is higher. Regarding the judgment of the prediction of reliability, Sugiyama and Inoue (1996) pointed out the relationship between multiple correlation coefficient (R) and reliability, which is shown in Table 8.

Table 8. The relationship between R and Reliability

Multiple correlation coefficient (R)	Reliability
$0.00 \sim 0.20$	Low relevance is shown in the predictive value
$0.20 \sim 0.40$	Relevance is shown in the predictive value
$0.40 \sim 0.70$	Strong relevance is shown in the reliability of the predictive value
$0.70 \sim 1.00$	Very strong relevance is shown in the reliability of the predictive value

Regarding "attractiveness" in Table 7, we can see the IPC of menu status (0.89) is higher and affects the relevance of attractiveness most when compared with other design factors. Therefore, the development of these design factors should be considered by designers to enhance user experience and let the effect of this feature be fully developed to satisfy the user experience need of customers. In contrast, the IPC of menu level (0.49) is lower, which means that the relevance between the design factor and attractiveness is lower. Therefore, without affecting other conditions for the entire design, this can be considered a the secondary priority for the development of design factors when the image of attractiveness is established.

CS contains the positive value and the negative value; the positive value means a positive correlation effect on user experience. When CS is higher, the effect is bigger. Taking "attractiveness" as an example, the "traditional" value (1.19) of the "menu status" is the highest. This means that the image of "attractiveness" can be established and properly evaluated when the "menu status" is designed in the "traditional" Way. In contrast, the image of "attractiveness" cannot be established or properly evaluated when the "menu status" is designed in the "hidden" way (−1.85). Therefore, the combination of "two-level" with "traditional" in design factors can sufficiently show the effect of the feature to satisfy the "attractiveness" of user experience for customers. In this "attractiveness," R is 0.89 and R2 is 0.80, which indicates a strong relevance of the reliability of the predictive value. By following this rule, the features of the design factor categories for the construction of user experience dimensions can be organized and concluded as criteria for the best design factor, as shown in Table 9.

Table 9. Laptop RWD main menu design factor compatibility list

Dimension		Design factor		R
		Menu level	Menu status	
UX	Attractiveness	Two-level	Traditional	0.89
	Perspicuity	Two-level	Traditional	0.88
	Efficiency	Two-level	Traditional	0.97
	Dependability	Two-level	Traditional	0.99
	Stimulation	One-level	Direct display	0.98
	Novelty	NA	Direct display	0.99

Table 10. The Quantification I analytic results of the tablet PC

Item	Category	Attractiveness		Perspicuity		Efficiency		Dependability		Stimulation		Novelty	
		CS	IPC	CS	IPC	CS	IPC	CS	IPC	CS	IPC	CS	IPC
Menu Level	One-Level	0.05	0.24	-0.13	0.50	-0.34	0.75	-0.14	0.82	0.13	0.32	-0.11	0.53
	Two-Level	-0.05		0.13		0.34		0.14		-0.13		0.11	
Menu Status	Traditional	0.68	0.97	0.84	0.97	1.64	0.97	1.37	1	-0.41	0.81	-2.7	0.99
	Hidden	-1.00		-1.29		-1.74		-1.86		-0.29		0.73	
	Direct Display	0.32		0.45		0.10		0.49		0.70		1.34	
Constant Term		0.84		1.51		0.77		1.11		0.79		-0.10	
		R= 0.96		R= 0.96		R= 0.98		R= 0.99		R= 0.81		R= 0.99	
		R^2= 0.93		R^2=0.94		R^2= 0.97		R^2= 0.98		R^2=0.66		R^2=0.98	

The Construction of Relevance Between Tablet PC and User Experience

We took the eight experimental web samples for the tablet PC as description variables and the averages of the six user experience dimensions as the purpose variables to analyze relevance, which can be seen in Table 10.

According to the quantification I analytic results in Table 10, the features of the design factor categories for the construction of user experience dimensions can be organized and concluded as criteria of the best design factor for tablet PCs, which is shown in Table 11.

Table 11. Tablet PC RWD main menu design factor compatibility list

Dimension		Design factor		R
		Menu level	Menu status	
UX	Attractiveness	One-level	Traditional	0.96
	Perspicuity	Two-level	Traditional	0.96
	Efficiency	Two-level	Traditional	0.98
	Dependability	Two-level	Traditional	0.99
	Stimulation	One-level	Direct display	0.81
	Novelty	Two-level	Direct display	0.99

The Construction of Relevance Between Smartphone and User Experience

We took the eight experimental webpage samples for the smartphone as description variables and the averages of the six user experience dimensions as the purpose variables to analyze relevance, which can be seen in Table 12.

Table 12. The Quantification I analytic results of the Smartphone

Item	Category	Attractiveness		Perspicuity		Efficiency		Dependability		Stimulation		Novelty	
		CS	IPC	CS	IPC	CS	IPC	CS	IPC	CS	IPC	CS	IPC
Menu Level	One-Level	-0.02	0.99	-0.08	0.78	-0.20	0.70	0.06	0.23	-0.26	0.60	0.08	0.33
	Two-Level	0.02		0.08		0.20		-0.06		0.26		-0.08	
Menu Status	Traditional	-2.81	1	-0.89	1	-1.81	0.99	-2.13	0.99	-1.69	0.96	-0.64	0.89
	Hidden	1.33		0.21		0.72		0.70		0.71		0.22	
	Direct Display	1.48		0.67		1.08		1.44		0.98		1.42	
Constant Term		0.47		1.63		0.85		1.34		0.52		-0.52	
		R= 0.96		R= 0.99		R= 0.98		R= 0.98		R= 0.96		R= 0.88	
		R^2= 0.93		R^2=0.99		R^2= 0.97		R^2= 0.97		R^2=0.92		R^2=0.79	

The quantification I analytic results in Table 12 can be organized and concluded as criteria of the best design factor for the smartphone, which is shown in Table 13.

Table 13. Smartphone RWD main menu design factor compatibility list

Dimension		Design factor		R
		Menu level	Menu status	
UX	Attractiveness	One-level	Direct display	0.96
	Perspicuity	Two-level	Direct display	0.99
	Efficiency	Two-level	Direct display	0.98
	Dependability	Two-level	Direct display	0.98
	Stimulation	One-level	Direct display	0.96
	Novelty	Two-level	Direct display	0.98

5   Conclusions and Suggestions

Currently, designers tend to focus on "humanity" when designing an interaction interface; therefore, they should regard people's feelings and incorporate them into the elements of the design to understand humanity, which creates value in the user experience, elevates a user's intention to use a system, and increases competitiveness. Based on this idea, this study concentrates on the cross-screen web browsing on mobile devices and uses different RWD design parameters as the research target to understand how the setting of "different RWD design parameters" can obtain the best browsing experience for users of different mobile devices. Finally, the best design criteria for "different RWD main menu design parameters" and "different user experience dimensions" of different mobile devices (laptop, tablet PC, and smartphone) can be organized and concluded. The following research results were obtained:

With a larger screen, the "traditional" form of the "main status" is better for laptops. By analyzing user experience dimensions, we can understand that it has better frequency of use but lacks stimulation and novelty. The "Two-level" form of the "main level" is better only on the premise of having a great amount of information for classification. It is suggested to use the "two-level" form to enhance not only attractiveness but also the value of perspicuity and efficiency of frequency of use.

The screen size and resolution between tablet PCs and laptops differ only slightly; therefore, the result of the "menu status" of different user experience dimensions for tablet PCs is similar to that of laptops. The "Two-level" way of the "main level" is also preferable and can elevate the frequency of use but cannot bring better values for attractiveness and stimulation.

With the smallest screen size, which obviously affects the layout of the web content, the "direct display" of the "menu status" of different user experience dimensions is best for smartphones. The second best is the "hidden" way, while the "traditional" way is the worst with a negative correlation. Therefore, it is strongly suggested not to use it.

Moreover, the "two-level" way of the "menu level" is better for frequency of use, but "one-lever" is better for dependability and novelty.

According to the above results, we can better understand that the screen size of different RWD devices can profoundly affect the main menu design parameters. The best design criteria of "different RWD main menu design parameters" and "different user experience dimensions" obtained in this study can be practically considered as references for web designers that develop interaction interfaces, as well as a reference for enhancing the value of interaction between the user and the webpage. These results can likely help designers to quickly obtain the design emphasis and manage user experience more delicately and precisely. Therefore, the value of user experience can be elevated to stimulate the user's intention to use the system and create competitiveness in the field.

In this study, the "two-level" way is mostly used in the "main menu" of RWD of different devices. We suggest using the "two-level" way on the premise of having a great amount of information for classification. This study does not use the variable to make the classification score of menu information; therefore, all details need to be examined and explored by other researchers in the future.

References

Albert, W., Tullis, T.: Measuring the User Experience: Collecting, Analyzing, and Presenting Usability Metrics, 2nd edn. Morgan Kaufmann, Newnes (2013)

Brooke, J.: SUS-A quick and dirty usability scale. Usability Eval. Ind. **189**(194), 4–7 (1996)

Butler, K.A., Jacob, R.J.: Human-computer interaction: introduction and overview. ACM (1997)

Chen, Y.-M.: Applied Business Research, 1st edn. Ting-Mao, Taipei (2011)

Davis, F.D.: Perceived usefulness, perceived ease of use, and user acceptance of information technology. MIS Q. **13**, 319–340 (1989)

Davis, F.D., Bagozzi, R.P., Warshaw, P.R.: User acceptance of computer technology: a comparison of two theoretical models. Manage. Sci. **35**(8), 982–1003 (1989)

Doyle, M.: Responsive Web Design Demystified (2011). https://www.elated.com/articles/responsive-web-design-demystified/. Accessed 26 Dec 2017

Ericsson: Ericsson Mobility Report June 2017. https://www.ericsson.com/assets/local/mobility-report/documents/2017/ericsson-mobility-report-june-2017.pdf. Accessed 20 Nov 2017

Ericsson: Ericsson Mobility Report November 2017. https://www.ericsson.com/en/mobility-report/reports/november-2017/enhancing-the-event-experience. Accessed 20 Nov 2017

Gardner, B.S.: Responsive web design: enriching the user experience. Sigma J. Inside Dig. Ecosyst. **11**(1), 13–19 (2011)

Garrett, J.J.: Elements of User Experience, The: User-Centered Design for the Web and Beyond. Pearson Education (2010)

Goto, K., Cotler, E.: Web redesign 2.0: Workflow that Works. New Riders (2004)

Hartson, R., Pyla, P.S.: The UX Book: Process and Guidelines for Ensuring a Quality User Experience. Morgan Kaufmann, Newnes (2012)

Hassenzahl, M., Tractinsky, N.: User experience-a research agenda. Behav. Inf. Technol. **25**(2), 91–97 (2006)

Huang, K.-L., Chen, K.-H.: A preliminary study on Kansei images and design elements associated with varied sensory channels for the interactive interface of SHD. J. Kansei **1**(2), 4–27 (2013)

Huang, K.-L., Chen, K.-H., Ho, C.-H.: Enhancement of reading experience: users' behavior patterns and the interactive interface design of Tablet readers. Library Hi Tech, **32**(3), 509–528 (2014a)

Huang, K.-L., Chen, K.-H., Ho, C.-H.: Promoting in-depth reading experience and acceptance: design and assessment of Tablet reading interfaces. Behav. Inf. Technol. **33**(6), 606–618 (2014b)

ISO: 9241-210: 2010 Ergonomics of human system interaction-Part 210: Human-centred design for interactive systems. International Standardization Organization (ISO), Switzerland (2009)

Kim, S.H.: Moderating effects of job relevance and experience on mobile wireless technology acceptance: adoption of a smartphone by individuals. Inf. Manag. **45**(6), 387–393 (2008)

Kincl, T., Štrach, P.: Measuring website quality: asymmetric effect of user satisfaction. Behav. Inf. Technol. **31**(7), 647–657 (2012)

Kotamraju, N.P., van der Geest, T.M.: The tension between user-centred design and e-government services. Behav. Inf. Technol. **31**(3), 261–273 (2012)

Kraft, C.: User Experience Innovation: User Centered Design That Works, 2nd edn. Apress, New York (2012)

Kuniavsky, M.: Smart Things: Ubiquitous Computing User Experience Design. Morgan Kaufmann, Newnes (2010)

López-Nicolás, C., Molina-Castillo, F.J., Bouwman, H.: An assessment of advanced mobile services acceptance: contributions from TAM and diffusion theory models. Inf. Manag. **45**(6), 359–364 (2008)

Lasseter, J.: Principles of traditional animation applied to 3D computer animation. Paper presented at the ACM Siggraph Computer Graphics (1987)

Laugwitz, B., Held, T., Schrepp, M.: Construction and evaluation of a user experience questionnaire. Paper presented at the Symposium of the Austrian HCI and Usability Engineering Group (2008)

Lewis, J.R.: Psychometric evaluation of an after-scenario questionnaire for computer usability studies: the ASQ. ACM SIGCHI Bull. **23**(1), 78–81 (1991)

Lewis, James R., Sauro, J.: The factor structure of the system usability scale. In: Kurosu, M. (ed.) HCD 2009. LNCS, vol. 5619, pp. 94–103. Springer, Heidelberg (2009). https://doi.org/10.1007/978-3-642-02806-9_12

Marcotte, E.: Responsive Web Design. A List Apart. Eyrolles (2011)

Marcotte, E.: Responsive Web Design: A Book Apart. Eyrolles (2017)

Morville, P., Rosenfeld, L.: Information Architecture for the World Wide Web: Designing Large-Scale Web Sites, 3rd edn. O'Reilly & Associates, Sebastopol (2006)

Partala, T., Kallinen, A.: Understanding the most satisfying and unsatisfying user experiences: emotions, psychological needs, and context. Interact. Comput. **24**(1), 25–34 (2011)

Peterson, C.: Learning Responsive Web Design: A Beginner's Guide. O'Reilly & Associates, Sebastopol (2014)

Roto, V.: User experience from product creation perspective. Towards a UX Manifesto, pp. 31–34 (2007)

Schepers, J., Wetzels, M.: A meta-analysis of the technology acceptance model: investigating subjective norm and moderation effects. Inf. Manag. **44**(1), 90–103 (2007)

Sugiyama, K., Inoue, K.: The Basic for Survey and Analysis by Excel: A Collection of Tools for Planning and Design. Kaibundo publishing, Tokyo (1996)

Taylor, S., Todd, P.A.: Understanding information technology usage: a test of competing models. Inf. Syst. Res. **6**(2), 144–176 (1995)

Venkatesh, V., Morris, M.G., Davis, G.B., Davis, F.D.: User acceptance of information technology: toward a unified view. MIS Q. **27**, 425–478 (2003)

How Do Older Adults View Online Health Webpages? Preliminary Results from Eye Tracking Data

Anushia Inthiran[1](✉) and Robert D. Macredie[2]

[1] Department of Accounting and Information Systems,
University of Canterbury, Christchurch, New Zealand
anushia.inthiran@canterbury.ac.nz
[2] Department of Computer Science, College of Engineering Design
and Physical Sciences, Brunel University London, Uxbridge, UK
robert.macredie@brunel.ac.uk

Abstract. In this paper, we describe how older adults view online health webpages with the use of eye tracking technology. A study was conducted using two pages from the medical encyclopedia section of MedlinePlus and a sample of 52 older adults. This research study provides visual information on how older adults view online health webpages with the use of fixation counts and heatmaps. Preliminary results indicate that older adults focused more on text than on images. Older adults often viewed information on the periphery of the webpages sparingly and did not pay much attention to metadata information pertaining to trustworthiness and credibility. Our results indicate the need to redesign online health webpages to support older adults viewing behavior. There is also a need to examine the use of images on health websites.

Keywords: Eye tracking · Fixation · Health webpage · Older adults
User study

1 Introduction

The results of a Pew survey indicate that older adults show a faster adaptation rate to using the Internet compared to the younger generation [1]. Higher Internet usage among older adults was found to be significant predictors of reduced loneliness, better life satisfaction and psychological well-being [2]. Older adults have embraced Internet applications for various reasons [1]. One common activity conducted by older adults on the Internet is searching for health information [1] in support of their own healthcare [3]. In particular, having more chronic medical conditions and engaging in formal volunteering increased the likelihood of Internet use for health-related tasks amongst older adults [4]. Older adults who used online means to obtain health information were found to be more participative in medical decision making [5].

However, older adults are a diverse demographic group [6] and may have a different perception of what a good webpage should look like in comparison to other demographic groups. The development of webpage guidelines for older adults supports this claim [7], hence making them an important group in relation to Internet-based

© Springer International Publishing AG, part of Springer Nature 2018
J. Zhou and G. Salvendy (Eds.): ITAP 2018, LNCS 10926, pp. 252–260, 2018.
https://doi.org/10.1007/978-3-319-92034-4_19

research. Unfortunately, older adults may experience a less that satisfactory search experience owing to physical and cognitive difficulties [8]. In other cases, older adults may find the process of searching for health information online to be cumbersome owing to interface [9], usability [9] and page design issues [6, 7]. As 'digital immigrants', older adults may lack digital literacy skills and knowledge of how effectively to 'surf the web' [11].

Whilst research studies have paid attention to the searching behavior [1, 3–5], page design and usability needs of older adults when searching on health websites [6–9], there are limited research studies conducted on older adults with the use of eye tracking data. Previous studies conducted by older adults with the use of eye tracking data was related to the viewing and use of a particular type of search interface [12], viewing behavior of images based on web content [12] and how reading patterns of health text messages can be used to predict recall ability [14]. This means that there is yet to be eye tracking data on what older adults look at during their viewing and reading of a single health webpage. Eye tracking data provides an objective source of interface evaluation and enables the understanding of visual presentations [15], so can be useful in the context of users viewing online health information. Information in relation to how older adults view a page is not available. This information is important as it provides evidence relating to aspects of a page that attracted the attention of older adults. Similarly, aspects of a page that did not attract the attention of older adults could mean that pertinent information was not seen or read. Indeed, a research study conducted on older adults with the support of eye tracking data has identified implications for the design of health webpages and associated interface components [16]. Results of another research study identified relationship between web content and image viewing behavior [13]; demonstrating the general value of the approach.

This study, therefore, considers older adults, using fixation counts – essentially data on the frequency with which a user looks at a specific area of the screen – to answer the research question: On which elements of a health webpage do older adults focus? A higher fixation count on an area indicates that it is noticeable or attracted the attention of the user [15]. These fixation counts are then visualized using heatmaps to provide accessible representations of the eye tracking data.

2   Related Work

Previous research studies indicate older adults experience challenges when searching on a health website. Amongst challenges experienced are issues in relation to understanding different components of the webpages and needing assistance in comprehending the function of text boxes [7, 8, 10]. In addition, results of a survey applying The National Institute of Aging Web guidelines on 125 health websites indicate that the sampled websites were not user friendly [16]. Results of these studies indicate that design and usability issues hampered older adult's ability to experience high search efficacy. However, little is known of an equally important aspect of human computer interaction which is the viewing behavior of older adults based on single webpages.

Aesthetics, visual appeal, beauty and utility are criteria's that cannot be ignored when viewing a webpage [17]. This is because these elements form a user's impression of the website. A positive impression meant that the website has met the users' needs [17]. Without a positive impression, a website is rendered pointless regardless of how usable the webpage is [17]. Thus, it is important to pay attention to page viewing behavior.

Results of a previous research study conducted with older adults with the use of eye tracking technology indicate older adults view and use faceted search interface elements more when searching for a severe health condition [12]. It is believed that the use of the faceted interface reduced cognitive load [12]. Results of another research study that compared older adults and younger adults viewing and reading behavior on health webpages indicate older adults spent less time viewing and reading text on health websites in comparison to young adults [13, 14]. On a webpage providing information on cancer, older adults spent more time fixating on illustrations on cognitive websites in comparison to affective websites in comparison to younger adults [13]. Older adults who fixated more on text recalled more information in comparison to young adults [14]. Other research studies comparing young adults and older adults viewing behavior on non-health based websites indicate on the average, older adults spent 42% more time looking at the content of the pages than younger adults. Older adults also spent 51% more time looking at the navigation areas. The pattern of fixations on almost all pages showed that the older adults looked at more parts of the page than did the younger adults [18]. Another research study conducted on non-health websites indicate, older participants had lower accuracy levels and took longer to complete tasks compared to younger participants. Older adults looked at central parts of the screen more frequently than younger participants. Older adults also looked at the peripheral left part of the screen less frequently and took longer to first look at the peripheral top part of the screen in comparison to younger adults [19].

Results of a recent research study describing older adults' viewing patterns for the favorable and unfavorable health webpages [20] indicate when viewing a favorable page, older adults seemed to pay attention to most aspects of the page; however, when viewing an unfavorable page, most sections of the page were not viewed. Specifically, the periphery of the webpage (top left, top right) were not viewed when a page was deemed unfavorable. The next difference observed concerned the manner in which text was read. When reading a favorable health webpage, attention was paid equally to all areas of the text [20]. However, when reading an unfavorable health webpage attention was largely paid to the text at the top of the screen. Surprisingly, whilst the images on favorable webpages were viewed; images on unfavorable webpages was not viewed at all [20]. Whilst previous research studies provide a wealth of information, what remains unknown is how do adults view single webpages? Do older adults pay attention to specific sections on a page and ignore other sections? This research study attempts to describe older adults viewing behavior of single webpages. Results will enable the design of health webpages that appeal to older adults.

3   Experimental Design

An exploratory study was conducted with 52 participants, all aged 55 years or over. There were 31 female and 21 male participants. The average age was 60.5 (SD = 4). All but two of the participants had previously performed an online health search (but none had used MedlinePlus, the site used in this study). This provides us with an opportunity to obtain 'fresh' viewing behavior patterns based on viewing a page for the first time. Participants were either working part-time (22 participants) or full-time (30 participants). Participants who had a medical education or had worked in a medical or an allied healthcare discipline were excluded from participating as their education and/or experience would influence viewing behavior of health webpages.

3.1   Webpage Selection

Webpages from MedlinePlus were selected pertaining to two health issues: high blood pressure (Fig. 1 Webpage 1 (left)[1]) and diabetic nephropathy (Fig. 1 Webpage 2 (right)[2]). These two topics represent common health issues experienced by older adults [21]. The webpages in Fig. 1 were taken from the medical encyclopedia page of the medical domain *MedlinePlus*. Both webpages had similar design underpinnings allowing for focus and analysis. This means both pages used the same font size, font

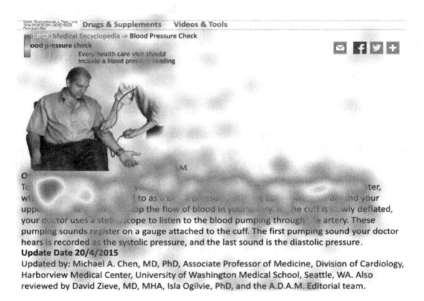

Fig. 1.   Heatmap for Webpage 1

---

[1] Original webpage at https://medlineplus.gov/ency/imagepages/19255.htm.

[2] Original webpage at https://medlineplus.gov/ency/imagepages/19713.htm.

type, color scheme and placement of text and images. The pages were also selected based on the variety of elements available on the page. Both pages had an image, an explanation to accompany the image, a piece of overview text, metadata at the bottom of the page containing information on reliability and update information (as shown in Fig. 1). Thus, the pages provided participants with a variety of interesting elements on which to focus.

3.2   Experimental Procedure and Data Collection

An explanatory statement was provided and participants were asked to sign a consent form. Participants were informed that they would be viewing two health webpages on the Tobii TX300 screen and their eye tracking data would be recorded. Participants were told to view and read the page as normally as possible. It is acknowledged that viewing a health page and searching for health information is usually performed with a specific search goal in mind, but for the purpose of this research study the intention was to obtain fixation points on the webpage or attention focus rather than to fulfill a search goal. Participants were told to view and read the page for a period of 10 s. This period was chosen as it is the average time spent on a webpage before deciding whether to stay on the page or to leave [22]. Calibration was first performed. Participants were then showed the first webpage for a period of 10 s, after which a blank page was automatically shown to participants. This was then followed by the next webpage. The blank page was shown for a total of 5 s to allow participants to 'rest their eyes'. Participants were informed that they had to keep looking at the screen when it was blank and that the next screen would appear soon after. The webpages were presented one at a time and the order was reversed for each participant. Heatmaps generated from a total of 104 recordings of user eye tracking data were taken into the analysis stage (52 participants*2 webpages).

3.3   Data Analysis

Areas of interest (AoIs) were identified for each page. Fixation percentages for each AoI were used for analysis. This is because fixation percentages represent the division of attention between the AoI's shown by users based on their eye movement. These AoIs were selected as they represented different elements of the page that could attract attention (image, text, social media links, metadata). Table 1 provides information on the AoIs.

Table 1. AoI for Table 1

AoI	Name
i.	Links (top left)
ii.	Image
Iii	Accompanying text
iv	Overview text
v	Update information
vi	Social Network (top right)

4   Results

Table 2 provides information on each AoI and its fixation percentages for the sample as a whole. Figure 1 presents these results as heatmaps for each webpage. AoI (v) was viewed the most with a fixation percentage of 93% for Webpage 1 and 70% for Webpage 2. This is followed by AoI (iii) and AoI (ii). AoI (i) and AoI (v) were viewed the least with fixation percentages of 7% and 5%, respectively. AoI (vi) was not viewed at all. Based on fixation percentages, participants paid attention to similar elements on each webpage, but there were some differences in the fixation percentages between the two webpages. For example, the image on webpage 2 was viewed more than the image in webpage 1. Similarly, the overview text in webpage 1 was viewed more than webpage 2. This indicates differences in viewing behavior (Fig. 2).

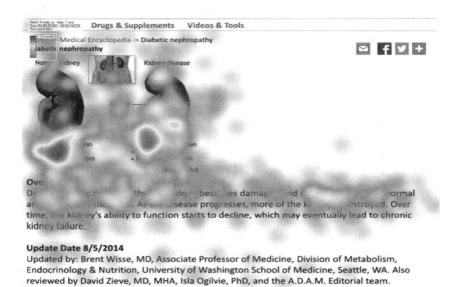

Fig. 2.   Heatmap for Webpage 2

5   Discussion

This section begins by discussing viewing behavior based on the fixation percentages, then seeks to provide an explanation of the differences in viewing behavior between the webpages. It appears that older adults prefer viewing text to images. As shown in Table 2, older adults fixated more on the overview text and accompanying text. However, a difference exists in the way that participants fixated on AoI (iii) and (iv). Participants fixated more on AoI (iv) for webpage 1 but more on AoI (iii) for webpage 2. This may be because the accompanying text (AoI (iii)) for webpage 2 contained information on a diseased and healthy kidney, whereas, the overview text for webpage

1 was more general in relation to the condition. We postulate that the strength and detail of the accompanying text on AoI (iii) (webpage 1) to the health topic was weak and this may have caused this text fixation difference. However, this interpretation requires further investigation. Reading patterns in Fig. 1 for AoI (iv) indicate that older adults do not demonstrate the F-pattern in relation to text reading [23]. Older adults seem to demonstrate a horizontal reading pattern for the first two lines of the overview text. In addition, the reading pattern for Webpage 1 indicates that more attention was paid to the initial parts of the first two sentences of the overview text (indicated by red fixation points) and a little more towards the end of the text on the first line. For Webpage 2, parts of the overview text were viewed almost equally. This may indicate that sections of the overview text contained keywords that attracted the attention of older adults for Webpage 1. Another explanation for this could be attributed to the details of the text. Information about high blood pressure (webpage 1) would be perceived as generally known by participants as opposed to diabetic nephropathy (webpage 2). Thus, for webpage 1 the reading pattern was focused on to the initial parts of the first two sentences whereas in webpage 2, the reading pattern was even throughout the text.

Table 2. Fixation percentages for Webpages 1 and 2.

AoI	Fixation percentage for Webpage 1	Fixation percentage for Webpage 2
i.	7	7
ii.	10	45
iii.	30	50
iv	93	70
v	5	5
vi	0	0

AoI (v) received the fewest views for each webpage. AoI (v) is an important element on each page as it provides metadata information on the author, reviewer and information update. These pieces of metadata information are pertinent when it comes to health information as it provides information to the reader on accuracy and correctness and the ability to trust information. Older adults only viewed this element of the webpage sparingly. We postulate that older adults may not be able to appreciate the importance of metadata information hence only viewed AoI (v) sparingly. Appreciation for metadata information would require higher levels of literacy or the ability to evaluate health information.

We note information on the peripherals of the webpage - AoI (i) was viewed sparingly whilst AoI (vi) was not viewed at all. This viewing behavior was demonstrated for both webpages. This aspect requires further investigation. However, a previous research study indicates that older adults may have trouble discriminating specific colour combinations (blue, green) and juxtapositions [24]. This could be a reason as to why AoI (vi) was not viewed.

There was also a difference in viewing behavior of the image in webpage 1 and 2. Older adults viewed the image in webpage 2 more than webpage 1. A previous research study indicates older adults spent more time fixating on illustrations on cognitive websites in comparison to illustrations on affective websites [12]. We note that the overview text content - AoI (iv) in webpage 1 narrates the process of taking blood pressure which fits the definition of an affective webpage (aimed to invoke a positive feeling) whereas the overview text content in webpage 2 is an example of a cognitive webpage (aimed to compliment text and support understanding) as information on kidney functions deteriorating is explained. Results in Table 2 indicate participants fixated more on the image on webpage 2 in comparison to webpage 1. Our results show similar findings with a previous research study [13].

This research study provides preliminary insights into the elements on which older adults fixate when viewing a health webpage. The results indicate that older adults viewed the two webpages similarly, but there were differences in the way that some equivalent elements were viewed for the different pages. The results raise interesting questions regarding older adults' attention to text, their seeming tendency to pay less attention to information on the periphery of webpages, the use of images on health webpages, and why metadata information was viewed minimally.

This research study has several limitations. We acknowledge that the sample size was small and only 2 webpages were used. As such, results cannot be generalized. In the next phase of the research, we intend to ask participants to explain their viewing behavior in order to provide rich information to contextualize the viewing behavior and to explore the subtle differences that were identified in this initial work. We also intend to run a second phase of the study with a larger number of webpages of similar design and with more participants with the aim of generating robust data, the analysis of which will inform design guidelines for health webpages aimed at older adults.

Acknowledgements. The authors thank participants for their participation.

References

1. Kernel, A.: A Hot Trend: The Internet, Social Media & The Elderly, The Huffington Post (2016). http://www.huffingtonpost.com/anita-kamiel-rn-mps/older-people-social-media_b_9191178.html. Accessed 10 Jun 2017
2. Heo, J., Chun, S., Lee, S., Lee, K.H., Kim, J.: Internet use of wellbeing of older adults. Cyberpsychol Behav. Soc. Netw. **18**(5), 268–272 (2015)
3. Medlock, S., Salami, S., Askar, M., Arts, D.L., Sent, D., Roil, S.D.E., Abu-Hanna, A.: Health information-seeking behavior of seniors who use the internet: a survey. J. Med. Int. Res. **17**(1), e10 (2015)
4. Flynn, K.E., Smith, M.A., Freese, J.: When Do Older Adults Turn to the Internet for Health Information? (2006)
5. Hall, A.K., Bernhardt, J.M., Dodd, V.: The digital health divide evaluating online health information access and use among older adults. Health Educ. Behav. **42**(2), 202–209 (2015)
6. Choi, N.G., DiNitto, D.: Internet use among older adults: association with health needs, psychological capital, and social capital. J. Med. Int. Res. **15**(5), e97 (2013). https://doi.org/10.2196/jmir.2333

7. Watkins, I., Xin, B.: eHealth literacy interventions for older adults: a systematic review of the literature. **16**(11) (2014). https://www.jmir.org/2014/11/e225/

8. Future of an ageing population: evidence review, Foresight, Government Office for Science (2016). http://www.ageing.ox.ac.uk/files/Future_of_Ageing_Report.pdf

9. Aula, A., Kaki, M.: Less is more in web search interface for older adults. First Monday, **10** (7) (2005)

10. Kules, B., Xin, B.: Older adults searching for health information on MedlinePlus – an exploratory study on faced online search interface (2011). https://doi.org/10.1002/meet.2011

11. McMillian, S., Macias, W.: Strengthening the safety net for online seniors: factors influencing differences in health information seeking among older. J. Health Commun. **3**(8), 778–792 (2008)

12. Kules, B., Xie, B.: Older adults searching for health information in MedlinePlus – an exploratory study of faceted online search interfaces. Proc. Assoc. Inf. Sci. Technol. **48**(1), 1–10 (2011)

13. Bol, N., Bergstrom, J.C.R., Smets, E.M.A., Loos, E.F., Strohl, J., van Weert, J.C.M.: Does web design matter? examining older adults' attention to cognitive and affective illustrations on cancer-related websites through eye tracking. In: Stephanidis, C., Antona, M. (eds.) UAHCI 2014. LNCS, vol. 8515, pp. 15–23. Springer, Cham (2014). https://doi.org/10.1007/978-3-319-07446-7_2

14. Bol, N., Bergstrom, J.C.R., Smets, E.M.A., Lools, E.F., Strohl, J., van Weert, J.C.M.: How are online health messages processed? using eye tacking to predict recall of information in Younger and Older Adults. J. Health Comm. **21**(4), 387–396 (2016)

15. Poole, A., Lindell, J.B.: Eye tracking in HCI and usability research. Encycl. Hum. Comput. Interact. (2006). https://doi.org/10.4018/978-1-59140-562-7.ch034

16. Making Your Website Senior Friendly, A Checklist, National Institute on Aging and the National Library of Medicine. https://www.nlm.nih.gov/pubs/checklist.pdf

17. Faraday, P.: Visually Critiquing Websites, 6th Conference on Human Factors on the Web (2000). http://facweb.cs.depaul.edu/cmiller/faraday/Faraday.htm

18. Tullis, T.S.: Older Adults' and the Web: lessons from eye tracking. In: International Conference on Universal Access in Human-Computer Interaction, pp. 1030–1039 (2007)

19. Romano Bergstrom, J.C., Olmsted-Hawala, E.L., Jans, M.E.: Age-related differences in eye tracking and usability performance: website usability for older Adults. Int. J. Hum.-Comput. Interact. **29**(8), 541–548 (2013)

20. Inthiran, A., Macredie, R.D.: Older Adults' perception of online health Webpages using eye tracking technology. In: Rocha, Á., Guarda, T. (eds.) Proceedings of the International Conference on Information Technology and Systems (ICITS 2018). ICITS 2018. Advances in Intelligent Systems and Computing, vol. 721, pp. 531–537. Springer, Cham (2018). https://doi.org/10.1007/978-3-319-73450-7_50

21. Vann, M.R.: The 15 Most Common Health Problems for Seniors, Everyday Health (2016). http://www.everydayhealth.com/news/most-common-health-concerns-seniors/

22. Nielsen, J.: How Long Do Users Stay on Webpages (2011). https://www.nngroup.com/articles/how-long-do-users-stay-on-web-pages/

23. Shrestha, S., Owens, J.W.: Eye Movement Analysis of Text-Based Web Page Layouts (2009). http://usabilitynews.org/eye-movement-analysis-of-text-based-web-page-layouts

24. Sanner, B.M. (d.u.) Creating Age Friendly Websites. http://www.changingthewayweage.com/Media-and-Marketers-support/Articles/creatingage-friendlywebsites.pdf

Confronting Common Assumptions About the Psychomotor Abilities of Older Adults Interacting with Touchscreens

Suhas Govind Joshi[✉]

Department of Informatics, University of Oslo, Oslo, Norway
joshi@ifi.uio.no

Abstract. This paper confronts commonly-made assumptions about older adults and their general levels of capability when interacting with technology by reporting from an evaluation involving 49 older adults ($M = 81$ years) where performance was studied during task solving on a touch-based interface. The tasks involved were derived from a set of corresponding psychomotor abilities that are commonly involved in interaction mechanisms associated with touchscreen devices: precision, steadiness, dexterity, speed, and coordination. The evaluation consisted of measuring the performance of participants as well as having them assessing their own performance. To provide empirical results on why it is argued that it can be dangerous to assume anything about the capabilities of older adults, multiple analyses of the gathered data were used to highlight individual, group-related, and general patterns. Important relations, levels of variance, and statistically significant effects are highlighted as the paper argues for how these particular results do not align with common assumptions. The discussion draws on both the empirical results as well as related research to advocate why designers should acknowledge individual capabilities to ensure maximized performance when designing enabling technology for older adults.

Keywords: Older adults · Touchscreens · Psychomotor abilities · Performance
Enabling technology

1 Introduction

As the body grows older, the psychomotor abilities usually involved in interaction with enabling technology [1, 2], such as dexterity and steadiness, often tend to deteriorate [3]. The impact of age on the ability to execute precise and coordinated movements can manifest itself in different ways, e.g., inaccuracy or nonlinearity. This has been particularly evident in studies on tracking using a computer mouse, e.g., in [4]. However, a wide range of enabling technologies for older adults relies on interaction mechanisms that assume specific psychomotor skills in the hands and fingers of the users. This has been particularly prevalent in the many new digital and non-digital equipment found in care facilities in Norway [1].

This paper aims to challenge common assumption made about the capabilities of older adults. More specifically, five distinct psychomotor abilities commonly used in

© Springer International Publishing AG, part of Springer Nature 2018
J. Zhou and G. Salvendy (Eds.): ITAP 2018, LNCS 10926, pp. 261–278, 2018.
https://doi.org/10.1007/978-3-319-92034-4_20

interaction mechanisms associated with touchscreens, e.g., during swiping or pinching, have been evaluated with 49 older adults ($M = 81$ years) and 20 younger adults in a control group. Our goal is not to compare older adults to younger generations, but rather to produce empirical evidence that supports our argument of why "solutionist" strategies [5] that consider all older adults as equal does not utilize the full capabilities of the user and does not realize the full potential to facilitate enabling interaction. As such, we report from an evaluation of self-assessment and measured performance during task solving of five tasks derived from a set of five corresponding psychomotor abilities, namely precision, steadiness, dexterity, speed, and coordination.

The results and analyses suggest that there is a high degree of variation in the capabilities and premises for interaction between the participants and that while older adults might not perform at the level of younger users, they still inhabit the potential to perform at near-perfect levels if provided with the appropriate interaction mechanisms. Multiple analyses studying statistically significant main effects are used to discuss the implications of observed variations. We also argue that the presented results demonstrating individual, group-related, and overall variance can challenge prevailing assumptions about older adults and their capabilities when interacting with touchscreens.

The findings presented in this paper are part of a broader research effort focusing on understanding more about older adults' capabilities when interacting with enabling technology [1]. While this paper concentrates on touchscreens, we bring in prior experience related to older adults and the use of psychomotor abilities to assess capabilities (from, e.g., [6]).

2   Related Work

This paper draws on past research from mainly HCI-related research communities as the focus is to report from an evaluation of common assumption made about older adults, their capability levels, and their readiness towards touch-based interfaces in particular. As such, most of the literature presented in this section addresses relevant topics found in the intersection between older adults and interaction with touchscreen devices. We also refer to results from our overarching research efforts to contextualize the presented results.

2.1   Studies on Psychomotor Abilities of Older Adults Using Touchscreens

Wood et al. [7] study the pattern of performance across interfaces for older adults. Their findings suggest that touchscreens may be challenging or inappropriate for activities requiring continuous contact when considering physical strain. The use of psychomotor abilities during assessment touches upon highly relevant issues, e.g., the study of the finger and motor dexterity during task-based evaluation. One of the input devices studied in [8] was touchscreens with finger input and their results on usage frequency provides a perspective on the breadth and depth of said technology. Caprani et al. [9] discuss several types of challenges such as psychomotor and physical challenges due to arthritis or stroke. Their research points to several challenges with touchscreen devices, e.g., difficulties with tasks requiring precision, speed, or positioning. The paper also raised interesting points on strategies and considerations for designing for disability, e.g., the challenge of adequately assessing and recruiting representative users. Rogers et al. [10] report from two experiments involving among others older adults performing tasks on both a touchscreen and a physical rotary encoder. There are interesting observations, statistically significant main effects, and experienced challenges reported in their paper. They also indicate that there was a deviation between expected patterns of performance and actual measured performance. In a related study, Pak et al. [11] also discuss the usability of touchscreens as an input device in the context of older and younger adults, and they also report results on performance. Other research inquiries have also studied the fit of the touchscreen in the context of older adults and smart homes, e.g., [12]. They raise pressing concerns such as how psychomotor challenges like tremor may affect both performance and perception of touch-based interfaces. The use of tablets to discuss touch-based interaction was also the case of [13] where senior citizens were guided through a series of tasks during an evaluation of performance on an iPad. Doyle et al. [14] present results from a long-term usability assessment of a touch-based communication device and the participants' attitude towards technology.

In [15], the author discusses direct, gestural input via multimodal touchscreen devices for older adults. In the proposed research outlining relevant lines of inquiry, several of the objectives are of relevance to this paper, for instance, ambidexterity issues when interacting with touchscreens or adaptations necessary due to motoric challenges such as arthritis or Parkinson's disease. Also in [16] do we see a study on benefits of multimodal interfaces tailored for older adults. Also [17] reports on the suitability of touch-based interfaces for older adults in the context of everyday life activities. Their results are anchored in user experiences of the users as they highlight the perceived experience of use. While their focus is not particular scoped to psychomotor abilities and related challenges, they do emphasize that physical changes, for instance, impaired motor skills, can make the use of certain types of technologies difficult. The authors of [18] present a study on tremor patients and their interaction challenges and opportunities with screen-based interfaces. Their target demographic includes older adults as tremor is considered a prominent trait associated with aging. They also emphasize the importance of acknowledging psychomotor abilities, in this case, fine motor skills, when assessing interaction opportunities. Specific examples such as frictional resistance are provided to highlight the relationship between abilities and appropriateness of different types of interfaces.

Other relevant studies include design recommendations suggest for touchscreens in the context of older adults [19]. Their emphasis on psychomotor abilities, for instance, manual dexterity, is highly relevant to the evaluation carried out in our study. They also conclude by stating that even design guidelines need to adapt design choices (e.g., the size and spacing of interface elements) to the abilities of the target demographic. Another study pointing out the lack of understanding of older adults and attempting to offer informal guidelines for the design of senior-friendly interfaces is [20]. Their main hypotheses answer interesting questions such as older adults' easiness of use when operating touchscreens and challenges with gestures such as pinching. Interaction mechanisms associated with touch-based technology, e.g., tapping, dragging, and pinching, are discussed in the paper and follows the same understanding as we adopted when designing the tasks for our evaluation. Page [21] also describes experiences with specific tasks such as navigation in the context of touchscreen and senior users. Another similar study on touchscreens and optimal reference levels is [22]. Chen et al. [23] also study interface accessibility and usability for older users with different backgrounds, including a range of physical challenges. A literature review found in [24] on older adults using touchscreen also contains relevant findings and recommendations on motor impairment and touchscreen interaction, e.g., arthritis. They highlight task types used during trials and experiments, typical interaction gestures, and data collection strategies.

3   Research Method

3.1   Empirical Context

This study reports from an evaluation of performance that was conducted at a local care facility in Oslo, Norway. More precisely, the evaluation consisted of a self-assessment and measured performance as older adults and a control group solved five specific tasks derived from a set of five corresponding psychomotor abilities. The evaluation initially consisted of four groups of 20 persons each. One of the four groups constituted the control group while the three others were experimental groups with representative users from the target demographic. The control group was used to indicate a comparable level of expected performance from a fully functional user for later analyses. The group consisted of faculty, Ph.D. candidates, and master students within the field of Interaction Design or Human-Computer Interaction. We conducted no pre-evaluation assessment of physical condition or psychomotor challenges, and the older adults were only spread across the three experimental groups based on gender to counteract any heavily skewed distributions of participants as the participant pool included 30 women and 19 men. The average age of the participating older adults was 81 years. However, several participants from the three experimental group were ultimately unable to attend due to health concerns or other commitments leaving the total number of participants at 69 out of which 49 were representative users. The final number of participants in each group is outlined in Table 1 below. While the sample size of older adults in this study is limited ($N = 49$), all participants were recruited from a more extensive study on enabling technology for older adults involving 542 participants ($M = 83$ years) [1]. The results presented in this paper align with previously discovered limitations and opportunities among this demographic, for instance, the prior findings on psychomotor abilities discussed in [6].

Table 1. Overview of groups, number of participants, and distribution of age

Group	Participants	Age distribution
Experimental group 1	16	72–83 ($M = 77.9, SD = 3.44$)
Experimental group 2	18	71–87 ($M = 79.2, SD = 4.38$)
Experimental group 3	15	78–89 ($M = 83.6, SD = 3.20$)
Control group	20	24–44 ($M = 32.7, SD = 6.07$)

3.2 Selection of Psychomotor Abilities and Tasks

The evaluation comprised five assessments of psychomotor abilities in hands and fingers: precision, steadiness, dexterity, speed, and coordination. These five abilities used to structure the evaluation were all borrowed from Fleishman's taxonomy of psychomotor abilities and skills [25, 26]. *Precision* refers to the ability to move and quickly repeat exact positions and tasks; *steadiness* refers to the ability to suspend the hand in air while moving; *dexterity* refers to finger dexterity (as opposed to manual dexterity) and the ability to make skillful movements with the fingers; *speed* refers to wrist-finger speed and the ability to quickly repeat movements; and *coordination* refers to the ability to coordinate movements when the body is not in motion. All these descriptions are based on the original taxonomy of Fleishman [25].

These five particular abilities were selected due to two main reasons: firstly, they allowed us to map common interaction mechanisms associated with touch-screen devices (e.g., drag-and-drop and swiping) back to one distinctive psychomotor ability; and secondly, they had all been previously used as a part of a similar study involving evaluation of psychomotor abilities [6]. We do not claim these five abilities to provide a holistic or definitive representation of psychomotor capability of older adults. However, we argue that these five factors in conjunction can indicate patterns of limitations and support a discussion of common assumptions about older adults interacting with technology. This particular study focuses on screen-based technology, but our past research efforts have concentrated mainly on tangible interaction and physical devices (see, e.g., [1]). Thus, the intention of expanding explored and evaluated technology is to further complement our general understanding of what we can expect from older adults' capabilities regarding readiness towards enabling technology.

During the evaluations, each participant performed a set of five simple tasks involving independent and coordinated movements and gestures that were calculated to a performance score ranging between 1 and 10. Each task mapped back to one of the five psychomotor abilities. The task order was also randomized to avoid learning effects, and each task relied on specific metrics to assess the performance of the participant. Table 2 gives an overview of the involved tasks, a brief description, and related evaluation metrics. The rightmost column indicates the level of performance required to achieve a perfect score of 10. The level of this upper bound was intended to represent the expected performance of a fully functional user and was calculated using the weighted average performance score of the 10 participants in a pilot evaluation. The goal of this pilot evaluation was to run through the test procedure as well as to help us normalize the difficulty of the tasks and determine the upper bounds. These 10 participants were recruited through similar means as the control group and consisted mostly of faculty, Ph.D. students, and master students. As such, the automatic calculation of performance required us to first evaluate the tasks with the pilot group without any upper bound. All performance scores for the participants in the pilot group were mapped post-evaluation once their weighted average scores were calculated. Their results are not included in this paper, but a paired sample t-test did not reveal any statistically significant difference from the performance of the control group.

Table 2. Overview and description of tasks, metrics, and upper bounds

Task/ability	Task description	Evaluation metric	Upper bound
Navigation and selection *(precision)*	Select a specific option from a set of selective menus such as drop-down bars without making wrong selections	Completion time in seconds and number of errors traced with mouse/touch events	Completion time of fewer than 10 s and maximum two errors
Reproducing hand positions *(steadiness)*	Reproduce a set of hand positions and swiping movements in front of the screen with minimal trembling	Tremble factor (0–1) decided by shaking and rapid movements traced using Leap Motion	Tremble factor of less than 0.85
Mimicking finger movements *(dexterity)*	Reproduce a set of three finger movements mimicking movements associated with pinch and zoom gestures as exact as possible	Mimic factor (0–1) decided by reproduction precision traced with Leap Motion	Mimic factor of 0.85 or above across all three finger gestures
Reaction *(speed)*	Click on the correct option among randomly appearing icons and dialogue windows as fast as possible	Reaction time in seconds and number of errors traced with mouse/touch events	Reaction time of fewer than 5 s on average and maximum one error
Drag-and-drop *(coordination)*	Drag a specific icon into a designated area without colliding with adjacent objects	Placement accuracy in relation to origin measured with percentage-wise deviation and dragging accuracy measured with number of errors	90% accuracy and maximum one collision error

In addition to the automatically calculated score based on performance, each participant was also asked post-completion to assess their own performance on a scale from 1 to 10. The intention with this self-assessment was to study the relationship between the self-perception of the users' performance and their actual performance, hence using a similar scale as the automatic calculation of performance score for a more natural comparison. The rest of the paper will refer to these two measurements as the *self-assessment score* and the *measured performance score*, respectively.

3.3   Testing Devices

The web-based system permitted assessment of performance independent of device or operating system, which in turn allowed us to offer all participants a selection of three compatible devices: a 9.7-in. 3rd generation iPad running iOS; a 10-in. Samsung tablet running Android; an 11-in. custom tablet running Windows. The custom tablet was pre-installed in the homes of most participants at a local care facility as part of the municipality's welfare technology initiatives and was used to offer residents social and recreational services. These three tablets helped us further reduce the statistical significance of any learning bias, familiarity challenges, or issues understanding the basic modes of operation. Figure 1 presents a screenshot from the web interface used during the evaluation on the left, and a photo from the empirical context where the evaluations were performed on the right (photo by C. Haug and F. H. Kvam).

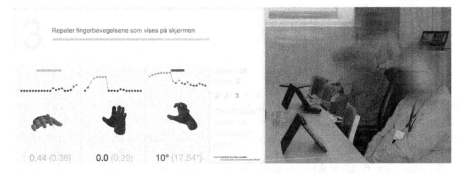

Fig. 1.   Screenshot of the web interface on the left and the empirical context on the right

4   Results

The purpose of the evaluation was first to identify a general level of expectancy of both self-perception and actual performance for older adults using psychomotor abilities as the unit of measurement and then later study group-related and individual variances. Thus, the results are reported in chronological order following the same sequence in which the various analyses were carried out.

4.1   Analyzing Average Scores for Self-assessment and Measured Performance

The first set of results we present is the examination of score distribution for each of the two sets of scores independently. This is intended as a general, descriptive depiction of the average trends between the control group and the three experimental groups. As the values indicated a difference between the control group and the experimental group, the descriptive statistics reported in this paper will mainly focus on separate analyses. Table 3 below presents two independent sets of univariate analyses of self-assessment and measured-performance, respectively. It should also be noted that while each of the three experimental groups was spread across the whole scale from 1 to 10, either in self-assessment, measured performance or in both, the control group had a minimum value of 4 and a maximum value of 10 for both types of measurement. A z-test for mean scores of self-assessment confirmed a statistically significant difference ($z = -11.103, p < .001$, two-tailed) when comparing all samples from the experimental group ($M = 5.420$, $SD = 2.319$) to the control group ($M = 7.880, SD = 1.647$). A similar comparison of measured performance ($M = 5.408, SD = 2.337; M = 8.010, SD = 1.521$) yielded a similar difference ($z = -12.207, p < .001$, two-tailed).

Table 3. Overview of groups and the descriptive statistics for the two sets of scores per group.

Group	Measurement	Mean	N	Std. Dev.	Std. Err. Mean
Experimental	Self-assessment	5.42	245	2.319	.148
	Measured performance	5.41	245	2.337	.149
Control	Self-assessment	7.88	100	1.647	.165
	Measured performance	8.01	100	1.521	.152

A factorial analysis of variance was performed *(group x ability)* for self-assessment and measured performance scores. Figures 2 and 3 present the estimated marginal means for these two sets of scores. Beginning with the self-assessment, the results revealed multiple main effects worth presenting. First, there was a statistically significant main effect for the groups, $F(3, 325) = 31.994, p < .001$. This suggests that the null hypothesis does not hold. Second, there was also a statistically significant main effect for the type of test, i.e., which ability that was tested, $F(4, 325) = 5.876, p < .001$. For the measured performance, the patterns were similar. There were statistically significant main effects for both groups and type of test: $F(3, 325) = 39.352, p < .001$ for groups and $F(4, 325) = 12.152, p < .001$ for the ability being tested.

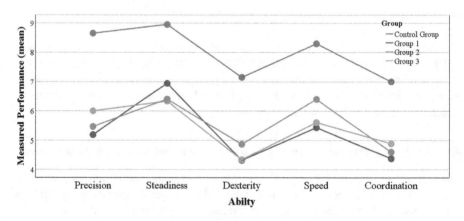

Fig. 2. Estimated marginal means for measured performance

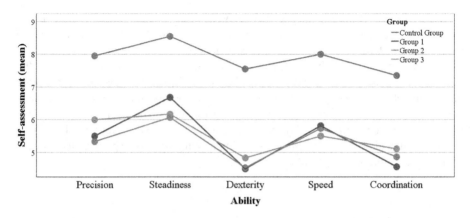

Fig. 3. Estimated marginal means for self-assessment

As reported previously with the z-test scores, the control group held a higher average score for both self-assessment and measured performance. While the control group in total only constituted 29% of the total participants, due to withdrawals amongst the older adults, they ended up as the largest group with 20 participants. Thus, when pairing each of the four groups, the better average score in the control group for both self-assessment and measured performance results in main effects for the group. If we isolate the three experimental groups, there is no longer a statistically significant main effect for groups for neither self-assessment nor measured performance. Levene's test for equality of variances was found to be violated for both sets of analysis, with $p < .05$ for self-assessment, and $p < .01$ for measured performance. A post hoc analysis using Bonferroni confirmed two essential factors. First, the control group statistically significant difference in both sets of scores against all the experimental groups. Second, none of the experimental groups showed any statistically significant difference against each other in the post hoc analysis.

To remain in line with the outlined topic of this paper, i.e., common assumptions about older adults and their psychomotor abilities, the rest of this result section will focus on comparing the control group against the whole experiment group as one. It will also look at the participants' individual scores when analyzing the effects of the abilities on performance.

4.2 Observing Gaps in Perception and Performance

The second set of results present inferential statistics on the relationship between the two score sets. Figure 4 shows a scatterplot of the relationship between the self-assessment made by the participants and the corresponding mean levels of measured-performance. The increased color intensity suggests a higher frequency. A test for Pearson Correlation confirmed a strong relationship between the two sets of scores ($r = .829$), indicating that an increased self-assessment would most likely also result in actually increased performance. For both groups, we saw a positive covariance (4.298 for the experimental group and 1.712 for the control group). While we do not find best-fit regression lines particularly relevant to our overarching research interest, the r^2-levels were also calculated: $r^2 = .482$ for the control group and $r^2 = .634$. One immediate conjecture about why we can account for a higher level of variability in the case of the experimental group would be that the overall sample size was more substantial and the spread of data points was more distributed. However, further analysis revealed another interesting relation: the experimental group saw a smaller gap on average between self-assessment and actual performance, i.e., they had a smaller distance on average between the self-assessment and the actual performance for each task performed. Thus, it is possible to speculate whether a more realistic understanding of own performance caused some of the differences in r^2-values.

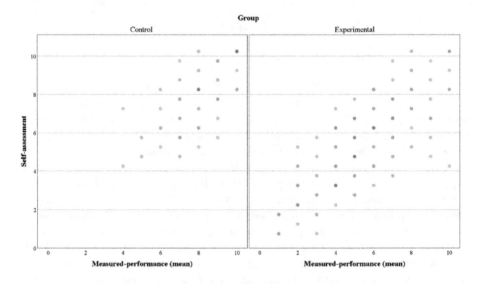

Fig. 4. The plotted relationship between self-assessment and measured performance

To investigate this further, the average difference between self-assessment and measured performance was calculated for each task for each participant. For the experimental group, the average difference between these two values was $M = 0.012$ ($SD = 1.486$), while it was $M = -0.130$ ($SD = 1.244$) for the control group. This result suggests that the older adults in the three experimental groups were marginally better at assessing their actual performance than the control group, albeit with the caveat of a smaller sample size for the control group. When only accounting for the largest discrepancy for each participant across all five tasks, the difference between the groups increased as the new mean values were $M = 0.100$ ($SD = 2.160$) and $M = -0.796$ ($SD = 2.150$), respectively. Only on a few occasions did the older adults overestimate their own performance (i.e., a positive difference between self-assessment and actual performance) while the over-estimation frequency was comparatively more common within the control group. Thus, we attempted to understand the causality of this difference by examining the particular intersections of groups and abilities tied to each task. When looking closer at the tendencies across both groups and abilities, there was not enough data to conclude with any directional difference between self-assessment and measured performance. This means that while the overall tendency suggests that the older adults may be better at not over-estimating their actual performance, there are no guarantees when examining a particular ability. This is illustrated in Fig. 5, where the interpolation line suggests a correct esti-mation, or an over- or underestimation.

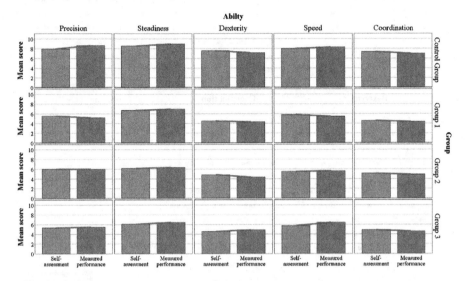

Fig. 5. The mean scores for self-assessment and measured performance *(ability x group)*

We see from the figure that for the control group, the self-assessment was only higher than the actual performance on two occasions, during the test of coordination and dexterity. As we have seen previously, these exact two tasks yielded a noticeable lower average score across all group. Only in one of eight rounds of testing did a group on average not overes-timate their own performance for these two tasks (*dexterity x group 3*). We also see how all groups, including the control group, overestimated their performance for coordination, despite this not being neither particularly tricky nor straightforward if measured by mean score and standard deviation. As such, the data does not suggest any relationship between over- or underestimation on the one hand, and the difficulty level of the task on the other.

4.3   Investigating the Role of Psychomotor Abilities on Measured Performance

While we discovered early that the older adults were unable to maintain measured performance score at the average level of the control group, we continued our study by examining the performance scores across the five tests to assess their significance. Figure 6 illustrates both self-assessment and measured-performance scores for the five types of abilities tested.

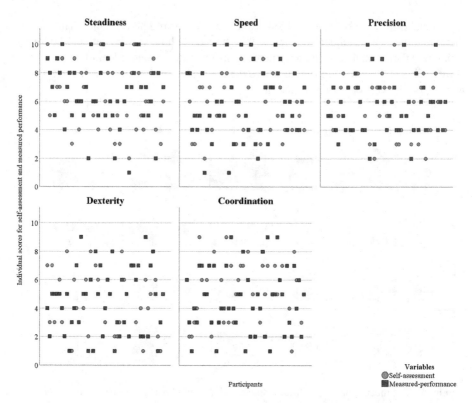

Fig. 6. All individual levels of self-assessment and measured performance across all abilities

An analysis of variance *(participants x ability type being tested)* showed a statistically significant main effect for the types of ability being tested, $F(4, 240) = 7.235$, $p < .01$. A Bonferroni post hoc analysis indicated that the two tasks testing dexterity ($M = 4.490$, $SD = 2.283$) and coordination ($M = 4.633$, $SD = 2.243$) yielded a clearly lower measured performance score than the rest. When compared against the highest-yielding task, steadiness ($M = 6.551$, $SD = 2.227$), the main effect was statistically significant at a .01 level. The rest of the comparisons were non-significant even at a .05 level.

If we zoom in on the results pertaining to one of the abilities, we can identify additional patterns that are relevant to the overarching topic of this paper. For instance, the ability coordination yielded a lower score than the average for both self-assessment and measured performance. However, this deviation was not due to consistent patterns of a lower level of performance. If we study the individual assessment and performance, we can see from a frequency table (as well as from Fig. 6) that there were multiple occurrences of extreme results in both directions – for both self-assessment and measured performance. Four individuals only scored 1 point, and there were also individuals who scored 9 points. As such, it is hard to comment on the expected performance without zooming into the specific ability required to complete a task and the particular individual doing it. Along with dexterity, coordination was also the only task with a statistically significant main effect of ability being tested when isolating the control group. Thus, these tasks can be considered relatively more challenging.

We do not have the appropriate data to analyze whether it was the ability being tested or the difficulty level of the task itself that caused this consistent pattern, but what we do have sufficient data to comment on is the extremities. Even for tasks that were both perceived and measured as relatively more laborious tasks, e.g., coordination, the experimental groups still saw participants both assessing and performing at near perfect levels (with a score of 9). For relative straightforward tasks such as steadiness, there were still low-performance scores registered (e.g., four instances of a score 2 or lower for measured performance). Thus, the data does demonstrate the challenge of assuming abilities of older adults in either direction. A final analysis of participants' performance pattern across these five tasks (that were presented in randomized order) did not reveal any statistically significant patterns of performance that would indicate causality between task order and performance.

5   Discussion

5.1   Searching for Causality by Unpacking Individual Performance Scores

From the first set of results (Figs. 1 and 2), we see that it is easy to conclude that older adults perform at a relatively lower average level and that downgrading any and all expectations regarding capabilities may seem like a viable strategy. Responding to the challenge of designing enabling technology by assuming a reduced capacity across cognitive, sensory, and motor capabilities for the whole demographic of older adults can be one approach [27]. Our goal is instead to remain positive and look for patterns that may suggest new lines of inquiry not building on disabilities but rather capabilities [1, 6].

The control group performed better than the older adults on average with higher minimum values for both self-assessment and measured performance. However, the control group represented a younger and more technology-oriented user group, and the comparison was not intended as a generational analysis (as seen in, e.g., [8, 10, 11]), but rather to have participants representing fully functional users for later comparison. This was important to study if older adults managed to perform well at specific tasks, but also to investigate how close they could potentially get to an optimal level of performance if presented with the right interaction opportunities.

Once we unpacked the individual performances in the last analysis (Fig. 6), we saw how participants were able to perform at the level of the control group if presented with the right type of interaction mechanism. There are empirical studies suggesting that touchscreens can yield positive experiences (e.g., [13]), but we argue that the correct order is to adapt the technology to the capabilities of the user rather than assuming anything about the users' expected performance. There are enough studies pointing to the effects motor impairment can have on interaction opportunities (e.g., [7–9, 18, 19]), and we have previously argued that this change in capability should be seen as an opportunity to shift the way the technology is presented rather than just summarizing it as a decline [1]. This study has demonstrated how performance varies with interaction mechanisms rather than with the touchscreen as an interface itself. Hence, we argue that there are many opportunities to remain on the same interface at a proficient level if the technology allows the users to adjust their interaction to their changing capabilities. Adaptation of technology has also been extensively discussed in prior studies, e.g., in [20, 24, 27].

5.2 Isolating Psychomotor Abilities

We want to stress that the results presented are not intended for the medical technology community, nor did the evaluation follow the same level of clinical practice for testing [28]. If compared to past studies, the average age of the older adults in this study stands out. However, our study is not without weaknesses regarding the strength of the results. One factor ignored was time, learning, and adaptation [14]. The study in [10] collected more detailed data points than most of our study did. For instance, we only had the same level of precision for time *(ms)* in the two tests using tracking with Leap Motion (steadiness and dexterity). Another important factor not addressed in this paper is how cognitive deficiencies may influence performance. Past studies have emphasized the role of cognitive deficiency in terms of reduced ability to interact with touchscreen [7, 9, 10, 12, 21, 24, 29]. All our tasks were also created to solely address psychomotor-related challenges. To minimize the chance of any severe cognitive issues, all tasks were intended to be single-purpose, short, and simplistic. However, we do emphasize that this study does not attempt to study effects of cognitive challenges as discussed by [10], who, for instance, considered working memory when designing instructions for activities.

The selection of tasks was revised several times and later polished during the pilot evaluation, but the means of measure may have been influential in terms of observed results. The point of a high degree of variance performance, e.g., captured through movement time, among older adults was also made by [10]. It should be noted that the post hoc analysis did not reveal any statistically significant difference between the three experimental groups, which does suggest that it is most likely the overall sampling rather than the distribution of participants into groups that should account for most of the observed variance.

Furthermore, our goal was also to allow everyone to join without any screening test (as seen in, e.g., [10]). Nor did we try to control variables like age differences, technological experience, or specific disability that could reduce the variance as proposed by [16, 20], or as we have done ourselves in past research [6]. However, this decision naturally challenges the "representativity" of the participants [9], but in our opinion, it simultaneously gives a more realistic expectation to those that consider "older adults" to constitute an appropriate scoping in terms of target users.

5.3 Reduced Performance Does not Equal Reduced Self-perception

The relationship between self-assessment and measured performance was studied in the search for patterns in the observed gap between the two sets of scores. This paper does not comment on related issues such as willingness to learn or adopt new practice which has previously been discussed by [8, 9, 17, 30], but the topics of self-perception, technology acceptance, and understanding of technology are all related issues. Only a few participants had previously participated in any of our research efforts (e.g., [6]), but that may have familiarized them with technology in a way that they would not have had the opportunity to do themselves. Prior experience with relevant technology may have a strong influence on the observed performance [24], and the same might be said for domain-related or social factors [8, 14, 23, 27]. Another main reason for including both self-assessment and measured performance was due to the performance scores not always revealing accurate perceptions or intentions behind specific actions. The gap between intended and actual use was also raised by [20].

The results of our analyses suggested that the participants mostly made excellent assessments of their performance. While we observed overestimation from the control group in some instances (Fig. 5), no notable patterns of either over- or underestimation emerged during the analysis that would help us predict future performance, even with similar tasks. The most important takeaway from this analysis would be that older adults, while performing at a lower average level, did not demonstrate any lower capacity to assess their own performance. In fact, the correlations suggested that the older adults were better at not overestimating their own performance when the tasks became statistical significantly more difficult – as seen in the case of dexterity and coordination.

5.4   The Challenge with General Assumptions

As mentioned in the introduction, this paper intends to broaden our understanding of how older adults are affected by changes in psychomotor abilities when interacting with technology. While this paper focuses on touch-based systems, our past efforts have focused on tangible and physical interfaces. The purpose of this specific study was to gather enough empirical evidence to demonstrate the dangers of assuming that older adults inhabit specific psychomotor capabilities regardless of whether they are positive or negative assumptions. Older adults remain a heterogeneous population in terms of being end-users of enabling technology [1]. It should be mentioned that we did not record any similar patterns as previously reported [6] despite using the same abilities and target demographic, albeit with an entirely different set of interfaces. The effects that the type of technology can have on performance have been discussed in past research [6, 31]. For instance, while we have seen an increase in performance in past research efforts when switching from touch-screens to physical interfaces (e.g., in [31]), the results of [10] suggest that this is not a guaranteed relation. Other studies also suggest that touchscreens can offer proficient usability in terms of readability, writing, and gesture control (e.g., [13]). We do not consider these results to be conflicting but rather empirical examples of how performance patterns for such a substantial demographic cannot be easily reduced down to universal truths. Even with similar results, the reported reasons behind the specific results may vary [7]. These arguments are also supported by other studies, e.g., [9, 16, 21].

Our general belief is similar to [10]: no single device will be consistently perceived as the best one. Allowing freedom of choice is about not only our responsibility but also a matter of liability in certain situations [27]. There are concerns related to both inappropriateness and ethical responsibility on the line when suggesting that a specific device will be suited for a particular context – especially in the case of users who might be more vulnerable or technology-dependent in their everyday life than others. The point of ethical considerations arising when designing or discussing technology in the context of lost abilities was also raised by [12, 28, 32]. This paper aligns with these past discussions and attempts to demonstrate why a "one solution fits all" [5] may cause challenges for individual users, and that there is a benefit of having a conscious attitude towards the variance in performance amongst older adults. A positive attitude may contribute with new ways of facilitating technology-related well-being for older adults (as seen, e.g., in [33]). Wrongful assumptions, even those with good intentions, may drastically affect the performance of the users. As also reported in [6], the results presented in this paper suggest that the distance between best and worst performance can be very high and that loss or reduction in one ability does not translate to an equal reduction for all other abilities. We advocate an approach that does not attempt to generalize the traits and capabilities of older adults but instead seek to adapt interaction mechanisms to the continuously changing abilities of all people, including those who fall into the category of older adults.

6   Conclusion

This paper has argued for why older adults should not be considered one large homogenous population with similarly reduced capabilities when interacting with technology. To support our belief of how common assumptions made about older adults can be wrong, we have reported results from an evaluation of psychomotor abilities carried out with 69 participants. Our evaluation highlighted both challenges and opportunities found when older adults engage in interaction with touchscreens using their hands and fingers. The evaluation studied self-assessed and measured performance during task solving of five tasks corresponding to a pre-selected set of psychomotor abilities commonly involved in interaction with touchscreens: precision, steadiness, dexterity, speed, and coordination. Statistical analyses of variations and tendencies were used to study both the self-assessment and the measured performance for the five psychomotor abilities. The discussion revolved around a comparison between the results found in this study and results from similar studies involving either older adults or psychomotor abilities as the unit of analysis. We have attempted to raise important concerns about individual capabilities and challenges with general assumptions about older adults as we argue against common assumptions often made in the context of older adults and enabling technology.

References

1. Joshi, S.G.: Designing for capabilities: a phenomenological approach to the design of enabling technologies for older adults (Doctoral dissertation). Ser. Diss. Submitt. Fac. Math. Nat. Sci. 1881 (2017)
2. Light, A., Pedell, S., Robertson, T., Waycott, J., Bell, J., Durick, J., Leong, T.W.: What's Special About Aging. Interactions 23, 66–69 (2016)
3. Smith, M.W., Sharit, J., Czaja, S.J.: Aging, motor control, and the performance of computer mouse tasks. Hum. Factor J. Hum. Factors Ergon. Soc. 41, 389–396 (1999)

4. Riviere, C.N., Thakor, N.V.: Effects of age and disability on tracking tasks with a computer mouse: accuracy and linearity. J. Rehabil. Res. Dev. **33**, 6–15 (1996)
5. Blythe, M., Andersen, K., Clarke, R., Wright, P.: Anti-solutionist strategies: seriously silly design fiction. In: Proceedings of the 2016 CHI Conference on Human Factors in Computing Systems, pp. 4968–4978. ACM, New York (2016)
6. Joshi, S.G.: Designing for capacities rather than disabilities. Int. J. Adv. Intell. Syst. **9**, 565–758 (2016)
7. Wood, E., Willoughby, T., Rushing, A., Bechtel, L., Gilbert, J.: Use of computer input devices by older adults. J. Appl. Gerontol. **24**, 419–438 (2005)
8. Olson, K.E., O'Brien, M.A., Rogers, W.A., Charness, N.: Diffusion of technology: frequency of use for younger and older adults. Ageing Int. **36**, 123–145 (2011)
9. Caprani, N., O'Connor, N.E., Gurrin, C.: Touch screens for the older user. In: Assistive Technologies. InTech (2012)
10. Rogers, W.A., Fisk, A.D., McLaughlin, A.C., Pak, R.: Touch a screen or turn a knob: choosing the best device for the job. Hum. Factor J. Hum. Factors Ergon. Soc. **47**, 271–288 (2005)
11. Pak, R., McLaughlin, A.C., Lin, C.-C., Rogers, W.A., Fisk, A.D.: An age-related comparison of a touchscreen and a novel input device. Proc. Hum. Factors Ergon. Soc. Annu. Meet. **46**, 189–192 (2002)
12. Culén, A.L., Bratteteig, T.: Touch-screens and elderly users: a perfect match? In: Presented at the ACHI 2013, The Sixth International Conference on Advances in Computer-Human Interactions (2013)
13. Werner, F., Werner, K., Oberzaucher, J.: Tablets for seniors – an evaluation of a current model (iPad). In: Wichert, R., Eberhardt, B. (eds.) Ambient Assisted Living. ATSC, pp. 177–184. Springer, Heidelberg (2012). https://doi.org/10.1007/978-3-642-27491-6_13
14. Doyle, J., Skrba, Z., McDonnell, R., Arent, B.: Designing a touch screen communication device to support social interaction amongst older adults. In: Proceedings of the 24th BCS Interaction Specialist Group Conference, pp. 177–185. British Computer Society, Swinton, UK (2010)
15. Hollinworth, N.: Improving computer interaction for older adults. SIGACCESS Access Comput. **93**, 11–17 (2009)
16. Lee, J.-H., Poliakoff, E., Spence, C.: The effect of multimodal feedback presented via a touch screen on the performance of older adults. In: Altinsoy, M.E., Jekosch, U., Brewster, S. (eds.) HAID 2009. LNCS, vol. 5763, pp. 128–135. Springer, Heidelberg (2009). https://doi.org/10.1007/978-3-642-04076-4_14
17. Häikiö, J., Wallin, A., Isomursu, M., Ailisto, H., Matinmikko, T., Huomo, T.: Touch-based user interface for elderly users. In: Proceedings of the 9th International Conference on Human Computer Interaction with Mobile Devices and Services, pp. 289–296. ACM, New York (2007)
18. Mertens, A., Jochems, N., Schlick, C.M., Dünnebacke, D., Dornberg, J.H.: Design pattern TRABING: touchscreen-based input technique for people affected by intention tremor. In: Proceedings of the 2nd ACM SIGCHI Symposium on Engineering Interactive Computing Systems, pp. 267–272. ACM (2010)
19. Jin, Z.X., Plocher, T., Kiff, L.: Touch screen user interfaces for older adults: button size and spacing. In: Stephanidis, C. (ed.) UAHCI 2007. LNCS, vol. 4554, pp. 933–941. Springer, Heidelberg (2007). https://doi.org/10.1007/978-3-540-73279-2_104
20. Kobayashi, M., Hiyama, A., Miura, T., Asakawa, C., Hirose, M., Ifukube, T.: Elderly user evaluation of mobile touchscreen interactions. In: Campos, P., Graham, N., Jorge, J., Nunes, N., Palanque, P., Winckler, M. (eds.) INTERACT 2011. LNCS, vol. 6946, pp. 83–99. Springer, Heidelberg (2011). https://doi.org/10.1007/978-3-642-23774-4_9

21. Page, T.: Touchscreen mobile devices and older adults: a usability study. Int. J. Hum. Factors Ergon. **3**, 65–85 (2014)
22. Lepicard, G., Vigouroux, N.: Touch screen user interfaces for older subjects. In: Miesenberger, K., Klaus, J., Zagler, W., Karshmer, A. (eds.) ICCHP 2010. LNCS, vol. 6180, pp. 592–599. Springer, Heidelberg (2010). https://doi.org/10.1007/978-3-642-14100-3_88
23. Chen, K.B., Savage, A.B., Chourasia, A.O., Wiegmann, D.A., Sesto, M.E.: Touch screen performance by individuals with and without motor control disabilities. Appl. Ergon. **44**, 297–302 (2013)
24. Motti, L.G., Vigouroux, N., Gorce, P.: Interaction techniques for older adults using touchscreen devices: a literature review. In: Proceedings of the 25th Conference on L'Interaction Homme-Machine, pp. 125:125–125:134. ACM, New York (2013)
25. Fleishman, E.A.: Toward a taxonomy of human performance. Am. Psychol. **30**, 1127 (1975)
26. Fleishman, E.A., Reilly, M.E.: Handbook of Human Abilities: Definitions, Measurements, and Job Task Requirements. Consulting Psychologists Press, Palo Alto (1992)
27. Blythe, M.A., Monk, A.F., Doughty, K.: Socially dependable design: the challenge of ageing populations for HCI. Interact. Comput. **17**, 672–689 (2005)
28. Rauhala, M., Topo, P.: Independent living, technology and ethics. Technol. Disabil. **15**, 205–214 (2003)
29. Astell, A.J., Ellis, M.P., Bernardi, L., Alm, N., Dye, R., Gowans, G., Campbell, J.: Using a touch screen computer to support relationships between people with dementia and caregivers. Interact. Comput. **22**, 267–275 (2010)
30. Heerink, M., Kröse, B., Evers, V., Wielinga, B.: Assessing acceptance of assistive social agent technology by older adults: the Almere model. Int. J. Soc. Robot. **2**, 361–375 (2010)
31. Joshi, S.G., Bråthen, H.: Lowering the threshold: reconnecting elderly users with assistive technology through tangible interfaces. In: Zhou, J., Salvendy, G. (eds.) ITAP 2016. LNCS, vol. 9754, pp. 52–63. Springer, Cham (2016). https://doi.org/10.1007/978-3-319-39943-0_6
32. Joshi, S.G.: Emerging ethical considerations from the perspectives of the elderly. In: Presented at the Ninth International Conference on Cultural Attitudes in computer-Human Interactions (2014)
33. Blythe, M., Steane, J., Roe, J., Oliver, C.: Solutionism, the game: design fictions for positive aging. In: Proceedings of the 33rd Annual ACM Conference on Human Factors in Computing Systems, pp. 3849–3858. ACM, New York (2015)

A Review of Age-Related Characteristics for Touch-Based Performance and Experience

Jing Liao, Jianan Lou, Qifei Wu, Min Zou, and Linfeng Zheng[✉]

Zhejiang University, Hangzhou, Zhejiang, China
zhenglinfeng@zju.edu.cn

Abstract. Touchscreens are considered as a friendly interface for elderly people. However, a gap between young users and older users was still observed in either interaction performance or user experience. Although previous studies have identified the gap is associated with age-related characteristics, most researches are focused on specific input or output elements. This heterogeneity of research subjects makes it difficult to understand, compare and to recommend proper techniques for a specific design. Accordingly, we provided a review, thoroughly describing the efforts on the touch-based system and the elderly population in the past decade and answering the following questions: (1) How to identify characteristics that sensitive to performance and experience? (2) How to accommodate for elderly's special interests? We also summarized the relevant design guidance, and provides novel perspectives of inclusive technical design for the elderly. Our work may enlighten those who is interested in the design of both hardware and software elements for the elderly.

Keywords: Elderly · Age-related characteristics · Touch-based system
Interaction performance · Interaction experience

1 Introduction

As a direct input, touchscreens eliminate control-display displacement, and are regarded to be able to reduce interaction time and boost accuracy. The older adults also have high subjective satisfaction and preference on touchscreens [1]. However, a gap between young users and older users was still observed in considerable experimental results of performance and self-reported experience [3].

The characteristics of older people relating to this gap are referred as age-related characteristics. Understanding the influence of age-related characteristics on performance are the prerequisites for setting design criteria for the older group [2]. Many researchers strived to explore relations of this heterogeneous group characteristics to behaviors and outcomes of interaction [1–11, 14, 15, 22–24, 29–41, 43–59]. Motti et al. reviewed experimental variables related to interaction performance and experience, i.e. the population involved, the kind of tasks that were executed, the apparatus, the input techniques, the provided feedbacks [3].

In this paper, we specified elderly's characteristics and determine factors (both experimental and practical) on performance and experience of using touchscreens. We summarized significant findings as design guidelines. Our work will guide for

© Springer International Publishing AG, part of Springer Nature 2018
J. Zhou and G. Salvendy (Eds.): ITAP 2018, LNCS 10926, pp. 279–296, 2018.
https://doi.org/10.1007/978-3-319-92034-4_21

researches on elderly-technology interaction in (1) design of empirical experiments exploring touch-based interaction; (2) implications of possible barriers during inter-action; (3) approaches to improving technology experience.

This review is organized as follows: Sect. 2 describes metrics of interaction per-formance and experience and emphasizes the role of age-related characteristics as a primal cause of generation gap. Section 3 surveys the elderly centered touch-based interaction techniques and Sect. 4 assesses them and provides guidelines considering the special interests for elderly group. Finally, we concluded our work in Sect. 5. Detailed settings of experiments involved in literature are appended in the Appendix (Fig. 1).

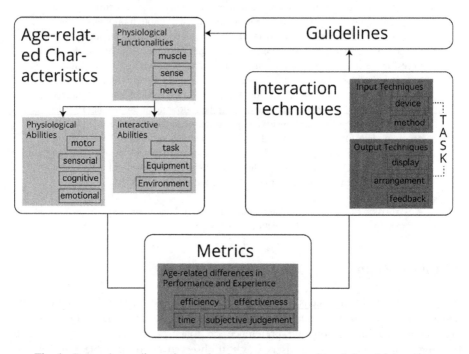

Fig. 1. Research paradigm of age-related characteristics and touch-based interaction

2   Age-Related Characteristics as a Primal Cause of Generation Gap in Elderly-Computer Interaction

A general conclusion is reached in human computer interaction community that users' abilities would strongly impact interaction performance and experience. We built a three-level of descriptions of aging characteristics: Physiological Functionalities, Physiological Abilities and Interaction Abilities, to explain physiological changes, effects of physiological changes and how these effects act during the elderly of using touch-based systems.

2.1   Three-Level Taxonomy of Age-Related Characteristics

Physiological Functionalities: Muscle, Sense and Nerve.

Muscle. Age-related muscular changes include declines in muscle strength and power [4–6], number and size of muscle fibers [7]. As a result, limb and finger tiredness are more frequently happened on older adults, particularly when working on devices i.e. tablet PC, where arms need to be kept in-air.

Sense. Aging may accompany with pathological changes in sensorial organs, such as opacities of the crystalline lens of the eye caused by cataract, local loss of visual function caused by diabetic retinopathy, and age-related macular degeneration (AMD) of the photosensitive cells at the retina [5]. These sensorial pathological changes may lead to degenerations of sensorial abilities required by interaction, then obstruct the elderly to use the general interfaces.

Nerve. Aging brings about neural changes, e.g. reduced speed of conduction of nerve signals [4, 7] and slower nerve signal processing [4], directly affecting motor, sensorial and cognitive abilities of older adults.

Physiological Abilities: Motor, Sensorial, Cognitive and Emotional.

Motor. In the context of touch-based interaction, motor degenerations include negative changes in strength, speed of upper limb muscles [5, 8], as well as reduced abilities, i.e. consistency of movement [5, 8, 9], coordination [9–11], endurance [6] and accuracy [5, 7]. Motor degenerations directly hindered older people in performing reaching, selecting, grasping, and gestural tasks [3, 5].

Sensorial. Primarily, sensorial degenerations in touch-based interaction are visual and tactile declines. Firstly, old people are at high risk of visual impairment incidents, reducing the depth-perception [6], field-of-view [7, 9], visual acuity [8], the ability to resolve detail [7, 9, 12], to detect [13] and focus on object [12], to discriminate color [5, 6, 9], to detect contrast [5, 9, 12, 14], and to estimate motion [9]. As vision being widely known as the main tunnel of perceiving external stimulus, difficulties in perception and utilization of visual feedbacks may be one of the important causes of poor performance of older people [15]. Secondly, tactile degenerations make older adults have difficulties in sensing the texture, quality and temperature of surfaces. Loss of tactile sensitivity may lead to not being able to rely on haptic interface to interact. Particularly, atrophic skin decreases the quality of fingerprint data, posing challenges on fingerprint-feature-based identification authentication [16, 17], which is widely used on smartphones.

Cognitive. Old adults have more difficulties in concentrating on tasks and filtering out irrelevant information [5, 11, 12, 18, 19], the abilities to know, understand and reason [11, 14], to respond [9, 10], to recall and learn [12, 22], to navigate [21, 23], and to recognize and use words [6, 12, 18]. However, higher-level cognitive abilities, i.e. visuospatial memory are less influenced by aging [24]. In general, declines in memory (both long-term and short-term [5, 9, 18, 19], and verbal memory [21]), processing abilities(e.g. visual processing) and intelligence (both fluid and crystallized) [3, 5], is three of significant cognitive degenerations. An interesting finding is that the fluid intelligence (the capacity to analyze, reason and solve problems) is widely considered to be decreased with age, while the crystallized intelligence (the ability to use skills, knowledge, and experience) is considered to be improved with age, because experiences tend to expand one's knowledge. But close relationships were determined between aging and declines in crystallized intelligence in e.g. pen interaction [5]. Cognitive abilities play an *increasingly* significant role in usability and acceptance of design for the elderly [20].

Emotional. Emotional degenerations of older adults are related to beliefs, attitudes, anxiety, fear, acceptability [9, 25, 26]. Older adults may have misconceptions that they cannot or do not use advanced technologies (e.g. computers, the Internet) [25]. A lack of beliefs in capability may prohibit some older people using technologies [27]. Fortunately, many emotional degenerations are highly related to computer literacy [9, 25, 26, 28]. Social media and social networks encourage older people using digital products and services, which improves their computer literacy [26, 28].

Interaction Abilities. Interaction abilities are physiological abilities associated with user performance and behaviors under specific experimental settings. By analysis of experimental results in literature, we found the interaction abilities rely on the task performed, the equipment and the task-being environment.

Task Dependency. Most studies observed age-related differences in, i.e. performance or behavior difference between younger group and older group. However, the measured ability is actually affected by task requirements defined in individual experiment. For instance, the efforts required by accomplishing tapping gestures is negatively related to the target size [29], but is positively related to the precision requirement [29, 30], the distance from the target [29] and complexity [31]. These factors interact with age and have complex effects on performance and experience.

Equipment Dependency. Equipment type, or interactive techniques may also have strong effects on practical interactions. Early touch-panels use capacitive touchscreen, which is prone to color distortions and becomes inaccurate when temperature or moisture changes. Thus, large studies conducted on capacitive touch-panels concluded that touch-based interaction is even worse than traditional mouse [32]. This contradict to outcomes yielded in subsequent experiments using high-stability and high-resolution touch-panels (e.g. Piezoelectric touchscreen and Infrared touchscreen).

Environment Dependency. The user being environments are into categorized in-virtuo (in the real environment, easy-to-control but poorly reflecting to the user's reality), in-situ (being able to provide high-realistic data, but may be highly biased by the observers and extremely costly) and in-simu (or in-sitro, a synthetic environment for a real environment to work under laboratory conditions of control) [33]. The closer to a real environment, more insights may yield from the experiments.

2.2   Metrics of Interaction Performance and Experience

Identifying evaluation metrics is of great significance, because metrics are practical for examining disparities between older and younger people and accessing experimental results of literature. In the context of touch-based interaction tasks, we defined the definition of time (both learning time and retention over time), effectiveness, efficiency and subjective judgement measures.

Time. Time can be considered as temporal duration required or related to perform pre-defined action(s). An action can be viewed as contact with the interface (e.g. reach and tap on a target) or any inclination provoked by interaction task (e.g. reaction). Elderly people may encounter difficulties in either performing an action or becoming aware of performing the action.

Effectiveness. Error, including error rate (or accuracy), error severity, recovering from errors, is a common measure of interaction effectiveness. Effectiveness could be evaluated at different levels. Take text entry task as example, the minimum string distance (MSD) can be used to evaluate sentence-level errors (incorrect word or word order), occurrence of insertions, substitutions and omissions to evaluate character-level errors.

Efficiency. Simply, the efficiency metric can be mathematically explained as an indicator of effectiveness per unit time. In previous example of text entry, efficiency metric can be the word-per-minute (wpm).

Subjective Judgements. Subjective judgements can be qualitative (e.g. interview) or quantitative (e.g. questionnaire). A general method is to ask participants to do self-evaluations on task-specific measures. Particularly, subjective results are not always consistent with objective measures. For instance, elder users may prefer an awkward way (poor measure of time, effectiveness or efficiency) to interact [34].

3   Studies on Elderly Centered Touch-Based Interaction Techniques

In this section, we discussed effects of input and output domains of touch-based interaction techniques on interaction according to tasks, to have deep examinations into consistencies and inconsistencies in elderly interaction performance and experience.

3.1   Interaction Tasks in Touch-Based Systems

The interaction task can be a good variable when analyzing designs of interaction for the elderly. Firstly, well-defined interaction tasks are good simulations of processes of interaction in real contexts. Secondly, the interaction performance and experience is highly related to tasks to be finished. Thirdly, most of retrieved literatures have clear definitions on the experimental task, so comparing these experimental results based on the interaction task is available.

Target Acquisition (TA). As one of the of the most basic manipulation, TA has been the most theoretically and experimentally studied. A typical TA movement consists of two control phases: (1) an initial large and quick directing phase and (2) a later small and slower acquiring phase [31]. Older adults may face more challenges in either (1) or (2) phases with respect to distinct contexts. Three problems of on-screen interaction are identified to be more challenging for older people: First, the fat finger' problem in finger-based selection task. The finger, hand, or arm may occlude part of, or even the whole target [35, 36]. Second, the 'slipping' in stylus-based selection. Older adults are easily slipping away from a target when tapping on smooth screen [37]. Third, difficulties in small targets selection [5, 35], because a more precise tapping is required to successfully select a target. Interestingly, target size also has detrimental influence on the efficiency of cognitive processes involved in the target acquisition task, especially for the elderly [38].

Text Entry (TE). TE has also been widely studied. It is particular challenging for older adults because of the nature of high complexity. The performance of text entry is highly affected by keyboard design [34, 41], predict system [34], nature of task [42, 43], and the workstation configuration [44]. Besides, TE performance has close relationships with user pre-experience [40]. Generally, older adults require more intuitive and easy-to-use entry method [34].

Keyboard Layout. Visual layouts and techniques do not improve TE performance, or even have negative effects [34, 39]. The input accuracy has no relationships with the familiarity of QWERTY layout [40]; Also, the input speed is found to be strongly related to previous QWERTY experience rather than keyboard layout [40]. Still, a carefully-designed keyboard, e.g. visual-adaptive keyboard, may provide comfortable and natural typing experience [41]. Additionally, old users can be benefited from adaptions that was hide from the interface. Findlater et al. designed a visual-adaptive keyboards that reshuffle layout of keys and a non-visual-adaptive keyboard that do not change visually rectangular layout but increase the chance that the user will press one visual key but output a different letter [41]. The non-visual-adaptive keyboard provided both typing speed and efficient/easy-to-use/preferred improvements [41].

Predict Variant and Working Condition. Surprisingly, old users are the least satisfied with Predict Words variant keyboard, and they performed comparable or even worse in general regarding input speed and error rate [34]. The reason suggested by self-report is that the text predict is too complex and need more practice in order to correctly use it. As for effects of typing in stationary or mobile condition, the text input speed decreases, the error rate and mental workload increases when user is walking [44].

Real Scenario Tasks (In-Situ Usage). Real scenario tasks can be defined as complete interaction 'transactions' happening in daily work, i.e. sending an email. Two problems may lead to a gap between experimental results and practical usage. The first problem is task inconsistency. Take TE as example, it can be divided into three in-situ tasks, copy, compose and describe [42]. Most in-vitro experiments asked participants copy sentences, but we think-and-write rather frequently than copy in practical conditions. Actually, older adults were found to pause more frequently during the fixed time allowed for typing (in self-judgement, they were also reported to spend more time thinking than younger adults) [42]. In other words, the difference between two age groups in speed of typing as being caused by longer inter-key times, e.g. thinking, not the actual tap times. The second problem is difficulties in controlling and determining variables in real scenario tasks. However, underlying factors may be identified since results are limited to less assumptions. For instance, the use of hands leads to increasing both time and error rate for older people, while it has no effects on the young [43]. But only a few studies considered this variant in experiments.

3.2   Input Techniques for Touch-Based Systems

Input techniques can be device-based (smartphones, tablets, tablet PCs, and table-size touchscreens), or method-based (finger-based and stylus-based techniques). A considerable of studies have thoroughly examined the input devices and methods for the older adults [7, 45, 46]. Most studies evaluated common techniques as tap, multi-tap, long-press, drag, drag-and-drop and free-drawing. Many novel input methods have also been proposed, e.g. Steadied-Bubbles [47] and SWABBING [48].

3.3   Output Techniques for Touch-Based Systems

Display: Size, Color, Contrast, Fonts. The effects of display size [29, 49], orientation [50], color [34], contrast [51, 52] and fonts [14, 53] were examined and were identified to have significant influence on performance and subjective evaluations.

Arrangement: Layout, Information Architecture. Arrangements strongly affect navigation task [20, 31, 54, 55], e.g. keyboard layout is strongly related to identifying location of keys [39]. Besides, arrangement of interface elements (information architecture) has a significant influence on speed, mental load and satisfactory during web browsing [31, 55].

Feedback: Visual, Acoustic, Tactile and Multimodal Feedback. Few studies conclusively discussed effects of output feedbacks on elderly. After examining relevant literature, we found many inconsistencies in findings. Although popular opinion is that providing feedback from these 'absent' channels will enhance user performance and satisfaction, and results of many empirical studies validated this hypothesis. However, some studies found that either visual (older adults were less sensitive to visual feedbacks [35]), auditory, or haptic feedback do not act important as expected on older users. We discussed these effects case-by-case, because each type of feedback has typical effects on interaction.

Visual Feedback. Visual feedback is usually designed to aid in pointing [29], navigation [54] and entry tasks [34]. The hovering techniques and the long-press on touchscreen, for instance, either help users affirming whether the desired target is accurately pointed, or suggest the possible behaviors after the target is selected. Another type of visual feedback is aimed at modeling feeling that naturally generated by other modalities, i.e. when clicking on a button, it looks like a real button is pressed. This type of visual feedbacks is widely used in computers, mobile devices and virtual environments [56]. But for older users, studies did not recommend the mechanism of creating pseudo-haptic feedback [57] through visual channel, especially in onscreen text entry task [34].

Acoustic Feedback. The auditory feedback is usually used as secondary channel to facilitate visual feedbacks. The presentation of multimodal feedback with auditory signals via a touch screen device enhances performance and remark of older adults [58]. Besides, auditory feedback can be designed to provide implications on word to be typed. For instance, introducing an enhanced auditory feedback (EAF) for Korean language entry task can provide subtle phonetic auditory feedback with the use of acoustic phonetic features of human speech [59]. Another potential of auditory feedback is to elicit emotions of users, based on evidence of the systematic relationships between acoustic features and emotions felt [60]. Providing pleasant sounds in augmented artifacts and interfaces is able to make the task slightly easier, to leave users feeling more in control [60], and to mitigate negative effects of tactile feedback of increasing cognitive efforts [29].

Tactile Feedback. One of the weakness of touchscreens typing is the lack of tactile feedback as provided from physical keyboard [8]. Researchers tried to compensate for this nature by providing proper haptic feedbacks, however, completely exploring these parameters is very complicated and of high cost of sensors and actuators at present. On the other hand, effects of providing feedbacks on touchscreen is also inconclusive. Some studies found haptic feedbacks aid performance, particularly for elderly and blind users [29, 58, 61, 63, 64]. One the other hand, haptic feedbacks were found to provide fewer help and to distract attention or affect older adults' stable grasp of the device [29, 59, 65]. That tactile feedbacks being so tricky is related to subjective satisfactory nature of sensitiveness and the currently incomplete simulation of physical feedbacks. Even if provided a small but unnaturally force, it will have strong negative effects on performance; as for satisfaction, significantly worse than those without tactile feedbacks [65]. Therefore, detailed design guidelines are needed in the design of haptic feedback. Nishino et al. provided a design guideline specific for implementing mutually discriminable tactile stimuli in practical applications [61]. But this guideline is still not sufficient for supporting designing efficient and natural haptic responses.

Multimodal Feedback. Multimodality has been recommended for elderly-technical system interaction for many years, conclusively for: (1) various modalities could compensate disadvantages more than interfere between each channel [62]; (2) various modalities can accommodate more characteristics of users and environments [66, 67]; (3) human's natural ability on utilizing and integrating between multimodalities is little affected by aging [66]. However, some studies show multimodal feedbacks yield worse performance than a unimodal feedback, if some modalities, e.g. improper tactile feedback, that has negative effects on performance are combined [68, 69]. And these negative effects of multimodal feedback may be gender-related [70].

4 Guidelines for Interaction Design on Elderly People

4.1 How to Identify Characteristics that Sensitive to Performance and Experience?

According to results of literature examination, effects of age-related characteristics on interaction performance and experience are summarized in Table 1. Contradictory results are labeled as '?', implying the effects have not been determined.

Table 1. Effects of age-related characteristics on performance and experience of touchscreen (+: increase; −: decrease)

		Time	Effectiveness	Efficiency	Subjective Judgement	Remark
Motor degenerations	Strength	?	−	−	?	
	Speed	+	?	−	−	
	Consistency	+	?	−	?	
	Coordination	+	?	−	−	
	Endurance	?	?	?	−	
	Accuracy	+	?	−	−	
Sensorial degenerations	Depth-perception	?	?	−	?	
	Field-of-view	+	?	−	?	
	Tactile	?	−	−	−	
	Detail resolve	+	−	−	?	
	Motion detect	+	−	−	?	
	Color discrimination	?	?	?	−	
	Contrast detect	?	?	−	−	
Cognitive degenerations	Concentration and Respond	+	?	−	?	
	Know, Understand and Reason	+	−	−	?	
	Recall	+	−	−	?	
	Learn	+	−	−	−	
	Navigate	+	?	−	−	retain previous strategies
	Recognize and use words	?	−	−	?	
Emotional degenerations	Attitude	?	?	−	−	based on results of surveys
	Belief	?	?	−	−	
	Anxiety	?	?	−	−	
	Fear	?	?	?	−	
	Acceptability	?	?	?	−	

According to Table 1, effects of motor and sensorial degenerations have been the most fully studied. It is reasonable, considering a large volume of the geriatrics studies provided implications on research. Although effects of many cognitive degenerations are identified, the underlying mechanisms remain a mystery. As Zhou et al. described in [20], the feature of big fonts, big buttons, large displays, and loud volume, is just the tip of the iceberg; below the water lie design modifications that reduce old adult's cognitive demands. Effects of emotional degenerations on performance and experience are not clear, and are also need to be further examined.

4.2   How to Accommodate for Elderly's Special Interests?

Based on the experimental results and the analysis of the literature, we summarized the approaches for accommodating the needs of the elderly:

Focus on Ability Rather Than Attribute. Age-related degenerations can be biological or chronological [24]. Chronological age is not enough for describing the age-related characteristics [71]. Vocal degenerations for instance, chronological vocal degenerations show strong relationships with aging, while biological vocal degenerations can be affected by overuse of vocal, consumption of tobacco and alcohols, psychological stress etc. [24]. We encourage focus on biological age-related degenerations in user backgrounds.

Consider Specific Tasks and Environments and Focus on Usage in Real Scenarios. Most studies conduct experiments under laboratory environments. The findings and recommendations are somewhat questionable when guiding for design in real scenarios because user performance and experience are highly dependent on experimental tasks and environments (Sect. 2.1).

Facilitate Learning of Interaction. Although having more barriers during interaction, the difference between the young and the elderly could be reduced with inclusive design approaches. Additionally, along with popularity of social media and social networks, effects of emotional degenerations are fading (Sect. 2.1). Older people are becoming increasingly interested in learning novel techniques for the purpose of entertainment, communication, social support etc. [26–28]. Designing solutions to help them learning is of great significance.

Be Prudent on Novel Interaction Techniques. Particularly, interaction performance and experience of older adults are highly related to the acceptance of technology. According to Zhou's acceptance model [20], a lack of knowledge on computers and experience may impede computer usage of the older adults. Low acceptance of older adults is also related to anxiety, diffidence and fear during interaction [11, 51].

Reduced Functionalities and Assistive Techniques for Special Needs as Secondary. Most of the researches focus on age-related difference during the interaction process. However, this gap also exists in learning to control and react to touch-based devices. For instance, the young adults and old adults show different learnability in navigation [21] and text entry tasks [34]. Unlike Millennials, older adults are not born with computer and the Internet. Tutorials or guidelines for general users probably not sufficient for an elder to get familiar with novel techniques. Learning to use assistive techniques will be a painstaking process for older people.

5   Conclusion

Building a thorough map of effects of age-related characteristics on touch-based interaction system become the crux of design for the elderly. In this work, we provided a literature review, specifying elderly's characteristics and determined factors (both experimental and practical) on performance and experience of using touchscreens. We also summarized the relevant design guidelines, and provided some novel perspectives of the inclusion design of technologies for the elderly. Research on elderly cognitive process during interaction, learning of interaction, and elderly-friendly feedbacks, remain the under-explored areas. This stimulates curiosity for future studies.

Acknowledgement. This paper is supported by the National Natural Science Foundation of China (61303137), the National Science and Technology Support Program (2015BAH21F01) and the Art Project for National Social-Science Foundation (15BG084).

Appendix

See Table 2

Table 2. Experiment settings in literature

Reference	Equipment	Task	Sample size (old + mid + young)	Age mean/SD	Environment
Chen 2017 [J]	21″ 1920×1080 touchscreen PC	One-directional-pointing; multi-directional-pointing, dragging-and-dropping	18(−) + 18 + 18	68.7/4.7	
Rodrigues 2016 [J]	Samsung ATIV Smart PC Pro 11.6″	Five variations of QWERTY entry: COLOR, WIDTH, PREDICT_WORD, SHIFTED, SIZE_INVISIBLE	20(5M15F) + 0 + 0	–/–	
Cáliz 2016 [C]	Szenio 10.1 capacitive multi-touch	Tap; Double tap; Long press; Drag; Scale up; Scale down and One-finger rotation in game	50(25M25F) + 0 + 0	–/–	
Smith 2015 [J]	Motorola Droid 4, FlexT9 Text Input suite, Version XT9, Version T9WRITE, Dragon Version 2	Physical QWERTY, onscreen QWERTY, tracing, handwriting and voice	25(9M16F) + 0 + 25	68.8/7.4	

(continued)

Table 2. (*continued*)

Reference	Equipment	Task	Sample size (old + mid + young)	Age mean/SD	Environment
Motti, 2015 [J]	Galaxy Note II (WXGA 1280×720 Super AMOLED); Galaxy Note 10.1(WXGA 1280×800 LCD)	Drag-and-drop	24(−) + 0 + 0	72.25/5.8	
Alshowarah 2015 [d]	Samsung Galaxy Ace S 5830, HTC wildfire, Samsung Galaxy Tab 2, Samsung Galaxy Note 10.1	–	22(−) + 31 + 50	–/–	
Acarturk 2015 [J]	iPad	Usability test on iPad use and email services	5(3M2F) + 0 + 5	72/2.35*	
Zhou 2014 [J]	Apple iPod Touch (3.5 in., 480×320), Dell Streak (5 in., 800×480), Samsung Galaxy Tab (7 in., 1024×600), Apple iPad (9.7 in., 1024×768)	Four daily task related to entry	32(7M25F) + 0 + 0	67.2/5.53	In-situ
Wulf 2014 [C]	iPad, 9.7″ 1024×768	Tap; drag; pinch; pinch-pan; rotate left and rotate right	20(9M11F) + 0 + 20	71.85/5.13	
Rodrigues 2014 [C]	Samsung ATIV Smart PC Pro 11.6″	–	–	–	
Muskens 2014 [C]	iPad 2.0	Four existing applications and one prototype	14(−); 12 (7M5F)	~69/–	Iin-simu
Motti 2014 [J]	Galaxy Note II (WXGA 1280x720 Super AMOLED), Galaxy Note 10.1 (WXGA 1280x800 LCD)	Drag-and-drop in a puzzle game	24(8M16F)	74.25/5.8	In-simu
Barros 2014 [C]	HTC Titan 4.7′, HTC Radar 3.8′	Vertical swipe; horizontal swipes; tap	9(2M7F); 9 (5M4F); 9(−)	80.7/–; 76.4/–; 84.4/–	
Schlick, Jochems 2013 [J]	Elo resistive 17″ TFT LCD(model 1715, 1280×1024)	Pointing; drag-and-drop	30 + 30 + 30	65.47/4.08	
Leah 2013 [C]	Apple iPad 3, Apple laptops	Pointing; dragging; crossing; steering	20(−) + 0 + 20	74.3/6.6	
Hwangbo 2013 [J]	4.3″ Android smartphone	Pointing	22(9M13F) + 0 + 0	70.55/–	

(*continued*)

Table 2. (*continued*)

Reference	Equipment	Task	Sample size (old + mid + young)	Age mean/SD	Environment
Nicolau, 2012 [C]	HTC Desire and ASUS Transformer TF101 Tablet	QWERTY entry	15(4M11F) + 0 + 0	79/7.3	
Mertens 2012 [M]	HP TouchSmart tm2-1090eg, 12.1 in. capacitive multi-touch, 1280×800	A new direct input technique based on swiping called swabbing	15(−) + 0 + 0	73.56/−	
Vella 2011 [C]	15″ TFT display, 1024×768	Clicking; dragging; clicking; magnetization	8 + 16 + 19 + 26 + 28	−/−	
Nishino 2011 [C]	A self-designed system on touchscreen	–	85(-) + 0 + 0	−/−	
Leung 2011 [j]	–	Icon usability test	18(−) + 18	−/−	
Bradley, 2011 [c]	Samsung Galaxy Tab	Daily tasks	–	−/−	in-situ
Moffatt 2010 [C]	Wacom Cintiq 12WX, 12.1″ pen tablet, 1280×800; Cintiq Classic pen	Pointing	12(6M6F) + 0 + 12	73/−	
Lepicard 2010 [C]	Dell Tablet PC Latitude XT2, 12.1″ inch LCD monitor,	Target selection	24(−) + 0 + 36	76.5/8.2	
Fezzani 2010 [J]	Apple Macintosh; Wacom DIP digitizer tablet; wireless pen	Pointing	14(6M8F) + 0 + 14	66.9/4.0	
Vigouroux 2009 [C]	15″ laptop, 1024×768 TFT display	Clicking; clicking and magnetization	15(7M5F3W) + 0 + 0	−/−	
Tsai 2009 [C]	ASUS MyPal A730W compatible PDA	Continuous-touch digit input	45(17M28F) + 0 + 0	67.6/−	
O'brien 2008 [J]	Dell 600-MHz Pentium 3	4 keyboard shapes, 3 keyboard arrangements text entry	24(−) + 0 + 24	69.67/4.27; 67.17/3.54; 68.33/2.88; 69.17/4.88	
Moffatt 2008 [C]	Fujitsu LifeBook T3010D Tablet PC	Tap; glide; entry	12(4M8F) + 0 + 12	72/−	
Moffatt 2007 [C]	Fujitsu 12.1″ tablet, 1024×768; inductive pen	Multi-dimensional tapping; menu	12(4M8F) + 12(3M9F) + 12	62.1/−, 76.3/−	

(*continued*)

Table 2. (*continued*)

Reference	Equipment	Task	Sample size (old + mid + young)	Age mean/SD	Environment
Li 2007 [C]	Hewlett-Packard iPAQ 5450, touch screen QWERTY keyboard	QWERTY text entry	63(20M43F) + 0 + 0	49.8/18.8	
Lee 2007 [C]	PDA(ASUS A730), Cell phone(Dopod 818)	Tasks in realistic environment	5(−) + 5 + 5	67.9/3.8	In-situ
Asano 2007 [J]	NTT DoCoMo P901i	Access all mobile Web sites and perform a task specific to each Web site	–	65.4/–	
Arning 2007 [C]	Toshiba Pocket PC e740, LCD-screen (Iiyama TXA3841, TN, 15″ 1024×768	"Create a new entry" and "change an existing entry")	32(16M16F) + 32 + 32	58.2/6	
Hourcade 2006 [C]	Compaq iPAQ 3950 PocketPC, 320×240; pen	Tap; touch	20(−) + 20 + 20	–/–	

References

1. Hertzum, M., Hornbæk, K.: How age affects pointing with mouse and touchpad: a comparison of young, adult, and elderly users. Int. J. Hum. Comput. Interact. **26**(7), 703–734 (2010)
2. Arning, K., Ziefle, M.: Barriers of information access in small screen device applications: the relevance of user characteristics for a transgenerational design. In: Stephanidis, C., Pieper, M. (eds.) UI4ALL 2006. LNCS, vol. 4397, pp. 117–136. Springer, Heidelberg (2007). https://doi.org/10.1007/978-3-540-71025-7_9
3. Motti, L.G., Vigouroux, N., Gorce, P.: Interaction techniques for older adults using touchscreen devices: a literature review. In: Proceedings of the 25th Conference on L'Interaction Homme-Machine, pp. 125–134. ACM, Talence (2013)
4. Chen, J., Or, C.: Assessing the use of immersive virtual reality, mouse and touchscreen in pointing and dragging-and-dropping tasks among young, middle-aged and older adults. Appl. Ergon. **65**, 437–448 (2017)
5. Hourcade, J.P., Berkel, T.R.: Simple pen interaction performance of young and older adults using handheld computers. Interact. Comput. **20**(1), 166–183 (2008)
6. Neerincx, M.A., Cremers, A.H.M., Kessens, J.M., van Leeuwen, D.A., Truong, K.P.: Attuning speech-enabled interfaces to user and context for inclusive design: technology, methodology and practice. Univ. Access Inf. Soc. **8**(2), 109–122 (2009)
7. Taveira, A.D., Choi, S.D.: Review study of computer input devices and older users. Int. J. Hum. Comput. Interact. **25**(5), 455–474 (2009)
8. Smith, A.L., Chaparro, B.S.: Smartphone text input method performance, usability, and preference with younger and older adults. Hum. Factors **57**(6), 1015–1028 (2015)

9. Holzinger, A., Searle, G., Nischelwitzer, A.: On some aspects of improving mobile applications for the elderly. In: Stephanidis, C. (ed.) UAHCI 2007. LNCS, vol. 4554, pp. 923–932. Springer, Heidelberg (2007). https://doi.org/10.1007/978-3-540-73279-2_103

10. Vigouroux, N., Rumeau, P., Vella, F., Vellas, B.: Studying point-select-drag interaction techniques for older people with cognitive impairment. In: Stephanidis, C. (ed.) UAHCI 2009. LNCS, vol. 5614, pp. 422–428. Springer, Heidelberg (2009). https://doi.org/10.1007/978-3-642-02707-9_48

11. Leung, R., McGrenere, J., Graf, P.: Age-related differences in the initial usability of mobile device icons. Behav. Inf. Technol. **30**(5), 629–642 (2011)

12. Asano, Y., Saito, H., Sato, H., Wang, L., Gao, Q., Rau, P.-L.P.: Tips for designing mobile phone web pages for the elderly. In: Jacko, J.A. (ed.) HCI 2007. LNCS, vol. 4550, pp. 675–680. Springer, Heidelberg (2007). https://doi.org/10.1007/978-3-540-73105-4_74

13. Gruber, N., Mueri, R.M., Mosimann, U.P., Bieri, R., Aeschimann, A., Zito, G.A., Nef, T.: Effects of age and eccentricity on visual target detection. Front. Aging Neurosci. **5**(2), 101 (2013)

14. Lee, C.-F., Kuo, C.-C.: Difficulties on small-touch-screens for various ages. In: Stephanidis, C. (ed.) UAHCI 2007. LNCS, vol. 4554, pp. 968–974. Springer, Heidelberg (2007). https://doi.org/10.1007/978-3-540-73279-2_108

15. Suleyman, A.S.: Effects of age on smartphone and tablet usability, based on eye-movement tracking and touch-gesture interactions. Doctoral Thesis (2015)

16. Modi, S.K., Elliott, S.J., Whetsone, J., Kim, H.: Impact of age groups on fingerprint recognition performance. In: 2007 IEEE Workshop on Automatic Identification Advanced Technologies, pp. 19–23. IEEE (2007)

17. Lanitis, A., Tsapatsoulis, N.: Quantitative evaluation of the effects of aging on biometric templates. IET Comput. Vis. **5**(5), 338–347 (2011)

18. Taljaard, D.S., Olaithe, M., Brennan-Jones, C.G., Eikelboom, R.H., Bucks, R.S.: The relationship between hearing impairment and cognitive function: a meta-analysis in adults. Clin. Otolaryngol. **41**(6), 718–729 (2016)

19. Barrantes, S.S.: Some aspects of ICT accessibility, usability and design methods with the young elderly (2006)

20. Zhou, J., Rau, P.-L.P., Salvendy, G.: Use and design of handheld computers for older adults: a review and appraisal. Int. J. Hum. Comput. Interact. **28**(12), 799–826 (2012)

21. Ziefle, M., Bay, S.: How to overcome disorientation in mobile phone menus: a comparison of two different types of navigation aids. Hum. Comput. Interact. **21**(4), 393–433 (2006)

22. Vella, F., Vigouroux, N., Rumeau, P.: Investigating drag and drop techniques for older people with cognitive impairment. In: Jacko, J.A. (ed.) HCI 2011. LNCS, vol. 6764, pp. 530–538. Springer, Heidelberg (2011). https://doi.org/10.1007/978-3-642-21619-0_65

23. Etcheverry, I., Terrier, P., Marquie, J.-C.: Assessing web interaction with recollection: age-related and task-related differences. Comput. Hum. Behav. **28**(1), 11–22 (2012)

24. Acartürk, C., Freitas, J., Fal, M., Dias, M.S.: Elderly speech-gaze interaction. In: Antona, M., Stephanidis, C. (eds.) UAHCI 2015. LNCS, vol. 9175, pp. 3–12. Springer, Cham (2015). https://doi.org/10.1007/978-3-319-20678-3_1

25. Morris, A., Goodman, J., Brading, H.: Internet use and non-use: views of older users. Univ. Access Inf. Soc. **6**(1), 43–57 (2006)

26. Vošner, H.B., Bobek, S., Kokol, P., Krečič, M.J.: Attitudes of active older Internet users towards online social networking. Comput. Hum. Behav. **55**, 230–241 (2016)

27. Dell, P., Marinova, D.: Are they acting their age? Online social interaction and identity in the elderly. In: Modsim International Congress on Modelling & Simulation Land Water & Environmental Management Integrated Systems for Sustainability, vol. 364, no. 3, pp. 2700–2706 (2007)

28. Wandke, H., Sengpiel, M., Soenksen, M.: Myths about older people's use of information and communication technology. Gerontology **58**(6), 564–570 (2012)
29. Hwangbo, H., Yoon, S.H., Jin, B.S., Han, Y.S., Ji, Y.G.: A study of pointing performance of elderly users on smartphones. Int. J. Hum. Comput. Interact. **29**(9), 604–618 (2013)
30. Grabowski, P.J., Mason, A.H.: Age differences in the control of a precision reach to grasp task within a desktop virtual environment. Int. J. Hum Comput Stud. **72**(4), 383–392 (2014)
31. Liao, M.J., Wu, Y., Sheu, C.F.: Effects of perceptual complexity on older and younger adults' target acquisition performance. Behav. Inf. Technol. **33**(6), 591–605 (2014)
32. Farhadi-Niaki, F., Etemad, S.A., Arya, A.: Design and usability analysis of gesture-based control for common desktop tasks. In: Kurosu, M. (ed.) HCI 2013. LNCS, vol. 8007, pp. 215–224. Springer, Heidelberg (2013). https://doi.org/10.1007/978-3-642-39330-3_23
33. Portet, F., Vacher, M., Golanski, C., Roux, C., Meillon, B.: Design and evaluation of a smart home voice interface for the elderly: acceptability and objection aspects. Pers. Ubiquit. Comput. **17**(1), 127–144 (2013)
34. Rodrigues, E., Carreira, M., Goncalves, D.: Enhancing typing performance of older adults on tablets. Univ. Access Inf. Soc. **15**(3), 393–418 (2016)
35. Tsai, W.-C., Lee, C.-F.: A study on the icon feedback types of small touch screen for the elderly. In: Stephanidis, C. (ed.) UAHCI 2009. LNCS, vol. 5615, pp. 422–431. Springer, Heidelberg (2009). https://doi.org/10.1007/978-3-642-02710-9_46
36. Zhou, J., Rau, P.L.P., Salvendy, G.: Older adults' text entry on smartphones and tablets: investigating effects of display size and input method on acceptance and performance. Int. J. Hum. Comput. Interact. **30**(9), 727–739 (2014)
37. Moffatt, K.A., Mcgrenere, J.: Slipping and drifting: using older users to uncover pen-based target acquisition difficulties. In: International ACM Sigaccess Conference on Computers and Accessibility, pp. 11–18. ACM (2007)
38. Fezzani, K., Albinet, C., Thon, B., Marquie, J.C.: The effect of motor difficulty on the acquisition of a computer task: a comparison between young and older adults. Behav. Inf. Technol. **29**(2), 115–124 (2010)
39. Cuaresma, J., MacKenzie, I.S.: A study of variations of Qwerty soft keyboards for mobile phones. In: Proceedings of the International Conference on Multimedia and Human-Computer Interaction, pp. 126.1–126.8. International ASET, Inc., Ottawa (2013)
40. Nicolau, H., Jorge, J.: Elderly text-entry performance on touchscreens. In: Proceedings of the 14th International ACM SIGACCESS Conference on Computers and Accessibility, pp. 127–134. ACM, Boulder (2012)
41. Findlater, L., Wobbrock, J.: Personalized input: improving ten-finger touchscreen typing through automatic adaptation. In: Proceedings of the SIGCHI Conference on Human Factors in Computing Systems, pp. 815–824. ACM, Austin (2012)
42. Nicol, E., Komninos, A., Dunlop, M.D.: A participatory design and formal study investigation into mobile text entry for older adults. Int. J. Mobile Hum. Comput. Interact. **8**(2), 20–46 (2016)
43. Lepicard, G., Vigouroux, N.: Touch screen user interfaces for older subjects. In: Miesenberger, K., Klaus, J., Zagler, W., Karshmer, A. (eds.) ICCHP 2010. LNCS, vol. 6180, pp. 592–599. Springer, Heidelberg (2010). https://doi.org/10.1007/978-3-642-14100-3_88
44. Yatani, K., Truong, K.N.: An evaluation of stylus-based text entry methods on handheld devices in stationary and mobile settings. In: International Conference on Human Computer Interaction with Mobile Devices and Services, pp. 487–494. ACM (2007)
45. Motti, L.G., Vigouroux, N., Gorce, P.: Improving accessibility of tactile interaction for older users: lowering accuracy requirements to support drag-and-drop interaction. Procedia Comput. Sci. **67**, 366–375 (2015)

46. Mclaughlin, A.C., Rogers, W.A., Fisk, A.D.: Using direct and indirect input devices: attention demands and age-related differences. ACM Trans. Comput. Hum. Interact. **16**(1), 1–15 (2009)
47. Moffatt, K., McGrenere, J.: Steadied-bubbles: combining techniques to address pen-based pointing errors for younger and older adults. In: International Conference on Human Factors in Computing Systems, CHI 2010, pp. 1125–1134. ACM, Atlanta (2010)
48. Mertens, A., et al.: Model based processing of swabbing movements on touch screens to improve accuracy and efficacy for information input of individuals suffering from kinetic tremor. In: Hippe, Z.S., Kulikowski, J.L., Mroczek, T. (eds.) Human – Computer Systems Interaction: Backgrounds and Applications 2. Advances in Intelligent and Soft Computing, vol. 98, pp. 503–522. Springer, Heidelberg (2012). https://doi.org/10.1007/978-3-642-23187-2_32
49. Jin, Z.X., Plocher, T., Kiff, L.: Touch screen user interfaces for older adults: button size and spacing. In: Stephanidis, C. (ed.) UAHCI 2007. LNCS, vol. 4554, pp. 933–941. Springer, Heidelberg (2007). https://doi.org/10.1007/978-3-540-73279-2_104
50. Wulf, L., Garschall, M., Klein, M., Tscheligi, M.: The influence of age and device orientation on the performance of touch gestures. In: Miesenberger, K., Fels, D., Archambault, D., Peňáz, P., Zagler, W. (eds.) ICCHP 2014. LNCS, vol. 8548, pp. 583–590. Springer, Cham (2014). https://doi.org/10.1007/978-3-319-08599-9_86
51. Sciarretta, E., Ingrosso, A., Volpi, V., Opromolla, A., Grimaldi, R.: Elderly and tablets: considerations and suggestions about the design of proper applications. In: Zhou, J., Salvendy, G. (eds.) ITAP 2015. LNCS, vol. 9193, pp. 509–518. Springer, Cham (2015). https://doi.org/10.1007/978-3-319-20892-3_49
52. Chen, W.: Gesture-based applications for elderly people. In: Kurosu, M. (ed.) HCI 2013. LNCS, vol. 8007, pp. 186–195. Springer, Heidelberg (2013). https://doi.org/10.1007/978-3-642-39330-3_20
53. Muskens, L., van Lent, R., Vijfvinkel, A., van Cann, P., Shahid, S.: Never too old to use a tablet: designing tablet applications for the cognitively and physically impaired elderly. In: Miesenberger, K., Fels, D., Archambault, D., Peňáz, P., Zagler, W. (eds.) ICCHP 2014. LNCS, vol. 8547, pp. 391–398. Springer, Cham (2014). https://doi.org/10.1007/978-3-319-08596-8_60
54. Barros, A.C.D., Leitão, R., Ribeiro, J.: Design and evaluation of a mobile user interface for older adults: navigation, interaction and visual design recommendations. Procedia Comput. Sci. **27**, 369–378 (2014)
55. Bergstrom, J.C.R., Jans, O.H.M.E.: Age-related differences in eye tracking and usability performance: website usability for older adults. Int. J. Hum. Comput. Interact. **29**(8), 541–548 (2013)
56. Witt, H., Lawo, M., Drugge, M.: Visual feedback and different frames of reference: the impact on gesture interaction techniques for wearable computing. In: International Conference on Human Computer Interaction with Mobile Devices and Services, pp. 293–300. ACM (2008)
57. Ott, R., Thalmann, D., Vexo, F.: Haptic feedback in mixed-reality environment. Vis. Comput. **23**(9), 843–849 (2007)
58. Lee, J.-H., Poliakoff, E., Spence, C.: The effect of multimodal feedback presented via a touch screen on the performance of older adults. In: Altinsoy, M.E., Jekosch, U., Brewster, S. (eds.) HAID 2009. LNCS, vol. 5763, pp. 128–135. Springer, Heidelberg (2009). https://doi.org/10.1007/978-3-642-04076-4_14
59. Park, Y., Heo, H., Lee, K.: Enhanced auditory feedback for Korean touch screen keyboards. Int. J. Hum Comput Stud. **73**, 1–11 (2015)

60. Lemaitre, G., Houix, O., Susini, P., Visell, Y., Franinovic, K.: Feelings elicited by auditory feedback from a computationally augmented artifact: the flops. IEEE Trans. Affect. Comput. 3(3), 335–348 (2012)
61. Nishino, H., Goto, R., Fukakusa, Y., Lin, J., Kagawa, T., Yoshida, K., Nagatomo, N.: A touch screen interface design with tactile feedback for practical applications. Int. J. Space Based Situated Comput. 3(1), 8–21 (2013)
62. Pitts, M.J., Burnett, G., Skrypchuk, L., Wellings, T., Attridge, A., Williams, M.A.: Visual–haptic feedback interaction in automotive touchscreens. Displays 33(1), 7–16 (2012)
63. Üzüm, B., Göktürk, M.: The effect of vibrotactile feedback on novice older adults in target selection tasks. In: Robertson, M.M. (ed.) EHAWC 2011. LNCS, vol. 6779, pp. 171–179. Springer, Heidelberg (2011). https://doi.org/10.1007/978-3-642-21716-6_18
64. Hoggan, E., Brewster, S.A., Johnston, J.: Investigating the effectiveness of tactile feedback for mobile touchscreens. In: Conference on Human Factors in Computing Systems, CHI 2008, Florence, Italy, April, vol. 2008, pp. 1573–1582 (2008)
65. De Boeck, J., Vanacken, L., Coninx, K.: Target Acquisition with force feedback: the effect of different forces on the user's performance. In: Altinsoy, M.E., Jekosch, U., Brewster, S. (eds.) HAID 2009. LNCS, vol. 5763, pp. 11–20. Springer, Heidelberg (2009). https://doi.org/10.1007/978-3-642-04076-4_2
66. Schierholz, I., Finke, M., Schulte, S., Hauthal, N., Kantzke, C., Rach, S., Sandmann, P.: Enhanced audio-visual interactions in the auditory cortex of elderly cochlear-implant users. Hear. Res. 328, 133–147 (2015)
67. Huyse, A., Leybaert, J., Berthommier, F.: Effects of aging on audio-visual speech integration. J. Acoust. Soc. Am. 136(4), 1918–1931 (2014)
68. Faeth, A., Harding, C.: Emergent effects in multimodal feedback from virtual buttons. ACM Trans. Comput. Hum. Interact. 21(1), 1–23 (2014)
69. Köpsel, A., Majaranta, P., Isokoski, P., Huckauf, A.: Effects of auditory, haptic and visual feedback on performing gestures by gaze or by hand. Behav. Inf. Technol. 35(12), 1044–1062 (2016)
70. Park, E., Joon, K., Pobil, A.P.D.: The effects of multimodal feedback and gender on task performance of stylus pen users. Int. J. Adv. Robot. Syst. 9(3), 1 (2012)
71. Motti, L.G., Vigouroux, N., Gorce, P.: Ease-of-use of tactile interaction for novice older adults. In: Zhou, J., Salvendy, G. (eds.) ITAP 2015. LNCS, vol. 9193, pp. 463–474. Springer, Cham (2015). https://doi.org/10.1007/978-3-319-20892-3_45

Acoustical Evaluation for the Renovation of Multipurpose Performance Hall

Wei Lin[1(✉)], Hsuan Lin[2], Kung-Huang Huang[3], and Chung-Tsung Wu[4]

[1] Department of Interior Design, Hwa Hsia University of Technology, Taipei, Taiwan
weilin@cc.hwh.edu.tw
[2] Department of Product Design, Tainan University of Technology, Tainan, Taiwan
te0038@mail.tut.edu.tw
[3] Shang You Construction Co. Ltd., Kaohsiung, Taiwan
sf.land@msa.hinet.net
[4] Chung-Tsung Wu Architectural Firm, Taipei, Taiwan
archwu@seed.net.tw

Abstract. Taipei Arts Promotion Center Hall carried out renovation works and acoustical evaluation was conducted in 2003. In the past 15 years of use, due to air humidity and material aging and other factors, may affect the room acoustics. The assessments mainly focus on the setting of the space in theater mode, this is the most frequently used setting by the owner. Auditorium impressions of different audiences are different due to the different characteristics of the reverberation time. Different auditory impressions may also reflect time, space, intensity and frequency characteristics and other factors in sound field. In the survey and assessment, field measurement is taken as the basis for assessment, and the real field hall is measured, which includes in-site measurement and computer simulation evaluation for chamber music performance. Finally, the article finally presents the relevant improvement and description.

Keywords: Multipurpose performance hall · Room acoustics
Computer simulation · In-site measurement

1 Introduction

Taipei Arts Promotion Center Hall is multipurpose auditorium and normally used for theater. First, the single-channel sound measurement for indoor sound field performance which is carried out based on the sound field performance evaluation, and the reinforcement sound system measurement is conducted consequently. In order to consider the performance environment of music acoustic (natural sound), once again entered the venue for the two-channel spatial impression of the objective measurement which was evaluated. Some researches presented suitable mid-frequency depending on theater mode, room volume and seating capacity [1]. In the Meanwhile, the musicians can also hear their own sound with the monitoring system, which can improve performance communication among musical band at pit. In addition to creating a good theater environments, the sound reinforcement system is another major focus of this study, the role

© Springer International Publishing AG, part of Springer Nature 2018
J. Zhou and G. Salvendy (Eds.): ITAP 2018, LNCS 10926, pp. 297–306, 2018.
https://doi.org/10.1007/978-3-319-92034-4_22

and function of electro-acoustic system in hall, speakers deliver music to listeners by the PA sound system, known as PA (Public address), however, it is not satisfied to meet various performance status, the system of sound reinforcement (SR) is also introduced in 1965, SR demands not simply transmit the sound, but also receive the brilliant sound from the source, high-quality of sound speaker lead music effect clearly without distortion which could reach the ears of the listener's. This paper presents the in-site measurement, acoustical simulation for the live house which is verified at exited performance space. A number of major acoustical features have been employed in order to provide a hall which meets the various criteria for a venue designed to accommodate a multi-purpose repertoire of events [2]. Schroeder the basic principles of computer simulation into the room acoustics was since 1960 [3]. Room acoustic modeling technique and especially the room acoustic computer models have developed over the last decades [4] and highly accurate prediction models are available today.. Image Source Models method is based on the principle that a specular reflection can be constructed geometrically by mirroring the source in the plane of the reflecting surface. In a rectangular box-shaped room it is very simple to construct all image sources up to a certain order of reflection [5]. The first computer model that was used for practical design of auditoria was a ray tracing model which is proposed by Asbjørn Krokstad [6]. Numbers of sound rays are traced from a source point up to high order reflections following the geometrical and optical law of reflection. Although the room acoustic modeling technique has originally been devoted to the acoustic prediction and design of auditoria, the problems are equally challenging in practical projects, and to a great extent, the same methods can be adopted. One fundamental problem is that the rooms can be very irregular, the diffusion of sound can be uneven and very different from the simple assumption of a diffuse sound field, and the sound absorption is unevenly distributed over the surfaces [7]; all together this means that the reverberation time can be significantly different from that calculated by the classical equations of Sabine and Eyring [8]. Another situation is that even if the reverberation time can be measured and predicted, it may not be relevant parameters to describe the acoustical condition of a room. For the instance, stage support is evaluated for the musician communication and IACC and LF are for sound specialness. In auditoria and performance spaces the room acoustic parameters are laid down in ISO 3382-1 [9]. The paper begins with the in-site measurements, following sections are dedicated to detailed studies concentrating on the computer adjustable. The results presented here not only have been used to verify the design scheme concept, simple field verifications have also achieved in the future renovation in order to characterize information of room acoustic. A room form was developed as prototype that had overall proportion and volume similar to the rectangular, bilaterally symmetrical, the location of measuring points is taken unilateral planning, the average distribution in the auditorium on the right, 1002 seats are distributed in the three level of floors during all assessment. Compared to first renovated completion the planning of the reverberation time (RT), the chamber music mode at middle frequency band is 1.52 s, the theater mode is 1.28 s. The volume of the hall is 5614 m^3, and equipped the hall with acoustical curtains by modifying its acoustical characteristics.

2   In-Site Measurement

The main measurement is the theater mode, which is the most frequently used setting by the Taipei Arts Promotion Center Hall. The general design conditions of the auditorium which is included are shown in Table 1. All the curtains on the stage are open (Broadband frequency usage), including the backdrop, the curtain and screen cover, auditorium floor and the third floor of the sound-absorbing curtain fully expanded. The measurement was set unoccupied state, all entrances and exits are closed. When the background noise is measured, the air-conditioning system is normally set for theater performance, and the field lighting in the auditorium are turned on. In the measurement process, to be consistent with the consistency of the state of the environment, the hall lighting and equipment fully open and use air conditioning equipment to stabilize the temperature and humidity changes.

Table 1.   List of general design conditions of the auditorium

Event	Theater mode
Room form	Rectangular hall
Seating capacity	1002 seats (Fist floor: 576 seats, second floor: 217 seat, third floor: 209 seats)
Hall dimensions	Width × Length × High: 32 m × 52 m × 15.6 m
Proscenium size	Width × Length: 14.8 M × 9.8 M
Stage size	Width × Length: 20.8 M × 24.4 M
Musical pit size	Width × Length: 16 M × 4 M
Auditorium volume	5614 M^3
Adjustable absorption	Heavy weight drapery

2.1   Measuring Equipment and Point Distribution Planning

Signal to noise ratio is sufficient and the frequency can reach more than 45 dB in the auditorium, the DIRAC was utilized for measurement as calculation station of the sound field measurement system. The sound source is set on the stage (S1), the receiving point is set to 10 points (M1-M10), the measurement points and instruments are located on the right side of the auditorium (See in Figs. 1 and 2). The omnidirectional sound source (S) is located 2-m above the center of the stage to the edge of the orchestra pit, 125-cm height above the ground, and the e-sweep signal is transmitted using a dodecahedron shape loudspeaker. The receiving points are distributed as a 0.5-in Microphone (B&K Type-2250), fixed with a microphone holder and 120-cm above the ground. The impulse response is calculated by the signals measured by a digital workstation (DIRAC) and filtered to obtain the decay curve by the inverse product. For the assessment of Spatial impression in the sound field, Inter-aural Cross Correlation (IACC) and early lateral energy fraction (LF) parameters were also evaluated, respectively. Sound reinforcement system are also conducted at the stage.

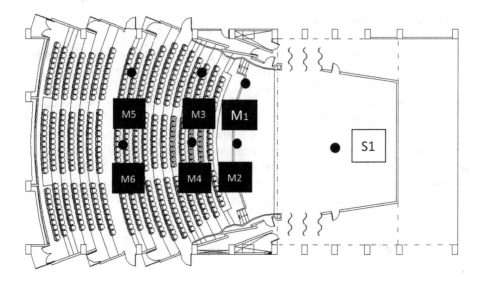

Fig. 1. Sound source and 6 receiving points are distributed in first floor of auditorium

Fig. 2. Photos of measurement instruments are illustrated

2.2 Results of Room Acoustic Measurement

In-site field measurement to the international standard ISO3382-1: 2009 (E) content and specifications described as the basis. In this field measurement, performance settings to the main theater mode, this is the most used frequency setting. Measurement parameters include the Reverberation time (T30), clarity (C80), Sound Strength (G), Stage support (ST), Inter-aural Cross Correlation (IACC) and early lateral energy fraction (LF). The results of in-site field measurement (theater mode), the reverberation time (RT) is 1.18 s at the middle frequency band (500 Hz, 1 kHz), and the recommended indoor perform-ance of the theater is 1.05–1.35. The measured results are consistent with the sound field performance. In addition, the spatial image of music performance, IACC and LF two parameters were measured, results are indicated 0.73 and 0.18, respectively. The two parameters pointed out that may not meet the sense of subjective hearing specialness in auditorium. Preliminary measurements results and recommendation of acoustical parameters are summarized in Table 2.

Table 2. Acoustical parameters with live music performance are listed

Parameter	500 Hz	1000 Hz	Overall average	Recommendation
T_{30} (s)	1.25	1.11	1.18	1.05–1.35
C_{80} (dB)	5.4	6.6	6.0	4.0–6.0 dB
G (dB)	1.1	1.3	1.2	1.0–3.0 dB
Solo (ST)	−18.3	−16.8	−17.6	N/A
Brass (ST)	−16.3	−16.1	−16.2	N/A
String (ST)	−15.4	−16.3	−15.9	N/A
IACC	0.82	0.63	0.73	≤0.45
LF	0.16	0.20	0.18	≥0.20

Based on the usage of the sound reinforcement system in the theater mode, this hall is associated a line array system providing a very high performance of loudspeaker capability and a wide range of sound energy distribution for the sound field. Measurement indicators include array speaker electrical audio frequency response and acoustic gain. In the measurement of electrical audio frequency response, consider the sampling frequency of the speaker response to the scope of requirements, IEC268-5 provides in the frequency band within the scope of the electrical audio frequency response, the proposed tolerance difference for frequency of sound pressure within ±5 dB. Consideration all 1/3 octave band range, the difference of 50 Hz to 1.6 kHz in each frequency needs to be within 10 dB. Measurement results except for points M1 and M2 meet the recommended value, the remaining points are greater than the standard value (≦ ±5 dB). Transmission gain measurement results −18.3 dB, did not meet the recommended value (≧ −8 dB).

3   Computer Simulation for Chamber Music

In order to meet the future renovation, except the theater mode, chamber music mode is conducted by computer simulation. When the musical perform, in addition to facing architectural space design, the tone, volume, reverberation may have a influence musical performance, may also have an impact on the live sound effects. To further confirm the performance hall planning goals and acoustic parameters of the correlation between topography, assess technology includes the design stage through to computer simulation. Since the establishment of and modifications to establish a database of digital material model parameters through information operations, then check the status of the sound quality of the sound field. As shown in Fig. 3, the coverage of 1st order reflections can be evenly distributed to the stage and the frontal audience by only proposed upper reflectors.

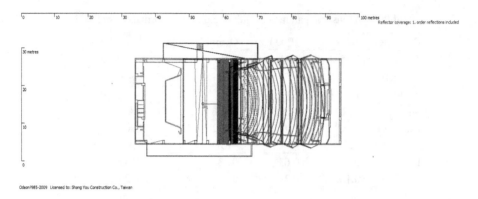

Fig. 3. Simulated 1st order reflection coverage from the upper reflectors

3.1 Computer Simulation Calculation

The simulation was performed by using the upgraded Odeon software package that can handle energy parameters of ray tracing calculation and was used to validate the schematic concept of using the curve reflectors. The number of rays was set to 10001 and the truncation time of calculation was set to 5000 ms. The source was on the central axis and 3-m from the front edge of the platform. Computer simulation of calculation is set as shown in Table 3.

Table 3. List of calculation for computer simulation

Scatter method	Lambert
Decimate late rays	ON
Transition order	1
Number of rays	10001
Max. reflection order	2000
Impulse response length	5000 ms
Angular absorption	All materials
Late reflection density	600/ms
Scatter method	Lambert

A diffusive bricks are attached and a 0.7 scattering factor are assigned to the side and rear walls. Occupied seating with medium upholstery was used for the audience and a 0.7 scattering factor was assigned. 650 m^2 heavy absorptive draperies for reinforcement music with a 0.4 scattering factor were introduced. Furthermore, acoustics parameters were proposed design target values by computer simulation for the energy parameters EDT, RT, C_{80}, D_{50} T_s and LF_{80}. Materials assignments in library of Computer simulation are as shown in Table 4.

Table 4. Materials assignments in library of computer simulation

Location	Materials	Frequency (Hz)							Scattering coefficient
		63	125	250	500	1 k	2 k	4 k	
Stage floor	Oregon Wood	0.15	0.15	0.2	0.1	0.1	0.1	0.1	0.1
Audience floor	Wood	0.15	0.15	0.11	0.1	0.07	0.06	0.07	0.1
Audience seat	Medium upholstered	0.24	0.25	0.47	0.63	0.75	0.78	0.83	0.7
Side wall	Diffusive Bricks	0.02	0.02	0.02	0.02	0.02	0.02	0.02	0.7
Reflector	Gypsum board	0.04	0.04	0.06	0.06	0.06	0.06	0.04	0.2
Stage opening	Drapery	0.28	0.28	0.26	0.46	0.71	0.75	0.7	0.3
Adjustable absorption	Heavy drapery	0.03	0.03	0.5	0.65	0.7	0.7	0.7	0.4

3.2   Results of Computer Simulation

A omni-directivity sound source provided by the software package and was used occasionally as references. The source was on the central axis and 1.5-m from the front edge of the platform. Due to the cross-shaped hall-room space and symmetry, averaging 8 measuring points are chosen one side of seating which were symmetrically distributed. Sound source in front of stage is set and simulated perspective and distribution of sound energy particles of schematic model is shown in Fig. 4. Preliminary obtain mono sound parameter, reverberation time (RT), early decay time (EDT) and music clarity (Clarity, C80) are discussed. Acoustical indices, such as RT30, C80, D50, Ts and EDT, are derived from the impulse response which is based on the International Standard ISO 3382 (Bradley 2004) [10]. Preliminary results of acoustical parameters were calculated by computer simulation were summarized in Table 5 when all the acoustical draperies are taken on. The reverberation time for the chamber music at mid-frequency is resulted about 1.42 s.

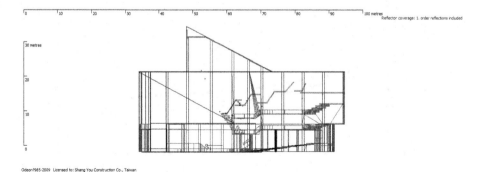

Fig. 4. Simulated perspective model and distribution of sound energy particles

Table 5. Acoustical parameters with music performance (Chamber music) are listed

Frequency	Parameter					
	125 Hz	250 Hz	500 Hz	1000 Hz	2000 Hz	4000 Hz
EDT (s)	1.95	1.73	1.66	1.51	1.38	1.20
T_{30} (s)	1.35	1.59	1.45	1.38	1.28	1.15
C_{80} (dB)	5.4	3.1	3.4	3.7	4.2	5.0
D50	0.54	0.56	0.56	0.58	0.60	0.70
Ts (ms)	82	74	70	64	57	39
LF_{80}	0.056	0.064	0.060	0.067	0.065	0.073

4   Preliminary Results

The result of reverberation time measurement was 1.18 s at middle frequency of this investigation, compared with the renovation in 2003, reverberation time measurement was 1.28 s at middle frequency (Theater mode), sound amplitude is decreasing to 0.1 s, mainly due to the hall 15 years of sound-absorbing material effect results. Although the use of the theater mode is currently influential, considering the future use of music performances, it is suggested that the middle band reverberation time should be 1.52 s (Chamber music mode), and it is suggested that details be elaborated and explained in the future detailed construction design. It is recommended that the amplitude range of the reverberation time range from 16% to 30%. The comparison of reverberation times (T30) among the different period derived from the measurement and simulation for the theater and chamber music mode are shown in Fig. 5.

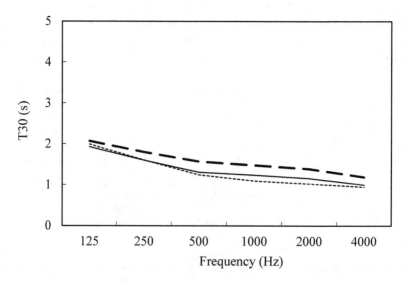

Fig. 5. Comparison of reverberation times (T30) at 1/1 octave frequency band among the different period time, year 2003 (Solid line) and year 2017 (Dotted line) derived from the measurement, respectively and simulation for the chamber music mode (Dashed line) are illustrated.

5   Discussion

The main assessments in Taipei Arts Promotion Center Hall carried out renovation works and acoustical evaluation was conducted in 2003 and 2017, respectively. In the past 15 years of use, due to air humidity and material aging and other factors, may affect the room acoustics. Theater mode is the most frequently used setting for the owner utilized. The auditorium impressions of different audiences are different due to the different characteristics of the reverberation time. In the survey and assessment, field measurement is taken as the basis for assessment, which includes in-site measurement and computer simulation for chamber music performance. Some preliminary results are abstracted as followed:

1. The result of reverberation time measurement was 1.18 s at middle frequency of this investigation, compared with the renovation in 2003, reverberation time measurement was 1.28 s at middle frequency (Theater mode), sound amplitude is decreasing to 0.1 s, mainly due to the hall 15 years of sound-absorbing material effect results.
2. Measurement results except for points M1 and M2 meet the recommended value, the remaining points are greater than the standard value ($\leqq \pm 5$ dB). Transmission gain measurement results -18.3 dB, did not meet the recommended value ($\geqq -8$ dB).
3. For Spatial image of music performance, IACC and LF two parameters results in 0.73 and 0.18, respectively. The two parameters pointed out that may not meet the sense of subjective specialness in auditorium. Upper divided reflector of the hall can compensate the insufficient of sense of hearing in specialness.
4. Although the use of the theater mode is currently influential, considering the future use of music performances, it is suggested that the middle band reverberation time should be 1.52 s (Chamber music mode), and it is suggested that details be elaborated and explained in the future detailed construction design.

Acknowledgements. The authors wish to thank Huang Kung Huang, Shang You Construction Co. Ltd. for the assistant of filed measurements and simulation, Professor Wei-Hwa Chiang, Dep. of Architecture, National Taiwan University of Science and Technology the kindly assistances during the measurement phase.

References

1. Barron, M.: Auditorium Acoustics and Architectural Design, 2nd edn. E & FN Spon, London (1993)
2. Chiang, W., Lin, W., Chen, Y.-R., Hu, H.-Y.: Variable acoustics design of a small proscenium concert Hall. J. Asian Archit. Build. Eng. (2008)
3. Schroeder, M.R., Atal, B.S., Bird, C.M.: Digital computers in room acoustics. In: 4th International Congress on Acoustics (ICA 4), Kopenhagen, Vortrag M21 (1962)
4. Rindel, J.H.: Modelling in auditorium acoustics. From ripple tank and scale models to computer simulations. Revista de Acústica **XXXIII**(3–4), 31–35 (2002)
5. Allen, J., Berkley, D.A.: Image method for efficiently simulating small-room acoustics. J. Acoust. Soc. Am. **65**, 943–950 (1979)

6. Krokstad, A., Strom, S., Sorsdal, S.: Calculating the acoustical room response by the use of a ray tracing technique. J. Sound Vib. **8**(1), 118–125 (1968)
7. Christensen, C.L., Rindel, J.H.: A new scattering method that combines roughness and diffraction effects. In: Proceedings of Forum Acusticum, Budapest, Hungary, pp. 2159–2164 (2005)
8. Siebein, G.W., et al.: Project Design Phase Analysis Techniques For Predicting the Acoustical Qualities of Buildings. University of Florida (1986)
9. ISO 3382-1:2009: Acoustics - Measurement of room acoustic parameters - Part 1: Performance spaces (1986)
10. Bradley, J.S.: Using ISO 3382 measures to evaluate acoustical condition in concert halls. In: International Symposium on Room Acoustics: Design and Science 2004, Kyoto, Japan (2004)

Viewing Angle, Depth and Directionality
of 2D and 3D Icons

Hsuan Lin[1]([✉]), Kuo-Liang Huang[2], and Wei Lin[3]

[1] Department of Product Design, Tainan University of Technology, Tainan, Taiwan
te0038@mail.tut.edu.tw
[2] Department of Visual Arts and Design, Nan-hua University, Chiayi, Taiwan
shashiliang@gmail.com
[3] Department of Interior Design, Hwa Hsia University of Technology, Taipei, Taiwan
weilin@cc.hwh.edu.tw

Abstract. The modern world is faced with an increasingly aging population, so the demand and market of the aged have expanded rapidly. The authors suggest researching the icons suitable for the elderly. The findings herein identify design elements of 2D and 3D icons and may serve as a reference for those engaged in icon design and research in the future. Therefore, this study probed comprehensively into the viewing angles, depth, and directionality of 2D and 3D icons. The useful references for further research and practical applications of website design.

Keywords: Icon · Viewing angle · Depth · Directionality

1 Viewing Angle of 2D and 3D Icons

1.1 Three-View Diagram

As a 3D object is observed, the position of the object in relation to the observer can be shown from different viewing angles. There are six viewing angles available: top, left, front, right, back, and bottom (Fig. 1). However, the front, top, and right viewing angles are the three frequently used. As the feature of an object differs, the viewing angle suitable for it varies. A designer will choose the viewing angle that can present the features and details of the icon more adequately.

1.2 Viewing Angle

A designer can present an icon from four viewing angles, or viewpoints: one-view, two-view, three-view, and offset from front [1], which are explained below.

One-View Diagram. The one-view diagram is the most commonly used for icons at present. This way, an object is presented from only one viewing angle, which is parallel with the viewer's sightline, usually from the front or the angle which can show the optimum features of the object (Fig. 2).

© Springer International Publishing AG, part of Springer Nature 2018
J. Zhou and G. Salvendy (Eds.): ITAP 2018, LNCS 10926, pp. 307–314, 2018.
https://doi.org/10.1007/978-3-319-92034-4_23

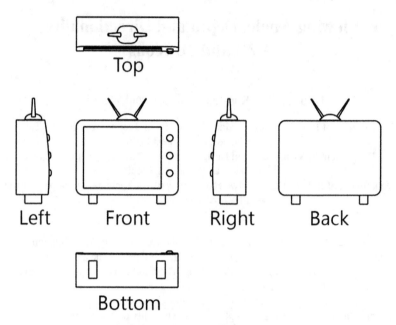

Fig. 1. Three-view diagram

Fig. 2. One-view diagram

Two-View Diagram. A two-view diagram presents an object from two viewing angles, from the front and the slight top or side, to show its two sides and highlight its features (Fig. 3).

Fig. 3. Two-view diagram

Three-View Diagram. A three-view diagram presents an object from three viewing angles, i.e., from the front, top and side, to show the object in an optimum and equal way (Fig. 4).

Fig. 4. Three-view diagram

Offset From Front. An offset from front diagram (Fig. 5) is similar to a two-view diagram (Fig. 3) in terms of presentation effects, for both are presented from two viewing angles. However, close examination reveals their difference. The offset from front diagram takes the front view as the major viewpoint and the slight top or side as the minor viewpoint [1]. The major viewpoint shows more features of the object than the minor viewpoint. The greatest difference between offset from front and two-view is that the former presents the object in a one-view diagram without contracting the major viewpoint. By contrast, the latter contracts the major viewpoint to present a two-view diagram. Therefore, when the object is presented in the offset from front viewpoint, a one-view diagram plus depth and shade is good enough to present a perspective.

Fig. 5. Offset from front

1.3 Depth

Depth is an important factor used to distinguish 2D icons from 3D icons. The factors affecting the way to present the depth of an icon are shade [1], shadow [1–3], depth/shallowness [1], and front/back. As an icon is presented in different levels of depth, the results are widely different. 2D icons show farness or closeness by means of front/back (Fig. 6), depth/shallowness (Fig. 7), distance (Fig. 8), and size (Fig. 9). However, 3D icons (Fig. 10) are presented in common ways; that is, their convexness or concaveness is shown in two ways. Moreover, some icons show 3D effect through 2D techniques; namely, shades are used to present convexness (Fig. 11) or concaveness (Fig. 12).

Fig. 6. Front/back

Fig. 7. Depth/shallowness

Fig. 8. Distance

Fig. 9. Size

Fig. 10. 3D perspective

Fig. 11. 2D convexness with 3D effect

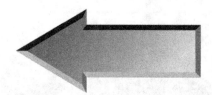

Fig. 12. 2D concaveness with 3D effect

1.4 Directionality

Icons can present directionality [1]. To be exact, 2D icons can show such two-dimensional directions as upwardness, downwardness, leftwardness, and rightwardness (Fig. 13). However, 2D icons can hardly present depth, i.e., inwardness and outwardness (Fig. 14), though the front of the arrow is larger than its back. By contrast, 3D icons can not only show upwardness, downwardness, leftwardness, and rightwardness (Fig. 15) but also inwardness and outwardness (Fig. 16).

Fig. 13. Upwardness, downwardness, leftwardness, and rightwardness of 2D icons

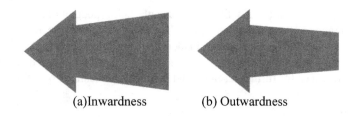

(a)Inwardness   (b) Outwardness

Fig. 14. Depth of 3D icons

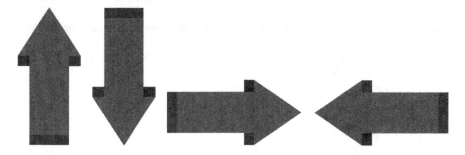

Fig. 15. Upwardness, downwardness, leftwardness, and rightwardness of 3D icons

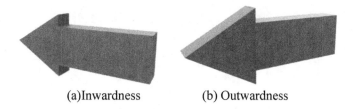

(a)Inwardness   (b) Outwardness

Fig. 16. Depth of 3D icons

2 Conclusions

Presentation of depth is an important factor influencing 2D and 3D icons. Viewing angles, depth, and directionality are important factors that affect viewers' judgment of depth. In general, there are four viewing angles used for icons: one-view, two-view, three-view, and offset from front. To present an icon in an optimum way, designers usually adopt the offset from front viewpoint. Thus, the main features of the object may be presented from the major viewpoint while the features from the minor viewpoint are less important, with only depth indicated. In addition, to present depth, 2D icons rely on front/back, depth/shallowness, distance, and size. As for directionality, 2D icons can show the direction on a two-dimensional axis without presenting depth (inwardness and outwardness). By contrast, 3D icons can easily present three-dimensional movements, including inwardness and outwardness.

The modern world is faced with an increasingly aging population, so the demand and market of the aged have expanded rapidly. The authors suggest researching the icons suitable for the elderly. The findings herein identify design elements of 2D and 3D icons and may serve as a reference for those engaged in icon design and research in the future. The useful references for further research and practical applications of website design.

References

1. Horton, W.K.: The Icon Book: Visual Symbols for Computer Systems and Documentation. Wiley Inc., New York (1994)
2. Sing-Sheng Guan, H.-Y.C.: A study on icon design applied kansei engineering. J. Sci. Technol. **13**, 33–43 (2004)
3. Guan, S., Tong, D., Hsieh, C.: A study of partial feature attributes affecting holistic kansei for icon design. J. Sci. Technol. **17**, 149–158 (2008)

A Study on Haptic Feedback Awareness
of Senior Citizens

Shuo-Fang Liu, Yu-Tzu Yang[⊠], Ching-Fen Chang, Po-Yen Lin,
and Hsiang-Sheng Cheng

Department of Industrial Design, National Cheng-Kung University,
No 1, University Road, Tainan City 701, Taiwan (R.O.C.)
4a21c067@stust.edu.tw

Abstract. The global population is moving toward an ageing population. Many countries are improving their technology to create smart cities suitable for the elderly. With the development of smart devices, people can make their life more convenient and can use phone APP to help the older with medical or health management. With the degeneration of their body, their sense of touch decreases, which in turn affects their feelings of haptic feedback for smart devices. Therefore, the study is aim to measure haptic feedback differences between elderly and young people, and to provide the manufacturers of mobile devices development as a basis for elderly have a good haptic feedback experience and improve the quality of use. The study was divided into two phases, a total of 58 participants recruited, of whom 27 people were 18 to 50 years old and 31 people over the age of 50, and through comparing haptic vibration feedback intensity by different vibration frequency and vibration time of mobile devices to explore whether there is any feeling difference between two ages.

Keywords: Elderly · Physiological function · Tactile · Haptic feedback

1 Introduction

As the world enters a society with more senior citizens, more and more elderly people embrace technological products (such as smartphone, computer, etc.) and use them to contact other people and learn new things. The frequency of use of high technology device by elderly people is not necessary less than that of young people. In addition, the design of smart devices can be combined with the software in medical related purposes which may help the elderly to have better connection with medical team to track their health condition and diet habits. It could provide an easier way to help the elderly to achieve their health management and improve their quality of lives [1–3].

Alongside the progress of science and technology, man-machine interaction provides people with richer experience, especially giving people a rich sensory experience in the side of visual, tactile, and auditory senses. In the daily life, it can be observed that the screen meets the visual needs and the speaker meets the auditory part. The current trend shows that science and technology is oriented towards the development of haptic feedback. The process of virtual reality and wearable devices reduces the size into the finger-grounded skin deformation device from the larger devices originally. The size

© Springer International Publishing AG, part of Springer Nature 2018
J. Zhou and G. Salvendy (Eds.): ITAP 2018, LNCS 10926, pp. 315–324, 2018.
https://doi.org/10.1007/978-3-319-92034-4_24

miniaturization provides the users an improved tactile experiences by using the three freedom dimensions of kinesthetic and skin tactile interaction to the fingertips [4, 5]. Taptic Engine developed by Apple assumes the responsibility for tactile sensation. Currently, sensory dimension is the haptic feedback mechanism that Apple is committed to developing [6]. The tactile vibration feedback from human senses is the earliest measurement and the most common-use tactile haptic feedback. The tactile perception is able to obtain many diversified information by sending different tactile form messages to the brain through touching on the different sizes of objects, shapes, materials, roughness, and temperature, and so on [7, 8].

The smart devices can be applied in the haptic feedback development to assist the visually impaired. The researchers creates the braille pattern on the touch screen with different frequencies and different length of vibrations to test if the visually impaired people is able to discriminate the differences [9]. The haptic feedback technology can be categorized into three major applications: confirmation, immersion, and enriched communication. 1. Confirmation: for example, making the users to be able to have an actual feeling on their fingers when they press the virtual keyboard which may avoid the over pressing problems. 2. Immersion: it can provide the users more actual experiences by integrating the Confirmation technology with the environment into the smart devices. 3. Enriched communication: the meaning of communication is included the hearing, vision, and tactile communications. Inputting the tactile vibration feedback can create live experiences to the users [10].

Although many senior citizens enjoy learning new technologies, during the learning process, they still feel some inadequacy. The reasons for this maybe (1) they are not familiar with the operation of a new technological product due to the complicated design of its hardware and software which is too complex and difficult to understand; (2) they have limited experience of using computer products and cannot use past experience to operate the device; (3) the deterioration of their body function (such as vision, tactile sense, hearing, etc.) makes them unable to successfully complete an action [11–13]. The skin is the largest organ of the body. The sense of touch can replace auditory and visual senses. Hence, although the elderly's physical functions are degrading, smartphones can enhance their tactile experience and make up for their weakened hearing and vision [14]. In terms of tactile sense, neurostimulation, such as light, sound, current, vibration, action, and thought, can be used as a way to stimulate the brain [15]. Most people undergo deterioration of sight at the age 40 to 50 [16]. Therefore, if haptic feedback can be enhanced, the elderly would be able to have a better smart phone experience. However, the sense for haptic feedback of the elderly people differs from general users due to the deterioration of their physiological function due to aging. In general, smart phone haptic feedback research is rarely done on the older generation. Therefore, this study focuses on the haptic feedback of the elderly and compares it with users of different ages so as to understand the differences in the haptic feedback between the elderly and other age groups in order to give senior citizens a satisfactory experience of smart devices.

2   Method

The aim of this study was to explore the differences in the haptic feedback between the elderly and the different age groups. Experiments were conducted with different haptic feedback samples accompanied. This study is divided into two experiments, and the individual recruitment of the older and the younger groups of participants were compared. The descriptions of Experiments are as follows:

- Experiment 1: The main purpose is to explore the intensity perception of different vibration frequencies under fixed vibration time. Participants should be based on personal perception of the same vibration time to compare different vibration frequency samples, and provide the feedback of which vibration strength is the greatest.
- Experiment 2: The main purpose is to explore the intensity perception of different vibration time under fixed vibration frequencies. Participants should be based on personal perception of the same vibration time to compare different vibration frequency samples, and asked them which vibration strength is the greatest as experiment 1.

2.1   Experimental Sample

Experiment 1

Three different vibration frequencies (80 Hz, 160 Hz, 200 Hz) were compared among three different vibration times (100 ms, 300 ms, 500 ms), as shown in Table 1.

Table 1. Experiment 1 sample.

Vibration time	100 ms	300 ms	500 ms
Vibration frequency	80 Hz	80 Hz	80 Hz
	160 Hz	160 Hz	160 Hz
	200 Hz	200 Hz	200 Hz

Experiment 2

Three different vibration times (300 ms, 500 ms, 1000 ms) were compared among three different vibration frequencies (160 Hz, 180 Hz, 220 Hz), as shown in Table 2.

Table 2. Experiment 2 sample.

Vibration frequency	160 Hz	180 Hz	220 Hz
Vibration time	300 ms	300 ms	300 ms
	500 ms	500 ms	500 ms
	1000 ms	1000 ms	1000 ms

2.2   Experimental Setup

- Participants: Two experiments were recruited the middle-aged or older and the young groups. In experiment 1, 22 participants were recruited (10 young people and 12 middle aged people). In the second experiment 2, 36 people were recruited (17 young people, middle-aged and older people 19 people).
- Apparatus: In experiment 1, two different devices were used to perform the experiments, 5.5 in. phone panel and 9.7 in. tab panel. The main idea is to know whether the two sizes have different effects on the participants. According to the results of the first experiment, we discover that perception of the participants on the tab panel is better than that the phone panel. Therefore, in the experiment 2, the experiment will be conducted only on the tab panel device. Two experimental motors are based on the most common type of tactile vibration motor which is model 301-101.945 of mobile devices.

2.3   Conducting Experiment

The apparatus as shown in Fig. 1. The motor was placed in the four corners of the sample. Then, the sample was placed on a stationary table to reduce the external factors caused by the hand. In addition, a noise pad was laid between the sample and the table to reduce the resonance or sound interference when the device was put on the table. The order of sensitivity of the hand is as follows: the most sensitive are the fingertips, followed by the knuckles, then the palms [17]. Therefore, this test allowed the subject to place the index finger of the dominant hand on the center of the screen sample (Fig. 2).

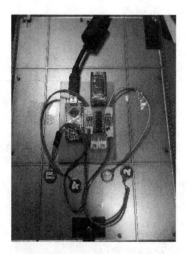

Fig. 1. Experimental devices

Fig. 2. Illustration of the experiment

2.4   Experimental Process

This study has two phases of experiments, below are process details based on the experimental sample settings.

Experimental 1 Process

The Sample see Table 1. In this experiment, to explore the effect of vibration frequency on intensity perception under the fixed vibration time. Participants will be in a fixed time vibration samples to compare the different vibration frequency of the intensity feelings for 9 times. For example, under 100 ms vibration time, the participants will experience the vibration frequencies of 80 Hz, 160 Hz and 200 Hz in random, and then ask them to sort the intensity of the vibration sample they feel. Using the answer of participants to compare with the experimental vibration frequency in sequence which is correct answer, as correct rate. Seeing sample in Table 1.

Experimental 2 Process

In experiment 2, different vibration times will be compared at the same vibration frequency, with a total of 9 comparisons per participant (see Table 2 for the sample). For example, under the vibration frequency of 160 Hz, the participants experience three groups of vibration which are 300 ms and 500 ms, 300 ms and 1000 ms, 500 ms and 1000 ms in sequence, and compare which feeling of vibration time is more intensive within each group. Using the answer of participants to compare with the experimental vibration time in sequence which we set the answer is that 500 ms is more intensive than 300 ms, 1000 ms is more intensive than 300 ms and so on, as consistency rate.

3   Result

3.1   Experiment 1

The participants were divided into the elderly group (total 12, the average age of 58.2 years) and the young group (total 10 people, the average age of 22.6 years). Those with related experiences (9 males and 13 females) in using smartphones or tablets were divided. The results showed that the elderly group had better tactile vibration feedback on the tablet than the smartphone. The results of the experiment 1 is shown on Table 3; the compliance rate of 40 Hz difference on smartphone is shown on Fig. 3; the compliance rate of 40 Hz difference on tablet is shown on Fig. 4.

Table 3. Experiment 1 results

	Phone	Pad
The young group rate	77.78%	80%
The elderly group rate	65.74%	81.48%
F rate	70.09%	76.92%
M rate	72.84%	86.42%
Compliance rate	71.21%	80.81%

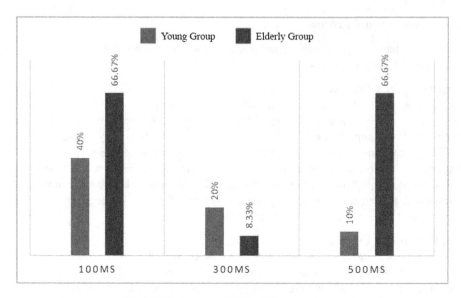

Fig. 3. Error rate at 40 Hz difference-phone

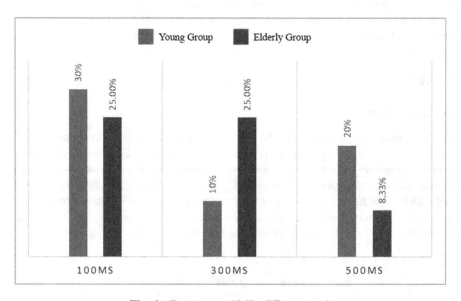

Fig. 4. Error rate at 40 Hz difference-pad

3.2   Experiment 2

The respondents from experiment 2 were recruited 36 people in total. There were 19 people in the elderly group (average age of 67 years old) and 17 people in the young group (the average age of 23 years old). The purpose of this experiment is to investigate if the users are be able to distinguish the differences the different time length of vibrations at the same vibration frequency condition from the mobile devices. Moreover, this experiment discussed about if the users will have stronger feeling from the longer time length of vibrations by calculating the consistency from each vibration samples of the respondents' perception of the strength and the differences of vibrating durations.

As shown in Fig. 5, when the vibration frequency was fixed under 160 Hz, 77.5% respondents from the young group and 71.9% respondents from the elderly group found that the longer duration of the vibration provided them stronger feeling ($\alpha = 0.1$, p value = 0.209). When the vibration frequency was fixed under 180 Hz, 77.5% respondents from the young group and 71.1% respondents from the elderly group found that the longer duration of the vibration provided them stronger feeling ($\alpha = 0.1$, p value = 0.138). When the vibration frequency was fixed under 220 Hz, 72.5% respondents from the young group and 63.2% respondents from the elderly group found that the longer duration of the vibration provided them stronger feeling ($\alpha = 0.1$, p value = 0.132).

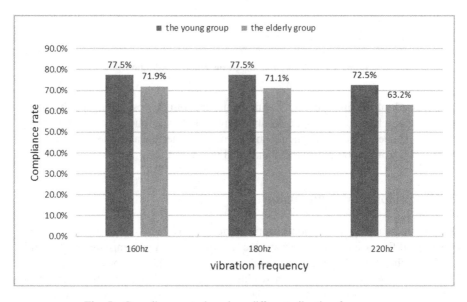

Fig. 5. Compliance rate based on different vibration frequency

Figure 6 is shown the results by using the duration as standard to compare. Taking 300 ms as the standard to compare with other durations, 76.5% respondents from the young group and 65.2% respondents from the elderly group were able to distinguish it clearly with others ($\alpha = 0.1$, p value = 0.07). Taking 500 ms as the standard to compare with other durations, 75.5% respondents from the young group and 61.4% respondents from the elderly group were able to distinguish it clearly with others ($\alpha = 0.05$, p value = 0.016). Taking 1000 ms as the standard to compare with other durations, 72.5% respondents from the young group and 78.3% respondents from the elderly group were able to distinguish it clearly with others ($\alpha = 0.1$, p value = 0.27).

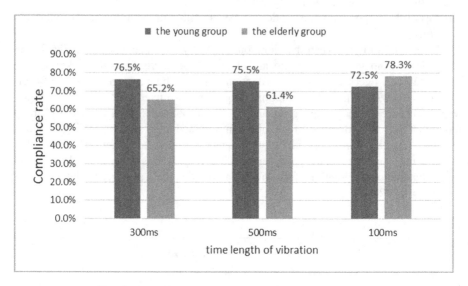

Fig. 6. Compliance rate based on different vibration time

The result of the differences of haptic feedback from the rest group and the control group is the perception of haptic feedback from the test group was generally lower. However, the perception of haptic feedback from the elderly was higher than the young group when using 1000 ms as the standard (Figs. 5 and 6).

4   Discussion and Conclusion

The response rate for smartphone haptic feedback was 71.2% and for tablets 80.8%, showing a difference of 9.6%. Perhaps the rate of vibration transmission is affected by the size of the panel. For those who are 20 to 50 years old, the correct answer rate is 77.7%; for those 50 years of age and older, the correct answer rate is 65.7%. From these data, the deterioration of the tactile sense of the elderly can be clearly compared. Their rate of haptic response differs from those below 50 years old by 12%. For tablets, the correct answer rate of 20 to 50 years old is 80%, while the correct answer rate of those 50 years of age or more is 81.4%. From these data, it can be observed that the elderly has a better sense for the haptic response for samples with larger area. 86% of the respondents like phones with a vibration mode. 81.82% of the respondents preferred the smart devices with vibration mode. This shows that most users like to have actual haptic feedback experience when using smart phones.

In addition, the study found that respondents had difficulty in distinguishing frequencies with a difference of 40 Hz (as shown in Figs. 3 and 4). Therefore, for future development of device with haptic feedback, it is necessary to put into consideration that the elderly might not feel the slight drop in haptic feedback due to tactile deterioration. On the tablet test, the elderly's the correct answer rate is nearly 20% higher than on the phone test. This maybe because the larger area of a tablet enables the elderly to distinguish the vibration better. Therefore, in future studies on the increase in haptic feedback experience, a larger sized tablet could be considered.

In experiment 2, when using 300 ms and 500 ms vibrating time as standards to compare with other durations, the elderly group's the compliance rate of perception of the vibration intensity and duration was lower than young group. It may imply that when the single vibration duration is low, the elderly may have more obvious feeling on the vibration intensity than the duration, which may make them easier to feel fatigue.

In experiment 2, the data showed the differences in haptic feedback perception among the elderly group and the young group. The young group had better perception than elderly group from the frequency of haptic feedback. However, the elderly group had better respond in 1000 ms test. For further discussion, from the data at 1000 ms which is under 180 Hz test, the tactile perception of the elderly group was almost 3% better than the young group. In the interview from the experiment 2, most respondents from the elderly group had more sensibility to the longer vibration feedback, and they also could feel the differences vibration feedback at the very first and second time at the same millisecond and the same frequency. Furthermore, the result of perception of haptic feedback of 1000 ms under 160 Hz was 6% higher than other frequencies and the perception feedback of 300 ms was higher than other frequencies under 180 Hz, which provide an opportunity to discuss the differences for the future study.

Most of the tactile experience on smartphones available on the market are not designed for the elderly. In the future, this study will add users of different ages in the research on haptic feedback and focus on the haptic feedback sensed by the elderly. To make products meet the needs of the senior citizens, there is a need for more experiments and samples to verify the frequency of vibration for the elderly's haptic feedback experience. This would make it easier for them to identify and learn to use smart devices. This study also provides future mobile device developers a reference on haptic feedback in order to give senior citizens a good user experience.

Acknowledgements. We are thankful for the financial support from The Ministry of Science and Technology (MOST), Taiwan. The grant MOST 106-2221-E-006-156.

References

1. Plaza, I., Martin, L., Martin, S., Medrano, C.: Mobile applications in an aging society: status and trends. J. Syst. Softw. **84**(11), 1977–1988 (2011). https://doi.org/10.1016/j.jss.2011.05.035
2. Hardill, I., Olphert, C.W.: Staying connected: exploring mobile phone use amongst older adults in the UK. Geoforum **43**(6), 1306–1312 (2013). https://doi.org/10.1016/j.geoforum.2012.03.016
3. Patrick, K., Griswold, W.G., Raab, F., Intille, S.S.: Health and the mobile phone. Am. J. Prev. Med. **35**(2), 177–181 (2008). https://doi.org/10.1016/j.amepre.2008.05.001

4. Claudio, S., Massimiliano, A., Vincent, D.: Wearable haptic systems for the fingertip and the hand: taxonomy, review, and perspectives. IEEE Trans. Haptics **10**(4), 580–600 (2017)
5. Schorr, A.B., Okamura, A.M.: Three-dimensional skin deformation as force substitution: wearable device design and performance during haptic exploration of virtual environments. IEEE Trans. Haptics **10**(3), 418–430 (2017)
6. Chamary, J.V.: The iPhone 7 Killer Feature Should Be Haptic Feedback (2015)
7. Gregg, E.C.: Absolute measurement of the vibratory threshold. Arch. Neurol. **66**, 403–411 (1951)
8. Hu, S.-S., Peng, Y., Wu, S.-P.: Ergonomics/Human factors (1983)
9. Ali, X., Cheng, I., Pouoyrev, I., Bau, O., Harrison, C.: Tactile display for the visually impaired using TeslaTouch (2011)
10. Immersion: Bridge between the real world and the digital world - tactile feedback (2013)
11. Rama, M.D., Ridder, H., Bouma, H.: Technology generation and age in using layered user interfaces. Gerontechnology **1**(1), 25–40 (2001)
12. Chang, C.-Y.: The Observation of operating electronic products and the performance of utilizing a touch panel for the elderly, p. 2008. Graduate Institute of Design Chaoyang University of Technology. Thesis for the Degree of Master (2008)
13. Tsai, W.-C.: A study on the product interface mode for the elderly. National Yunlin University of Science & Technology in Partial Fulfillment of the Requirements for the Degree of Master of Design in Industrial Design (2004)
14. Sanders, M.S., McCormick, E.J.: Human Factors in Engineering and Design. McGraw-Hill, New York (1998)
15. Doidge, N.: The Brain's Way of Healing (2016)
16. Saxon, S.V., Etten, M.J., Perkins, E.A.: Physical Change and Aging: A Guide for the Helping Professions, 5th edn. Springer, New York (2010)
17. Johansson, R.S., Vallbo, A.B.: Tactile sensory coding in the glabrous skin of the human hand. Trends Neurosci. **6**, 27–32 (1983)

Cognitive Aging and In-Car System Operations: A Proposal for an Age-Friendly System Using a Cognitive Model-Based Approach

Miki Matsumuro[✉] and Kazuhisa Miwa

Graduate School of Informatics, Nagoya University,
Fro-cho, Chikusa-ku, Nagoya, Japan
muro@cog.human.nagoya-u.ac.jp, miwa@is.nagoya-u.ac.jp

Abstract. In recent years, advanced driving support systems have been introduced in automobiles. When drivers use such systems, they have to engage in two parallel tasks: driving a car and operating the system. Older people have some difficulties in engaging in this dual task. This paper examines the relationship between these difficulties and the decline in time perception using a computational cognitive modeling approach. The results of the simulations demonstrated that the declining ability to perceive time led to poorer driving performance; however, it did not affect the amount of time needed to complete a secondary task.

Keywords: Dual task · Driving · Cognitive aging · Time perception
Cognitive modeling

1 Introduction

Advanced driver assistance systems (ADAS) such as adaptive cruise control (ACC) and lane keeping assist (LKA) have recently been developed. Such systems help older drivers in particular to drive their car. To use the ADAS or other in-car devices (e.g., car navigation system, air conditioning), the drivers have to operate buttons and levers in their car to enable them and to change settings while controlling their car. However, older drivers have difficulties engaging in such dual task. In this study, we investigate how cognitive aging affects the ability to enable or set the ADAS while driving a car using cognitive modeling.

1.1 Driving and Aging

Many previous studies have investigated the effect of aging on driving performance [1–3]. The researchers in most studies measured older drivers' abilities to control the car, such as the response time while braking and behavior at an intersection. However, a dual task driving situation requires other cognitive abilities beyond those required when just driving a car.

© Springer International Publishing AG, part of Springer Nature 2018
J. Zhou and G. Salvendy (Eds.): ITAP 2018, LNCS 10926, pp. 325–334, 2018.
https://doi.org/10.1007/978-3-319-92034-4_25

For older drivers, the dual task situation is more difficult than for younger drivers because the cognitive abilities required for performing the dual task are affected by aging [4]. Should they encounter a dangerous situation once, it is possible that older drivers will give up on using the useful support systems. It is, therefore, important to specify what type of cognitive aging would result in what type of danger. This research focuses on the impact of cognitive aging in time perception.

1.2 Dual Task and Time Perception

When people conduct a dual task, they process each task alternately by switching their goal. This means that they process only one goal-focused task at a time.

The situation investigated in this study involves the primary task of driving the car and the secondary task of changing the system state. Namely, the driving goal is the main goal and the enabling goal is the secondary goal. When drivers pursue the driving goal, they control the car; similarly, when they pursue the enabling goal, they operate the in-car device to change the state of the system.

Kujala and Salvucci (2015) investigated drivers' cognitive processes in a similar situation [5]. The drivers switched their goal from the primary one (i.e., driving) to the secondary one (a task other than driving) when the main task was stable. They switched back to the main task at two points of time: (1) following the achievement of the sub-goal of the secondary task and (2) when a certain period of time had lapsed.

Previous studies demonstrated that older people have difficulties performing dual tasks [6,7]. One possible cause of this impaired performance is a decline in time perception. The internal clock of older people tends to be slower than that of younger people [8,9]. This decline in time perception affects when the older drivers switch back to the driving goal, especially their judgment whether a certain period of time is passed. Based on their internal clock, older people may not estimate how long they engage in the enabling goal correctly (i.e., they estimate shorter), and as a result, they may not to switch back to the driving goal with sufficient rapidity. In this study, we investigate the effects of declining time perception on the performance of dual tasks in the driving situation.

2 Task

Our target task in this study was to change the state of the ACC from an off to a "set" state. The ACC is one of the ADASs that automatically adjusts the car's speed and helps to maintain a certain distance from the vehicle ahead.

The virtual car driven by our model was based upon the Levorg by Subaru. Figure 1 shows the devices in the Levorg related to the ACC. The state of the ACC is changed by using three of the six buttons on the steering wheel, two of which were used for the task in this study. The ACC monitor in the instrumental panel displays the current state of the ACC.

Fig. 1. Buttons for controlling the ACC and the ACC monitor.

To change the state of the ACC from off to "set", the driver must push two buttons in order. First, they push a "cruise" button, which takes the ACC into the standby state. Then, by pushing a "set" button, the ACC switches to the set state and starts adjusting the speed of the car.

3   User Model

3.1   Cognitive Modeling

A cognitive modeling approach was used to investigate the effect of aging on task performance. A cognitive modeling approach uses a computer model of human cognitive processes, which can perform a task by simulating human action. We constructed a user's cognitive model that could enable the ACC and drive the car. Then, the value of the parameters related to the time perception were modified, and the changes in performance observed. The purpose of this study was not to evaluate the effectiveness of the model or parameter settings, but to observe what happened when the computer model aged virtually.

3.2   Adaptive Control of Thought–Rational

We used the Adaptive Control of Thought–Rational 7.0 (ACT–R) to construct the user model. ACT–R is a cognitive architecture consisting of multiple modules as shown in Fig. 2, which can replicate human cognitive processes, including both internal and external processes [10].

The ACT–R model receives perceptual stimuli from the environment through perceptual modules and changes the environment using motor modules. We added steering and pedal modules to control the car, and a device-operation module to push the buttons in the car.

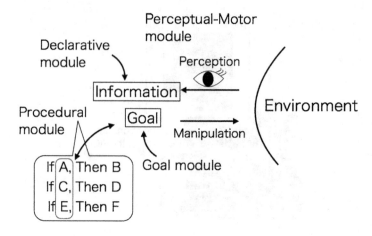

Fig. 2. Structure of ACT–R.

The ACT–R has two memory modules: declarative and procedural modules. The procedural module includes the production rules (i.e., "IF ···, THEN ···"). The declarative module stores declarative knowledge. The ACT–R selects the subsequent action based on the current goal, knowledge retrieved from the declarative module, and information from the environment. A selected production rule is activated, and the ACT–R model adds the operations to the environment.

3.3   Declarative Knowledge

We provided the user model with two types of declarative knowledge needed to achieve the task. One was the knowledge of instructions shown in Table 1, which were used as the sub-goals of the enabling goal. Each knowledge of the instruction entailed an operation to be conducted and the object to be used. In addition, the knowledge of the function of the buttons was used to identify whether a button was the target one.

Table 1. Sub-goals for enabling ACC.

Sub-goal	Declarative knowledge		Explanation
	Operation	Object	
Sub-goal 1	Push	Cruise	Push the Cruise button
Sub-goal 2	Check	Standby	Check whether the ACC state is Standby
Sub-goal 3	Push	Set	Push the Set button
Sub-goal 4	Check	Set	Check whether the ACC state is Set

3.4 Model's Behavior

We constructed our user model based on an ACT–R model by Kujala and Salvucci (2015) [5]. Their model simulated a process of searching for a target music title from an in-car display while driving a car. Their model switched goals from the primary driving goal to the search goal when the driving was stable. The stability of driving was evaluated by assessing the vehicle's lateral position in the lane and its lateral velocity [11]. It switched back to the primary driving goal when the sub-goals of the search goal (i.e., finding the target or finishing searching a current page) were achieved, or when the model was aware of the passage of time.

An overview of our user model is shown in Fig. 3, which was designed to alternately activate a driving goal and an enabling goal. We prepared four sub-goals for the enabling goal as shown in Table 1. Our user model switched between the two goals in a similar manner to that described in the study by Kujala and Salvucci (2015) [5].

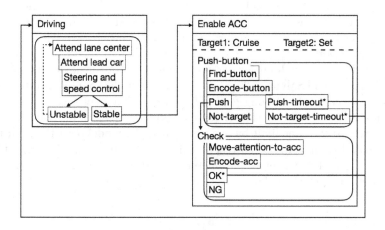

Fig. 3. Schematic overview of the user model.

The user model enabled the ACC through the following procedures. First, it retrieved an instruction and set it as the current goal. When the sub-goal was the retrieved instruction which value of the operation was "push," the model moved its attention to one of the buttons on the steering wheel. The function of the attended button was retrieved. If the function was the target one (i.e., a value of the object), the model pushed the button; if not, the model moved its attention to the next button. When the sub-goal was the retrieved instruction which value of the operation was "check," the model moved its attention to the ACC monitor and read it, to check whether the state of the ACC was the state required to meet its goal.

3.5   Manipulation of Time Perception

The ACT–R model was able to perceive the duration of time by counting internal ticks [12]. Based on the human cognitive mechanism, as the ticks counted increased, the tick interval became longer. An interval for the nth tick (t_n) was calculated using the following equations:

$$t_0 = start + \varepsilon_1$$
$$t_n = a * t_{n-1} + \varepsilon_2$$

where $start$ was the initial tick interval, and ε_1 and ε_2 were noise; parameter a decided how slow the ticks became as time passed.

To simulate the decline in time perception of an aged person, the value of this parameter a (hereinafter, referred to as the "interval parameter") was increased. As the value of the interval parameter increased, the estimated time for a certain period of time became shorter (i.e., decline in time perception). The default value of the interval parameter was 1.10, which increased by 0.08 till 1.26; namely, 1.10, 1.18, and 1.26 were used as the interval parameter values. The interval parameter of 1.10 was the default model not affected by cognitive aging. The other two longer interval parameters simulated the progressive effects of aging on time perception.

We decided the time limit for one operation of the in-car device based on the model by Kujala and Salvucci (2015) [5]. When the model counted a certain ticks, it switched back to the driving goal. The initial number of ticks was 17 ticks. When the model returned to the driving task under stable driving conditions, the model increased the time limit by one tick; if not, the model reset the limit to its initial value. The initial limit corresponded to 0.5 s, 1.0 s, and 2.5 s respectively, with each value of the interval parameter as 1.10, 1.18, and 1.26. For all other parameters, we used the default values of ACT–R.

4   Simulation

4.1   Procedure of One Trial

The driving environment of our model was a straight three-lane highway. The model drove its car in the middle lane without changing lanes. During the first 10 s, the model only controlled the vehicle to ensure its driving was stable. Each model began the dual task to enable the ACC after 10 s had passed. The model performed the dual task following the leading vehicle, driving at about 100 km/h. Each trial was terminated 10 s after the model changed the ACC state to "set". The time duration for the model to conduct the dual task was analyzed. Additionally, to investigate vehicle control performance we added angles to the steering angle based on a synthetic sine wave.

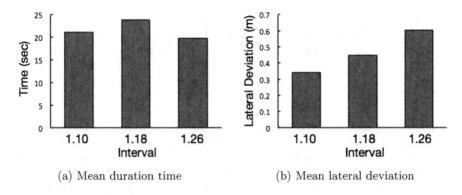

(a) Mean duration time   (b) Mean lateral deviation

Fig. 4. Mean duration time and lateral deviations.

4.2 Simulation Results

We ran each model 100 times. Figure 4 shows the time duration needed to enable the ACC as well as the lateral deviations. The value of the interval parameter had no effect on time duration.

The lateral deviation was an index of driving performance while setting the ACC state, which assessed the deviation from the mean lateral position. The lateral deviation was found to increase as the parameter value increased. When the interval parameter was increased from 1.18 to 1.26 (0.107) the lateral deviation changed larger than that when it increased from 1.10 to 1.18 (0.157).

4.3 Modification of Environment

As we described above, three of the buttons had no relation to the ACC, one of which activated a lane keep assist system, with the other two used to change driving modes. We ran our user model in an environment where those three buttons were removed. Figure 5 shows the duration times and lateral deviations

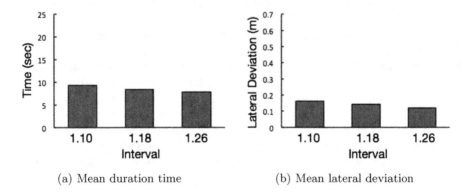

(a) Mean duration time   (b) Mean lateral deviation

Fig. 5. Mean duration time and lateral deviations in the modified environment.

in the modified environment. Both values were found to reduce dramatically, and the aging effect disappeared, meaning that in each case the sub-goal was achieved before the model focused too long on the enabling goal.

5   Discussion

The model developed investigated how a decline in the ability to perceive time affects driving performance in a dual task scenario. The simulation results showed that while cognitive aging affected the control of the car position in the lane, it had no effect on the time taken to change the state of ACC from off to "set".

This relationship between time perception and lateral deviation was explained based on the goal switching behavior. The user model had to switch back to the driving goal frequently, or their car strayed over the line and crashed into other cars. When the model attended to the in-car device, they could not acquire information from the driving environment.

Older people, as well as the older models in this study, have difficulty estimating how much time has passed due to the decline in time perception that results from cognitive aging [4,8]. Therefore, they may continue the operation of the in-car device and neglect to control the car due to a lack of awareness of how much time has passed. The mean time duration from switching to the enable goal to switching back to the driving goal was 0.503, 0.737, and 0.941 s, for each value of the interval parameter, 1.10, 1.18, and 1.26.

Driving is not the only situation where the effects of time perception can be observed. Older people neglect their main tasks for a longer period of time in other dual task situations.

5.1   Time Perception and Time for Enabling

A decline in time perception did not affect the duration of time needed to complete enabling the ACC. This is because of the trade-off relationship between enabling the ACC and controlling the car. The model's goal switching had the features shown in Fig. 6. This diagram was constructed based on the models' process logs.

The amount of time needed to achieve all sub-goals (the sum of the gray bars) did not differ since the interval parameter did not affect the ability to operate the ACC (e.g., find the button and check the ACC state). As each engagement by the default value model for the enabling goal was relatively short, each adjustment of the car's position (i.e., driving goal) was completed in a short time. In contrast, the larger value (older) model engaged in the enabling goal over a longer time interval, during which the car deviated from the center of the lane; consequently, each adjustment (i.e., driving goal) required a longer period of time. For these reasons, only the lateral deviation was affected by the interval parameter setting.

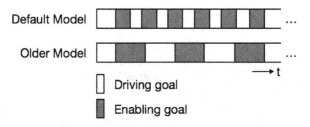

Fig. 6. Conceptual goal switching diagram. The white bars show the duration while the model engaged in the driving goal, and the gray bars show that while it engaged in the enabling goal. The total gray bar areas are identical in the two models.

5.2   Advantages of Cognitive Modeling

As demonstrated in this study, cognitive modeling can be a useful method to investigate the human cognitive process during complex activities. It is impossible to explore the effects of only one factor, such as time perception, based upon naturalistic observations of complex human activities such as driving. However, by using cognitive modeling, we can investigate how a certain factor affects a target activity. Note that there are many other factors to be considered, time perception is not the only one that affects driving performance.

Cognitive modeling also can verify the functionality of new interfaces based on the user's cognitive processes. In this study, we tested the situation with fewer buttons, where the lateral deviation was small and constant, despite the decline in time perception. However, it is difficult to merely reduce the number of buttons, because recent vehicles have numerous functions that the driver must control. Our study suggests that further consideration of the positioning and grouping of buttons may help older people to use the driving support functions more effectively.

6   Conclusion

The simulation results suggested that the older people tended to concentrate for too long on the non-driving task; as a result, the lateral deviation increased. An additional simulation demonstrated that by removing the unrelated buttons, the effect of aging was eliminated. Car designers need to develop a user interface that makes it easier to switch back to the primary driving goal.

Acknowledgment. This study was partly supported by Tateishi Science and Technology Foundation (TSTF).

References

1. Bunce, D., Young, M.S., Blane, A., Khugputh, P.: Age and inconsistency in driving performance. Accid. Anal. Prev. **49**, 293–299 (2012)
2. Green, M.: "How long does it take to stop?" Methodological analysis of driver perception-brake times. Transp. Hum. Factors **2**, 195–216 (2000)
3. Vichitvanichphong, S., Talaei-Khoei, A., Kerr, D., Ghapanchi, A.H.: What does happen to our driving when we get older? Transp. Rev. **35**, 56–81 (2015)
4. Verhaeghen, P., Steitz, D.W., Sliwinski, M.J., Cerella, J.: Aging and dual-task performance: a meta-analysis. Psychol. Aging **18**, 443–460 (2003)
5. Kujala, T., Salvucci, D.D.: Modeling visual sampling on in-car displays: the challenge of predicting safety-critical lapses of control. Int. J. Hum. Comput. Stud. **79**, 66–78 (2015)
6. Aksan, N., Dawson, J.D., Emerson, J.L., Yu, L., Uc, E.Y., Anderson, S.W., Rizzo, M.: Naturalistic distraction and driving safety in older drivers. Hum. Factors **55**, 841–853 (2013)
7. Bédard, M., Leonard, E., McAuliffe, J., Weaver, B., Gibbons, C., Dubois, S.: Visual attention and older drivers: the contribution of inhibition of return to safe driving. Exp. Aging Res. **32**, 119–135 (2006)
8. Baudouin, A., Vanneste, S., Pouthas, V., Isingrini, M.: Age-related changes in duration reproduction: involvement of working memory processes. Brain Cogn. **62**, 17–23 (2006)
9. Craik, F.I., Hay, F.: Aging and judgments of duration: effects of task complexity and method of estimation. Atten. Percept. Psychophys. **61**, 549–560 (1999)
10. Anderson, J.R.: How Can the Human Mind Occur in the Physical Universe?. Oxford University Press, New York (2009)
11. Salvucci, D.D.: Predicting the effects of in-car interface use on driver performance: an integrated model approach. Int. J. Hum. Comput. Stud. **55**, 85–107 (2001)
12. Taatgen, N.A., Van Rijn, H., Anderson, J.: An integrated theory of prospective time interval estimation: the role of cognition, attention, and learning. Psychol. Rev. **114**, 577–598 (2007)

Optimal Data Entry Designs in Mobile Web Surveys for Older Adults

Erica Olmsted-Hawala[1(✉)], Elizabeth Nichols[1], Brian Falcone[1],
Ivonne J. Figueroa[2], Christopher Antoun[3], and Lin Wang[1]

[1] U.S. Census Bureau, Washington D.C., USA
{erica.l.olmsted.hawala,elizabeth.may.nichols,
brian.falcone,lin.wang}@census.gov
[2] HCSC Blue Cross Blue Shield, Chicago, IL, USA
Ivonne_j_figueroa@bcbsil.com
[3] University of Maryland, College Park, MD, USA
antoun@umd.edu

Abstract. Growing numbers of people are using their mobile phones to respond to online surveys. As a result, survey designers face the challenge of displaying questions and their response options and navigation elements on small smartphone screens in a way that encourages survey completion. The purpose of the present study was to conduct a series of systematic assessments of how older adults using smartphones interact with different user-interface features in online surveys. This paper shares results of three different experiments. Experiment 1 compares different ways of displaying choose-one response options. Experiment 2 compares different ways of displaying numeric entry boxes, specifically ones used to collect currency information (e.g., prices, costs, salaries). Experiment 3 tests whether forward and backward navigational buttons on a smartphone survey should be labeled with words (*previous, next*) or simply indicated with arrow icons (<, >). Results indicate that certain features such as picker-boxes that appear at the bottom of the screen (iOS devices), fixed formatting of numeric-entry boxes, and icon navigation buttons were problematic. They either had negative impacts on performance (response times and/or accuracy) or only a small percentage of participants preferred these design features when asked to compare them to the other features.

Keywords: Mobile survey design · Mobile guidelines · Older adults
Drop-downs · Currency inputs · Mobile navigation controls

1 Introduction

More and more often people are using smartphones to interact with the electronic world [1]. In February of 2018, 77% of all U.S. adults had a smartphone and 46% of U.S. adults over the age of 65 years old had a smartphone [1]. Where in the past people may have waited until they were in front of their desktop PCs to conduct a search, fill out a form, or answer a survey, adults "on the go" are increasingly using their smartphones for such activities. While the majority of adults answer internet surveys on their PC's

J. Zhou and G. Salvendy (Eds.): ITAP 2018, LNCS 10926, pp. 335–354, 2018.
https://doi.org/10.1007/978-3-319-92034-4_26

there are some indications that responding to a survey on a smartphone is on the rise. For example, the American Community Survey, an ongoing monthly U.S. survey, has seen a steady increase in mobile respondents since 2011 when it was just under one percent through today where it is just under eight percent [2]. For private-sector surveys, almost one third of survey responses occur on mobile phones [3, 4]. It is likely that adults responding to internet surveys while on mobile phones will continue to increase over time.

At the U.S. Census Bureau, as at other survey organizations, we are interested in developing mobile web surveys that reduce measurement error while also improving the user experience. With the smaller screen real estate of the smartphone, the user interface must be adapted for the smaller space. Yet, the small amount of touchable space available on the screens of smartphones can be challenging for both survey respondents and for developers of online surveys. Evidence suggests that mobile surveys lead to lower response rates because respondents break off (i.e., don't finish the survey) as well as longer survey completion times [5, 6]. For a review on the impacts of using mobile phones to answer online survey, see [7].

An additional challenge of creating mobile web surveys is that many different age groups are now using smartphones [1]. While the older adult population is more resistant to new technology generally [8] they are using smartphones in their daily lives [9, 10] and they too need to be accommodated in the design of online surveys.

At present, there has been little empirical research on how to best design surveys on smartphones for older adults. Current literature is typically focused on the general population and not specifically for surveys [11, 12]. There is evidence that for touch screens, older adults do better with larger buttons, but this study was on kiosk-type touch screens, not on the smaller display of smartphones [13]. Within the healthcare field, the use of mobile phones by older adults to aid in managing home health has begun but is not fully tested for its effectiveness or usefulness [14]. In fact, there is some evidence that the designs of the mobile health applications cause barriers to the older adult population in terms of uptake and use [15].

It is possible that older adults may interact with smartphones differently than younger adults. For example, research shows that accurately touching a target takes longer for older adults than for younger adults, commonly referred to as the tradeoff between speed and accuracy [16, 17]. In addition, as adults age, the sensory changes with respect to touch and vision can impact what older adults are able see and touch when interacting with a small screen that contains a variety of information [18]. Literature has shown that older adults generally have reduced vision, mobility, and certain cognitive capacity such as memory, compared to younger adults [19–21].

The purpose of the present study was to conduct a series of systematic assessments on a mobile phone to determine how older adults use different user-interface designs to answer online survey questions and to identify better performing and preferred designs. The results of these assessments could be used as guidelines for developers. Our rationale was that if we develop guidelines for a mobile web survey interface that older adults can successfully complete, then younger adults would do at least as well because of their superior perceptual and motor capability. The initial impetus for the work was based on observations made while participants used mobile phones to fill out surveys during earlier, unrelated usability tests.

The rest of the paper lays out the methods we used and the specifics of each of the three experiments including hypothesis, results and conclusions.

2 Methods

In this paper we discuss results from three different experiments from a larger ongoing research study that includes multiple experiments aimed at establishing a set of mobile web survey guidelines for developers. For more information on this entire research project please see [22]. Below are highlights of methods relevant to the three experiments described in this paper.

2.1 Sample

We aimed to get a study sample of persons aged 60–75. We prescreened to include only participants who had at least 12 months of experience using a smartphone under the assumption that these participants were more typical of respondents who choose to use mobile devices to complete online surveys than those with less experience using smartphones. Additionally, we prescreened participants to include only individuals who had an education of 8th grade or more, who were fluent in English, and who had normal vision or corrected to normal with glasses or contacts. The participants were a convenience sample recruited from senior and/or community centers in and around the Washington DC metropolitan area between November 2016 and February 2017.

Experiment 1 was conducted with a pool of 30 participants, and Experiments 2 and 3 were conducted on a different pool of 32 respondents. Participants in each pool reported an average of familiarity with using the smartphone of 3 on a 5-point scale where 1 was "Not at all familiar" and 5 was "Extremely familiar." See Table 1. We consider significance to be at $p = 0.05$ or less.

2.2 Data Collection

One-on-one sessions were conducted at senior/community centers. For each session a given participant completed between 4 to 6 experiments, only some of which are the subject of this paper. Each experiment was run at a "station" with a different Census Bureau staff member (i.e., test administrator (TA)) manning the station. As participants were recruited, the first station's TA explained the purpose of the testing, had the subject sign a consent form, conducted the prescreening, and assigned the participant a unique ID number. Then the participant went to the next station where another TA worked one-on-one with the participant to complete one or two experiments. Once the participant finished the experiment(s) at one station he/she moved to the next station where a different TA worked with him/her on the next experiment. Each experiment took about 10 min to complete. At the end of the session, the participant was given $40 for their time.

Table 1. Participant demographics for 3 experiments

Experiment	Average age (Standard Error (SE))	Gender (Male/Female)	Smartphone usage [1 – Not Familiar to 5 – Extremely familiar] (SE)
Experiment 1 (n = 30)	68.8 (0.87)	10M/20F	3.96 (0.17)
Experiments 2 and 3 (n = 32)	70.5 (0.79)	7M/25F	3.56 (0.18)

The experiments were preloaded as applications (commonly referred to as apps) on Census-owned iPhone 5S. Each station had its own iPhone. The TA opened the experiment, entered the participant's unique ID and based on that ID selected the condition to administer. For each experiment, conditions were pre-assigned to IDs using a randomized (or quasi[1]-randomized) order. From there, participants were handed the iPhone with the app loaded to the correct starting location and the TA followed the individual protocol for that experiment. This included instructing participants not to talk aloud during the session, and to complete the survey to the best of their ability as though they were answering the survey at home without anyone's assistance. All three experiments were video-recorded using QuickTime with the phone plugged into a MacBook laptop.

3   Experiment 1: "Choose-One" Response Option Design

3.1   Designs Tested in the Experiment

Experiment 1 focused on "choose-one" questions. Survey designers have a number of options when designing for a question with a set number of answer choices where the user is told to choose only one answer. The most common design is a "radio button" design where the response choices are on the same screen as the question itself, as shown in Fig. 1. For that design users answer the question by touching the appropriate response choice on the screen. They can change their answer by touching another response choice. Another response-option design solution is to use an "open-text" field as shown in Fig. 2. When a respondent answers these questions, touching the open-text field brings up the character keyboard or numeric keypad and then the respondent can enter the response as shown in Fig. 3. That design is typically used when the answer is easily typed, such as a number, or when the set of answers is so large that it would be unwieldy to place them all on the screen, such as street names.

---

[1] Prior to collecting data, a random assignment computer algorithm was used to assign conditions for each experiment. A few of the assignments in Experiment 1 were manually manipulated so there were an equal number of participants assigned to each condition.

Fig. 1. Radio button design

Fig. 2. Open-text field design

Fig. 3. Open-text field w/keypad

A third design solution for choose-one questions is a "dropdown" format. Drop-downs are often implemented when there is limited space on the screen or when there is a long list of response options and the response options are well known, like the list of states in the U.S. On mobile webpages, the default dropdowns display differently depending upon the operating system. For both operating systems, the user must first touch the dropdown field to see the choices, Fig. 4 shows what the screen looks like for both operating systems before the user taps the response box. Figure 5 shows what happens in the iOS when the user taps the response box: the list displays in grey at the bottom of the screen, and is called a "picker," Fig. 6 shows what the screen looks like on the Android, when what is called a "spinner" opens and displays a view more similar to a PC dropdown, with a list of choices displaying over the screen. Once a selection is made, the answer choice appears in the dropdown field and the other choices disappear as shown in Fig. 7. Dropdown designs are quite different from radio button designs. With dropdowns, the user will not know the available response choices until he or she "opens" the dropdown; with radio buttons, the user does not have to do anything to see the answers – they are already displayed on the screen.

In Experiment 1, we compared three different designs for choose-one questions using a 12-question survey and a between-subjects design. The three conditions were the iOS picker (Fig. 5); the Android spinner (Fig. 6), and a radio button/keyboard design (Figs. 1 and 2).

We hypothesized that the iOS picker design would cause more difficulties for users as compared to the other two designs because the response options (Fig. 5) appear in gray font at the bottom of the screen and are easily missed.

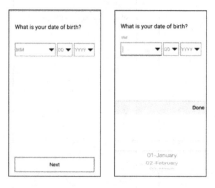

Fig. 4. Initial view   **Fig. 5.** iOS picker   **Fig. 6.** Android spinner   **Fig. 7.** Final view

3.2 Adaptation of Survey Questions with the Three Alternative Designs

A set of 12 questions on a range of topics was selected and an app was created that displayed the 12 questions in each of the three formats described above. Participants were randomly assigned to one of the three formats, and there were 10 participants in each condition. Each participant completed the 12-question survey in the assigned condition. The 12 "choose-one" questions included some with a small number of response options (i.e., 5 or fewer) and some questions with a large number of response options (i.e., more than 5). Some questions had familiar responses in the sense that the respondent could probably predict the response options based on the survey question (e.g., question about a respondent's sex), some had ordinal responses (e.g., age categories), while other questions had response options that a respondent would probably not know prior to reading through them. We varied the response option types to be able to control for the type of question, in case particular types of "choose-one" questions performed better in one design compared to another. Table 2 provides the questions with their response option characteristics.

For the radio button/keyboard design condition, questions 2–5 and 7–12 used radio buttons. Question 6 was an open-text field that brought up a keyboard when the participant touched the field. The first question, date of birth, was also an open-text field, which when touched, brought up a keypad as shown in Fig. 4 above. We used open-text fields for those two questions because in practice, survey designers rarely, if ever, use radio buttons for states or dates. For the iOS and Android dropdown conditions, dropdowns were used for all 12 questions.

Each question was on a separate screen with forward and backward navigation buttons in a fixed location at the bottom of each screen. After completing the survey, the participant then answered a satisfaction question. The satisfaction question asked, "How easy or difficult was it to complete this survey?" with a rating scale from 1 to 5 where 1 was defined as "Very Easy" and 5 was defined as "Very difficult." Finally, the respondent interacted with a date of birth question using each of the designs – first the picker, then the spinner, and then open-text field using the number keypad. After interacting with the date of birth question with the three designs, respondents answered a preference question that collected the respondent's design preference for that question.

Table 2. Question and question characteristic

Questions 1–6	Questions 7–12
1. Date of birth (Familiar and >5 choices)	7. Citizen of more than one country (Familiar and <=5 choices)
2. Age range (Ordered and >5 choices)	8. Fuel for heating home (Unique and >5 choices)
3. Sex (Familiar and <=5 choices)	9. Eyesight rating (Ordered and <=5 choices)
4. Marital status (Unique and <=5 choices)	10. Work status (Unique and >5 choices)
5. School level obtained (Ordered and >5 choices)	11. Opinion question (Ordered and <=5 choices)
6. State attended high school (Familiar and >5 choices)	12. Preference for reporting (Unique and <=5 choices)

3.3 Evaluation Criteria

For each condition, we measured respondent burden (operationalized as time-on-task and the number of touches on each screen of the survey); accuracy of data entries (by comparing any discrepancies between the entered data and data provided to a screening paper questionnaire administered prior to the mobile phone survey); satisfaction and preference by the responses provided within the experiment. We then compared these measures between conditions.

We modeled time to complete at the question level using a mixed model. Modeling at the question level increases the number of observations from 30 to 30 × 12 or 360 and allows us to account for different question characteristics. In the model, we controlled for the condition, and the characteristics of the question as outlined in Table 2 above, and any interaction between condition and those characteristics. To control for any participant effect because each participant would contribute up to 12 times (one time for each question), we included a random effect for the participant. We also modeled the log of time because the residuals from the first model were slightly skewed. As a check we also modeled time with controlling for the question number instead of the question characteristics.

We modeled the number of touches on the screen in the same manner, but without the log transformation.

Because of an error in the app, we did not collect data for one radio button/keyboard design participant and only partial data were saved for another participant assigned to the Android condition. In total, we had 344 observations for each model instead of the expected 360.

We had self-reported measures of sex, age range, date of birth for month and year, and education from the demographic information collected via a paper questionnaire at the beginning of the one-hour session. We compared that data, which we considered truth, to the data reported within the experimental survey. Any survey data that matched was considered accurate; and data that did not match was considered an error. Based on that assignment, we tabulated the accuracy rate for the four questions for each condition. We tabulated satisfaction scores for each of the three conditions. For these analyses, we conducted a Chi-square test of independence. And, finally we tabulated the preference data for the date of birth question. Again, because of missing data, we only collected data from 28 participants; we were missing these data from one radio button/keyboard condition and one Android condition.

3.4   Results

Respondent Burden as Measured by Time to Complete. The average time to complete a question using the iOS picker condition was nearly 21 s (Standard Error (SE) = 1.3), compared to 15 s (SE = 1.0) for the Android spinner, and 13 s (SE = 1.6) for the radio button/keyboard entry. Modeling time to complete, we found that questions using the iOS picker design took significantly longer on average to answer than the radio button/keyboard design (p = 0.02) while we did not find a difference in time to complete for questions using the Android spinner design compared to the radio button/keyboard design (p = 0.60). There were no significant interactions between the condition and the question characteristics. When modeling the log of time, the pattern of results was unchanged. When modeling time with the question number instead of the question characteristics, the pattern of results was unchanged.

Respondent Burden as Measured by the Number of Touches per Screen. The average number of touches per question for the iOS picker condition was 6.5 (SE = 0.3), compared to 3.5 (SE = 0.1) for the Android spinner, and 2.6 (SE = 0.2) for the radio button/keyboard entry. Modeling the number of touches needed to answer the question without any interactions, we found that questions using the iOS picker design required significantly more touches to answer than the radio button/text design (p < 0.01) and the Android spinner design took significantly more touches to select an answer than the radio button/keyboard design (p < 0.01). However, when interaction terms between the condition and the question characteristics were added, there was a significant interaction between the conditions and question characteristics (p < .01). The effect of the iOS picker design on the number of touches per question was particularly large for questions that had many response options.

Accuracy of Responses by Condition. We found no significant differences in accurate reporting by condition. The accuracy rate for all 28 participants was 100% for each condition for the sex question and the age range question. For date of birth, the accuracy rate was 100% for the radio button/keyboard design; 89% for the iOS design and 78% for the Android design. The iOS and Android conditions had 100% accuracy for education, but the radio button design's accuracy rate was 67% for that field. Even with these differences, there was no significant difference in accuracy rates for date of birth (χ^2 = 2.3, p = 0.3, n = 27) or education (χ^2 = 7.1, p = 0.1, n = 28) by condition.

Satisfaction Scores by Condition and Response Option Preference. Satisfaction was measured on a 5-point scale where 1 was very easy and 5 was very difficult. The average satisfaction score was 1.3 (SE = 0.3) for the iOS picker; 1.1 (SE = 0.1) for the Android spinner; and 1.0 (SE = 0) for the radio button/keyboard design. We found no differences in satisfaction scores by condition (χ^2 = 3.98, p = 0.4) and with the exception of one participant who rated the iOS picker as difficult, the participants found the designs easy to use. However, once participants were able to use each of the designs, they overwhelmingly preferred the keypad design for the date of birth question, with 22 of the 28 participants selecting only that design as their preferred response option design. Their preference was not based on the design they used during the main portion of the experiment (χ^2 = 3.1, p = 0.8).

4   Experiment 2: Layout of Currency Fields

4.1   Designs Tested in the Experiment

In Experiment 2 we investigate alignment and formatting of currency fields on mobile devices. Surveys that ask for monetary information and online banking apps vary in both of these aspects. Part of this research was inspired by what we had seen when respondents were answering questions that included monetary amounts on the American Community Survey. During usability studies participants attempted to add in the dollar sign and decimal place even though it already appeared on the screen.

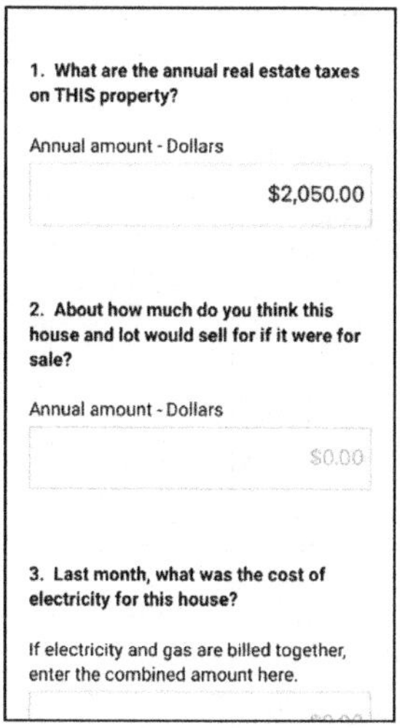

Fig. 8. Right alignment 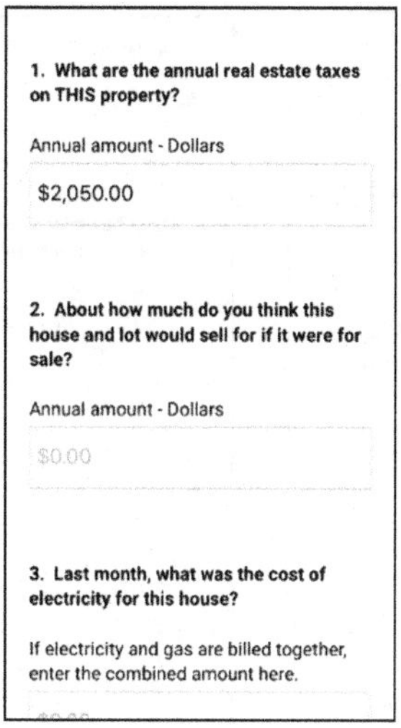   **Fig. 9.** Left alignment 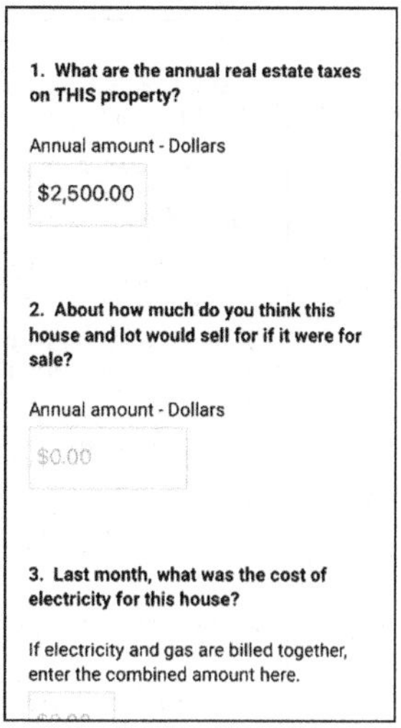   **Fig. 10.** Center alignment

One aspect of response options for currency data is 'alignment' – that is, where in the response field the numbers appear once the respondent begins entering the numbers. For this study, we chose three variations in alignment to test. First is what we call right alignment, where currency data are entered into a response field with the numbers coming in on the right, like the numbers on most calculator displays. See Fig. 8. Second is what we call left alignment where the numbers representing currency amounts are treated more like text, coming in from the left. See Fig. 9. Third is what we called center alignment where the field itself gets longer or shorter based on the number of digits the respondent enters, such as on apps like Cash© or Paypal©. See Fig. 10 for an example of center alignment. Our hypothesis was that left-alignment would not perform as well as the other alignment types because in earlier usability studies we had noticed users miss the cents display when currency was left-aligned.

Another aspect of the response option for currency data is "formatting" by which we mean the way the currency cues (e.g., dollar sign and cents, including the decimal point) are displayed on the screen, either fixed and always present on the screen or where the application itself is programmed to react to the users' data entry.

We examined three different alternatives for formatting of currency fields. First is what we called the fixed formatting, when the dollar and cents symbols are fixed in place and always present in the field. See Fig. 11. Second is what we call post-entry formatting where formatting occurs only after the user has entered the number in the field; this is indicated when the respondent taps "Done" on the keypad. At that point, the program rounds to the nearest dollar and enters (.00) and ($) into the field. In Fig. 12, the amount in the field at the top of the screen is what was shown after the participant selected "Done," and the amount in the field at the bottom is what was shown as the participant touches the numbers on the keypad, prior to selecting "Done."

Fig. 11. Fixed ($) and (.00) permanently on screen

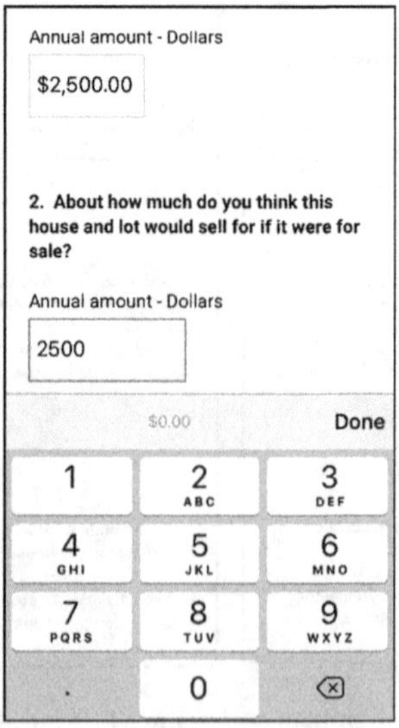

Fig. 12. Post-entry formatting

And finally the third formatting type is what we called automatic formatting where a dollar sign and/or the cents symbol automatically appear in real time as the user enters the currency numbers. (Note, there is no figure image example of this as it would have to be a video.)

Our hypothesis was that the fixed formatted design would cause more problems for users. The rationale for this was that we had noticed in earlier usability testing studies that respondents often fail to notice the static dollar sign and decimal place for cents and consequently attempted to add that data in. The alternate designs that we tested used some form of automatic or real time formatting that we hypothesized respondents would notice more readily.

4.2 Adaptation of Survey Questions with Alternative Alignment and Formatting of Monetary Fields

The two design elements (alignment and formatting) each had three versions, and we fully crossed them in a 3-by-3 design We chose questions for this experiment that are asked in the American Community Survey.

The five questions included the following:

- Cost of real estate property taxes;
- Cost of the lot and house;
- Cost of electricity for the previous month;
- Annual cost of water and sewer for the house and
- Cost of the gross annual income.

Using a within-subjects design, participants were presented with all nine conditions in counterbalanced and randomized order. See Table 3.

Each condition required that the participant enter currency for five questions (for a total of 45 trials). Each condition had the same five questions and for each condition the five questions appeared on the same screen. This required the participant to scroll to answer all five questions. For example, Fig. 8 above shows the first three questions in Condition 5 (e.g., right alignment with post-entry formatting of the ($) and (.00)). Figure 11 on the other hand shows the first three questions in Condition 1 (e.g., left alignment, fixed formatting). The fourth and fifth question require scrolling and so are below the fold of the screen.

Table 3. Experiment 2 properties of each condition

Condition	Alignment	Format of ($) and (.00)	# of questions on screen
1	Left	Fixed	5
2	Right	Fixed	5
3	Center	Fixed	5
4	Left	Post entry	5
5	Right	Post entry	5
6	Center	Post entry	5
7	Left	Automatic	5
8	Right	Automatic	5
9	Center	Automatic	5

For each condition participants were provided identical pieces of paper, mocked up as an actual bill, with the exact amounts to be entered for each question. The amounts were formatted with common features such as commas, cents, and dollar signs. Regardless of condition, the keyboard that popped open allowed users to manually enter the numbers and period but not the dollar sign or commas.

4.3   Evaluation Criteria

Following each condition, participants rated the ease of entering currency using a 5-point Likert scale where 1 was "very easy" and 5 was "very difficult." Finally, the participant was asked which of the three different types of formatting (fixed, post-entry, auto-formatting) they preferred. We examined the difference in satisfaction, accuracy, and respondent burden as measured by time-on-task, accuracy, satisfaction and subjective preference for participants on the currency data tasks for each condition.

A repeated measures ANOVA (2X2) was conducted in SAS©. There were two Generalized Linear Models. We modeled the log of time controlling for currency formatting (fixed, post-entry, auto-formatting) and currency alignment (left, right, center). We modeled total accuracy controlling for currency formatting (fixed, post-entry, auto-formatting) and currency alignment (left, right, center).[2]

Chi-square tests were used to determine differences in difficulty ratings between the nine conditions and differences in preference between currency formatting (fixed, post-entry, and auto-formatting).

4.4   Results

Time (Efficiency). Modeling the log time to complete, we found no main effect of currency formatting (fixed, post-entry, auto-formatting) on time per page ($F(2, 30) = .85$, $p > .05$) and no main effect of currency alignment type (left, right, or center) on time per page ($F(2, 30) = .17, p > .05$).

Accuracy (Effectiveness). A repeated measures model was used to determine if total accuracy per page is influenced by currency formatting and currency alignment. Each condition had five questions and a score of 1 was given to the correct responses. To calculate the variable total accuracy, we calculated a sum value for the five questions per page. A perfect score per page would have a score of five. Total accuracy for fixed entry was $M = 4.06$, $SE = .17$; total accuracy for post-entry was $M = 4.57$, $SE = .17$; and total accuracy for auto-formatting was $M = 4.26$, $SE = .17$.
Comparison tests (Tukey) reveal a significant difference between fixed entry and post-entry groups only (difference between means = .51, $p < .05$). This suggests that there was a difference in total accuracy between the groups—entering numeric data for post-entry resulted in higher accuracy compared to fixed formatting. There was no difference between fixed entry and auto-formatting or between post-entry and auto-formatting.

---

[2] We checked for significant interactions and found none, so we use a main effects model.

Results reveal a main effect of currency alignment type (left, right, or center) on total accuracy per page (F(2, 30) = 3.99, $p < .05$). Total accuracy per page for left alignment was $M = 4.46$, $SE = .17$, total accuracy per page for right alignment was $M = 4.05$, $SE = .17$, and total accuracy per page for center alignment was $M = 4.41$, $SE = .17$. Comparison tests (Tukey) reveal a significant difference between left and right alignment (difference between means = .41, $p < .05$) only but no significant difference between left and center alignment, or right and center alignment.

Difficulty Rating (Satisfaction). Two chi-square tests were used to determine an optimal currency formatting (fixed, post-entry, auto-formatting) and currency alignment type (left, right, center). Chi-square results reveal no difference in satisfaction ratings between currency formatting ($\chi^2(4) = .67$, $p > .05$). Chi-square results also reveal no difference in satisfaction ratings between currency alignment types ($\chi^2(4) = 1.6$, $p > .05$). There were no ratings lower than 3, suggesting that overall, participants did not find the task too difficult.

Preference. A chi-square test was conducted to determine if there was a significant difference in participant's subjective preference between currency formatting only. The chi-square was not significant ($\chi^2(2) = 5.6$, $p = .06$). Four participants preferred fixed entry compared to 14 for post-entry and 12 for auto-formatting.

5   Experiment 3: Forward and Backward Navigation Buttons

5.1   Designs Tested in the Experiment

Experiment 3 focused on navigation buttons. Forward and backward navigation buttons are a necessity in the design of online mobile surveys. These buttons are what allow respondents to move to the next page and progress through a survey or move back to a previous page to fix a mistake on a question they have already answered. Due to the importance of forward and backward navigation on the successful completion of a mobile web survey, it is imperative that the function of these buttons is clear. Due to the limited screen size on mobile devices, buttons are often labeled with icons rather than text labels because they can be smaller and take up less space. However, this practice has the potential to make the function of these buttons ambiguous to populations not familiar with them.

In a study by [23], they tested the success of novice computer users in initially learning to use an end user application program on a desktop computer over the course of two 90 min sessions separated by one week to test knowledge retention. The interfaces for this application implemented buttons labeled with only icons, only text, or a combination of icons with text. The icon-only labeled buttons performed the worst out of the three interfaces in all performance measures in the first session. However, by the end of the second session, the icon-only was not significantly different from the other groups. This research suggests that buttons labeled with icons rather than text will not be understood by total novices.

Fig. 13. Icon navigation button label

Fig. 14. Text navigation button label

Further, in a study by [24], they tested modern icons from mobile phones with both younger (age 20–37) and older adults (age 65+) and found that older adults have more problems using existing mobile device icons. It was also found that text labels help both young and old adults to initially use icons. They suggest on the basis of their findings that mobile device icons should be labelled at least initially, especially for older adults.

This was a between-subjects design with a single experimental factor, navigation button labels. This factor had two levels:

- Level 1: Labelled with text
- Level 2: Labelled with icons

Two different versions of a short five question survey were developed where the forward and backward navigation buttons were labeled using one of these two methods. In the text labelled condition, the forward button was labelled with "Next" and the backward navigation was labelled with "Previous". In the icon labelled condition, the forward button was labelled with ">" and the backward button was labelled with "<". Sixteen participants completed the survey in the text labelled condition and sixteen participants completed it in the icon labelled condition. See Figs. 13 and 14 for examples of both labeling conditions.

5.2   Adaptation of Survey Questions

The survey questions were based on real questions that are used in government surveys. Four of the questions were yes/no questions and included the following:

- Have you completed a secondary (high) school diploma or equivalent?
- Last week were you employed for pay at a job or business?
- During the past 12 months, did you take any work related training, such as workshops or seminars?
- Do you have a currently active professional certificate or a state or industry license?

The fifth was a question on race and can be seen in Figs. 13 and 14.

5.3   Evaluation Criteria

The app collected behavioral measures, which included trial navigation response times, optimal navigation deviations, and difficulty ratings. Trial navigation response times was the length of time it took participants to find and tap the navigation buttons. The time was recorded starting from the point that the participant tapped a response option for each survey question and ended when they tapped any navigation button or link. In this way we were able to isolate the time spent navigating and not the time spend interpreting and answering the question. Deviations from an optimal navigation path were recorded as any buttons tapped that were not the forward navigation button. The purpose of this was to identify whether participants had difficulty interpreting the button labels to move forward. Finally, difficulty ratings were recorded at the very end of the survey with a short 5-point rating scale for participants to rate the difficulty of completing the short survey from "very easy" to "very difficult." At the very end of the session, participants were shown both design conditions printed on a piece of paper and asked to choose which one they would prefer to assess overall preference.

It is assumed that any differences in trial navigation response times between conditions resulting from a lack of understanding of the navigational icon labeling would disappear or decrease after the first trial due to a learning effect. Therefore, an independent samples t-test was conducted for the response times for the first trial only and another t-test was conducted for the average of the remaining four trials (after learning occurs) response times. It is well known that response time data is susceptible to skewness due to the fact that it is bounded at zero to the left side but not on the right. There can be lapses in attention or distractions which can result in large outliers that may reduce the power of hypothesis tests of response time means between conditions [25]. To address this, we applied a log transform of the response time data before conducting these analyses. Additionally, three extreme outliers were identified in the first trial after visual inspection of the raw response time data. Video recordings from the sessions were reviewed and it was confirmed that the three outliers in the first trial had selected a response option, which started the timer, and then began to speak with the TA about the content of the question instead of immediately trying to navigate to the next question. These extreme values were excluded from the first trial t-test because we were able to confirm that they resulted from human error.

Optimal navigation deviations were expected to be rare so this was collapsed across all trials and whether a deviation occurred at all at any point during the survey was simply coded as 1 or 0. Due to the low expected values, the assumptions for a Chi-squared test could not be met and a Fisher's exact test was conducted instead.

A Chi-squared test was conducted for satisfaction ratings and overall preference.

5.4   Results

First Trial Completion Time (Efficiency). An independent sample unequal variances t-test was conducted to identify any significant differences between labeling conditions on the time it took to navigate forward after the first survey question. The results of this test found that the icon condition ($M = 4.16$, $SE = 1.17$) was significantly slower to navigate forward than the text condition ($M = 1.53$, $SE = 0.16$) after selecting a response option when participants saw the navigation button for the first time; $t(16.42) = 2.43$, $p < .05$. See Fig. 15.

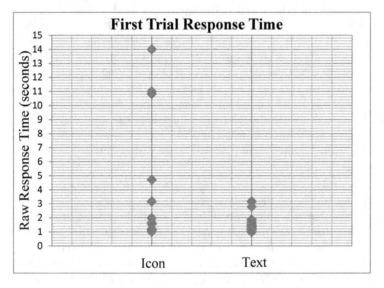

Fig. 15. Scatterplot split by labeling conditions of the raw response times for the first survey question.

Average Trial Completion Time (Efficiency). An independent sample t-test was conducted to identify any significant differences between labeling conditions for the mean time it took to navigate forward after a response option was selected. The results of this t-test found that there was not a significant difference between the icon ($M = 1.76$, $SE = 0.27$) and text ($M = 1.36$, $SE = 0.11$) conditions in the average time it took to navigate forward after selecting a response option; $t(30) = -0.05$, $p > .05$. See Fig. 16.

Optimal Navigation Deviations (Effectiveness). A Fisher's exact test was conducted to identify whether the number of participants who tapped an incorrect button to navigate forward differed significantly between label conditions. The results of the Fisher's exact test found that there was not a significant difference between groups ($p > .05$) for optimal navigation deviations. There were no deviations at all in the text-labeled group and there were two deviations in the icon-labeled group.

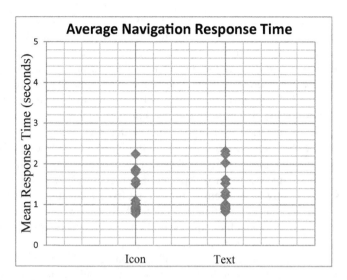

Fig. 16. Scatterplot split by labeling condition showing the mean navigation response times excluding the first trial.

Satisfaction (Satisfaction). A Chi-squared test was conducted to determine whether difficulty ratings were significantly different between labeling conditions. The results of this test did not yield any significant differences ($\chi^2(2) = 1.04$, $p > .05$). Difficulty ratings were virtually identical between groups with almost all participants reporting a rating of 1 (very easy).

Overall Preference (Satisfaction). A Chi-squared test was conducted to determine whether there was a significant difference between proportion of participants that preferred one labeling design of the other. The participants were shown both designs and were asked to choose which one they would prefer to use in a survey or both/neither. The results of the Chi-squared test found that a significant number of the older adults preferred the text labeled navigation buttons ($\chi^2(2) = 19.75$, $p < .001$). Almost 70% of the 32 participants preferred the text labeled navigation buttons compared with just over 20% that preferred the icons.

6 Overall Discussion and Implications for Future Research

The basis of this research was to learn more about how to design mobile surveys for older adults. For the first experiment, the data suggest that the iOS picker took longer and was preferred less than the other designs, which supports the hypothesis. We observed a significant increase in respondent burden as measured by time-on-task and by number of touches to the screen for the iOS picker design compared with a radio button/keyboard design. There were a high number of touches per question on questions with many response options when using the iOS picker. This finding matched our observation that the wheel at the bottom of the screen went fast and a lot of participant manipulation was needed to select from long lists such as months, days, years, and states. When asked to compare three different designs, participants overwhelming selected the keypad entry design as the preferred mode to enter date of birth. Thus we recommend designers avoid using the default iOS picker design for response options and instead opt for the Android spinner style or the radio button/keyboard design. To accomplish this for iOS systems, developers will need to implement additional programming to override the default iOS design. For date of birth, a common survey question, a keypad is preferred over dropdowns for this user group.

In the second experiment we observed that left-aligned currency resulted in higher accuracy which did not match the hypothesis. The data also suggest that currency formatting was least effective when it appeared as fixed format, which is in line with our hypotheses. Currently at the Census Bureau the fixed formatting is used in many online surveys because auto-formatting will not work if the respondent has JavaScript turned off. This will be something that should be investigated as more tools are developed and programming for web-based surveys evolve.

Finally, in the third experiment the hypothesis that the navigation button labeled with text words would outperform the button labeled with only an icon was supported by the data. We recommend always labeling the forward and backward navigation buttons using text rather than icons for older adults. It was found that older populations may not be as familiar with the functionality associated with common internet UI elements such as the forward and backward arrow icons. The icon labeled buttons were simply ambiguous to some participants upon their first encounter with them as was seen by the longer response times on the first survey question and errors that only occurred when an icon was present versus a text label.

In contrast to some of the literature on healthcare and older adults that show the use of apps and mobile phones to cause barriers to older adults, [15], this work shows that older adults are able to answer survey questions on a mobile phone and that some designs outperform others. This work is in line with the general conclusion that found that older adults are interested and able to learn how to use mobile phones in their daily lives and that improvements to the design will aid in their performance [26]. Designers should take these recommendations into consideration when optimizing survey response choices for mobile phone and older adults. Future work should look at comparing how young and middle aged adults perform on these same tasks to see if there are any differences.

Acknowledgements. This report is released to inform interested parties of research and to encourage discussion. The views expressed are those of the authors and not necessarily those of the U.S. Census Bureau. We would like to thank Andrew Roberts and Joanne Pascale for their reviews of an earlier draft of this paper.

References

1. Pew Research Center.: Mobile Fact Sheet (2018). http://www.pewinternet.org/fact-sheet/mobile/
2. Horwitz, R.: Personal Communication. U.S. Census Bureau (2018)

3. Cunningham, J., Neighbors, C., Bertholet, N., Hendershot, C.: Use of mobile devices to answer online surveys: implications for research. BMC Res. Notes **6**, 258 (2013). https://doi.org/10.1186/1756-0500-6-258

4. Pew Research Center: Tips for Creating Web Surveys for Completion on a Mobile Device (2015). http://www.pewresearch.org/files/2015/06/2015-06-11_tips-for-web-surveys-on-mobile.pdf

5. Antoun, C., Couper, M., Conrad, F.: Effects of mobile versus PC web on survey response quality: a crossover experiment in a probability web panel. Public Opin. Q. **81**(S1), 280–306 (2017)

6. de Bruijne, M., Wijnant, A.: Comparing survey results obtained via mobile devices and computers: an experiment with a mobile web survey on a heterogeneous group of mobile devices versus a computer-assisted web survey. Soc. Sci. Comput. Rev. **31**(4), 482–504 (2013)

7. Couper, M.P., Antoun, C., Mavletova, A.: Mobile web surveys: a total survey error perspective. In: Biemer, P., et al. (eds.) Total Survey Error in Practice, pp. 133–154. Wiley, New York (2017)

8. Zhou, J., Rau, P., Slavendy, G.: Use and design of handheld computers for older adults: a review and appraisal. Int. J. Hum. Comput. Interact. **28**(12), 799–826 (2012)

9. Parker, S., Jessel, S., Richardson, J., Reid, M.: Older adults are mobile too! Identifying the barriers and facilitators to older adults' use of mHealth for pain management. MC Geriatr. **13**(43) (2013)

10. Zhou, J., Rau, P.-L.P., Salvendy, G.: A qualitative study of older adults' acceptance of new functions on smart phones and tablets. In: Rau, P.L.Patrick (ed.) CCD 2013. LNCS, vol. 8023, pp. 525–534. Springer, Heidelberg (2013). https://doi.org/10.1007/978-3-642-39143-9_59

11. Hoober, S.: Design for Fingers and Thumbs Instead of Touch. UX Matters (2013). https://www.uxmatters.com/mt/archives/2013/11/design-for-fingers-and-thumbs-instead-of-touch.php

12. Hoober, S.: Common Misconceptions About Touch. UX Matters (2013). https://www.uxmatters.com/mt/archives/2013/03/common-misconceptions-about-touch.php

13. Jin, Z.X., Plocher, T., Kiff, L.: Touch screen user interfaces for older adults: button size and spacing. In: Stephanidis, C. (ed.) UAHCI 2007. LNCS, vol. 4554, pp. 933–941. Springer, Heidelberg (2007). https://doi.org/10.1007/978-3-540-73279-2_104

14. Joe, J., Demiris, G.: Older adults and mobile phones for health: a review. J. Biomed. Inf. **46**, 947–953 (2013)

15. Fletcher, J., Jensen, R.: Mobile health: barriers to mobile phone use in the aging population. Online J. Nurs. Inf. (OJNI) **19**(3) (2015). http://www.himss.org/ojni

16. Goggin, N., Meeuwsen, H.: Age-related differences in the control of spatial aiming movements. Res. Q. Exerc. Sport **63**(4), 366–372 (1992)

17. Ketcham, C., Seidler, R., van Gemmert, A., Stelmach, G.: Age-related kinematic differences as influenced by task difficulty, target size, and movement amplitude. J. Gerontol. Psychol. Sci. **57B**(1), 54–64 (2002)

18. Wallace, S., Graham, C., Saraceno, A.: Older adults' use of technology. Perspect. Gerontol. **18**(2), 50–59 (2013)

19. Craik, F.I.M., Salthouse, T.A.: The Handbook of Aging and Cognition. Lawrence Erlbaum Associates, Mahwah (2000)

20. Fisk, A.D., Rogers, W.A.: Handbook of human Factors and the Older Adult. Academic Press, San Diego (1997)

21. Salthouse, T.: When does age-related cognitive decline begin? Neurobiol. Aging **30**(4), 507–514 (2009)

22. Wang, L., Antoun, C., Sanders, R., Nichols, E., Olmsted-Hawala, E., Falcone, B., Figueroa, I., Katz, J.: Experimentation for developing evidence-based UI standards of mobile survey questionnaires. In: Proceedings of the 2017 CHI Conference Extended Abstracts on Human Factors in Computing Systems, pp. 2998–3004. ACM Press, Colorado (2017)
23. Wiedenbeck, S.: The use of icons and labels in an end user application program: an empirical study of learning and retention. Behav. Inf. Technol. **18**(2), 68–82 (1999)
24. Leung, R., McGrenere, J., Graf, P.: Age-related differences in the initial usability of mobile device icons. Behav. Inf. Technol. **30**(5), 629–642 (2011). https://www.learntechlib.org/p/52032/
25. Whelan, R.: Effective analysis of reaction time data. Psychol. Rec. **58**(3) (2008). Article 9
26. Wright, P., Bartram, C., Rogers, N., Emslie, H., Evans, J., Wilson, B., Belt, S.: Text entry on handheld computers by older users. Ergonomics **43**(6), 702–716 (2000)

Is Co-creation Superior to User Centred Design? Preliminary Results from User Interface Design for Inclusive Public Transport

Maurice Rekrut[1(✉)], Johannes Tröger[1], Jan Alexandersson[1], Daniel Bieber[2], and Kathleen Schwarz[2]

[1] DFKI GmbH, Saarbrücken, Germany
{rekrut.maurice,troger.johannes,alexandersson.jan}@dfki.de
[2] ISO Institut e.V., Saarbrücken, Germany
{bieber,schwarz}@iso-institut.de

Abstract. Mobility is a basic need which is especially critical for older people and persons with physical impairments. Within the scope of a long-term effort, we have established a human-based, technology-aided support service that helps mobility-impaired passengers to use public transport by engaging so-called mobility guides. A mobility guide is a person that supports passengers, for instance door-to-door. In order to interact with the system, e.g. ordering trips and guides, passengers can use a smartphone app or a webpage. Following a user-centered approach, we conducted monthly meetups – regulars' tables – in order to maintain contact and passengers' engagement with the goal of eliciting feedback about the UIs' usability and to jointly discuss new features. However, both quality and quantity of feedback as well as engagement reduced over time. In this paper, we describe and discuss the positive effect of replacing the regulars' tables with co-creation based meetings with a small dedicated group of passengers – co-developers. Results of the first co-developer workshops indicate substantial improvements in factors like engagement and quality of feedback resulting in concrete enhancements of the UIs.

Keywords: Co-creation · Co-developer · User-centered design
Public transport

1 Introduction

Since 2011, we are concerned with improving public transport experience and usage for persons that are momentarily excluded from using it due to their age or a range of different mobility impairments[1]. In previous efforts, we developed and validated a human-based technology aided service in the city of Saarbrücken, the capital of the federal state of Saarland[2], Germany [1]. Currently, mobisaar aims at extending this

---

[1] See http://www.mobisaar.de/mobia and http://www.mobisaar.de/ .
[2] See https://en.wikipedia.org/wiki/Saarland: Saarland has a population of about 1 Mi. habitants and an area of 2.6 km² → a density of 390/ km².

© Springer International Publishing AG, part of Springer Nature 2018
J. Zhou and G. Salvendy (Eds.): ITAP 2018, LNCS 10926, pp. 355–365, 2018.
https://doi.org/10.1007/978-3-319-92034-4_27

service to include rural regions of the federal state of Saarland. The pilot service was established 2014 and is based on human support provided by so-called *mobility guides* together with a technology component. The main purpose of the mobility guides is to accompany and support passengers who cannot use public transport on their own, due to physical limitations or perceived obstacles. Mobility guides help to overcome everyday hurdles occurring during the use of public transport, such as gaps or unlevelled entry and exit points between transport vehicles and pavement, complicated ticketing systems. In general, the guides foster a feeling of security among clients as experienced and trained public transport companions.

The technology component consists of software for intelligent positioning, scheduling and coordination of the mobility guides as well as user interfaces (UIs) for both guides and passengers. The coordination software directs the guides to the requested point of service, see Fig. 1. The passenger UIs have been implemented such that all passengers can interact with it. In addition to traditional telephone calls, personalised and adaptable user interfaces running on smartphones – APPs – allow users not only to order trips, but to receive real-time support during the trip. This functionality includes a bus/tram tracking service as well as notifications and alerts. The long-term goal of the system is to deliver coordinate personalised interaction and service that allows – in principle – everyone to use public transport.

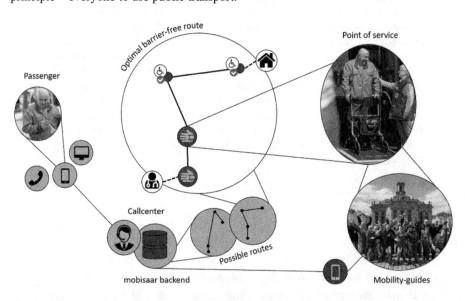

Fig. 1. Overview of the mobisaar system. The passenger can request the service via telephone, website or app. The "mobisaar backend" matches the request by searching for suitable mobility-guides and barrier free public transport routes. The guides are directed to and sufficiently informed about passenger, place and time of the requested service by his smartphone app.

The service targets a broad range of people from different social backgrounds with different requirements, living in areas with varying public infrastructure. We followed a user-centred design (UCD) approach [4, 5] to tailor the developed solution to the needs of these different people. UCD is an iterative methodology that puts the user in the centre of the development process thus supporting the creation of solutions solving real needs. Additionally, our efforts are implemented and continuously improved so that passengers can evaluate and contribute to the improvements of the service.

The basic methodology of UCD was adapted as described in [1] to enable a continuous improvement of the system and in particular, to adapt the user interfaces to the changing requirements as the service evolves over time. To achieve a maximum output and feedback from the users, as well as to engage them deeply in the project and create stronger personal commitment to the project, we ran so-called *regulars' tables* that were held on a monthly basis. We invited the mobisaar users to an informal meeting, serving coffee and cake, to discuss their experiences with the use of the service. Not only app users were invited but the whole customer group, whoever was interested to share their experiences and opinions. For a detailed review of positive effects of these regular's tables see [14].

The regulars' tables managed to create the desired strong commitment and engagement in terms of regular use of the service. In terms of experience exchange however, the broad open set-up often led to undirected feedback session with more or less repeating topics. The main discussion points arising in each of the sessions evolved into complaints about bus drivers and the insufficient expansion of public transport within the users' hometowns. Furthermore, the heterogeneous group of people and the large number of participants led to private discussions and inattentiveness to the main theme. These inattentive phases appeared increasingly during the parts of the meetings dealing with the app and the web interface. This was further aggravated by the fact that not all people attending the regulars' tables were actually using these interfaces. A call centre was established to ensure access via telephone [1, 3] and to avoid exclusion of passengers that shy away from technologies like the internet or smartphones. Technology-disinclined users were therefore separated from those actually using the app for discussing the current state of the application and suggesting improvements. By creating a more calm and focused environment, the sessions produced more directed feedback. Nevertheless, our passengers did not productively work out possible solutions themselves. Instead, developers took feedback home and re-evaluated new designs/mock-ups at the following regular's table. These suggestions were often either accepted straight away without any critical regard or plainly rejected. A vivid and active participation of the users could therefore not be achieved but would have been necessary for producing better solutions.

This is partly due to the fact that in UCD, researcher and users are still very much separated as the user is not part of the development team [10]. Therefore, we decided to proceed with rather active development methodology involving the users in a more hands-on co-creative way - as co-developers.

Co-creation can be classified as a participatory design approach. Although first descriptions of the approach occurred already in the 1970s [13] it took researchers until the 2000s to discover the need for new methodologies moving beyond pure user-centered to participatory approaches. Prahalad and Ramaswamy defined the term co-creation for the first time in 2000 [8] identifying an evolution of the customer's role from a passive to a more active one in the value creation process. In 2002, Sanders coined the term postdesign [10], a new method moving away from designing for the user towards designing together with them. The method aims at blurring the borders between the different roles involved in the development process, between designer, researcher and the user, actively including all parties. The work tries to fit participatory design into a methodology by giving it a new name, nevertheless it lacks a strong definition for it. Spinuzzi discovered the lack of clearly defined methodological approach for participatory design in literature in 2005 [13] and started reviewing studies concerning this topic starting back in the 1970s. He defined three initial stages that all reviewed approaches have in common:

- **Stage 1: Initial exploration**
  In this stage, designers meet the users and familiarize themselves with the context of the activity. This exploration includes the technologies used, but also includes workflows and procedures, routines, and other aspects.
- **Stage 2: Discovery processes**
  In this stage, designers and users employ various techniques to understand and prioritize organization and envision the future qualities of the activity, enhanced by the new solution. This work is often conducted on site.
- **Stage 3: Prototyping**
  In this stage, designers and users iteratively shape technological artefacts to fit visions of Stage 2. Prototyping involves one or more users.

These stages should be iterated several times.

As mobisaar is a follow-up project to a finished research project, building on experiences and a solution developed under the methodology of UCD, a complete repetition of all 3 stages mentioned above was beyond scope especially as stages 1 and 2 had been extensively worked out in Mobia already [3]. The clear aim of this work was to take the existing solution and co-creatively refine and co-develop it further to meet the new requirements [9]. Therefore, we focus on stage 3 on an iterative basis including all underlying concepts and tools of co-creation [11, 12, 15] as described in Sect. 2 below.

A literature research shows that co-creation methodologies applied in the field of public services including public transport often utilize social media and features within smartphone applications as a feedback channel. These approaches neither include face-to-face interaction with users nor hands-on prototyping of new solutions [2, 6, 7]. As this approach does not fit our needs in mobissar, we have adapted our methodology. According to lessons learned, we prefer relying on a close and persistent relationship to our target group as described in the following section.

2   Materials and Methods

Co-developers
The literature reveals problems with several participatory approaches. Concerning feedback channels, a face-to-face solution was preferred over social media channels. Beside the fact that the target group is rarely active to completely inactive on social media platforms, close contact including meetings turned out to be crucial for the development of the interfaces and the service itself as experienced and published in [14]. Another strategy unsuitable for the framing conditions in our effort is the frequent change of

participants over multiple co-creation cycles, e.g. inviting people for a one-time feed-back and co-creation session.

An important aspect is the regular use of our service and user interfaces to a long-term evaluation of the applications in different real-world scenarios over a longer period of time. Introducing new people into the system and the complex scenarios arising with the use each time would not lead to fruitful results. In the frame of our efforts we therefore define co-developers as follows:

A **Co-Developer** is an active user of the system who takes part in regular meetings to deliver feedback and participate in the development process by delivering suggestions as well as prototypical implementations in an experimental frame accompanying the project over a significant period of time.

We further defined prerequisites tailored to the special requirements of our project: A Co-Developer:

- is an active user of the mobisaar service (8 times per month)
- has a smartphone or at least PC with internet access
- is aged 50+
- faces mobility impairment when using public transport

Recruiting was done via newspaper articles. In order to address those willing to participate actively in the development process, the expression *co-developer* was stressed, chosen deliberately and mentioned repeatedly. A monthly ticket for the public transport covering the whole federal state of Saarland was offered to facilitate an active participation in the public transport. The search lead to numerous responses resulting in a heterogeneous group of co-developers representing different residential areas within our test region – Saarland, differing in age, smartphone experience level, and experience in other public transport apps.

Co-developer Workshops
The workshops primary goal has been to provide a basis for regular exchange concerning passengers' experiences with the user interfaces. One intention was discussing problems with the app in daily use. Co-developers' suggestions should be worked out with a focus on interactive sessions to implement these changes in a prototypical way. In the attempt of combining these two sessions, we merged a plain feedback approach with an active co-creation approach using pen and paper prototyping. Other tools of participatory design like collages, cognitive and context mapping, and storyboards, have not been used as we are in an advanced stage of the project where the service and technology is up and running. Future functionalities however and the establishment of profound changes in interaction principles should be talked through and worked out in a concep-tual stage with one of these tools.

To encourage active participation and ensure every opinion to be heard, the group size was limited to a maximum number of 4 co-developers per instructor. The classroom like atmosphere created within the regulars' tables with one presenter in the front and the participants rowed up facing the projection screen was relaxed to a round table approach. The instructor sat at the top of the table while the co-developers took a seat around it, facilitating face-to-face discussions with room for pen and paper prototyping in the middle.

For the regular cycle we agreed on two-hour workshops every 6 weeks. We started with a complete redesign of the application informed by other popular public transport applications on the market, while maintaining the main design principles developed in Mobia and mobisaar. Our Co-Developers did not receive any introduction to the app and were left alone for the first six weeks to evaluate the app with a focus on usability and easy comprehension.

First results of the Co-Developer Workshops as well as general impressions concerning the adapted methodology compared to the previous approach (regulars' tables) are reported in the next section.

3   Results and Discussion

Until the point of publishing three co-developer workshops were held and the number of co-developers stabilized at a group of 6 people aged between 45 and 82. The presented results are based on these first three workshops, while the meetings continue on a regular basis.

In general, the co-developer approach delivered the desired team-like atmosphere. Starting from the term "co-developer", the participants demonstrated higher commitment to the project and its solution compared to the previous approach with the regulars' tables. While during the preparation of each regulars' table it was a gamble to guess how many registered participants would actually show up, the co-developers were a lot more reliable. This facilitates planning and the selection of appropriate tools and methods for the workshop taking into account the expected number of participants. Furthermore, the developed group dynamic was an astonishing result. As the co-developers are a heterogeneous group of people bringing along different smartphone skills, some had minor problems with the use of the app in daily life. Without the instructors' impulse, the experienced participants teamed up with the unskilled ones and arranged trips together to explain basic usage of the app. Compared to the regulars' tables, this was a big success, as at each regulars' table a refresher about the app and its' use for some of the participants was a crucial and time-consuming part.

The small group size allowed each co-developer to bring in his/her own feedback which was one of the main advantages over the regulars' tables. Regulars' tables turned out to provide a platform for those who wanted to speak out problems often not related to the app/solution or the service in general which often dominated the discussions. Unfortunately, it may be that valuable opinions and feedback got lost in these complaint-oriented sessions.

Choosing users with smartphone experience could be seen as a limitation, as experienced user might tend to envision new solutions too strongly rooted in existing public transport applications. This would lead the development not necessarily in the direction of the special context requirements in mobisaar. As an example, the interaction principle of multiple confirmation dialogs to prevent triggering unintended actions in the app, bothered one of the participants. This navigation mechanism was a relic from the former project focusing mainly on older, less-tech-savvy smartphone users who asked for more safety layers when ordering help through the app. Nevertheless, the person voicing the complaint himself understood the reasons behind this approach and considered it as useful for unexperienced users. This way of thinking from different points of view, on the one hand regarding the own experience and on the other hand taking the view point of other target group un-experienced user, was well established throughout the workshop and all co-developers and provided creative solutions.

In the following we will highlight three detailed cases that arose during one of the first co-developer workshops starting with identifying a problem, developing conceptual ideas for a solution and finally working it out together with the users in pen and paper mock-ups. These mock-ups have later on been implemented in first prototypes by the software developers to present and discuss them at the next co-developer workshop.

Case 1 – Communication Passenger - Mobility Guide

One of the co-developers uses the mobisaar-Service and the application for his way home from work. The co-developer is working in a bigger office building with several entrances and the mobility guide receives only the main address. The mobility guide and the user did not find each other on several occasions. In contrast to most of the problems mentioned at the regulars' tables, the co-developer already came up with solutions he could imagine for this problem and discussed them together with the group.

Fig. 2. Examples of pen and paper mock-ups created in our first session. For each of the views positive points were placed left and the negative points on the right. The feedback was followed by an interactive pen and paper prototyping session to directly apply changes. The created screens were attached at the bottom section to summarize the process at a glance.

Earlier, a direct communication via telephone and sharing the phone numbers of the mobility guides was rejected due to privacy reasons. Therefore, it was agreed to use a messaging solution instead. For privacy reasons the co-developers came up with the idea of an input field for additional information during the process of booking a trip. Within this message, the user can inform about certain circumstances concerning the start/ endpoint of the trip or any other additional details. This idea was further developed with the group via pen and paper mock-ups (example see Fig. 2) and for a following meeting it was implemented by the software developers in a prototype, see Fig. 3.

Fig. 3. Prototypes created after the co-developer workshops from the pen and paper prototypes, to present and discuss them with the users at the next workshop. From left to right the mockups represent the results from the evaluation of case 1, 2 and 3.

Case 2 – Information about the Surroundings
In another instance, the passengers claimed that their journey would profit from more information on the suggested locations in the autocomplete of departure and destination selection, especially for places not visited before. The rationale behind this was that it would provide insights on the surrounding area. The proposed solution was an "info-button" appearing in the application at each geolocation, i.e. start, end or any stop in between of a route. Furthermore, it was suggested that additional information should be provided in form of a picture and a map highlighting the position. Showing cultural offerings or shopping possibilities nearby was recognized as useful but categorized with lower priority and postponed to future workshops. Pen and paper mock-ups resulted in a prototype depicted in Fig. 3.

Case 3 – Personalization
Following design principles for the elderly we ensured an easy to use and "secure" interaction concept. This included several confirmation dialogs preventing unintended

interactions. One of the co-developers described this fact as disturbing and mentioned as an example the steps needed to book a trip with the service. Subsequent to entering trip details, such as departure, destination etc., the system calculates and presents an overview of possible routes. The user selects one of these suggestions and is presented a detailed overview of the trip with all the stations and stops in between and the passenger can select where a guide is necessary. To continue the process, the passenger has to scroll to the bottom of the page and click a button, with the intention having to check the route and all points of service again. Having clicked the button, another confirmation dialog appears, summarizing the trip and the points of services asking the user if he really wants to send a request for the given route. In the group a discussion arose about the necessity of that many dialogues. Although all of the co-developers agreed that they do not really need it, they also agreed that it might be helpful for users less experienced with smartphones. In the end, it was the idea of the group to use personalization and show an adapted view of the interface depending on the smartphone experience level. Developing the concepts behind personalization itself might have covered a whole developer workshop. Therefore, we started with the development of a simpler screen for a more direct way of booking routes. Instead of switching to the detailed view after selecting one of the suggested routes and proceed with the confirmation dialog, the confirmation dialog should be shown directly and the selection/deselection of guides for the stops along the way should be possible from within this view. If more details are needed, the user can switch to the detail view by clicking a button in the footer (see Fig. 3).

Ultimately, using the co-developer framework we were able to increase efficiency thus saving a lot of unproductive time. Furthermore, regulars' tables require intense preparation where the feedback collected at the previous meetings had to be transformed into several mock-ups. These solutions had to be presented often resulting in ceiling or floor effects: either flat rejection or flat acceptance.

On the other hand, in the co-developer approach the participants created solutions themselves based on their own feedback. Typically, this resulted in one concrete mock-up that the software developers had to implement until the next session.

Although saving time in general, the active and engaged participation lead to time constraints within the workshop itself and not all parts of the app scheduled for discussion could be worked out in detail. For future workshops the time frame should be extended covering probably half a day.

4   Conclusion

The paper proposes a participatory approach called "co-developers" to extend the methodology of user-centred design applied within the mobisaar project aiming for public transport for everyone. The solution consists of a human-based service in form of mobility guides – persons available within the public transport supporting anyone that cannot use public transport of any reason. The second component is a technology that coordinates the guides such that they are available as needed for the passengers. From a development methodology point of view, the regulars' tables have been established as tool for the advancement of user interfaces and provided valuable insights. Active participation however was a rare commodity so that personal requirements arising with the use of the app in daily life were not discussed in detail as desired. Presentations of solutions for known issues provided by the developers during the regulars' tables resulted in flat rejection or acceptance without providing nuanced feedback. Hence, the value of the design and suggestions could not be assessed. To overcome these and similar problems and engage users deeper into the development process, we introduced the concept of co-developers.

Building on common participatory design approaches, the concepts of close personal contact to the target group was a crucial aspect. Considered important especially by elderly persons, as experienced in the regulars' tables, this concept was maintained within the co-developer approach. The expression "co-developer" resulted in the desired team-like atmosphere and increased engagement of the users. Compared to the regulars' tables the co-developers showed a stronger commitment and a kind of feeling of responsibility emerged in their role as "developers". This reliability facilitated the planning and the selection of appropriate tools and methods for the workshop.

The biggest benefit however was the saving of time due to the active participation of the co-developers. Whereas for the regulars' tables known issues were collected and worked out as several possible solutions by the developers in advance, the co-developers produced solutions themselves in the form of mock-ups. In contrast to the regulars' tables, the co-developer workshops led to discussion rounds taken into account different points of view resulting in one solution to implement for the developers until the next meeting.

Two hours meeting time every six weeks was chosen based on the experiences of the regulars' tables. This turned out to be too little mainly due to the increased output delivered by the co-developers. Future workshops will be extended to half a day every fourth week. To support co-developers tagging ideas and problems occurring in daily life, as well as collecting feedback in advance to the workshops in a standardized way, we plan to hand out diaries.

Furthermore, a concept to include functionalities establishing profound changes within the interfaces needs to be developed, as the current co-developer approach with prototyping sessions only evaluates existing UIs. Methods like cognitive or context mapping could be used to develop such profound features in a process of co-creation on a conceptual stage, whereby most suitable tools still need to be evaluated.

Acknowledgements. This research has been funded by the Federal Ministry of Education and Research of Germany in the projects "Mobia – mobil bis ins Alter" (grant number 16SV5697) and "mobisaar – Mobilität für alle" (grant number 16SV7431). We are grateful to our project partners and colleagues that have made this work possible, see http://www.mobisaar.de.

References

1. Alexandersson, J., et al.: Oil in the machine: technical support for a human-centred service system for public transport. In: Wichert, R., Klausing, H. (eds.) Ambient Assisted Living. Advanced Technologies and Societal Change, pp. 157–167. Springer, Cham (2015). https://doi.org/10.1007/978-3-319-11866-6_13
2. Alves, H.: Co-creation and innovation in public services. Serv. Indus. J. **33**(7–8), 671–682 (2013)
3. Bieber, D., Alexandersson, J., Schwarz, K.: Das Mobia-Projekt: Die Kombination von Dienstleistung und Technologie für den ÖPNV. In: Proceedings of the 6th German AAL-Kongress with Exhibition: Lebensqualität im Wandel von Demografie und Technik, Berlin, Germany (2013). (In German)
4. Gulliksen, J., Göransson, B., Boivie, I., Blomkvist, S., Persson, J., Cajander, Å.: Key principles for user-centred systems design. Behav. Inf. Technol. **22**(6), 397–409 (2003)
5. ISO/DIS 9241–210.: "Ergonomics of Human System Interaction-Part 210: Human-Centred Design for Interactive Systems." International Standardization Organization (ISO), Switzerland (2009)
6. Nunes, A.A., T. Gonçalves, T. Galvão, T.: A prototype for public transport service co-creation using social media: results from usability testing. In: International Conference on Exploring Service Science 1.3 (2013)
7. Nunes, A.A., Galvão, T., e Cunha, J.F.: Urban public transport service co-creation: leveraging passenger's knowledge to enhance travel experience. Procedia-Soc. Behav. Sci. **111**, 577–585 (2014)
8. Prahalad, C.K., Ramaswamy, V.: Co-opting customer competence. Harvard Bus. Rev. 79–87 (2000)
9. Rekrut, M., Alexandersson, J., Britz, J., Tröger, J., Bieber, D., Schwarz, K.: "mobisaar" – a technology-based service providing mobility for everybody in public transport. In: The SIforAGE International Conference, Barcelona (2016). In press
10. Sanders E.B.-N.: From user-centered to participatory design approaches. In: Design and the Social Sciences: Making connections, 1.8 (2002)
11. Sanders, E.B.-N., Stappers, P.J.: Co-creation and the new landscapes of design. Co-design **4**(1), 5–18 (2008)
12. Sanders, E.B.-N., Simons, G.: A social vision for value co-creation in design. Open Source Business Resource December 2009
13. Spinuzzi, Clay: *The Methodology of Participatory Design*. Tech. Commun. **52**(2), 163–174 (2005)
14. Tröger, J., Alexandersson, J., Britz, J., Rekrut, M., Bieber, D., Schwarz, K.: Board games and regulars tables extending user centred design in the mobia project. In: International Conference on Human Aspects of IT for the Aged Population. LNCS, vol. 9754, pp. 129–140. Springer, Cham (2016). https://doi.org/10.1007/978-3-319-39943-0_13
15. UX Magazine, *"Creativity-based Research: The Process of Co-Designing with Users"*. https://uxmag.com/articles/creativity-based-research-the-process-of-co-designing-with-users. Accessed 20 Jan 2018

Online Learning for Long-Query Reduction in Interactive Search for Experienced Workers

Kaoru Shinkawa[(✉)], Toshinari Itoko, and Masatomo Kobayashi

IBM Research - Tokyo, 19-21 Hakozaki, Nihonbashi, Chuo, Tokyo 1038510, Japan
{kaoruma,itoko,mstm}@jp.ibm.com

Abstract. For domain specific document searches like job matching, long queries are often given as a detailed information of targets. Previous studies found that higher quality results can be obtained by searching with an optimal subset of words excerpted from a long query. To excerpt the optimal subset of words, query reduction using machine learning techniques has been studied. Supervised learning requires training data with annotation, which is especially difficult for in-domain data because of its specific terminology. In this study, we propose a model that integrates machine learning techniques and manual processing for long-query reduction. We integrated our model into a job matching system that collects manual "interactions" and used them as training data to learn query reduction. Furthermore, we evaluated our model with actual job offerings and expert profile data obtained from a recruitment agency. We found that our proposed model outperformed the baseline in precision, recall, and F-measure. The result suggests that our model could be used for query reduction of interactive search systems of specific domain data.

Keywords: Long query · Query improvement · Job matching
MAP estimation · Interactive interface

1 Introduction

In document search applications for domain experts such as job matching and patent search, long queries are often given, which include detailed descriptions about search targets. For example, recruiters of job matching agencies will search for candidate resumes on the basis the text in job offerings. Intellectual Property experts will search for similar patents on the basis of an invention's disclosure document.

Previous studies found that we can obtain higher quality search results if we obtain an optimal subset of word sets from a long query, and use them as the query instead of the original [1]. Extracting an optimal subset of word sets from long query essentially reduces the unimportant words of long queries. There are two approaches for reducing the words from long queries, automatic and manual. For automatic approaches based on supervised learning, we need relevant

J. Zhou and G. Salvendy (Eds.): ITAP 2018, LNCS 10926, pp. 366–376, 2018.
https://doi.org/10.1007/978-3-319-92034-4_28

documents [2] and manual annotation [3] as learning data, which is difficult especially for in-domain data. Therefore, many approaches based on unsupervised learning for in-domain data have been proposed [4]. On the other hand, several manual approaches have also been proposed [5–8]. Unlike in a typical web page retrieval, quality is more important than retrieval speed in document retrieval performed by domain-specific experts. Therefore, manual interactions that improve the quality of search results could be acceptable to users.

We propose a model that integrates automatic and manual approaches. We developed a straightforward and simplified user interface so that users can fully interact and acquire the best reduced queries. Automatic reduction is used to generate initial queries, thereby reducing the burden of user interaction. Furthermore, we proposed a user interface that embeds hidden learning data collections during search interactions. It functions like a shopping cart on an online shopping website, which you can store selected documents in a list. A user can review the created list later and adjust the list before completion. Since the list at the completion state can be considered to be a document list relevant to the query, the system collects learning data without making the user aware of it.

To investigate whether our proposed model can improve given queries, we integrated our model into the job matching system of a Japanese recruitment agency and analyzed it using real job offerings and simulated interaction data. Through the analysis, we demonstrated how word sets in queries are improved and suggested that our model can be used for the query reduction of interactive search systems of specific domain data.

2   Related Works

Numerous efforts have been made towards improving the long-query issues. Bendersky and Croft proposed an automatic techniques for query reduction, which involved learning to identify key concepts in long-queries using a variety of features [3]. However, their method requires manual annotation to identify a key noun phrase in each query.

Other studies that have key phrase extraction methods that use supervised machine learning techniques was first introduced by Turney [9] and later explored by several other researchers [10, 11]. They treated a document as a set of phrases, which must be classified as either positive or negative examples of key phrases. This approach requires documents with key phrases attached as learning data. Although this approach is reported to be effective, it is difficult to obtain domain-specific learning data in the early phases of a real production environment.

An unsupervised technique that involves the interaction of dropping unnecessary terms from long queries was proposed by Kumaran and Carvalho [4]. However, the interaction could be an additional burden for ordinary document searches.

Query expansion is an another approach for improving search queries. Cui and Wen have proposed a use of query logs as a training data for adding keywords to the original query [12]. It has been suggested as an effective way to resolve the short query and word mismatching problem. Kumaran and Allan [13] combined query reduction and expansion methods to improve original queries.

In this study, we focus on a query reduction technique for processing long-query which assume to be a major query type for job recruitment purpose. We propose a model for query reduction involving both automatic and manual approaches that enables online learning in a production environment.

3   Query Reduction Model

We propose a new model of query reduction to improve the quality of verbose queries. This model uses past search "interactions," such as word deletion, word addition, and word weighting, collected by a document search engine to learn new keyword deletion procedures.

The model estimates the ideal word set S of a long query by using past interaction data. We define Q as a word set of every words included in a given long query. We calculate P_w as a probability of word w ($w \in Q$) not being included in the ideal query on the basis of the maximum a posteriori (MAP) estimation method. MAP is an estimate of an unknown quantity, that equals the mode of the posterior distribution. The MAP can be used to obtain a point estimate of an unobserved quantity on the basis of empirical data.

We defined N_w and D_w as the total count of occurrence and total count of deletion of word w in past interaction logs, respectively. The weight assigned to word w is defined as W_w, in which the default value is 1. E_w is the sum of the weights assigned to word w when the weight is smaller than 1, which can be describes as $E_w = \sum_w (1 - W_w)$. M_w is the sum of the weights when each weight is larger than 1, and can be described as $M_w = \sum_w (W_w - 1)$. Probability P_w is calculated as:

$$P_w = \frac{D_w + E_w + \alpha - 1}{N_w + \gamma M_w + \alpha + \beta - 2}, \tag{1}$$

where α and β are beta distribution parameters and γ is a bias parameter.

We calculate score S_w as:

$$S_w = k(1 - P_w) - P_w, \tag{2}$$

where k ($k > 1$) is an additional cost of word addition compared to that of keyword deletion. We considered this additional cost since addition requires more procedures compared to deletion. Words in an ideal word set S are selected by defining the threshold of S_w.

4   Interactive Search Interface

We introduce the user interface of our document search system and how it collects interaction log data that can be used as learning data for our model. Our interface is based on the system proposed in [8]. Our system is implemented as a web application that consists of two pages as shown in Figure. 1. Users interact with the system as follows. (1) On the search page, users input a verbose query and click

A

Job offering
(Search query)

Search button

Results

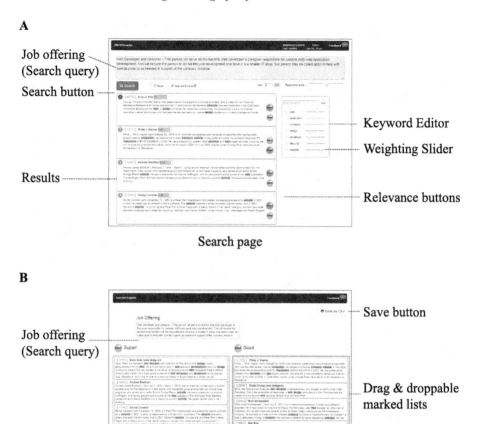

Keyword Editor

Weighting Slider

Relevance buttons

Search page

B

Save button

Job offering
(Search query)

Drag & droppable
marked lists

Matching page

Fig. 1. User interface of interactive search system. (A) Search page to input query and retrieve relevant documents. This interface also include the Keyword Editor field to add/delete/change weight for keywords. (B) Matching page to confirm and adjust selected documents. It is a drag-and-droppable interface to adjust the candidate lists before completion.

"Search" to get the initial result. The top ten keywords scored by term frequency-inverse document frequency (TF-IDF) are used for the initial query by default, which appears in the "Keyword Editor." The top ten ranked documents are shown as the result. (2) Users look through the documents, identify which are relevant, and click either of the "Relevance" buttons "Good" (probably a good match) or "Super!" (best match) in accordance with the degree of their relevance. (3) If users think they have not found a sufficient number of relevant documents, they can edit the query words in the "Keyword Editor," i.e. delete a word, change the weight of a word, or add a new word. When any of the query words are edited, the search result is updated automatically. Users repeat steps 2 and 3 until they are satisfied with

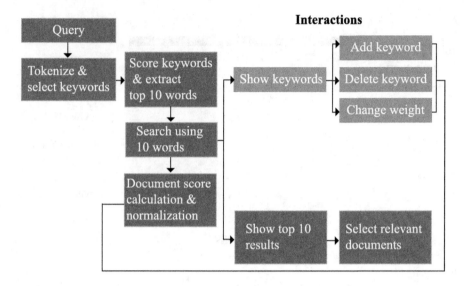

Fig. 2. System flow of the interactive interface. Highlighted boxes represent interactions operated in the "Keyword Editor".

the final result. Users then click the "Selected Experts" button, which navigates them to the "Matching" page to review their search results. (4) On the "Matching" page, two lists of selected documents that are marked as "Good" and "Super!," respectively, are shown. Users can review and adjust the documents in the lists by dragging and dropping them between the lists. (5) Users save and download the confirmed documents lists by clicking the "Save" button (Fig. 2).

Our interface is designed on the basis of a typical web search interface and enhanced to make keyword editing and relevant document selection efficient with the Keyword Editor and Relevance buttons/Matching page, respectively. The Keyword Editor enables visual editing of query words more efficiently than directly editing space-separated query text e.g. "wordA^2.0 wordB" where numerical value after caret represents a weight of a word. The Relevance buttons and Matching page provide a functionality very similar to the "Add to Cart" button on online shopping websites. These concepts may not be considered new as user interfaces but their introduction is very important in the sense that they enables the collection of data regarding which words will contribute to the finding of relevant documents. The system logs every user's click of Search, Save and Good/Super!. Those logs are significantly different from typical click logs collected from web search systems in that they cannot be used to determine when the retrieval process starts and finishes just as whether any results were found. In our system, every completed search starts with Search and finishes with the Save operations, so we can precisely define a query session as a user's interactions for a topic. In addition, we can identify "definitely relevant" documents from the documents in the Super! list at the time of clicking the "Save" button. We can also identify the query words used to find the relevant documents by tracking the logs when the documents are marked as Good/Super!.

5   Preliminary Experiments

To investigate our proposed reduction model, we evaluated our model using data obtained from a job recruitment agency. In this section, we first describe the job offering and profile data used for analysis. We next explain the procedure of collecting learning data. Finally, we will describe how we measured our model with obtained results.

5.1   Profile Data Used in Experiment

We used the profile data of registered experts and job offerings data obtained from a job recruitment agency located in Tokyo, Japan. Approximately 30% of their registered workers are over 60 years old, which is very high compared to that of a general recruitment agency. Their recruitment process is mainly divided in two parts, "Registration" and "Recommendation". The Registration process is performed as follows. (1) Experts register themselves via the website. They input their profile information such as previous job experience, skills, career, and personal connections in a simple text format. (2) Recruiters in the agency hold online or face-to-face meetings with the registered experts to obtain their additional profile information. (3) Recruiters input the additional information into the system in a simple text format. The Recommendation process is performed as follows. (1) A recruiter in the agency holds a hearing with a company regarding their business needs. (2) The recruiter searches for registered experts who would meet the company's business needs. (3) The recruiter recommends the matched experts to the company, then proceed with face-to-face interviews.

The expert profile data generated during the Registration process are considered as target documents, and business need (job offering) data generated during the Recommendation process are considered as queries for searching. We extracted 3,000 experts' profiles and ninety job offerings to evaluate our proposed reduction model.

5.2   Procedure

To investigate our proposed reduction model, we collected interaction data of the simulated search process. The authors manually simulated the interactions of recruiters by reviewing the results of searched resume documents. The search engine is built on Solr/Lucene, where the Japanese morphological analyzer, "kuromoji," is used. After the tokenization and part-of-speech tagging by "kuromoji" is complete, noun words are filtered and stored as a data collection. Dictionaries and stop words are defined on the basis of feedback from recruiters. When a query is given, resume documents are ranked by the BM25 similarity algorithm [14]. BM25 scoring utilizes both word frequency and document length normalization. For a given query Q containing keywords $q_1, ..., q_n$, (q_i, D) is $q_i's$ word frequency in the document D, $|D|$ is the length of D in words, and avgdl is the average document length in the text collection. The BM25 score of D for Q is calculated as:

$$Score(D,Q) = \sum_{i=1}^{n} IDF(q_i) \times (\frac{f(q_i,D) \times (k_1 + 1)}{(f(q_i,D) + k_1 \times (1 - b + b \times \frac{|D|}{avgdl}}). \qquad (3)$$

k_1 and b are free parameters, and we used Lucene's default values $k_1 = 1.2$, $b = 0.75$ for this experiment. $IDF(q_i)$ is the inverse document frequency weight of a query word computed by:

$$IDF(q_i) = log\frac{1 + N - n(q_i) + 0.5}{(n(q_i) + 0.5)}. \qquad (4)$$

5.3   Measurement

We measured the correctness of the query reduction results by leveraging the commonly-used machine learning measurements: precision, recall, and F-measure. As a preprocessing condition, job offering text obtained from the recruitment agency was used as an original long query and words that were considered to be important were selected manually from the query. We collected the interaction data until we reached the list of selected keywords as described in the previous section. Selected words were confirmed by reviewing the result of the retrieved documents. These interaction data are used as training data.

When a new long query is given, all words in the query were rearranged in descending order on the basis of the scores calculated by the proposed algorithm using the interaction log. The top ten words were evaluated using the precision, recall, and F-measure measurements as an index.

6   Results

We analyzed our proposed algorithm using the job offerings and profile data of the recruitment agency. We obtained ninety job offerings with interactions data and cross-validated ten subjects using other eighty as a training data. Specifically, we selected each ideal word set from eighty subjects, and keyword operation were recorded as training data by using the user interface of the job matching system. Keyword scoring was performed for the other ten subjects using the training data. We evaluated the top ten keywords by comparing them with manually selected ideal word sets using average precision, recall and F-measures. The beta distribution parameters α and β were set to 2. Bias parameter γ was set to 1. The additional cost of word addition compared to keyword deletion k was set to 5 on the basis of the exploratory experiments.

The result showed that our proposed model outperformed in all measures compared to the baseline, which is the TF-IDF scoring. (baseline: precision = 0.35, recall = 0.44, f-measure = 0.37, proposed model: precision = 0.54 ± 0.06, recall = 0.59 ± 0.07, f-measure = 0.55 ± 0.06) (Fig. 3). Figure 4 and Table 1 shows

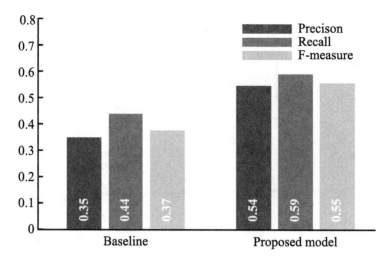

Fig. 3. Comparison of the precision, recall and F-measure between baseline (TF-IDF) and the proposed reduction model.

the transition of the precision, recall, and f-measure measurements by changing the amount of training data from ten to eighty subjects. Recall improved right after leaning ten subjects, while precision gradually improved on the basis of the amount of learning data.

Table 1. Values of the precision, recall, and F-measure measurements by changing the amount of training data.

Training data	Precision (SD)	Recall (SD)	F-measure (SD)
Baseline (TF-IDF)	0.347	0.439	0.374
10 offerings	0.475 (0.078)	0.643 (0.131)	0.522 (0.068)
20 offerings	0.484 (0.078)	0.595 (0.086)	0.521 (0.081)
30 offerings	0.514 (0.056)	0.603 (0.076)	0.543 (0.061)
40 offerings	0.518 (0.066)	0.609 (0.080)	0.549 (0.071)
50 offerings	0.525 (0.061)	0.607 (0.084)	0.551 (0.069)
60 offerings	0.530 (0.067)	0.601 (0.084)	0.551 (0.072)
70 offerings	0.542 (0.072)	0.596 (0.097)	0.557 (0.080)
80 offerings	0.544 (0.064)	0.587 (0.075)	0.554 (0.064)

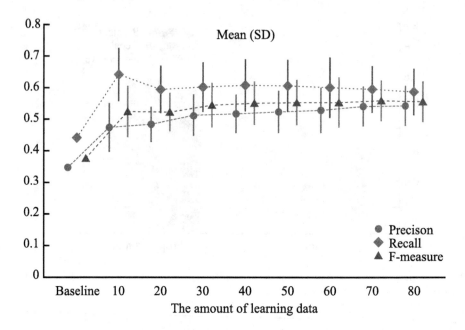

Fig. 4. Transition of the precision, recall, and F-measure measurements by changing the amount of training data.

7   Conclusion

In light of the demand for query improvement of in-domain data searching, we focused on a long-query reduction method and proposed a model that enables the reduction of unimportant keywords on the basis of past search interactions collected by a document search engine. We also proposed a user interface that embeds hidden learning data collections during search interactions. To investigate our proposed model, we integrated our model and interface into the job matching system and analyzed them with the data obtained from a recruitment agency.

We found that our proposed model outperformed in all measures (precision, recall, and F-measure) compared to that of the baseline. We also found that recall improves with a relatively small amount of training data, which in this case was that of ten subjects. The cost of keyword addition is considered to be larger than that of keyword deletion, therefore, the result would be preferable for the user. Precision gradually improves on the basis of the amount of training data, suggesting that the quality of the query improves as the interaction logs get collected via the search system. As a result, as the recruiter repeats a series of job matching processes (inputting job offerings, keyword operations, and selecting candidates), the default keyword set extracted from the original query will be gradually improved without any additional actions to create training data. The keyword operations during searches for experts can be considered to reflect domain knowledge related to specific industries and business processes. In other words, a set of domain knowledge required for job matching will be extracted from keyword operations of experienced recruiters. Using keyword operations of experienced recruiters as training data, we hope to help improve the performance of inexperienced recruiters.

Acknowledgments. This research was partially supported by Japan Science and Technology Agency (JST), under Strategic Promotion of Innovative Research and Development Program (This acknowledgement shall be retained in any derivative works that you publish). We sincerely thank Circulation. Ltd. for providing the data used in this study and appreciate their valuable comments and suggestions.

References

1. Kumaran, G., Allan, J.: A case for shorter queries, and helping users create them. In: HLT-NAACL, pp. 220–227 (2007)
2. Lease, M., Allan, J., Croft, W.B.: Regression rank: learning to meet the opportunity of descriptive queries. In: Boughanem, M., Berrut, C., Mothe, J., Soule-Dupuy, C. (eds.) ECIR 2009. LNCS, vol. 5478, pp. 90–101. Springer, Heidelberg (2009). https://doi.org/10.1007/978-3-642-00958-7_11
3. Bendersky, M., Croft, W.B.: Discovering key concepts in verbose queries. In: Proceedings of the 31st Annual International ACM SIGIR Conference on Research and development in Information Retrieval, pp. 491–498. ACM (2008)
4. Kumaran, G., Carvalho, V.R.: Reducing long queries using query quality predictors. In: Proceedings of the 32nd International ACM SIGIR Conference on Research and Development in Information Retrieval, pp. 564–571. ACM (2009)
5. Ruthven, I.: Interactive information retrieval. Ann. Rev. Inf. Sci. Technol. **42**(1), 43–91 (2008)
6. Koenemann, J., Belkin, N.J.: A case for interaction: a study of interactive information retrieval behavior and effectiveness. In: Proceedings of the SIGCHI Conference on Human Factors in Computing Systems, pp. 205–212. ACM (1996)
7. Henninger, S., Belkin, N.J.: Interface issues and interaction strategies for information retrieval systems. In: Conference Companion on Human Factors in Computing Systems, pp. 352–353. ACM (1996)
8. Shinkawa, K., Saito, K., Kobayashi, M., Hiyama, A.: Towards extracting recruiters' tacit knowledge based on interactions with a job matching system. In: Zhou, J., Salvendy, G. (eds.) ITAP 2017. LNCS, vol. 10298, pp. 557–568. Springer, Cham (2017). https://doi.org/10.1007/978-3-319-58536-9_44
9. Turney, P.D.: Learning algorithms for keyphrase extraction. Inf. Retr. **2**(4), 303–336 (2000)
10. Frank, E., Paynter, G.W., Witten, I.H., Gutwin, C., Nevill-Manning, C.G.: Domain-specific keyphrase extraction. In: IJCAI 1999, pp. 668–673 (1999)
11. Hulth, A.: Improved automatic keyword extraction given more linguistic knowledge. In: Proceedings of the 2003 Conference on Empirical Methods in Natural Language Processing, pp. 216–223. Association for Computational Linguistics (2003)

12. Cui, H., Wen, J.-R., Nie, J.-Y., Ma, W.-Y.: Probabilistic query expansion using query logs. In: Proceedings of the 11th International Conference on World Wide Web, pp. 325–332. ACM (2002)
13. Kumaran, G., Allan, J.: Effective and efficient user interaction for long queries. In: Proceedings of the 31st Annual International ACM SIGIR Conference on Research and Development in Information Retrieval, pp. 11–18. ACM (2008)
14. Robertson, S., Zaragoza, H.: The Probabilistic Relevance Framework: BM25 and Beyond. Now Publishers Inc., Hanover (2009)

Eye Movements and Reading Behavior of Younger and Older Users: An Exploratory Eye-Tacking Study

Mina Shojaeizadeh[(⊠)] and Soussan Djamasbi

User Experience and Decision Making Laboratory,
Worcester Polytechnic Institute, 100 Institute Road, Worcester, MA 01609, USA
{minashojaei, djmasbi}@wpi.edu

Abstract. Baby boomers and millennials form two major user groups that tend to exhibit different behaviors when viewing online information. Because important online information is often communicated via text, understanding the differences in the way textual information is scanned by these two user groups allow designers to better meet the needs of each group. Our results showed that saccadic amplitudes were strong predictor of user age groups when they were reading a relatively long and difficult text passage. These results help to improve online reading experience by examining metrics that can unobtrusively capture and compare the overall reading experience of younger and older users. The results are also relevant to research in designing advanced decision tools that use eye tracking to detect cognitive effort to respond to user needs.

Keywords: Eye tracking · Baby boomers · Generation Y · User performance
Online reading · Eye movements

1 Introduction

Baby Boomers, born between 1946 and 1964 (age in 2017, 53 to 71) are the second largest generation in the U.S. With 74.9 million people in 2015, they make up 26 percent of the total U.S. population [1]. People 65+ represented 14.5% of the population in the year 2014; they are expected to grow to be 21.7% of the population by 2040 [2]. The internet provides a number of benefits for older adults. It is used as a means of communication via E-mail, chat rooms, discussion groups, and direct messaging. The Internet also contains a wealth of medical information that can be particularly useful for older adults when health becomes a greater issue and concern [3]. Important online information is often conveyed via text-based communication. Thus, examining the reading behavior of older users and comparing it to those of younger users allow designers to better meet the need of both user populations. Additionally, recent research calls for designing advanced systems that can respond to user needs in real time. To achieve this goal, various studies are needed to identify eye movements that can reliably detect user experience [4]. To address this need, in this study we examined eye movement factors that are likely to reflect the overall reading experience of baby boomers and younger generation. To this end, an eye tracking study was

© Springer International Publishing AG, part of Springer Nature 2018
J. Zhou and G. Salvendy (Eds.): ITAP 2018, LNCS 10926, pp. 377–391, 2018.
https://doi.org/10.1007/978-3-319-92034-4_29

conducted with 20 participants including 10 young generation and 10 baby boomers. The task required each participant to read a text passage about law and to provide answers to a set of questions about the passage, while the participants' eye movements were recorded by a high speed eye-tracking device. The main objective of the study was to investigate a range of eye movement data that prove to be important in reading behavior and to examine whether these eye movements can reliably predict user age group and performance. This investigation not only facilitates a better understanding of the differences in reading behavior between the two generations but also contributes to research that aims at designing advanced system [4]. Identifying eye movement metrics that reliably predict a user's age group can help designing adaptive systems that can respond to older and younger users appropriately in real-time.

2   Theoretical Background

2.1   Baby Boomers and Young Generation: Differences in Online Experiences

Literature indicates that older users may expend more cognitive effort when processing online information. For example, past research demonstrate that older adults are slower in cognitive processing from younger people [5]. Based on the cognitive theory of aging, slowdowns of cognitive processing in older adults can explain the age related differences between older and younger adults [6, 7]. Furthermore, research shows that because of a numerous factor such as social, cognitive, psychological, and physical factors as well as overall differences in life experience, baby boomers often have different usability issues as compared to young adults [8].

Existing psychological eye-tracking literature has also reported older adults exhibit more cognitive effort during reading. For instance, it is known that older adults read more slowly and make more fixations and regressions than younger readers [9–11]. Examining eye movement characteristics, Rayner et al. [12] asked young and old adults to read sentences containing target words that varied either in frequency (low-frequency vs. high-frequency target words) or in predictability (low-predictable, medium-predictable, or high predictable target words) to determine whether frequency and predictability interact with age when these target words are read. They learned that older adults make more fixations, longer fixations and more regressions (backwards movements to re-read text). Another study, comparing older and younger adult's differences, suggests that older adults perform at a reasonable level; they are as successful in reading as younger adults, but it seems that they make more effort in reading as demonstrated by longer fixation durations [13].

A similar finding occurred from a study looking at expert older users working at an investment company, Fidelity. In their first study, they examined the behavior of expert older adults (50–69) while working in the office and used the web daily, compared to younger colleagues (20–39) [14]. The results showed that older adults spent on average 42% more time looking at the content of the pages than did the younger adults. Older adults also spent 51% more time looking at the navigation areas as compared to the younger adults. Their results also suggest that older participants distributed their gaze more widely across the pages and read more of the text than younger users did. In another study, researchers examined preferences for web page presentation, and reported that baby boomers had longer fixations on large images and search bars as compared to their younger counterparts [15]. Similarly, in another study, Zaphiris and Savitch [16] compared older (58–87) and younger (19–27) web users browsing health information sites of varying depth of hierarchy, and observed that older adults looked at more of the page and spent longer considering which link to choose. However, the researchers found no significant difference in reading speeds. Chadwick et al. [8], conducted two usability studies to investigate the differences between older and younger adults in completing a task using a prototype employee/retiree benefits Fidelity's website. In their first study, researchers examined whether there were differences in how older adults interacted with the Web and whether changes in text size would affect performance. Users completed tasks on the website using various text sizes. Researchers learned, from the results of the study, that older users (55 years or older, mean = 69.2) had significantly more difficulty using the Web than younger users (55 and younger, mean = 35.9). In their second study new participants performed the same tasks on a version of the site that was redesigned to address the usability problems encountered by older users in the first study, with the purpose of improving the performance of older adults. They concluded that performance improved significantly for both older and younger users, they also observed that older users read more text and often read all of the text on a screen [8]. Additionally, they found that older adults were particularly cautious and not confident about clicking on links that were nouns, like Accounts. When they changed those links to actions, like Go to Accounts, both older and younger users were faster and more confident.

A different study [17] examining the differences between old and young adults in reactions to a set of homepages through a laboratory experiment captured users' reactions using self-report measures and eye tracking. The results of this study showed that both generations reported similar aesthetic preferences, and both generations preferred pages that had images and little text. However, the two generations also displayed differing online viewing behavior and preferences. For instance, eye tracking data revealed that Baby Boomers had significantly more fixations on web pages that they found less appealing and their fixations covered more of the pages than Young Generation. In addition, Baby Boomers reported a significantly higher tolerance for clutter (more web components) on a page [17].

Another study [28] looked at the differences between older and younger users in information search behavior. Participants were asked to complete a search task related to health information on three different websites. The study investigated whether age or other factors such as gender, educational background and frequency of internet use had an impact on navigation patterns, the use of the search box, effectiveness, efficiency and user satisfaction. According to the findings of the study, older users were less likely to make use of the search box than younger users. In addition, younger users were more successful in accomplishing the search task and were much faster than their older counterparts in completing the task. Although the results showed that there were some difference between older and younger users in fulfilling an information search task the most impactful factor on information search behavior was not always age. For example, when comparing the navigation patterns of older people using internet daily with those of younger age group no significant differences were observed between the two groups.

2.2   Eye Movements and Information Processing

Fixation and saccade are two major eye-movements that represent the information processing behavior [23]. Fixation are a collection of relatively stable gaze points on a part of stimuli that are close to each other in proximity and time. Saccades refer to small rapid movements of the eye when it jumps from one fixation to another [27]. Due to their nature, fixations reflect our attention to a part of stimuli that the eyes are fixated on [19, 24]. A number of studies have associated fixation related metrics such as fixation count and fixation duration as measures of information processing. For example, the number of fixations within an area of investigation (AOI) has been used to compare cognitive processing of millennials and baby boomers when viewing a web page [17]. Eye movements have been also used to understand how textual information is processed [18, 19]. For example, Campbell et al. [20] and Gustavsson [21] used eye movements to detect whether a person was reading a text or not. Similarly, eye movements were used to detect whether users read or skim textual information [22]. When reading English, fixation duration is around 200–300 ms, with a range of 100–500 ms and saccades range in duration between 10–20 ms for short between word saccades, and between 60–80 ms for longer saccades from end of one line to the beginning of another line [23]. Majority of saccades during reading English are made from left to right, however, in skilled readers, about 10–15% of the saccades are regressive, they are backward saccades to the previously read words or lines [23]. In general, saccades during reading are divided into two categories: (1) Progressive saccades in the direction of reading text, (2) Regressive saccades, or backward saccade to the opposite direction of reading [23]. Short within-words regressions can be due to problems in processing the currently fixated word [23]. Longer regressions (more than 10 letter spaces back along the line or to another line) are because of the difficulties in comprehension, or may be because the text is particularly difficult and the reader cannot understand the text [23].

2.3   Research Question

The discussed literature suggests that (1) eye movements can be used to understand the cognitive processing during reading, and that (2) there is significant differences between younger and older adults' online reading and web experience. Our research question is whether we can distinguish the age group of a user (younger/older) from eye-movements data when they read textual information. As Loos and Bergstrom [29] aptly put it, to better serve older and younger users it is important to have a deeper understanding of the differences in behavior between these two populations and to investigate how differently older adults interact with online information as compared to their younger counterparts.

Because important information is often communicated via text, in this study grounded in cognitive linguistic literature, we focused on examining the differences between older and users in reading textual information only, in particular, whether we can predict user population (older vs. younger) via eye movements. In this study, we also investigated the relationship between eye movements and performance. We addressed our research questions by designing an eye tracking laboratory experiment. Eye tracking is a natural method for examining how people process information. Eye tracking is broadly used in HCI research and facilitates accurate measurement of online user experience unobtrusively. In particular, researchers have used eye tracking to gain a more complete understanding of the older adults' needs when using websites and mobile applications [29]. The following section provides the methodology used in conducting the eye tracking experiment and the methods used in analyzing the eye movement data.

3 Methodology

This section provides a brief review of the laboratory experiment that was conducted to collect eye movement data used in this study. Furthermore, it provides details on the method used to process the eye-movement data captured from a number of participants who completed a cognitive task online.

3.1 Task and Participants

The task selected for this study included reading a passage and answering to three questions about the passage. The passage was selected from a pool of GRE sample practice passages available on www.majortest.com. The topic of passage was about law and included 553 words. The passage yielded an overall readability score of 16.1 (Flesh-Kincaid grade level = 16.5, Gunning Fog Index = 20.1, Coleman-Liau Index = 9.7, SMOG Index = 15.8, Automated Readability Index = 18.1) which corresponded to a rather difficult reading level. As in prior research [26], the readability score was measured using the online tool: https://readable.io/text/. Participants were recruited among college students and staff from a northeastern university at US. Out of 20 participants, ten were among young generation (age range of 18–30) and the other ten were baby boomers (age range 53–70). Each participant received incentive for their participation in the study.

3.2 Eye-Tracking Study

A commercially available eye tracking device, Tobii X300, was used to collect eye movement data of each participant during reading. This remote eye tracking device can capture eye movements unobtrusively at the rate of 300 samples per second. The eye tracker was calibrated for each participant before starting the task. This process requires participants to observe a moving dot on the eye-tracking screen. Tobii software version 3.4.5, and I-VT filter with 30°/sec saccadic velocity threshold was used to process raw gaze data into fixations and saccades.

3.3   Eye-Movement Preprocessing

Studies suggests that older user are more "patient" than younger users when they view online material. They are likely to expend more cognitive effort when scanning a web page and tend to scan more areas on the web page [8, 17]. This difference in behavior is likely to be observed via saccadic eye movements when processing textual information. Willingness to expend more cognitive effort is likely to reveal itself in saccadic eye movements, which represent effort to move the eyes from one area of interest and refocus it on another area of interest. The list of saccadic eye movement metrics that we used in our study are displayed in Table 1.

Table 1. List of eye tracking metrics

1	Regressive Saccade Count	4	Average Progressive Saccade Amplitude[a]
2	Progressive Saccade Count	5	Average Regressive Saccade Amplitude[a]
3	Average Saccade Duration		

[a]*Saccade Amplitude* (measured in degree) refers to the visual angle that a gaze travel during a saccade

Eye movement data obtained from the eye tracking software included the x and y-coordinates of the participant's eye location on the screen (pixel), whether the eye movement was a fixation or saccade, and the duration of fixation or saccadic event in milliseconds. Additionally, the software provided the visual angle (measured in degree) that a gaze travel during a saccade (saccade amplitude). Table 2 displays the algorithm that we developed to calculate regressive and progressive saccades using x and y-coordinates of two consecutive fixation points. According to Rayner [25] regressive saccades are backward saccades to a word or a line which were occurred earlier in the text, and hence they can be computed based on the positional information of consecutive fixations [12, 23]. We calculated regressive saccades as those in the opposite directions of reading (to the negative of x- and y-direction with respect to the top left corner of the screen delineated as x = 0 and y = 0).

In this study we were interested in examining overall page scanning behavior. Thus, we excluded shorter regressive saccades that are typically only three character long [25].

3.4   Regression Analysis

To investigate whether the difference in cognitive effort during reading a passage online between older and younger users can be detected through saccadic eye-movements data, a regression analysis was performed using the eye movements given in Table 1 as independent variables. Equation 1 shows the regression model used in this study.

$$f(x) = \sum_{i=1}^{5} a_i x_i + b, \tag{1}$$

Where f(x) is a binary dependent variable: $f(x) = \begin{cases} 1, & babyboomer \\ 0, & younggeneration \end{cases}$

x_i represents each of the eye metrics shown in Table 1, and a_i are the coefficients corresponding to each metric, and b is the intercept.

Table 2. Regressive and progressive saccade tracking procedure

Locate the origin of the gaze x-y coordinate from eye-tracking system[a].

If

    { absolute changes in Y values of the most recent consecutive gaze points (k-1 and k) is less than a predefined threshold, TH_{inline}[b],

$$|Y_{gaze}(k) - Y_{gaze}(k-1)| =< TH_{inline} \quad (1)$$

    then check for the changes in X values of those gaze points, $X_{gaze}(k)$ & $X_{gaze}(k-1)$,

        • If $X_{gaze}(k) - X_{gaze}(k-1) < -TH_{inline\_Regress}$[c],

        {It indicates regressive saccade}

        • Else If $X_{gaze}(k) - X_{gaze}(k-1) > 0$

        {it indicates progressive saccade}

    }

Otherwise[d]

    {check if the reader is looking at the point upper than its previous gaze or lower.

        • If $Y_{gaze}(k) - Y_{gaze}(k-1) < -TH_{inline}$,

        {It indicates regressive saccade}

        • If $Y_{gaze}(k) - Y_{gaze}(k-1) > 0$

        {It indicates progressive saccade}

    }

End

[a] (The origin (0.,0) is on top left corner of the screen in Tobii X300, which means reading a text from left to right would return gaze points with increasing x values, and reading from top of the text down toward next lines would return gaze points with increasing y values)

[b] TH_{inline} is the maximum pixel difference between each lines of the text on interface, which checks whether the reader is in the same line or went to a new line.

[c] $TH_{inline\_Regress}$ is number of pixels that include 3 letter character. This threshold is adopted from Reyner et al. 2009).

[d] The reader is reading from a different line: $|Y_{gaze}(k) - Y_{gaze}(k-1)| > TH_{inline}$

Saccadic eye movements are representative of reading difficulty [23], hence, we expected to detect a correlation between performance and saccadic metrics. To investigate this possibility, we used the following regression model.

$$f(x) = \sum_{i=1}^{5} a_i x_i + b, \tag{2}$$

Where f(x) is refers to performance measured as the number of correct answers to three multiple choice questions.

As in Eq. 1, x_i represents each of the eye metrics shown in Table 2, and a_i are the coefficients corresponding to each metric.

4   Results

Mean and standard deviation of variables of interest are displayed in Table 3. As the values in Table 3 indicate, younger users on average had longer (in duration) and more saccadic eye movements. This behavior is consistent with previous research that suggests younger users, compared to older users, exhibit less patient viewing behavior [17]. Although as we will discuss further in the discussion section some research suggest that experience may moderate the impact of age on web user experience [13, 28]. Our results also showed that older people had larger saccade amplitude, which indicates that in order to process the provided information their eyes traveled longer distances to scan the text. This eye movement behavior, consistent with previous research [17], suggests a greater degree in willingness to expend cognitive effort to read textual information.

Table 3. Mean and standard deviation for the eye movement variables for each age group

	Younger users	Older users
Regressive saccade count	124.3	106.9
Progressive saccade count	480.7	455.7
Avg. Saccade duration (msec)	28.51 (±3.25)	25.50 (±3.23)
Avg. Progressive saccade amplitude (degree)	3.65 (±0.34)	4.20 (±0.34)
Avg. Regressive saccade amplitude (degree)	4.94 (±1.90)	5.06 (±1.26)

Table 4 displays the results of regression analysis as modeled by Eq. 1. As the results show the two groups did not differ significantly in regressive saccades. However, the progressive and regressive saccade amplitudes, as well as saccade duration and progressive saccade counts were significantly correlated with the age group of the users. The results also show a stronger effect for the relationship between progressive and regressive saccade amplitudes and age of the users (as attested by the stronger p value and larger beta value). These results suggest that saccadic eye movements may serve as a reliable predictor of users' age group.

Table 4. Results of regression analysis for different age groups as dependent variable and eye movements as independent variables $R^2 = 0.87$, Adj $R^2 = 0.83$

Eye movement metric	t-stat	P-value	Beta
Regressive saccade count	1.27	0.22	−0.1
Progressive saccade count	**2.47**	**0.02**	**0.19**
Avg. Saccade duration	**2.14**	**0.04**	**0.12**
Avg. Progressive saccade amplitude	**8.38**	**7.9E−7**	**−0.59**
Avg. Regressive saccade amplitude	**5.88**	**3.9E−5**	**−0.40**

As mentioned earlier after reading the passage each participant was asked to provide answers to three questions about the passage. To further explore the differences between young generation and baby boomers we looked at the difference in performance of these two groups using two sample t-test. The results revealed no significant difference between the two age groups in performance. The results of the t-test support the results reported in Table 3, showing no significant differences in regressive saccades between the two groups. The observed behavior support previous research that showed while older adults were slower in cognitive processing, they performed relatively similar to younger adults [8].

Table 5. Results of regression analysis for performance as dependent variable and eye movements as independent variables $R^2 = 0.61$, Adj $R^2 = 0.15$

Eye Movement Metric	t-stat	P-value	Beta
Regressive saccade count	0.93	0.37	0.32
Progressive saccade count	0.36	0.73	0.13
Avg. Saccade duration	0.02	0.99	−0.00
Avg. Progressive saccade amplitude	0.42	0.68	0.13
Avg. Regressive saccade amplitude	1.96	0.07	0.60

We were also investigated the relationship between eye movements and performance. In other words, we examined whether we can use eye movements to predict the reading comprehension performance of users. To do so, we ran a regression on performance as the dependent variable and saccadic eye movement variables (Table 2) as independent variables. Therefore, in the regression analysis we used performance as a categorical variable with different values of {0, 1, 2, 3}, where zero corresponds to no correct answers at all, and three corresponds to answering all the questions right. Since the performance of the two groups was not significantly different, we did not separate the two age groups. The results of regression analysis are shown in Table 5.

As the results in Table 5 show only one of the eye metrics, meaning, average regressive saccade amplitude (t-stat = 0.02, p-value = 0.07, B = 0.71) was almost significant. Thus, our results suggest that regressive saccade amplitude, given a larger sample size, may serve as a predictor of reading comprehension.

5   Additional Analysis

In the previous section we examined saccadic eye movements that may predict user age group and/or reading comprehension. We used saccadic eye movements because we expected that younger and older users show differences in the way they scan the text for reading. In this section we look at possible differences between the two user groups in regards to fixations. Note that consistent with prior research, fixations with durations shorter than 100 ms were filtered out from the fixation data [25].

(a) Young Generation   (b) Baby Boomers

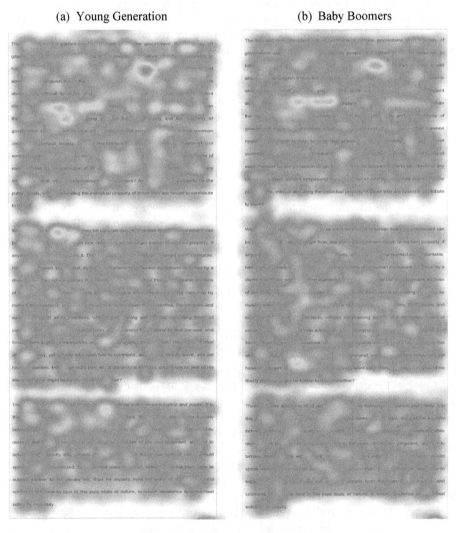

Fig. 1. Heat map of aggregated gaze duration – a comparison between (a) young generation and (b) baby boomers

Figure 1 shows the heat map of aggregated gaze duration between the two groups of users, (a) for young generation and (b) for baby boomers. Green corresponds to minimum gaze duration, and red corresponds to maximum gaze duration (10.58 s in this heat map), which is the aggregation of gaze duration over all the participants who read the passage. The heat maps of total gaze duration do not seem to reveal significant differences between the reading behaviors of the two groups of users.

In addition to qualitative analysis using heat maps we also conducted a regression between different age groups as dependent variable and fixation eye metrics as independent variables. The result of regression analysis is given in Table 6. As the results show fixation metrics, such as average fixation duration and average fixation count, were not significantly correlated with the age group of the users.

Table 6. Results of regression analysis for different age groups as dependent variable and eye movements as independent variables $R^2 = 0.033$, Adj $R^2 = -0.08$

Eye movement metric	t-stat	P-value	Beta
Fixation count	0.44	0.66	0.05
Average fixation duration	−0.66	0.52	−0.08

6 Discussion and Conclusion

In this research we examined the differences between young and old adults in online reading experience by comparing their eye movement behavior. Past research indicates that older adults are likely to expend more effort when processing information [5, 8–12, 17, 28].

Building on the previous research we examined whether we can detect differences between the two user groups reading textual information. Because we were examining overall reading behavior (over the entire text passage) we expected to see differences in saccadic eye movements. The results show that saccadic eye movements (both regressive and progressive), as well as saccade duration and saccade counts in reading was a significant predictor of the user age group. Our results extend previous literature in reading [e.g., 23, 25]. First, in our study we focus on overall passage reading rather than sentence or word by word processes. Second, our results suggest that saccadic metrics may serve as a strong predictor of users' age group. Third, the results indicate that average regressive saccade amplitude may serve as a predictor of reading comprehension. These findings have important implications for capturing online and/or screen reading experience of textual information. For example, it can be used to examine the impact of text simplification on reading experience [26] for one or both age groups.

Fixation metrics such as fixation duration or fixation count were not significant in identifying the differences between the two age groups in our study. We also did not observe any major differences between the aggregated fixation duration of the participants on the passage, according to Fig. 1. This may be because in this study we focused on passage level reading experience and not on the sentence or word level analysis. For example, we did not consider the effect of word predictability or word frequency in fixation duration during reading. Additionally, our sample size was small; by expanding our sample size we may also see significant differences in fixation metrics between old and young users.

Our analysis examining the relation between performance and eye movement revealed that reading comprehension performance was almost significantly correlated ($p = 0.07$) with regressive saccade amplitude. Because, regressive saccades represent cognitive effort in reading, these results show that regardless of age group, the more people were willing to go back and reread information the better they performed the task. It is likely that with a larger sample size the relationship between regressive saccade and performance becomes stronger. Further research with a larger data set is important because it can help to determine whether we can predict a user's reading performance from their eye movement behavior.

Overall our findings are consistent with previous literature that have indicated that there are differences between young and old adults in online reading and web experience [5, 7, 12–14, 17, 28]. For example, Rayner et al. [12] investigated the differences between older and younger adults in reading and learned that older adults make more fixations, longer fixations and more regressions. We also saw significant differences between regressive saccadic eye movements among younger and older adults during reading (Table 4). Another study, comparing older and younger adult's differences in web usability [28] showed that there is some difference between older and younger users when they search for information on the web, as far as the effectiveness, efficiency and user satisfaction are concerned. Overall, our results showed that user population (younger vs. older) when they read textual information can be predicted using the eye movement data. We add to the previous research by investigating the eye movements that are representative of cognitive processing during online reading, and by focusing on the passage level reading rather than sentence level reading, and by comparing the reading behavior of younger and older adults on a relatively long and difficult text passage.

7   Limitations and Future Research

As in any other research our study is not without limitations. Such limitations, however, provide opportunity for directing future research efforts. For example, future studies, including some of our own planned experiments, are needed to test text passages with different content other than law to see whether similar results are obtained. Expanding population to a larger number can also help enhancing the generalizability of our results.

Our results showed that regressive and progressive saccadic amplitude predict user age group. The text used in our study was relatively difficult. Future research, comparing saccadic metrics between the two age groups for text passages with various difficulty levels, is needed to see whether saccade amplitude is a robust predictor of user age when reading online text.

Prior research demonstrates that experience can impact behavioral differences between younger and older users in web usability [13, 14, 28]. According to Loos and Hill et al. [13, 28] daily internet experience usage seems to have greater impact on web usability and navigation patterns of older people than their age. In this study, we did not control for web experience because we focused on reading textual information only. That is, we did not include web components such as navigation bar or links in our experiment. Further research is needed to replicate our study as web content to test whether the inclusion of other web components and their related tasks (e.g., navigations, visual search behavior, etc.) can impact our results and to test how web experience can influence results observed in our study.

In the current study all participants were recruited from university environment and they all had college level reading background. Since research shows that experience has an impact on web usability [13, 28] we plan to take into consideration user's self-reported level of reading experience in our future analysis and examine its possible effects on user experience.

8   Contributions

Effective communication of textual information is key in providing many important online services for both older and younger users. Our results showed that progressive and regressive saccadic amplitudes as well as saccade duration and progressive saccade counts were strong predictor of user age groups. These results suggests that we can potentially predict the age group of the user and/or their reading performance unobtrusively via their eye movements. However, future research is needed to extend our results. There is evidence that familiarity with the web can moderate age effects on web usability [13, 28]. Whether familiarity with web impacts the age related eye movements effects during reading observed in this study when reading text heavy websites needs further research. This information would be of great value to research in designing advanced systems that can use eye movements to respond to user needs [4].

References

1. Baby Boomers and Credit. https://insight.harlandclarke.com/wp-content/uploads/2017/06/HC-Baby-Boomers-and-Credit-white-paper-2017.06.pdf. Accessed December 2017
2. ACL. https://aoa.acl.gov/Aging_Statistics/Index.aspx. Accessed April 2017
3. Grahame, M., Laberge, J., Scialfa, C.T.: Age differences in search of web pages: the effects of link size, link number, and clutter. Hum. Factors 46(3), 385–398 (2004)
4. Fehrenbacher, D.D., Djamasbi, S.: Information systems and task demand: an exploratory pupillometry study of computerized decision making. Decis. Support Syst. 97, 1–11 (2017)
5. Fisk, A.D., Rogers, W.A., Charness, N., Czaja, S.J., Sharit, J.: Designing for Older Adults: Principles and Creative Human Factors Approaches, 2nd edn. CRC Press, Boca Raton (2009)
6. Salthouse, T.A.: The processing-speed theory of adult age differences in cognition. Psychol. Rev. 103, 403–428 (1996)
7. Kemtes, K.A., Kemper, S.: Younger and older adults' on-line processing of syntactically ambiguous sentences. Psychol. Aging 12, 362–371 (1997)

8. Chadwick-Dias, A., McNulty, M., Tullis, T.: Web usability and age: how design changes can improve performance. In: Proceedings of the 2003 Conference on Universal Usability, pp. 30–37 (2003)
9. Kemper, S., Crow, A., Kemtes, K.: Eye-fixation patterns of high and low-span young and older adults: down the garden path and back. Psychol. Aging 19, 157–170 (2004)
10. Kliegl, R., Grabner, E., Rolfs, M., Engbert, R.: Length, frequency, and predictability effects of words on eye movements in reading. Eur. J. Cogn. Psychol. 16, 262–284 (2004)
11. Solan, H.A., Feldman, J., Tujak, L.: Developing visual and reading efficiency in older adults. Optom. Vis. Sci. 72, 139–145 (1995)
12. Rayner, K., Reichle, E.D., Stroud, M.J., Williams, C.C., Pollatsek, A.: The effect of word frequency, word predictability, and font difficulty on the eye movements of young and older readers. Psychol. Aging 21(3), 448–465 (2006)
13. Hill, R.L., Dickinson, A., Arnott, J.L., Gregor, P., McIver L.: Older web users' eye movements: experience counts. In: Proceedings of the SIGCHI Conference on Human Factors in Computing Systems (CHI 2011), pp. 1151–1160. ACM, New York (2011)
14. Tullis, T.S.: Older adults and the web: lessons learned from eye-tracking. In: Stephanidis, C. (ed.) UAHCI 2007. LNCS, vol. 4554, pp. 1030–1039. Springer, Heidelberg (2007). https://doi.org/10.1007/978-3-540-73279-2_115
15. Capozzo, D., Groezinger, R.L., Ng, K.-F.F., Siegel, M.J.: Appeal of Web Page Layout and Characteristics Based on Age: Usability Research through Eye Tracking at Fidelity Investments Inc. Worcester Polytechnic Inst., Worcester (2008)
16. Zaphiris, P., Savitch, N.: Age-related differences in browsing the Web. In: SPARC Workshop on "Promoting independence through new technology", Reading, England, UK (2008)
17. Djamasbi, S., Siegel, M., Skorinko, J., Tullis, T.: Online viewing and aesthetic preferences of generation Y and baby boomers: testing user website experience through eye tracking. Int. J. Electron. Commer. 15(4), 121–158 (2011)
18. Salojarvi, J., Puolamaki, K., Simola, J., Kovanen, L., Kojo, I., Kaski, S.: Inferring relevance from eye movements: Feature extraction. Technical report A82. Helsinki University of Technology (2005)
19. Iqbal, S.T., Bailey, B.P.: Using Eye Gaze Patterns to Identify User Tasks. The Grace Hopper Celebration of Women in Computing (2004)
20. Campbell, C.S., Maglio, P.P.: A robust algorithm for reading detection. In: Paper Presented at the Proceedings of the 2001 Workshop on Perceptive User Interfaces, pp. 1–7 (2001). http://doi.acm.org/10.1145/971478.971503
21. Gustavsson, C.J.: Real Time Classification of Reading in Gaze Data (Masters Thesis). School of Computer Science and Engineering. Royal Institute of Technology, Stockholm, Sweden (2010)
22. Buscher, G., Dengel, A., Elst, L.V.: Eye movements as implicit relevance feedback. In: Paper Presented at the CHI 2008 Extended Abstracts on Human Factors in Computing Systems, Florence, Italy, pp. 2991–2996 (2008). http://doi.acm.org/10.1145/1358628.1358796
23. Rayner, K.: Eye movements in reading and information processing: 20 years of research. Psychol. Bull. 124(3), 372–422 (1998)
24. Kenneth, H., Marcus, N., Richard, A., Richard, D., Halszka, J., Weijer, J.V.: Eye tracking: a comprehensive guide to methods and measures. Oxford University Press, New York (2011)
25. Rayner, K.: Eye movements and attention in reading, scene perception, and visual search. Q. J. Exp. Psychol. 62, 1457–1506 (2009)

26. Djamasbi, S., Shojaeizadeh, M., Chen, P., Rochford, J.: Text simplification and generation Y: an eye tracking study. In: SIGHCI 2016 Proceedings, p. 12 (2016). http://aisel.aisnet.org/sighci2016/12
27. Goldberg, J.H., Kotval, X.P.: Computer interface evaluation using eye movements: methods and constructs. Int. J. Ind. Ergon. **24**, 631–645 (1999)
28. Loos, E.: In search of information on websites: a question of age? In: Stephanidis, C. (ed.) UAHCI 2011. LNCS, vol. 6766, pp. 196–204. Springer, Heidelberg (2011). https://doi.org/10.1007/978-3-642-21663-3_21
29. Loos, E.F., Romano Bergstrom, J.: Older adults. In: Romano Bergstrom, J., Schall, A. J. (eds.) Eye Tracking in User Experience Design, pp. 313–329. Elsevier, Amsterdam (2014)

Semantic Understanding and Task-Oriented for Image Assessment

Cheng-Min Tsai[1(✉)], Shin-Shen Guan[2], Wang-Chin Tsai[3], and Zhi-Hua Zhang[1]

[1] Department of Visual Arts and Design, Nanhua University, Chiayi, Taiwan, R.O.C.
ansel.tsai@gmail.com
[2] School of Design, Fujian University of Technology, Fuzhou, China
[3] Department and Graduate School of Product and Media Design, Fo Guang University,
Yilan, Taiwan, R.O.C.

Abstract. This study focuses on image perception issues based on humans' visual assessment. Semantic understanding and task-oriented are also considered in image assessment. The brightness and colorfulness attributes are selected to be the image assessment tasks in the study. The Linear Regression (LR) analysis and Non-Linear Regression (NLR) analysis methods are used to establish the image assessment models, which also compares their prediction ability. The visual assessment experiment was comprised of 90 participants. Four images were selected from the ISO standard by the focus group. The results showed that "brightness" and "colorfulness" remained stable in the predictive models of the LR and NLR methods. The results also demonstrated very high prediction ability in brightness and colorfulness in both the linear and non-linear models. The brightness attribute directly relates to the image's lightness, and the colorfulness attribute directly relates to the image's saturation. The simple semantic understanding and the single task oriented that assessed the brightness and colorfulness of the images are also very important in the image assessment experiment.

Keywords: Brightness · Saturation · Visual assessment · Linear regression

1 Introduction

According to Newell's information processing system (IPS), three levels, which include physical implementation, algorithmic manipulation, and semantic understanding, should be considered in information processing [1]. Maeder and Eckert [2] also found three levels including mathematical, psychovisual, and task-oriented, which are part of the cognition processing system (CPS) with oriented human cognition. However, the first level (physical implementation in the IPS and mathematical in the CPS) is primarily intended to consider the physical attributes such as the image fidelity of processed images relative to the original images. The second level can be considered the base of the human visual system, which includes algorithmic manipulation in IPS and psychovisual in CPS. The most important level is the top level, which includes the cognition processes (semantic understanding in IPS and task-oriented in CPS). The top level is widely researched by implementing human factor research to perform empirical studies.

© Springer International Publishing AG, part of Springer Nature 2018
J. Zhou and G. Salvendy (Eds.): ITAP 2018, LNCS 10926, pp. 392–400, 2018.
https://doi.org/10.1007/978-3-319-92034-4_30

Many studies have started to examine assessments of image information and visual assessment through human visual systems based on the perspective of human factor engineering and perception psychology.

Table 1, three levels, including image compression, human visual system, and image assessment/visual quality, were used to assess image quality issues. According to Tsai's research framework, the perceptual image quality corresponds to the three levels of IPS and CPS models based on a user-centered approach (see Fig. 1) [3].

Table 1. The three levels of image assessment.

Levels	Research items	Researcher
Image assessment and visual quality	Brightness, colorfulness, naturalness, preference, information-theoretic, visual assessment, visual perception, perceptual image quality	Tsai *et al.* (2016) [3]; Tsai *et al.* (2009) [4]; Sheikh and Bovik (2006) [5]; Ginesu *et al.* (2006) [6]; Fedorovskaya *et al.* (1996) [7]; Kurita and Saito (2002) [8]; Chalmers (1997) [9].
HVS (Human visual system)	Region of interest (ROI), contrast sensitivity function	Tsai *et al.* (2016) [3]; Maeder (2004) [10]; Watson (2002) [11]; Janssen and Blommaert (2000) [12].
Image compression/Coding	Signal process, compression, coding, algorithms, restoration, reproduction, moving picture quality	Nguyen *et al.* (2006) [13]; Civanlar (2004) [14]; Oda *et al.* (2002) [15].

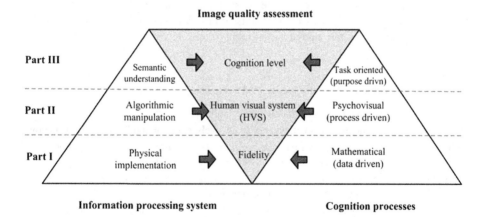

Fig. 1. The framework of perceptual image quality assessment [3].

The top level shows that image assessment items consider the cognition issues. It is also directly related to semantic understanding and the task-oriented concept. Tsai *et al.* (2016) [3] said that the important items for image assessment at the cognition level include brightness, colorfulness, naturalness, preference, and total image quality. Although these attribute items correspond to cognition issues, sometimes it was difficult to assess the total image quality with visual assessment. The previous study figured out the key points, which were not only that the results of "perceptual image quality" and "perceptual color quality" were directly correlated, but also that the "perceptual color quality" was easier than the "perceptual image quality" in image assessment. In addition, the time required to assess perceptual image quality was significantly higher than the time needed to assess perceptual color quality, and the results showed that the concept of perceptual image quality is broader and vaguer in the cognitive processes of subjects compared to the concept of perceptual color quality. Two different kinds of phrases, "color quality" and "image quality," correspond to the semantic understanding of the observer. Furthermore, the tasks for evaluating "perceptual color quality" were significantly clearer and more specific than the tasks for evaluating "overall image quality." Table 2 shows the top eight attributes corresponding to the image quality. The attributes —brightness, colorfulness, naturalness, preference, sharpness, contrast, fidelity, and total image quality—were selected and discussed by 33 master program students in the department of design. Brightness and colorfulness are the top two attributes, which directly corresponds to the image assessment concept.

Many studies in the past decade have started to assess image information and visual quality through human visual systems based on human factor engineering and perception psychology [10, 12, 16, 17]. Because the model should be easy to apply to image industrics and practical issues, most studies use the simple linear regression analysis method to construct the model. However, many assessment items used to evaluate an image are complex for semantic understanding, such as preference [18, 19], naturalness [20], and total image quality [6, 10]. Thus, this study questions whether the linear analysis method is sufficiently accurate and easy to apply based on simple assessment items. Semantic understanding and task-oriented are the most important issues in image assessment. Thus, the aim of this study focuses on discussion of clear semantic understanding and single task-oriented in the image assessment issues based on the cognition level

Table 2. The attributes related to the image quality concept.

Attributes	Related items (semantic understanding)
Brightness	Tone of light/shadow, gray scale levels, detail of highlight, detail of shadow
Colorfulness	Saturation, color balance, memory color for objects, skin color, color scale levels in shadow, chorma, hue angle, reality color
Naturalness	Skin color, object color, main subject color, nature color, preference, sharpness, texture, color appearance, image fidelity
Preference	Personal experience, the object attribute, acceptable color, acceptable texture, image content. Color tone
Sharpness	Clear, sharp image, sharp edge
Contrast	Acceptable color, brightness contrast, color contrast, total image contrast
Fidelity	Nature color, preference, sharpness, main subject color, memory color, memory texture
Total image quality	Gray scale levels, detail of highlight and shadow, saturation, color balance, skin color, preference, sharpness, texture, color appearance, image fidelity, nature, main subject color, memory color, memory texture

approach. As the clear semantic understanding and single task-oriented concept, brightness and colorfulness are selected to discuss in this study. In the role of psycho-attributes and physical attributes, the brightness relates to the lightness of image and the colorfulness relates to the chroma and hue angle.

2   Research Method

2.1   The Scale of Physical Attributes

A previous study checked the scale of physical attributes, which is appropriate for an experiment of image quality. Serial psychophysical experiments were conducted to examine the differences of each physical attribute by visual assessment. In the results of the previous study, the range of image adjustments in lightness was set from 60% to 140%, and the best was 100%. The range of image adjustments in chroma was set from 80% to 155%, and the best was 115%. The range of image adjustments in hue angle was set from −20° to 20°, and the best was 0°. The range of image adjustments in contrast was set from −5 to +3, and the original value was zero [4].

2.2   The Image Stimuli of Previous Study

Four images were used in the previous study, and each image was modulated by four physical attributes including lightness, chroma, hue angle, and contrast (see Fig. 2). All images were also processed according to color conversion and physical adjustment based on the CIECAM02 function by the Boland C++ program. To display the image for visual assessment tasks, the modulated images were represented on the screen by Visual Basic 6.0 software [3, 4].

Fig. 2.   Image stimuli set for main experiment.

2.3   Experiment Design and Participants

Each observer was seated facing a calibrated 30 inch Sharp LCD-TV with fixed luminance and color temperature control on 120 cd/m² and about 6500 k. The laboratory light was fixed luminance and the color temperature was controlled by 233 lx and abuts 6500 k. The resolution of screen was multiply 1360 by 768 pixels. Each trial randomly showed an image, and the background color was set by a mid-grey color having L^* about 60. The serial order in which the images were projected was randomized by the computer so that the image order changed every trial. Totally, that about 40 min for finish the experiment. The experimental environment has set as the same as to the environment of pervious study [4]. The scale of physical attributes and the image stimuli of experiment were according to the previous studies [3, 4]. 90 observers participated in the visual assessment experiment. All the observers possessed normal color vision according to the Ishihara color vision test.

2.4   Multi-collinearity Testing

In terms of Multi-Collinearity testing based on the Person correlation coefficient analysis for check the correlation coefficient between brightness and colorfulness. 90 observers participated in the results show that there were very low correlation coefficient between brightness and colorfulness ($r = .154$, $p < .001$). In the other words, that may have no linear relationship between those two attributes.

3   Data Analysis and Results

Due to the stepwise regression method in linear analysis can achieve the greatest predictive power of dependent variables with a minimum number of variables. Stepwise regression method also uses the relative strength of every explanatory variable and dependent variable to determine which independent variables can be incorporated into regression equations [21]. Thus, this study implemented the stepwise regression method to establish a regression prediction model by using SPSS 17 statistic software. The data adopted to establish the regression model in this stage was obtained by randomly selecting the 81 participants (about 90%) from the original 90 participants. The remaining one-third of the 9 participants (about 10%) were reserved for model verification [21]. The sample size of participants conforms with the minimum sample size criteria of holdout data, which is 2 K + 25. Since there are four independent variables, K equals to 4. Thus, 33 participants conformed with the minimum sample size criteria [21]. The total number of observation from experiments were 26,244 (4 images × 81 scale adjustment variations × 81 participants). Finally, 81 averaged samples were set for linear and non-linear regression analysis.

3.1   Linear Regression Result for Brightness

The Lightness variable in Model I can explain that Brightness has reached a variance of 94.0% ($F_{(1,79)} = 598.340$, $p < .001$). The Lightness variable also has an explanatory power of 88.3% when represented by adjusted R^2. Chroma variable was added into Model II, which can individually explain that Brightness only possesses a variance of 2.5% ($F_{(2,78)} = 395.649$, $p < .001$). Contrast variable was added into Model III, which individually explained Brightness with only 0.4% for variance ($F_{(3,77)} = 351.579$, $p < .001$). Hue Angle variable was added into Model IV. This variable can explain Brightness individually, and it revealed the minimum R^2 with a variance of 0.4% ($F_{(4,76)} = 281.019$, $p < .001$). All four independent variables aforementioned reached the significance level for regression model

($p < .001$). Therefore, the four independent variables in Model IV can explain Brightness with a variance of 96.8% in total. The adjusted R^2 was also 93.3% (see Table 3). So the regression equation for Brightness is shown as Eq. (1).

Table 3. Explanatory power and cross-validation of two prediction models with linear regression by stepwise method.

Linear model	Brightness	Colorfulness
Including independent	Li	Ch
Variables	Ch	Ha
	Co	
	Ha	
Adjust R²	.933	.810
F	281.019	171.616
Sig.	.000	.000

Li: Lightness, *Ch*: Chroma, *Ha*: Hue angle, *Co*: Contrast

3.2   Linear Regression Result for Colorfulness

The Chroma variable in Model I can explain that colorfulness has reached a variance of 89.4% ($F_{(1,79)} = 314.086, p < .001$). The colorfulness variable has an explanatory power of 79.6% when represented by adjusted R^2. Hue angle variable was added into Model II, which can individually explain that colorfulness only possesses a variance of 1.4% ($F_{(2,78)} = 171.616, p < .001$). All the two independent variables aforementioned reached the significance level for regression model ($p < .001$). Therefore, the two independent variables in Model II can explain colorfulness with a variance of 90.3% in total. The adjusted R^2 was 81.0%. So the regression equation for colorfulness is shown as Eq. (2).

$$\begin{aligned} \text{Brightness} = &\,5.736 \times \text{Lightness} + 1.067 \times \text{Chroma} \\ &+ 2.210 \times \text{Contrast} + 0.919 \\ &\times \text{HueAngle} - 0.706 \end{aligned} \tag{1}$$

$$\begin{aligned} \text{Colorfulness} = &\,4.060 \times \text{Chroma} + 1.175 \times \text{HueAngle} \\ &+ 0.706 \end{aligned} \tag{2}$$

3.3   Cross-validation of the Linear Regression Prediction Model

Cross-validation was also implemented at the same time to examine the correlation between the actual value of participants' evaluation and the prediction value posted to the computing process of the model. The analysis using Pearson's correlation coefficient discovered that the participants' evaluation outcome obtained from the brightness prediction model had 94.6% correlation (prediction ability), while the prediction model for colorfulness had 82.9% prediction ability.

3.4   Results of Non-linear Regression Analysis

The stepwise regression method has also used to non-linear regression analysis. The results of regression analysis shows (see Table 4), the six independent variables in brightness's model can explain that Brightness has reached a variance of 98.5% ($F_{(1,79)}$ = 402.972, $p < .001$). The adjusted R^2 was also 96.8%. The seven independent variables in colorfulness's model can explain that colorfulness has reached a variance of 97.6% ($F_{(1,79)}$ = 207.606, $p < .001$). The adjusted R^2 was about 94.8%. It's also very high prediction ability that compare to the results of linear regression.

Table 4. Explanatory power and cross-validation of two prediction models with non-linear regression by stepwise method.

Non-linear model	Brightness	Colorfulness
Including independent	*Li*	*Ch*
Variables	*ChHaCo*	*Ch²*
	Li²	*LiCh²HaCo*
	Li²Ch²Ha²Co	*LiCh²Ha²Co²*
	LiChHaCo	*Li²ChHaCo*
	Li²ChHaCo	*LiChHaCo*
		ChCo
Adjust R²	.968	.948
F	402.972	207.606
Sig.	.000	.000

Li: Lightness, *Ch*: Chroma, *Ha*: Hue angle, *Co*: Contrast

4   Discussion

The image assessment tasks for diverse observers are difficult to collect as stable data and results. Both the semantic understanding in the IPS model and the task-oriented in the CPS model were considered high-level processing based on cognition level. It's an important issue for image assessment research. Clearly a semantic allows observers to understand the assessment task when they assess a complex image, such as the brightness attribute directly related to the image's lightness, tone, highlight/shadow, grayscale levels, and so on. Specifically, the single task-oriented, which assesses the brightness of the images, is very important in the image assessment experiment. For example, the colorfulness attribute directly relates to the image's saturation, color balance, memory color for objects, skin color, color scale levels in shadow, chroma, hue angle, and reality color. All of these items were considered by the observers when they assessed the images. Tsai *et al.* (2016) [3] point out that naturalness, preference, and total image quality also corresponded to diversity factors with cognition issues, but they were more complex when assessing the total image quality by visual assessment. In contrast to brightness and colorfulness, the "semantic understanding" should be more difficult for observers who are assessing total image quality.

The aim of this study is to focus on the clear semantic understanding and single task-oriented issues in image assessment. Thus, brightness and colorfulness were selected to discuss in this study. This study also finds the simple function based on brightness and colorfulness prediction models. They are easy to apply or to reconstruct the research. The results demonstrated a very high prediction ability in brightness and colorfulness whether the linear ($Adjust\ R^2 = .933$ in brightness prediction model, $Adjust\ R^2 = .810$ in colorfulness prediction model) or non-linear ($Adjust\ R^2 = .968$ in brightness prediction model, $Adjust\ R^2 = .948$ in colorfulness prediction model) models were used. Since the model should be easy to apply to images, industries and practical issues are the main purpose. The results show that a clear semantic understanding and single task-oriented are important in the experiment, which could help observers go through a simple image assessment process. It could also help researchers get clear data and nice results.

Acknowledgements. The authors would like to thanks TTLA (Taiwan TFT LCD Association) for supporting this research and providing insightful comments. The authors would also like to thanks all observers for helpful in the experiments.

References

1. Newell, A.: Unified Theories of Cognition. Harvard University Press, Cambridge (1990)
2. Maeder, A.J., Eckert, M.: Medical image compression: quality and performance issues. In: Pham, B., Braun, M., Maeder, A.J, Eckert, M.P. (eds.) New Approaches in Medical Image Analysis, Proceedings of SPIE, vol. 3747, pp. 93–101 (1999)
3. Tsai, Cheng-Min, Guan, Shing-Sheng, Tsai, Wang-Chin: Eye movements on assessing perceptual image quality. In: Zhou, Jia, Salvendy, Gavriel (eds.) ITAP 2016. LNCS, vol. 9754, pp. 378–388. Springer, Cham (2016). https://doi.org/10.1007/978-3-319-39943-0_37
4. Tsai, C.M., Guan, S.S., Juan, L.Y.G, Lai, Y.Y.: The scale on different physical attributes of images. In: 11th Congress of the International Colour Association on Proceedings, Sydney, Australia (2009)
5. Sheikh, H.R., Bovik, A.C.: Image information and visual quality. IEEE Trans. Image Process. **15**(2), 430–444 (2006)
6. Ginesu, G., Massidda, F., Giusto, D.D.: A multi-factors approach for image quality assessment based on a human visual system model. Sig. Process. Image Commun. **21**, 316–333 (2006)
7. Fedorovskaya, E.A., Ridder, H., Blommaert, F.J.: Chroma variants and perceived quality of color images of natural scenes. Color Res. Appl. **22**(2), 96–110 (1996)
8. Kurita, T., Saito, A.: A characteristic of the temporal integrator in the eye-tracing integration model of the visual system on the perception of displayed moving images. In: IDW 2002 Conference VHF2-1 on Proceedings, pp. 1279–128 (2002)
9. Chalmers, A.N.: Colour difference and colour preference in video imaging. In: 8th Congress of the International Colour Association on Proceedings, Kyoto, Japan, pp. 634–637 (1997)
10. Maeder, A.J.: The image importance approach to human vision based image quality characterization. Pattern Recogn. Lett. **26**, 347–354 (2004)
11. Watson, A.B., Malo, J.: Video quality measures based on the standard spatial observer. In: IEEE ICIP, pp. 41–44 (2002)
12. Janssen, T.J.W.M., Blommaert, F.J.J.: A computational approach to image quality. Displays **21**, 129–142 (2000)

13. Nguyen, A., Chandran, V., Sridharan, S.: Gaze trackign for region of interest coding in JPEG 2000. Sig. Process. Image Commun. **21**, 356–377 (2006)
14. Civanlar, M. R.: Content adaptive video coding and transport. In Proceedings of the IEEE 12th Signal Processing and Communications Applications Conference, pp. 28–30 (2004)
15. Oda, K., Yuuki, A., Teragaki, T.: Evaluation of moving picture quality using the pursuit camera system. Euro Display **6**(3), 115–118 (2002)
16. Egmont-Petersena, M., de Ridderb, D., Handelsc, H.: Image processing with neural networks - a reivew. Pattern Recogn. Lett. **35**, 2279–2301 (2002)
17. Sheedy, J.E., Smith, R., Hayes, J.: Visual effects of the luminance surrounding a computer display. Ergonomics **48**(9), 1114–1128 (2005)
18. Choi, S.Y., Luo, M.R., Pointer, M.R., Rhodes, P.A.: Investigation of large display color image appearance i: important factors affecting perceived quality. J. Imaging Sci. Technol. **52**(4), 040904-1–040904-11 (2008)
19. Choi, S.Y., Luo, M.R., Pointer, M.R., Rhodes, P.A.: Investigation of large display color image appearance ii: the influence of surround conditions. J. Imaging Sci. Technol. **52**(4), 040905-1–040905-9 (2008)
20. Choi, S.Y., Luo, M.R., Pointer, M.R., Rhodes, P.A.: Investigation of large display color image appearance- iii: modeling image naturalness. J. Imaging Sci. Technol. **53**(3), 301104-1–301104-12 (2009)
21. Hair, J.F., Black, W.C., Babin, B.J., Anderson, R.E., Tatham, R.L.: Multivariate Data Analysis, 6th edn. Prentice Hall, Englewood Cliffs (2006)

Intergenerational Communication and Social Participation

Mobile Digital Storytelling in a Brazilian Care Home

Ana Raquel Abrahão[1], Paula Fernanda Carlos da Silva[1], David M. Frohlich[2(✉)],
Theti Chrysanthaki[2], Aline Gratão[1], and Paula Castro[1]

[1] Gerontology Department, Federal University of Sao Carlos/UFSCar, São Carlos, Brazil
[2] Digital World Research Centre, University of Surrey, Guildford, UK
d.frohlich@surrey.ac.uk

Abstract. Digital stories are short personal films made up of a series of still images with voiceover, music and text. The technical barriers to creating such stories are falling with the use of mobile apps which make it easy to assemble story elements as audiophoto narratives on a smartphone or tablet. In this case study, we explored the potential of mobile digital storytelling in a care home context. It was used for four weeks as form of multimedia communication between formal and informal carers inside and outside the home, and a care home resident suffering from dementia. The home was located in São Carlos, Brazil as part of a larger international project called Time Matters (UK and Brazil), in which Time stands for 'This is me'. Fifteen digital stories were made by participants in the trial, which is about one for every visit of the researchers to the care home. Stories focused mainly on the resident; capturing aspects of everyday life discussed in **Visit conversations** (4), documenting **Social events** (3) inside or outside the home, recording **Therapy sessions** (3) with the resident or **Health reports** (3) by professional carers, and forming **Media albums** (2) of the residents' art or life. In general, the technology was most useful for facilitating richer conversations with the resident and other participants, and stimulating greater expressivity and creativity in the resident herself. The desire to document the resident's *current* life and interests in the home for later reminiscence by their family, stands in contrast to conventional reminiscence therapy and related digital systems. These use media artefacts to stimulate reminiscence of residents' *past* life outside the home.

Keywords: Digital storytelling · Mobile · Multimedia narratives · Photo sharing
Dementia · Care home · Family and friends · Informal carers · Formal carers
Reminiscing · Memory · Communication

1 Introduction

Despite extensive scientific funding and research, dementia remains one of the biggest challenges of national and international health care [25]. In the year 2010, the cost of dementia in the world totalled $604 billion: equivalent to 1% of gross domestic product (GDP) [26].

© Springer International Publishing AG, part of Springer Nature 2018
J. Zhou and G. Salvendy (Eds.): ITAP 2018, LNCS 10926, pp. 403–421, 2018.
https://doi.org/10.1007/978-3-319-92034-4_31

As the disease progresses, several factors may result in relocation to a care home, especially when their informal caregivers struggle to cope with the increasing burden of care, and their own aging process [2]. Moving to a care home is a difficult period, being a stressful time for both the person with dementia and their families and friends [21]. Residents of these institutions during their first four weeks of admission often feel anxiety, depression and loneliness [13]. Relatives who used to be informal caregivers also experience grief and ambiguous loss when they are separated from their loved ones. As a result, these caregivers usually require a significant role and remote involvement with resident care [8].

With the advance of the disease, the need for meaningful remote and co-present interaction and enjoyable activities with the resident becomes even more important. Caregiver inability to understand and be understood by the person they are caring for is one of the most commonly mentioned communication barriers for both formal (professional team) and informal (family/friends) caregivers [22]. Surprisingly little attention or communication technology has been applied to this problem. In a review of 66 technology studies to meet the needs of people with dementia and their caregivers, [27] concluded that: "The findings show that research on the role of technology in dementia care is still in its infancy."

One exception is the use of reminiscence therapy with residents at which family and friends may (or may not) be present [30]. This usually involves life review and the handling of physical media artefacts in 'memory boxes' to stimulate the residents' memory and conversation about the distant past [4, 28]. Other occupational therapies involving art, craft, music and drama are also used, but these are difficult to fit into busy care schedules and seldom involve the use of new technology. Email and text-based channels of communication may supplement phone contact between remote family and friends and modern care homes, but residents themselves are unlikely to be able to use these effectively as their disease progresses.

One technology which has not been fully considered in this context is that relating to 'digital storytelling'. Digital stories are short personal films made up of a series of still images with voiceover, music and text [17]. These can now be made quite simply on smartphones and tablets, using apps to assemble these media elements into 'audio photo narratives' [9]. A number of popular photo sharing systems are now including such facilities for making video stories out of photographs (e.g. Instagram Stories, Snapchat Stories, iPhoto Memories, etc.). The possibility of using digital stories as a form of multimedia communication between dementia sufferers in a care home and their formal and informal carers, could provide a richer channel of both co-present and remote interaction between them. It might also extend earlier attempts to use multimedia content in reminiscing activities (see below), by offering it to formal and informal carers as well as dementia sufferers. We test these predictions in a small-scale field trial in Brazil, after reviewing related work in the area.

2   Related Work

Reminiscence is a mental process that involves the recovery of significant autobiographical memories [6]. Therefore, as an intervention strategy, it is a psychological process of recovering personal experiences, lived in the past that are used for therapeutic purposes [19]. Although the clinical value of reminiscence has not yet been demonstrated, reminiscing may offer opportunities for mental stimulation, amelioration of the behavioural and psychological symptoms of dementia [3, 30]. The sense of personal identity, continuity, self-esteem and efficacy are restored as the individual manages to self-orientate with the past and maintain social connectivity with the present, despite her/his dementia [16].

The production of collages, gift boxes and albums of life story are popular recollection support activities. Despite its many benefits, the reminiscence interventions using old photo albums are often perceived as intensive activities for dementia patients [12]. Nevertheless, narrative is one of the best non-pharmacological interventions for patients with dementia [5].

Moreover, digitizing family photo albums can help with individual care planning for the care home resident. The use of innovations for creative expression through digital narratives can help in memory, communication, and influencing sensory aspects, participation and quality of life [23]. Case studies [15] show that drama therapy using life history improves communication between older institutionalized patients and caregivers.

In the early stages of dementia, bright colours, interesting sounds and flashing objects can attract attention more than other activities. A multi-sensory approach to interaction and care is particularly important when a person has advanced dementia. Several authors have begun to design and test multimedia systems which stimulate dementia sufferers with digital media of various kinds. This includes both university and industry initiatives to digitize memory cues for reminiscing and communication.

In the university category, researchers from the Universities of Dundee and St Andrews in Scotland developed a system called *CIRCA* for presenting multimedia stimulation to dementia sufferers to stimulate conversation [11]. This was found to support reminiscence and put them on an equal conversational footing with caregivers [1]. Researchers at Pace University in the USA challenged their computer science students to design services for dementia and Alzheimer patients. These included mobile apps for families to share photos, video clips and music with loved ones remotely [31]. Although not targeted at people with dementia, Waycott and colleagues from the University of Melbourne, Australia, developed and tested digital story sharing with older housebound adults. In one study they examined the sharing of video stories over the internet or via a community display [7]. In another study, they developed a photo display system called *Enmesh* which allowed older adults living at home to share photo-and-text stories with each other and their remote carers [29]. Both studies showed participants were willing to create story content and benefitted from deepening relationships with carers and peers.

Finally, a number of commercial systems for reminiscing have come onto the market in recent years. For example, *MyLife*, *InteractiveMe* and *RemindMeCare* are all touch-screen systems designed for care home use in profiling residents with personal and internet media relating to their interests and past. Care home staff, family and friends are expected to input data in collaboration with residents, who can then access the materials alone or with others. No formal evaluations have yet been published, although the market success of these systems provides some indication of value to users.

3 Methods

Given that mobile digital storytelling has never been carried out before in a care home setting, we set about testing the approach with an existing system of our own, with a single resident and their formal and informal caregivers. A simple field trial was conducted using the *Com-Phone Story Maker* app as a 'technology probe' [14] to uncover the benefits and requirements for future systems, customised for this context. *Com-Phone* is part of the Community Media (*Com-Me*) toolkit designed to support multimedia communication in communities with low levels of literacy (http://digitaleconomytoolkit.org). It is an open source Android app available free on the Google Play store. It allows users to assemble photo narratives on a smartphone or tablet and annotate each photograph with voiceover and/or text in a multimedia slide show [10]. Three screen shots of the interface are shown in Fig. 1. The narratives can be saved as movies and uploaded to social media sharing systems such as YouTube. Full details of its capabilities are given in the user manual for Com-Phone from the website above. For our study, we created a Portuguese language version of the app and made it available within a single care home, acting as a case study.

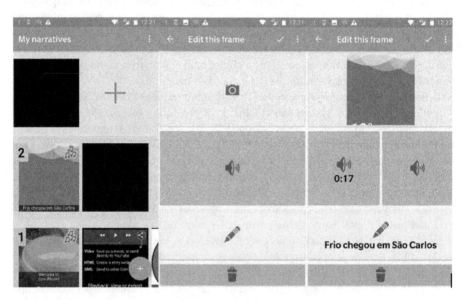

Fig. 1. The *Com-Phone* interface, showing the home screen (left), the options for an individual frame (middle) and a frame populated with image, sound and textual content (right).

The case study was conducted in a private care home, having about 24 residents and 26 care staff, in São Carlos, in the countryside of São Paulo state in Brazil, in 2017. All the residents of this care home have neurocognitive impairment and present dependency for daily living activities of levels 2 or 3 (in a 0–3 Katz scale, being 3 totally dependent) [18].

One female resident aged 60 with dementia was invited to participate following the inclusion criteria of presenting important neurocognitive impairment but still having communication skills remaining, with score of ten on the Mini Mental State Exam (MMSE) [20]. After that, we invited the resident relatives and carers to participate. Final participants were: two family members, one sister and the brother-in-law; and two care-givers, one manager and the nutritionist. Four Brazilian researchers (Abrahão, da Silva, Castro and Gratão) also participated in the fieldwork. The study protocol (875.356/2014 and 2.069.671/2017) received ethics approval from the Federal University of Sao Carlos Ethics Committee and all volunteers signed a consent form.

The procedure used in the trial is illustrated at Fig. 2. After a baseline interview, the participants attended a half-hour workshop about digital storytelling and the Com-Phone app, and then used tablets and smartphones to create their stories over the next four weeks. A Portuguese version of the app was installed on an Android tablet kept in the care home for the duration of the trial, and also on the Android smartphones of the researchers and the resident's sister. A principle researcher and author (Abrahão) led the fieldwork in the trial and attended all care home visits. She was occasionally accompanied by another field researcher on a subset of visits (da Silva, Castro or Gratão). In fact, these researchers became important participants in the study itself because the technology proved difficult to hand over to other participants for unassisted use. During the trial period, the researchers met the resident for twelve one-hour sessions (usually scheduled every 2 days). They also met family members and care home staff four times to support story creation and upload onto YouTube. Every week the researcher uploaded the narratives at YouTube for sharing them.

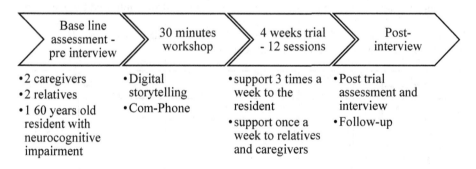

Fig. 2. Trial procedure

After the four-week trial period, participants answered questions in two post-trial interviews (soon after and follow-up) about their experiences with the software, as well as about the values of the system in supporting communication. Because of the significance of the field researchers in the trial and their involvement in both therapy and story creation sessions, they were also interviewed as additional 'participants' by UK author four (Chrysanthaki) who did not attend any of the sessions in Brazil.

4   Results

The data were analysed with frequency and thematic analysis in the following way. First, we collected 15 digital stories made by participants in the study, over one month from 24th May to 26th June 2017. These stories comprise multimedia narratives in sound, image and text. Stories were assembled into a 'story-book' transcript with English translation in the form of a PowerPoint slide show with associated sound. This was eventually printed (without translation) as a photobook which was given back to the care home resident as a memento of the study. The storybook was also used to code the technical characteristics of stories as described in Sect. 4.1 below. Unfortunately, the content of the 15th story was lost due to a failure of the authors' phone, which had to be reset. We include it in the analysis so far as we can, without knowing the exact characteristics or including it in the storybook transcript.

Second, we recorded all pre and post-trial interviews with participants and field researchers, and created both Portuguese and English transcripts. These were subject to separate content analyses for each type of participant; generating four different perspectives on the technology intervention from the care home resident, care home staff, family and friends, and researchers themselves. The results of these analyses are given in Sects. 4.2, 4.3, 4.4 and 4.5 below, summarising answers to similar questions asked and themes which emerged in each type of interview as salient to participants themselves.

4.1   Story Characteristics

The best way of introducing the characteristics of stories made in the trial is to describe a typical story, such as that shown in Fig. 3. This comprises five frames containing one image each, in which some of the frames have additional text, voiceover or music. The total duration of the story was one minute, 45 s (1:45) and was authored by one of the

Table 1. Characteristics of recorded stories (key to authors: RS = Researcher, HR = Home resident, FF = Family or Friend, FC = Formal Carer).

Story number	Primary author	Co-authors	Platform	Story type	Story content	No. Frames	No. Images	No. Voice overs	No. Music clips	No. Texts	Duration (Min:Sec)
1	FF	HR	Phone	Media album	Family makes a photo album for resident						
2	RS	HR, FF	Tablet	Visit conversation	Resident made her first story and had 3 visitors	6	6	2	0	5	00:31
3	RS	FC	Tablet	Health report	Resident was not feeling well	2	2	2	0	2	01:13
4	RS	HR, FF	Phone	Visit conversation	Discussing forthcoming birthday party	7	7	7	0	0	02:17
5	RS	HR	Tablet	Media album	Resident exhibits her art work	20	20	0	1	7	02:57
6	FF	RS	Phone	Social event	Resident goes to a dentist appointment	2	2	2	0	2	00:29
7	FF	RS	Phone	Social event	Sister-in-law's birthday party	5	5	1	0	5	00:39
8	FF	RS	Phone	Social event	Resident's birthday party	8	8	1	1	2	01:02
9	RS	HR, FF	Phone	Therapy session	Cognitive training session	7	7	6	0	0	03:52
10	RS	FF	Tablet	Health report	How the resident felt the past week	1	1	1	0	0	00:30
11	RS	HR, FF	Phone	Visit conversation	Talking on a family visit	5	5	2	2	2	01:45
12	RS	HR	Phone	Therapy session	Cognitive stimulation through craft	9	9	2	1	0	01:17
13	RS	FC, FC	Phone	Health report	Resident care history and diet	2	2	2	0	1	01:19
14	RS	HR	Tablet	Therapy session	Learning to use whatsapp voice calling	5	5	2	0	2	00:39
15	RS	HR, FF	Phone	Visit conversation	Saying goodbye with photos	10	10	3	0	0	01:29
					Mean	6.53	6.53	2.2	0.4	2.2	01:25

field researchers with help from the resident and her sister. Creation was done on the sister's phone. The features of this story approximate to an average story of 6.53 frames and images, with 2.2 voiceovers and text messages and 0.4 music clips, all with an average duration of 1:25. Most stories were authored by the researchers in collaboration with other participants on either a phone or tablet. The distribution of these characteristics across the story corpus is shown in Table 1, together with a description and classification of their content and authorship.

This particular story is not very story-like, which is also typical of the corpus. It was recorded during a visit to the resident of her sister and brother-in-law, by a researcher who was also present. The researcher begins the story by recording a short conversation with the resident about what she is wearing for the visit, perhaps prompted by the fact she is wearing a warm woollen hat, scarf and cardigan indoors with her legs covered by a blanket. The first three frames show this in pictures and sound before showing the exchange of a prescription between the resident and her sister, and a group shot of all visitors around the resident's chair (researchers in white). In effect, the 'story' is a **visit conversation** illustrated with photographs, text and music in no particular order, and serves as a reminder for all parties of the time they had together. Four other story types could be observed in the corpus. These were **social events** beyond a regular visit, **therapy sessions** documenting progress in some ongoing cognitive or sensory-motor training programme, **health reports** by formal carers, and **media albums** containing

Fig. 3. A typical story (number 11)

collections of artwork or media of various kinds. These appeared to have different functions and appeal depending on who they were made by and made for. Therefore, we illustrate them below in relation to the perspectives of different trial participants.

4.2 Resident Perspective

The formal post-trial interview with the resident was difficult because the resident found it tiring and wasn't able to answer many of the questions. However, she was much more talkative in the story creation sessions. So findings in this section are brief and taken mainly from these sessions and the content of stories themselves.

The resident's favourite stories were the social events, specifically her dentist appointment (story 6) with her brother-in-law and sister. The two frames of story 6 are in Fig. 4. She may have felt a sense of freedom because of the trip outside the care home to the dentist office, excitement due to being with her family and she got a gift (toothbrush) from the dentist. She told us that she would like to share this story with her extended family, in the post interview.

Maria a caminho do dentista!   Maria na cadeira do dentista!

Fig. 4. Going to the dentist (story 6)

Story 5 was also noteworthy for the resident. In this one, a story was created as a kind of media album to showcase the resident's artwork with music clips. It is worth mentioning that she has hypergraphia and repeatedly draws simple nature pictures such as apples and flowers, making them almost without interruption every day. She also colours different pictures made by others as a gift, for example, the painting of a cake drawing, because her birthday was due soon.

In this sense, simple everyday actions are special to her, and most of the stories are about these routine activities. She likes to win little gifts and mementos, shoes or even school supplies, such as paper clips described on story 4.

In addition, the resident therapy sessions were also theme for many stories, as for example the cognitive stimulation activities with smells and colours on story 9 and tactile therapy in story 12.

The resident was unable to perform the activities alone using the Com-Phone application and required help for commands and direct aid for using the features of the app, as described in the second story. She had co-participation in carrying out the stories and tried to interact with another app (*WhatsApp*) (story no. 14). However, she had positive interaction with researchers, was responsive and communicative during the meetings, as portrayed in the story 4. In effect, the main benefit of the technology to the resident was in the process of story creation which was done collaboratively with either the researchers, her family or both.

She greatly enjoyed the family and researcher visits in their own right, and welcomed the opportunity to create multimedia artefacts about her life with their help. In fact some of the stories are about the resident's relationship with the researchers, such as the last Story 15 in which she says goodbye and says to them: *"Don't forget me"*.

4.3   Family and Friend Perspective

The family participants showed great interest in trying new ways of communication with the resident. They made about half of the 15 stories and were very engaged with the process and possibilities of the trial. The extended family visited the resident on festive dates, while the close family members such as the sister responsible for the resident, visited on average three times a week for four weeks.

The resident's sister and brother-in-law needed aid to interact with the application in the beginning of the project, but gradually became more independent in making stories themselves. At the end of the study, they needed help only to upload the stories to the study YouTube channel.

The sister did not choose just one favourite story, but pointed out all the stories with family reunions. She said that every story has its own meaning. These were stories of social events, such as story 8 describing the resident's birthday when the largest number of family members and friends were gathered. The sister is the primary author of this story, which contains eight frames, seen in Fig. 5, with photos taken by her own family. Family, friends and caregivers reunion was what made the story so important and meaningful for her, according to her post interview comments: *"The most beautiful is when we are all gathered... was her (resident) birthday here at the care home, with all the carers, the care home owner, a party that symbolizes happiness, friendship, joy, because every year of life is a new opportunity."*

On the first voice recording, the resident and her sister are naming and saying the relation of each of the people in the photos, which the resident does not meet often, the other siblings and mother. She is happy because all these people had gone to visit her. The song on the following frames is Roberto Carlos' musical track "Happy birthday to you", whom is one of the resident's favourite singers since childhood.

The family appreciated the possibility of sharing day-to-day activities with the resident and her artwork, by means of digital narratives, according to a statement from the post-trial interview: *"We took more pictures of her, didn't we? We took more of her daily*

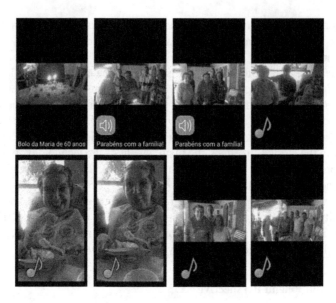

Fig. 5. HR birthday party (story 8)

routine in the clinic, like the little flowers that she likes to draw… Bringing her the pictures, the colours, because she cannot walk and she does not go out of the clinic. So we are bringing some of the beauty, a little joy, the positive energy also that I think this is to live: it's sharing." The sister reports that regular conversation on her visits is repetitive, covering topics such as food, paintings the resident has done, people she has seen. But there was a sense with the storytelling technology that a wider range of topics are introduced through photographs and the things different people say about them.

When asked what she would like to do with the stories after they are made, the sister mentions their historical value for her and the rest of the family, and sharing with younger generations such as her daughter (the resident's niece). The family have an awareness that the stories will be even more precious in the future when the personality or the person of their loved one is lost: *"It is history. It means that it was what we lived; moments, souvenirs and memories. So we have to keep it in the heart…"* These memories are not just those of the resident herself in happier times before the care home, but of the times spent with her in the care home, good and bad, and the care given to her by the family itself. *"I have as recorded, I have as photos, very important to remember also that I was here with my sister for the best steps (crying)"*.

In this connection, it is also worth mentioning that the family liked to watch the stories related to formal caregivers, to see the care that is being provided to the resident and thus establishing a better communication with the formal caregivers.

4.4 Formal Carer Perspective

The formal caregivers who work in the institution failed to participate in most story-making sessions and didn't create stories pro-actively. Probably the task of making the stories brought more demands, increasing the burden of care. Another issue observed by the researchers was the lack of support and guidance of the care home management. For these reasons the care home staff did not keep track of all the stories being made in the trial and did not have a favourite as such.

However, they did make three stories collaboratively with the lead field researcher (Abrahão). The researcher interviewed them about the resident and recorded their talk on *Com-Phone*. She later added image files to the frames. In these conversations, the formal caregivers made comments about the resident, how she arrived at the institution to live, her health condition, her diet (story no. 13) and about what happened in her day-to-day care (stories 3 and 10).

For example, story 13 depicts the story of the resident with the institution when she arrived at the care home, including the rehabilitation after a surgery due to a hip fracture (see Fig. 6). At first, she could not walk and had limited locomotion, but after a while with physiotherapy and adequate diet, the patient was able to walk with the aid of a walker. In the first frame of story 13 the care home manager discusses the state of the resident when she joined the home. *"The resident arrived in a very difficult condition in order to have a quick recovery. She had surgery to put on a prosthesis after a trochanter fracture, but she suffered rejection... the prosthesis was removed, and later the movements rehabilitation was very difficult because without articulation it is almost impossible to walk. But today she still presents difficulty to walk, even on account of coping with her weight. But she walks normally today, like any other person with the disability that she has, without the trochanter."* In the second frame of the story, the nutritionist discusses her diet. This is important due to the resident's tendency to gain weight caused by knee joint problem, reduced mobility and low physical activity level. *"Her diet is normal, except that she is using skim milk, non-fat yogurt, we are not giving dessert candy, she is eating more fruit and we have reduced the calories of all her meals a little, that's all."* Together the resulting story summarises the early care of the resident in a way which may be useful to other staff or to the resident's family and friends.

Fig. 6. Health **report story** (story 13)

When asked about the value of the system in the post-trial interviews, the manager was sceptical that the resident would be able to use it, and didn't see the need to record health reports herself since she speaks to the family almost every day. The nutritionist felt that the system might be evolved into a game which could help the resident communicate better, but did not see a professional value in it for herself or her colleagues.

4.5   Researcher Perspective

There were four Brazilian researchers in total involved in the study recruitment and data collection (Abrahão, da Silva, Castro and Gratão). They usually visited the care home in pairs. Their roles varied and evolved over time depending on story theme, participant and project requirements. During the first session, after meeting and consenting all participants involved (resident, family/relatives/staff), researchers acted as facilitators in the digital technology training workshop. Using content from their story of arrival to the care home and weather example, the purpose of this workshop was to teach both the resident and the family members what digital story telling was and how they could use the app using the tablet and/or the smartphone to make their own stories. It was soon realised by the researchers that the tablet was the most appropriate technology platform for the resident whilst family members decided to use their personal mobile devices for the duration of the study. After the training session, using pictures from her phone and in collaboration with the resident, the resident's sister decided to make their own first story. *"They were doing it together. The main practice person was the sister who was putting everything in but she was showing the resident, the brother in law. They seemed to be doing it together. The resident actually chose one of the pictures". (Researcher)*

The researchers' role in this instance was just to observe the resident with the family interacting with the new technology and assist them when in need. For example, the resident's sister requested some help for uploading the media from her phone and for posting the finished story on YouTube channel. Uploading did not seem to work directly from the sister's phone. Furthermore, since the resident did not use the internet, she couldn't view any stories on YouTube. These technology issues acted as a barrier to the development of a culture of digital story sharing on the project. Stories tended to be made locally in the care home or at the sister's house, and then shared face-to-face on a tablet or phone during a family or researcher visit. Further technology use and access problems prevented the resident from privately reviewing stories on the tablet.

During the second visit, and whilst family members were also present, the resident started using the tablet for the first time. With a step by step guidance by the researcher, the resident took photos of the researcher, selfies with herself holding the tablet, created an audio and created a whole story by herself. Researchers felt that the resident was really efficient and intuitive in using the touchscreen whilst family members felt really pleased that the resident could create the content on her own and learn how to use the tablet. Family members would even take the opportunity to change the task (story making) and use the *Com-Phone* technology for other cognitive task performance (colour identification task, reminiscence). The main difficulty identified by researchers for a resident with dementia in the use of *Com-Phone* technology was the 'click and hold' function: *"If you click it, just touch one click you open the frame to watch the video, if you click and hold you are going to add the story. On the day this was the main difficulty and the access to the whole story. She did not overcome this difficulty. She was not able to click when she wanted to watch it and click and hold when she wanted to add it."* After the end of each session, the tablet was returned to the researcher as the care home did not want to leave the technology with the resident or care home staff. Lack of access to the tablet in between visits was an indication of the lack of care home staff engagement with the study in the absence of research staff. It also compromised the ability of care home staff and resident to develop a sense of ownership and familiarity with technology and the growing repository of stories.

Researchers spent most of their time with the resident and helped her with the story making process as a joint act. During this time, they developed a close relationship with the resident and learned via this task who she was and what made her happy and motivated: *"When she usually draws it is flowers and apples. When it is something different, someone else has drawn for her to colour inside. She considers them as presents. She does not like books for colouring. She likes people to draw for her... We talked about what she draws, what she likes and she asked us to put some music with the drawings and then she watched all the photos. She watched the presentation and she enjoyed it very much. She laughed throughout. She asked us if she could have it and we said yes, she could have it all in an album at the end".*

Stories became a means of communicating the resident's likes and dislikes (e.g. photo frame layout) and her daily routines and activities within the care home. For example, towards the end of the 9th session the resident talked to the researchers about how she liked to eat in the kitchen as eating on the porch or dining room was too isolating. Walking to kitchen though was challenging so she asked them to take a picture of her favourite object 'the walker'. This eventually appeared within story 8.

The use of the storytelling technology helped researchers to facilitate rich conversations with the resident and their relatives, and stimulated greater expressivity and creativity in the resident herself. On the last day of the visits, the sister brought in a picture of the resident as a child. Although the resident liked seeing herself as a child what she loved mostly was a frame that she asked the researcher to create which captured both herself now and her picture as a child.

Creating digital stories not only gave the residence a sense of purpose but also for family members it was a mean of connecting their loved one with the world and her relatives/friends outside the care home environment. During the 7th session the researcher was asked to help the family put a story together about a birthday party they attended so they could share it with the resident. They brought photos, texts to put on the smartphone and asked the researcher to post it directly on the You Tube channel:

"resident was watching as the story was being made. The sister also provided some narratives and was explaining to resident 'who is who' and how the people were after some time that she has not seen them, what they are doing and how the party went".

In other instances (on visit days of cognitive training) and usually in the absence of relatives, the researchers' role in the digital story making process was different. Researchers became the core authors of stories usually to document in real time or narrate an incident that involved resident's engagement (bonfire, 2nd birthday party with interns) or non-engagement with a task (Visit 3, resident's refusal to do the cognitive training). Similarly, the researchers created stories about their interviews with care home staff.

For the researchers using digital story telling technology in this context was a new and exciting learning experience. When asked about what they liked the most in the study they argued that they enjoyed the interaction with the resident, the family and the opportunity they both had via the study to access and learn how to use the technology:

> *"What I liked the most was the interaction. I feel that I was able to enter the life of the resident. The family's life as well but mainly the resident's life because I went inside the care home. I also liked the technology part because it was new and the resident did not know it and she learned how to use it. Sometimes she would not even look and she would continue to draw but she was listening and then she was asking us to put it again, and again and again. She enjoyed more listening than watching. She started to talk with the stories as if someone was asking a question. She answered again as if the person was there but she realised it was a story, She still talked to it anyway."*

One researcher focused more on the benefits of the technology in bridging the gap between the relatives and the resident in the care home: *"Talking to the sister was my favourite one as she was the only one who verbalised the communication problem because the resident feels it and if she had access to the phone she would talk a lot to her family."* The researcher felt the technology provided another way for the sisters to talk.

5   Discussion

At the outset of the study we noted the distressing nature of admitting a family member with dementia into a care home, and the need for **remote** involvement of family and friends in their care. We also cited research showing problems in communication with dementia sufferers and the need for meaningful and enjoyable **co-present** activities with them, particularly as the disease progresses. In the context of a relative lack of technology support for these problems, we cited multimedia systems for the support of co-present **reminiscing** conversations. We wondered if digital storytelling could extend this approach as a more general form of multimedia communication between care home residents with dementia and their formal and informal carers.

The short answer to this question is that we have found a strong value in the co-present creation and sharing of digital stories for a resident and her close family who visit regularly to spend time with her in the care home. Surprisingly, and in contrast with computer-supported reminiscing therapy, the most common and valuable stories were those relating to the resident's current rather than past life. These served to elicit richer conversations with the resident in the process of creating the stories, and acted as mementos for the family themselves to look back on in the future. Other values were evident in the findings, together with additional discoveries about the design, integration and management of storytelling technology in this context. These will now be discussed under the headings of Technology and Values, before outlining their implications for Future Research.

5.1 Technology

Surprisingly few usability problems were discovered with the *Com-Phone* app, even when used by the resident herself. It quickly became evident with her that a tablet was more suitable for interaction than a smartphone, because of the larger size of the fonts and display. But only a click-and-hold action was singled out for criticism, since this could be invoked accidentally with different consequences for story creation than a single click. With help from the researchers, the resident learned to contribute to the media design of stories, and enjoyed sharing them with others as they played full-screen.

Of far greater significance were problems of integration of the storytelling app with other software on the tablet and social media services on the web. Being able to select a photo or sound clip from the tablet relied upon knowledge of the repository structure for media on the device, and a means of navigating it. Even more difficult was uploading a completed story to the YouTube channel created for the trial. This had to be configured on the device to point to the right account, and simply never worked from the sister's smartphone. Unfortunately, this was where the sister made all her independent story content relating to her own activities that she wanted to share with the resident. Even if this had worked, the resident has no independent access to the YouTube channel anyway and wouldn't have been able to see such stories without assistance. This compromised the remote sharing of stories in the trial and meant that we didn't really test this value.

A final lack of integration of the technology was with the care home management. For busy staff, new technology is a burden to master and maintain. This is even more true in a small-scale field trial where the technology will be removed at the end of the trial. Consequently, in this case, the staff chose not to engage with it and even refused to keep the tablet in the care home between researcher visits. This meant that the staff did not really test its value for themselves or allow the resident access to stories independently. If the first author (Abrahão) had not taken over the role of maintaining and using the tablet with the resident, the trial would have collapsed. In effect, she took over some aspect of care for the resident in this decision, and even became facilitator for the care home staff to record stories about the health of the resident. We will return to this point in Sect. 5.3 below because it has consequences for how care homes might accommodate such technology in their day-to-day care of residents. For now, it is sufficient to note that the cooperation of care home staff is as important as the technology itself to its long-term success.

5.2 Values

The range of values experienced by participants in the trial can be illustrated in connection with the five different types of stories they created. By far the greatest values were associated with the **visit conversation** and **social event** stories which made up nearly half the stories. Together these began to form a multimedia journal or diary of the resident's life in and out of the home, with special trips to the dentist and birthday celebrations making up the highlights. While these were fun for the resident to make and share, they had deeper meaning for the family. The resident's sister was aware that they were documenting her own care of her sister in the home, and the happy moments that she planned to look back on in the future. Given the progression of dementia over time and the gradual loss of memory and personality of the sufferer, this is not a surprising observation. However, it does reinforce the value of these stories for future reminiscing by family and friends.

The documentation of **therapy sessions** and **health reports** by the researchers, sometimes on behalf of care home staff, formed another set of stories. These were valued by the resident's family as a record of professional care given, and also as a testimony of character through adversity. The latter was illustrated most dramatically in health story 13 featured in Fig. 6, which contained two bland photographs but a powerful narrative about how the resident had overcome mobility problems on admittance to become mobile with the use of a walker (now her favourite object).

The final category **of media album** stories was also valued by the resident as a record of her many drawing and art works, and by family and friends who saw these as reflecting her personality. The use of digital media technology to essentially digitise and collate art works for archiving and broader review is a latent value which might be developed further in the future. It begins to connect with other forms of occupational therapy performed in care homes involving arts and crafts, and might be seen either as a method of capturing the outputs of those, or as a form of digital media art in its own right.

Moving away from a focus on the story **outcomes** in the study, there is much that can be said about the **process** of story creation and sharing that took place. Perhaps the strongest value of the technology discovered in the whole trial was its ability to draw the resident and her visitors into richer and more creative conversations about her life than usual. This was true for the researchers as much as for family members, who expressed delight in getting to know the resident on a deeper level through the kinds of conversations involved in story making. One reason for this may be that stories were essentially photo narratives with an average of 6 photos per story. This meant that participants were always looking to illustrate activities and ideas visually, as scaffolding for voice or text annotation. Another reason is that the images and stories themselves became points of conversation, and could be recycled with other visitors in different ways. The fact that they were always created and shared collaboratively, points to the highly social nature of the technology and some new possibilities for enhancing this in the future, as described below.

5.3   Future Research

A number of implications for the design of digital storytelling technology follow from these observations, and we begin with these here. An **end-to-end solution** is needed for care homes, which allows stories to be remotely shared as easily as they can be made. This should either attend to integration with existing ICT systems in the care home, or alternatively provide a self-contained solution that operates without dependence on existing infrastructure. The former route is likely to be less expensive, but more challenging across the diversity of systems currently in place. Once achieved however, this solution should begin to address the requirement of remote communication between the care home and the family and friends of residents. This may unlock new values such as the sharing of social events outside the home that residents are not able to attend, and the reception of health reports by family and friends reassuring them of resident care in their absence.

Given that story creation was collaborative and involved interesting conversations with the resident, much more could be done to support this. **Larger displays** might be used in tabletop orientation or via projection on a wall, to facilitate better media browsing and larger group review. Indeed, a latent possibility exists to share or even make stories locally with other residents. This was not tested in our trial but would reinforce the capture and sharing of *current* care home life by the whole population of residents.

The assembly of individual stories into a larger 'book' was used as a mechanism for analysis in the trial. This was surprisingly effective in educating the remote UK researchers about the life of the resident, and something that the family appreciated as a memento in both digital and printed form. Future developments might pay greater attention to the packaging of story collections as **digital or physical mementos**, and explore augmented paper technologies that allow media assets to be linked and played back from printed photos and photobooks [24].

Other implications for care home management and research follow from our findings. We recommend the establishment of a **new staff role** in care homes focussed on the mental health and wellbeing of residents, rather than their physical health. A large part of this role should involve liaison with family and friends, addressing *their* need to feel involved in the life of the resident as well as the resident's need for an active social network. This was essentially the role played by Abrahão in our study. We think digital storytelling technology has a role to play in this process, but only if it can be embraced and managed by 'wellbeing staff' who see it as an integral part of their professional work.

Finally, our findings imply that research on reminiscing in dementia care should take a new direction. This should focus on documenting the current life of dementia sufferers, and support for future reminiscing by family and friends. More attention should be paid to the kinds of conversations involved in creating multimedia stories of the everyday lives and activities of people with dementia. These appear to have the potential to increase social engagement and creativity in dementia sufferers, and to deepen the topics of conversation that can be had with them by family, friends, care staff and strangers. The current case study did not record such conversations but reports their benefit anecdotally from the comments of participants. Future studies should examine this systematically with a larger population.

Acknowledgements. We would like to acknowledge funding from the University of Surrey and FAPESP for the SPRINT UK and Brazil network on *Assistive Media for Health and Wellbeing in Ageing*. This allowed us to travel and collaborate on the *Time Matters* project together: https://www.surrey.ac.uk/digital-world-research-centre/funded-projects/time-matters. The reported work was led in Brazil by Castro and contributes to the student dissertations in Gerontology of Abrahao and da Silva, at the Federal University of São Carlos. We also thank the resident, family and staff of the care home involved in the study for their time and insights in the research.

References

1. Astell, A.J., Ellis, M.P., Bernardi, L., Alm, N., Dye, R., Gowans, G., Campbell, J.: Using a touch screen computer to support relationships between people with dementia and caregivers. Interact. Comput. **22**(4), 267–275 (2010)
2. Bauab, J.P., Emmel, M.L.G.: Mudanças no cotidiano de cuidadores de idosos em processo demencial. Revista Brasileira de Geriatria e Gerontologia **17**(2), 339–352 (2014)
3. Brooker, D.: Understanding dementia and the person behind the diagnostic label. Int. J. Person Centered Med. **2**(1), 11–17 (2012)
4. Butler, R.N.: The life review: an interpretation of reminiscence in the aged. Psychiatry **26**(1), 65–76 (1963)
5. Cabrera, E., Sutcliffe, C., Verbeek, H., Saks, K., Soto-Martin, M., Mehyer, G.: RightTimePlaceCare Consortium: non-pharmacological interventions as a best practice strategy in people with dementia living in nursing homes. A systematic review. Eur. Geriatr. Med. **6**(2), 134–150 (2015)
6. Cappeliez, P., Guindon, M., Robitaille, A.: Functions of reminiscence and emotional regulation among older adults. J. Aging Stud. **22**, 266–272 (2008). https://doi.org/10.1016/j.jaging.2007.06.003
7. Davis, H., Waycott, J., Zhou, S.: Beyond YouTube: sharing personal digital stories on a community display. In: Proceedings of the Annual Meeting of the Australian Special Interest Group for Computer Human Interaction, pp. 579–587. ACM, December 2015
8. Frank, J.B.: Evidence for grief as the major barrier faced by Alzheimer caregivers: a qualitative analysis. Am. J. Alzheimer's Dis. Other Dementias® **22**(6), 516–527 (2008)
9. Frohlich, D.M.: Fast Design, Slow Innovation: Audiophotography Ten Years On. Springer, London (2015). https://doi.org/10.1007/978-3-319-21939-4
10. Frohlich, D., Robinson, S., Eglinton, K., Jones, M., Vartiainen, E.: Creative cameraphone use in rural developing regions. In: Proceedings of the 14th International Conference on Human-Computer Interaction with Mobile Devices and Services, pp. 181–190. ACM, September 2012
11. Gowans, G., Campbell, J., Alm, N., Dye, R., Astell, A., Ellis, M.: Designing a multimedia conversation aid for reminiscence therapy in dementia care environments. In: CHI 2004 Extended Abstracts on Human Factors in Computing Systems, pp. 825–836. ACM, April 2004
12. Guse, L., Inglis, J., Chicoine, J., Leche, G., Stadnyk, L., Whitbread, L.: Life albums in long-term care: resident, family, and staff perceptions. Geriatr. Nurs. **21**(1), 34–37 (2000)
13. Hodgson, N., Freedman, V.A., Granger, D.A., Erno, A.: Biobehavioral correlates of relocation in the frail elderly: salivary cortisol, affect, and cognitive function. J. Am. Geriatr. Soc. **52**(11), 1856–1862 (2004)
14. Hutchinson, H., Mackay, W., Westerlund, B., Bederson, B. B., Druin, A., Plaisant, C., Roussel, N.: Technology probes: inspiring design for and with families. In: Proceedings of the SIGCHI Conference on Human Factors in Computing Systems, pp. 17–24. ACM, April 2003
15. Jaaniste, J., Linnell, S., Ollerton, R.L., Slewa-Younan, S.: Drama therapy with older people with dementia—does it improve quality of life? Arts Psychother. **43**, 40–48 (2015)
16. Kitwood, T.: On being a person. In: Dementia Reconsidered: The Person Comes First, pp. 7–19 (1997)
17. Lambert, J.: Seven Stages: Story and the Human Experience. Digital Diner Press, Berkeley (2013)

18. Lino, V.T.S., Pereira, S.R.M., Camacho, L.A.B., Ribeiro Filho, S.T., Buksman, S.: Cross-cultural adaptation of the independence in activities of daily living index (Katz index). Cadernos de Saúde Pública **24**(1), 103–112 (2008)
19. Lopes, T., Afonso, R., Ribeiro, Ó.: Impacto de intervenções de reminiscência em idosos com demência: revisão da literatura. Psicologia, Saúde & Doenças **15**(3), 597–611 (2014)
20. Lourenço, R.A., Veras, R.P.: Mini-Exame do Estado Mental: características psicométricas em idosos ambulatoriais. Rev Saúde Pública **40**(4), 712–9 (2006)
21. Melrose, S.: Reducing relocation stress syndrome in long term care facilities. J. Pract. Nurs. **54**(4), 15 (2004)
22. Neves, R., Pereira, C.: Os idosos e as TIC–competências de comunicação e qualidade de vida. Kairós. Revista da Faculdade de Ciências Humanas e Saúde **14**(1), 5–26 (2011). ISSN 2176-901X
23. Pereira, C.M., Neves, R.: Os idosos na aquisição de competências TIC. Educação, Formação & Tecnologias **4**(2), 15–24 (2012). ISSN 1646-933X
24. Piper, A.M., Weibel, N., Hollan, J.: Audio-enhanced paper photos: encouraging social interaction at age 105. In: Proceedings of the 2013 Conference on Computer Supported Cooperative Work, pp. 215–224. ACM, February 2013
25. Pot, A.M., Petrea, I.: BUPA/ADI report: Improving dementia care worldwide: Ideas and advice on developing and implementing a National Dementia Plan. Bupa/ADI, London (2013)
26. Relatório ADI/Bupa, Demência nas Américas: Custo atual e futuro e prevalência da doença de Alzheimer e outras demências [Internet]. 2013 Out [citado em 2017]. Disponível em. https://www.alz.co.uk/sites/default/files/pdfs/dementia-in-the-americas-BRAZILIAN PORTUGUESE.pdf
27. Topo, P.: Technology studies to meet the needs of people with dementia and their caregivers: a literature review. J. Appl. Gerontol. **28**(1), 5–37 (2009)
28. Wang, J.J.: Group reminiscence therapy for cognitive and affective function of demented elderly in Taiwan. Int. J. Geriatr. Psychiatry **22**(12), 1235–1240 (2007)
29. Waycott, J., Davis, H., Vetere, F., Morgans, A., Gruner, A., Ozanne, E., Kulik, L.: Captioned photographs in psychosocial aged care: relationship building and boundary work. In: Proceedings of the SIGCHI Conference on Human Factors in Computing Systems, pp. 4167–4176. ACM, April 2014
30. Woods, B., Spector, A.E., Jones, C.A., Orrell, M., Davies, S.P.: Reminiscence Therapy for Dementia. The Cochrane Library (2009)
31. Yamagata, C., Coppola, J. F., Kowtko, M., Joyce, S.: Mobile app development and usability research to help dementia and Alzheimer patients. In: 2013 IEEE Long Island Systems, Applications and Technology Conference (LISAT), pp. 1–6. IEEE, May 2013

The Use of Social Media Among Senior Citizens in Portugal: Active Ageing Through an Intergeneration Approach

Inês Amaral[1,2(✉)] and Fernanda Daniel[2,3]

[1] Centro de Estudos de Comunicação e Sociedade,
Universidade do Minho, Braga, Portugal
[2] Instituto Superior Miguel Torga, Coimbra, Portugal
{inesamaral, fernanda-daniel}@ismt.pt
[3] Centro de Estudos e Investigação em Saúde,
Universidade de Coimbra, Coimbra, Portugal

Abstract. Societal narratives arise from shared social constructions that corroborate social discourse about a given subject or object. Social representations endorse the image that society creates about people, objects, and events. The Internet constitutes a world of mediated social interactions, where communication is decontextualized several times for the distribution of disaggregated. Practices within the new social tools demonstrate individual behaviour-based that occurs in online networks. The new computer-mediated communication platforms and social media are used to create bonds and social capital from decontextualized social representations. This paper maps social representations of old age through the appropriation of social media tools, analysed from a digital storytelling perspective across images published in Instagram platform using semantic indexing techniques. A dataset of Instagram images draw through the hashtag #aavoveiotrabalhar, which is connected to an intergenerational active ageing project, will be analysed. The main aims are to identify dominant discourses and to understand if it is possible to generate engagement from the deconstruction of age and gender stereotypes.

Keywords: Active ageing · Social media · Social representations

1 Introduction

In contemporary societies the socially constructed nature of the ageing phenomenon [1] is embodied in the discursive "requalification" of ageing linked to a positive terminological plurality of adjectives [2]. The term "active ageing" is the successor to concepts such as "healthy ageing" or "successful ageing" [3–6]. In fact it was produced and has been conveyed essentially through political discourse. In 1997 the World Health Organization, inspired by the United Nations Principles for Older Persons, presented the concept of "active ageing", defined as "the process of optimizing opportunities for health, participation and security in order to enhance quality of life as people age" [7].

© Springer International Publishing AG, part of Springer Nature 2018
J. Zhou and G. Salvendy (Eds.): ITAP 2018, LNCS 10926, pp. 422–434, 2018.
https://doi.org/10.1007/978-3-319-92034-4_32

Like other European countries, Portugal is also a country with a considerable aged population. In the last Census (2011) [8], the population over 65 was 19%. Currently the population over 65 years old represents 20,9% [9]. According to PORDATA, in 2016 the longevity index was 48.8% and the ageing index was 148.7. The last metric represents the relationship between the elderly population and the young population, meaning that there are 148.7 elderly people per 100 young people in Portugal. The average life expectancy in Portugal is 80.6 [10]. According to the annual estimates of the resident population, the Portuguese female population above the age of 65 is 23.2%.

The process of construction of social representations is social because it happens in a particular social context and determining composed of ideologies, values and shared social categorization systems through communication and social interaction; as well as produces and translates social relations [11]. The changing nature and transformative of the society leads to the construction of shared social representations associated with a collective identity [2, 11], which assumes the media as an element of social connection. A multiplicity of discourses propagated by the media and digital media systematically create and recreate identities about social groups producing social representations anchored to stereotypes [12].

The paradigm of 'active ageing' proposes a redevelopment of old age, promoting positive conceptions, and an extension of the social and economic participation of older people against the persistence of stereotyping that associates this stage of life the uselessness, illness and dependence. Taking into account the importance of the digital world in the interaction and the construction of social identities, this paper aims to understand how it is represented the "old age" in digital storytelling and if cyberspace can be, for its disaggregated distribution of contents, a reconstruction tool of meanings and serving less conventional representations of old age and ageing. "What representations of old age and elderly are prevalent in the digital world?" is the research question that guides this paper.

The new paradigm of communication is social-oriented and based on social media platforms, social networks and user-created content. Therefore, it is focused on the social use of technology. All elements become collective, in the sense in which they are shared: content, distribution, interaction, practices, context [13]. The purpose of this paper is to analyse social representations of old age in social media through a hashtag connected to an intergenerational active ageing project that aims to deconstruct stereotypes of age and gender.

1.1 Social Representations in Cyberspace

As the Internet is a markedly symbolic space [13], information and the context of interaction have become major elements in the process of reformulating spatial temporal notions and social representations [13, 14]. The concepts of user generated content and user- generated media make it possible to maximize the notion of participation in the Internet through the formation of social networks. In the context of this kind of structure, threaded networks [14] and hashtag networks are essential for understanding the development of new practices and, therefore, relationships based on content streaming's, designed by appropriations of social representations. Conversations on social networks and social media platforms enable the analysis of content systems, interactions and social representations based on the perspective of distributed outputs that induces collective consumption [15].

In the context of Communication Sciences, research on social networks in cyberspace uses multiple theoretical and methodological approaches [16]. One issue that should be emphasised is the fact that it is possible to identify and study social networks on platforms with diverse characteristics and purposes and where different aspects can be analysed. Most research on online social networks and social media has focused on social networking platforms and studied the potential of information transmission; social capital and temporal patterns for messages [17].

Social networks on the Internet derive from the appropriation of technical tools, transforming them into channels of content and conversation circulation based on different social representations of the world. There are patterns of connectivity in and on network that have metamorphosed the digital culture [13]. The concepts of user-generated content and user-generated media make it possible to maximize the notion of participation in the Internet through the formation of social networks of contents that are constantly changing, in a logic of viral speed, where social representations are decontextualized, disaggregated and consumed collectively. In the context of this type of structure, semantics is essential for understanding the development of new practices and, consequently, relationships based on streaming of contents, drawn by appropriations of social representations [13].

Social media embody a world of mediated social interactions, where communication is recontextualised several times for the distribution of disaggregated and the semantic indexing. Practices within the new social tools demonstrate individual behaviours based on and in networks. In this sense, the behaviours, attitudes and values are presented in permanent mutation. The social media are used to create ties and capital from decontextualized social representations. Image publishing platforms, by disaggregated content distribution, change the user perspective. Collective narratives are materialized in decontextualized images. The social era and the beginning of the massification of the *prosumer* [13, 16]-the consumer converted into a user, substantially alter the patterns of consumption.

Cyberspace, as it constitutes a new space of sociability, also generates new practices and forms of social relations based on social representations of the world with their own codes and structures [13]. However, these codes will not be entirely new, but rather a reformulation of the already known forms of sociability, now adapted to the new spatial-temporal conditions [14]. At a time when the notion of consumption is changing with the passage from "going online" to "being online" [13], and digital discourse is a pressing sociocommunication reality in social change, we consider it urgent to rethink in the light of contemporaneity the idea posed by Jean Baudrillard [18] that consumption translates to systematic manipulation of signs. Based on the assumption that those who are not represented in the media universe are not socially relevant, we agree that traditional media and digital media currently represent reconfigured Greek "ágora", where everything is discussed and decided and where everyone wants to participate. The media play a crucial role in defining and reinforcing the cultural characters of a society. Among its potential attributions are the modelling of conceptions about ageing and the place and role of the elders.

1.2 Gender Representations and Stereotypes

Family in the contemporary world is in profound change. Since the twentieth century, the family organisation has undergone reconfigurations due to changes in the social role of women. The traditional model of the masculine lost the strength that characterized it [3]. There have been some changes in the attribution of roles to men and to women within and outside the family. Even though, the media continues to perpetuate gender conceptions that determine the conventional gender roles where male is associated to the public life and business, and female to domesticity, private life and affections. There is a certain mystification based on normalization of the act of ageing [3], referring the elderly to a perpetuation of these gender roles to a stage where they are labelled as "retired" and therefore inactive [1].

In determining a social construction of gender roles and attributes in relation to biological sex, there are historical and cultural factors of our society that lead to social representations of masculine and feminine that are distinguished and hierarchized in terms of importance [3, 19]. Oakley [20] proposed the term gender to refer to the socially constructed character of the differences between men and women, thus rejecting the naturalizing and essentialist explanations for inequality. Different social representations are created on the attributes and personal characteristics, competences, interests and motivations of men and women, in the scope of work and the family, that translate into social practices in keeping with these representations [19, 20]. However, and traditionally, roles and responsibilities are assigned to men in the public domain, livelihood and outcome orientation, competitiveness, independence and strength, and women's roles are anchored in the private domain, the care of others /domesticity, based on more emotional, relational and aesthetic characteristics [19].

Social representations of gender determine "who does what" on the basis of "how women are" and "how men are" [19]. These representations are normative and impose themselves in the definition of different capacities, roles and functions between women and men [3]. According to these gender roles and stereotypes, the male group, considered the dominant group, is not limited to one role or function as with women. These are seen as dependent and submissive beings whose characteristics refer them to the family and domestic field [19]. These representations will be reflected in the roles played by men and women in the various spheres, as well as in the expectations of their behaviour.

Gender issues tend to be invisible in older people [19] and the media perpetrate this assumption as a normalization, and consequent sociability, of the condition of being old [21]. There are a large number of studies related to research on how the senior public is represented in literature, print media and even cartoons. Given its great impact on society is in this logic of corroboration of the media image of the elderly, television is the most investigated medium [21]. In one of the first studies on the representation of the elderly in television, Gerbner et al. [22] identified that there is an attribute that is perpetuated in all analyses into this matter regardless of time or space to unfold. It refers to a tendency for underrepresentation of older television characters, contrasting this situation with its growing significance in population demography [21, 22].

Several authors have focused on the study of the representation of the elderly in advertising, concluding that this social group are subject to a tendency under-representation in television advertising. Numerous studies underline that within the underrepresentation of the elders, the female gender is even less represented than the masculine [21, 23]. This situation is further reinforced by the fact that women over 50 are incomparably more vulnerable than men to a categorization of pejorative stereo-types [24]. Lindsey [25] also argues that in age-based cultures, media discourses present gender intersected with social class and race. In this regard, Kjaersgaard [26] consider that the low representation of the elderly in media, particularly in advertising, focuses on a certain type of sexism that celebrates the younger women and tends to devalue or even ignore the older ones.

Bailey et al. [27] refers that "stereotypical representations of girls as sexualized objects seeking male attention are commonly found in social networking sites". However, as gender became invisible through the ageing process, this idea is not connected to the elderly. As elderly are seen as a homogeneous group, though as a group they get more diverse the older they become [28–30], their social representations in digital media is anchored to society's traditional perceptions of them. As Aroldi et al. [31] stated, "media play different roles at different moments of this social construction of a shared identity, and that these roles are strongly affected by a lot of variables, both socio-cultural and technological".

1.3   Digital Media: Inclusion, Active Ageing and Inter-generational Approaches

The trend of population ageing in contemporary European societies determines the need to pay attention to the heterogeneous nature of the situation and experiences of elderly people. In fact, diverse life experiences are connected to different forms of ageing [32]. The promotion of "active ageing" implies optimizing health, safety, independence, mobility and participation opportunities in order to achieve the highest quality of life for the elderly [7]. Digital media may represent an opportunity for inclusion and improve quality of life of citizens, especially for senior individuals. However, demographic and socio-cultural changes push the elderly towards social and digital exclusion.

Low levels of media and digital literacy (competences that enable people to understand the media and use digital tools effectively) induce a condition of sub-citizenship [2] that is anchored to the difficulty of mobilizing civic knowledge, digital capital, and participation in public life. In the Portuguese case, in 2016 there were 26% of the population who have not used the Internet, mostly among the elderly and less educated [27]. According to a OberCom report from 2014 [33], the rate of Internet use in Portugal declines significantly with age, with a percentage of 31% users in the 55–64 age group and only 11,6% in the age group over 65 years of age. Social exclusion is a reality for millions of people around the world and this social phe-nomenon can lead to a global sense of injustice [2] as it enhances distorted media representations as a contributing factor to the categorization of "disadvantaged groups" that can be characterized in a multidimensional scale, which includes indicators of the absence of social rights.

This idea may be address from an inter-generational approach [34]. Age and generations are central concepts within this perspective [35]. Comunello et al. [34] reflected on "generational semantics" that "are produced by senior citizens to interpret their own relationship with ICT deals with the perception of both personal abilities and socially expected performances and might be shaped by their own perception of age and ageing". In this sense, media environments may be considered as "generational contexts" [36] following the idea that different age-based groups arrange the technological experience in a similar way according to cultural backgrounds [37] and interactions. Therefore, it may shape a social construction of a "generational identity" [37] that arises from discursive practices and appropriations of the media and digital media.

Trentham et al. [38] concluded that the senior citizens might resist to ageism through social media contradicting the dominant narratives of their inability to adapt to the world of technology. boyd [39] argues that social media "allow people to gather for social, cultural, and civic purposes and they help people connect with a world beyond their close friends and family". The engagement of citizens may depend on this tools that can be inclusive instruments to advocacy and promote social change. This is the aim of several projects of active ageing, anchored an intergenerational approach. In Portugal, the project "A Avó Veio Trabalhar" ("Grandma Came to Work") brings together women over 65 years to produce design objects.

1.4   Active Ageing Project "Grandma Came to Work"

The proposal of the project is to get away from the traditional offers of social programs for the elderly and intends to reintegrate senior citizens from an area of the city of Lisbon into community life. Through creative challenges, the members develop design work. Currently the project has 70 participants, has a physical store and two work centers. "A Avó Veio Trabalhar" ("Grandma Came to Work") uses the Internet, in particular social media, to disseminate the project nationally and internationally. The average age of project members is 75 years. It is not a project for women only, although these are in the majority. The participants are involved in various projects in the city, such as the DOC Lisboa film festival, the cultural weekend "Silent Festival" and even the Lisbon LGBT march. The work developed allows the elderly to fit into community life and also in the modernization process of that particular geographical area. The members of the project regularly participate in handicraft fairs and design at national and international level. The intergenerational approach also aims at the deconstruction of age and gender stereotypes.

2   Method

The aim of this paper is to map symbols and social representations of "old age" in cyberspace through the analysis of semantically indexed in the photo sharing service Instagram. We conducted a study that relied on the hashtag "#aavoveiotrabalhar" ("grandma came to work") to call Instagram API and collected the data through the tool Visual Tagnet Explorer. The script has extracted all media items posted 2014-12-17 (16:38:41) and 2017-12-11 (09:15:35). The dataset is composed by 500 media items posted by 78 unique users with the hashtag #aavoveiotrabalhar. The tool also retrieved statistics, activity metrics and metadata.

The process of collective narrative was collected from the public stream of Instagram by the semantic indexation to the hashtag. The methodology combines quantitative analysis with a descriptive and documentary analysis of semantic classification of images collected and interactions generated in order to map a collective narration process. The main goals of this study are: (1) map the dominant discourse about the hashtag in analysis; (2) analyse most engaged media items correlating these with the dominant discourse; (3) identify the most common hashtags used with "#aavoveiotrabalhar".

3   Results and Discussion

The day with more posts published with the hashtag #aavoveiotrabalhar was 26th July 2017 (International Grandparents Day, $n = 43$). The frequency of publication is essentially related to events in which project members participate. Most posts with the hashtag #aavoveiotrabalhar are published by the project mentor and project profile.

There are no comments in 54.6% of posts, as showed in Table 1. The engagement generated by the posts in terms of comments is reduced. Only 1.2% ($n = 6$) of the posts get more than 10 comments.

Table 1. Comments on posts.

Comments	n	%
0	273	54.6
1	106	21.2
2	52	10.4
3	19	3.8
4	15	3.0
5	10	2.0
6	9	1.8
7	4	.8
8	5	1.0
9	1	.2
11	1	.2
12	1	.2
15	1	.2
17	1	.2
23	1	.2
35	1	.2
Total	**500**	**100.0**

The engagement analysed from the likes is significant, with 49.8% of the posts having more than 28 likes. All posts received likes with an average of 42.54 (*Mode* = 13; *Std* = 53.286; minimum value = 1, maximum value = 506) (Table 2).

Table 2. Number of likes (categorized into quartiles).

Likes	n	%
<=18	125	25.0
19–27	126	25.2
28–45	126	25.2
46+	123	24.6
Total	**500**	**100.0**

A post with 267 likes and without hashtags in the caption is from a granddaughter that posted a message when the project was in danger of ending. Two other posts have 435 and 501 likes and also no hashtag in their messages announcing the presence of the project in a design event. The post that has more likes (506) is from a Portuguese vintage store and also doesn't have hashtags in the caption ("A cup of tea, please!"), which accompanies the photograph of a piece of embroidery that covers a cup. The posts with more likes mobilised in their captions the hashtags that are presented in Table 3.

Table 3. Hashtags in the captions of the top ten posts according to likes.

Likes	Hashtags
160	#popinlisbon #popinthecity #popinlisbonne #aavoveiotrabalhar
171	#aavoveiotrabalhar
172	#oldisbeautiful #oldisthenewyoung #aavoveiotrabalhar #fashion #fashionista #diva #granny #91yearsold #lisbon #follow4follow #followforfollow #follow
175	#haconversa #oldisthenewyoung #aavoveiotrabalhar #lata_65
178	#aavoveiotrabalhar #vamoscorrercomoovento #iamnotamorningperson #coffee #magazines #hellokristof #lisbon
186	#oldisbeautiful #oldisthenewyoung #aavoveiotrabalhar #follow4follow #followforfollow #follow #picoftheday #lisbon #portugal
207	#oapartamento #wildling
263	#AAvoVeioTrabalhar #Lanidor
303	#lovelyhumansofportugal #aavoveiotrabalhar
381	#AAvoVeioTrabalhar #Design #ProjetodeAprendizagem #Lisboa #Maquilhagem

Interestingly, the most called hashtags on messages are related to events (e.g. #popinthecity), deconstruction of old stereotypes (e.g. #oldisthenewyoung or #lovely-humansofportugal), trademarks (e.g. #Lanidor). However, there is evidence of gender-ization in hashtags like #fashionista #diva #granny. It is also important to point out that there is concern about indexing the streaming content of hashtags with more users to publicize the project (e.g. #follow4follow or #picoftheday).

Table 4. Hashtags of the posts.

Filters	n	%
aavoveiotrabalhar	325	10.7
oldisthenewyoung	123	4.0
Oldisbeautiful	92	3.0
Gerador	50	1.6
ig_captures	46	1.5
Ignant	46	1.5
Huntgram	45	1.5
myfeatureshoot	45	1.5
p3top	38	1.2
Handmade	36	1.2
Embroidery	32	1.0
Lisboalive	30	1.0
Lisbon	30	1.0
oh_mag	29	1.0
Pixeispt	29	1.0
Tarefadodia	25	.8
Instiesgerador	24	.8
Igerslisboa	23	.8
Lisboa	22	.7
Lisbonlovers	22	.7
bordadosobrefotografia	21	.7
Igersportugal	21	.7
Fermenta	20	.7
follow4follow	20	.7
followforfollow	20	.7
Igerslx	20	.7
Instapic	20	.7
Others	1797	59.7
Total	**3051**	**100.0**

In the "Hashtag" field, the user can enter keywords. It is possible to verify that some are common with those that are also used in captions when comparing Tables 3 and 4. The most commonly used hashtag is the one that identifies the project (#aavoveiotrabalhar). Also issues related to geotagging (#Lisbon, #lisbonlovers) and location (Fermenta - name of the project store) are evident. The #oldisthenewyoung ($n = 123$) and #oldisbeautiful ($n = 92$) hashtags again stand out as forms of deconstruction of idadaist stereotypes. The streaming indexing of hashtags with many followers is also evidence in this table (#ig_captures, #Ignant, #Huntgram, #myfeatureshoot, #p3top, # oh_mag, #Pixeispt, #Igerslisboa, #igersportugal, #followforfollow, #followforfollow, #Igerslx #Instapic). The characterization of the works produced in the project (#Handmade, #Embroidery, #bordadosobrefotografia), the association to projects of entrepreneurship (#gerador) and events (#Lisboalive) are also present in the mobilisation of hashtags (Table 4).

Table 5. Filters on images posted.

Filters	n	%
Normal	255	51.0
Gingham	84	16.8
Crema	32	6.4
Clarendon	26	5.2
Slumber	18	3.6
Lark	17	3.4
Juno	14	2.8
Aden	10	2.0
Ludwig	9	1.8
Reyes	6	1.2
Sierra	5	1.0
X-Pro II	5	1.0
Valencia	4	.8
Lo-fi	3	.6
Amaro	2	.4
Hefe	2	.4
Mayfair	2	.4
Perpetua	2	.4
Rise	2	.4
Hudson	1	.2
Skyline	1	.2
Total	**500**	**100.0**

Most images have no filters ($n = 255$, 51%), which allow to understand a representation of the project participants in a realistic perspective. It should be noted that images with filters ($n = 245$, 49%) correspond mostly to products created by project members and events in which they participate (Table 5).

4   Conclusion and Limitations

This paper aimed to map social representations of "old age" in digital narratives semantically indexed in Instagram in order to answer to the research question: "What representations of old age and elderly are prevalent in the digital world?". The dominant discourse present in the 500 analysed posts is clearly related to the ideas of empowerment, stereotype deconstruction and promotion of active ageing. In an age where the notion of ageing is undergoing change, with powerful social and individual impacts, digital discourse is a major socio communicational factor in social change. Images and representations of old age are social constructions in a constant state of change, related to socio-economic and political contexts, and the collective digital narratives have the same influence on the self- and hetero- categorisation of the elderly as the offline discourses. This explains how the digital discourse can transform the social representations old age and participate in the creation of new identities and social relations that impel change in the concept of ageing held by contemporary societies.

In cyberspace, the social dimension of a shared construction of meanings and representations replaces the physical place. The idea of territory is diluted in simulacra of presence, feelings of belonging, permanence and own codes. The technique, through the tools of computer-mediated communication, creates mechanisms of interaction that are assumed as spaces of collective narratives and shared social representations [13]. We have verified this aspect in the study. Indeed, the hashtags used in streaming analysed classified images, allowing the creation of shared social construction. The hashtags are assuming the logic of the semantic Web as a new social practice. In fact, "Do-It-Yourself media tools" as a way to enhance network connectivity can introduce a new modality of sociability, as they enable new forms of communication and interaction [13]. The semantic Web itself is already changing the media and landscape of the Internet, as we know it. The involvement of users, meanings, actions and social contexts in collective environments are increasingly built on the basis of object-oriented sociability. From the multiple hashtags published in the streaming analysed, we find that the most predominant ones relate to events, deconstruction of stereotypes related to old age, and trademarks. In the process of collective narrative of #aavoveiotrabalhar there is a central discourse promoting active ageing through the deconstruction of preconceived ideas about the elderly (#oldisthenewyoung, #Oldisbeautiful, #lovelyhumansofportugal), in particular of older women (#fashionista, #diva, #granny). The induction of social change is done through social representations presented in a realistic perspective of images (images with no filters: $n = 255$, 51%), where the participants of the project appear as protagonists in different contexts of real life, regardless of age (#91yearsold, #lata_65). Social change and changes in the traditional social representations of the elderly can be potentially altered by projects such as the one presented in this paper.

The main limitations of this study are related to quantitative perspective analysis. In future studies, it will be interesting to analyse captions of images and comments in a qualitative content analysis approach. It would also be interesting to study through the analysis methodology of social networks ties and communities, which are created by the indexed content in order to understand how this induces new relationships and social practices that may promote social change.

References

1. Debert, G.: A reinvenção da velhice: socialização e processos de reprivatização do envelhecimento. USP, São Paulo (1999)
2. Amaral, I., Daniel, F.: Ageism and IT: social representations, exclusion and citizenship in the digital age. In: Zhou, J., Salvendy, G. (eds.) ITAP 2016. LNCS, vol. 9755. Springer, Cham (2016). https://doi.org/10.1007/978-3-319-39949-2_15
3. Daniel, F., Caetano, E., Monteiro, R., Amaral, I.: Representações sociais do envelhecimento ativo num olhar genderizado. Análise Psicológica 34(4), 353–364 (2016)
4. Baltes, P.B., Baltes, M.M.: Successful Aging: Perspectives from the Behavioral Sciences, vol. 4. Cambridge University Press, Cambridge (1993)

5. Rowe, J.W., Kahn, R.L.: Successful aging. Gerontologist **37**(4), 433–440 (1997)
6. Loos, E.F., Ivan, L.: Visual ageism in the media. In: Ayalon, L., Tesch-Roemer, C. (eds.) Contemporary Aspects on Ageism. Springer, Berlin (accepted)
7. WHO: Active Ageing: A Policy Framework, Geneva, Switzerland (2002)
8. INE: Censos (2011), http://censos.ine.pt/. Accessed 08 Dec 2017
9. PORDATA, https://www.pordata.pt/Portugal/Popula%C3%A7%C3%A3o+residente+total +e+por+grandes+grupos+et%C3%A1rios-513. Accessed 08 Dec 2017
10. PORDATA, https://www.pordata.pt/Portugal/Indicadores+de+envelhecimento-526. Accessed 08 Dec 2017
11. Daniel, F., Antunes, A., Amaral, I.: Representações sociais da velhice. Análise. Psicológica **33**(3), 291–301 (2015)
12. Amaral, I., Fonseca, F., Daniel, F., Monteiro, R.: Ageism: media discourses during the Portuguese elections. Atención Primaria **48**, 103–104 (2016)
13. Amaral, I.: Redes Sociais na Internet: Sociabilidades Emergentes. Editora LabCom. IFP, Covilhã (2016)
14. Ackland, R.: Web Social Science: Concepts, Data and Tools for Social Scientists in the Digital Age. Sage (2013)
15. Huberman, B.A., Romero, D.M., Wu, F.: Social Networks that Matter: Twitter under the Microscope (2008)
16. Boyd, D., Ellison, N.: Social network sites: definition, history, and scholarship. IEEE Eng. Manage. Rev. **3**(38), 16–31 (2010)
17. Ackland, R.: Social network services as data sources and platforms for e-researching social networks. Soc. Sci. Comput. Rev. **27**(4), 481–492 (2009)
18. Baudrillard, J.: Mass Media Culture. Revenge of the Crystal: Selected Writings on the Modern Object and Its Destiny (1968)
19. Daniel, F., Simões, T., Monteiro, R.: Representações sociais do «Envelhecer no masculino» e do «Envelhecer no feminino». Ex aequo **26**, 13–26 (2012)
20. Oakley, A.: Sex, Gender and Society. Temple Smith, London (1972)
21. Ribeiro, R.: A representação dos idosos na publicidade televisiva dos canais generalistas portugueses: verdades, estereótipos e ideologias (Master dissertation). University of Minho, Braga (2012)
22. Gerbner, G., Gross, L., Signorielli, N., Morgan, M.: Aging with television: Images on television drama and conceptions of social reality. J. Commun. **30**(1), 37–47 (1980)
23. Kaushik, A.: Gender differentiation in the portrayal of the elderly in indian media. Indian J. Soc. Work **75**(2), 301–320 (2014)
24. Signorielli, N.: Aging on television: Messages relating to gender, race, and occupation in prime time. J. Broadcast. Electron. Media **48**(2), 279–301 (2004)
25. Lindsey, L.: Gender Roles: A Sociological Perspective. Routledge, New York (2015)
26. Kjaersgaard, K.: Aging to Perfection or Perfectly Aged? The Image of Women Growing Older on Television (2005)
27. Bailey, J., Steeves, V., Burkell, J., Regan, P.: Negotiating with gender stereotypes on social networking sites: from "bicycle face" to Facebook. J. Commun. Inquiry **37**(2), 91–112 (2013)
28. Stone, M.E., Lin, J., Dannefer, D., Kelley-Moore, J.A.: The continued eclipse of heterogeneity in gerontological research. J. Gerontol. Ser. B **72**(1), 162–167 (2017)
29. Loos, E.F.: Designing for dynamic diversity: representing various senior citizens in digital information sources. Observatorio (OBS*) J. **7**(1), 21–45 (2013)
30. Loos, E.F.: Senior citizens: digital immigrants in their own country? Observatorio (OBS*) J. **6**(1), 1–23 (2012)

31. Aroldi, P., Fortunati, L., Gebhardt, J., Vincent, J.: Generational belonging between media audiences and ICT users. Broadband Soc. Generational Changes **5**, 51–67 (2011)
32. Walker, A.: Commentary: the emergence and application of active aging in Europe. J. Aging Soc. Policy **21**(1), 75–93 (2008)
33. OberCom: A Internet em Portugal: Sociedade em rede 2014. OberCom, Lisboa (2014)
34. Comunello, F., Fernández-Ardèvol, M., Mulargia, S., Belotti, F.: Women, youth and everything else: age-based and gendered stereotypes in relation to digital technology among elderly Italian mobile phone users. Media Cult. Soc. **39**(6), 798–815 (2017)
35. Bolin, G., Skogerbø, E.: Age, generation and the media. Northern Lights **11**, 3–14 (2013)
36. Mannheim, K.: The problem of generation. In: Mannheim, K. (ed.) Essays on the sociology of knowledge, pp. 276–320. Routledge & Kegan Paul, London (1952)
37. Colombo, F., Fortunati, L. (eds.): Broadband Society and Generational Changes, vol. 5. Peter Lang, Frankfurt (2011)
38. Trentham, B., Sokoloff, S., Tsang, A., Neysmith, S.: Social media and senior citizen advocacy: an inclusive tool to resist ageism? Polit. Groups Identities **3**(3), 558–571 (2015)
39. Boyd, D.: Social network sites as networked publics: affordances, dynamics, and implications. In Papacharissi, Z. (ed.) A Networked Self: Identity, Community, and Culture on Social Network Sites, pp. 39–58. Routledge, New York (2011)

New Media, New Commodification, New Consumption for Older People

Karine Berthelot-Guiet[✉]

CELSA Sorbonne Université, Paris, France
karine.berthelot-guiet@sorbonne-universite.fr

Abstract. This paper intends to explore how the commodification of items linked to assisted living for older people educate the rest of the population to aging issues, especially when people are staying at home. We will work on the popularization capacity of advertising and commercial discourses in this respect. Classical ads, advertorials, common mass consumption promotional leaflets and catalogs, along with the uses of new media and online shopping enable the massification of a consuming class of elderly people. Advertising acts as information-education for the general audience, preparing younger senior to accept more easily assisted-living goods and even encouraging them to change their habits in advance. This is particularly obvious in marketing and off and online media productions that use three main communication strategy to reach baby boomers: 1/address to the main population in order to reach baby boomers senior working sometimes on taboo facts linked to aging, 2/work on offer and messages addressing a double target (young senior and their parents) or 3/changing the representations of old people in communications by promoting a new stereotypy of "longer young seniors" or "silver generation".

Keywords: Advertising · Baby boomers · Elderly · Consumption · New media

1 Elderly, New Frontiers for New Media and Advertising

Aging as a New Consumption Eldorado

In countries with growing aging population, Elderly people have become a huge political, social and economical stake. On a demographic point of view, the whole population is ageing and the so familiar pyramid shape of population demography will evolve towards a cylinder shape around 2050. This is a major change in all fields since lesser young people will have to provide economical help for elders, and this could be a problem. At the same time, especially in European countries and USA, a great part of social, economical, political power will be on the side of senior people who appear as groups that need to be understood since they are a kind of promise [1–3]. In some of these countries, for the first time, two generations in a same family reach together the limit of senior-age, being both part of the older part of the population, the senior «kids» being 60 to 70 or plus and their senior parents being 80 to 90 and more. The younger ones being most of the time involved in taking care of the oldest. It appears that the challenge for the system of consumption, including marketing, media and advertising,

© Springer International Publishing AG, part of Springer Nature 2018
J. Zhou and G. Salvendy (Eds.): ITAP 2018, LNCS 10926, pp. 435–445, 2018.
https://doi.org/10.1007/978-3-319-92034-4_33

is to understand fully these new populations of consumers as being plural, with different ways regarding some new needs linked to aging, in terms of food, way of life, media consumption or home adaptation.

These different ages of life are still often categorized as one, as a whole, especially when it comes to new ways of consumption, new media and IT products consumption. It is now the time to distinguish the «Older» senior population from the younger one. Especially since the newcomers in this class of age are experienced users of classical and new media as much as IT devices and will go on like this, inventing on the go new uses and new or adapted forms of sociability, mixing traditional and online media [2, 4, 5]. Uses regarding consumption, advertising and media are very different between the different generation of senior and each of them has to deal with specific needs of consumption regarding health, care, grandparenthood, leisure and everyday life, including the question of assisted living.

In this respect, adapted and/or assisted living is a main consumption challenge that touches all generations of Elderly, the younger ones having to manage their parents into this step and they themselves, as very well trained, experienced consumers, from the baby boomers generation, start to find their own way to consume through aging, as the «best in class» in consumption they always have been. We will try to analyze these assumptions of what marketing professionals could call different senior targets in brand and media discourses through a socio-semio-communicative approach that enables to analyze how representations circulate across society through different media and commercials.

Rise of New Classes of Consumers: *Silver* more than *Older*

As it is now well known, marketing, media and advertising people work on groups of people eligible as consumers, that is to say people having the purchasing power and the will to purchase [2, 4, 6]. Until not so long ago, senior citizens, especially retired people were considered as poorly purchasing people, stuck to habits, at least suspicious towards innovation, especially IT ones, even unable to adapt to new technologies, new products and rejecting them. In this respect, as we labeled it, «once Elderly were no target at all» [4]. Till less than fifteen years ago, older people were thought as too stuck to old ways and habits and difficult to convince because of a great suspicion towards advertising. Since then, this point of view started to change in society in general and in the mind of marketing professionals [4, 7, 8]. Being more and more numerous, having a longer life expectancy, working later and having bigger pensions, Elderly started to turn into an interesting «new frontier» for products like banking products, life and health care insurances or pre-arranged funerals, then leisure products came into the scope (travel etc.) and finally everyday and IT products [5, 7, 9–12].

The context has changed during the last decade since it has become obvious that more and more people reach the age of being called *senior* and stays in this category for decades. Furthermore, the *baby boomers* have massively joined the group. This category of people is well known for their great ability in all consumption fields since their great number and their incomes have made of them the dream target for sales since they were young. In fact, the idea of teenagers as a marketing target emerged with this generation [13]. France is now the place where a new configuration is more and more numerous:

parents and children being together retired with a two-step system of consumption. French marketing people even created the expression of *silver economy* (in English) to refer to this supposed treasure [14]. The American case is partly different since senior people are working longer and staying longer in regular consumption with different needs regarding the physical problems linked to aging [3, 15].

Because nowadays senior marketing target (60–79) is constituted of people and consumers very different from the previous senior, their parents, which are still alive and constitute the Elderly marketing target (80–…). This two ages of life are, on a consuming point of view very different, they don't need the same things, they don't have the same income and the youngest one tend to take care of the oldest and have to deal with their parents who are reluctant towards assisted living expenses. Nevertheless, assisted living products and services tend to become an everyday commodity and a mass consumption issue.

The Senior and Elderly marketing target are seen as a «new frontier» because of the economical weight they represent. We intend here to question and analyze in what respect media and advertising discourses can drive the acculturation of baby boomers and elderly to the buying and use of assisted living products and services. But first of all, speaking about marketing and target requires a theoretical and methodological clarification regarding our specific point of view in research linked to communication sciences which are different from business and management sciences as well from psychology or sociology. Using the next-presented method, we will approach the following research questioning trying to have a first exploratory approach on how marketing and advertising people try to address, on an off-line, to baby boomers, taking into account their very complex situation in between generations, feeling not or not so old and dealing with their parents great age.

2 Communication Sciences: Point of View and Methods

2.1 Media and Communication Studies

The scientific point of view here will be framed by the specificity of French Information and Communication Sciences contemporary approaches [16, 17]. Especially the part of French communication sciences which are dedicated to the description and analysis of social, media and market discourses and how they circulate among different social and media spaces building their public exposure. Brand discourses are considered as social discourses assuming market mediation. We are not in a psychological or sociological point of view, we won't take in charge what people think or say and we won't be able to work on processes of choice. Our approach will concentrate on public discourses, through media or professional communications: corporate communication, advertising, journalistic discourse and, more widely media communication. These communication productions provide a specific point of observation and can give a way to reach practices.

In this frame, methodology can be considered on an epistemological point of view. This communication sciences approach takes in charge what people publicly say they do or think, especially advertising professionals and what is present in fact in media productions. This implies to work on openly commented uses in order to reach practices and, then, it enables to go towards both uses and representations that accompany or guide them. It also gives access to creative appropriation users may develop. This perspective is not on the reception side since it is not media uses studies, but it is however on the side of the receiver. The point is to be in a socio-semiotic point of view, looking for the negotiation in interpretation and creative appropriation.

A Semiotic-Based Method: Socio-Semio-Communicational Analysis [18, 19]
Another important point is the idea of creative methodology in research. Each research needs the search and find of the proper set of qualitative methods, that is to say not based on statistics or not able to be presented with quantitative results, in order to question it, theoretically, in a proper way. Using already existing set methods is not enough, and most of the time it is necessary to conduct a theoretical analysis before choosing the proper set and architecture of mingled methods.

A last we think that *micro* scale approaches are necessary and very useful especially when one want, in the end, to reach *macro* analysis. The accumulation of small scale, very detailed, analysis on small elements, going towards, in a second step big corpuses of small elements, enables to reach precious and unexpected results which would not have been attained with a direct *macro* analysis. This methodological point of view is based on the idea that the smaller are your research objects, the bigger and wider can be the conclusions.

In view of the foregoing, our theoretical position regarding methodology is one of a socio-semio-communicational approach. Working on contemporary brand discourses and both formal and strategic transformations at work, the need for an adaptable methodology that will respect the complexity of research objects is obvious. The method needs to cope with the on going and never ending metamorphosis of brand discourses, advertising, and it has to enable the analysis of forms, given professional aims and discourses, and social discourses. Regarding brand discourses, the method starts form the point that these discourses are semiotic forms and communication *tive*/apparatus [20]. In this respect, they aim to recommend some uses.

In order to be able to fully analyze these discourses, it is necessary to provide a global and specific context understanding based on different aspects: technical and material conditions of production, socio-economic logics at work dealing with economics, sociology of organizations, variety of professional players (advertising, communications, marketing, media professionals and State regulation and consumer groups). From this, it is possible to build an analytical method that is the result of a semiotic approach of discourses, forms, formats and contents using methods or part of methods coming from discourse analysis, semiotics, economy, sociology, anthropology and regarding the organization of companies, agencies and business as well as culture in the wider sense. The method is a socio-semio-communicational point of view, looking for negotiation and interpretation of messages.

Regarding new media, new commodification and elderly people we will concentrate mainly on French media and advertising discourses. We will use content analysis mixing socio-semiotic analysis, visual semiotics, semio-linguistic analysis and discourse analysis on three kind of elements: gathered elements from French and international brands being specifically dedicated to older population, media and new media discourses dealing with the same brands or themes in a socio-semio-communicational approach to brand discourses.

In order to analyze fully these productions, we need a both comprehensive and specific context understanding the specificities of the market of *Elderly,* globally and internationally and, more specifically, about the French market and society regarding older people. In this respect, one has to know that the French society is specific regarding retirement and pensioning, since people usually stop working between 60 and 65 years old with a universal and «pay as you go» pension system that enable them, most of the time, to have a stable situation and a good income on a monthly basis.

3 Aging Turning Commonplace Through Commodification and Its Discourses

Educating Everybody To Sell To Senior

As already seen, the baby boomers constitute the first generation that massively reaches the qualification of *senior*, being at the same time involved in grandparenthood and in caregiving for their own parents reaching advanced age with very specific health and life care needs. In this respect, baby boomers can be seen, in a marketing point of view, as a double target: they are consumers who loves traveling, leisure activities alone or with grand-kids and, at the same time, they are the one helping their parents in a new consuming path, the one of assisted living on order to stay as long as possible at home.

As a matter of fact, the older generation is entering the time of life when assisted living is involved on different scales: from staying at home with adaptations to nursing homes with or without residential care. The older ones are reluctant to change their way of life before being obliged to, mostly because of health and security issues. They prefer to stick to their usual ways because buying specific home appliances linked to assisted living is a proof of disability and one of their main argument could be condensed into «as long as I can do it… ». In this respect, even if they are, in fact, potential consumers for a full range of specific products, they are not so easy to address directly. That is why brand communications, advertising, advertorials, and so on, will mostly try to reach their children since they are the ones being able to make them buy specific products and appliances. But the problem is that some of the baby boomers already have body changes due to aging and sometimes, on another scale, could need some of these products or services. Brand discourses face a kind of a dilemma: they need to speak about aging and adapted products to people that will be repelled if they feel to much involved for themselves too.

The problem can be circumvented by presenting in media the products related to aging and/or assisted living as mass consumption products, regarding a wide range of people of different generations, completely standardized in order to normalize their consumption and open new markets. In this respect brand managers use the educational capacity of advertising [21, 22] in traditional and new media. Education can be thought as a paradoxical effect of brands and advertising, but it is one of their long-standing missions that began at the end of the nineteenth century when brands of soap or toothpaste started to educate people to body and dental hygiene in order to sell their products better. In this respect, the fact that an object or service becomes a good, its *commodification,* acts as a sign of its normalization since there is no need to go in a specialized or dedicated to professionals store. When a supermarket chain like French *Intermarché* starts to exhibit in its weekly promotion advertising catalogues, delivered in every mailboxes, assisted living products in between shampoo, baby food and shoes, these small products linked to assisted living mixes with promotions on food, kid products and adult clothes. It gives to the main population the information that these products can be bought at any time, by everyone, in a well-known and familiar neighborhood store and, at the same time, it provides the information that this kind of products are now common, part of everyday life. And they go further, implying that it is normal to need as to buy these goods along with the groceries and, at the same time, that it is strange not to buy them if you need them (Fig. 1).

Fig. 1. Intermarché hypermarket advertising catalog

The presence, almost on a daily basis of this kind of products in mass consumption communications, is a first step towards the education of the whole population and it can help older people to accept and eventually buy themselves or with the advise and help of their senior children, these goods. But the commodification and the massification have to act deeper and be more present in everyday advertising and media in order to really reach and educate down to the baby boomers, being themselves *senior* who are not really thinking of themselves as old people especially since they are caregivers for their elders. New ways of communicating relaying on this generation great knowledge of consumption have to be found using both traditional and new media.

Advertising is once again used as a user's manual for life. It brings into full light former taboo topics related to aging an one can see on TV, computers and tablets, especially at mass viewing hours and largely general public, news or women magazines. This is the case for health issues like cholesterol, diabetes etc. and their numerous everyday products such as special Omega-3 enriched margarines. It also goes toward more delicate subjects such as bladder control problems for both women and men. This is not the kind of topic people usually talk about, even with their own family. Since a significant number of senior of all ages are concerned by the problem, advertising tackles this issue directly by generalizing the point, speaking very directly about it and extending it to very young senior women and men. At the same time, brands use advertorials in magazines on and off-line in order to explain the phenomena and build a common knowledge about it, as French brand *Tena* and international brand *Always* do. These ads are targeting more «young» senior than their parents.

They do two things at a time, saying that age issues services and products are mass products, they will be consumers as ever and not «turning old» and the offer will be both sanitary safe and aesthetically acceptable (Fig. 2).

Fig. 2. Tena and Always print advertisings

Aging in Consumption as Aging in Beauty: Stereotypes and Taboos

This opens a new field of expectation for marketing people who develop a single new target of *senior baby boomers* and specific products are regularly launched such as magazines, radios, TV broadcasts and programs, websites, specific food and so on. These new *seniors* appear in more and more commercials for cars, insurance, banking, and rather expensive goods. We can say that brands and advertising are using a stereotype to change a stereotype for a new one. Advertising makes the work of stereotypy, choosing carefully nice looking not so old people, very dynamic, beautifully tanned, hair magnificent gray or white, doing easily physically and intellectual demanding activities [4, 8, 18, 19]. The new generation of senior appear as a most acceptable socio-marketing built artifact using a stereotype to replace the previous one of old people as turned towards past. This new representation spread by commercials depicting people looking forward future with confidence and buying power. Being senior is no more about aging but about staying young. Baby boomers appear to stay «younger later» and most of all they still have money to spend after retirement (Fig. 3).

Fig. 3. Young senior stereotypy in mass advertising

Brand managers and advertisers begin to be well aware about how baby boomers become old and most of all how they dealt, all their lifelong, with IT change, from radio to TV, from tape-recorder and CD's to streaming, from video-recorder to DVD and blue-ray players and then router boxes. At work, they started everyday use of computers and web services and keep on using once retired, coping with new devices as often as necessary. They commonly use travel applications to buy plane tickets and hotel reservations. The newcomers in the senior class of age are totally users of IT devices and will go on like this for a while, inventing new uses and new sociabilities.

It is a challenge to be able to keep these very well trained, experienced consumers that do not stick to international brands as oldest people do. And the main issue will be to provide safety, comfort and aesthetics at the same time and show it in advertising on and offline.

As a matter of fact, it appears that baby boomers start to plan assisted living devices before needing them, using the experience built while convincing and helping their parents. When older senior people change, *in extremis*, their old bath tube for a plastic built in a day shower when they are no longer able to step over the side of the bath when entering or leaving it, the younger ones plan to change their entire bathroom to something more adapted but still stylish. Some brands are playing on these two sides like the French store specialized in home decoration *Leroy Merlin*. On their website one can find a two step proposition with different offers regarding aging and home adaptation. The first one is for very old people needing instant change in their bathroom because of a physical degraded condition; it's built in a day shower with practical issue and no aesthetical concern. The second one is presented as a guide to go towards aging beautifully and harmoniously in a redesigned bathroom, adapted with style and value to future issues linked to great age (Fig. 4).

Fig. 4. Leroy Merlin Website about adapted bathtub and bathroom (01.02.2018)

Other options can be analyzed in the press, off and online, dedicated in France to *senior* persons. The two main publications are *Pleine Vie* (meaning *living fully*) and *Notre Temps* (meaning *nowadays*). *Pleine Vie* gives a great place to consumption as a main topic, especially on its website where *consumption and finance* is section in itself. That implies that aging with fulfillment is linked to consumption and that advices are given about the good or best way to consume. *Notre temps* has the same point about consumption and goes further on its website since the third element, presented as an information, is an advertorial dedicated to a conference about *silver economy* obviously training senior people to think about themselves as consumer, and more, as a specific kind of consumer, designated with the gratifying word *silver*. This is a three months marketing operation delivering three videos featuring the same «self-invested» expert who is CEO of a French company *Indépendance Royale,* specialized in home adjustments for elder people like walk-in showers, stair lifts, specialized beds etc. These three conferences are dedicated to French demography, International demography, Digital and Senior and, as they are advertising at core, we can say that they prepare good consumers feeding them with facts and statistics leading to the idea that baby boomers generation is *THE* senior consumer generation not in the idea of aging, but of being smart consumers. Some other marketing discourses speak about a *new generation* of senior.

The point now is to keep in touch with this generation through their uses of new media.

4 Conclusion and Limitations

As a conclusion after this exploratory research regarding how marketing and advertising people try to address, on an off-line, to baby boomers, taking into account their very complex situation in between generations, feeling not or not so old and dealing with their parents great age, we have discovered three main communications strategy to reach baby boomers: 1/address to the main population in order to reach baby boomers senior working sometimes on taboo facts linked to aging, 2/work on offer and messages addressing a double target (young senior and their parents) or 3/changing the representations of old people in communications by promoting a new stereotypy of "longer young seniors" or "silver generation". These is in fact a first approach and we need now to conduct specific and extended research on the three of them in order to provide a global reflexive approach on communications toward Elderly but also in order to understand how the rise of this new class of consumers is changing the whole system of advertising and media discourses putting former taboo themes in full light and how on and off-line discourses play their parts. There is a research to conduct on the circulations among different discursive spaces of the new stereotypies of aging to do, taking into account how economic, sometimes state driven topics or denominations like "silver économie" in France has travelled along different media spheres and ends perfectly naturalized, as presented by Roland Barthes [XZ], that is to say given as perfectly normal while hiding the ideology at work. In other words, the full extent of this research will enable starting with commercial discourses to deal with the ideologies at work within society regarding aging.

References

1. Pison, G.: Le vieillissement démographique sera plus rapide au Sud qu'au Nord. Population et sociétés. **457**, 1–4 (2009)
2. Colombo, F.: Ageing, media and communication. In: Paper Proceedings, ICA, Puerto Rico, 21–25 May, pp. 1–13 (2015)
3. Beard, J., Biggs, S., Blomm, D., Fried, L., Hogan, P., Kalache, A., Olshansky, J.: Global Population Ageing: Peril or Promise? PGDA Working Paper 89 (2012). http://www.hsph.harvard.edu/pgda/working.htm
4. Berthelot-Guiet, K.: Elderly and IT: brand discourses on the go. In: Zhou, J., Salvendy, G. (eds.) ITAP 2016. LNCS, vol. 9755, pp. 186–193. Springer, Cham (2016). https://doi.org/10.1007/978-3-319-39949-2_18
5. Colombo, F., Aroldi, P., Carlo, S.: New Elders, Old Divides: ICTs, Inequalities and Well Being amongs Young Elderly Italians, Comunicar, Media Educ. Res. J. **45**(XXVIII), 47–55 (2015)
6. Colombo, F.: The long wave of generations. In: Colombo, F. Fortunati, L. (eds.) Broadband Society and Generational Changes. Peter Lang, Francfurt, pp. 19–36 (2011)
7. Defrance, A.: Penser, classer, communiquer. Publicité et catégories sociales, Hermès **38**, 155–162 (2004)
8. Loos, E.F., Ivan, L.: Visual ageism in the media. In: Ayalon, L., Tesch-Roemer, C. (eds.) Contemporary Aspects on Ageism. Springer (accepted)

9. Loos, E.F., Designing for dynamic diversity: representing various senior citizens in digital information sources. Observatorio (OBS*) J. **7**(1), 21–45 (2013)
10. Loos, E.F., Ekström, M.: Visually representing the generation of older consumers as a diverse audience: towards a multidimensional market segmentation typology. Participations **11**(2), 258–273 (2014)
11. Berthelot-Guiet, K.: Mort de pub, stéréotypie des discours publicitaires, 5, Effeuillage Revuc, pp. 28–31 (2015)
12. Feillet, R., Bodin, D., Héas, S.: Corps ages et medias: entre espoir de vieillir jeune menace de la dependence. Etudes de communication, Languages, Information, Mediations **35**, 149–166 (2010)
13. Berthelot-Guiet, K.: La marque médiation marchande ou mythologie adolescente, In: Lachance, J., Saint-Germain, P., Mathiot, L. (eds.) Marques cultes et culte des marques chez les jeunes: Penser l'adolescence avec la consommation, Presses Universitaires de Laval, Laval, pp. 23–38 (2016)
14. La filière Silver Economie. www.entreprises.gouv.fr/politique-et-enjeux/la-silver-economy, consulté le 3 janvier 2018
15. Mather, M., Jacobsen, L.A., Pollard, K.L.: Aging in the United States. Popul. Bull. **70**(2), Population Reference Bureau (2015), www.prb.org
16. Jeanneret, Y., Ollivier, B.: Les sciences de l'information et de la communication, HERMES, 38. CNRS Editions, Paris (2004)
17. Jeanneret, Y.: Critique de la trivialité. Les médiations de la communication, enjeux de pouvoir, Le Havre, Editions Non Standard (2014)
18. Berthelot-Guiet, K.: Paroles de pub. La vie triviale de la publicité, Le Havre, Éditions Non Standard (2013)
19. Berthelot-Guiet, K.: Analyser les discours publicitaires. Armand Colin, Paris (2015)
20. Foucault, M.: Le jeu de Michel Foucault, entretien avec Colas, D. Grosrichard. In: Le Gaufey, A., Livi, G., Miller, J., Miller, G., Millot, J.-A., Wajeman, C., Ornicar: Bulletin périodique du champ freudien **10**, 62–93 (1977). Repris in: Dits et Ecrits II. 1976–1979, Paris, Gallimard, pp. 298–329 (1994), texte n° 206, p. 299
21. Cochoy, F.: Une Histoire du Marketing. Discipliner l'Économie de Marché. Paris, La Découverte (1999)
22. Berthelot-Guiet, K.: Grandir en publicité: marques et mythes d'enfance, In: Bahuaud, M. et Pecolo, A. (Dir.) Naître et grandir en terres publicitaires, Jeunes et Médias, 9 (accepted)
23. Barthes, R.: Mythologies. Editions du Seuil, Paris (1957)

Technology: A Bridge or a Wall?
The Inter(intra)generational Use of ICTs
Among Italian Grandmothers

Simone Carlo[1(✉)] and Catarina Rebelo[2]

[1] Università Cattolica del Sacro Cuore, Largo Gemelli 1, 20121 Milano, Italy
simone.carlo@unicatt.it
[2] Instituto Universitário de Lisboa (ISCTE-IUL),
Centro de Investigação e Estudos de Sociologia (CIES-IUL), Lisboa, Portugal
ana_catarina_rebelo@iscte-iul.pt

Abstract. Our research aims to investigate the role played by media and ICTs in building intergenerational and intragenerational relations for the grandparents. The project aims to understand how grandmothers use Facebook and digital devices (computers, laptops, tablets, smartphones) within the family and the friend networks, the role of communication technologies for entertainment and the resistance and difficulties in using ICT for elderly. Data for research analysis was collected through four focus groups conducted with 28 Italian grandmothers living in Milan, Italy.

Our focus groups show an intricate scenario: although the trigger to start to use new digital technology comes from family and people belonging to different generations, the daily use of the ICTs reveals a complex relationship with children and grandchildren regarding technological issues, which often characterized by incompatible netiquette, different competences and lack of learning assistance.

As more elderly are going online and widening their online interactions, further research should be pursued to understand how older people use digital technologies to communicate with peers and to point out the differences between elderly digital use for intra and intergenerational communication.

Keywords: Elderly · ICTs · Generations · Grandmothers · Family

1 Introduction

The aging of population is a global trend and a big challenge for societies, as the major transformations it produces implicate almost every sector of society. It is a global phenomenon as, even if in different stages and speeds, it implicates virtually every country in the world. While more advanced in countries that developed earlier it became also an undergoing process in many countries where the development has occurred later [1]. The fertility decline, together with the improved longevity, are the key factors explaining this process. By 2030, according to the UN forecasts [1], the proportion of elderly people will be more than 25% of the population in Europe and Northern America.

© Springer International Publishing AG, part of Springer Nature 2018
J. Zhou and G. Salvendy (Eds.): ITAP 2018, LNCS 10926, pp. 446–464, 2018.
https://doi.org/10.1007/978-3-319-92034-4_34

Followed by Oceania with 20% of the population, 17% in Asia, Latin America and Caribbean, and 6% in Africa.

Concomitant to the population aging, the mediatization by technology also continues to proliferate producing important transformations in every aspect of society including how we live and how we relate to others.

In this context, it becomes critical to understand how latter life is being experienced in this mediatized society. As the elderly experienced these transformations later in life, they may felt changes in a greater extent, which increase the relevance to understand how the elderly manage to adapt their everyday life to the social transformations resulting from the process of proliferation of digital devices and mediatization. The role of family and intergenerational communication within family seems to have a great impact on the appropriation of ICT between the elderly, especially grandmothers. It is thus important to further analyze the ICT practices within this group.

Taking into account these assumptions, a qualitative study was conducted with the aim to understand:

- What are the social contexts of ICT's use in the daily life of the grandmothers?
- What are the role of ICT on grandmother's intergenerational and intragenerational relationships dynamics?

2   Context, Theoretical Framework and Research Methodology

2.1   ICT and the Elderly

The interest on how the elderly relate with digital technologies has grown in the past few years with a significant increase of the studies devoted to the issue. The digital divide is the reasoning behind most of these studies, following the observation of the data on Internet use, where age is recurrently a key configuration of the digital divide within many societies [2]. The digital divide literature argues that being excluded from the society mediated by technology affects not only the economic inclusion as all the other aspects of life, as education, community issues, cultural and entertainment, personal interactions and political participation [3]. At the beginning the concept was focused only on the access variable, making a distinction from those who have and those who have not access to technology. The concept then developed to an understanding that the digital exclusion would not end with full access [4, 5], not only because there are different levels of access [6] but mainly because the access to digital technologies by itself, do not promote the inclusion of the people who does not have the "technical skills, status markers, and content structures that are fast becoming key institutional features of the Internet age" [5, p. 144]. Thus, the debate on digital divide was refocused from the access to the different uses and skills to benefit from the access to digital technology [4].

Senior citizens are currently, however, a most growing group of people going online [2, 7]. Loos [9] points out for the danger of using age as an ultimate explanatory variable of digital exclusion and argues that more than a problem of age, it is a problem of lack of experience with digital technology. Colombo [10] argues that factors such as the social network of the individuals, their professional status and their former jobs should be taken in consideration more than the causal impact of age. In fact, some studies shown that there are not empirical evidences that the young people do not have problems with technology [11–13]. And some studies about population of the Netherlands show that content skills tend to increase in older users [11, 12]. As the studies on the seniors and ICT are strongly conditioned by the socio-cultural and socio-economic variables and contexts, they are country relative [14]. Italy, for example, if compared to more digi-talized countries, seems to have a delay on Internet adoption of around ten years [15].

Another frequent premise on studies about seniors and technology is that the Internet, and particularly Social Network Services (SNS), would benefit the quality of life of the elderly. Factors as the decrease of social relations and the mobility loss are viewed as common processes in latter age that contribute to a greater exposition to isolation and loneliness [16]. In this context, SNS are seen as tools capable of strengthen the social networks of the elderly, making them less vulnerable to situations of isolation and lone-liness [16, 17]. General socio-economic benefits and facilitated access to services such as researching services, bank and shopping [18], access to cultural and recreational activities and the enhancing of inter-generational solidarities [19] and access to infor-mation such as health information [20] are also pointed out as potential benefits for seniors being online. Other studies drown attention for the fact that the use of the Internet by senior citizens are not just about benefits, it involves also some risks [15] that should be taken into consideration.

Although the elderly are a fast growing group of Internet users, in many countries senior digital exclusion are still one of the most expressive feature of digital exclusion. The reasons pointed out by the elderly for not use the Internet are predominantly the lack of motivation and interest [19, 21–23] and the idea that elderly "often do not consider the internet a technology that is appropriate or relevant for people of their age group" [24].

Levy and Benaji [25, p. 62] have pointed out that negative stereotypes about older people impact on their "cognition, behavior and health without their awareness". After a lifelong exposure to ageist stereotypes, they can be directed inward, on the form of "implicit age self-stereotypes" or the beliefs of older individuals about the senior popu-lation [25–27].

In a study about how senior Internet users position themselves against to different others Kania-Lundholm and Torres [28] shown how senior citizens that are active users see it as a privilege and constructed as exceptional and that "they refer to their age as one of the aspects that informs their usage [28, p. 28].

Also, intergenerational relations seem to have a great impact on the use of the Internet by senior citizens. This issue enters the debate both as a start and an ending point as maintaining contact with children and grandchildren seems to have both a positive outcome from the elderly being online and as a motivation for the senior citizens start to use the Internet.

2.2   Grannies Online

Senior citizens and woman are both two of the demographic groups reported as less likely to be online on the digital divide literature. Lack of perceptions of benefits for going online is one of the central issues on the reasons presented by the elderly for not use Internet. However, the possibility to connect with family members, especially the younger ones is a strong benefit perceived by the elderly to go online [29]. Intergenerational relations, maintaining contact with children and grandchildren seem to be a reason for elderly to start to go online and result in strengthen intergenerational relations [22]. "Forced adoption" [30] or "pressure to adopt" [31] are some of the expressions used to describe the process by which senior citizens adopt a technology persuaded by family members, either children, grandchildren, nieces and nephews or others. Although it is an external pressure, it is not necessarily felt as negative by the elderly [32].

Since the beginning of the studies of technology on the domestic space [32] that family, and specially children have been identified as elements that foster adults' adoption. Sawchuk and Crow [31] mentioned a desire to belong and the desire to understand and connect with grandchildren as a special motivation for grandmothers to changing perspectives towards what they don´t understand and as a reason to keep up with practices they did not feel comfortable with. Being highly involved in the everyday life of their family and particularly the children and grandchildren is presented as a main point of the relevance of the use of social media for grandmothers [36]. Specially in a context which they may not related much to the contents they find online, as "when marginalized groups do log on, there is often scare content that applies to their lives and their communities." [33, p. 20].

This intergenerational communication mediated by technology gives visible shape to the different set of values and behaviors between generations towards communication. Sawchuk and Crow [34] identify how elderly understand distraction and interruption as rudeness or impoliteness in the case of the use of the cell phone. Ivan and Hebblethwaite [33] also highlight how grandmothers use the shared presence on Facebook with their grandchildren to act as a role model, rising issues of decency and privacy.

In addition to the ability to connect with family, other perceived benefits by the elderly identified by Quinn et al. [29] are the ability to surpass some age related limitations, such as mobility, being able to contact with distant friends and the cognitive benefits of learning something new.

Senior users reportedly integrate ICT in a weighted way, making choices around different options accordingly to their needs and lifestyles [30, 34].

In terms of use of Facebook seniors seem to have a relatively passive use [17, 33], the platform is seen as a place to get updates, keep in contact and monitor the situation but in a passive way. For Erickson [17] the lack of trust reported by the elderly on Facebook is not focused on the persons they can contact with but on the nature of the technology and their limited comprehension of it.

For distant grandmothers, although Facebook is not a preferred platform to communicate with the family, it has a key complementary role. It is used as a complementary platform for everyday reminiscing [35] offering an opportunity to keeping update about the everyday life of the families and functioning as a trigger for conversations via other platforms [33]. For instance, personal photos posted at Facebook can generate "photo-talk" [36], talk around them in conversation on via other channel.

Telephone and video-chatting, however, seems to be the favorite platforms for distant grandmothers to talk with their relatives because of the deeper feel of connections and personal relationship they provide [33]. Forghani et al. [36] argue that the adoption of video-mediated technologies at home is motivated by the desire for closeness.

But this sense of closeness brought by the technology raises questions about the risk of replacement of face-to-face connection and interaction. For Erickson [17] the awareness raised by Facebook does not replace face-to-face interaction, it often results in emotional support through other channels.

It terms of the risks perceive by the elderly about ICT they seem to relate with the type of use. The more experienced elderly users perceive more risks, but also more opportunities [37]. Among the perceived risks by the elderly are the fear of making technical mistakes, exposure to offensive content, data theft, or wasted time on the Internet [37].

2.3   Objectives and Methodology

The main research objective was to understand the role played by the ICTs in the daily life of the grandmothers. A crucial importance was given to the role played by the intergenerational and intragenerational relations in shaping media use and learning style of the elderly. Specifically, the research wanted to investigate:

– the possible relationships in place between the grandmothers, children and nephew, with the aim of understanding the dynamics of intergenerational exchange, and how grandmothers experience the use of Internet as a tool to facilitate family communication with family members.
– the possible relationships in place between the grandmothers and their friends with the aim of understanding the dynamics of intragenerational exchange, and how grandmothers experience the use of Internet as a tool of communication and entertainment and leisure activities with friends.

Data for our research analysis was collected through four focus groups, with approximately two hours, conducted with 28 Italian grandmothers living in Milan, Italy, in February and March 2017. Participations were recruited first by a snowball approach through acquaintances and then in collaboration with a local association of elderly. The average age of the focus-group participants was 72 (minimum 65, maximum 81). The grandmother's selection criteria was being 65 years old or older and user of digital technology. The questions asked to participants focused on their subjective experience and were organized around five main topics: how they communicate with their family, how they communicate with their friends and acquaintances, the role of digital technologies in their leisure activities, the difficulties faced when using them and what would they change about these technologies.

3   Learning Processes and Family Role

Every interviewed grandmother has got and uses at least one device for digital communication (computer, laptop, tablet, smartphone). From the interviews clearly emerges that often the digitalization process and ICT usage is not a recent event in grandmothers' life: according to many of the interviewed grandmothers learning how to use digital technologies happened some years ago, this by using the computer at work.

The majority of our grandmothers are teachers or employees in retirement; they lived in time the digitalisation processes during the second half of the 90s.

Children's education and the need to give children tools for school and homework were an additional incentive to the approach to the information technology and the digital world. The computer has often entered grandmothers' houses when their children attended university or school. For some grandmothers it was an opportunity to get closer to the information technology and the digital world.

In some cases grandmothers taught basics of computer usage to their little children:

In fact, my daughter learned to use the PC with me, I approached her to the PC. Now things are different, maybe for so many functions I lose and I have to ask her (65, FG2)

Grandmothers who own a computer for many years (for work reasons or because they bought it when children attended school) still use it nowadays to do research or to send emails, but they know they use it less than before, since the smartphone, tablet and mobile arrival. In the last few years, grandmothers perceived that the real change has been the arrival of the Internet and the smartphone but especially the computer usage in relationships and entertainment terms, not just related to work and to help children with their homework.

As regarding the theme of the family role in stimulating the technologies, the possibility/necessity to keep in touch with their younger relatives (children and grandchildren) is still the initial incentive to adopt technologies.

Familiar relationships support and stimulate the initial usage of the ICT, but in some cases it is not a serene relationship: grandmothers perceive a sort of family pressure concerning the update and learning of new digital services: a "commitment to be up with the times" but especially to be connected with the familiar web:

I've always refused to use the IPhone, then my children and husband have almost forced me, and since then when I use the smartphone I also use WhatsApp, it's quite comfortable I do not really like telecommunications. But I use it, even because otherwise I would feel cut off even from my family (FG1, 71)

If the first digitalisation processes (computer and feature phone during the 90s/2000) were bounded to the work sphere and to children education, during the "second digital wave" (the Internet and smartphone) the role of the family is fundamental, both in supporting/pressing the adoption (provide technologies to keep in touch with family) and, in some cases, in supporting a "reaction" of the elderly people, who want to show relatives to still be able to learn and to be at the same level of the other (younger) members of the family.

According to some grandmothers, in particular the oldest ones, the adoption of digital technologies is told as a "personal" challenge towards the family and the society in general (and also a personal challenge in feeling still active):

I always wanted to keep up with the times and at some point I decided to buy the smartphone. My son asked me to do what with smartphone but I had decided to buy it. Also because in everyday life I saw everybody using the new technology and I did not want to be outdone. Apart from the fundamental importance of being always reachable... (79, FG1)

For some grandmothers, in particular, learning to use the computer and other digital devices (especially through organised courses for elderly) is an occasion to show their independency, modernity and activity. The beginning of these courses offers an opportunity for grandmothers to feel active and independent (also towards husbands and children).

Many interviewed grandmothers tell how often the basics to use "new" digital technologies came from children, but rarely, from grandchildren, in the case of older grandmothers with adult grandchildren. In particular, children saw in the digitalisation of the elderly an "inclusion" opportunity in children/grandchildren world:

> My daughter taught me to use all these things because I used to reject them... if it was not for her, she is very technical. It was a way to get me closer. (71, FG1).

After this learning phase, it seems there is not an attention of the younger generation in answering grandmothers' additional doubts and questions. It seems that the introduction in the "new" digital world mainly happens in delimited and unexpected moments (perhaps towards the present of a smartphone or the new service casual download), but it is not combined with a daily following assistance. Numerous grandmothers expressed a certain difficulty in receiving help from children and grandchildren:

> In fact, children when they have time to teach are so fast they do not understand that we may need to take note, to answer calmly... they now have this use speed in themselves and they don't think that for us is different... (76, FG2)

In particular, grandmothers consider their grandchildren to be rushed and not able to explain with attention the complex steps of the ICT usage. Indeed, grandmothers request certain patience in teaching, the respect of their learning times, and comprehension of the different literacy level. These are often requests, that fall on deaf ears: several interviewed grandmothers perceive, often with lots of frustration, they do not have always available children or grandchildren to count on for doubt related to the use of the computer and smartphone:

> I don't ask to my children because they don't explain me anything, I prefer to go to the shop or to a friend who knows more than me. (73, FG4).

It is interesting to notice that elderly people consider younger generation less able to understand elderly people "times" in learning new digital technologies. To this "generational" problem we can also include another problem related to familiar dynamics: children and grandchildren are often perceived as impatient in teaching.

Facing a detached and unpleasant familiar environment, learning can also happen (as an alternative or as an integration) by means of information technology courses organised by public or private authorities, which are able to offer basic information technology knowledge that can be integrated, if possible, with children and grandchildren pieces of (often sporadic) advice.

These courses in particular are appreciated for the ability teachers (often elderly teachers if not adult) have to teach with calm how to use the computer and the smartphone. Rather than the informal and not organised (and often rushed) learning of children and grandchildren, several interviewed grandmothers seem to prefer a "classical" and formal learning process, based on the "teacher-learner" relation, on the classroom dimension, homework, final exam and based on the certificate.

4   Being on the Internet

With "being on the Internet" we mean grandmothers' reflection elements concerning the role of the Internet in their daily life and the digital services use (or not use). It is interesting to notice that interviewed grandmothers' reflections regarding the role of the Internet are linked to the comparison with "younger generations".

It seems to constantly emerge in grandmothers a worry concerning young people use of the Internet, but also a certain pride of a more "adult" and balanced approach to technologies, which is more thoughtful and reflective than the use children and grandchildren do.

Interviewed grandmothers give importance to the use of the digital technologies they consider to be "correct" and "appropriate", and they are very reflective about it. In particular, they say they consider with attention both when to use technologies and, with a wider choice of means of communication, which means and services to use for a certain aim (playful, formal, intimate).

Concerning the "when to use the ICTs" issue, interviewed grandmothers consider exaggerated the use young people do of new technologies. A use which is often judged inappropriate because in contests in which the ICTs should not be used, for example in public spaces:

Several grandmothers affirm, with certain strength, to face "correctly" (in a wisely and moderate way) the use of technologies rather than the younger generations that often use them in an antisocial and deregulated way, in some cases at the edge of pathology and dependence. Grandmothers demonstrate to have a particular attention in using the technologies in an appropriate way, at the same time the interviewed intensely criticise the use younger generations (both children and grandchildren) do of technologies. Grandmothers consider very important to have limits in the use of technologies, even though they perceive that the Internet, smartphone and computer have features that support an extended use. The worry for an excessive use of the Internet is both a criticism towards grandchildren and children, but also a personal risk in a reflective way. Grandmothers think that being elderly, experienced and responsible, the risk is limited for them, on the other hand the worry for younger people is higher.

They strongly criticise the unaware and superficial way the younger generations use of ICTs, affirming to be more "prepared" to face with maturity so powerful tools. Being elderly people and having more experience in general concerning "things in life" helps to use the ICTs in a more balanced way:

Their generation and more the next one are kind of superficial... I see my grandchildren who, although they still cannot read, are able to use, decide, look... I also think that it's a matter of generation. Young people are more skillful in using but somewhat more unprepared (71, FG2)

Grandmothers express a strong criticism, sometimes, concerning the use their children and grandchildren do of the ICTs. In particular there is a certain worry regarding intimate pictures children and grandchildren often publish, with the aim to show private life and feelings:

> *I think my children have no problem [to post personal photos]. They were born in another time; we are more suspicious. (81, FG2)*

Elderly people perceive to be less "competent" than younger generations, but they feel to use technologies with more common sense and measure. On one side grandchildren's ability to use technologies is considered positive and admirable (*"they are so young but already so active"*), on the other side a worry emerges and they distance themselves from an excessive use of technologies. Young people's knowledge is perceived as a source of opportunities, especially material and practical ones, but at the same time it is also perceived the risk to loose the cultural substance that other "analogic" content have (the reading of a book for example) and the human dimension of communication and relationships:

> *From the practical point of view, young people can take advantage by the use of these technologies. They certainly have a boost in practical terms but not in terms of human relationships. (71, FG1)*

Between the strong critical element regarding children and grandchildren use of the ICTs, there is a perception that the digital is coming along with the replacement of offline and "real" relationships with "virtual" ones. In particular, face-to-face relationship or "traditional" means of communication such as the telephone are considered, by our grandmothers, to be the more suitable means of communication to express important things and feelings: Whatsapp messages or emails are considered too superficial to be used for complex issues, leading to misunderstandings. Verbal communication is still considered more suitable (even though in some cases it is mediated by a telephone), rather than written communication:

> *I belong to a generation in which it is more important a phone call or a meeting when you have something to say or share, rather than sending a video or photo (71, FG2).*

According the interviewed grandmothers, the excessive use of the smartphone makes the verbal communication and the experiences in "real" contexts more difficult. In grandmother's perception, young people use of social network risks to make more difficult intimate relationships with their own coetaneous:

> *In fact, the problem for young people is exactly this... being linked, for example, to games, friends on FB, Instagram... and to be detached from reality. They have maybe 3,000 friends on FB and two friends nearby (76, FG2)*

The criticism towards "young" and grandchildren is also extended to their children, daughter-in-law and son-in-law, who are considered to be at risk in the process of replacement of "real" friendships with "virtual" ones, the replacement of lived/remembered experiences with the ones memorised on the smartphone, the replacement of "here and now" and the use of the smartphone:

> *And for young people, I also mean people of 40, 45, 50 years... [...] they have lost a lot of sense of reality in my opinion. Because everyone looks at it, everyone is taking pictures, but a cell phone more in memory cannot contain... with the result that in the end you lose the real memory of your remembering. (71, FG2).*

There is the anxiety of always being connected, between difficulties already mentioned in the use of technology and between the negativities considered in the digital world. The anxiety seems to be, already once, imputed to the younger generations, to children and grandchildren.

I call my daughter "mother anxiety" because of these technologies and because they always have to communicate everything (76, FG3)

nowadays going out without our smartphone is a catastrophe (72, FG3)

This anxiety sometimes makes grandmothers pride of their partial disconnection, and their necessity to have moments in which the smartphone is turned off:

Some time in the evening I switch off my cell phone because I do not want to be dependent to, and everyone knows that if anything is needed, they can be found on the fixed telephone (71, FG2).

5 The ICTs and Familiar Relationships Among People Belonging to Different Generation

In the previous paragraph we underlined how grandmothers widely criticise the ICTs and their "wrong", excessive, unaware use. Nevertheless, interviewed grandmothers consider the digital tools to maintain intimate and distant relationships with family members fundamental. This concerns grandmothers, whose children and grandchildren live far away and who find in digital channels tools able to "stimulate" proximity and feel, even though virtually, the pleasure of a "physical" and intimate relationship with distant relatives (children and grandchildren). In particular, grandmothers find in digital tools a possibility, from distance, to observe grandchildren growth, sending pictures:

I'm seeing my nephew growing up, I actually see her two or three times a year when I go there, but I feel really close. For me it's an emotion every time, every Sunday, she does not talk yet but starts playing… it's just a joy (66, FG1)

Elderly people with grandchildren and children, who live far from them, consider digital communication services necessary and fundamental and allowing to build intimate (mediated) relationships with their dear ones, even though they consider them personal face-to-face relationship "substitute":

However, if these instruments were not there, it would have been even more difficult. Because even when it comes to small messages or small videos, they are always very important to us (76, FG2).

Therefore, if digital communication tools are considered to be central for the maintenance and care of distant relationships with children and grandchildren, the ICTs role is more problematic in building intimate relationships among people belonging to daily contests (children and grandchildren), especially if seen regularly. In building/maintenance intimate relationships, face-to-face relationships and the necessity to see and talk to each other is also considered central in a transversal way. Despite this certainty, clearly emerges that for the majority of our grandmothers digital communication tools (Whatsapp in particular) are still useful to build a connection, not necessarily intimate, but work and instrumental, and are fundamental to maintain sentimental relationships with children (in a more residual way) with grandchildren.

Physical contact, see and talk to each other, "touch" children and grandchildren is still the main way to demonstrate affection, to feel the pleasure of given and received love, but digital channels and services (Whatsapp especially) have the ability to build a thick web of daily messages, a light, playfully and jokingly communication with the aim to keep in touch with relatives through "little things daily exchange":

> It's a daily exchange of small things, the other night my daughter made the tortellini with my mother-in-law, she sent me the picture, to see... we get involved... (71, FG1)

On one hand there is a wide scepticism regarding digital tools ability to "create" a relationship with relatives, on the other hand communication technologies are considered excellent tools to consolidate an already existing intimate relationship, "reinforcing" bonds:

> I think there must be a basic predisposition, a very good relationship that is so humanly strengthened. (72, FG1)

According to our interviewed grandmothers, digital channels have not created a drop in meeting moments and they have not substituted face-to-face relationships, but they have created new (little, daily, interstitial) relationship moments between a meeting and the other. This concerns channels that create a spread, arranged intimacy in the often frenetic life interstices of children and grandchildren.

Indeed, interviewed grandmothers consider asynchronous digital communication channels (Whatsapp in particular, but also emails) useful because less invasive than the telephonic contact: indeed grandmothers have a certain worry to disturb their children, who are considered to be always too busy (or distracted and unpleasant).

Whatsapp use is central from this point of view, as a technology included in children crack times and it is considered to be a less invasive technology, which does not disturb and allows children (and grandchildren) to be free to answer when they want:

> WhatsApp because the children do not often respond, the only solution is to send them a nice message they might answer to, they say they will call later (71, FG2).

On one hand Whatsapp is considered a suitable tool for familiar relationships "interstitial" management, on the other hand the criticism against Facebook is wider, especially because it is not considered able to express in the best way oneself feelings. Indeed, Facebook is considered a too "public" place of "exhibition", rather than the more private Whatsapp. In particular, concerning grandchildren's pictures, grandmothers agree that Facebook can put at risk minor's privacy and be dangerous. Whatsapp is for this reason preferred because there is no danger that people who do not belonging to relative and friends web can see published pictures.

Grandmothers perceive they do not have control on the list of addressee and the audience of published images. Worries on Facebook are fomented by children and by social and medial speeches regarding this service but also by the negative behaviour children have against the medium that brings to limit and control grandchildren use of it. Facebook does not seem to be a "safe" environment to share personal material and feelings, because it is considered to be a public environment unlike Whatsapp, which is the communication medium "for the family" and in general dedicated to the private sphere, and which allows to share in a protected way grandchildren's pictures, through closed "family" groups:

> *Photos of children or some family situations I'm not used to sharing them with so many people,*
> *I'd just like to share them with them, with the family group that's been created on WhatsApp*
> *(76, FG2)*

Despite strongly criticising Facebook, a significant number of interviewed grandmothers has got a Facebook account and uses it. A wide part of grandmother's Facebook web is composed of relatives, children and grandchildren. Grandmothers strongly refuse to publish "intimate" and "familiar" contents, but they demonstrate to often use Facebook in a lurking way, to be updated on children and grandchildren lives, without interacting with them.

> *I see their photos there. My grandchildren, my daughter, publish a lot... I use it basically to see,*
> *I enjoy seeing what they do. For example, my grandson who was in the mountains and published*
> *the world cup skiing race that I liked... (81, FG2).*

It is interesting to notice that for some grandmothers, Facebook is a necessary window opened on the world of their own children, on their private and professional life, on their activities and their lives updates. From this point of view, Facebook is used as a tool to follow from "closer" children lives, who are often considered to be too busy to daily orally update parents on their lives (private or professional):

> *My son is involved in musical activities and so I use FB to get know about what he is doing. It's*
> *not that he does not want to tell me things but maybe he sometimes ignores me... (72, FG1)*

As a matter of principle, grandmothers strongly criticise when children or grandchildren publish intimate contents on Facebook, but in substance they consider those contents useful to "understand better" their own children and grandchildren. Being on Facebook is a way to comprehend grandchildren's character, to understand if they have worries, if they are happy or sad, it is a way to understand their feelings, through their status vision and their pictures on Facebook:

> *Sometimes it's a bit like reading the secret diary as we did once. Now you look at Facebook (70,*
> *FG2)*

According to some grandmothers, feeling the necessity to be "updated" through Facebook on movements, news of their grandchildren (who are considered to be way "further" than children) is a sign of incommunicability between grandparents and grandchildren or it is a sign of an asymmetrical relationship. Facebook use is for some grandmothers an attempt to keep in contact with grandchildren and to enter (glance?) their world, apart from real confronting and updating occasions, considered to be too little.

The advent of digital technologies brought positive aspects in our interviewed grandmothers' perception, both related to the possibility to keep in touch with their familiar web. However, negative elements emerge constantly connected to the use of the Internet and the difficulty and challenges brought by the use of these tools in familiar relationships. In some situations and contests, the presence of digital tools is a digital barrier to interpersonal relationships and an obstacle to the dialogue and interpersonal relationships with children and grandchildren, this facing a different netiquette, a different way to "being on the web" among grandmothers, children and grandchildren:

> *For example my daughter in the evening almost cannot talk because she is always at the phone, speaks, looks, reads... and she does not listen to me (70, FG2)*

In every situation and familiar and intimate contest, the invasive presence of smartphones is considered by our grandmothers an often insurmountable barrier, which is added to the difficulty to dialogue especially with their grandchildren, because they perceive to have little to share and say with them:

> *I have two grandsons and when I visit them at their houses, they are always using their smartphones and they don't participate to the conversation...We don't know anymore our grandsons (67, FG3)*

Regarding relationship with grandchildren, grandmothers often perceive to be secondary compared to the thick twist of conversation that guys have with their coetaneous or their parents. There is the impression that grandchildren call often, they send lots of text messages, they write, read and they engage with the smartphone but that they dedicate just a little percentage of the amount of time spent online to digital relationships with grandparents:

> *The grandchildren then use cell phones with their grandparents just to ask for something. When there is a need, then it is a continuous message (FG2)*

6   ICTs and Relationships Among Friends Belonging to the Same Generation

In the previous paragraph we described how interviewed grandmothers use digital services to build/maintain intimate relationships with their relatives alive, in particular with children. Our interviewed elderly ladies claimed not to be just grandmothers, but alive and active people regardless of their familiar relationship and their "grandmother" identity. Our elderly ladies wanted to underline that they have a thick and significant web of friends, and they have interests and hobbies. The ICTs are tools considered to be fundamental to manage their own web of friends, with the aim to keep in touch with their acquaintances. The ICTs are not just a useful tool to manage intimate and familiar sphere, but are always more useful tools to take elderly ladies' minds off, to spend time having fun, to support their free time, often spent with friends.

Comes out with perseverance from our interviewed ladies, that our grandmothers use intensively digital tools (Whatsapp firstly) to keep in touch with their web of friends. Often it is not a particularly extended web, but made up of a few, trusted people, with whom they shared decades of friendship and they find in digital tools a (new) efficient (and funny) channel of communication.

Some grandmothers underline how the intensity of communication with friends is superior than the one with relatives, both in terms of frequency and often in terms of value (fun, engagement) given by communication.

Interviewed grandmothers underline how communication technologies do not substitute "face-to-face" relationships and meetings in person, but they are integrated and they add a joking level relationship with friends, to continue between a meeting and the other. In particular, grandmothers underline how Whatsapp did not substitute personal relationships but it solidified them, multiplying occasions and ways to be in touch with friends, between an appointment and the other.

> But even with friends, it is not that personal relationships stop, we maybe send a video to laugh... then everything remains as it is, if we have a relationship we still prefer to see each other (71, FG1).

Not only: digital communication services allow to organise in a simpler way meetings and events. This favoured, in some grandmothers' perception, meeting moments with friends.

The most popular and used service with friends is Whatsapp, in particular through group organisation divided for "activities", to demonstrate the extreme activism of our interviewed elderly ladies. According to our grandmothers, Whatsapp has also the function to keep stable the bond with geographically "far" friendships that are kept "alive" during periods in which they do not see each other regularly. In particular, Whatsapp is necessary to keep in touch with friends they see during summer, during Christmas occasion and who live in their native cities or in resort places.

Among the positive Whatsapp elements there is the ability to offer space for a light humour, sometimes stupid, because it is able to fill grandmothers' daily life with happiness. Participants appreciate the playful element of this medium of communication between friends of the same generation, this can bring carefreeness and lightness but not only:

> They add something. They mostly add humour, we do so much more laughs... and a bit of affectivity (71, FG1)

The most important register in communication among people of the same generation is represented by the sense of humour, rather than feelings. If the use of Facebook for intimate and familiar relationship is generally criticised by our grandmothers (because of its public dimension and because of following dangers), several interviewed women underline the playful and recreational use of Facebook, in particular in relationships with friends:

> Even in the case of FB, everything depends by the way it is used. I like it, once a day I use it, just to do best wishes, to communicate with some friends, to post some photos if I go somewhere, to share with friends... it is also a way to communicate.. (66, FG1)

Regarding the role of Facebook to extend the personal social web, grandmothers show a strong scepticism about digital technologies and their ability to recover old lost friendships. Grandmothers show fatalism concerning the end of past relationships and they think Facebook just reactivates, in an artificial way, friendships and relationships ended many years before and that are still considered valid for some reasons.

Most of the time the recover of old friendships happens just at an online "conversation" level (Facebook chat in particular) or just accounts lurking of people they used to know. Therefore, there is a general diffidence to transform the "contact" recover in real new meetings:

I've found almost all my former students, they've written… and I like to see that one is married, the other has a son… their lives. It is not that we write, sometimes we see a picture… we wonder what they were doing. That's fine for me. (68, FG1)

Technologies are considered useful to reinforce still current but weak friendships. This is the case of colleagues, with whom there is still a current relation (in some cases grandmothers are in retirement since not many years) but that became weaker in the last few years, due to several familiar responsibilities (in particular grandchildren care):

I also have the group chat of ex-colleagues, but we also have lunch once a month. […] But this beautiful practice was born to meet us every month for about 3 years and WhatsApp was also able to resume contacts with someone who was lost and re-found thanks to the group (71, FG1)

According to some grandmothers Facebook has a positive role in recovering memories and relationships of past friendships. According to some other, not only is Facebook useless, but it risks to make worse, more complex, too thick and extended their social web, in a moment of life in which it is more important to pause on little and important personal relationships.

I find FB a waste of time. …between messages, comments and so on… you should spend all day. For me it really became just stressing. Parents of the pupils, then friends, acquaintances… I find it exaggerated. I finally decided to give up (71, FG1)

Nevertheless, grandmothers agree that a limit in the quantity of communication with friends is necessary: often the number of received messages is considered to be excessive, contents are recurring ("goodnight", "good morning") and elderly people live with inconvenience the impossibility to read every message or to answer to everyone. In these occasions, Whatsapp risks to pass from being a positive relational tool, to be a source of anxiety and strong criticism. If the number of received messages is considered excessive, it can be a symptom that who sends them is investing too much time in digital relationships, to the detriment of face-to-face ones:

They put a bit of sadness on me. In addition to being harassing, because of the thousands of useless messages, they make me sad because I think those who act like this, maybe he/she only too alone… (66, FG1)

7   Conclusions

Our study lead to new insights on the role of ICT on the everyday life of the grandmothers, especially regarding how intergenerational and intragenerational relations shape their process of uptake, learning and use of "new" media.

- What are the social contexts of ICT's use in the daily life of the grandmothers?

Interviewed grandmothers often characterised to be long-time digital users, with a past experience with computer, even though minimal and work related, from the late 90's. In line with the results of previous researches [30, 31], despite these past experiences, "new" digital technologies, as computers connected to the Internet and smartphones with data connection, seem to have entered our interviewed grandmothers' lives thanks to family pressure. This shift from a work related and child homework assistance computer use to a more entertainment, communication and relational centred use seems to characterize a second phase of their digitalization. Children – and also husbands in a residual way - have in some cases pushed grandmothers to use digital tools for safety reason and to control grandmothers' activities, for example, by qualifying grandmothers to send pictures while looking after grandchildren. The learning of these new technologies is immediately perceived as convenient, or even as a real social duty, for communicate efficiently within their family setting.

Grandmothers', however, often see technology as a "pray" escaping from the complete comprehension and complete control. Technology is sometimes considered dangerous, excessive and intrusive, able to "throw away" and ruin beautiful moments, as when the smartphone is intrusive and spoils face-to-face relationships, and to waste younger generations' time.

Elderly grandmothers are in general confident of their abilities to avoid those dangers, and they proudly affirm that their adult age, their experience with "complicated things in life", their wisdom and moderation, can keep them distant from risks and excesses of the digital communication.

- What are the role of ICT on grandmother's intergenerational and intragenerational relationships dynamics?

Several previous researches have underlined how processes of media literacy and appropriation are influenced by (positive) forms of intergenerational exchanges, especially in family contexts [15]. Our interviews show a more intricate scenario: although the trigger to start to use new digital technology comes from family and people belonging to different generations, the daily use of the ICTs reveals a complex relationship with children and grandchildren regarding technological issues, which often characterized by incompatible netiquette, different competences and lack of learning assistance. For this reason, elderly people seems to favour formal and structured ICT courses directed to them rather than the informal and not organized assistance provided by the younger relatives. This seems also to reinforce the development of some ICT uses linked the leisure dimension and to the relationship with friends.

Digital channels (Whatsapp in particular) become therefore not (only) *media* for communicate within the family boundaries but emancipatory tools, that allow to continuously nurture, reinforce and warm up long-standing friendships in a simpler and faster way and, for this reason, more compatible with the busy lives of some active grandmothers. Our interviewed grandmothers have demonstrated both an intense social activity, and the use of ICT as a backdrop where they articulate fun interactions and collective moments with friends.

Therefore, our research confirm how communication technologies can promote relationships between family members belonging to different generations and offer occasions to show (in a more or less clear way) love and intimacy. But in our research it's also clear how elderly consider digital services more and more important in offering a playful, light, leisure and entertaining environment where they can build satisfying friendships with people belonging to the same generation and with the same way to "being on the Internet".

8   Limitations and Future Works

The amount and features of our focus group participants exclude any possibility of generalization of our results. The interviewed grandmothers represent a not common profile of Italian elderly. They are middle and middle-upper class, involved in the associative context of one of the richest Italian city (Milan): our grandmothers are a wealthy and active niche of the Italian elderly population. As more elderly are going online and widening their online interactions, further research should be needed to understand how older people use digital technologies to communicate with peers and to point out the differences between elderly digital use for intra and intergenerational communication. Further researches should also explore the differences between uses in elderly with different social and cultural backgrounds.

References

1. United Nations, Department of Economic and Social Affairs, Population Division: World Population Ageing 2015 (2015)
2. Eurostat: People in the EU: who are we and how do we live? Eurostat Statistical Books (2015)
3. Warschauer, M.: Technology and Social Inclusion Rethinking the Digital Divide. The MIT Press, Massachusetts (2004)
4. DiMaggio, P., Hargittai, E.: From the 'digital divide' to 'digital inequality': Studying internet use as penetration increases. In: Princeton University Center for Arts and Cultural Policy Studies, Working Paper Series, no. 15 (2001)
5. Witte, J.C., Mannon, S.E.: The Internet and Social Inequalities. Routledge, New York (2010)
6. Norris, P.: Digital Divide: Civic Engagement, Information Poverty, and the Internet Worldwide. Cambridge University Press, New York (2001)
7. Madden, M.: Older adults and social media. Pew Internet & American Life Project (2010)
8. Prensky, M.: Digital natives, digital immigrants part 1. Horizon 9(5), 1–6 (2001)
9. Loos, E.: Senior citizens: digital immigrants in their own country? Observatorio (OBS*) 6(1), 1–23 (2012)
10. Colombo, F.: Aging, Media, and Communication. In: Nussbaum, J.F. (ed.) Communication Across the Lifespan, pp. 107–123. Peter Lang, New York (2016)
11. Loos, E., Haddon, L., Mante-Meijer, E.: Generational Use of New Media. Ashgate Publishing Ltd., Farnham (2012)
12. Van Deursen, A.J., Helsper, E.J.: A nuanced understanding of Internet use and non-use among the elderly. Eur. J. Commun. 30(2), 171–187 (2015)
13. Roberto, M.S., Fidalgo, A., Buckingham, D.: De que falamos quando falamos de infoexclusão e literacia digital? Perspetivas dos nativos digitais. Observatorio (OBS*) 9(1), 43–54 (2015)
14. Helsper, E.J., Reisdorf, B.C.: The emergence of a "digital underclass" in Great Britain and Sweden: changing reasons for digital exclusion. New Media Soc. 19(8), 1253–1270 (2016)
15. Colombo, F., Aroldi, P., Carlo, S.: New elders, old divides: ICTs, inequalities and well-being amongst young elderly Italians. Comunicar 23(45), 47–55 (2015)

16. Leikas, J., Saariluoma, P., Rousi, R. A., Kuisma, E., Hannu Vilpponen, H.: Life-based design to combat loneliness among older people. J. Commun. Inf. **8**(1) (2012)
17. Erickson, L.B.: Social media, social capital, and seniors: the impact of Facebook on bonding and bridging social capital of individuals over 65. In: AMCIS Proceedings, Paper 85 (2011)
18. Neves, B.B., Amaro, F., Fonseca, J.R.S.: Coming of (old) age in digital age: ICT usage and non-usage among older adults. Sociol. Res. Online **18**(2), 1–14 (2013). 6
19. Dias, I.: O uso das tecnologias digitais entre os seniores, Motivações e interesses. Sociologia, Problemas e Práticas **68**, 51–77 (2012)
20. Espanha, R.: Saúde e Comunicação numa Sociedade em Rede – o caso Português. Monitor, Lisboa (2009)
21. Morris, A., Goodman, J., Branding, H.: Internet use and non-use: views of older users. Univ. Access Inf. Soc. **6**(1), 43–57 (2007)
22. Selwyn, N., Gorard, S., Furlong, J.: The information aged: Older adult' use of information and communications technology in everyday life. School of Social Sciences, Cardiff University, Wales, Working Paper Series, paper 36 (2003)
23. Lugano, G., Peltonen, P.: Building intergerational bridges between digital natives and digital immigrants: attitudes, motivations and appreciation for old and new media. In: Loos, E., Haddon, L., Mante-Meijer, E. (eds.) Generational Use of New Media, pp. 151–170. Ashgate Publishing Ltd., Farnham (2012)
24. Eynon, R., Helsper, E.: Adults learning online: digital choice and/or digital exclusion? New Media Soc. **13**(4), 534–551 (2011)
25. Levy, B.R., Banaji, M.R.: Implicit ageism. In: Nelson, T.D. (ed.) Ageism: Stereotyping and Prejudice Against Older Persons, pp. 49–75. MIT Press, Cambridge (2002)
26. Gendron, T.L., Welleford, E.A., Inker, J., White, J.T.: The language of ageism: why we need to use words carefully. Gerontologist **56**(6), 997–1006 (2016)
27. Levy, B.R.: Eradication of ageism requires addressing the enemy within. Gerontologist **41**(5), 578–579 (2001)
28. Kania-Lundholm, M., Torres, S.: The divide within: older active ICT users position themselves against different 'others'. J. Aging Stud. **35**, 26–36 (2015)
29. Quinn, K., Smith-Ray, R., Boulter, K.: Concepts, terms, and mental models: everyday challenges to older adult social media adoption. In: Zhou, J., Salvendy, G. (eds.) ITAP 2016. LNCS, vol. 9755, pp. 227–238. Springer, Cham (2016). https://doi.org/10.1007/978-3-319-39949-2_22
30. Quan-Haase, A., Martin, K., Schreurs, K.: Interviews with digital seniors: ICT use in the context of everyday life. Inf. Commun. Soc. **19**(5), 691–707 (2016)
31. Sawchuk, K., Crow, B.: "I'm G-Mom on the phone" remote grandmothering, cell phones and inter-generational dis/connections. Feminist Media Stud. **12**(4), 496–505 (2012)
32. Haddon, L.: Explaining ICT consumption: the case of the home computer. In: Hirsch, E., Silverstone, R. (eds.) Consuming Technologies: Media and Information in Domestic Spaces, pp. 82–96. Routledge, London (1992)
33. Ivan, L., Hebblethwaite, S.: Grannies on the net: grandmothers' experiences of Facebook in family communication. Revista Română de Comunicare şi Relaţii Publice. **18**(1), 11–25 (2016)
34. Colombo, F., Aroldi, P., Carlo, S.: "Stay tuned": the role of ICTs in elderly life. In: Riva, G., Ajamone, M.P., Grassi, C. (eds.) Active Ageing and Healthy Living: A Human Centered Approach in Research and Innovation as Source of Quality of Life. IOS Press, Amsterdam (2014)
35. Cosley, D., Sosik, V.S., Schultz, J., Peesapati, S.T., Lee, S.: Experiences with designing tools for everyday reminiscing. Hum. Comput. Interact. **27**(1–2), 175–198 (2012)

36. Forghani, A., Venolia, G., Inkpen, K.: Media2Gether: sharing media during a call. In: Proceedings of the 18th International Conference on Supporting Group Work, pp. 142–151, November 2014. ACM
37. Carlo, S., Vergani, M.: Risk and benefit perceptions: resistance, adoption and uses of ICT among the Italian elderly. In: Zhou, J., Salvendy, G. (eds.) ITAP 2016. LNCS, vol. 9754, pp. 155–166. Springer, Cham (2016). https://doi.org/10.1007/978-3-319-39943-0_15

Design Empowerment for Older Adults

Yumei Dong and Hua Dong[✉]

Tongji University, Shanghai 200092, China
donghua@tongji.edu.cn

Abstract. Ageing is commonly considered as a serious social problem. Older adults are often regarded as the consumers of social welfare rather than creators and they are thought to be "incapable" and "worthless". This article advocated a strength-oriented or empowerment-oriented perspective. Based on different empowerment models, this paper proposed an influence and process model of empowerment. It provided a framework to map the strengths of "incapable" people (as traditionally believed) and barriers to empowering them, and a practical reference to take action for empowerment during which participation was emphasized. Cases of empowerment for older people was introduced and analyzed following the framework of the model by which we provided a reference of empowerment-oriented practice for researchers and practitioners.

Keywords: Design empowerment · Older adults · Participation · Strengths

1 Introduction

The ageing of populations is rapidly accelerating worldwide. For the first time in history, most people can expect to live into their 60s and beyond [1]. On the one hand, this shows the dramatic development of human society. On the other hand, it also brings new challenges. From a stereotype viewpoint, ageing is often considered as a serious social problem. Older adults are regarded as the consumers of social welfare rather than creators and they are thought to be "incapable" or "worthless" [2, 3]. The public always neglects older adults' diverse capabilities and their positive impacts on the society. Consequently, the government and families tend to hold a negative view when dealing with the age-related issues, which seriously hampers the functioning and self-actualization of older adults and makes them a burden to both the government and their families [4, 5].

However, a report by WHO provides evidence that age and physical decline are not linearly related, as traditionally believed [6]. Older people in fact are diverse in their capabilities. Some older people are equivalent to middle-age people in physical functioning [7]. With the right policies and services in place, population ageing can be viewed as a rich new opportunity for both individuals and societies. Therefore, there is a necessity to change the paradigm from problem-based to strength-based stance which encourages practice with a focus on individuals' potential and capacities rather than their limits [8, 9]. The strengths and empowerment perspective places emphasis on individuals' inner and environmental strengths and resources of people and their environment rather

© Springer International Publishing AG, part of Springer Nature 2018
J. Zhou and G. Salvendy (Eds.): ITAP 2018, LNCS 10926, pp. 465–477, 2018.
https://doi.org/10.1007/978-3-319-92034-4_35

than their problems and pathologies. From this perspective, the focus to work with older people is to help them maintain agency and create a supportive environment for them [10].

Empowerment theories have been applied to many disciplines such as management, social work, nursing and education. Many models are developed for empowerment research and practice. In recent years, researchers and practitioners in design discipline show a growing interest in this field. In the social background of ageing, the question of how design can help to empower older people calls for answers from both theoretical and practical perspective. Manzini proposed the concept of "enabling ecosystem" and suggested that design activities should focus on facilitating users and stakeholders and help people to solve their problems by their own rather than provide design solution for them directly [11]. However, how to facilitate, enable or empower people from a design perspective is unclear and the theory of design empowerment is lacking.

In this paper, we compared and analyzed different empowerment models and developed one for the design discipline. In order to demonstrate how this model can be applied in design, several cases of design empowerment for older people were analyzed using this model.

2   Empowerment Models

2.1   1-A Linear Empowerment Process Model

Conger and Kanungo developed an empowerment model in 1988 that focused on the process and action to empowering subordinates in the organization management context [12]. In order to differentiate it with the later empowerment process model by Cattaneo and Chapman [13], we refer to *The Linear Empowerment Process Model* based on its linear process.

This model divides empowerment in five stages that include the psychological state of empowering experience, its antecedent conditions, and its behavioral consequences. The five stages are shown in Fig. 1. The first stage is the diagnosis of conditions within the organization that are responsible for feelings of powerlessness among subordinates. This leads to the use of empowerment strategies by managers in Stage 2. The employment of these strategies is aimed not only at removing the external conditions responsible for powerlessness, but also (and more important) at providing subordinates with self-efficacy information in Stage 3. As a result of receiving such information, subordinates feel empowered in Stage 4, and the behavioral effects of empowerment are noticed in Stage 5.

This process can by roughly divided into 3 stages—diagnosis, intervention and results. In intervention stage, we can see both measures targeted on internal and external factors are taken. This process gives a detailed and practical guideline for organizational management based on identification of factors effecting empowerment.

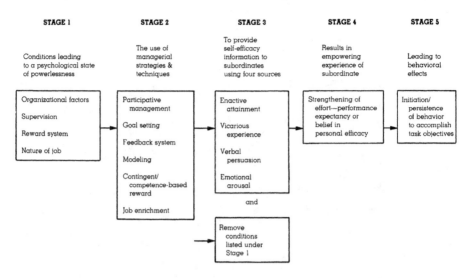

| STAGE 1 | STAGE 2 | STAGE 3 | STAGE 4 | STAGE 5 |

Fig. 1. The linear empowerment process model by Conger and Kanungo (1988)

2.2   The Contextual-Behavioral Empowerment Model

Fawcett and his colleague developed the contextual-behavioral model of empowerment in 1994 [14]. It includes three dimensions: the person or group, the environment, and the level of empowerment. It is assumed that the level of empowerment results from the interaction between personal (group) factors and environmental factors. The personal dimension represents the degree of personal or group's strength-from vulnerable to strong. People with physical disability or less knowledge and experience may be less empowered and vice versa. The environment factors including opportunity, discrimination, information access may facilitate or restrict the empowerment outcome and status. The surface of the model depicts the level of empowerment that will be effected by the dynamic interplay of personal and environmental factors (Fig. 2).

With this model, Fawcett and his colleague identified 4 main strategies encompassing 33 specific enabling activities, or concrete tactics for promoting community empowerment. Those strategies include enhancing experience and competence, enhancing group structure and capability, removing social and environmental barriers and enhancing environmental support and resources [15].

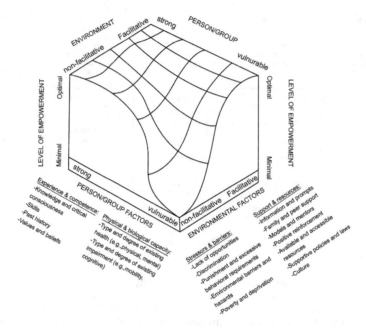

Fig. 2. The contextual-behavioral empowerment model by Fawcett and his colleague (1994)

2.3 The Social Work Model for Empowerment-Oriented Practice

The social work model for empowerment-oriented practice with older people was developed in 1994 by Coxs and Parsons and introduced to Japan in 1997 [16, 17]. This model

Table 1. A practice framework of empowerment-oriented practice with the elderly developed by Coxs and Parsons.

4 dimensions	Conceptualization of problems and focus of interventions		
D-1	Personal	Personal individual aspects	Individual needs, difficulties, values, and attitudes
D-2		Personal common aspects	Common problems; Personal strengths and weaknesses; The developing of social support
D-3	Interpersonal	Micro environmental and organizational aspects	Social, health, and economic services; Problems with service delivery; The developing of skills related to obtaining services, communicating with professionals, and participating in related advocacy and change activities
D-4	Political	Macro environmental aspects	Political, economic, and social factors and social policy

provides a framework containing both a theory base and a practice framework. The empowerment practice includes a 4-dimensional conceptualization of problems and focus of interventions from micro to macro aspects (Table 1).

The practical part of this model empathizes on understanding of the personal, interpersonal, and political aspects of at-risk population's situation and developing interpersonal support network. It stresses recognizing and working with the strengths and resource of clients including respect for diversity, which transfers the traditional problem-based paradigm to a strength-oriented paradigm. What is more, it encourages participation and a partnership in action [18].

2.4   The Iterative Empowerment Process Model

The iterative empowerment process model was built on the understanding that an increase in power is an increase in one's influence in social relations at any level of human interaction, from dyadic interactions to the interaction between a person and a system. Six components are identified, namely meaningful and powerful goal, self-efficacy, knowledge, competence, action and impact. The model defines empowerment as an iterative process in which a person who lacks power sets a personally meaningful goal oriented toward increasing power, takes action toward that goal, and observes and reflects on the impact of this action, drawing on his or her evolving self-efficacy, knowledge, and competence related to the goal. In this model, the author underlines the importance of social context. Social context influences all six components and the links among them.

As shown in Fig. 3, the process is not linear, and a person may cycle through components repeatedly with respect to particular goals and associated objectives. The successful outcome of the process of empowerment is a personally meaningful increase in power that a person obtains through his or her own efforts [13].

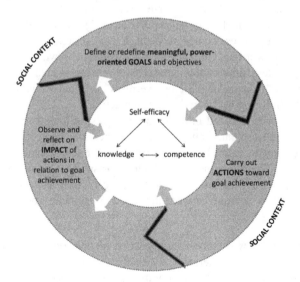

Fig. 3. The iterative empowerment process model by Cattaneo and Chapman (1988)

2.5 Comparison of These Models

The four models above provide rich information for empowerment. Comparing these models, we can see the different focus in the following three aspects.

Factors or Process. Some models lay emphasis on describing the influence factors of empowerment, while others pay more attention to provide a practical guideline step by step. For example, the contextual-behavioral empowerment model identified and clarified personal and environmental factors that affect the behaviors and outcomes associated with empowerment. Although it proposes many strategies for empowerment at the same time, most of them were based on certain factors that do not show a practical sequence. How to apply them in practice is unclear. In comparison to the factors model, Conger and Kanungo's linear empowerment process model and Cattaneo and Chapman's iterative empowerment process model provide the practical guideline step by step. By a clear process, the practitioners can take empowerment-oriented actions. However, without a comprehensive recognition of influence factors of empowerment, the action may not work.

Different Dimensions of Factor Categories. Different models divide influence factors in different way. The social work model for empowerment-oriented practice clarified the influence factors into 4 dimensions, which can be divided into 3 categories—personal, interpersonal, and political aspects. While in the contextual-behavioral empowerment model, the factors are divided into two categories, personal/group factors and environmental factors, even though the environmental categories can also include the political environmental factors. This model also discriminates the positive aspects (supports) and negative (stressors and barriers) aspects in its environmental factors, which shows a specific direction for action. For example, to deal with negative factors, the practitioners may try to restrict or remove them and verse vice.

Besides the 4 models which distinguish different categories by different criteria, Rich et al. examined different types of empowerment [19] and grouped them into 4 categories, namely "formal empowerment" (or societal empowerment, in which the larger political decision-making system allows some measure of meaningful local control), "intrapersonal empowerment", "instrumental empowerment" (via individual citizen participation) and "substantive empowerment" (via group action).

Different terms were utilized in order to distinguish different influence factors or dimensions of empowerment. Some terms described the categories from different perspectives and some terms include other terms in their scope, which makes the clarification ambiguous. We divide these terms into two aspects. One refers to the domain of empowerment, such as personal, intrapersonal, and environmental aspects. The other refers to the properties of empowerment that make a distinction between the positive and negative factors.

Linear or Iterative. In two empowerment process models, one presents the process in a linear form while the other is iterative. By the iterative empowerment process model, Cattaneo and Chapman argued that the components of the model influence each other in dynamic ways. In other words, the action of empowerment and reflection on impact after action will affect the initiative goals, thus start a new round of empowerment action. They cited Kieffer's idea to convince readers.

"The longer participants extend their involvement, the more they come to understand. The more they understand, the more motivated they are to continue to act. The more they continue to act, the more proactive they are able to be. The more proactive they are able to be, the more they further their skill and effect. The more they sense their skill and effect, the more likely they are to continue [20]".

Therefore Cattaneo and Chapman suggested take empowerment-oriented action in an iterative way. Since power is a rational construct, it is a relative concept rather than an absolute concept. We believe empowerment as a process has not a definite end.

3   An Influence Factors and Process Model of Empowerment

3.1   Introduction of the Model

Based on the review of the prior four models, a process model of empowerment based on the influence factors was developed. As shown in Fig. 4, this model described empowerment from both spatial and temporal dimensions.

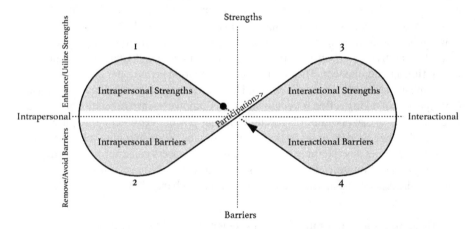

Fig. 4. A process model of empowerment based on the influence factors

From a spatial dimension, this model identifies the influence factors of empowerment, including both the **intrapersonal and interactional** aspects. Intrapersonal aspects refer to the factors influenced by individuals' internal condition such as knowledge and experience which may subsequently influence personal confidence and competence. Interactional aspects refer to the external factors including "person to person interaction" (interpersonal) and person to environment interaction (environmental, societal and political).

Additionally, distinguished from a problem-based paradigm to solve age-related issue, this model addresses the positive factors of older adults based on a strength-oriented paradigm and utilized **"strengths"** and **"barriers"** to replace "problems".

These two pairs of criterion–intrapersonal/interactional and strength/barriers divide the factors' space into 4 subspaces, namely intrapersonal strengths, intrapersonal barriers, interactional strengths and interactional barriers.

From a temporal dimension, this model presents an iterative empowerment process. In order to empathies the agency of vulnerable people, this process encourages practitioners to start from working on intrapersonal factors. From a strength-oriented principle, people's strength should be paid more attention in action. Therefore, an expected process of empowerment may start from enhancing intrapersonal strength and removing intrapersonal barriers to enhancing interactional strength and removing interactional barriers based on comprehensive identification of those factors. It should be noted that not all the steps must be addressed in practice, sometimes it only need to focus on one or two steps of them.

Participation is the key component of this model. Rappaport endorsed the Cornell Empowerment Group's definition of empowerment as involving respectful, caring and reflective participation in a community group in order to gain equal access to and control of resource [21]. Zimmerman considered participation in community organizations is one way to exercise a sense of competence and control. Participation in a variety of community organizations has reported an increase in activism and involvement, greater competence and control, and a decrease in alienation [22]. Maton and Salsem's paper also viewed empowerment in general terms as a process enabling individuals, through participation with others, to achieve their primary personal goal [23]. Based on the prior viewpoints on empowerment, participation is crucial for people to be empowered.

In the iterative empowerment process model, Cattaneo and Chapman adopted the term **action** as a component. They argue that participation is improper because it is only one of an almost limitless range of action. However, we think participation is precisely a specific way of taking action for empowerment. Empowerment as a relational construct describes a status that one controls resource and has power over others. It requires interaction with other people, organizations and resources. Someone may take actions by themselves without any interplay with others and this process can improve self-efficacy. Without participation, self-efficacy cannot transfer to social impact. However, empowerment addresses on social practice to promote social change [24].

3.2 Designing Participation as Empowerment

The above model illustrates the influence factors of empowerment and a generic process to empower people. How design can play an important role in this process? We consider participation as an essential aspect for empowerment-oriented design.

Reviewing empowerment in the design discipline, we find that empowerment related to participatory design frequently.

In the context of participatory design, users are encouraged to participate and exercise power in the design process. Correia and Yusop considered users' democratic participation and empowerment as the core aspects of the Participatory Design [25]. Ertner et al. had conducted a review on 39 papers from the PDC (Participatory Design Conference) proceedings of 2008 and found 21 papers in which an enunciation of empowerment was evident [26]. In order to empower users via design participation, many approaches and tools were utilized and suggested. Visualization was suggested as a mediator for user participation and empowerment in neighborhood design [27]. Narratives have the ability to create imaginary worlds for the public and increase their active participation in social life via enabling social dialogue [28, 29]. Olivia's research identified crafting activities as a way to allow older adults to participate in the design process [30].

Design outcomes can also be a mediator to encourage participation in empowerment-oriented design. Users can experience power by open-ended solution. Storni's research shared a project on self-care technology for diabetes in which a mobile journaling tool was developed to enable the personalization of self-monitoring practices [31]. With this product, people with diabetes can participate in tracking the effects of their actions, thus improving a sense of control. In this case, users' participation is an essential part of the solution. Therefore, the key of designing empowerment is designing participation. An open-ended and flexible solution may welcome participation with lower threshold and less restriction.

4   Cases of Design Empowerment for Older Adults

In this section, we illustrate four cases of design empowerment for older people.

A-Gingko house is a western restaurant with the value proposition of supporting senior employment enjoying life. In this restaurant, 90% of the employers are older people. Those people with rich life experience can amuse people when providing catering services for guests. Before joining the work, older people are required to attend repetitive training in order to overcome the problem of senior's bad memory. The working duration is adjusted to 4–5 h one day with the consideration of their physical ability. All the vegetable in Gingko House comes from an organic farm where most of the employers are also older people who has many years of farming experience. Staffs transporting vegetables from the farm to the restaurant are also retired drivers [32].

B-"The Innocent Big Knit" is a public welfare program for helping people to overcome their loneliness in later life. This program asked older people and younger people to knit little woolly hats. They then put those hats on the drinks of smoothies. For every behatted smoothie sold, Age UK will receive 25p to help fund vital national and local services that combat loneliness for older people, in particular keeping people warm and well in winter. The idea snowballed and so far the people of the UK have knitted an astonishing 6 million hats. Together they've raised over £2 million for Age UK [33].

C-"Hosting a Student" is a co-housing program between independent elderly people and university students from outside Milan. Its initiative is based on a very simple idea: find lodging for students in the homes of elderly people who have a spare room. The young people do not pay rent as such, but contribute to the expenses of house-sharing by paying a monthly sum of about € 250–280, as well as performing practical tasks and providing company for the elderly person who, in addition to suffering less from loneliness, can enjoy the satisfaction of still feeling useful. Since 2004 over 650 house-sharing agreements have been established of which only eight were discontinued due to incompatibility [11, 34].

D-AARP Foundation Experience Corps is an intergenerational volunteer-based tutoring program to provide both older adults and children with opportunities to enrich their lives through literacy. This program inspires and empowers adults aged 50 and above to help students who have difficulties in reading in primary schools. Volunteers provide an average of 6–15 h of support each week throughout the school year. After one year, many students who work with Experience Corps volunteer tutors achieve as much as 60% improvement in critical literacy skills compared to their peers [35].

4.1   Mapping the Influence Factors to the Model

The above 4 cases identified different strengths and barriers of older people. Many activities in these cases are based on these strengths and barriers. We mapped them in the framework of the above model (see Fig. 5).

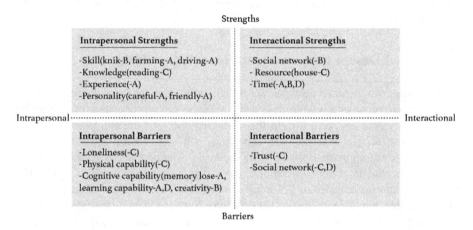

Fig. 5. Strengths and barriers mapping

How to enhance or utilize the intrapersonal strengths and remove or avoid the intra-personal barriers are evident in the case of "Gingko House". For example, people who are employed by this restaurant are equipped with many skills such as farming and driving. Farming can be identified as a special strength of older people since farming is gradually lost in the rapid process of urbanization and the youth have few chances to learn it. These skills are identified and facilitated to produce value while matching to suitable work. Additionally, it is reported that guests speak highly of the senior waiters because of their rich experience since they might understand guests' unique need better. What is more, some intrapersonal barriers of older people are also identified. With consideration of their memory loss and physical power limitation, the restaurant provided repetitive training and adapted staff time rota to a shorter duration.

In the case of "Hosting a Student", most efforts are made based on identification of interactional factors of senior people. In Italy and many other countries, some older people often have a house with spare rooms. Meanwhile, they live alone in town and need help in everyday activities. The "Hosting a Student" program utilized their resource and bridge them with the needs of students who can not afford a relatively higher house rent but have spare time to company the elderly. However, the difficulty to enhance mutual trust between the older people and students is evident. In this case, The association Meglio Milano carried out a careful cross-analysis – of their psychological profiles – in order to match people who will be able to live their everyday lives together in the best possible way, and afterwards also provides support to avoid and solve tensions and misunderstandings [36].

4.2 Designing Participation

All of the four cases place great emphasis on designing participation. For example, "The Innocent Big Knit" provided many approaches calling for participation both online and offline. In order to lower the barrier of participation, many patterns of woolly hats were post on the website for beginners to easily find a pattern which is proper for their level. Video tutorials are also shown in website. In order to attract more expert participants, the organizers launched annually competition which allows participants to vote for their favorite hats. The winner hats will be promoted in Facebook. Offline activities included knitting together in senior house and at home. The website reported a story that an old mother teach her two daughters knitting hats at home. This report shows a Parent-Child Interaction scenario which attract much attention of participants.

"AARP Foundation Experience Corps" also provided diverse activities for participation. The organizers arranged a 30-hour training course for the senior volunteers during which they can build new social network and form mutual support group in 7–10 members. Each group will enter a primary school to help the young students in reading. Volunteers were encouraged to participate in regular meetings which allow them to make planning, discussion and socialize together. Those social participation activities proved to be beneficial for enhancing their physical and cognitive capabilities.

5   Conclusion

The shift from a problem-based paradigm to an empowerment-oriented paradigm shows a positive transformation to view population ageing. In the background of ageing society, the benefits of empowerment-oriented paradigm is widely accepted by many researchers and practitioners in many fields such as phycology, social work, and organization management. Many practices around the world also show the advantages for both senior individuals and the society. However, when this concept was introduced to the design discipline, it is important to think about how design can play a unique role for empowerment.

This paper proposed a design empowerment model which provides a framework to identify and map the influence factors of empowerment. This framework also gives a step-by-step guideline for practitioners to take action. More importantly, we argue participation as a key component in the process of empowerment since it bridges the action on the internal (intrapersonal) aspect with the external (interactional) aspect. We also argue that the key of designing empowerment is designing participation. The four cases provide a reference for empowerment for older people in practice. By these cases, we identified specific strengths and barriers and show the strategies to design for participation such as lowering the barriers to participation, attracting diverse participants in different capability levels and building networks between participants.

However, we have not provided a comprehensive list of strengths and barriers in the model. A survey will be conducted among older adults in the future to identify more strengths and barriers.

References

1. Dey, A.B.: World report on ageing and health. Indian J. Med. Res. **145**(1), 150–151 (2017)
2. Guo, A.: Old-age social security research from a multi-discipline perspective. Sun yat-sen University Press, Guangzhou (2011)
3. Prince, M.J.: Apocalyptic, opportunistic, and realistic discourse: retirement income and social policy or Chicken Littles, Nest-Eggies, and Humpty Dumpties. In: Ellen, M.G., Gloria, M.G. (eds.) The Overselling of Population: Apocalyptic Demography, Intergenerational Challenges, and Social Policy. Oxford University Press, Toronto (2000)
4. Gao, S.: Financial burden of population aging and countermeasures. Local Finance Res. **1**, 75–77 (2011)
5. Wu, P.: The dilemma and solution of one-child family in China Rural in the trend of the aging of population. Soc. Work **9**, 87–89 (2012)
6. WHO: World report on ageing and health (2016)
7. Peeters, G., Dobson, A.J., Deeg, D.J., et al.: A life-course perspective on physical functioning in women. Bull. World Health Organ. **91**(9), 661–670 (2013)
8. Cox, E.O.: Empowerment-oriented practice applied to long-term care. J. Soc. Work Long-Term Care **1**(2), 27–46 (2001)
9. Moyle, W., Parker, D., Bramble, M.: Care of Older Adults: A Strengths-Based Approach. Cambridge University Press, UK (2016)
10. Chapin, R., Cox, E.O.: Changing the paradigm: strengths-based and empowerment-oriented social work with frail elders. J. Gerontol. Soc. Work **36**(3), 165–179 (2001)
11. Manzini, E.: Design, When Everybody Designs: An Introduction to Design for Social Innovation. The MIT Press, US (2015)
12. Conger, J.A., Kanungo, R.N.: The empowerment process: integrating theory and practice. Acad. Manag. Rev. **13**(3), 471–482 (1988)
13. Cattaneo, L.B., Chapman, A.R.: The process of empowerment: a model for use in research and practice. Am. Psychol. **65**(7), 646–659 (2010)
14. Fawcett, S.B., White, G.W., Balcazar, F.E., et al.: A contextual-behavioral model of empowerment: case studies involving people with physical disabilities. Am. J. Community Psychol. **22**(4), 471–496 (1994)
15. Perkins, D.D., Zimmerman, M.A.: Empowerment theory, research, and application. Am. J. Community Psychol. **23**(5), 569–579 (1995)
16. Cox, E.O., Parsons, R.J.: Empowerment Oriented Social Work Practice with the Elderly. Books/Cole Pub. Co., Pacific Grove (1994)
17. Inaba, M.: Aging and elder care in Japan: a call for empowerment-oriented community development. J. Gerontol. Soc. Work **59**(7–8), 587–603 (2016)
18. Gutierrez, L.M.E., Parsons, R.J.E., Cox, E.O.E.: Empowerment in Social Work Practice. A Sourcebook. Empowerment in social work practice. Brooks/Cole Pub. Co., Pacific Grove (1998)

19. Rich, R.C., Edelstein, M., Hallman, W.K., et al.: Citizen participation and empowerment: the case of local environmental hazards. Am. J. Community Psychol. **23**(5), 657–676 (1995)
20. Kieffer, C.H.: Citizen empowerment: a developmental perspective. Prev. Hum. Serv. **3**(2), 9–36 (1984). https://doi.org/10.1300/J293v03n02_03
21. Rappaport, J.: Empowerment meets narrative: listening to stories and creating settings. Am. J. Community Psychol. **23**(5), 795–807 (1995)
22. Zimmerman, M.A.: Empowerment theory. In: Rappaport, J., Seidman, E. (eds.) Handbook of Community Psychology, pp. 43–63. Springer, Boston (2000). https://doi.org/10.1007/978-1-4615-4193-6_2
23. Maton, K.I., Salem, D.A.: Organizational characteristics of empowering community settings: a multiple case study approach. Am. J. Community Psychol. **23**(5), 631–656 (1995)
24. Freire, P., Moch, M.: A critical understanding of social work. J. Prog. Hum. Serv. **20**(1), 92–97 (2009)
25. Correia, A.P., Yusop, F.D.: "I don't want to be empowered": the challenge of involving real-world clients in instructional design experiences. In: Tenth Anniversary Conference on Participatory Design, pp. 214–216. Indiana University (2008)
26. Ertner, M., Kragelund, A. M., Malmborg, L.: Five enunciations of empowerment in participatory design. In: Conference on Participatory Design, PDC 2010, pp. 191–194. DBLP, Sydney (2010)
27. Senbel, M., Church, S.P.: Design empowerment the limits of accessible visualization media in neighborhood densification. J. Plann. Educ. Res. **31**(4), 423–437 (2011)
28. Anzoise, V., Piredda, F., Venditti, S.: Design Narratives and Social Narratives for Community Empowerment. In: STS Italia Conference. A Matter of Design: Making Society Through Science and Technology, Italy, pp. 935–950 (2014)
29. Prost, S., Mattheiss, E., Tscheligi, M.: From awareness to empowerment: using design fiction to explore paths towards a sustainable energy future. In: ACM Conference on Computer Supported Cooperative Work & Social Computing, pp. 1649–1658. ACM, New York (2015)
30. Olivia, K.R.: Exploring the empowerment of older adult creative groups using maker technology. In: CHI Conference Extended Abstracts on Human Factors in Computing Systems 2017, pp. 166–171. ACM, New York (2017)
31. Storni, C.: Design challenges for ubiquitous and personal computing in chronic disease care and patient empowerment: a case study rethinking diabetes self-monitoring. Pers. Ubiquit. Comput. **18**(5), 1277–1290 (2014)
32. Gingko House Homepage. http://www.restaurant.org.hk. Accessed 9 Jan 2018
33. The big knit Homepage. http://www.thebigknit.co.uk/about. Accessed 9 Jan 2018
34. MeglioMilano project page. http://www.meglio.milano.it/en/progetti/prendi-in-casa/. Accessed 9 Jan 2018
35. AARP Homepage. https://www.aarp.org/experience-corps/. Accessed 9 Jan 2018
36. Cipolla, C.: Relational services and conviviality. In: Satu Miettinen (Org.). Designing Services with Innovative Methods. 1 edn., pp. 232–243. TAIK Publications/University of Art and Design Helsinki, Helsinki (2009)

The Role of New Media in Communicating and Shaping Older Adult Stories

Simone Hausknecht[✉]

Simon Fraser University, Burnaby, Canada
shauskne@sfu.ca

Abstract. Older adults are finding new ways to communicate their stories and one way is through digital storytelling. This study examined a selection of ten older adults' digital stories to explore how they used multimedia in their stories. It was found that older adults use media in different ways to express their life narratives. The stories either followed the narration across a lifespan or centered around a single event. Stories often brought the topic into a reflection on life as a whole. Images were used to display historical pictures of people and places, or they were used in more implicit expressions such as visual metaphors. A further examination of a reflective journal of one individual's process in creating the digital story, and the multimedia choices used, was also examined. The visual and aural choices made by the participant suggest that they were made to enhance the story; however, the media appeared to simultaneously shape the participant's understanding of their story. The act of putting images and sound together with a life narrative can serve not only to enhance the story, but to shape its telling and the storyteller's understanding.

Keywords: Digital storytelling · Older adults · Multimedia · Lifelong learning
Reflection

1 Introduction

Storytelling is a crucial part of our lives. It has a long history of playing an important role in how we learn, communicate, and perceive our life [1]. Each event we experience could be segmented into a small story within the larger story of who we are. These life stories help to form our identity and allow us to make meaning of the world and our place within it [2]. Older adults may benefit from reflecting upon life and sharing these stories; for example, sharing stories may increase self-awareness [3]. Sharing a life narrative serves as an opportunity to reflect upon an experience, and the telling of the experience may reshape the memory and the meaning of the events [4].

Within a technological society, there are many possibilities for expressing life stories with new media. Multimedia can be used and can play a role in how storytellers convey themselves. The advantages of using multimedia for storytelling range from having a digital platform to share stories easily, to layering with different artistic expressions that create diverse moods and meaning [5]. New media also provides an opportunity to share

© Springer International Publishing AG, part of Springer Nature 2018
J. Zhou and G. Salvendy (Eds.): ITAP 2018, LNCS 10926, pp. 478–491, 2018.
https://doi.org/10.1007/978-3-319-92034-4_36

stories with a larger audience [6]. Furthermore, information shared through an audio-visual approach can be more effective then text based [7].

Older adults are increasingly using technology in communication, including telling snippets of life story through social media and other platforms. Recently, the Pew Research Center [8] reported that 34% of seniors use social media in the United States, including such platforms as Facebook, Twitter, and Instagram. Furthermore, younger seniors, particularly those that are more affluent and highly educated, have similar rates of technology ownership and use to those under 65. However, there is still a significant digital divide for those seniors not within this category. Using new media as a form of communication and expressing their story could be important to allowing older adults' stories to be heard, and it may help to facilitate intergenerational connections [9]. Further, a multimedia approach may allow for diversity and depth of narrative expression.

One form of new media story that has risen in popularity is digital storytelling. Digital storytelling is a layering of visuals, narrative, and sound that are combined in a digital platform and presented as a short film [10]. The current project examines ten older adults' digital stories created during an 8–10-week course. It aims to explore the different approaches older adults take to layering images, sound, and narrative. This paper also examines one participant's reflective journal during the course to explore the process of choosing and reflecting on multimedia choices.

1.1 Narrative Knowing

Various researchers and theorists have explored the role of narrative in our lives and its role in shaping understanding and identity (e.g. 1, 2, 11). For example, Bruner [11] takes a distributed intelligence perspective on knowledge arguing that "cultural products, like language and other symbolic systems, mediate thought and place their stamp on our representations of reality". Our experiences, and the meaning we form from them, are often organized into a narrative structure [11]. Bruner [11] outlines a series of features present in the narrative construction of reality.

1. *Narrative diachronicity*: Narrative events occur over time. However, this sense of time is characterized by the significance of the event and how the storyteller decides to frame it.
2. *Particularity*: Narrative includes a particular event; however, the particulars also may have some generic aspects.
3. *Intentional state entailment*: Characters within a narrative have specific intentions (beliefs, values, desires, etc....) that they act with within a specific environment.
4. *Hermeneutic composability*: Narratives are constructed from a series of events that are interpreted as a story with meaning.
5. *Canonicity and breach*: A story usually requires a breach of the normal set of events; thus, something interesting should happen.
6. *Referentiality*: Narratives are only a representation of a reality; they are narrative "truth". Therefore, they don't need to be exactly true, but they must appear believable.

7. *Genericness*: Narratives can be classified into a genre to guide our understanding of human difficulties.
8. *Normativeness*: Stories, although they deal with a breach of the norm, are essentially about social norms.
9. *Context sensitivity and negotiability*: Narratives that are told undergo a negotiation between the readers perspective and background knowledge and the storyteller's version. This partially happens through an understanding that the story is context dependent and the reader agrees to suspend disbelief.
10. *Narrative accrual*: Narratives are cumulative, one leads to another. In the case of life narratives, the life story does not consist of a single event but is gathered from many stories.

1.2   Multimedia Storytelling

The way in which we share and understand story is constantly changing within a world that is driven by new media. Throughout history, storytelling has been multimodal in its expression [12]. However, storytelling no longer only occurs while sitting around the fire using our body and expression to portray meaning, but it also occurs over and with technology. Multimedia is not new as a tool for storytelling, but with each generation and with each expansion of technology new ways of communicating life narratives arise. For example, with the invention of slides came the social activity of the slide show, where individuals would invite guests over and go through a series of photographs. These could be related to holidays or other events; thus, the slide presenter would tell a story using the images as a guide.

While including images in storytelling can be seen in slide shows, picture books, and photo albums, today's new media communication is increasingly including photos in social media storytelling, such as Instagram and Snapchat [13]. At the present time, much of this activity takes place online through social media and other sites. Users will often post photos, with brief descriptions of meaning or events. Yet, social media as a way to publicize a personal story has met some resistance by older adults [14]. In a study by Xie et al. [14], they found the main barriers were related to privacy issues; however, these attitudes changed with a course designed around social media use.

Music has also been used as a vehicle to tell a story. Many of the structures seen within musical compositions can be considered comparable to those within a plot structure of a story [15]. Within the romantic era, composers would often have a story to be read or imagined that accompanied the musical score, creating a story with an emphasis on sound. With new media, music within narrative presentations (such as film and video games) often contributes to a large proportion of how we experience music today [16]. It is often a distinct part of the understanding of new media storytelling.

Using new media to combine images, sound, and narrative into expressions of life narratives expand many of the creative and communicative options for older adults. Creating stories with new media gives older adults a voice and allows them to be content producers, sharing their understanding of the world to multiple audiences [6]. The different multimedia pieces bring with them different representations of and for reality and knowledge [17]. Thus, choosing the visual representations of story and the musical accompaniment requires a consideration of what the storyteller wants to highlight. In a study by Subramaniam and Woods [18] that used digital stories to engage six older adults with dementia, it found that the multimedia layer, particularly music, was very important to sharing their life narratives. Furthermore, a study by Hausknecht et al. [19] found that older adults also increased digital literacy skills through the act of telling their stories on a multimedia platform. In a further analysis of focus group interviews, they found that older adults gained valuable depth in story expression through including the multimedia layer [20]. A multimedia approach to storytelling may provide older adults with opportunities to explore meaning and re-imagine life narratives.

1.3   Research Questions

1. In what ways do older adults incorporate multimedia into digital stories?
2. What is the process involved in choosing multimedia components?

2   Method

Over a two-year period (2014–2016), multiple offerings of an 8–10-week digital storytelling course for older adults were implemented. A selection of ten older adult digital stories were chosen from different groups who attended one of the offerings. The stories were analyzed for specific content and examined how older adults used multimedia elements in the creation of their stories. In the second part of the analysis, one story was chosen to examine in depth. The analysis of this story examined a reflective journal that was kept during each week to develop a more thorough understanding of the storyteller's process in choosing different multimedia to represent their story.

2.1   Participants

The participants (N = 10) were chosen from a range of participants from different iterations of the digital storytelling courses. The researcher selected ten representative digital stories to analyze, examining choice of story and multimedia aspects. Story selection was based on choosing from a range of age groups (all participants selected were from ages 55–95), with a sample from each decade and from different courses. Over half of the participants in our study were immigrants and most were female. One participant was chosen who had completed a detailed reflection journal of their process. This in-depth example of the process of choosing media was from a female immigrant in her 70s.

2.2   Summary of Course

Each offering of the course was an 8–10-week digital storytelling program for older adults and was offered through centers, care homes, and libraries across Metro Vancouver. The design of the course used principals from creative writing, film, and suggestions from the Digital Storytelling Cookbook [10]. The course consisted of two phases, the first being focused around writing story and the second focused on the digital aspects and creating a digital artifact. The theory behind the design was to give learners an understanding of, and practice in, creating a solid story they are happy with, that can be shared and explored within a group setting before participants were in front of a computer adding the digital aspects [19]. This was important to the social and emotional benefits that a shared story experience might have [19]. However, within the first half of the course, participants were shown various digital stories and given information on choosing imagery and music. They were then required to create a storyboard, so although they were not necessarily on the computers initially, they were encouraged to continually consider their story in terms of its multimedia representation (For details on the course see [19, 21]).

2.3   Analysis

The ten stories chosen were analyzed for story topic, temporality of story content, visual and aural choices. Bruner's framework [11], outlined earlier, was also considered in the analysis; specifically, regarding *narrative diachronicity* (also called temporality here*), particularity and genericness* (genre and content), *canonicity and breach* (adversity/conflict), *hermeneutic composability* and, *intentional state entailment*. This analysis was done through watching each of the stories and making notes on these aspects. For the analysis of the process of the one story, the reflective journal was used to understand the process of choosing different multimedia aspects. The findings in the journal were scrutinized with the digital story to form a better understanding.

3   Results

Stories ranged from three to eight minutes in length. Each story was a fully developed piece that used photos and some form of sound.

3.1   Story Analysis

Temporality and Content of Digital Stories. The ten stories were examined for their temporality, whether the narrative expanded over a lifetime, a specific time (e.g., childhood) or a single event (Table 1). As Bruner [11] points out, narrative diachronicity can be very different from our sense of time; however, the events are understood as how they relate over a point in time. The current set of stories are written by older adults; and thus, they had extensive options for the time of life they wanted to focus on. Stories that took place across a persons' life tended to have a specific theme that tied the stories together; for example, a love of dance, a pen, a person (grandparent), or a place. Within these stories, the older adult storytellers often started with a comment on childhood, and then continued through to adulthood, and concluded with thoughts of their current selves. However, the common theme tied each of these moments together over the narrative timeline.

Table 1. Story topic and temporality

Category	Topic	#	Example items
Adversity in story	Family	1	Challenging family relationships
	Health	2	Overcoming health issues or looking after someone else who has a health problem.
	Gender	3	Being a female widow and needing to challenge roles (women as a coach, as a worker)
	Race	3	Struggles of immigrant minority as a child
	Fear	1	Fear of robber and physical harm
Story across time	Main event	4	Baseball game, Robbery, Fixing a boat over summer, piano recital
	Across specific time	3	The effect a childhood place had on life as adult, growing up in China town and an influential person, living with a family as a student
	Across time	3	Dance as a constant passion from childhood to adulthood and how it helped overcome health issues
			A pen given in childhood and its significance across time, memories and reflection on grandmother

Where the individual told a specific story about an event, it often focused on a point in their adult life where there was a breach in the normal set of events and something exciting was happening; for example, a baseball game where the other team attempted to cheat, struggling to fix up a boat after a husband's death, and a robbery. However, even if the focus was on a single event, the storyteller included a reflection about the story's current meaning to their life. Interestingly, in our sample, the oldest participants chose this form of narrative.

Story Type. Narratives incorporate both genericness and particularity [11]. Within "The Digital Storytelling Cookbook", Lambert [10] discusses the genericness of personal stories that digital storytellers often tell, such as a story about someone important (character stories, memorial stories), a story about events (adventure story, accomplishment story), a story about a place, a story about what a person does (recovery story, love story) and a story about discovery. However, when analyzing the ten stories within the study, they rarely fit in one category alone.

The stories all displayed a breach to normal events and often incorporated overcoming some form of adversity or challenge (Table 1). When the stories were about other people they often discussed the challenges that those individuals overcame. Most of the stories focused on, or in the very least touched upon, moments of hardship encountered and how these were overcome. The challenge of such aspects as race and gender were often seen within the stories of the past. Only one of the ten stories focused on a humorous event that did not highlight overcoming adversity; however, it had a clear rising action and tension and breach of normal events (in a humorous way).

All stories had intentional state entailment [11], in that the intentions of characters were clearly displayed regardless of their role. Most stories incorporated people in their lives who are important. However, the extent that this was done depended upon the story events and topic. It also depended on how important the people were to the meaning of the story. Thus, in cases where the story was what Lambert [10] might call "a story about someone important" there was a heavy focus on the person and the meaning the person brought to the storyteller's life. For example, in one story told by a man who immigrated to Canada as a child, the story was based around a prominent figure in the community that he admired.

In instances where the storyteller was the main character, the emphasis was less on the person or people and more on their value to the story of self. For example, in one story a woman discusses her love of dance and struggles with health, yet an older women's dancing group (and those within it) are important to her recovery. Within another story, the antagonist of the story who bet the woman she couldn't fix her boat became the motivation for her doing so. The focus was on the accomplishment of the storyteller; however, the accomplishment was not possible without the challenge or support of the other person.

3.2   Imagery and Sound as Media

The ten stories were examined for the storyteller's choice of photos. Some of the decisions on photo choice were dependent on whether the participants had personal photos available or whether they had to find or create these. Within the courses, there is a day designated to discussing, and giving examples, of implicit and explicit information through photo choice. For example, when narrating about a person, did the person use a picture of that person (explicit representation); thus, the photo was a literal representation of what the person narrated. On the other hand, if they used implicit imagery, the participants used images to represent something other than the literal meaning of what they were saying within the narration; for example, an image of a dark cloud to represent a feeling of depression.

All participants used images such as photos of their family, places, objects and childhood memories that they were discussing. This type of imagery was the most common imagery used. These photos often enhanced the impression of time and the history of the people within them or provided a visual of the noun they were discussing. All participants had at least one photo of themselves during the time period described. There was one participant who used photos that were almost all explicit to the story. Where participants did not have a photo, they sometimes drew a picture; for example, one participant drew a map and took a photo of this to show where they were talking about.

Most of the older adults combined both styles of visual representation. Thus, they layered the narratives with photos of family, places, and objects that were mentioned in the story, but also used symbolic photos to represent different emotions and moods, such as a tree when discussing growth. Occasionally participants used videos or moving images within the story, but this was less common. Digital storytellers were taught a number of editing techniques. All of the participants used the zoom in and zoom out feature on at least one photo. This may be due to the ease of creating this effect or that it was taught early on.

Sound as a Medium. Music was used in most stories; however, the amount it was featured varied (Table 2). In some designs there was only a single song that was featured, giving the story a sense of consistency whereas in other stories there were music shifts. Most of the musical shifts coincided with a change in the mood of the story; for example, an upbeat song was used when a person had a life breakthrough. Occasionally, music was used as a part of the narrative; for example, in a story about a piano recital, a variety of piano compositions were used throughout the narrative, yet when the storyteller mentions twinkle little star then the music turns to twinkle little star. Where storytellers used varied music throughout, they seemed to use moments of silence to emphasize serious points within the story. One storyteller didn't use music but included sound effects.

Table 2. Visuals and sound used

Category	Number	Example items
Imagery, photos, visuals	All	
– Explicit	10	Photos of people, houses, places
– Implicit	9	Photos that act as visual metaphors such as a dark cloud for depression
Videos	3	Video of dancing and water twirling, lights, bike
Music, sound	All	
– No music	1	
– Music (single song)	2	One song or theme creating consistent mood
– Music (varied)	8	Music varies throughout, creating varying moods
– Sound effects used	5	Airplane, seagulls, background voices

Sound effects were not used as often, but still played a specific role in some participants' stories. When they were used, they were often used to bring the listener/viewer to a particular place. For example, discussing a gathering and using background voices as if at a party, seagulls when discussing an event on the harbour, and the sound of an airplane when talking about immigrating as a child.

3.3   A Study of the Process of Working Through Multimedia Story Creation

A case study from one of the stories was conducted examining process based on weekly reflective journals and the digital story created. Each week in the course session, participants were asked to reflect upon specific aspects of creating a story. In this instance, an elder storyteller kept a journal of the process. The researchers examined the story and journal to determine the participant's process.

Story Details. The story spans over a lifetime starting with a focus on the storyteller's grandmother and childhood memories and ending with a reflection upon her role as a grandmother. Throughout, the story explores the idea of the storyteller's perspective as a carefree child, her mother's perspective, her grandmother's perspective, and finally her perspective as a reflective older adult. In her journal, she comments on the process of needing to re-explore her relationship to, and understanding of, her grandmother. She commented "I'd had only negative reflections of grandmother, but thanks to this project, my thoughts of her have been tempered by adult recollections and reflection".

The story also took place across various settings. As she is an immigrant, her childhood memories and family history spans over China and Singapore and then the setting shifts to Canada. Although this is not the main focus of the story, it is prominent in her reflections within the narrative of the story as she discusses her grandmother's Chinese heritage and some of the rituals she remembered her grandmother doing, such as dressing in her Chinese funeral clothes or getting Gua Sha treatments.

Imagery Process and Choice. In this case, the storyteller used both explicit and implicit representations in her choice of imagery to give her story life (Fig. 1). A variety of photos were used throughout, some with symbolic or metaphorical meaning. Other photos were family photos, such as herself as a child and photos of her grandmother and mother. Within her short story a combination of imagery is used. In the reflection journal, she specifically outlines her choices and the meaning she hoped to convey (Fig. 1); for example, a frozen leaf "to represent grandmother, my dry withered memory of her, my cold attitude."

Images chosen were explicit, implicit or visual metaphors – to express or convey abstract thought, states of mind – e.g.

Black/green abstract spiral – to depict confused mind trying to dig deeper into memory & understand

Balancing rock – something heavy that fell into place & is impossible or difficult to remove, like grandmother being foistered on my parents

Covered female face with only one eye uncovered – to represent women not allowed to speak

Condensation on window – to convey death – grey, grim, forlorn, ending

Frozen leaf – to represent grandmother, my dry withered memory of her, my cold attitude

Dew on single flower – to symbolize a coming to life – my "dead" lifeless grey-coloured attitude to grandmother has come to life with beautiful colour

---

Fig. 1. Reflective journal image choice

The choice of photos was not simply guided by the story and mood she wanted to create, but while searching for photos they influenced the telling of the story. In one journal excerpt (Fig. 2), the storyteller describes how as she was searching for photos to use for the story, the images began to shape her story. Choosing the photos seemed to help clarify the structure of the story. She began to play with ideas of juxtaposition and meaning. She describes how her grandmother's absence in family pictures also gave her a deeper understanding of the woman. The two photos of her mother and grand-mother side by side in different dress made her consider that "there was a cultural divide between her and my mother" (Fig. 2).

Photographs of childhood:

To some extent, the phrasing & wording of my narrative were shaped by the photos I had.

As I brought them out & studied them, with the memories of grandmother running through my mind, thoughts came. I saw her complete absence in my childhood photos, which reinforced the memory that she was not a part of our family life. This led me to ask why, which led me to the possibility that there was a cultural divide between her and my mother. The photos of the two women, one dressed in the Straits-born/Peranakan attire of sarong-kebaya & the other in traditional mainland Chinese black silk stared at me & brought out this thought.

The photos of me & my own grandkids at the end echoed my childhood photos in the first part of the story & I think, nicely book-ending the details of my grandmother.

Fig. 2. Reflection journal excerpt on photographs of childhood

Music and Sound. The storyteller uses a variety of music to create different moods throughout the digital story, no sound effects were used. Music was used to "reflect and express different moods" within the story (Fig. 3). The storyteller suggests that she uses points of no background music "to give greater significance to the voice and words said" (Fig. 3).

As I went through the music sites, I found and downloaded several pieces which seemed to reflect & express the different moods of my narrative – light, lively music to go with my "carefree childhood" 1st paragraph, then quieter & reflective, then quiet & somewhat "oriental" in tone.

I'd wanted to use sound effects but decided not to, thinking they would make the narrative a little choppy & contrived.

I thought the background music enhances the moods/tones of the various parts of the narrative. I left gaps without music to give greater significance to the voice & words said, & I tried to start the music at significant junctures too.

Fig. 3. Reflective journal on music choice

4   Discussion

Storytellers explored a diverse range of stories that either captured an event within their lives or a more extensive reflection. They often chose stories where the storyteller (or other protagonist) had to overcome some form of adversity. Thus, the canonical breach [11] was evident through one or more difficulties interrupting the norm. Narrative diachronicity [11] was often displayed as either a single event or a theme across many years, usually starting in childhood and ending at their reflection of their current life situation and who they are now.

In what ways do older adults incorporate multimedia into digital stories? In this sample of older adult digital stories, a variety of approaches are shown to capture life stories with new media. At times participants seem to focus more extensively on the narration and story element, whereas others played with imagery and film to add depth to expressions. Imagery and sound were incorporated in different ways to emphasize certain aspects of the story or to explicitly show a place, person, or object. This seems to be one of the most important uses of imagery for the storytellers in this study. Memories are often associated with photos and this gave older adults an opportunity to share these within the story format. Many storytellers also used imagery to present a more metaphorical meaning, particularly to give expression to the emotional experience. Music and sound were also used in different ways to highlight meaning. In many of the stories a variety of music was used to show a shift in tone or mood. Whereas, sound effects were used to recreate a specific place or feeling. The use of multimedia seems to allow older adults to communicate with multiple layers of expression within their stories.

In a previous digital storytelling project with immigrant women, Brushwood Rose and Granger [22] found that the multimodal approach to storytelling created unexpected shifts in the original meaning of the story. Within the current paper, this shift in understanding can be seen within the participant's journal as she works through her relationship with her grandmother. The storyteller is influenced by the images she finds. As mentioned in her comments, the photos played an integral role in shaping the story, but also reflecting upon the meaning of the story within her life. In the storyteller's description of working through the multimedia story, narrative and imagery begin to play off each other. Whereas the music played the role of enhancing mood and expression.

Within each of the stories, the storytellers often brought the story back to some reflection about self or about life. They seemed to convey a number of messages and lessons learned. The reflective aspects of recounting life histories has a capacity to give the teller an opportunity for self-reflection [3]. The choices made for creating the multimedia story were thought out thoroughly. This seemed to require the teller to continually reflect upon their story and reexamine its meaning to the storyteller's life.

With recounting the story, the storyteller begins to be more than one person at a time and contains a multiplicity [12]. Thus, the storytellers within the study share their reflection on what the story means now to their moral understanding, who they are, or reconceptualization of what the event meant to their life direction. They become the person in the story (another self) and the person they are now. This idea was prominent in the participant's reflective journal and story as she was looking through the eyes of a carefree child, an adult who understands hardships in life, and as a caring grandmother. All of these aspects were brought together in the story; however, the images of her grandmother and reflecting on the different images and music seem to have required the participant to explore all of these multiplicities in detail and give them a visual and a sound.

What is the process involved with choosing multimedia? For the participant examined in this study, the process involved a reciprocity with the multimedia shaping the narrative of the story as much as the narrative being used to choose the multimedia. The participant underwent an extensive process of considering their emotions and the mood they wanted to display. The old photos viewed made them think of their story in relation to the photos representation of reality and form new meaning. Bruner [11] discusses how we narrate our lives within "cultural tool kits" and the symbol system of cultures. It may be that when the narrator is faced with choosing visual and aural material to enhance their story, they must renegotiate their understanding based on the addition of the media. Thus, if narratives are symbolic cultural tools [11] and multimedia also hold representations of and for reality [17], when storytellers include multimedia into their stories, they must negotiate with the new knowledge of that representation.

5   Conclusion and Limitations

This study was a smaller exploratory analysis of a larger project; and thus, it was limited by the number of stories selected to examine. The researcher is planning to conduct a larger study analyzing the stories in further detail. Furthermore, as the older adults were part of a course some of what they included in their stories related to the instruction. It would be interesting to explore the choices of multimedia in online environments where limited instruction is given. Finally, the older adults represented in this study were those who came to a course held in the community. This eliminates some participants who may be homebound or uninterested in community courses.

Older adults' use of digital storytelling is growing and may be an increasingly beneficial way to express their understanding of their life history. The ways in which they integrate multimedia and use technology differs; however, they tend to use both imagery and sound in thought-provoking ways to enhance meaning. The process as seen in this instance, and others [20], can be very emotionally powerful for the storytellers. Reflecting back upon life can create a situation where the storytellers must redefine their relationship to the story (and in this case, the people within). Furthermore, including multimedia aspects in the retelling and reshaping of the story may have an influence on how it transpires. Creating digital stories may require storytellers to further investigate events and lead to increased depth of understanding as the storyteller must put sound and imagery to their memories.

Acknowledgements. We wish to thank the Social Sciences and Humanities Research Council of Canada (SSHRC) and the AGE-WELL Network of Centres of Excellence (NCE) for supporting this project financially.

References

1. Bruner, J.: Life as narrative. Soc. Res. **71**(3), 691–710 (2004)
2. Polkinghorne, D.E.: Narrative and self-concept. J. Narrative Life Hist. **1**(2), 135–153 (1991)
3. Birren, J.E., Deutchman, D.E.: Guiding Autobiography Groups for Older Adults: Exploring the Fabric of Life. Johns Hopkins University Press (JHU Press), Baltimore (1991)
4. Davis, A., Weinshenker, D.: Digital storytelling and authoring identity. In: Technology and identity: Research on the development and exploration of selves in a digital world, pp. 47–64 (2012)
5. Lambert, J.: Digital Storytelling: Capturing Lives, Creating Community. Digital Diner Press, Berkeley (2006)
6. Burgess, J.: Hearing ordinary voices: Cultural studies, vernacular creativity and digital storytelling. Continuum: J. Media Cult. Stud. **20**(2), 201–214 (2006)
7. Bol, N., van Weert, J.C., de Haes, H.C., Loos, E.F., Smets, E.M.: The effect of modality and narration style on recall of online health information: results from a web-based experiment. J. Med. Int. Res. **17**, 4 (2015)
8. Pew Research Center. Internet and Technology: Tech adoption climbs among older adults (2017). http://www.pewinternet.org/2017/05/17/tech-adoption-climbs-among-older-adults/. Accessed 14 Dec 2017
9. Chonody, J., Wang, D.: Connecting older adults to the community through multimedia: an intergenerational reminiscence program. Activities Adaptat. Aging **37**(1), 79–93 (2013)
10. Lambert, J. Digital Storytelling Cookbook. Berkeley, CA. (2010)
11. Bruner, J.: The narrative construction of reality. Crit. Inq. **18**(1), 1–21 (1991)
12. Ochs, E., Capps, L.: Narrating the self. Annu. Rev. Anthropol. **25**(1), 19–43 (1996)
13. Vivienne, S., Burgess, J.: The remediation of the personal photograph and the politics of self-representation in digital storytelling. J. Mater. Cult. **18**(3), 279–298 (2013)
14. Xie, B., Watkins, I., Golbeck, J., Huang, M.: Understanding and changing older adults' perceptions and learning of social media. Educ. Gerontol. **38**(4), 282–296 (2012)
15. Maus, F.E.: Music as narrative. Indiana Theory Rev. **12**, 1–34 (1991)

16. Wingstedt, J., Brändström, S., Berg, J.: Narrative music, visuals and meaning in film. Visual Commun. **9**(2), 193–210 (2010)
17. Pea, R.D.: Seeing what we build together: distributed multimedia learning environments for transformative communications. J. Learn. Sci. **3**(3), 285–299 (1994)
18. Subramaniam, P., Woods, B.: Digital life storybooks for people with dementia living in care homes: an evaluation. Clin. Interv. Aging **11**, 1263 (2016)
19. Hausknecht, S., Vanchu-Orosco, M., Kaufman, D.: Sharing life stories: design and evaluation of a digital storytelling workshop for older adults. In: Costagliola, G., Uhomoibhi, J., Zvacek, S., McLaren, B. (eds.) Computers Supported Education. Communications in Computer and Information Science, vol. 739, pp. 497–512. Springer, Cham (2017). https://doi.org/10.1007/978-3-319-63184-4_26
20. Hausknecht, S., Vanchu-Orosco, M., Kaufman, D.: Digitizing the wisdom of our elders: Connectedness through digital storytelling. (In review)
21. Hausknecht, S., Vanchu-Orosco, M., Kaufman, D.: New Ways to Tell My Story: Evaluation of a Digital Storytelling Workshop for Older Adults. In: CSEDU, vol. 2, pp. 231–239 (2016)
22. Brushwood Rose, C., Granger, C.A.: Unexpected self-expression and the limits of narrative inquiry: exploring unconscious dynamics in a community-based digital storytelling workshop. Int. J. Qual. Stud. Educ. **26**(2), 216–237 (2013)

Promising Practices in Collaborative Digital Literacy and Digital Media-Making with Older Adults

Constance Lafontaine[✉] and Kim Sawchuk

Concordia University, Montreal, QC H3G 1M8, Canada
`admin@actproject.ca`

Abstract. For the past seven years, the Ageing, Communication, Technologies (ACT) team (http://actproject.ca/) has been creating workshops and events that engage older adults, many who have limited access to digital tools and technologies, in digital media-making projects. We collaborate with elders in a variety of Montreal settings, from public libraries, to public housing and organizations founded and run by seniors developing ways to both meet their individual wish to engage with digital media, as well as their collective desire to "take a class" that is social and sociable. Building on our past work on "precarious ageing and media-making", as well as the impetus to "mediatize" older adults and organizations, we focus on both the concept of promising practices and the specific insights of those who lead these workshops: the students and professionals employed by ACT, all of whom are young adults, between the ages of 18 and 35. We begin by offering a set of five "promising practices" for collaborative digital media making with seniors. From our point of view, promising practices are not prescriptive, but rather a way of contesting some of the imperatives and normativities subsumed by the idea of "best practices". We conclude the paper by describing the key principles to our contextualization of "best practices" in terms of digital workshops for seniors.

Keywords: Promising practices · Aging · Digital literacy

1 Introduction

For the past seven years, the Ageing, Communication, Technologies (ACT) team (http://actproject.ca/) has been creating projects that engage older adults in digital media-making and digital literacy workshops. We have collaborated with elders in a variety of Montreal settings, from public libraries, to public housing and organizations founded and run by seniors. Many of these participants have limited access to digital tools and technologies. In all cases, we have taken on the challenge to meet their individual desire to engage with digital media while "taking a class," or partaking in an activity that is social, sociable and enjoyable. By organizing and facilitating these workshops, we have recognized that working with different groups and in different settings can drastically change learning contexts, and we need to be attuned to learning dynamics that are in flux over time.

© Springer International Publishing AG, part of Springer Nature 2018
J. Zhou and G. Salvendy (Eds.): ITAP 2018, LNCS 10926, pp. 492–504, 2018.
https://doi.org/10.1007/978-3-319-92034-4_37

Building on our past work on precarious ageing and digital literacy [1], as well as on the pressures to "mediatize" older adults and organizations [2], we reflect upon lessons learned over the course of several varied workshops, from the basics of learning the internet, to digital scanning and photography, to making blogs. We offer insights on what has worked and what has not, presenting these ideas as a set of "promising practices". In this paper, we focus on both the concept of promising practices and the specific insights of those who lead these workshops: the students and professionals employed by ACT, all of whom are young adults, between the ages of 18 and 35. This is distinct from our previous discussions, which have been based primarily on conversations and surveys with the older adults who are workshop participants. For this paper, we have interviewed the young workshop leaders about their experiences in leading these digital workshops over several years. These interviews form the basis for intergenerational knowledge sharing and collaborative digital media making with older adults over 65.

From these interviews, we articulate five points: flexibility, meaning of technological devices, boundary setting in workshops, openness of outcomes, and the celebration of shared success. These are points that our interviewees identified as key elements for organizing and facilitating a successful workshop or series of workshops, and together, these points can be thought of as an interlocking set of promising practices. We conclude the paper by drawing from our reflexive comments about workshop practices to flesh out three key principles that inform and contextualize our approach to using the term promising practices, and more broadly our approach to sharing methods and processes related to digital workshops for seniors.

2   Methodology

2.1   ACT and Its Approaches to Digital Workshops with Seniors

ACT is a seven-year research project that is funded by the Social Sciences and Humanities Research Council of Canada (SSHRC). ACT was launched in 2013, but we have been developing and leading digital literacy and digital media-making projects with seniors since 2011. These projects have been essential to building long-term relationships with community organizations serving the needs of older adults in the Montreal area. In this paper, we draw specifically from our long-term connections to some of these organizations, including digital literacy workshops in Montreal low-income housing buildings in partnership with Groupe Harmonie, digital media projects done in collaboration with activist group Respecting Elders: Communities Against Abuse (RECAA), and various creative projects undertaken with the community group Notre-Dame-de-Grâce Seniors Citizen Council (NDGSCC), and the Atwater Library and Computer Centre (ALCC), each of which serves a large population of seniors. We also include in the scope of this paper podcasting and video-making workshops that were components of "aging activisms capsules," undertaken with colleagues at Trent University [3]. These projects vary widely based on the needs, interests and proclivities of the seniors with whom we often co-design workshops, as well as the mandates of the organizations and groups with which we collaborate. Since 2013 only, we estimate that we have given over 300 individual workshops, and well over 500 seniors have participated in them.

We typically run two basic types of workshops: those focused on enhancing the basic digital skills of our participants (like using the Internet), and others focused on participatory media making as a way to enhance the learning of digital skills through collective projects. The former workshops have entailed "technical drop-in sessions" that are held on a monthly basis, where seniors bring their devices to troubleshoot or learn new computing tricks on ACT's devices. An individual can attend only once or can choose to return several times for more sustained learning. Through lessons, conversations and engagements with devices and software, participants learn the basics of the Internet or they are invited to ask "tech mentors" for assistance in addressing specific issues or problems. Our second type of workshop typically involves projects with significant creative components. Examples include recent workshops on building a food blog, workshops on taking, processing and exhibiting digital photography, workshops on telling, recording and sharing stories about the city, and a video series about participants' lives. What these workshops have in common is that the learning of digital technologies is accomplished by focusing on a collective, shared goal using a community-arts approach, usually over several sessions over the span of a few weeks or months. Often, these workshops culminate with an exhibition or vernissage of some sort.

The increasing scope of ACT's involvement with community groups and digital literacy workshops since 2011 has meant that over twenty young people have been employed at ACT. These young adults have held various roles in these projects: research assistant, workshop facilitators, tech mentors, coordinators and leaders. These individuals are MA or PhD students, postdoctoral fellows, or recent graduates turned professionals. They have worked at ACT and collaborated with community organizations for several years, often throughout the duration of their graduate degrees and even beyond.

For a number of students, employment with ACT has represented the first time they engage with the topic of aging and the topic of later life as part of their formal education. Partaking in an intergenerational digital literacy workshop is often their first experience of working with older adults, and the first time they are pressed to reflect on digital media and ICTs from this perspective. Although support through regular meetings and other means of training is provided, learning to be a facilitator for ACT team has been a proactive and collective project-one in which we have tested, succeeded, failed and tried again together, through various iterations of projects, and slowly built the contours of promising practices along the way.

2.2   Interviews with ACT Workshop Facilitators

To understand what current facilitators might share with future facilitators, we undertook semi-directed interviews with four current and past employees of ACT. We interviewed Kendra Besanger, Kelly Leonard, Ashley McAskill, and Magdalena Olszanowski, hereby identified by their first names only. We approached these particular four individuals for two reasons. First, they all had been in charge of one or more intergenerational digital workshop over the past three years. Second, they had been working (or had worked) at ACT for a significant amount of time, with the durations ranging from two to six years. Third, they had each been involved in more than one form of workshop, and thus could offer insight into the diverging contexts in which ACT workshops unfold.

We used an interview template that included ten open-ended questions that were common to all, and then asked further questions in relation to specific projects they had facilitated. In answering their questions, the participants were invited to draw from concrete examples from their experiences. As co-authors of this paper, we also have interviewed each other, and discussed our own experiences facilitating and organizing workshops. These six interviews are used to identify some thematically dominant themes that outline five promising practices for running either a technical workshop or a more collaborative community-based arts workshop. They also inform our conceptualization of the undertheorized term 'promising practices'.

3 Theorizing 'Promising Practices'

3.1 Questioning Best Practices and Prescriptive Approaches

We use the term promising practices deliberately, and in response to the prevalence of best practices in the current literature in the social sciences and the humanities. The term "best practices" originates from the field of management and the model has been taken up in various areas of public policy, as well as in several academic disciplines [4]. Best practice guides often discuss the insights gleaned from what has been previously implemented elsewhere, and what has been proven to work [4]. The term best practice, for Bretschneider et al., implies that the practice in question is considered "best when compared to any alternative course of action and that it is a practice designed to achieve some deliberative end" [5]. Best practices are, as such, recognized as being superior to any considered alternative, and are often geared towards efficient attainment of a well-identified objective or set of objectives.

As Overman and Boyd argue, one of the strengths of best practices is that they allow practitioners and researchers to distill complex situations, and turn them into a readable and prescriptive format. This is often done "by avoiding negative analysis and focusing instead on possibility and change" [6]. What this approach does, however, is cast aside discussions of failure, which can be just as informative, illuminating and rich as stories of success.

There are a number of other theoretical and methodological issues that can be raised in response to the development and widespread use of best practices (see those compiled by Veselý, for instance), including a lack of common methodologies for identifying best practices. As Bardach suggests, the term "best practices" can be misleading, as it implies that all other options have been tested out and considered, which is rarely, if ever, the case [7]. In addition, it is not always evident how one set of best practices can be transferred to a different setting [6]. The specificity and context of the original terrain of study or original "case study" is usually not relayed in a way that provides a complete or satisfactory picture of the original context and existing conditions. Despite what the term boasts, best practices do not necessarily reveal an optimal path that can be applied in diverse settings. The idea of best practices thus sets up a normative course of action that may very well be inappropriate for the context at hand.

3.2   Towards Promising Practices

In her study of caregiving institutions across a variety of countries and contexts, Canadian age studies scholars Pat Armstrong, with Baines, Daly and Braedley, uses the notion of promising practices, or "ideas worth sharing," to articulate a set of contextual possibilities for caregiving [8–10]. To demonstrate the range of caregiving possibilities, Armstrong and her team have produced an intentionally accessible series of small books, or "bookettes," of what they term promising practices in long term care. The bookettes do not lay out a set of conditions to measure the efficacy of care. Rather, they articulate a range of practices for caregiving in a number of different countries. With each case being distinct, they collectively provide a vantage into the ways caregiving can be reimagined and implemented within institutional settings. These bookettes of promising practices incorporate vignettes and storytelling culled from "flash ethnographies" of long-term care residences that researchers visited for a short period of time. The bookettes, and their vignettes, effectively document different forms of caregiving that are not prescriptive. They contest the idea of universally applicable solutions, and engage with complicated sites and situations. It is worth quoting at length Armstrong and Braedley's description of their approach to promising practices:

> Too much research looks for universal patterns and solutions, eliminating variation and conflicting interests. In contrast, we seek to recognize differences and identify ideas worth considering by those on whom they have an impact, allowing them to do so in ways that take their particular context into account. We also seek to recognize conflicting approaches and interests, looking for ways to balance them rather than ignore them or choose one side. This is why we talk about promising practices rather than best practices or a single, right way [10].

Following Armstrong's lead, it is possible to imagine the potentials for using interviews and observations to articulate promising practices for enhancing and sharing different digital literacy and digital media-making workshops with seniors. Although we are not doing a "flash ethnography" that is either "institution by institution" or "project by project," we are inspired by the potential of the term promising practices, for those doing community engaged research using digital media tools with older adults.

Promising practices, in the context of digital media-making with older adults, present a vision of what participatory collaborations with older adults can do to bridge digital and intergenerational divides. As Magdalena reminds us in her interview, taking a prescriptive approach to teaching technologies can have an undesirable outcome. As she explains, too rigid a set of expectations "might reinforce their fear and discomfort with technology, or reinforce their assumption that they are unable to learn to use technologies" precisely because they cannot learn through rigid or recognized teaching models.

In this context, we contend that the ideas of sharing promising practices means representing the insights gathered from empirical first-hand experience. These practices are guidelines that are not fixed, but are used to initiate a reflection on the multiplicity, context-specificity and fallibility of approaches. Describing a promising practice must pay attention to the open-ended character of research relationships and collaborations. Outlining promising practices, to recapitulate, entails engaging in a collective and reflexive exercise to document and open up a repertoire of approaches and tools that can avail themselves to practitioners and researchers. Promising practices challenge cookie-cutter approaches, and instead promote experimentation and collaborations on-the-ground, and allow for the building of relationships of trust. We build upon this these ideas, and upon this definition of promising practices, for the remainder of this article. From the interviews conducted with participants, we present five overarching promising practices, that gain specificity and context through their explanation. The practices we put forth in the context of this paper contribute not only to our understanding of how to create meaningful intergenerational digital literacy workshops, but to enhance the conceptualization of promising practices within the social sciences and humanities.

4   Five Promising Practices for Digital Workshops with Seniors

4.1   Be Flexible

One promising practice is learning to balance organization and open-mindedness, and imbuing each aspect of the project with flexibility. Seniors are not a homogeneous group, particularly in a highly multilinguistic and multiracial city like Montreal. Workshop participants who come to ACT typically arrive at a session not only with different linguistic and cultural backgrounds, educational and workplace experiences—they come with a wide variety of experience using media that has been accrued over years. Many have accumulated a multiplicity of devices over time, and have variegated experiences with technologies, digital and otherwise.

Given this great potential variety within the population of older participants, we have learned, in the words of one facilitator, Ashley, to "expect the unexpected". Expecting the unexpected is particularly critical when working in "the field" rather than a classroom setting—in our case in senior's housing complex or a community centre. Ashley adds that "you may arrive with your toolkit, and realize that you'll have to try out lots of different tools, and maybe these won't work either". This point highlights several dimensions of why being flexible when working with seniors on site matters.

While a typical advertisement for a workshop may promise the delivery of a particular set of learning outcomes—say to learn how to take, edit, and print a digital photograph—when giving workshops to seniors, one needs to be in conversation with the participants and adjust accordingly. Kendra noted that "you have to be genuinely willing to include their vision of the workshop into their plans, and work towards that vision". As digital activist Virginia Eubanks pithily writes in Digital dead end, it is important to value what participants bring to the table individually [11].

Being flexible, not only with learning outcomes but with a work plan, means being responsive to unforeseen contingencies. Workshops must leave the time and space to discover new things, that are unexpected by the participants. Further, participants may either have trouble putting into words what they do not know, or conversely, they may underestimate what they do know. As Magdalena put it "people don't know what they don't know". She further asserts that it is important to be aware of this fact, and to "read between the lines and to surmise their technology needs in alternate ways".

While all of the facilitators interviewed emphasized that it was important to come prepared with an agenda and a plan for a workshop that includes a set of goals and steps to achieve those goals, each of them had contingency plans to help with different kinds of potential learning styles within this already heterogeneous population. Some people like to learn through written instructions, others by oral directions, visuals, or by trying to use a device. Further, having supplementary materials is important. For Magdalena, giving a sheet "primer" at the beginning of a workshop allows for room in the workshop to take tangents, without feeling like she has not covered the basics. For Kelly, a worksheet with the information that could be taken away meant that people who do not want to sit through a workshop, and just want a worksheet, could still have access to basic information.

One of the key themes that emerged in interviews with these facilitators, which we too have observed, is the import of being mindful of "time". This emerged in interviews in several respects. While there is the myth that seniors have much time on their hands, many had sudden appointments with medical practitioners, which are always more important than our workshops. Facilitators also stressed that it was important to make it clear to people that they can drop out of the project at any point and that they will not be penalized for doing this. Yet at the same time, this volatility in membership can pose problems in meeting a project's stated objectives.

Working with groups sometimes means that things can take longer than expected, and part of meeting people where they are means respecting the time it takes for them to experiment with devices and to learn with them. "You shouldn't necessarily set expectations for how things need to happen, because then you miss on a lot of good surprises." Ashley further emphasized that it was important to "make time" to let things happen, and often this means letting the group take the lead and help steer the project in the way they wanted.

4.2   Address What Each Technological Device Means Culturally

Digital devices are not only technical objects, but cultural objects that are imbued with histories of meaning, and individual anxieties and fears. Attention to the symbolic power of technology needs to be built into the workshop, and it can be helpful and revelatory to encourage conversations on this matter. If one is not attuned to the complex nature of technology, one risks missing something important. As Kendra suggests, "sometimes, people need to talk about their fear of or their uneasiness with a technology before a workshop can proceed". She adds that at first, she did not think to ask questions like "are you comfortable with a microphone". Kendra describes how she learned to be a better facilitator when she acknowledged the discomfort of a participant in a digital storytelling workshop. This participant felt uncomfortable with a microphone propped up in front of her; the device made her uneasy, though she expressed that she wanted to be recorded. The facilitators found an arrangement that allayed these fears by putting the microphone behind her. This incident launched ongoing conversations about microphones being objects of power within the context of that workshop. Different anxieties, decades of perspectives about complex social and personal implications of technologies often surface, reminding facilitators that technologies are not neutral tools.

Universities often have better equipment than individuals, and sometimes the most cutting edge of technologies may not be the most appropriate: they only remind people of what they cannot afford. In some instances, it has been helpful to eschew the use of the latest and greatest, an ethos followed by the ALCC, whose workshops with seniors use the least expensive equipment possible. Instead of choosing the best device, a favoured alternative has been to use point-and-shoot cameras. Instead of purchasing one camera, we are able to afford purchasing one camera per participant and the facilitators were then able to lend out these cameras to the participants between workshops. This gave them the chance to practice their newly-acquired skills but more importantly to play and experiment with the devices without having the feeling that someone was looking over their shoulder. Yet, the devices themselves also offered challenges. These smaller cameras were more difficult for participants to use because the buttons were small and difficult to manipulate from an affordance perspective.

Again here, there is not one solution or best practice—balance and context are key. For some facilitators, these workshops are a way to let participant have access to more expensive or professional tools that they might not otherwise buy. Some seniors are keen to try out more expensive and complicated digital cameras. As Magdalena describes, "participants do enjoy using the DSLR [digital single-lens reflex camera] because it gives them a certain access to a camera that is professional, and that they otherwise would not have access to". However, she is at the same time aware of what this can mean for participants and emphasizes that "it's important to demystify the technology and to show how certain functions correspond between devices". This expensive equipment can also deter participants from playing around with the device for fear of risking breaking it. Magdalena's experience suggests that when dealing with the meaning of technologies in these situations, that ultimately facilitators must "make sure that the equipment that is not overwhelming to people".

4.3 Navigate Social Boundaries

For the facilitators, key to setting up workshops for older participants was the process of creating a sense of familiarity and openness between participants and facilitators, and challenging the hierarchy of a typical teacher-learner rapport. This, however, needs to happen while navigating sometimes difficult social dynamics provided by varied workshop settings. As Kelly points out, she found that this hierarchy was somewhat challenged from the onset for facilitators in these intergenerational settings, "because they are older, I feel uncomfortable being in a role where I say 'you should do this'". Further, facilitators adopted workshop themes that would engage the participants and their experience (like recording stories about living in the city, for instance). This was specifically done so as to promote knowledge sharing, and not knowledge transfer, and to assert the roles of seniors in the workshop as knowledge bearing assets within a digital technologies workshop setting. Ashley, mentioned the importance of "trust building" and "creating lasting relationships" in her approach, and building the conditions for people to feel encouraged to ask questions and for knowledge to be shared in a reciprocal way.

Ashley further notes that it can be important to set limits to the level of familiarity one seeks to cultivate in a workshop, and not doing so can make the workshop dynamic unravel. Similarly, Kendra remarks that "we're not part of their everyday life," and we cannot expect that bringing together strangers, friends, or individuals with histories of conflict with one another will generate the same workshop dynamic. For instance, in working in low-income housing buildings, where tenants are living together out of necessity and not out of choice, facilitators have encountered conflicts between tenants, and have often had to find workaround solutions to deal with situations of conflict. Facilitators developed tactics for dealing with moments of friction, like bounding conversations more strictly to the subject matter at hand, or relying on knowledgeable community partners for input and guidance.

Conversely, the facilitators' experiences have been different when they worked with groups of seniors who choose to congregate and spend their spare time together. Working with RECAA, an activist group of older adults, can be quite different than working with seniors in social housing. As we have argued elsewhere, eating together, engaging socially and building friendships are essential building blocks to their activist project, and these activities structure the way they engage with their activist project [10]. As such, the digital literacy projects ACT has undertaken with RECAA entailed workshops that usually followed potluck-style lunches. These lunches became a way for facilitators and participants to get to know each other, but also to build the social connections that would carry over into the workshop.

Magdalena emphasized another balance that needs to be struck in setting the tone for a workshop. It is important to navigate a line between using language that is simple, and that risks being infantilizing, and using language that is too advanced, and that risks being alienating. This line is one that can change from group to group, depending on the skill levels of the participants and facilitators alike. Further, others pointed to the fact that it was important to be open with one's own lack of knowledge about technology, and thus show to the participants that learning to use the latest device or software is not so easy, and that we are all learning all the time. For example, Kelly explains: "sometimes, they ask me questions, and I do not know the answer. I tell them 'I need ten minutes to figure it out, and then I could explain it to you'". She adds "they usually laugh, they say 'See! The young people they can't figure it out either!'".

4.4   Be Open to Different Outcome and Successes

Part of building flexibility is opening up the workshop to have different possible measures of success and different possible outcomes. As previously discussed, while the facilitators noted the need to have a set of goals at the beginning of the workshop, they all emphasized the importance of parting with some of them along the way, when they no longer fit with the trajectory of the workshop.

This is illustrated especially well by an example from Kelly. She explains that she worked with a man from Serbia in the context of workshop in a low-income housing building. He participated in a workshop on learning to navigate the Internet and it became clear that the only thing he really wanted to do online was find his childhood home on Google Maps. "We wanted to show him how he could do this on his own, but he wasn't interested in doing this". She explains that "we found it for him and he then talked to us about his childhood home and neighbourhood for some time. I think he was just happy to show us his home, and his town, and sharing this with us and the other participants seemed to be important to him". Kelly recognized that this man wanted to engage with the digital, but wanted to do so in a way that would allow him to connect to people around him. The workshop became a place where he could see his former home, but also a place where he could break his social isolation.

Success in the context of digital workshops for seniors does not usually mean that the participant will become a regular user of a technology or that they will become proficient 'super users'—though this has happened on occasion. To define success as technology adoption or use would be to misunderstand the diversity of reasons that push seniors to follow the workshop in the first place. In ACT's experience, workshops are valued as a place to learn but they are just as valued as creative and social spaces. In this sense, as Kendra emphasizes, it is important to ask participants what they want to get out of the workshop, and to constantly be attuned to this when thinking about outcomes.

Facilitators also noted the need to be open to victories and successes that were not foreseen. ACT, in collaboration with partner Groupe Harmonie, organized a digital photography workshop that took place in the common room a low-income building was especially difficult for the facilitators, Ashley and Kelly. There was much enthusiasm for the workshop, and five participants joined it at the beginning. However, a conflict arose, and one participant was diagnosed with a serious illness. These conditions diffused participation and the workshop eventually dwindled to two facilitators and one participant, an older African woman who had been living in the building for about a year. There was question at this time as to whether ACT should cancel the workshop series, but it was decided that it was important to move forward. This woman created a series of digital photographs and exhibited her collection in the common room of the building. If one were to match the outcome of the workshop against narrowly-established goals about teaching digital camera skills to the seniors of a single building, one might miss seeing how the project actually succeeded. The facilitators and the participant organized a vernissage to open the exhibit and put the spotlight on this woman's work. To everyone's surprise, the event drew a crowd of over fifty individuals, most of whom were from the building itself. This enthusiasm was an anomaly in a building where interpersonal conflicts were rampant, where the common room is often shunned and locked, and where participation in social events is meagre. A few months later, we learned that the woman who had completed the workshop had remarked that, while she was the subject of significant racism in a building of Caucasian inhabitants, the workshop had significantly lessened these racial barriers with the other tenants. The photography workshop had made her feel more at home in her building—a success well outside the bounds of what facilitators could have imagined for a digital photography workshop.

4.5 Share and Celebrate Successes, Whatever They Are

Over the last few years, we conclude digital media-making workshops with the organization of public events such as the photography vernissage described above. We have also hosted launches for podcasts, "listening parties" for digital stories, and screenings for video capsules. These events often include "Q & A" sessions with the participants, biographical notes about the seniors, and interpretive information about each collection or piece on display. Participation in a workshop is never contingent on sharing one's work publicly or on participating in the final exhibit. Nevertheless, nearly all workshop participants have partaken in the public exhibit over the last few years, and in doing so, have collaborated towards its organization through its curation, and by having an input on the venue, guest list, theme, and so forth.

In preparing public events, it is important not to bog down the curation stage with narrow aesthetic ideals, or to seek technical perfection. Several facilitators who had worked with digital photography pointed out that it was okay if not all the final images turned out perfect, or if they were conventionally beautiful images. What was most important is that they had been taken as part of the workshop, had reflected the participants' vision for their own work, and had been chosen by the workshop participants because they were proud of them.

This practice of organizing public events has been especially fruitful in the low-income housing setting, where building residents can participate in a social event together, and see their common room cleaned up, decorated and repurposed into an exhibition space. In addition to neighbours, friends and family members of the workshop participants are invited, and they often come to the exhibitions to celebrate the work of their loved ones. Members of ACT often attend, as do community partners, and past workshop participants. The exhibit has served as a way of highlighting the work of the seniors, and also the work of the facilitators, and it has provided for all a common and shared goal towards which everyone can work over the course of a workshop series. Further, it has been a ground for creating conversation about digital technologies and aging, and of reaching out to prospective participants for future workshops, and even building further connections within the Montreal community.

5   Conclusions and Implications for Future Research

In this paper, we have articulated five promising practices gleaned from ACT's work organizing and facilitating intergenerational digital workshops for communities of older adults in Montreal. Drawing from interviews conducted with facilitators, we identified five practices that we have mobilized in our workshops with seniors. These practices emphasize the importance of flexibility, of positioning devices and technologies culturally, of navigating social boundaries, of having plural measures of success while remaining open to different outcomes and, finally, of celebrating successes, whether they be big or small. We built upon on these approaches to challenge the rigidity of best practices and instead foreground the term promising practices. In this light, we outline below three principles that guide our understanding of promising practices in the context of digital workshops for seniors.

First, our approach to promising practices is inspired by a commitment to accounting for the heterogeneity of later life. Older adults live in different contexts informed by their social positionings, and they engage with technologies in vastly different ways. We understand that in the context of digital literacy or digital media-making workshops, what works in one setting often does not in another for a wide array of reasons-ranging from the workshop spaces, [12] to the level of interest of the participants, to mobility and physical access, to the weather, among countless others. Promising practices, then, make us attuned to the uniqueness of encounters, and seek to instill within us an awareness that a holistic approach to thinking about context is essential.

Second, our approach to promising practices connects to our commitment to emphasizing process over results, to engaging earnestly with failures, and to challenging normative measures of success in digital literacy. There is much to gain from not shying away from thinking and writing about failure, and this goes well beyond knowing and sharing information about what not to do. What could be considered failure for some in the context of intergenerational workshops on new technologies can still offer a wealth knowledge about people and the contexts for learning, knowledge sharing and co-creating. Some failures also reveal paths towards unexpected successes, and can put into focus that learning to use a device or technology is far from being the only or most important outcome of such projects. In this sense, promising practices are committed to a plurality of processes and outcomes.

Third, promising practices are open-ended, and signal a commitment to collaboration and long-term engagements. Promising practices imply that they are constantly in flux, always being tried and tested, and potentially tweaked or overhauled. Researchers, and in our case, workshop facilitators and coordinators, are not the sole keepers of knowledge about how best to structure our own workshops, and finding methods that show promise is always a process that involves conversations and negotiations with colleagues, research partners and workshop participants. The open-ended nature of promising practices for our research group has also reflected a commitment towards building relationships with community partners and seniors that extend beyond the parameters of a single project or workshop.

In fleshing out our own set of promising practices based on interviews with workshop facilitators, we have deliberately outlined five practices that emphasize the openness, contextuality and responsiveness we collectively value in teaching digital technologies to seniors. These are traits that we also find to be lacking in the prescriptive best practices model, that claims transferability and predictability of outcomes. The facilitators interviewed in the context of this paper offer not univocal approaches, but varied and complementary ideas that are attuned to the specificity of each teaching and learning context.

References

1. Sawchuk, K., Lafontaine, C.: Precarious ageing: questioning access, creating InterACTion. In: Dias da Silva, P., Alves, A. (eds.) TEM Proceedings of the Technology and Emerging Media Track (2015)
2. Sawchuk, K.: Tactical mediatization and activist ageing: pressures, push-backs, and the story of RECAA. Mediekultur **29**(54), 18 (2013)
3. Aging Activisms (2017). http://www.agingactivisms.org/about
4. Veselý, A.: Theory and methodology of best practice research: a critical review of the current state. Cent. Eur. J. Public Policy **5**(2), 98–117 (2011)
5. Bretschneider, S., Marc-Aurele, F.J., Wu, J.: "Best practices" research: a methodological guide for the perplexed. J. Public Adm. Res. Theor. **15**(2), 309 (2005)
6. Overman, E.S., Boyd, K.J.: Best practice research and postbureaucratic reform. J. Public Adm. Res. Theor. **4**(1), 67–84 (1994)

7. Bardach, E.: A Practical Guide for Policy Analysis: The Eightfold Path to More Effective Problem Solving. Chatham House Publishers, New York (2000)
8. Baines, D., Armstrong, P.: Promising Practices in Long Term Care: Ideas Worth Sharing. Canadian Centre for Policy Alternatives, Montreal (2015)
9. Armstrong, P., Daly, T.: Exercising Choice in Long-Term Residential Care. Canadian Centre for Policy Alternatives, Montreal (2017)
10. Armstrong, P., Braedley, S.: Physical Environments for Long-Term Care: Ideas Worth Sharing. Canadian Centre for Policy Alternatives, Montreal (2016)
11. Eubanks, V.: Digital Dead End: Fighting for Social Justice in the Information Age. MIT Press, Cambridge (2002)
12. Sawchuk, K., Lafontaine, C.: Activist aging: the tactical theatrics of RECAA. In: Chazan, M., Baldwin, M., Evans, P. (eds.) Unsettling Activisms: Critical Interventions on Aging, Gender and Social Change. Women's Press/Canadian Scholars' Press (forthcoming)

Evaluating a Smartphone-Based Social Participation App for the Elderly

Nina Lee[1(✉)], Katie Seaborn[2], Atsushi Hiyama[2], Masahiko Inami[2], and Michitaka Hirose[3]

[1] Department of Industrial Design, National Cheng Kung University, Tainan, Taiwan
p38051054@mail.ncku.edu.tw
[2] Research Center for Advanced Science and Technology, The University of Tokyo, 4-6-1 Komaba, Meguro, Tokyo 153-8904, Japan
{kseaborn,hiyama,inami}@star.rcast.u-tokyo.ac.jp
[3] Graduate School of Information Science and Technology,
The University of Tokyo, 4-6-1 Komaba, Meguro, Tokyo 153-8904, Japan
hirose@cyber.t.u-tokyo.ac.jp

Abstract. Hyper-aging societies are looking for ways to support their elderly populations and mitigate aging-related societal challenges. One way to do this is by increasing elders' social participation in the workforce and their communities. Towards this end, an opportunity-matching app for Japanese elders called GBER (Gathering Brisk Elderly in the Region) was created and deployed in a large Japanese city. In this paper, we report on the results of a usability and user experience (UX) study that evaluated a new version of the app's user interface (UI), which was redesigned for smartphones based on feedback from current users and by taking an elder-centric design approach. The study, which involved representative elderly users, revealed several insights about the use of flat UI design, conceptual transferability of common app iconography, information reading patterns, and persona and scenario methodology. It also confirmed the diversity of Japanese elders interests and skills, providing further empirical support for the need for an opportunity-matching service like GBER.

Keywords: User interface · Smartphone · Aging · Elderly · Senior workforce
Senior community · Social participation

1 Introduction

Societies around the earth are aging rapidly, and Japan is leading the march. As a hyper-aging country [12, 14], Japan has a rapidly increasing population of elderly citizens and one of the lowest birth rates in the world. It is speculated that by 2040 over one third of the population will be over 64 years of age [3]. This is already having important and widespread effects on Japanese society, especially healthcare and social systems, that are sure to be reflected elsewhere as other countries' aging rates catch up. As such, how to manage the realities of a hyper-aging society while supporting elders is becoming a crucial social, technological, and research concern.

© Springer International Publishing AG, part of Springer Nature 2018
J. Zhou and G. Salvendy (Eds.): ITAP 2018, LNCS 10926, pp. 505–517, 2018.
https://doi.org/10.1007/978-3-319-92034-4_38

One way to both support elders and society at large is by increasing elders' participation [4, 12]. Participation is defined as a combination of social interaction—the micro scale acts of speaking with and being around people—and community engagement—the macro scale behaviors of being present in community spaces and going to community events. Several factors can affect whether and how elders participate in society. In many industrialized nations, people are expected, if not required, to retire once they reach a certain age; in Japan, this is 60 or 65 years of age. As we get older, we also tend to encounter issues with mobility that assistive tools and devices, such as wheelchairs, may not be able to reverse and may introduce new issues, such as environmental barriers. Finally, relationships can weaken or break down, such as in the event of family moving far away or when elderly friends pass away. In the face of reduced participation and a desire to regain a sense of community presence, many elders in Japan take on part-time jobs or volunteer positions; however, these can be difficult to find and may not match the elder's interests [11].

One avenue for tackling these issues is technology. Elders, in Japan and elsewhere, are becoming an increasingly tech-savvy population. Smartphones, in particular, are becoming a popular choice among seniors in Japan; as of 2014, 39.4% of younger elders (50+59) and 22.5% of older elders (60+) own smartphones [2]. Following this trend, a research team at the University of Tokyo created GBER (short for Gathering Brisk Elderly in the Region), a cross-platform app that matches elders to activities, jobs, and events in their community [1]. The purpose of the app is to improve elders' participation by providing them with curated, personalized opportunities near where they live. The current version of the app was designed using a combination of research-backed guidelines, expert design, and interview with a group of assumed users. At present, 106 elders in Kashiwa city, Tokyo are registered users of GBER.

This paper describes the results of a usability and user experience (UX) study conducted around improving the current GBER app's user interface (UI) design. The current users of the app informally provided feedback about the UI, revealing three main issues. First, it is difficult to imagine what kind of service will be provided under each menu displayed on the top page. Current top page displays a set of abstract icon with brief description by text. Displaying information which does not directly concern each user on top page made user reluctant to interact with further contents in lower hierarchy. Second, finding activities is not tied to the user's availability: users must add their schedule, then go to a different calendar to see booked and recommended events. Third, gathering preference information from users is tedious. Users must fill out a lot of questionnaire forms consecutively, which can be tiresome. With these issues in mind, a new version of the UI was designed and user tested with six elderly Kashiwa residents. The aim of this study was to ensure that the new design addressed these issues in a user-friendly and easy to use fashion, towards the overarching goal of to accelerate elderly participation in GBER service. The main contribution is a series of usability and UX insights on an activity-finding and schedule-based smartphone app design for Japanese elders.

2   Related Work

In the wake of widespread smartphone use, researchers and designers have begun to assess their usability, UX, and accessibility for elderly users. Indeed, there is now some evidence to suggest that elderly users have different kinds of experiences and needs when it comes to the design of smartphone interfaces. Salman *et al.* [13] revealed and categorized some usability issues related to effectiveness (e.g., inability to complete the task), efficiency (e.g., time required to carry out task), and user satisfaction (e.g., not using the feature phone again). This implies there were a gap between developers (who were mostly young) and elderly users' mental models, where developers made design decisions based on their own understanding, which may not al-ways reflect those of elderly users. Other research has shown that elderly users might experience difficulties in navigation, easily getting lost when walking through dialogs that are composed of several phases requiring navigation, selection, input, output, confirmation, and so on [7]. Harada *et al.* [6] investigated the issues and challenges that elderly people may encounter when using smart devices in certain kinds of interfaces, such as map apps and address books. In these interfaces, elderly users were found to make unintentional taps due to parts of their hand accidentally making contact with the touchscreen on the device. Additionally, they sometimes took action without noticing important information or being aware of their mistake, and then received unexpected feedback as a result. During our study, we made sure to watch for these kinds of issues in the redesigned GBER interface.

Some studies have conducted experiments to generate guidelines for how to ad-dress known issues about elderly people using smartphones. Kobayashi *et al.* [10] suggested that an input target should be larger than 30px to make it easier for elders to tap. Since smart-phone screen sizes and resolutions have changed much in the seven years since this study was published, we decided to redesign using the official iPhone guidelines. As such, most clickable elements on the redesigned GBER UI are at least 44pt in width or height in the iPhone X. Their study also noted that elderly preferred dragging operations rather than tapping. Further, they suggest that applications should avoid multi-mode interfaces— similar interfaces that show different statuses for one screen or view—as much as possible, since elderly users are less likely to notice changes in the modes and thus can become confused. For example, in their study, there were multiple modes for thumbnails, such as by events and by persons, and the participants had difficulty understanding which mode was active. In the redesigned GBER app, multiple views for the same or similar tasks were removed or merged into one, such as the calendar feature.

The ideal model of technology usage for elderly might involve breaking tasks down into small pieces to avoid elderly users feeling overloaded or getting lost easily. For instance, it is difficult for elderly users to use social networking applications on smart devices because they often require a sequence of actions during form completion. Hiyama *et al.* [9] proposed "Question First," an interaction model based on the inter-action modes of phone calls and emails. Elderly users were able to become familiar with the idea of social networking by simply answering questions on the application. The similar concept of micro-tasking can also be found in a study about elderly workforce matching [8]. The authors proposed a "spatial mosaic" framework for management of time, space, and skills related to elderly workforce matching. The current GBER service was based on this particular framework, and in the redesign, we applied the UI principles to the GBER UI. For example, the event recommendation and question cards were designed with a simple operation for the user: answering one survey question at a time by simply clicking a preset response option. This could make it easier to collect the user's data for the matching system. We will describe this and the other changes we made in more detail in the next section.

3 System Design

The main purpose of GBER as a service app is matching elderly people to jobs or activities that suit their interests and abilities. By collecting user behavior through GBER's in-app questionnaires, the system knows how to recommend opportunities to each individual user. Users need to manage and review their booked activities on the service. The following are the main actions possible using GBER:

1. Jobs and activities exploration based on time and location
2. Questions interface ("Q&A") for user profiling
3. Schedule interface for reviewing and managing booked jobs and events
4. Recommended opportunities information feed
5. Group-based communication and a personal profile page

A mid-fidelity prototype of the redesigned interface was developed using InVision, a web-based prototyping tool that generates realistic, interactive prototypes without the need for coding. The InVision prototype was presented to users on an actual iPhone X device. The following sections detail the parts of the prototype that were redesigned and tested in the user study. See Fig. 1 for a visual reference to the redesigned screens detailed below, and Fig. 2 for the equivalent screens on the current, live version of GBER.

Fig. 1. Key redesigned screens in the new GBER app UI. From left to right: (a) the home page; (b) the Q&A system in action; (c) the calendar page; and (d) the event search page.

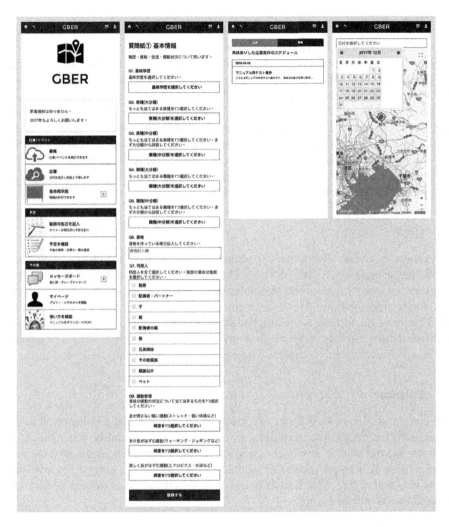

Fig. 2. Original screens in the current version of the GBER app. From left to right: (a) the home page, featuring the long, vertical menu; (b) the long version of the questionnaire; (c) the calendar page with a list display; and (d) the event search page with a calendar filter.

3.1 Tab Bar Navigation

Elderly users have difficulty understanding menu hierarchies [2], so it is recommended that the main navigation be placed identically on all pages [7]. Critical functions, like searching activities and scheduling, should always be accessible, from any screen in the app. Scrolling menu content should be reduced to a minimum as well. The tab bar fits these guidelines, so it was used in the new design (see any screen in Fig. 1).

3.2   Home Page

The aim of the new design (Fig. 1a) is to reduce the effort placed on the user in terms of getting access to the information they need across different situations. The home page design used several design strategies and patterns to reduce the information load yet provide the necessary information. A "feed" approach was used so that the user does not need to look for information by changing pages or by clicking any button: everything is accessible in one page. The card-based design creates a minimized information unit. Showing what is next on the schedule and recommending what can be next can shorten the experience of finding activities and opportunities in schedule calendar or map. By making home page general purpose—not tied to any specific feature—the design and the usage of the service becomes more flexible.

3.3   Q&A

Previous research has shown that extracting information from the elderly about their technology experiences is difficult [1, 9]. The current version of GBER users a series of long questionnaires to get information about users' activities and interests for the opportunity-matching algorithm. However, metrics showed that only about a third of users filled these out [1]. Instead, we redesigned the questionnaires as question cards (Fig. 1a) to divide the original long series of questions into smaller chunks that should be quicker and less overwhelming to complete. These pop up periodically on the home page.

3.4   Calendar

The current version of GBER has two kinds of information that are displayed in the calendar but these have different purposes: one is the user's availability, which they have to input, and the other is any booked events. For the former, this means that the user must go through a longer process of inputting information, with many steps involved. In the new design (Fig. 1c), the user does not need to input their availability: they can just add events at their leisure.

3.5   Map

To achieve the goals of involving users in activities in their region and making sure that the events are accessible, it is important to let users know where the event will be. The map interface needs to allow users to explore where and when events will take place. The difficulty is ensuring that this view provides enough information for the user to browse each possible event. The user will need to explore the available activities and then decide which to apply to given several pieces of information. In the new design (Fig. 1d), an easier solution is explored for elderly users to get access to events information. Specifically, information cards featuring events nearby and soon to happen are displayed at the bottom of the map view. Control filters are provided for fast exploration.

While the redesign was informed by informal feedback from current GBER users, we needed to ensure that the changes made would be beneficial. We also wished to know more about potential GBER users so as to attract more users and refine the service. Next we describe the user study we conducted towards this end.

4   Method

A user study was conducted to assess the usability and UX of the new GBER UI. The study followed a common approach [15] with a representative user testing an in-progress, mid-fidelity version of the UI through two scenario- and task-based "missions," completed by all participants. A think-aloud protocol [5] was followed to give us access to participants' thoughts as well as what they were looking at in the UI while using it. A split-part (pre- and post-testing) semi-structured interview was conducted to better understand participants' experiences with, knowledge on, and opinions about smartphones, community participation, and the GBER app.

4.1   Participants

Six Japanese elders (3 women and 3 men) aged 62 to 73 (mean age = 67) who were residents of Kashiwa city took part in the study. See Table 1 for demographics and usage information. Participants were not GBER users but all used smart devices, primarily smartphones. They also used map apps, particularly Google Maps, although only half used calendar apps. Participants were recruited through Second Life Factory, the elderly community located in Kashiwa city, which uses current GBER to improve social participation the member. Participants were compensated by Second Life Factory; and they were provided with refreshments and given access to the GBER app. The protocol was covered under the University of Tokyo ethics guidelines.

Table 1. Participant demographics and information on GBER and technology use

ID	Age	Gender	GBER user	Smart device	Map apps	Calendar apps
P1	73	Male	No	Smartphone, PC	Google Maps	Yes
P2	65	Female	No	Smartphone	Google Maps, Yahoo Maps	No
P3	62	Male	No	Smartphone	Google Maps	Yes
P4	65	Female	No	Tablet, Sony	Google Maps	No
P5	66	Female	No	Smartphone, Macbook	Google Maps	No
P6	73	Male	No	iPhone	Google Maps	Yes

4.2   Procedure

Participants were asked to meet the researchers at the University of Tokyo Kashiwa campus. They were greeted, lead to the study room (enclosed meeting rooms with a main table and chairs) and introduced to the study. They were then asked to sit at the table in front of a smartphone containing the new GBER prototype (Fig. 3). The facilitator then asked about demographics, technology use, and knowledge of GBER. After offering refreshments, the facilitator then introduced the participant to the new prototype and provided two "missions" tailored to assess the three redesigned features: the homepage; finding activities; and the new Q&A setup. An assistant then began to record video of the participants' interactions with the new prototype. The participant was guided through the tasks making up each mission by the facilitator. The facilitator took notes and prompted the participant to think aloud using neutral comments and questions, such as "Tell me more about that," "What are you thinking right now?" and "What are you looking at?" After finishing the missions, the participant was interviewed by the facilitator again about aspects related to the new GBER prototype. They were then debriefed and thanked for their participation.

Fig. 3. A participant interacts with the GBER prototype featuring the redesigned UI.

4.3 Missions and Tasks

Two missions addressing the three key issues covered by the redesign were provided to participants verbally by the facilitator. Each was framed as a scenario with a persona [15] and comprised of several tasks, where the participant was asked to imagine themselves as the user and carry out the action they believed would complete each task. The two missions were:

1. *Activity-Finding and Schedule:* Searching out new activities, viewing scheduled activities, and managing the schedule. An example task is: Your friends ask you for dinner next Wednesday, so you need to check if you are available at that time.
2. *Q&A:* Finding, understanding, and responding to the new Q&A system. An example task is: You notice that you are able to join some events tomorrow, so you try to find

an event to join through the searching feature. After you find some events, chose one and apply to it.

4.4 Instruments

Two sets of questions were used for pre- and post-test semi-structured interviews. The questions were split before and after to balance out the flow of the study. The first set of questions asked about demographics (age, gender) as well as GBER use, if the participant was already a user of GBER (e.g., *How do they use GBER, via smartphone, PC, or other? How often?*). The second set of questions asked about perceptions of participation, barriers and challenges to pursuing activities and hobbies, and general smartphone-related issues. Specifically:

- How would you rate your social participation on a scale from 1 to 5, where 1 is very low, 5 is very high?
- What kinds of activities you attend regularly, before and currently?
- Is there anything that makes it difficult for you to pursue your activities, hobbies, or interests? Please give an example.
- What activities do you want to do but cannot, and why? What is the difficulty?
- Do you use a calendar app? Which one? What do you use it for? Are you still using it? (If not, why not?) [The same was asked about map and message/SNS apps.]

4.5 Data Analysis

Written notes and answers to interview questions were transcribed. Video was reviewed to fill in blanks in the notes. Two analysts looked through the data several times for behavioral patterns and points where there were errors, confusion, and breakdowns. These were recorded in a qualitative matrix.

5   Results

5.1 Usability and UX Results

A summary of key results is presented in Table 2. Overall, while all participants were able to complete the missions and tasks, most required guidance, and there were clear areas where usability broke down for a substantial number of elders.

Although they were asked to find the next upcoming event, four of the participants pressed buttons on the recommendation card instead. P4 said that she had no interest in the upcoming event. P2 and P4 said that they were interested in the recommended event and kept pressing the "apply" button on the recommendation card. P6 found the upcoming event the first time and clicked on the information card to read the details, then said he did not see how this information benefited him.

Table 2. Matrix of the key user study results.

ID	Clicked "recommended" and ignored the upcoming card	Clicked the "cross" icon to finish the "add event" task	Used the tab bar to access the calendar	Used tab to find activities	Swiped to find out more information
P1	✓	✓	✓		
P2	✓		✓		✓
P3			✓	✓	
P4	✓	✓			
P5	✓	✓	✓		✓
P6					

Four participants were able to use the calendar icon in the tab bar as intended. P4 and P6 were not able to figure out how to navigate the calendar; they were looking for the entry of the schedule around the upper zone of the screen, not looking down at the tab bar. P2 encountered a bug and P6 was uncertain and give up on the task. The other three participants clicked on the cross icon to close the form. Only P3 used the "save" button on the bottom of the "add event" form page.

In terms of activity-finding, the majority struggled to complete the task, with the exception of P3. Only P3 successfully found and used the middle icon in the tab bar to get to the activities page without direction. P6 clicked another icon on the tab bar and then found themselves on another screen that was not what he wanted. When participants were asked to find an event to join, they kept looking at the event card at the bottom (see Fig. 1d). None used the red pins on the map to see if there was another event to join; instead, they pressed on the "I am interested" button. P2 and P3 used swiping gestures to slide between screens; even when the researchers told them that swiping was not possible and guiding them in terms of how to navigate, they kept trying to swipe between screens.

5.2 Activities and Barriers to Access

The difficulties in terms of pursuing activities that were reported by participants were highly specific and as such there were no patterns. For example, P1 said he was lazy, while P2 and P4's difficulties were about lacking time and money. P3 wanted to start his own business but did not know how. The self-rating of participation in social activities was high (median = 4). Two participants rated themselves as 5, or "very high," one gave a rating of 3, or "medium," and the rest of the participants rated their participation as 4, or "high."

6 Discussion

Overall, participants were intrigued by the new interface and experienced moments of joy. For instance, most participants enjoyed the emoji feedback and the level of detail presented in the events. However, there were several areas of confusion and usability breakdowns, such that it was challenging for some participants to finish certain tasks.

A common behavior that we observed suggests that our elderly participants were attracted to colors. Most participants kept pressing colorful elements or reading colorful text rather than the black and white elements and text, even though they were the right elements to interact with. This suggests we have to be careful about using flat design because it is hard for elderly to conceptually distinguish between visually similar elements, in our case flat-style tags and buttons. Importantly, this is not a visual perception issue (i.e., contrast, visual acuity), as older adults were able to perceive and read the elements in question. In effect, they were interpreting cues of the visual elements as the same, suggesting they were the same kind of element. Previous research has already indicated that older adults may prefer skeuomorphic rather than flat UI designs [cite]. Our results suggest that there is more than preference at play: flat design may not be as usable as alternatives. However, future work will need to explore this in greater depth. We will assess a skeuomorphic style for the interactive elements, like buttons, so the users might not miss them; also, non-button elements will be presented with colors or borders.

Some typical smartphone icons, like the calendar icon, were clear to participants, but some were not. This became apparent in two tasks requiring use of the tab bar navigation: checking the calendar schedule and exploring activities. Most participants successfully found the calendar (Fig. 1c) through the tab bar, but only one used the tab bar to access the activity-finding page (Fig. 1d), even though both tab bar buttons were placed next to each other in the tab bar. Further, all participants did not understand why and how the red pins on the activity-finding screen worked, even though all were Google Map users. This suggests that there was a mismatch between their mental model of what to expect on an activity-finding screen and what was actually on the screen. With these results alone, we can only speculate about the underlying cause: it could be the label ("recruiting") or presence of the map (elders do not associate maps or locations with activities). We will redesign the event boxes to have clearer clues of how to navigate or get access to other events. These clues will directly point out what users need to do to find out more information. For example, they may provide instruction text to guide first-time users to follow along.

There is a bit of evidence to suggest that certain visual design patterns overwrote the dominant right-to-left, top-to-bottom cultural reading pattern. When participants were asked to change screens using the tab bar or when they were expected to use the interactive elements at the bottom of the screen, they typically spent some time searched around the upper zone of the screen, exploring the bottom zone only after they realized what they needed was not there. However, this behavior changed when they were on the activity-finding page (Fig. 1d). Participants kept looking at the event box at the button and did not explore or interact with the elements in the upper zone (the map, filters, and search control). The most important action elements, like save buttons, may be moved to the upper zone, or perhaps be visually redesigned to more strongly draw the user's attention.

We also discovered an issue in our user study methodology that, in our experience, seems to be particular to our elderly participants. Specifically, it was hard for elders to pretend to be a persona. Even after we spent some time explaining what personas are and why we needed them to pretend (e.g., to save time, because the prototype was unfinished), they did not seem to understand and/or did not want to pretend In the first task, where participants were asked to find a booked event in the app, some said that they did not want to apply to that event or had not applied to it. One participant pressed on colorful elements, attempting to change the status of the interface. Half of all participants told us their real schedule or plans instead of carrying out the task of checking the schedule and adding an event. The facilitators needed to keep explaining that the tasks were pretend so that the study could go on. While it is unclear why, there are alternatives that we and others can explore in the future. One idea is to start with no preset persona (essentially, ensure a robust prototype design and have the participant carry out all necessary tasks before the main tasks). Another idea is to create customized personas based on the participants themselves (if we can get access to demographics information about them before the study).

The diversity of reasons for not participating or barriers to participation highlight the need for a service like GBER and motivate us to continue developing the platform, especially the matching algorithm.

7   Conclusions

We designed a new version of the GBER social participation app that was inclusive of elders' needs and abilities and then evaluated it with representative users. Through user testing supplemented by semi-structured interviews, we were able to glean new insights into elders' perceptions, behaviors, daily life, and use of smartphones, as well as their impressions on and ability to use GBER. The elders in our cohort—Japanese residents of Kashiwa city—were a tech-savvy group with diverse interests and a strong desire to participate more fully in their communities. The redesigned GBER app shows promise, but further design iterations are needed. Even so, we can propose some general findings and indications from our results. Even when elders are familiar with map and calendar apps, this familiarity may not translate to similar design patterns. Moreover, we must be careful with the use of flat design by ensuring that elements such as tags and buttons are clearly visually distinguishable. Finally, it may be difficult for elders to imagine themselves as personas going through scenarios, so alternative usability procedures may be needed. We will be applying these insights in the next design iteration and then release the new version, after which we will conduct further user testing with GBER users "in the wild." Future research will evaluate not only the usability and UX of the new GBER app but also its ability to improve the social participation of the elderly over a longer period of time and in situ.

Acknowledgements. This paper is based on results obtained from a project commissioned by the New Energy and Industrial Technology Development Organization (NEDO) and the Japan Science and Technology Agency (JST) under the Strategic Promotion of Innovative Research and Development Program. We thank Second Life Factory for their cooperation. We also thank the Institute of Gerontology at the University of Tokyo for hosting the study. We are grateful to our research assistants Seito Matsubara and Kao-Hua "Maark" Liu for helping us run the study. Finally, we thank our elderly participants for their time, effort, and insights.

References

1. Arita, S., Hiyama, A., Hirose, M.: GBER: a social matching app which utilizes time, place, and skills of workers and jobs. In: Companion of the 2017 ACM Conference on Computer Supported Cooperative Work and Social Computing, pp. 127–130. ACM, New York (2017)
2. Berenguer, A., Goncalves, J., Hosio, S., Ferreira, D., Anagnostopoulos, T., Kostakos, V.: Are smartphones ubiquitous?: An in-depth survey of smartphone adoption by seniors. IEEE Consum. Electron. Mag. **6**, 104–110 (2017). https://doi.org/10.1109/MCE.2016.2614524
3. e-Stat Statistics of Japan
4. Friedman, H., Martin, L.R.: The Longevity Project: Surprising Discoveries for Health and Long Life from the Landmark Eight Decade Study. Hay House, Inc., London (2011)
5. Gambier, Y., van Doorslaer, L.: Handbook of Translation Studies. John Benjamins Publishing, Amsterdam (2010)
6. Harada, S., Sato, D., Takagi, H., Asakawa, C.: Characteristics of elderly user behavior on mobile multi-touch devices. In: Kotzé, P., Marsden, G., Lindgaard, G., Wesson, J., Winckler, M. (eds.) INTERACT 2013. LNCS, vol. 8120, pp. 323–341. Springer, Heidelberg (2013). https://doi.org/10.1007/978-3-642-40498-6_25
7. Hellman, R.: Universal design and mobile devices. In: Stephanidis, C. (ed.) UAHCI 2007. LNCS, vol. 4554, pp. 147–156. Springer, Heidelberg (2007). https://doi.org/10.1007/978-3-540-73279-2_17
8. Hiyama, A., Kobayashi, M., Takagi, H., Hirose, M.: Mosaic: collaborative ways for older adults to use their expertise through information technologies. ACM SIGACCESS Access. Comput. **110**, 26–33 (2014). https://doi.org/10.1145/2670962.2670966
9. Hiyama, A., Nagai, Y., Hirose, M., Kobayashi, M., Takagi, H.: Question first: passive interaction model for gathering experience and knowledge from the elderly. In: 2013 IEEE International Conference on Pervasive Computing and Communications Workshops (PerCom Workshops 2013), pp 151–156. IEEE (2013)
10. Kobayashi, M., Hiyama, A., Miura, T., Asakawa, C., Hirose, M., Ifukube, T.: Elderly user evaluation of mobile touchscreen interactions. In: Campos, P., Graham, N., Jorge, J., Nunes, N., Palanque, P., Winckler, M. (eds.) INTERACT 2011. LNCS, vol. 6946, pp. 83–99. Springer, Heidelberg (2011). https://doi.org/10.1007/978-3-642-23774-4_9
11. Kobayashi, M., Ishihara, T., Kosugi, A., Takagi, H., Asakawa, C.: Question-answer cards for an inclusive micro-tasking framework for the elderly. In: Kotzé, P., Marsden, G., Lindgaard, G., Wesson, J., Winckler, M. (eds.) INTERACT 2013. LNCS, vol. 8119, pp. 590–607. Springer, Heidelberg (2013). https://doi.org/10.1007/978-3-642-40477-1_38
12. Obi, T., Ishmatova, D., Iwasaki, N.: Promoting ICT innovations for the ageing population in Japan. Int. J. Med. Inf. **82**, e47–e62 (2013). https://doi.org/10.1016/j.ijmedinf.2012.05.004
13. Salman, H.M., Wan Ahmad, W.F., Sulaiman, S.: Revisiting the usability of smartphone user interface for elderly users. In: Saeed, F., Gazem, N., Patnaik, S., Saed Balaid, A.S., Mohammed, F. (eds.) IRICT 2017. LNDECT, vol. 5, pp. 155–162. Springer, Cham (2018). https://doi.org/10.1007/978-3-319-59427-9_17
14. Tamiya, N., Noguchi, H., Nishi, A., Reich, M.R., Ikegami, N., Hashimoto, H., Shibuya, K., Kawachi, I., Campbell, J.C.: Population ageing and wellbeing: lessons from Japan's long-term care insurance policy. Lancet **378**, 1183–1192 (2011). https://doi.org/10.1016/S0140-6736(11)61176-8
15. Interaction Design - beyond Human-Computer Interaction. http://www.id-book.com/. Accessed 23 Feb 2018

Play It Again, Grandma: Effect of Intergenerational Video Gaming on Family Closeness

Loretta L. Pecchioni and Sanela Osmanovic[✉]

Department of Communication Studies,
Louisiana State University, Baton Rouge, USA
{lpecch1, sosman3}@lsu.edu

Abstract. Population aging, one of the sturdiest demographic trends of the past few decades, is leaving a substantial mark on the relationships and the structure of family. Three and even four generations are now in a position to spend significant parts of their lives together, making it increasingly important to form and maintain strong bonds among older and younger adults in families. One way to achieve this is through shared activities appealing to both sides of the age spectrum. In this study, we examined the potential of joint video gameplay to build or restore intergenerational family relationships. Participants (n = 183), mainly grandparents and grandchildren, were asked to play video games together over a period of six weeks. Before and after the treatment, participants completed a modified version of the questionnaire on the inclusion of the other in self as the measure of relationship closeness, as well as responded to a series of open-ended questions post-treatment. Results indicate a significant increase in the inclusion of other in the self. A comparison group (n = 88), tasked with having conversations with the same stipulations, yielded considerably less significant results. These findings suggest that video games as a shared activity hold the potential to positively impact family relationships by increasing relationship closeness, and thus improve the lives of both younger and older generation.

Keywords: Older adults · Video games · Inclusion of other in self
Intergenerational gaming · Family relationships · Interpersonal relationships

1 Introduction

The need for entertainment, competition, and challenge is part of human nature—that is how we discovered music, dance, and ultimately games [1]. People have always played games, from the ancient Senet board game, through more hazardous gladiator challenges of the Roman Empire, to contemporary leisure activities such as sports and video games [2]. Huizinga explained that playfulness and games are fundamental elements of civilization, critical for human cultural advancement, where each of us is *homo ludens*—man the player—and games are "a regularly recurring relaxation, the accompaniment, the complement, in fact an integral part of life in general" [1, p. 26]. This is becoming increasingly more prominent today, as the digital age has brought on

© Springer International Publishing AG, part of Springer Nature 2018
J. Zhou and G. Salvendy (Eds.): ITAP 2018, LNCS 10926, pp. 518–531, 2018.
https://doi.org/10.1007/978-3-319-92034-4_39

the tremendous rise of video games. Games are now pervasive, expanding into many aspects of modern life, from Internet search engine logos to mobile phones, from television to computers. Play is at our fingertips, instantly ready to begin as soon as we decide whether we want to dance to professional choreography, lose in scrabble to grandma who lives on the other side of the country, compete in tennis in our living rooms, fly a fighter jet, or go on a heroic adventure to save the world. While they started off as exercises for a narrow interest group in the last third of the 20th century, the technological revolution of the new millennium brought on the proliferation and accessibility of new computer devices, which in turn broadened video game development to encompass wider audiences, ultimately changing gaming from a marginal subculture to a major component of the mainstream culture [3, 4].

1.1   Sociability of Video Games

While games have historically been seen as collective activities [1], video games are generally perceived as a solitary endeavor [2]. Play with others, however, has been the backbone of video gaming since the beginning; after all, the first video game, *Pong*, was created for two players [5]. The Entertainment Software Association market report [6] revealed that some 54% of gamers play with others, while 45% say it helps their family spend time together. Further research found that the choice of gaming partners influences player's emotional state [7]. Specifically, playing with or against a friend produced deeper engagement, greater social presence, and higher levels of physiological arousal than playing with a stranger or against the computer. While friends use interaction through multiplayer games as a means to maintaining and enhancing their relationships [8], co-playing video games with parents was found to decrease the level of aggressive behavior, and increase prosocial behavior in adolescents [9].

1.2   Effect of Joint Video Gaming on Intergenerational Relationships

More recent studies have focused on the effect of joint video gaming on intergenerational relationships within families, particularly those between grandparents and grandchildren [10–13]. Distinct due to a usually large generational gap, positive grandparent-grandchild relationships have been shown to produce positive psychosocial outcomes for both parties, where grandchildren gain a source of family values, beliefs, and history, as well as social support, and grandparents gain a source of pride and the feeling of being young again [15]. Studies focusing on video games and the aforementioned relationships uncovered that intergenerational gameplay within families yielded social interaction and connectedness, with both younger and older adults finding video games a good platform for bonding [10, 11]. Young adults reported playing video games with older family members mainly as a means of maintaining or deepening the relationship, spending time together, and talking about simple and complex topics in a setting they find comfortable and comforting. Older adults found video gaming with younger family members enjoyable, fun, and bonding, highly rating the informal daily contact and the common ground joint gameplay creates between the two generations [11]. Both generations cherish the social interaction and the confederacy of collaborative play, while younger adults unanimously emphasized the desire to play more with the older adults in their families [11–15].

1.3   Relationship Closeness as Self-other Overlap

In order to understand the family interaction, in which individuals come to accommodate each other, video gaming within families has to be observed as a process in which people and technology adapt to each other over time through design, concession, and interaction. Understanding the aspects of our interactions with and around video games has much to offer to research on interpersonal communication and the adaptation of old social practices into new lifestyles. This is especially true in intergenerational gaming, where older adults who tend to have well-established rituals of social interaction come together with young adults, who have their rituals of social use of technology.

To empirically examine the effect of video gaming on family relationships, especially those among younger and older generations, we considered one of the relationship schemas imperative both to family communication and relational maintenance, inclusion of other in the self (IOS) [17]. Inclusion of other in the self is a measure of relationship closeness "in terms of differing degrees of overlap between the differentiated region that represents the self and the region that to the individual represents the other" [17, p. 597]. In other words, relationship closeness is seen as "people's sense of being interconnected with another" [17, p. 598]. The self-other overlap construct stipulates that individuals are motivated to form and maintain close relationships owing to an intrinsic yearning to grow, to expand their sense of the self [17]. Inclusion of other in the self develops as the person is motivated to embrace the resources, perspectives, and identities of their relationship partner [17]. Through this process, each individual not only welcomes other's knowledge and capabilities, but also begins experiencing the world from their point of view to some degree, which is exceptionally important in relationships with a significant generational gap. In a sense, one becomes closer with their relationship partner as the partner becomes more of a part of the self.

In relationships with a high degree of self-other overlap, an individual shares the other person's perspectives, identities, and resources [17]. In the context of family relationships, young adults who report high IOS with the parent are likely to share beliefs and values, use "we" language, and receive more support from the older adult [18]. Studies have shown that IOS is associated with relational maintenance, where the "model has proven fruitful in understanding the cognitive underpinnings of a variety of relationship phenomena such as the fundamental motivations to enter and maintain relationships" [19, p. 390]. Thus, it stands to reason not only that both younger and older adults are motivated to form stronger bonds, but also that the resulting higher IOS also may be associated with greater closeness in family relationships—that is, the sense of interconnectedness among family members—and with it, relationship satisfaction. With this, we postulated that:

H_1:   Regularly playing video games together is positively associated with a higher perceived IOS for both the older and younger adults.

1.4 Purpose of the Study

The aim of this study was to explore the effects of intergenerational video gaming on the bonds between older and younger family members. At the heart of the inquiry was the potential of the shared leisurely activity to build or maintain relationship closeness between family members, especially of different generations, through the increase in self-other overlap. To assess the effect of sharing the activity of playing video games as opposed to simply bonding over a conversation, we employed a mixed-methods longitudinal design to collect both survey data on self-other overlap and detailed personal accounts of the effects of gaming on dyadic family relationships. For comparison purposes, the same design was used to collect data on the effects of regular conversations on intergenerational family relationships, removing the shared gaming factor. The results of this investigation are presented below.

2 Method

To fully understand player interactions and relationship development in and around video gameplay, data were collected through a longitudinal study, using both quantitative and qualitative methods as described below. The participants were recruited from classes at two large universities in southern United States after receiving approval from the appropriate Institutional Review Board. Each participant was asked to select an adult, age 55 and above, from their immediate family circle who would consent to participate in the six-week study. Participants were divided into two broadly defined groups: younger adults (ages 17–35) and older adults (ages 55 and older). The broad demarcation of older adulthood was made with the study's focus on intergenerational family relationships in mind. Younger adults were tasked with selecting the game or games to be played, with input from the older family member where possible. For this study, data were gathered across two experimental groups. The first group, experimental group 1, was tasked with playing video games with their selected family member at least three hours a week, whether in a mediated or co-located setting. To control for the effect of gaming as a shared activity, a comparison group, experimental group 2, was asked to talk to their selected family member at least three hours a week, whether by mediated channels or in person. The data from the dyads were collected over a period of six weeks. Younger adults received partial course credit while older adults did not receive any compensation for taking part in the research.

Group 1 Participants. The sample consisted of 182 participants: 89 older adults, 58 females and 31 males (M = 1.65, SD = .48), ages 55–77 (M = 59.43, SD = 4.57), and 93 younger adults, 51 females and 42 males (M = 1.59, SD = .50), ages 17–28 (M = 20.39, SD = 2.05). The older cohort (n = 89) comprised 75 (84.27%) grandparents, 11 (12.36%) parents, 2 (2.25%) stepparents, and 1 (1.12%) aunt. The younger cohort (n = 93) comprised 77 (82.80%) grandchildren, 13 (13.98%) children, 2 (2.15%) stepchildren, and 1 (1.08%) niece.

Group 2 Participants. The sample consisted of 88 participants: 49 older adults, 32 females and 17 males (M = 1.65, SD = .48), ages 55–71 (M = 59.57, SD = 3.73), and 49 younger adults, 28 females and 21 males (M = 1.57, SD = .50), ages 18–25 (M = 20.84, SD = 1.71). The older cohort (n = 49) comprised 44 (89.79%) grand-parents, and 5 (10.20%) parents. The younger cohort (n = 49) comprised 44 (89.79%) grandchildren, and 5 (10.20%) children.

Data Collection. Considering the pretest-posttest nature of the study, self-completed questionnaires were used to collect standardized and thus comparable information from the participants. All questionnaires were web-based, administered using the Qualtrics survey tool. Web surveys were employed for being easily available and accessible, with the possibility to prompt for missing data or explain potentially difficult sections, which is important given the age of some of the participants and lack of funding for the study. For the same reason and also given the potentially mediated nature of the study, the questionnaires were used to collect narrative data as well, allowing for a broader accessibility. The survey was distributed online. It took approximately 30 min to fill out, with the narrative section approximated at 10 min, depending on the level of detail of the response and typing proficiency of the respondent. All participants were tasked with completing the survey at the beginning and the end of the study.

The pre-test survey consisted of four sections. The first section contained questions on demographic information (including gender, age, and relationship status) and the relationship between the two family members (i.e., parent-child or grandparent-grandchild) participating in the study.

For group 1, the second section comprised questions on previous gaming experiences (e.g. "Have you ever played video games?", "What games do you play most frequently?"). In the survey, video games were defined as all digital games, including applications embedded in mobile devices or accessible through social media. To assure understanding, pertinent examples were provided for game types, e.g. *FarmVille*, *Candy Crush*, card games. For group 2, the second section comprised questions on the modes and frequency of communication with their family members in general (e.g. "Which family member do you talk to the most?", "What means of communication do you usually use?").

For group 1, the third section was available to those who positively responded to the query on previous gaming experience with family members and consisted of questions related to that experience (e.g. "With which family member do you play video games most frequently?", "Within the past three months, how often have you played video games with this family member?"). For group 2, the third section comprised questions on the modes and frequency of communication with the family member who co-participated in the study (e.g. "How often do you talk?", "What means of communication do you usually use?"). Both groups were then asked to complete the fourth section of the survey which addressed the self-other overlap, coded per its respective scale, detailed below.

Self-other Overlap. The fourth and final survey section comprised the measure of relationship closeness as an overlap between the other and the self. The self-other overlap was measured using Aron, Aron, and Smollan's pictorial Inclusion of Other in the Self (IOS) instrument, presented in Fig. 1 [17]. The IOS scale asserts that in a close relationship, an individual acts as if there is a degree of inclusion of the other within the self so that, for example, close friends believe they are interconnected with each other. The IOS scale consists of a set of Venn diagrams, each representing varying levels of overlap ranging from slight to almost entirely overlapping. One circle in each pair is labeled "self" and the other circle is labeled "other." The participants were instructed to select the pair of circles that best depicted the nature of perceived overlap with the family member with whom they were participating in the study. The IOS scale has been extensively validated in both experimental and observational studies, with $\alpha = .87$ for family relationships [17].

Please circle the picture below which best describes your relationship

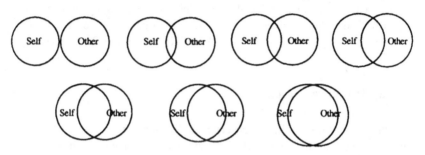

Fig. 1. The Inclusion of Other in the Self (IOS) scale

The post-test survey, completed after six weeks of video gaming and interaction, consisted of four sections. The first section contained questions on demographic information and the relationship between the two family members participating in the study. For group 1, the second section comprised questions on games played, gaming type (collaborative, cooperative, or other) and location (collocated, remote, or other) during the experiment. For group 2, the second section contained questions on the modes and frequency of communication with the selected family member during the study (e.g. "How often did you talk?", "What means of communication did you usually use?"). The third section comprised repeated self-other overlap measures.

Digital Postcards. The fourth and final section of the post-test survey was designed for narrative data collection, consisting of digital postcards asking the participants to share their experience of the six-week study in their own words. Participants were asked to reflect on their gaming/conversation rituals, the expectations, outcomes, and future plans in relation to joint gaming or conversations. Questions to aid in reflecting on the experience and writing the postcards were provided on the same page.

Data Analysis. Responses to the scaled items for both groups were examined using pretest-posttest statistical analysis. Narrative data was examined using careful, line-by-line content analysis, investigating the context, perspectives, and overall character of the responses. Emerging patterns and themes were uncovered by searching for word repetitions, then analyzing keywords and their context. Themes were grouped and assigned colors, and the narrative data was highlighted accordingly. Detailed analyses of pretest-posttest surveys and the narrative data for both groups are presented in the next section.

3   Findings

Based on the responses from our participants, we answer our questions about if and in what ways intergenerational game playing may affect the perceptions of self-other overlap as the measure of relationship closeness between family members. Both older and younger adults in group 1 largely reported positive outcomes from playing video games with family members—while enjoyment was an important aspect, maintaining connections with each other and with the home were repeatedly emphasized. The changes in self-other overlap were also noted, as both gained more insight into each other's lives, knowledge, and thoughts. The effects on group 2 were significantly smaller.

3.1   Group 1: Gaming Group

Group 1 Previous Video Gaming Experience. The majority of the older adults who participated in the study—63 or 70.8%—reported never having previously played video games. None of the remaining 29.2% identified as active gamers or playing video games on a regular basis, but stated they had either tried video games in the past or play sporadically. Their gaming experience included a wide variety of games and platforms, from mobile apps to exergames and sports simulations, to more complex first-person shooters. Younger adults who participated in the study predominantly (82, 88.2%) reported playing or having played video games, of which 29 (31.2%) identified as active gamers who play six or more hours per week. They too reported having played or playing a variety of games on different platforms.

The hypothesis postulated that regularly playing video games together is positively associated with a higher perceived self-other overlap for both the older and younger adults. To assess this hypothesis, a paired t-test was employed to determine whether there was a statistically significant mean difference between the perception of inclusion of other in self before and after the six-week gaming treatment. The results of the paired t-tests are presented in Table 1.

Table 1. Results of pretest and posttest IOS for younger and older adults for Group 1.

Variable/Results	N	Pretest-posttest diff. of M	SD	t	p
Inclusion of other in self for younger adults	93	1.44	.71	19.46	.000
Inclusion of other in self for older adults	89	1.30	.79	15.58	.000

Among younger adults, there was a statistically significant difference between pretest (M = 3.81, SD = 1.40) and posttest (M = 5.25, SD = .99), t(92) = 19.45, p < .0001, CI.95 1.29, 1.59. Cohen's effect size (d = 1.19) suggests a large increase in the perception of self-other overlap. The difference in the perception of inclusion of other in the self between pretest (M = 4.22, SD = 1.95) and posttest (M = 5.53, SD = 1.39), t(88) = 15.58, p < .0001, CI.95 1.14, 1.46, was also significant for older adults. Cohen's effect size for older adults (d = 0.77) suggests a moderate to high increase in the perception of self-other overlap. The hypothesis was thus supported for both test groups, with younger adults experiencing a more significant change.

3.2   Group 2: Conversation Group

Testing the conversation treatment group data for the same effects yielded significant outcomes, albeit much smaller. A paired t-test was employed to determine whether there was a statistically significant mean difference between the perception of inclusion of other in self before and after the six-week conversation treatment, finding a clear increase in the self-other overlap for both groups. The results of the paired t-tests are presented in Table 2.

Table 2. Results of pretest and posttest IOS for older and younger adults for Group 2.

Variable/Results	N	Pretest-posttest diff. of M	SD	t	p
Inclusion of other in self for younger adults	49	.36	.91	2.84	.007
Inclusion of other in self for older adults	49	.22	.59	2.68	.010

Among younger adults, there was a statistically significant difference between pretest (M = 4.27, SD = 1.38) and posttest (M = 4.63, SD = 1.52), t(49) = 2.84, p = .007, CI.95 .12, .63. Cohen's effect size (d = 0.25) suggests a small increase in the perception of self-other overlap. The difference in the perception of inclusion of other in the self between pretest (M = 4.49, SD = 1.12) and posttest (M = 4.71, SD = 1.29), t(49) = 2.68, p = .0101, CI.95 .06 .39, was also significant for older adults. Cohen's effect size for older adults (d = 0.18) suggests a small increase in the perception of self-other overlap.

3.3   Comparison Between the Groups

For both groups, the inclusion of other in the self pretest-posttest analysis follows the same trend, if not quite with the same effect size, as evident from Fig. 2.

As we can see, the conversation group started off with a higher perception of self-other overlap and experienced a distinctively smaller increase over the course of the study. It is important to note that in both groups, younger adults underwent a steeper increase than older adults.

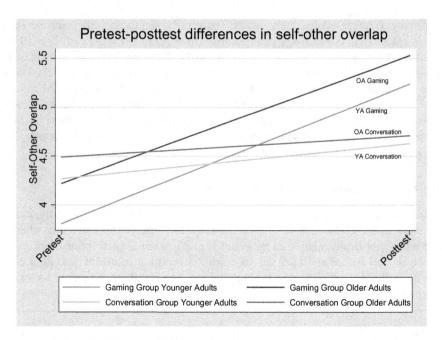

Fig. 2. Differences in IOS between pretest and posttest for both groups

3.4   Group 1: Qualitative Findings

In the final part of the closing survey, gaming group participants were asked to describe their six-week joint gaming experience—which games they played, did they compete or collaborate, what was the usual gaming ritual, what stood out to them the most, how did they feel about it at the beginning and the end of the study, will they continue playing video games together.

Time spent together and the resulting sense of closeness were in the center of most responses. As one female participant (57) noted:

My daughter is my oldest child so we have an extremely close bond. Now that she's older, it's hard for us to do fun things together even though we live in the same city. Even though it was a silly phone game for school, I appreciated the extra time we were able to spend together and I was surprised at the amount of time we actually spent engaged in conversation while doing this project. I think that more than anything that time actually made our relationship stronger.

Younger adults shared similar experiences, as a male participant (19) elaborated:

I found that we exchanged text messages more often during this time because my dad is a big trash talker. My dad and I already are very close but I'd say that this added an extra element to our relationship! It was great doing something together and it gave us something out of the norm to look forward to!

For some, it was about feeling physically closer to their family member, said one grandmother (63):

> With these video games, as simple as it may sound, reconnects you again no matter how far. While I played, it made me think of her, and when she played, it made me feel like we were connected even thought we were not in the same city. It made me feel close to her and we enjoyed it.

A younger female participant (18) concurred:

> I liked that we were playing together. It was a nice since the game put us both in position to have conversations about the game and other things in her and my life at the moment. She is about 900 miles away from me so it was a nice way to keep connected and share in each other's lives.

More than two-thirds of both older and younger adults (74.2% and 69.9% respectively) cited more frequent communication and spending more time together as the outcomes of the six-week joint gaming, while 24 (25.8%) younger adults and 31 (34.8%) older adults specifically cited an effect on the sense of interconnectedness or relationship closeness. A female participant, age 74, said:

> Playing games with my grandson keeps me sharp. We joke and talk and compliment each other on good moves. I love that he treats me as an equal and doesn't hold back. Playing games has brought us closer, in my opinion. Doing this with [my grandson] is now one of the joys in my life. I feel that playing games together has taught us both different things, we have learned from each other and about each other.

Participants' narratives provided a deeper understanding of their experiences, and perhaps an insight into potential moderating elements that occurred during the study. Primarily, both younger and older adults found new ways of connecting to their family members, whether through more frequent conversations, broader selection of topics, shared subjects, or pure entertainment. Gathering around the novel activity allowed participants the space to talk and listen in a relaxed environment, and they largely reported bonding and enjoyment, with older adults also placing emphasis on learning and acquiring new skills.

3.5   Group 2: Qualitative Findings

Unlike the gaming treatment group, for the conversation group time spent together and the resulting perception of closeness were not the focus of most narrative responses. As a matter of fact, only 10 (20.4%) younger adults and 14 (28.6%) older adults specifically referred to increased relationship closeness in their digital postcards. For some, as one female participant (21) noted, this is simply because three hours of talking per week was not beyond their usual routine:

> I live with my parents, so I see them every day. My [extended] family is also close, and we talk on the phone daily. There are times when I think they are too involved in my life and I get annoyed, but then I remember how lucky I am to have them. This assignment did not really make me go out of my way, although I did spend more time than usual talking to my grandma. She lives 10 min from my parents, so we just added our phone conversations with hanging out or shopping during the weekend.

For others, however, it was a bonding experience, as observed by one son (22):

I actually started calling my mom a couple of times a week to talk. I get along with her much better than with my dad and am more comfortable sharing things about myself and my life. I think she liked it too because I initiated the weekly phone calls and now she does it more. We definitely grew closer and she knows more about what's going on with my life than my brother.

Older adults shared similar stories and relished spending time with their family members, as a male participant (62) explained:

[My grandson] and I decided to do our "talking" during the weekend since we both have busy weeks, and he was at my door on Saturday nights with a half a gallon of ice cream and a war movie. Next weekend, I am barbecuing. We do talk when he is here, mainly about my late wife, or about his school and life. I like that it's brought us closer. He has grown to be a good man, and I am proud of him.

For one older female participant (59), it was about feeling better together:

When I was younger, I envisioned my kids and grandkids living near. Well, fate has a funny way of changing your life. When I fell ill 2.5 years ago, I had to move in with my daughter and her family. It's been difficult on everyone: I despise losing my independence and my daughter despises losing her freedom. But we love and respect each other and make it work. Helping my granddaughter with this school project, we talked to each other like two adults for the first time. We both opened up and I feel we are closer than ever before.

To summarize, in some measure, both younger and older adults appreciated the experience, connecting over deeper conversations, broader selection of topics, and newfound shared interests. For some, talking three hours a week was not outside the norm, while for others it created both opportunities and challenges. Opportunities were found in discovering more about family members, be it positive or negative. Challenges arose for both cohorts in having their voices heard during the conversation, dealing with arguments, boredom, and the lack of common topics that would move the chats from the realm of mundane. Majority of the participants do not plan on continuing with weekly conversations with family members, preferring that chats arise naturally.

4   Conclusion

In this study, we hypothesized that regularly engaging in a social activity—in this case, regularly playing video games together—will be positively associated with a higher perceived self-other overlap for both older and younger adults in the family. This was certainly true—while they played video games, in the background their relationships changed. The shift materialized in the significant upward slope of self-other overlap for both groups, indicating an increase in the perception of relationship closeness. This outcome suggests that playing video games together indeed creates a platform for the expansion of family relationships. Narrative accounts supported these findings. The opportunity for conversation and bonding attracted both younger and older adults. The older cohort, largely consisting of individuals who have never played video games before, found the experience entertaining, interesting, and gratifying. The younger cohort enjoyed the opportunity to display their expertise to older family members while in turn discovering more about them and receiving the benefit of an interested listener and adviser. Younger adults also gained greater awareness of their older gaming partners' knowledge and capabilities, while older adults saw their relationships with post-adolescents as more rewarding. The significance of these findings lies in the apparent ability of video games to serve as a bridge between generations, helping (re)form and maintain relationships that, when tended, can have a profound influence on the lives of both younger and older adults.

The findings of the comparison group were less stellar. While there was certainly an increase in the self-other overlap after the six-week conversation treatment, it was very modest. According to the illuminating narrative reports, the cause may be in the lack of motivation as most of the participants did not find the weekly conversations particularly rewarding. While the gaming dyads gathered around a fun activity, which added a dose of excitement and an environment that not only allowed for sharing stories but creating them too, the conversation group were left to their own devices, finding topics and ways to push through arguments and awkward pauses. As a matter of fact, accounts that reviewed the conversation experience positively, and saw it as bonding mostly also engaged in some shared experiences, such as shopping, watching a show, or pet sitting. The slightly higher increase in self-other overlap for younger adults possibly resulted from increased motivation as their participation in the study was a part of the class credit.

Overall, it can be said that the gaming group experienced larger effects post-treatment. For both younger and older adults, positive emotions such as happiness and enjoyment coalesced with—and stemmed from—the bonding, the conversations, the feeling of being closer to loved ones and of maintaining relationships across distances. They used the platform to spend time together, and have fun, talk, and generally take part in each other's lives.

Ironically, not all was fun and games in this group. Despite positive outcomes, only half of the older adults and less than half of the younger adults plan to continue playing with their family member. The cause of this lack of motivation to continue is clear—younger adults have considerably underestimated the technical abilities of their older family members, as well as their capabilities in mastering new forms of electronic entertainment. Thus, younger adults largely selected games based on old tabletop models, such as *Trivia Crack* and *Words with Friends*. Such games have a minimal learning curve and are less involving, which in turn led to older adults becoming bored towards the end of the six-week gaming period, and younger adults already being disinterested in these unchallenging apps. While some concerns about game accessibility may be valid, as many older adults do dread the fast response time requirements and the complex controls, this concern should be addressed and removed as an obstacle in enjoying the many worlds and stories video games provide.

5 Implications

With each year, the aging population grows [20]. In the same time, especially in the Western world, it seems that the use of technology has led to people living in the same space but rarely spending "quality time together," actually interacting and bonding. While popular media continuously emphasize the importance of meaningful interactions among family members and friends for the strength of the relationships, resulting in calls for sharing meals without distractions, with the wide introduction of personal computers, tablets and smartphones, the silence and distance are becoming more pervasive. However, as this and other recent studies show, the same technology can be used to counter this effect and enhance lives across generations. With careful design and consideration of current and potential players, video games have the capacity to positively impact families and social life in general, bridging the distance and drowning the silence [10, 12, 21].

6   Limitations

As with any research, this project has its limitations. First, the participants were selected using a sampling procedure of convenience rather than randomized sampling of a larger population. Furthermore, all participants are from the United States, which affects the generalizability of the findings. In addition, for younger adults the participation was a part of the course requirement, which may have impacted their perception of the project—must vs. want—and thus the level of their participation and satisfaction. Finally, the selection of the games was left to younger participants, who chose games based on their perception of the older adults' abilities and skills. Future research should address the limitations to this study, as well as examine more specific aspects of variable influences, examining the effect of specific games, of existing relationships, family patterns, and emotional and physical states. These additional motivations are important to gaining a more complete picture of shifts in family relationships and how video games can be used to help balance them.

References

1. Huizinga, J.: Homo ludens, a Study of the Play-Element in Culture. Roy, Oxford (1955)
2. Radoff, J.: Game On: Energize Your Business With Social Games. Wiley, New York (2011)
3. Castronova, E.: Synthetic Worlds: The Business and Culture of Online Games. University of Chicago Press, Chicago (2005)
4. Juul, J.: A Casual Revolution: Reinventing Video Games and Their Players. MIT Press, Cambridge (2010)
5. Kent, S.: The Ultimate History of Video Games: From Pong to Pokemon. Three Rivers Press, New York (2001)
6. ESA: 2017 Essential facts about the computer and video game industry (2017). http://www.theesa.com/wp-content/uploads/2017/04/EF2017_FinalDigital.pdf
7. Ravaja, N., Saari, T., Turpeinen, M., Laarni, J., Salminen, M., Kivikangas, M.: Spatial presence and emotions during video game playing: does it matter with whom you play? Presence Teleoperators Virtual Environ. 15(4), 381–392 (2006)
8. Wohn, D.Y., Lampe, C., Ellison, N., Wash, R., Vitak, J.: The "S" in social network games: Initiating, maintaining, and enhancing relationships. In: Proceedings of 44th Annual Hawaii International Conference on System Sciences. IEEE Computer Society, Kauai (2011)
9. Coyne, S.M., Padilla-Walker, L.M., Stockdale, L., Day, R.D.: Game on… girls: associations between co-playing video games and adolescent behavioral and family outcomes. J. Adolesc. Health 49(2), 160–165 (2011)

10. Osmanovic, S., Pecchioni, L.: Beyond entertainment: Motivations and outcomes of video game playing by older adults and their younger family members. Games Cult. Spec. Edn. Games Ageing **11**, 130–149 (2015)
11. Osmanovic, S., Pecchioni, L.: Family matters: the role of intergenerational gameplay in successful aging. In: Zhou, J., Salvendy, G. (eds.) ITAP 2016. LNCS, vol. 9755, pp. 352–363. Springer, Cham (2016). https://doi.org/10.1007/978-3-319-39949-2_34
12. de la Hera Conde-Pumpido, T., Loos, E.F., Simons, M., Blom, J.: Benefits and factors influencing the design of intergenerational digital games: a systematic literature review. Societies **7**, 18 (2017)
13. Zhang, F., Kaufman, D.: A review of intergenerational play for facilitating interactions and learning. Gerontechnology **14**, 127–138 (2016)
14. Lin, M., Harwood, J., Bonnesen, J.L.: Conversation topics and communication satisfaction in grandparent-grandchild relationships. J. Lang. Soc. Psychol. **21**(3), 302–323 (2002)
15. Costa, L., Veloso, A.: Being (grand) players: review of digital games and their potential to enhance intergenerational interactions. J. Intergenerational Relat. **14**(1), 43–59 (2016)
16. Loos, E., Zonneveld, A.: Silver Gaming: Serious Fun for Seniors? In: Zhou, J., Salvendy, G. (eds.) ITAP 2016. LNCS, vol. 9755, pp. 330–341. Springer, Cham (2016). https://doi.org/10.1007/978-3-319-39949-2_32
17. Aron, A., Aron, E.N., Smollan, D.: Inclusion of Other in the Self Scale and the structure of interpersonal closeness. J. Pers. Soc. Psychol. **63**(4), 596–612 (1992)
18. Agnew, C.R., Van Lange, P.A.M., Rusbult, C.E., Langston, C.A.: Cognitive interdependence: commitment and the mental representation of close relationships. J. Pers. Soc. Psychol. **74**, 939–954 (1998)
19. Mashek, D.J., Aron, A., Boncimino, M.: Confusions of self with close others. Pers. Soc. Psychol. Bull. **29**(3), 382–392 (2003)
20. UN: World Population Prospects. Key Findings and Advanced Tables. 2017 revision. United Nations, New York (2017)
21. Loos, E.F.: Designing meaningful intergenerational digital games. In: International Conference on Communication, Media, Technology and Design, Istanbul (2014)

The Big Meaning of Small Messages: The Use of WhatsApp in Intergenerational Family Communication

Sakari Taipale[1]([✉]) and Manuela Farinosi[2]

[1] Department of Social Sciences and Philosophy, University of Jyvaskyla, Jyvaskyla, Finland
sakari.taipale@jyu.fi
[2] Department of Humanities and Cultural Heritage, University of Udine, Udine, Italy
manuela.farinosi@uniud.it

Abstract. This study explores the use of WhatsApp instant messenger in extended families in two countries, Finland and Italy, that represent different family and communication cultures. Qualitative research material was collected in 2014/2015 from families consisting of three or more generations and living either in the same or different households. A directed approach to qualitative content analysis was applied in the analysis of the research data. The results of the study show that WhatsApp is considered to facilitate family interaction across generations. The success of WhatsApp in the family context accounts for two main factors: first, for the possibility to reach the whole family at once; and secondly, for its capacity to promote "phatic communion" via small messages. While utilizing various communicative modalities of WhatsApp (text and voice messages, photos, videos), family members take into account others' preferences and communication skills.

Keywords: Extended family · WhatsApp · Instant messaging
One-to-many communication · Phatic communion · Reach
Intergenerational relations

1 Introduction

This study investigates instant messaging as a form of everyday family communication. Particular focus is given to the use of WhatsApp which is currently one of the most popular instant messaging applications in many countries [1]. The study seeks to answer the question: What is the importance of small messages exchanged via WhatsApp for the sense of social coherence in extended families? In this research, extended families consist of family members representing two or more generations who may live in the same or different households [2, 3]. What makes WhatsApp an attractive communication tool for such families is that it allows both one-to-one and one-to-many interaction, and provides multiple modalities for intergenerational family communication (e.g. voice, text, photos, and videos).

The study argues that the big meaning of small WhatsApp messages emerges from both its technical properties and social affordances. WhatsApp makes it possible to reach

© Springer International Publishing AG, part of Springer Nature 2018
J. Zhou and G. Salvendy (Eds.): ITAP 2018, LNCS 10926, pp. 532–546, 2018.
https://doi.org/10.1007/978-3-319-92034-4_40

more than one family member at time, sometimes the entire family. Multiple modalities allow the choosing of the most suitable mode of communication according to personal and joint preferences of the sender and the receiver(s). Second, the study argues that extended families have harnessed WhatsApp especially for daily phatic communion [4]. That is to say that instead of the exchange of highly relevant and important information, small WhatsApp messages helps to sustain the social bonds between family members whose daily agendas and schedules are often incompatible.

Empirical evidence provided in the study is drawn from qualitative research material collected from Finland and Italy in 2014–2015. Finland is a Northern European country where families and households are characteristically smaller than in Italy that is located in Southern Europe. Both countries were among the forerunners in the adoption and use of mobile phones in Europe. The research material is analyzed following the principles of a directed approach to qualitative content analysis.

The next section provides a short overview of the WhatsApp application and its recent success. Thereafter, prior research of instant messaging in families is presented and definitions for the key theoretical concept of the study are provided. Qualitative methodology and data used in the study are presented before the results section. The study concludes by summarizing the answers to the research question and discussing the limitations of the study.

1.1 WhatsApp's Growth and Success

WhatsApp is an instant messaging application that runs on mobile communication devices equipped with an Internet connection. It allows sending text, picture, voice and video content, for one person at a time or to several persons using chat groups. WhatsApp can be categorized as a real-time – or near-real-time – communication tool.

In addition to these primary functions, WhatsApp makes possible following the success of a message delivery, such as checking when contacts are available and when they are typing messages. WhatsApp indicates with a 'tick' mark when the message has been successfully delivered and with two 'ticks' when it has been received and read. Similarly, WhatsApp shows whether other users are currently online and when they last were logged in. The user, however, can disable the latter feature. Previous studies have documented that this micro-scale peer-monitoring is commonly used to check whether a person is available, without a real intent to contact them [1, 5].

Following the release of WhatsApp in 2009, its popularity has grown globally. According to Statista [6], the total number of WhatsApp users elevated from 200 million to 1.3 billion between April 2013 and July 2017. However, available user statistics are somewhat diverse, incompatible, and unavailable for some countries, despite consistently demonstrating an increase in user rates.

In the context of Nordic countries, the Audience Project [7] report shows that WhatsApp was clearly more popular in Finland than in any other Nordic country in 2016. In Finland, WhatsApp was ranked as the most popular social media tool, while in other countries it did not come close to the top. In the last quarter of 2016, 68% of smartphone owners in Finland were reported to use WhatsApp. Finns were also very active WhatsApp users, as 49% stated using it several times every day and 29% at least once every day. In comparison, in Sweden the same figures were 25 and 16%, respectively. The same report shows that women (42%) used WhatsApp more than men (32%) in Finland, and that WhatsApp was the most popular social media in all age groups. The penetration rates varied being the highest among 15–25 year-olds (70%), and the lowest for 56+ year-olds (18%). In fact, the growth in the number of users is pronounced compared with 2014, when just more than a third (37%) of Finns reported using WhatsApp [8]. For Italy, the penetration numbers are not so readily available. According to Cosenza, 22 million Italians used WhatsApp in 2017, which is about a third of the total population. While the profile of users is diverse, ranging from the young to the old, the average time spent on WhatsApp in Italy was 11.5 h a month. However, those who use WhatsApp several times a day were typically between the ages of 15 and 24 [8]. Deutsche Bank estimated that the penetration rate of WhatsApp among Italian smartphone users was 68% in 2015 [9].

1.2 Instant Messaging in Families

Online instant messengers remained for a significant time a communication media mainly utilized by teenagers for peer-to-peer communication and young adults for work-related interaction [10–13]. Recent studies have also continued to highlight children's preference to communicate with their peers (and not parents) through mobile and social media tools [14]. As WhatsApp is sneaking into the technological reservoir of older family members, its untapped potential for family communication across generational boundaries begins to unfold.

A majority of prior research deals with the gratifications of instant messengers and similar media tools [15]. Church and de Oliveira [18] studied 20 to 60 year-old Spaniards, and found that immediacy, a sense of community and free use were considered as the main gratifications of WhatsApp, although SMS was still regarded more reliable, invoking less privacy concerns. O'Hara et al. studied the use of WhatsApp among 17 to 49 year-old Britons with various occupational backgrounds including both individuals and couples [1]. They suggest that WhatsApp is constitutive of commitment and faithfulness included in social relations, and serves the needs of social bonding more than functional exchange of information.

The migration of instant messengers from desktop computers and laptops to smartphones multiplied the total number of users and diversified their socio-demographic profile. Smartphones did not only add mobility to instant messaging but they also extended a range of available modalities from sole text-based messaging (e.g. IRC and AOL's Instant Messenger) and voice calls to photos, voice messages and Internet calls [17, 18]. The possibility to choose between various modalities makes WhatsApp a suitable tool for connecting people with differing communicative preferences, and by so doing it may help to overcome social differences between family generations.

In extended families instant messengers have to be positioned into intricate parent-child relationships. On the one hand, these relationships reflect children's opposing needs for autonomy and parental care. Studies show that mobile communication in general serves both ends; they work as an "umbilical cord" between children and parents [20] and as a medium to gain a bigger degree of independence [19]. On the other hand, the social roles of parent and child are easily inverted in relation to digital technology use. Daily family practice reflects parent's dependency on their children's technological assistance and caretaking [3].

A possibility to sustain and nurture family connections from afar has caused researchers to argue that new communication technologies and social media have produced "networked families" or new relational families [21–25]. However, studies exploring the ways in which families use mobile instant messengers, and their group chat functions in particular, to stay connected are few. One of the few comes from Rosales and Fernández-Ardèvol, who show that while WhatsApp is commonly used across all age groups in Spain, the ways in which smartphones are used relates to interests and communication needs that change as we grow older – more than to age-differentiated skills [26]. Siibak and Tamme argue that Estonian families appreciate new web-based communication tools especially because they offer a way to feel close [27]. The same authors remind that web-based communication technologies serve family relations also when people live in the same household. Portable communication devices and applications are widely used to coordinate activities and share information in the physical proximity of others [27].

Siibak and Tamme maintain that Estonian families favor synchronous chat groups and other closed online spaces in family communications. This is an important observation since prior research reiterates that face-to-face conversations and telephone calls predominate family communication and local relationships [28–31]. However, it begins to unfold now that some new forms of social media facilitate more group and small community interaction than early forms of social networking sites, in which multiple audiences easily collapse into one and compromise the privacy of conversations [32].

Therefore, compared with traditional person-to-person communication channels (like voice calls and SMS) instant messengers are particularly useful for staying in touch with closely related people and communities that favor enclosed and private communication spaces to public or semi-public social media platforms [16]. Close-knit communities, like families, do not seek to reach vast audiences, but are neither limited to private one-to-one communication.

1.3   A Technology of Middle Reach and Phatic Expression

Baym argues that the success of social networking sites is based on their wide, but selective reach [31, p. 30]. She has borrowed the notion of reach from Gurak, who describes it "as the partner of speed" and maintains that digitized contents cannot only travel with speed, but they can also reach large audiences. As Baym acknowledges, media technologies vary in their ability to attain, support, or reach audiences of different sizes. The reach of face-to-face contacts is the narrowest, but the qualities of in-person communication, are also insurmountable. In-person communication involves a range of nonverbal, facial, and bodily cues that are difficult to mediate to their fullest extent using any technological mean. Personal mobile communication tools allow both narrow reach of the closest friends and family members (using phone calls and SMS), but also a wide reach of acquaintances and even strangers (through Twitter, Instagram, Facebook and so on).

But as Graham notes, Byam's observations are based on early forms of ICT and social media [33]. Instant messaging applications like WhatsApp, that feature a closed group chat function, seem to fall in-between these two ends; WhatsApp makes it possible to reach, sustain, and manage middle reach audiences as well. The extended family serves as a good example of such a middle-range community, since it typically involves both close family members, (like siblings and parents), but also distant family members and relatives, (like stepparents and half-siblings), in addition to grandparents living further away. Previous research that relies on rather straightforward distinctions between weak and strong ties easily views contemporary families as a weak nexus of individually networked family members; families that have to make more of an effort to stay connected than the previous generations did [24].

WhatsApp and similar mobile instant messengers have introduced a new layer to mobile communication, which allows easy communication within families. WhatsApp affords a possibility for rather secure communication for dyadic family relationships and for the entire family communities, who want to discuss private family matters, to exchange emotions, provide care and support without revealing this intimacy in public. Family WhatsApp use does not bring separate individual networks together, but it conjoins family members who all know each other.

In this connection, the "sharing as caring" mantra obtains perhaps a deeper and fuller meaning than anywhere else. While small acts of sharing, such as social media statutes updates, "post sharing", and "liking", might be sufficient to establish and maintain weak ties in Twitter, Instagram, or Snapchat, strong family ties are never established purely online. The strength of family ties is based on a great amount of time, emotion, intimacy, and reciprocal services family members invest in intra-family relationships [34]. Family WhatsApp groups offer a particular channel to maintain and nurture these strong family ties whether near or afar, providing both synchronous and asynchronous modes of communication that helps the juggling of individual daily agendas and timetables. Considering that the notion of sharing points to a set of values that are typically feminine, such as openness, and mutuality [35], it is not so surprising that WhatsApp is used more widely among women than men.

These affordances of closed WhatsApp chat groups resonate well with the particularities of contemporary extended families, which are geographically dispersed, non-hierarchical, and change their composition over time. These affordances have made WhatsApp a very fit medium for one-to-group communication, and allowed constant family connectivity [15]. Family members, who used to, as Rainie and Wellman write, "mostly dance sole but take part in a few duets and household ensembles" [24, p. 162], can now use a WhatsApp chat group to keep their own band together and play their joint favorite songs non-stop.

The meaning of sharing photos, video clips, and exchanging small text and voice messages is perhaps best captured through the concept of phatic communion. The term was coined by Malinowski, who showed that seemingly meaningless and purposeless talk, greetings, and small talk have an important social function establishing, maintaining and renewing, social bonds between interlocutors [4]. More recently, Miller argued that online media cultures promote mainly social and networking-driven communication at the expense of functional and informational contents, and dialogic intents [37]. In fact, the design of many social media platforms encourage the use of only a short expression by limiting the number of characters a user may use (e.g. on Twitter). This promotes the use of visual material, and provides new ways of expressing emotion with one-click. Wittel pessimistically argues, that in the end all this contributes to the flattening of communication and even to the flattening of social bonds [36].

2   Method

2.1   Data Collection Procedure

The data was gathered using the Extended Group Interview (EGI) method [3, 38]. The EQI was designed to study intergenerational relations in extended families, and it was premised on the collaborative nature of the ethnographic enquiry. The "extended" refers to the study of extended families instead of nuclear families. It also points to the need for various methods of conducting interviews, ranging from in-person to electronically mediated ones, in geographically dispersed extended families. EGI allows reaching a number of family members by stretching out the interviews from one specific place and time into a series of interviews.

In this study, college students (hereafter, *key informants*) were given the assignment to first observe ICT-related communication in their families for one week and then interview at least five of their family members (hereafter, *informants*) on ICT usage. The key informants were instructed to interview at least one of their parents and one grandparent, if that was possible. They were free to choose the three remaining interviewees as long as that they were of different ages. Some key informants extended the interviews to cover their cousins, aunts and uncles, especially in Italy, and others interviewed their spouses and own children. The limitation of the EGI method had been reported in earlier publications [3, 38].

Based on the fieldwork, the key informants wrote three reports, with a minimum of 300 words each, in which they were asked to describe: (1) what ICT tools and applications were used to stay in touch with family members; (2) how the key informants consider their ICT skills in relation to one another; (3) how ICT shapes the roles within their family. ICT was defined broadly as different kinds of digital communication devices or services that are used to stay in contact and communicate with family members (e.g. mobile phones, e-mails, Facebook, Twitter, WhatsApp, Instagram).

2.2   Informants

The empirical research data consists of 66 student reports based on extended group interviews (EGI) collected from Finland, Italy and Slovenia in 2014/2015. In Slovenia, WhatsApp was largely concentrated on peer-to-peer usage at the time of data collection. Only one Slovenian family reported using it for family communication. For this reason, the analysis is limited to Finnish and Italian families (N = 43).

College students from three universities served as key informants. In Finland, the key informants were social sciences and communications studies students at the University of Jyväskylä, who were recruited through university e-mailing lists. In Italy, the students were undergraduate and graduate students of the Multimedia Communication study programme, who likewise were invited to take part in the study via email. In Slovenia, the key informants were students of the Social Informatics graduate programme at the University of Ljubljana. Unlike in other countries, Slovenian key informants completed interviews and reporting as a compulsory assignment as part of an ongoing course.

The key characteristics of the participants of the study are included in Table 1. The total number of informants in this study is 397, including the 66 key informants. A majority of the key informants were females (45). Their ages range from 20 to 38, being slightly higher on average in Finland (28) than in Italy (24). The key informants interviewed and observed altogether 162 female and 168 male family members. The key informant also provided information on whether or not they shared the same household with their family informants. A geographical distance between the key informants and informants was inquired to estimate the need for electronically mediated family communication, and to discern country differences in the dispersion of family members. The distances between family members were slightly shorter in Italy than in Finland, where the key informants most often lived in their own households.

Table 1. Characteristics of key informants and informants by country

	Finland	Italy	Slovenia
Key informants (n)	*22*	*21*	*23*
Gender (n)			
Male	3	10	8
Female	19	11	15
Age (years)			
Range	20–38	21–28	23–30
Mean	28	24	28
Informants (n)	*111*	*104*	*115*
Gender (n)			
Male	50	51	61
Female	61	53	54
Relationship with the key informant (n, (mean distance))			
Parent	36 (150 km)	31 (111 km)	42 (58 km)
Sibling/stepsibling	26 (217 km)	18 (219 km)	27 (141 km)
Grandparents	10 (239 km)	21 (164 km)	22 (90 km)
Others	39	34	25

2.3   Method of Analysis

The research material was analyzed following the principles of a directed approach to qualitative content analysis [39]. This method is based on a deductive category application and is also known as theory-driven approach because it usually starts with a theory or prior incomplete research findings as guidance for initial coding. During the analysis, the parts of the report that dealt with instant messaging and WhatsApp in particular were extracted. The notion of "reach" and "phatic communion" provided an initial coding frame and helped focus on parts of the reports that were relevant in terms of the aims of the study. These initial categories were then reanalyzed to promote clustering around common themes. What was found to be constructive of "reach" and "phatic communion" in the context of family WhatsApp use emerged straight from the research material without any specific pre-determined categories. When reporting results, pseudonyms are used to guarantee the anonymity of the informants. The ages of informants were manually inserted afterwards by the researcher, and they are presented within parentheses.

3 Results

3.1 Reaching the Family

National differences in the use of WhatsApp for intra-family communication are pronounced. They relate to different communication cultures and housing arrangements, such as a higher age of moving out in Italy when compared with Finland. These are directly connected to physical distances between grown-up children, their parents, and grandparents. The physical distance reinforces the need for electronically mediated family communication. In addition, a prevalent pricing model for wireless internet connection may encourage or hinder the shift from voice calls and SMS to online-based communication. In Finland, mobile broadband connections usually includes an unlimited amount of data transfer at a flat rate, while the flat rates in Italy typically include a limited amount of data transmission. Despite these differences, a common incentive for using WhatsApp in family communication was cost saving. Several key informants reported that in their families sending messages and making voice calls via WhatsApp was considered free-of-charge, and hence a cheaper option than making normal phone calls or sending SMS/ MMS which can be charged as per use (e.g., In Finland, Carla, 23 and Ella, 24; In Italy: Alice, 23 and Elisa, 26).

In Italy, a large part of family WhatsApp use took place between younger family members of approximately same age. Furthermore, this communication was not restricted to the closest family member only (e.g. the key informants Alessandro, 20; Bruno, 27; Matteo, 24), but WhatsApp was also used to reach cousins and second cousins (Silvia, 25), and in some cases also uncles and aunts, who were typically less than 20 years-older than the key informant (Melissa, 25; Monica, 25; Enrico, 24).

Families in which everyone uses WhatsApp were most numerous in Finland. Many Finnish key informants described WhatsApp as a new daily mode of family communication (e.g. Jenny, 28; Sara, 25), although they had typically created a family chat group quite recently. One of them is Emma (24), who describes the pivotal role of the WhatsApp group for daily family communication as follows:

> Me and my core family's (parents, 52 and 53, sister, 19) main channel of communication is nowadays a WhatsApp chat group. We created this group about half year ago, and it has become very active. Someone sends photos and messages every day for the group and everyone follows it actively. The biggest difference to the past is that my parents have learnt to use the instant messaging service WhatsApp.

A major advantage of WhatsApp chat groups is that they allow the majority of the family to be reached at once. Finnish key informant Emilia (24) express this as follows: "Recently, we created a WhatsApp chat group for the family, through which we can easily reach the entire family when we need to contact everyone at once." WhatsApp had clearly become more common in Italian families as well. Monica (25) from Italy describes WhatsApp as something novel for her family that is mainly used by her mother (53) and all the children (25 and 19):

> We all use WhatsApp, the smartphone application, primarily for instant messaging. My father (58) is a geek and enjoys technology. He likes to keep up to date but, due to his age or to scarcity of time, is not able to use this application as proficiently as the others. To my mother (53), although she is not the oldest of the respondents, WhatsApp is a novelty because a smartphone was bought for her only recently. My aunts and uncles, instead, regularly use WhatsApp with family and friends, and also for sending photos… I personally use WhatsApp with all the respondents but especially with my mother, because I want her to learn the use of this application and I wish to share with her some parts of my life, since we live far away from each other.

The end of this quote illustrates the "sharing as caring" aspect of family WhatsApp communication. Perhaps not so surprisingly it is a practice that mostly occurs between mothers and their daughters. This gendered aspect of WhatsApp communication is illustrated by several Finnish key informants too. For example, the Finnish key informant Emma (24) describes that her mother (52) was for a long time against acquiring a smartphone. But when she finally got a smartphone from her employer and learnt to use, it was the mother who "initiated the idea of creating a WhatsApp chat group for the family". Another Finnish key informant Emilia (24) encapsulates the central role of mothers in family WhatsApp communication writing: "No longer mom (52) needs to call once a week to ask news from her offspring, as we exchange news every day".

The mother's central role in family communication is also accentuated by comparing it to father's limited communication skills and practices. While Finnish key informant Julia (21), her sister (19) and mother (54) praise "that WhatsApp is the best communication means, as it can be used to send messages for free over a mobile network, and what's best, sending photos is easy and free", they have chosen other ways to stay in touch with the father (59). According to Julia, she, her sister and mother "always call [him] as he has not installed WhatsApp on his smartphone and his messages in general are unclear". Julia specifies that her father does not punctuate the messages, he makes spelling mistakes and sends jokes others do not understand. Some Italian key informants also elaborate the differences between mothers and fathers with respect to their WhatsApp communication. The Italian key informant Silvio (21) writes that:

> To keep in touch with my mom (50) I can use calls, SMS, WhatsApp and email, since she has been able to integrate herself almost completely into the world of technology, also using a smartphone. My dad (54), on the other hand, is still at a lower step, and I can communicate with him only through calls, SMS and more recently with emails.

These extracts indicate that even in the cases where the entire family can be reached through WhatsApp, mothers are typically considered as the main operators of family communication. At the same time, it is also considered problematic that fathers remain a bit distant if they do not use instant messengers (e.g. in Finland, Teresa, 26). In this light, WhatsApp family communication appears as a new form of immaterial labor, in particular of care work, which still involves more women than men [40].

The importance of WhatsApp communication for the social coherence of family is clearly articulated by both Finnish and Italian informants; WhatsApp facilitates intergenerational connections and togetherness within the extended family. A younger brother (11) of Finnish key informant Sofia (24) expresses this as follows: "Thanks to WhatsApp, we write and stay in touch with each other more". Similarly, the Finnish key informant Emma (24) summarizes her interviews writing that "We discussed that all have noticed how we are much more in touch with other family members after adopting WhatsApp than before it." Even a nine-year-old sister of the key informant Maria (24) maintains that the advantage of WhatsApp chat group is that "you can know how other family members are doing, even if they are afar".

In some families where parents had not started using WhatsApp, it was anticipated that their presence in this platform "would facilitate family communication", like the little brother (12) of Finnish key informant Marika (29) puts it. A sister (21) of Finnish Sofia expresses the same concern as follows: "parents (51 and 48) are excluded, we have own small circle. Parents are bitter as that they don't see the pictures... The relationships would be saved, if they only had WhatsApp."

3.2   Short, Fast and Trivial

The role of WhatsApp as a medium of phatic communion emerges strongly from the reports of both Finnish and Italian key informants. Most often, it appears implicitly as downplaying of the importance of small WhatsApp messages, which in practice, however, seems to form the backbone of electronically mediated family communication. The report of the Finnish key informant Ella (24) is illustrative in this sense. She writes that "at times, the contents of messages are not really important and full of information, and then WhatsApp is the best choice". Similarly, the sister (25) of Finnish key informant Teresa (26) feels that "WhatsApp has made us closer as we can speak about trivial matters and have fun even if we are physically in different places." While the benefits of reaching the entire family are perhaps most pronounced when geographical distance prevents regular in-person contact, WhatsApp is also actively used for intra-household communication. For instance, Italian key informant Claudia (21) writes that WhatsApp is the principal application when a "simple and fast application" is considered for daily communication with relatives sharing the same household with her.

Another characteristic of phatic expression via WhatsApp relates to its adaptability to different kinds of communication needs and preferences. Family members can accommodate each other's favorite communication modes when they want to facilitate intra-family communication and keep the family connected.

> With my partner (23) and little brother (23) we communicate with a mobile phone mainly using WhatsApp messages and Facebook Messenger... WhatsApp messages among a younger generation are usually the easiest and fastest ways to connect. Also the free use of the given application is a major reason for its usage. (Karin, 27, Finland).
> It must be said that WhatsApp makes everybody agree, and in my opinion, it acts as a connection between different generations, because it allows short and fast communications, those preferred

by my mother, but also longer casual chats with a lot of links and images, the kind of communication preferred by my sister. (Monica, 25, Italy).

The two extracts above show that WhatsApp promotes, on the one hand, short and fast communication often valued by younger generations. Such expression typically includes chat jargon and the use of emoticons. On the other hand, WhatsApp does not exclude longer forms of expressions either like some other social media platforms do (c.f. Twitter's 140-character limit). Furthermore, the extracts reveal individual variation and thus challenge some stereotypes of generation-specific communication styles. As in Monica's family, it is sometimes the members of the older generations who favor short and fact-based expression, while children go for longer chats.

3.3 Multimodality Spiced by Playfulness

A great deal of the popularity of WhatsApp accounts for its ability to transmit different types of contents. Sometimes, this seemingly purposeless exchange of photos and other media contents between family members is the easiest way for social bonding and feeling together. In Finland, key informant Carla (23) explains that in her family "WhatsApp is preferred especially when one wants to send photographs to another". Parents have also eagerly started exchanging photos and video clips to stay connected as the following extracts from Italy demonstrate:

> Lately, especially in relation to the festive seasons, I have noticed an increase in the use of WhatsApp by my parents (both 52), although they still employ it only for communications of minor importance or the exchange of photos and funny videos (Antonio, 30, Italy).
> With my sister, the cousins of my age, and my mother (51), I also sometimes use WhatsApp, it is very popular, convenient, and easy to use for sending videos and photos. (Mario, 24, Italy).

This multimodality of communication brings about some new aspects to family communication. First, the use of one's own voice in messages and self-taken photos makes communication a bit more personal compared to texting. Italian key informant Alice (23) describes this by writing that that even though her "parents (55 and 56) didn't immediately understand the meaning of WhatsApp groups, they found voice messages a new way to send a message more personal than a text message". Second, there is a certain playfulness that is included in the exchange of funny videos and photos, which encourages social bonding that is the ultimate end of phatic expression. For example, Italian key informant Francesco (25) writes as follows:

> I installed WhatsApp upon request by my father (n.a.), who wanted to clog my smartphone with "fun" videos... It is interesting to note that while I use WhatsApp for any kind of communication, the generation of my father and my mother (57), instead tends to view it more as a "game" in the sense that they employ it almost exclusively for communication of scarce importance or for the sharing of entertainment contents, relying on SMS and calls for everything else.

Parents' engagement in multiple new communication modalities provided by WhatsApp may also indicate their willingness to connect with their children. Similarly, children's willingness to take part in family WhatsApp groups and children's readiness to adjust their communication manners to those of the parent speaks for the same aspiration to reconnect. In closed family WhatsApp groups, intergenerational communication can be less reserved and deficiencies in one's own communication skills can be more easily revealed to other family members than in public online forums, where the risk of "losing face" is more likely. Hence, it is "quite common to send greetings and funny videos to smile together" as Italian key informant Claudia (21) summarizes the use of WhatsApp in her family.

4   Conclusion and Discussion

This study analyzed WhatsApp as a technology of "middle-reach" that can potentially serve the social coherence of extended families and intergenerational family relations. The research material provided many answers to the question: What is the importance of small messages exchanged via WhatsApp for the sense of social coherence in extended families?

First, WhatsApp provides a functional platform for facilitating intergeneration communication, especially between young people and their late-middle age parents, as it allows reaching the whole family at once. As parents have begun sending photos, video clips, and voice messages, it can be even argued that WhatsApp is marking a shift away from the straightforward division between "texting teenagers" and their "talking parents". Especially the mothers of the key informants have keenly engaged in instant messaging with their grown-up children in Finland and Italy, extending their role as family caregiver, to the electronically mediated communication and online world. The role of fathers in WhatsApp communication is much more limited, yet still existent.

Second, the importance of small messages relates to WhatsApp's capacity to promote "phatic communion". In family WhatsApp communication, social bonding via multiple modalities, such as small text messages, photos, and video clips, often appears as a superior form of communication to the exchange of messages with a high information value. In dyadic family relations, WhatsApp's many modalities allows the choosing of the most desired and most suitable mode of communication for every family member individually. Furthermore, WhatsApp provides a relatively safe environment for one-to-group communication. According to the informants, especially WhatsApp group chats facilitate intra-family communication and strengthen the social cohesion of geographically dispersed families. Sometimes small WhatsApp messages do have also functional value. They are utilized to exchange information and coordinate daily agendas and schedules among the family members living under the same roof.

It is worth noticing the interviews did not reveal any evidence about skipped-generation communication, in which children and grandparents would be directly in contact with one another via WhatsApp. While some grandparents and children exchange messages via WhatsApp on one-to-one basis, family chat groups have mainly remained as a communication channel for two successive family generations at time. Future research should be targeted to explain to what extent the relative lack of grandparent-grandchildren interaction and the absence of multigenerational WhatsApp groups accounts for the lower digital skills of grandparents, or is this current situation just a reflection of the pre-digital forms of intergenerational communication in which relations with own parents are naturally more intense than those with grandparents.

Lastly, the design of research material collection entails also some limitations that should be kept in mind while reading and interpreting the results. While the key informants were able to gain information that might not be accessible to an outside interviewer, their double role as co-researchers and the members of the studied families is not problem-free [38]. It is also likely that the self-selection of the key informants has bearings on the contents of the research material. Furthermore, the collected research material does not represent the whole diversity of social class backgrounds as college students tend to come from highly educated families.

Acknowledgements. This research has received project funding from the Academy of Finland (no. 265986), and it was carried out within the Academy of Finland's Centre of Excellence in Research on Ageing and Care (CoE AgeCare).

References

1. O'Hara, K., Massimi, M., Richard, H., Rubens, S., Morris, J.: Everyday dwelling with WhatsApp. In: Proceedings of the 17th ACM Conference on Computer Supported Cooperative Work & Social Computing, pp. 1131–1143. New York, ACM (2014)
2. Litwak, E.: Occupational mobility and extended family cohesion. Am. Sociol. Rev. **25**, 9–21 (1960)
3. Taipale, S., Petrovčič, A., Dolničar, V.: Intergenerational solidarity and ICT usage: Empirical insights from Finnish and Slovenian families. In: Taipale, S., Wilska, T.-A., Gilleard, C. (eds.) Digital Technologies and Generational Identity: ICT Usage Across the Life Course, pp. 69–86. Routledge, London (2018)
4. Malinowski, B.: The problem of meaning in primitive languages. In: Ogden, C.K., Richards, I.A. (eds.) The Meaning of Meaning, pp. 435–496. Routledge, London (1923/1994)
5. Statista.   https://www.statista.com/statistics/260819/number-of-monthly-active-whatsapp-users
6. Audience Project. Insights: Social media and Apps in the Nordics. https://www.audienceproject.com/wp-content/uploads/social_media_and_apps_nordics.pdf
7. Taloustutkimus: Social media survey for YLE. http://www.yle.fi/tvuutiset/uutiset/upics/liitetiedostot/yle_somekysely.pdf
8. Cosenza, V.: Utenti delle app di messaggistica in Italia. Vincos Blog, 10 July 2017. http://vincos.it/2017/07/10/utenti-delle-app-di-messaggistica-in-italia/
9. Stern, C.: Messaging will be Facebook's 'next major wave of innovation and financial windfall'. Business Insider, 24 June 2015. http://www.businessinsider.com/facebooks-next-big-profit-driver-is-messaging-2015-6?r=US&IR=T&IR=T
10. Lenhart, A., Rainie, L., Lewis, O.: Teenage life online: the rise of the instant-message generation and the Internet's impact on friendships and family relationships (2001). http://www.pewinternet.org/2001/06/21/teenage-life-online/
11. Nardi, B.A., Whittaker, S., Bradner, E.: Interaction and outeraction: instant messaging in action. In: Proceedings of the 2000 ACM Conference on Computer Supported Cooperative Work, pp. 79–88. ACM, New York (2000)
12. Grinter, R.E., Palen, L.: Instant messaging in teen life. In: Proceedings of the 2002 ACM Conference on Computer Supported Cooperative Work, pp. 21–30. ACM, New York (2002)
13. Bouhnik, D., Deshen, M.: WhatsApp goes to school: mobile instant messaging between teachers and students. J. Inf. Technol. Educ. Res. **13**, 217–231 (2014)

14. Johnston, M.J., King, D., Arora, S., Behar, N., Athanasiou, T., Sevdalis, N., Darzi, A.: Smartphones let surgeons know WhatsApp: an analysis of communication in emergency surgical teams. Am. J. Surg. **209**, 45–51 (2015). https://doi.org/10.1016/j.amjsurg. 2014.08.030

15. Nag, W., Ling, R., Jakobsen, M.H.: Keep out! Join in! Cross-generation communication on the mobile internet in Norway. J. Child. Media **10**, 411–425 (2016)

16. Church, K., de Oliveira, R.: What's up with WhatsApp? Comparing mobile instant messaging behaviors with traditional SMS. In: Proceedings of the 15th International Conference on Human-Computer Interaction with Mobile Devices and Services, pp. 352–361. ACM, New York. https://doi.org/10.1145/2493190.2493225

17. Ling, R., Baron, N.S.: Text messaging and IM: linguistic comparison of American college data. J. Lang. Soc. Psychol. **26**, 291–298 (2007)

18. Baron, N.S.: Always On: Language in an Online and Mobile World. Oxford University Press, Oxford (2007)

19. Ling, R.: Children, youth, and mobile communication. J. Child. Media **1**, 60–67 (2007)

20. Ribak, R.: Remote control, umbilical cord and beyond: The mobile phone as a transitional object. Br. J. Dev. Psychol. **27**, 183–196 (2009)

21. Horst, H.A.: The blessings and burdens of communication: cell phones in Jamaican transnational social fields. Glob. Netw. **6**, 143–159 (2006)

22. Wilding, R.: 'Virtual' intimacies? Families communicating across transnational contexts. Glob. Netw. **6**, 125–142 (2006)

23. Madianou, M., Miller, D.: Mobile phone parenting: reconfiguring relationships between Filipina migrant mothers and their left-behind children. New Media Soc. **13**, 457–470 (2011)

24. Rainie, L., Wellman, B.: Networked: The New Social Operating System. MIT Press, Cambridge (2012)

25. Lim, S.S. (ed.): Mobile Communication and the Family. Springer, Dordrecht (2016). https://doi.org/10.1007/978-94-017-7441-3

26. Rosales, A., Fernández-Ardèvol, M.: Beyond WhatsApp: older people and smartphones. Revista Română de Comunicare şi Relaţii Publice **18**, 27–47 (2016)

27. Siibak, A., Tamme, V.: "Who introduced granny to Facebook?": An exploration of everyday family interactions in web-based communication environments. Northern Lights Film Media Stud. Yearbook **11**, 71–89 (2013)

28. Fortunati, L., Taipale, S.: Mobile communication: Media effects. In: Rössler, P., Hoffner, C.A., van Zoonen, L. (eds.) International Encyclopedia of Media Effects, pp. 1241–1252. Wiley, New York (2017)

29. Chen, W., Boase, J., Wellman, B.: The global villagers: comparing internet users and uses around the world. In: Wellman, B., Haythornthwaite, C. (eds.) The Internet in Everyday Life, pp. 74–113. Blackwell, Malden (2002)

30. Quan-Haase, A., Wellman, B., Witte, J.C., Hampton, K.N.: Capitalizing on the net: social contact, civic engagement, and sense of community. In: Wellman, B., Haythornthwaite, C. (eds.) The Internet in Everyday Life, pp. 291–324. Blackwell, Malden (2002)

31. Baym, N.K.: Personal Connections in the Digital Age, 2nd edn. Polity, Cambridge (2015)

32. Marwick, A.E., Boyd, D.: I tweet honestly, I tweet passionately: Twitter users, context collapse, and the imagined audience. New Media Soc. **13**, 114–133 (2011)

33. Graham, A.: Personal connections in the digital age. Consumption Markets Cult. **20**, 293–296 (2017). https://doi.org/10.1080/10253866.2015.1135538

34. Granovetter, M.S.: The strength of weak ties. Am. J. Sociol. **78**, 1360–1380 (1973)

35. Johns, N.A.: The social logics of sharing. Commun. Rev. **16**, 113–131 (2013). https://doi.org/10.1080/10714421.2013.807119

36. Wittel, A.: Toward a network sociality. Theory Cult. Soc. **18**, 51–76 (2001). https://doi.org/10.1177/026327601018006003
37. Miller, V.: New media, networking and phatic culture. Convergence **14**, 387–400 (2008). https://doi.org/10.1177/1354856508094659
38. Hänninen, R., Taipale, S., Korhonen, A.: Refamilisation in the broadband society: the effect of ICTs in family solidarity in Finland (forthcoming)
39. Hsieh, H.F., Shannon, S.E.: Three approaches to qualitative content analysis. Qual. Health Res. **15**, 1277–1288 (2005). https://doi.org/10.1177/1049732305276687
40. Fortunati, L., Taipale, S., de Luca, F.: What happened to body-to-body sociability? Soc. Sci. Res. **42**, 893–905 (2013). https://doi.org/10.1016/j.ssresearch.2012.12.006

Impact of Online Social Media Communication and Offline Geographical Distance on Elder Users' Intergenerational Isolation: From Technology Affordance Perspective

Xiaolun Wang[1], Jie Gu[2(✉)], Anan Hu[3], and Hong Ling[3]

[1] Nanjing University of Science and Technology, Nanjing, China
[2] Shanghai Academy of Social Sciences, Shanghai, China
gujie@sass.org.cn
[3] Fudan University, Shanghai, China

Abstract. Social media technology has become an integral part in elders' daily communication. While there is an intense interest among HCI scholars to design effective function and interface to assist elder users' digital communication, a theoretical understanding to guide this design is lacking. To address this research gap, this study examines the effect of social media communication on elders' perception of intergenerational isolation. From the perspective of technology affordance (functional vs. emotional), we examines both the role of online usage behavior of social media (frequency and form) and offline intergenerational distance (geographical distance). 107 interview-based survey results show that: (1) Elders with a higher level of functional affordance are willing to try diverse social functions to communicate with their children, while emotional affordance will increase elders' intergenerational communication frequency; (2) Communication frequency can reduce elders' perceived intergenerational isolation, but diversity of communication forms cannot; (3) Unexpectedly, geographical distance significantly decrease elders' perception of intergenerational isolation, because of the mediator role of increased intergenerational communication frequency and forms in social media. Our research has profound theoretical and practical implications.

Keywords: Technology affordance · Intergenerational isolation · Social media
Elder people

1 Introduction

With the development of social media technology, more and more elder users have begun to use the new tool to maintain social connection (Xie 2003). According to the annual report of WeChat (the most popular social media in China) in 2017, there are more than fifty million active elder users per month (Zhong 2017). Hence, both practitioners and researchers have recognized the importance of social media in elders' digital life. While there is an intense interest among HCI scholars to design effective function and interface

© Springer International Publishing AG, part of Springer Nature 2018
J. Zhou and G. Salvendy (Eds.): ITAP 2018, LNCS 10926, pp. 547–559, 2018.
https://doi.org/10.1007/978-3-319-92034-4_41

to assist elder users' digital communication, a theoretical understanding to guide this design is lacking. To address this research gap, we aim to unravel the underlying mechanism through which social media communications influence elder users' life feelings, in order to provide more targeted services for them.

Then, whom do elder people mainly communicate with in social media? In Chinese society, children take the role as middlemen to motivate, facilitate and help parents to learn to use social media (Zhou and Gui 2017). Thus, children always ranked first in parents' contact list. Against this backdrop, this study attempts to focus on a unique perspective: intergenerational communication between elder users and their adult children.

Based on technology affordance theory, social media provide both functional affordance and emotional affordance for its users (Hutchby 2001). Intuitively, social media facilitate intergenerational communication and reduce elders' perception of intergenerational isolation due to its functional affordance to anytime- and anyplace-communication. However, prior literature is not consistent about the belief. Although technology enables communication, it does not necessarily improve communication efficiency. Tian (2016) found that the use of social media aggravated elder people's feeling of isolation instead. Highly underestimated in prior research, emotional affordance facilitated by social media may be a possible reason for the above inconsistence. From the perspective of technological affordance, a series of questions were proposed by this study: *Will technological affordance of social media (functional and emotional affordance) reduce elder people's perception of intergenerational isolation? In specific, how does technological affordance impact intergenerational communications via social media (frequency and form), and then change elder people's feelings?*

In addition, offline factors have been largely ignored in prior research when the research interests mainly lie in digital communication within social media. Geographical distance decreases the chance for intergenerational face-to-face communication, therefore has a negative impact on their offline communication. However, how the offline geographical distance impacts digital communication through social media is still a question to be answered. Focusing on this point, we proposed the following questions. *For those family who live apart (i.e., longer geographical distance), will they have more intergenerational communications via social media (frequency and form) or not? Can elder people's perception of intergenerational isolation be reduced through the use of social media (mediator effect)?*

Overall, this study aims to examine the effect of social media communication on elders' perception of intergenerational isolation. From the perspective of technology affordance (functional vs. emotional), we examines both the role of online usage behavior of social media and offline intergenerational distance (geographical distance).

We recruited 10 confederates to conduct face-to-face survey-based interview for elder people over 55 years old, and got a final sample of 107. SmartPLS was used to analyze our data. The results show that: (1) Elders with a higher level of functional affordance are willing to try diverse social functions to communicate with their children, while emotional affordance will increase elders' intergenerational communication frequency; (2) Communication frequency can reduce elders' perceived intergenerational isolation, but diversity of communication forms cannot; (3) Unexpectedly, geographical distance significantly decrease elders' perception of intergenerational isolation, because of the mediator role of increased intergenerational communication frequency and forms in social media. Our research has profound theoretical and practical implications for scholars, HCI practitioners, elders and their children.

The rest of the paper is organized as follows. We first review technology affordance theory, impact of social media technology and intergenerational support on elder users. Then we propose our research model and hypotheses. After that, we report on research method and data analysis. Finally, we discuss the implications and limitations of this study.

2 Literature Review

2.1 Technology Affordance Theory

In 1986, Gibson defined affordances as "possibilities of action" provided to the animal or the individual by the environment. This theory was soon adopted by IS researchers and a similar new term "technology affordance" appeared, which means the opportunities for action provided to a user by a computerized system (Markus and Silver 2008; Bloomfield et al. 2010). In other words, technology affordance is mainly helpful for examining what a specific technology can do to users (Argyris and Monu 2015).

As such, Hutchby (2001) identified two types of affordances: functional affordance and relational affordance. Similarly, Mesgari and Faraj (2012) distinguished technology affordance into materiality and sociality ones. An official report from Chinese Academy of Social Sciences also proposed that technology affordance of social media can be classified into functional affordance, emotional affordance, social participation affordance, and identity affordance (CASS 2017). Based on the above literatures, we summarized and categorized technology affordance into two groups. (1) *Functional affordance* comes from the relationship between technology and user, which reflects the possibilities for actions brought to the user by the technical features (Markus and Silver 2008). (2) *Emotional affordance* refers to the emotional relationship between users realized by technology (Hutchby 2001), which reflects the relational and sociality nature of affordance.

In this paper, we attempt to adopt technology affordance theory to explain how and why elder people begin to use social media, especially the different role of functional and emotional affordances.

2.2 Impact of Social Media Technology on Elder Users

With the development of technological and social change, many transformations are underway in terms of how elder people communicate with the aid of social media. Although elder people are with lower technical capability compared with younger ones, they are taking a more positive attitude about social media, and gradually learn to use this new technology (Xie 2003).

Summarized from previous literatures, social media technology provides two aspects of impact on elder users: functional impact and emotional impact. First, social media facilitate online communications for elder people, which can be an alternative to conventional communication channels in providing low-cost, synchronous talks and other easy to access service (McCormack 2010). In other words, elder users can obtain practical or technical benefits when using social media. Taking mobile instant messaging service (MIM) as an example, older adults can use various functions of MIM, such as sending messages, voice chatting, updating status, browsing news, and so on (Deng et al. 2010). Second, Harley and Fitzpatrick (2009) addressed the "social, cultural and spiritual impact" of social media to elder users. Social media makes their life meaningful and colorful, because they can share life stories and have frequent communications with friends, relatives, and especially their children. More deeply, their mental or psychological needs can be satisfied with the help of social media (Deng et al. 2010).

Therefore, in consistent with technology affordance theory, social media have both functional and emotional impacts on elder users. However, except for "what" impact social media have on older adults, a more important question is "why" and "how" elders use social media. We are among the first to fill the research gap in this field.

2.3 Impact of Intergenerational Support on Elder People

The primary responsibility of adult children is to care for and provide support on their elder parents (Silverstein et al. 2006). Silverstein and Bengtson (1997) proposed several types of intergenerational support for elder people, including financial, practical, and emotional support. Among them, financial support is exchanges of money and materials, practical support is exchanges of instrumental assistance (e.g., daily care), while emotional support means exchanges of heart-to-heart communications. In previous research, all of the intergenerational supports are proved to be helpful to elder people's health and happiness (Zunzunegui et al. 2001).

With the development of technology, social media become the mediators to help form a "distant but close" family relationship (Zhou and Gui 2017). Intergenerational communications can not only happen in face-to-face circumstances, but also in online context. Then, a new question appears: what is the relationship between online and offline emotional support? Are they complementary or exclusive on elders' psychological feelings? Relevant literatures mainly reported positive results. Elder people who use social media communicate almost twice than those who don't, and have a stronger feeling of emotional satisfaction (CASS 2017).

However, several gaps remain in previous research about online emotional support. First, they only focus on communication frequency but not communication form. Second, as an important component in intergenerational support, the impact of online emotional support should not only be limited to traditional factors like loneliness and health, but also be extended to elders' intergenerational feelings like isolation. Third, although our purpose is to investigate the role of online emotional communication, offline factors should also be paid attention to, especially those objective offline factors which can reflect intergenerational relationship. We attempt to solve the above problems in this study.

3 Research Model and Hypotheses

3.1 Research Model

Our research model is shown in Fig. 1. Elders' perception of technological affordance impacts the way they use social media, and then changes their perception of intergenerational isolation. Meanwhile, since online intergenerational support usually happens when elders and children live apart, offline geographical distance would also play an important role during the process.

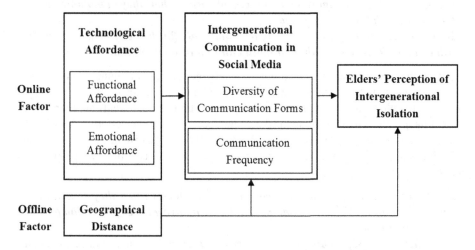

Fig. 1. Research model

3.2 Online Factors: Technological Affordance, Intergenerational Communication in Social Media, and Elders' Perception of Intergenerational Isolation

From the technology affordance perspective, social media, as one of the most popular technology, provide both functional affordance and emotional affordance for its users (Hutchby 2001; Mesgari and Faraj 2012). In this paper, we apply this dyadic classification to a special group: elder people. First, with multiple functions (e.g., voice chat, friend cycle, et al.), social media have gradually involved into older adults' daily life. Elder people can communicate with their children through text, voice or video format conveniently without limitation of time and space. They can also share picture, videos, or essays to adult children and have a deep discussion with them. Therefore, functional affordance of social media increases both the intergenerational communication frequency and form for elder people, we hypothesize H1a and H1b:

H1a: When elder people perceive higher functional affordance of social media, they are more likely to use more communication forms (e.g., text, video, friend cycle, et al.) when they communicate with their adult children in social media.

H1b: When elder people perceive higher functional affordance of social media, they will communicate more with their adult children in social media.

Different from functional affordance, emotional affordance of social media satisfies the psychological needs of elder people. Through the communications in social media, older adults can feel the care from and show the care for their children (CASS 2017). Therefore, to obtain more emotional happiness, elders are willing to have more frequent and diversified intergenerational communications. We propose H2a and H2b:

H2a: When elder people perceive higher emotional affordance of social media, they are more likely to use more communication forms when they communicate with their adult children in social media.
H2b: When elder people perceive higher emotional affordance of social media, they will communicate more with their adult children in social media.

With the development of social media, intergenerational communication becomes more convenient to be realized. Just as Zhou and Gui (2017) argued, social media is the mediator to help form a "distant but close" family relationship. Parents are more likely to feel happy and satisfactory about their intergenerational connection (CASS 2017). Therefore, online communications in social media shorten the distance between parents and children, and bring a lower feeling of intergenerational isolation, we propose H3 and H4:

H3: When elder people use more communication forms when they communicate with their adult children in social media, they will have a lower perception of intergenerational isolation.
H4: When elder people communicate more with their adult children in social media, they will have a lower perception of intergenerational isolation.

3.3 Offline Factors: Geographical Distance, Intergenerational Communication in Social Media, and Elders' Perception of Intergenerational Isolation

It is very important to maintain family connections with the help of human-computer interaction technology (Ling 2008). Especially for family members who live apart, social media help them to communicate more and feel the "virtual co-presence" or "connected presence", which overcome long geographical distance to some extent (Baldassar 2008). In other words, "long-distance" families have more frequency and forms of intergenerational communications to maintain their intimacy (Kang 2012). So, we propose H5a and H5b:

H5a: When elder people live further from their adult children, they are more likely to use more communication forms when they communicate with their children in social media.
H5b: When elder people live further from their adult children, they will communicate more with their adult children in social media.

However, although social media supplement traditional face-to-face communications to help family members living apart connect (Lam 2013), elder people's feeling of loneliness and intergenerational isolation can only be released to some degree. The role of online emotional support is supposed to be weaker than direct offline cares. For instance, when children live away from their parents, they cannot accompany and help the elders immediately when they are sick, sad or boring. In other words, geographical distance constrains the interaction between family members, and increases the perception of intergenerational isolation (Crimmins and Ingegneri 1990), just as H6 hypothesizes:

H6: When elder people live further from their adult children, they will have a higher perception of intergenerational isolation.

4 Research Method and Data Analysis

4.1 Data Collection

Considering the difficulty in collecting data from elder population, 10 confederates were recruited and trained to conduct face-to-face survey-based interview. The target subjects of our investigation are Chinese elders above 55 years old who use social media for daily communication. This study chose WeChat as our target social media technique as it is widely adopted among Chinese elders.

As we aim to examine intergenerational communication, our interview subjects need to have at least one child. In the investigation, four parts of questions were designed. (1) Subjects' basic information including their demographic information, economic state and family; (2) Subjects' perceived functional affordance and emotional affordance that are facilitated by WeChat; (3) Subjects were asked to nominate one of their children. Then they answer questions that were specified to their relationship with the nominated child. These questions included their intergenerational online communication through WeChat, how far their children live apart, economic support and daily care from the child; (4) Subjects' subjective perception of intergenerational isolation.

At this stage, valid data from 107 elder social media users were collected. Among them, 47 were male (44%) and 60 were female (56%). Average age of subjects was 61.

4.2 Instrument Development

An important step in data collection is to develop an instrument (e.g., questionnaire) to measure each latent constructs in the model (Xu and Chen 2006). To ensure the validity of the instrument, we adopted existing quality questions whenever possible. We also made necessary adaption of adopted items to our research context. In addition to research constructs, several control variables were also designed and tested. Demographic information such as gender and age are controlled. We also asked and controlled subjects' communication frequency with their nominated child via other channels, such as telephone call, email, short message or offline contact. Drawing on prior literature, we add economic support and daily care into our research model as control variables because they are found to be critical components in intergenerational support (Silverstein and Bengtson 1997).

Items for subjective constructs were measured based on a seven-point scale. In the survey-based interview, functional affordance was measured as multi-item formative construct, while emotional affordance and intergenerational isolation were measured as multi-item reflective constructs. For objective constructs, that is, diversity of communication forms, communication frequency, geographic distance, daily care, economic support and communication frequency through other channels, only one item was used. For example, geographic distance was measured as five levels (Living together, does not live under the same roof but in the same city, living in different cities but in the same province, living in different province and living abroad). Items for elder's perception of intergenerational isolation comes from PSI (parenting stress index) proposed by Abidin (1995).

4.3   Evaluating the Measurement Model

Although our research model only contains two multi-item reflective constructs, we still first checked the validity of the measurement model before hypothesis testing. Confirmatory factor analysis (CFA) is the conventional statistical method to test the convergent validity of a measurement model. The set of criteria includes (1) loading of each item is significant, (2) the average variance extracted (AVE) for each item should be greater than 0.5, and (3) the composite factor reliability (CFR) and Cronbach's alpha are greater than 0.7. Table 1 reports the results of convergent validity for our sample. All criteria were satisfied.

To satisfy discriminant validity, inter-construct correlation is required to be less than the square root of AVE. The underlying rationale is that an item should be better explained by its intended construct than by other constructs. Results indicate satisfactory discriminant validity. In summary, our measurement model confirmed both convergent validity and discriminant validity. With that, we could proceed to test the causal relationships among all factors.

Table 1.   The convergent validity of the measurement model

Construct	Item	Std loading	T-value	AVE	CFR	α
EA	EA1	0.924	34.35	0.836	0.953	0.934
	EA2	0.963	89.49			
	EA3	0.908	34.53			
	EA4	0.859	29.68			
II	II1	0.875	20.14	0.767	0.930	0.899
	II2	0.875	19.32			
	II3	0.883	22.02			
	II4	0.870	17.20			

EA: Emotional Affordance; II: Intergenerational Isolation

4.4 Hypothesis Testing

Due to there is one formative construct (FA) in our research model, PLS was used for data analysis. We first fitted the full model to test our proposed hypotheses. Then we conducted examined the mediator role of intergenerational communication via social media when controlling for geographical distance.

Table 2. Analysis results

	DCF	CF	II	
	DCF	Model 2	Model 3	Model 4
FA	0.472** (2.446)	0.064 (0.305)	−0.056 (0.904)	−0.052 (0.764)
EA	−0.070 (0.541)	0.283* (1.936)	−0.039 (1.038)	−0.048 (1.145)
GD	0.196** (2.551)	0.280*** (3.532)	−0.148 (1.33)	−0.102 (0.840)
DCF			−0.097 (0.913)	−0.085 (0.800)
CF			−0.162* (1.711)	−0.190* (1.672)
CF-O				−0.005 (0.048)
ES				0.051 (0.448)
DC				0.053 (0.397)
GENDER				−0.114 (1.141)
AGE				0.099 (0.942)
R-Square	**0.243**	**0.235**	**0.062**	**0.084**

*p < 0.10, **p < 0.05, ***p < 0.01. Values in parentheses are t-statistics. FA: Functional Affordance; EA: Emotional Affordance; GD: Geographic Distance; DCF: Diversity of Communication Forms; CF: Communication Frequency; CF-O: Offline communication Frequency; ES: Economic Support; DC: Daily Care

Table 2 showed the model fitting results. Results suggested that elder users' high level of perceived functional affordance of WeChat increased the diversity of communication forms. Thus H1a was supported. This result may suggest that functional affordance is closely associated with elder users' explorative behavior in technology usage. However, the effect of functional affordance on communication frequency was insignificant. Thus H1b was not supported. The effect of emotional affordance was exactly opposite. Emotional affordance imposed an insignificant effect on the diversity of communication forms, but its effect on communication frequency was significantly positive. Thus H2a was not supported while H2b was supported. Compared to functional affordance that addresses the human-technology interaction, emotional affordance is more about the human-human communication. Thus a high level of emotional affordance motivates elder users to use social media more frequently in order to maintain their social relationship, no matter which communication form is used.

Communication frequency showed a significant effect in reducing elders' perceived intergenerational isolation. However, the expected effect of diversity of communication forms was not detected. Thus, H4 was supported but H3 was not supported. Therefore, whichever communication form is used, elder's perception of intergenerational isolation can be only impacted by communication frequency.

Then, we focus on how offline factors impacts elders' online behaviors. The effect of geographic distance on the diversity of communication forms and communication frequency was both significantly positive. This result indicated that the more distance elder parents were apart from their children, the more they rely on social media to strength their connection. Thus H5a and H5b were both supported.

After controlling the effect of intergenerational communication via social media technology, the direct effect of geographic distance on intergenerational isolation was insignificant. However, from Table 3, we see that geographic distance and intergenerational isolation are significantly related. So, we test their relationship without adding in variables about social media communications, and find a significant negative effect between them ($\beta = -0.181^*$, $p < 0.1$), which is contrary to Hypothesis 6.

Table 3. Mediator effect of communication frequency

Mediator	Test procedure	Path	Unstandardized B	SE B	Mediator effect (Sobel Test)
CF	II = f(GD)	(c)	−0.181	0.108	Supported
	CF = f(GD)	(a)	0.370	0.092	
	II = f(GD, CF)	(c')	−0.111	0.115	
		(b)	−0.190	0.114	

A possible reason for the unexpected result may be that the effect of geographic distance was mediated by communication frequency. The positive effect of geographic distance on communication frequency and the negative effect of communication frequency on intergenerational isolation combined to lead to its direct negative influence. Following the well-recognized mediator testing procedure (Baron and Kenny 1986), we tested the mediator effect of communication frequency for the main effect of geographic distance. The results in Table 3 indicated that communication frequency significantly mediated the effect of geographic distance (ab/s(ab) = |−1.66| > 1.64), thus support our explanation.

5   Discussion and Implications

5.1   Discussion of Findings

Our results reflect interesting findings. First, while prior research emphasized the importance of functional affordance, our finding suggested that its effect in elders' technology-supported intergenerational communication is limited. Indeed, elders with a higher level of functional affordance are willing to try diverse social functions to communicate with their children. However, the increased communication diversity does not reduce their perceived intergenerational isolation.

Second, instead of functional affordance, we find that it is elder users' emotional affordance with social media technique that influences their intergenerational relationship. Emotional affordance is found to increase elders' intergenerational communication frequency, which significantly reduces their perceived intergenerational isolation. While prior research paid attention to functional affordance, this study suggests that the importance of emotional affordance in elder users' technological usage has long been underestimated.

Third, the anytime- and anyplace-feature of social media breaks through the barrier of geographic distance in intergenerational communication. Geographic distance decreased face-to-face communication. In the traditional offline world, the decrease of face-to-face communication may have a negative impact on intergenerational affection. With the help of social media technique, however, elders have an alternative and more convenient way to keep contact with their children, and might even strengthen their intergenerational relationship. We found that an increase of geographic distance motivates elders to resort to social media techniques, resulting in significant increase of both social media communication frequency and diversity. Afterwards, communication frequency further decrease elders' perception of intergenerational isolation. We summarized our research findings in Fig. 2, all significant relationships are marked in red dotted line.

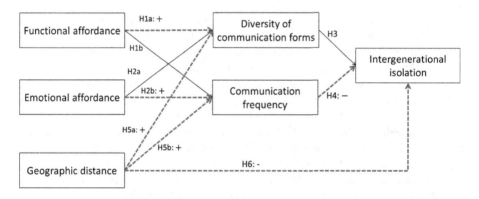

Fig. 2. Data analysis results (Color figure online)

5.2 Theoretical and Practical Implications

This study has profound theoretical and practical implications. Theoretically, this research improves our understanding of elder users' intergenerational communication in social media. First, through the perspective of technological affordance, we propose the dual effect of social media in its functional and emotional affordance to enhance intergenerational communication. Second, we are among the first to integrate offline intergenerational distance with online intergenerational communication, and proved that geographic distance doesn't always increase intergenerational isolation, which provides a different finding with previous literatures.

In practice, this study offers practical guidance of social media design for elder users and alerts people to pay more attention to elders' feeling of intergenerational isolation. For instance, social media should enable the "priority" feature that allows elder users to put their chat box with children at the top of the interface. This feature is used to help elder users to communicate more with their children (increase communication frequency). Besides, except for promoting technical functions, HCI practitioners should pay more attention to elder users' emotional need. An elder-friendly interface is thus in call for social media design. Content providers are also called to offer more content that fits elders' interest. For adult children, especially those who live far away from their parents, should take advantage of technique-mediated communication tool, and have more heart-to-heart intergenerational talk which shortens the objective geographic distance. For elder people, except for trying diverse forms of communication in social media, communicating more with their children is more important for them to release their feeling of isolation.

5.3 Limitations and Future Research

First, our cross-sectional investigation only reflects a static state of elders' social media usage. To have a better understanding of the evolution of elders' digital usage and their technique-supported intergenerational interaction, long-term follow-up surveys are necessary in the future.

Second, while the diversity of communication forms is positively influenced by both functional affordance and geographic distance, its effect on intergenerational isolation is unfortunately insignificant. A series of questions emerge here. (1) Does communication diversity means nothing for elder users? (2) If multiple communication forms are useless for elders, should HCI practitioners reduce communication options to make the interface simpler? The answer for the above questions may depend on whom elder users are communicating with. Although the diversity of communication forms shows no influence in reducing intergenerational isolation, it may benefit elders' peer communication with their friends of the same age. Future research will be conducted to examine elders' peer communication through social media.

Last, communicating more does not mean communicating better. In this research, we only focus on communication frequency, but did not further investigate the content of communication, which should be considered in future research.

Acknowledgement. This work was supported by the Fundamental Research Funds for the Central Universities, 30918013104; National Science Foundation of China (grant #71702103); Research Foundation in Nanjing University of Science & Technology (grant #AE89955), and the China Ministry of Education-China Mobile research grant (#MCM20150402).

References

Abidin, R.R.: Parenting Stress Index (PSI) Manual, 3rd edn. Pediatric Psychology Press, Charlottesville (1995)

Argyris, Y.A., Monu, K.: Corporate use of social media: technology affordance and external stakeholder relations. J. Organ. Comput. Electr. Commer. **25**(2), 140–168 (2015)

Baldassar, L.: Missing kin and longing to be together: emotions and the construction of copresence in transnational relationships. J. Intercultural Stud. **29**(3), 247–266 (2008)

Baron, R.M., Kenny, D.A.: The moderator-mediator variable distinction in social psychological research: conceptual, strategic, and statistical considerations. J. Pers. Soc. Psychol. **51**(6), 1173–1182 (1986)

Bloomfield, B.P., Latham, Y., Vurdubakis, T.: Bodies, technologies and action possibilities: when is an affordance? Sociology **44**(3), 415–433 (2010)

CASS (Chinese Academy of Social Sciences): Live here (2017)

Crimmins, M.E., Ingegneri, D.G.: Interaction and living arrangements of older parents and their children: past trends, present determinants, future implication. Res. Aging **12**(1), 3–35 (1990)

Deng, Z., Lu, Y., Wei, K.K., Zhang, J.: Understanding customer satisfaction and loyalty: an empirical study of mobile instant messages in China. Int. J. Inf. Manag. **30**(4), 289–300 (2010)

Gibson, J.J.: The Ecological Approach to Visual Perception, 2nd edn. Lawrence Erlbaum, New Jersey (1986)

Harley, D., Fitzpatrick, G.: YouTube and intergenerational communication: the case of Geriatric. Univ. Access Inf. Soc. **8**(1), 5–20 (2009)

Hutchby, I.: Technologies, texts and affordances. Sociology **35**(2), 441–456 (2001)

Kang, T.: Gendered media, changing intimacy: internet-mediated transnational communication in the family sphere. Media Cult. Soc. **34**(2), 146–161 (2012)

Lam, S.S.K.: ICT's impact on family solidarity and upward mobility in translocal China. Asian J. Commun. **23**(3), 322–340 (2013)

Ling, R.: New Tech, New Ties: How Mobile Communication is Reshaping Social Cohesion. MIT Press, Cambridge (2008)

Markus, M.L., Silver, M.S.: A foundation for the study of IT effects: a new look at DeSanctis and Poole's concepts of structural features and spirit. J. Assoc. Inf. Syst. **9**(10/11), 609–632 (2008)

McCormack, A.: Individuals with eating disorders and the use of online support groups as a form of social support. CIN-Comput. Inform. Nurs. **28**(1), 12–19 (2010)

Mesgari, M., Faraj, S.: Technology affordances: the case of Wikipedia. In: AMCIS 2012 Proceedings (2012)

Silverstein, M., Bengtson, V.L.: Intergenerational solidarity and the structure of adult child/parent relationships in American families. Am. J. Soc. **103**(2), 429–460 (1997)

Silverstein, M., Gans, D., Yang, F.M.: Intergenerational support to aging parents: the role of norms and needs. J. Fam. Issues **27**(8), 1068–1084 (2006)

Tian, H.: Mobile media and daily life in minority village. Doctoral Dissertation. Central China Normal University (2016)

Xie, B.: Older adults, computers, and the Internet: Future directions. Gerontechnology **2**(4), 289–305 (2003)

Xu, Y., Chen, Z.: Relevance judgment: what do information users consider beyond topicality? J. Am. Soc. Inf. Sci. Technol. **57**(7), 961–973 (2006)

Zhong, P.: Big data for WeChat 2017. Home of IT (2017). https://www.ithome.com/html/it/333802.htm. Accessed 13 Feb 2018

Zhou, B., Gui, S.: WeChat and distant family intergenerational communication in china: a study of online content sharing on WeChat. In: Xue, K., Yu, M. (eds.) New Media and Chinese Society. CCCA, vol. 5, pp. 185–206. Springer, Singapore (2017). https://doi.org/10.1007/978-981-10-6710-5_11

Zunzunegui, M.V., Beland, F., Otero, A.: Support from children, living arrangements, self-rated health and depressive symptoms of older people in Spain. Int. J. Epidemiol. **30**(5), 1090–1099 (2001)

The Comparative Study of Emotional Interaction Design of Empty Nesters in Urban and Rural Areas in China

Xinghui Xu and Xiaoping Hu[⊠]

School of Design, South China University of Technology,
Guangzhou, People's Republic of China
348329431@qq.com, hxp523@163.com

Abstract. This paper studies the causes for the loneliness of empty-nesters in rural and urban areas in China, analyzes their loneliness-solving methods with different living habits and living environments, and lists their different ways of emotional interactions. The purpose of this study is to verify the differences in the emotional needs of empty nesters in rural and urban areas, providing reference value for the emotional interaction products of them, hence better communicating with surrounding people and things. Based on questionnaires and field interviews, this study analyzes how they vent loneliness and thus determines their emotional demands, and eventually design an emotional interaction model for the elderly. The study found that the differences in emotional needs of rural and urban empty-nesters are more reflected in neighborhood relations and entertainment ways. Attaching importance to these differences can better help distracting them from loneliness. The findings can also be applied to other product designs that relate to the elderly's emotions.

Keywords: Urban and rural areas · Empty-Nesters · Sense of loneliness
Emotional needs · Emotional interaction model

1 Introduction

In China, with the deepening of aging population degree, the number of empty nesters is also increasing. The National Committee of Seniors predicts that by 2015–2035, Chinese elderly population will grow at an average rate of 10 million per year. In rural areas, a large number of migrant workers go to urban areas for work and rural empty-nest phenomenon becomes more and more serious [1]. In the cities, many teenagers study or work in other cities and settle there, resulting in a large proportion of empty nest, it has become a social issue that can not be ignored [2]. According to the data disclosed in the "White Paper on the Development of China's Pension Industry", it shows that as of the end of 2016, the population aged 60 or above has reached 230 million in China, accounting for more than 16% of the total population. At present, the empty nesters has almost reached 100 million, the decrease of the family pension calls for the aid of social pension subsidy. It indicates that under the rapid economic development in China, the problem of empty nesters has become increasingly prominent.

© Springer International Publishing AG, part of Springer Nature 2018
J. Zhou and G. Salvendy (Eds.): ITAP 2018, LNCS 10926, pp. 560–570, 2018.
https://doi.org/10.1007/978-3-319-92034-4_42

Empty nesters are tend to feel depressed and lonely [3]. According to the survey, it showed that the empty nesters suffering from psychological problems reached 60%. And those who reached the disease level, requiring medical attention, psychological intervention accounts for 10%−20%. Wenqu psychology network pointed out that the lack of elderly television programs, fitness and recreation facilities resulted in the poor spiritual life of the elderly, together with the insufficient social activities and children's care, which can easily lead to mental illness of the elderly.

For relieving loneliness of the empty nesters, the market has launched a series of technological and intellectual products for distracting them from loneliness, improving the living quality of them. In the design field, it has become mainstream to design products for the elderly, however they focus on their material level more than the spiritual level, or one-sided analysis on their emotions. In 2012, American cognitive psychologist Donald Norman put forward the concept of "emotionalization" of product design. With the advent of experiencing economy era, "emotionalization" has become one of the major design trends of current Internet products. Nowadays, people have higher requirements for the innovative design of products, however there are very few products that can really satisfy people's emotional needs.

As two different groups, urban and rural empty nesters have enormous differences in economic ability, living habits and living environment, leading to the distinctions of emotional sustenance. Based on these distinctions, this article discusses the needs of emotional interaction product.

2 Data Collection

2.1 Questionnaire Design

Firstly, the daily lives of the elderly were classified, in order to select the appropriate scenarios for research. As shown in Fig. 1, it indicated the main scenario of the empty nesters' emotional interaction.

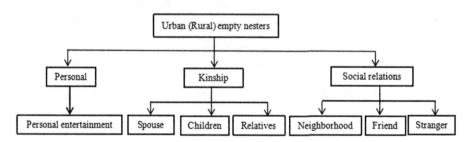

Fig. 1. The main scene of empty-nesters emotional needs.

To sum up the above scenarios about emotional interaction: (1) Given that the elderly may be widowed or living with their spouses, the spouse blank is excluded; (2) Both children and relatives have genetic relationships with the elderly, they can be classified as one group. (3) Friends and neighborhoods enjoy a large overlap ratio, so they can also be grouped into one category. (4) The strangers getting in touch with during outgoing (traveling, etc.) can be grouped separately. Therefore, personal recreation, children, neighborhoods (communities) and outgoing (tourism) were selected as four scenarios to figure out the proportion of the elderly's emotional demands for these scenarios, as shown in Table 1.

Table 1. The weight distribution of emotional demand scenarios.

Weight	Emotional demand scenarios			
	Personal entertainment	Children (relatives)	Neighbors (friends)	Strangers (travel, etc.)
Urban elderly	30%	20%	20%	30%
Rural elderly	20%	30%	30%	20%

The questionnaire design was based on the above four scenarios (as shown in Table 2), it collected information about the interactions between empty nesters in rural and urban areas under different scenarios, and explored the impact of them on the emotion of the elderly. Besides, the questionnaire also included the following descriptions of emotional needs: "For the purposes of this study, we categorized the emotional demands of a certain person or something in daily life into three levels from 0 to 2, the demands level increased sequentially, 0 - totally not needed, 2 - urgently needed." These descriptions were shown to participants before the questions were asked in Table 1, for establishing a basic emotional demands system.

Table 2. Questionnaire of emotional needs.

Category	Factor	Question statement	Response scale
Personal entertainment	Listen to the music	Do you like listening to music?	0-never; 1-occasionally; 2-often
	Reading books and newspapers	Do you like reading and reading newspapers?	0-never; 1-occasionally; 2-often
	Play the game	Do you like to play games?	0-never; 1-occasionally; 2-often
	Take a walk (walk the dog, etc.)	Do you like walking?	0-never; 1-occasionally; 2-often
	Exercise	Do you like to exercise?	0-never; 1-occasionally; 2-often

(*continued*)

Table 2. (*continued*)

Category	Factor	Question statement	Response scale
Children (relatives)	Voice call	Do you like to make voice calls with their children?	0-never; 1-occasionally; 2-often
	Video call	Do you like to make video calls with their children?	0-never; 1-occasionally; 2-often
	Daily interactions	Do you want to know the daily life of your children?	0-never; 1-occasionally; 2-often
	Photo sharing	Do you like sharing your daily photos with children?	0-never; 1-occasionally; 2-often
Neighbors (friends)	Playing CARDS	Do you like playing cards with your neighbors?	0-never; 1-occasionally; 2-often
	Square dancing	Do you like dancing square dance with your neighbors?	0-never; 1-occasionally; 2-often
	Shopping	Do you like to go shopping with your neighbors?	0-never; 1-occasionally; 2-often
	Chat	Do you like to have a chat with your neighbors?	0-never; 1-occasionally; 2-often
Strangers (travel, etc.)	A new friend	Do you like making new friends?	0-never; 1-occasionally; 2-often
	Photo sharing	Do you like sharing travel photos?	0-never; 1-occasionally; 2-often
	Write a diary	Do you like to write a travel diary?	0-never; 1-occasionally; 2-often

2.2 Sample Profile

This study was implemented in China, through questionnaire and interview, 60 copies of the elderly samples were collected as shown in Table 3, urban and rural empty nesters each accounted for 30 copies. This session could be applied to test the influence of personal information (age, gender, number of children, level of education) on the elderly.

Table 3. Participant profile (N = 60)

Characteristics	Category	N	%
Age	60–70	21	35.0%
	70–80	20	33.3%
	80–90	15	25.0%
	Over 90 years old	4	6.7%
Gender	Male	28	46.7%
	Female	31	51.7%
	Other or unknown	1	1.7%
Number of children	1	17	28.3%
	2	24	40.0%
	3	7	11.7%
	4 and above	12	20.0%
Education level	Primary school and below	11	18.3%
	Middle school	13	21.7%
	High school	15	25.0%
	University degree or above	21	35.0%

3 Results

3.1 Questionnaire Results

This questionnaire surveyed 30 urban empty nesters and 30 rural empty nesters respectively. The final statistical results are shown in Table 4.

Table 4. Investigation data on the emotional needs of urban and rural empty nesters.

Category	Factor	Urban elderly (N = 30)			Rural elderly (N = 30)		
		0-never	1-occasionally	2-often	0-never	1-occasionally	2-often
Personal entertainment	Listen to the music	5	7	18	15	9	6
	Reading books and newspapers	6	12	12	20	6	4
	Play the game	10	13	7	23	5	2
	Take a walk (walk the dog, etc.)	3	8	19	8	5	17
	Exercise	6	7	17	11	11	8
Children (relatives)	Voice call	2	17	11	1	11	18
	Video call	5	9	16	21	8	1

(*continued*)

Table 4. (*continued*)

Category	Factor	Urban elderly (N = 30)			Rural elderly (N = 30)		
		0-never	1-occasionally	2-often	0-never	1-occasionally	2-often
	Daily	1	8	21	2	10	18
	Photo sharing	2	11	17	4	11	15
Neighbors (friends)	Playing CARDS	10	12	8	2	8	20
	Square dancing	4	8	18	23	6	2
	Shopping	3	17	10	10	11	9
	Chatting	10	12	8	1	8	21
Strangers (travel, etc.)	Make friends	5	15	10	16	7	7
	Photo sharing	4	12	14	5	10	15
	Write a diary	3	18	9	21	7	2

Average and analyze the above statistics, and the results are shown in Tables 5 and 6. The Importance Degree of each factor (I) = Weight (W) * Demand value (D) (take I > 0.25 as effective value).

Through the comparison, the following conclusions are found: old people living in urban areas require more variety in personal leisure and entertainment, while the demand of whom in rural areas are relatively simple. As to the communication with their children, the urban elderly prefer to chat through the video, while the rural elderly prefer to contact with their children by phone. Both of them are longing to share photos with children, and have more daily interaction with them. Concerning to the neighborhood relation, the elderly in the city would like to dance with their friends in the community square or go shopping, on the other hand, rural elderly prefer to play cards or chat. When it comes to tourism, urban elderly prefer to make new friends when going out and like to write travel diaries. However, rural elderly have less demand for tourism, and their only wish is to have a photo as souvenir.

Table 5. Data analysis of emotional demand factors of urban empty-nesters.

Category: weight (W)	Factor	Urban elderly: Average value (A)	Importance (I = W * A)
Personal entertainment: (30%)	Listen to the music	1.43	0.429**
	Reading books and newspapers	1.20	0.360*
	Play the game	0.90	0.270*
	Take a walk (walk the dog, etc.)	1.53	0.459**
	Exercise	1.37	0.411**
Children (relatives): (20%)	Voice call	1.30	0.260*
	Video call	1.37	0.274*
	Daily interactions	1.67	0.334*
	Photo sharing	1.50	0.300*
Neighbors (friends): (20%)	Playing CARDS	0.93	0.186
	Square dancing	1.47	0.294*
	Shopping	1.23	0.246
	Chat	0.93	0.186
Strangers (travel, etc.): (30%)	A new friend	1.17	0.351*
	Photo sharing	1.33	0.399*
	Write a diary	1.20	0.360*

*I > 0.25, **I > 0.4.

Table 6. Data analysis of emotional demand factors of rural empty-nesters.

Category: weight (W)	Factor	Rural elderly: Average value (A)	Importance (I = W * A)
Personal entertainment: (20%)	Listen to the music	0.70	0.140
	Reading books and newspapers	0.47	0.094
	Play the game	0.30	0.060
	Take a walk (walk the dog, etc.)	1.30	0.260*
	Exercise	0.90	0.180
Children (relatives): (30%)	Voice call	1.57	0.471**
	Video call	0.33	0.099
	Daily interactions	1.53	0.459**
	Photo sharing	1.37	0.411**
Neighbors (friends): (30%)	Playing CARDS	1.60	0.480**
	Square dancing	0.33	0.099
	Shopping	0.97	0.291*
	Chat	1.67	0.501**
Strangers (travel, etc.): (20%)	A new friend	0.70	0.14
	Photo sharing	1.33	0.266*
	Write a diary	0.37	0.074

*I > 0.25, **I > 0.4.

3.2   The Construction of Emotional Interactive Model

According to the results of the questionnaire, the comparison of different emotional demands between urban and rural empty-nesters, and the relevant information of emotional interaction, the emotional interaction model of elderly can be constructed, as shown in Fig. 2. The model builds the emotional interaction process of them from 5 aspects, which are the person who express the emotion (Who), the person who receive the emotion (To Whom), Interactive Content, In Which Channel, and With What Effect.

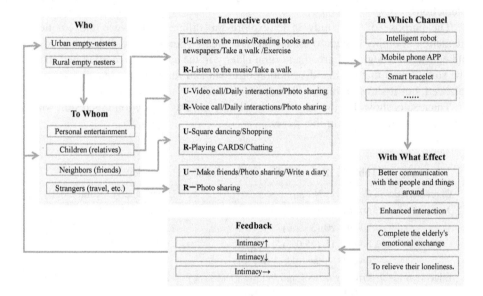

Fig. 2. The emotional interaction model of empty nesters.

In order to present the emotional interactive effect of the elderly more directly, intimacy value can be set in the interaction process. Through feedback, the model will inform the elderly about their current emotional status or remind their children or other relatives that they should enhance emotional interactions with the elderly. For example, the following information can be transferred to children:

- No interaction today, intimacy value decreases;
- Interact for twice, intimacy value remains stable;
- Interact for three times, intimacy value increases.

By information like these, the emotional status of the elderly can be monitored efficiently, informing their friends and relatives their emotional demands.

3.3   Other Influential Factors

This section was completed through interviews. Some questions were raised about the old people's personal information, in order to find out other personal characteristics that may affect the emotion of them. The study found that age and education had great impact on the emotional interaction of them. The empty nesters that are comparatively younger would like to pay more attention to personal space and they are more fond of traveling, and they also enjoy making new friends and sharing photos during tourism. The more educated elderly emphasize more on the quality of personal life, which is especially reflected in the interest of reading. Besides, the number of children and the gender of the elderly did not significantly affect the content of their emotional interactions.

The purpose of this study is to explore the difference between the emotional interaction of empty nesters in urban and rural areas. Therefore, the distribution of age and educational degree of urban and rural elderly in the sample is recorded in Table 7. The study found that the age distribution of urban and rural elderly remains generally balanced, but it shows a big gap in education level.

The results show that the education level may have an impact on this result, which is not discussed in detail in this paper.

Table 7. Data distribution for age and education level.

Characteristics	Category: N (%)	Urban elderly	Rural elderly
Age	60–70: 21 (35.0%)	10	11
	70–80: 20 (33.3%)	11	9
	80–90: 15 (25.0%)	8	7
	Over 90 years old: 4 (6.7%)	1	3
Education level	Primary school and below: 11 (18.3%)	2	9
	Middle school: 13 (21.7%)	3	10
	High school: 15 (25.0%)	7	8
	University degree or above: 21 (35.0%)	18	3

4   Discussion and Conclusion

4.1   The Emotional Needs of Empty Nesters

With the development of science and technology and the progress of society, people have met their material needs and now begin the pursuit of spiritual demands. For empty nesters, a special group, emotional interaction products that focus on emotional needs of them play an important role in releasing their loneliness and reducing mental illness.

In the course of questionnaire survey and interviews, it is found that empty nesters have an independent but lonely life. Although they are eager to communicate freely with others, there are few chances and occasions for them. That is why they become unsociable as time goes on. This research is based on the daily living habits and environment of the empty nesters in urban and rural areas with a hope of being closer to the life of every group. The urban empty nesters, in terms of personal recreation and travel, have much more needs than those living in rural areas, while the rural elderly pay more attention to the neighborhood relationship than the urban elderly. Though, both of them have strong emotional needs from their children. All these demands on emotional interaction deserve our attention.

4.2 The Design of Emotional Interaction Product

The research includes five parts, i.e. people with the need to express emotion, the object, content, the way and final effects of emotional interaction, and recommends a feedback channel. By doing these, a model of emotional interaction product design was established. In this model, the differences in the emotional needs of empty nesters in urban and rural areas are reflected in the interactive content on this step.

Emotional interactions in the product design cover two aspects: the emotional interactions between the user and the product, and the emotional interactions between people with the assistance of proper products. In the process of designing emotional interaction products, we should pay more attention to the emotional states of empty nesters, and conduct a further research on their daily behaviors and their emotional changes. We also should implant multiple emotional factors into the product in this process, thus creating more methods and opportunities for the lonely elderly to make emotional interactions, for the goal of successful emotional interaction between people and people, or between people and objects. The results of this study can provide references for the design of emotional interaction products for the empty nesters in urban and rural areas, realizing the commercialization of emotional interaction model through interactive mode.

4.3 The Possibility of Further Study

Ageing population and empty nesters belong to connotative, extensive, comprehensive and social issue, which involve knowledge concerning medical science, psychology, sociology and design science. This study, functioned as a basis exploration, provides reference and basis for the relevant research on emotional interaction for urban and rural empty nesters. However, systematic and deeper study remain further development. The objects of this study are set between empty nesters in urban and rural areas. Through this contrast, this study is to promote the largest interaction and communication extent between empty nesters and other people, so that they can eliminate loneliness when they are living by themselves, and improve their satisfaction to life.

Apart from living environments (urban or rural areas), this study finds that influential factors of emotion also include age and education, which probably lead to different emotional demand, while further discussion is needed concerning their influence on emotional interaction.

In China, similar to rural empty nesters, there are many vulnerable groups who haven't received enough attention, for instance, urban empty nesters, left-behind children and migrant workers. Like rural empty nesters, they live apart with their family, and cannot be taken good care of, what's more, they badly suffer from missing family, and their emotional demand cannot be met. The exiting problems among these groups can also be solved by design. The emotional interaction product design is currently in preliminary phase, theoretical research and design remain to be perfected. If further research and design can be done about emotional interaction product, with reference to other vulnerable groups, it is believed that the problem in regard to emotional vacancy of vulnerable groups can be solved, and it will bring tremendous benefit to the development of our country's modernization.

References

1. Juan, W.: Analysis on the quality of life and mental health of the elderly in urban empty nester. J. Chifeng Coll. (Nat. Sci. Edn.) **33**(02), 150–151 (2013). (in Chinese)
2. Fu, B., Li, Y.: Study on the emotional demand of left-behind elderly in rural areas. J. Lanzhou Inst. Technol. **22**(01), 101–104 (2015). (in Chinese)
3. Du, J.: Study on the spiritual life of empty nesters in the community. Hebei University (2014). (in Chinese)
4. Liu, X.: Study on the emotional needs of the elderly in urban empty nesters. Changchun University of Science and Technology (2013). (in Chinese)
5. Lu, M., Guo, C.: The current situation and research review of the mental health of the empty nesters. Prog. Psychol. Sci. **21**(02), 263–271 (2013). (in Chinese)
6. Di, X., Zhou, Y.: Sociological analysis of the emotional expression of the elderly in rural empty-nester. J. Anhui Agric. Univ. (Soc. Sci. Edn.) **21**(05), 5–10 (2012). (in Chinese)
7. Yi, G.: Research on the design of psychological comfort product system for the elderly in urban empty nesters. Jiangnan University (2012). (in Chinese)
8. Jian, C.: Research on the emotional needs of rural empty nesters and their emotional support. Central South University (2008). (in Chinese)
9. Isi, Y.: Design and research of emotional interactive products. Zhejiang University (2014)

Gamified Design for the Intergenerational Learning: A Preliminary Experiment on the Use of Smartphones by the Elderly

Weihan Xu[✉] and Xiao Liu

School of Economics and Management, Nanjing University of Science and Technology,
Nanjing 210094, China
whxu@163.com

Abstract. With the development of Web2.0, smartphone is one of the most typical and popular communication tools adopted by the public. As digital natives, young people has a high degree of absorptive and learning ability for those emerging technologies. In contrast, due to "technical panic" for smartphone, the elder groups face a few problems, such as technostress, learning barriers, and less interests. Intergenerational learning, as an informal communication and learning style within the family or in a larger community, delivers knowledge, skills, abilities, social norms and values among generations systematically. It is a mixed approach combining both formal and informal features, which integrates and involves the young generation with their predecessors in an appealing manner.

In this paper, we consider that the intergenerational learning dominated by young people would effectively help elder generation to use smartphone, which also has a significant impact on intergenerational relations and intergenerational barriers. Intergenerational learning is not limited to offline communication in which knowledge is delivered in words or written form, but it also includes the facial communications based on smartphones learning. In addition, it also mentions that game-based learning, or gamification plays an important role in improving the enthusiasm and effectiveness of study for the aged in process of intergenerational learning. This paper explores the phenomenon of reverse socialization of the elderly using smartphones which includes the reasons and the impact on intergenerational learning. Furthermore, it also attempts to analyze the change of attitude of both the youth and the elders during the process, which will yield some practical implication for the implementation of intergenerational learning.

Keywords: Intergenerational learning · Reverse socialization · Gamification

1   Introduction

At present, our country is in an era of rapid web2.0 and rapid social change. As the worldwide technological revolution has led to the changes in the mode of production and economic structure, it has also profoundly affected the changes in family intergenerational relations and family socialization process. With the popularization of the use of mobiles communication equipment, people's living habits, learning styles,

© Springer International Publishing AG, part of Springer Nature 2018
J. Zhou and G. Salvendy (Eds.): ITAP 2018, LNCS 10926, pp. 571–580, 2018.
https://doi.org/10.1007/978-3-319-92034-4_43

communication channels, modes of thinking and social relations have been greatly changed. Young people, as digital natives, have a high degree of acceptance and ability to learn new emerging technologies and devices. In contrast, the elder, as digital immigrants, are slow to learn and use hard-to-learn mobile communication equipment e.g. smartphones, less interests and difficult to accept the problem. The impact of young people on adult parents have become even more pronounced. In other words, we are in a "pre-symbolized" society called by Margaret Mead that the elder have to learn from their children that they have no experience [1]. In the case of using smartphones, what is undeniable is that young people use significantly more than their parents, especially in the field of daily life. The "Report on the Internet Utilization of Minors in China 2013–2014" published in 2014 shows that parents who take the initiative to consult minors about Internet knowledge have 56.1% and 22.7% of them, sometimes and often. There is a phenomenon of intergenerational learning in reverse socialization between parents and children, that is, elders ask knowledge and skills to their younger. The emergence of this phenomenon has broken the monopoly of elders over knowledge and authority over a long period of time. The adolescent generation is not only a passive recipient of knowledge and authority, but also an active agent for knowledge creation and dissemination. It also has great influence on parents, children and families.

Furthermore, from the perspective of human-computer interaction, we believe that the reverse socialization of intergenerational learning can be well reflected in the introduction of gamification into the use of smartphone by the elderly. Hamari et al. indicate that gamification is a desired way to support user engagement and enhance positive patterns in service use [2]. Deterding et al. highlight that the affordances implemented in gamification will lead to some positive outcomes of product/service use [3]. To our best knowledge, since the discovery of this phenomenon in our country, only a small amount of direct research on intergenerational studies has been published in conferences and periodicals. There is almost no application of gamification to this research. Therefore, we would like to explore whether the youth-dominated reverse social intergenerational learning can better motivate the elders to use smartphone, especially the influence of gamification on teaching. In this paper, some of our experiments adopted gamification design and observed the learning process of using smartphone by young people to teach the elderly. We conducted a preliminary experimental with 15 elderly people who have never had a smartphone before. We aim at answering these two questions:

RQ1: How does the influence of the intergenerational learning on the elderly's use of smartphone?

RQ2: How does the influence of gamification design on the process of intergenerational learning about the smartphone use by the elderly?

2   Literature Review

2.1   Intergenerational Learning

Intergenerational learning is first and foremost an interdisciplinary term in the fields of psychology, medicine and public policy [4]. With the development of information technology, it gradually penetrates into the fields of management science, pedagogy and information science. The concept of intergenerational learning is divided into three stages: the earliest can be traced back to the older generation, such as family, elder or grandparent, to extend the wisdom and values to the next generation, but did not form a standardized rule [5]. For example, Hoff defines intergenerational learning as a process that is very common among generations in the family and that delivers the knowledge, skills, guidelines and values to the next generation of systems [6]. Secondly, in order to solve the problem of being young as a result of geographical divisions due to work and family needs the gap between one generation and the older generation, the definition of intergenerational learning is no longer confined to the relationship between family members, extended to the family outside, that is, New Extrafamilial Paradigm [7], such as Ropes believes that intergenerational learning in business organizations is an interactive way that can promote the relations between generations and acquire new knowledge, new skills and new ideas [8]. In 1999, the UNESCO Institute of Education held a meeting in Dortmund to broadly define the intergenerational learning as a purposeful, continuous exchange of resources and learning tools between the older generation and the younger generation [9]. The intent is to adapt the concept to multiple perspectives and to promote cooperation. Bostrum believes that when people from different generations are learning together, there is an interaction of knowledge, skills, attitudes and values [10]. At this stage, researches on early childhood education, education for the aged, family relations and other aspects have begun to be explored [11–13]. Generation study in the modern sense began to emerge. Generation study gradually became a key area of focus for European and American countries. Intergenerational Program, Learning Practice [14] and Intergenerational initiative embody the meaning of intergenerational learning. Hatton-Yeo and Batty recognize that learning is a process that runs through life and that people may have different needs and interests at different stages of their lives, with the potential to share learning and transcend generations [15].

Therefore, the key to "intergenerational" terminology lies not between generations, but between interpersonal relationships. Finally, with the rapid development of instant messaging tools, the younger generation gradually occupies the leading position in knowledge transfer. Intergenerational learning not only includes lines under the communication, but we should also try to embed information and communication technologies, computer collaboration technologies and various smart devices in the process of knowledge transfer, so that the development of intergenerational education can get rid of the limitations of geographical, time, educational level and other factors to enhance learning convenience, innovation and scalability, while emphasizing the content of learning. We should also pay attention to the cultivation of intergenerational information literacy [16–18]. Klamma et al. defined intergenerational learning as "the process-based experience and experience of one generation with another generation" and emphasized that intergenerational learning should not be confined to face-to-face communication and ignoring the drive of emerging information technologies effect [19].

2.2   Reverse Socialization

Research on reverse socialization began in the mid-1950s and has been more than half a century old. The concept of reverse socialization was first proposed in the field of household consumption. There are two kinds of English expressions of reverse social-ization: "reverse socialization" and "retroactive socialization", but the two expressions are nearly 20 years before and after the proposal is made. The concept of "retroactive socialization" was first proposed by Riesman and Roseborough, meaning that children can learn consumer-related skills from peers and the media and influence his or her parents with those skills [20]. However, in the nearly 20 years since, very few studies have adopted this concept. Bell, who first proposed the idea of the two-way influence of parents and children in socialization, was considered a mountain to the study of reverse socialization, yet Bell himself did not come up with the concept of reverse socialization [21]. Ward proposed the concept of reverse socialization as the process by which children may influence their parents' knowledge, skills and attitudes about consumption [22]. Since then, the term "reverse socialization" has been widely adopted to denote reverse socialization.

The author thinks that reverse socialization includes two kinds of processes: one is the active learning process of the socialized subject to the object, and the second is the influence and pressure from the socialized subject that have a direct or indirect influence on the attitude and behavior of the socialized subject influences. The domestic (Main-land) reverse socialization research began in the late 1980s, Zhou put forward the concept of "cultural feedback" [23]. The concept of "localization of culture" has also become synonymous with the study of reverse socialization in China. At present, there are three kinds of perspectives for the definition of reverse socialization in China: From a sociological point of view, reverse socialization is the socialization of the previous generation by young people and youth, that is, the socialization of knowledge and skills that traditional recipients put into practice for educators [24]. From a cultural point of view, reverse socialization is Margaret Mead called "after metaphorical culture", "meta-phorical culture" is also a youth culture, which means that youth has become the authority of life groups, the elders to the cultural form of youth learning, also known as youth model culture. The third uses the concept of cultural nurturing proposed by Zhou, referring to cultural nurturing, which is a process of extensive cultural assimilation to the younger generation in the era of rapid cultural change [23].

3   Research Design

We conducted a preliminary experiment to investigate our research questions raised above. The purpose of this experiment is to let the experimental subject use some func-tions of the smartphone independently after learning, specifically for "use camera", "add address list", and "dial" these three basic functions of smartphone. After that, we eval-uated the results based on the completion of the tests.

3.1 Participants

First of all, this paper selected nine groups of families to participate in this experiment. Each family is composed of the elderly who has not been exposed to smartphones, and their children who can use smartphones. Meanwhile, we ensured that the selected elderly have a certain willingness to learn how to use smartphones before the experiment, and their cultural level is similar, which reduces interference caused by conflict, stereotype and learning ability.

3.2 Data Collection

After screening suitable experimental subjects, 15 groups of elderly were randomly divided into three groups: A, B and C. Each group contained 5 elderly families, including group A as control group, group B and group C as experimental groups. During the experiment, elderly of group A learn three functions of the smartphone by themselves through the manual and independent exploration. Elderly of Group B learn through reverse socialization intergenerational learning, and their children teach them by the traditional way of oral teaching and specific operation. Elderly of group C learn through reverse socialization intergenerational learning with gamification designs. Here, different from the teaching style of the group B, gamified styles are designed as following methods: In the intergenerational learning process, children describe to their parents the situation related to the daily life preferences or habits of the elderly to enable elderly to integrate into the situation, such as "playing chess", "watching flowers" and so on, which can trigger the demand of using "use camera", "add address list" and "dial", to make the teaching more realistic and practical. After elderly are familiar with the operation of smartphone, they repeated training by setting different situations to enhance proficiency, and by setting the countdown, operation is completed within the time limit to strengthen the memory of the operation process of the elderly. At the same time, children need to offer encourage or rewards constantly during the teaching, in order to improve the elderly to complete the learning achievements. After the 3 days, 3 h a day of learning and training, we arranged the same requirements of using smartphone to 15 groups of elderly people, and let them use the same smartphone in 10 min to finish, and after that we evaluated the overall completion degree and time of the test results, and then analyze it.

After the end of the experiment, we interviewed the elderly in 30–60 min per person around the contents of their learning experience, the feeling of using smartphone, and will to continue using smartphone in the future, and sought their advice on the use of smartphones and the way to learn, finally we recorded the interview results and carried on the analysis.

4 Results and Discussion

First of all, we analyzed the results of the experiment. From the view of finish time, the elderly of group C learning through gamified intergenerational learning finish respectively in 2′58″, 3′11″, 3′26″, 3′54″ and 4′04″, followed by the elderly of group B learning by traditional intergenerational learning are respectively 3′59″, 4′19″, 4′38″,

4′56″ and 5′02″, and the elderly of group A learning by themselves are respectively 5′18″, 5′44″, 6′21″, 8′06″ and 10′00″ (experiment time is 10 min). We can see that the group C significantly completed the fastest time, group B is the second, while the elderly of group A are generally slow, and even one of them had not completed at the end of the experiment. From the view of degree of completion, group C and group B completed the requirements accurately, while only two of group A completed the requirements and last one only completed the "use camera" and "dial", and did not complete the "add address list" timely. It can be seen that the group A learning by themselves compared to the group B with children's participation, group B is significantly faster and finish better than group A, which shows that the effect of reverse socialized intergenerational learning is better, and proves the importance of children's participation in the teaching of using smartphones for the elderly. At the same time, the comparison between groups B and group C shows that the overall speed and speed of each item of group C are generally faster than group B, which can be seen that the gamification designs of learning effect is significant, and there is an obvious improvement in the proficiency of elderly people using smartphones, and proves that the reverse social intergenerational integrated into gamification designs has a positive effect on the elderly using smartphones (Table 1).

Table 1. Testing timetables for the use of smartphones for older people

Group	Learning style	Num.	Finish time	Use camera	Add address list	Dial	Average time
A	Self-taught	1	8′ 06″	1′ 46″	4′ 53″	1′ 27″	7′ 06″
		2	5′ 44″	1′ 39″	3′ 06″	0′ 59″	
		3	10′ 00″	3′ 42″	——	2′ 49″	
		4	5′ 18″	1′ 21″	2′ 58″	0′ 59″	
		5	6′ 21″	1′ 38″	3′ 42″	1′ 01″	
B	Traditional intergenerational learning	6	4′ 19″	1′ 14″	2′ 50″	0′ 15″	4′ 35″
		7	5′ 02″	1′ 18″	3′ 01″	0′ 43″	
		8	4′ 56″	1′ 31″	3′ 04″	0′ 21″	
		9	3′ 59″	1′ 06″	2′ 35″	0′ 18″	
		10	4′ 38″	1′ 22″	2′ 53″	0′ 23″	
C	Gamified intergenerational learning	11	3′ 54″	1′ 03″	2′ 32″	0′ 19″	3′ 31″
		12	4′ 04″	1′ 21″	2′ 19″	0′ 24″	
		13	3′ 26″	1′ 15″	2′ 04″	0′ 07″	
		14	2′ 58″	0′ 59″	1′ 51″	0′ 08″	
		15	3′ 11″	1′ 01″	1′ 58″	0′ 12″	

Secondly, after finishing interviews, the answers to the three questions about "learning experience", "using experience" and "will you continue to use" are summarized in Table 2.

Table 2. A summary of interview

Group	Learning experience	Using experience	Continue to use
A	The self-learning of smartphones is difficult. Without other people's help, the function and operation of mobile applications can only be learned through the text on the instructions, which is difficult to understand and remember	There are few function introduction and operation guidance in mobile phone application. It is troublesome to search directions again when using, and many contents are not introduced in the instructions. It does not take care of all the kind of people who use it	They may not continue to use. The operation is more difficult than the convenience provided by the smartphone function, and they don't know whether the practicability is high, so they tend to use the landline, camera and so on
B	In the children's teaching can be more intuitive to understand the function and operation, but it is a little boring, and if not repeated operation they are easy to forget the details of the operation	After understanding the functions and operations, the mobile phone is easier to use, but it is limited to the mobile phone functions that have been taught	In some ways such as emergency contact, it will be useful, and it is very likely that it will continue to be used, to be prepared, and to be used when needed
C	The gamified learning process is more interesting. Besides the introduction of function and operation, learning is more relaxed, it also provides many kinds of situations that may be faced, and has a better understanding of the practicability of smartphones	With situational memory, smartphones are more proficient in use and they will try other functions	They will continue to use, think that smartphones are very convenient, in many situations, they will think of smartphones at the first time to solve problems rather than other alternatives

As for the use of smartphones and the way to learn using smartphones, the elderly also give some suggestions in the interview. After combining with the existing theories of intergenerational learning, gamification and reverse socialization, this paper innovates and lists the following suggestions:

(1) Participation of children. Children play a vital role in the process of reverse socialized intergenerational learning. With the company of children, elderly people are more likely to accept new things. Beginners are hard to avoid learning difficulties, but before their children, there is no emotional distress, such as loss of self-confidence, etc. Also, their children are more patient and can greatly improve their self-efficacy of smartphones.

(2) Gamified learning. Through the gamification elements, such as increase the sense of presence by increasing the situation used in the experiment. It let elderly people know what is the use of the smartphone's function and where it is used, and highlight

its practical significance. It also adds interest to the boring teaching operation directly, and cater to the interests of the elderly and the needs of their life to make the utility of smartphone deeply rooted in the hearts of the elderly people to achieve better teaching effect. Meanwhile it can integrate into the youth culture, to make the gap between the cultures and habits of the intergenerational closer.

(3) Help and prompt the specific application. Because many manual introduces the smartphone hardware level operation and some basic operation, and it is considered that the users have had the relevant empirical basis, but it does not consider the elderly who had never contact with the smartphone and its application. It is possible to set up a more obvious help interface for teaching and guidance in the application to reduce the operation error which lead to elderly people's using problems.

(4) The audiovisual of guide. For an instruction manual with whole words, the elderly are difficult to see the instructions on it because of the presbyopia and other vision problems. Video teaching with specific steps and voice interpretations is more acceptable to the elderly, which can reduce the error between the understanding and operation, and can be repeated to watch and reduce the difficulty of learning.

In summary, combined with the reverse socialization and intergenerational learning theory, in the future, we can try to develop specialized smartphone function teaching software, and let children participate in the learning process, make elderly learn smartphone effectively by watching the video, and with gamification designs like setting situation. And then it can improve the use of smartphones in the elderly group, and achieve the purpose of intelligent old-age care.

5   Conclusion and Implications

From the gamification point of view, our goal was to investigate the impact of the reverse socialization of intergenerational learning on promoting the use of smartphone for the elderly. We conducted a quasi-experiment to respond to our research questions. The research findings show that, first, the 15 elders were divided into three groups, guidance and gamification design of young people as a control experiment variables, the data found that the C group was the best effect, B followed by the second, the last group A; Second, we compare A with B, B with C, found that guidance and gamification of young people are helpful for the elderly to use their smartphone; Third, it is interesting to note that, the gamification design should be viewed as a journey rather than an event, our presume can be combined with other research studies. Since elders may get boring after a period time of usage, the gamification design should make the whole learning process more novel and unique. In other words, gamification design is one of the keys to the success of this experiment. In addition, our study was not without limitations. The theoretical mapping between application of theory and the gamification design in experiment needs further literature supports and discussion. The stereotypes and lifestyle habits of some elders may be the problems that affect and limit the experiment. In summary, our research gives a guidebook that will help young people to teach their elders to use their smartphone to enhance intergenerational relationships. In future studies, we will use this guidebook to dig deeper into the motivations of the reverse socialization of intergenerational learning to validate our findings.

References

1. Mead, M.: Culture and commitment: a study of the generation gap. Leonardo **6**(2), 411–413 (1970)
2. Hamari, J., Koivisto, J., Sarsa, H.: Does gamification work? – A literature review of empirical studies on gamification. In: Hawaii International Conference on System Sciences. IEEE Computer Society, pp. 3025–3034 (2014)
3. Deterding, S., Dan, D., Khaled, R., et al.: From game design elements to gamefulness: defining "gamification". In: International Academic Mindtrek Conference: Envisioning Future Media Environments, pp. 9–15. ACM (2011)
4. Gadsden, V.L., Hall, M.: Intergenerational learning: a review of the literature, 43 (1996)
5. Newman, S., Hatton-Yeo, A.: Intergenerational learning and the contributions of older people. Ageing Horiz. **8**(10), 31–39 (2008)
6. Hoff, A.: Intergenerational learning as an adaptation strategy in ageing knowledge societies. In: Education, Employment, Europe, pp. 126–129 (2007)
7. Newman, S., Hatton-Yeo, A.: Intergenerational learning and the contributions of older people. Ageing Horiz. **8**(10), 31–39 (2008)
8. Ropes, D.: Intergenerational learning in organizations. Eur. J. Training Dev. **37**(8), 713–727 (2013)
9. Hattonyeo, A., Ohsako, T., Foundation, B.J.: Intergenerational Programmes: Public Policy and Research Implications: An International Perspective. UIE and Beth Johnson Foundation (1999)
10. Hattonyeo, A.E., Ohsako, T.E.: Intergenerational programmes: public policy and research implications–an international perspective. Adult Educ. 73 (2000)
11. Corrigan, T., Mcnamara, G., O'Hara, J.: Intergenerational learning: a valuable learning experience for higher education students. Eurasian J. Educ. Res. **52**(52), 99–118 (2013)
12. Newman, S.: Intergenerational Programs: Past, Present, and Future. Taylor & Francis, Washington, D.C. (1997)
13. Campbell, R., Kaplan, M., Kusano, A., et al.: Intergenerational programs: support for children, youth, and elders in Japan. J. Asian Stud. **58**(1), 200–202 (1999)
14. Mitrofanenko, T., Muhar, A., Penker, M.: Potential for applying intergenerational practice to protected area management in mountainous regions. Mt. Res. Dev. **35**(1), 27–38 (2015)
15. Hatton-Yeo, A., Batty, C.: Evaluating the contribution of intergenerational practice to achieving social cohesion. In: Promoting Social Cohesion Implications for Policy and Evaluation (2011)
16. Shi, Y., Zhao, Y., Zhu, Q.: Intergenerational learning: an emerging field to bridge digital natives with digital immigrants. Libr. Inf. **2**, 63–71 (2017). (in Chinese)
17. Bailey, A., Ngwenyama, O.: Bridging the generation gap in ICT use: Interrogating identity, technology and interactions in community telecenters. Inf. Technol. Dev. **16**(1), 62–82 (2010)
18. Hill, R.L.: Keeping in touch: talking to older people about computers and communication. Educ. Gerontol. **33**(8), 613–630 (2007)
19. Klamma, R., Spaniol, M., Jarke, M., et al.: ACIS: intergenerational community learning supported by a hypermedia Afghan sites and monuments database. In: IEEE International Conference on Advanced Learning Technologies, pp. 108–112. IEEE Computer Society (2005)

20. Ekström, K.M.: Parental consumer learning or 'keeping up with the children'. J. Consum. Behav. **6**(12), 203–217 (2007)
21. Bell, R.Q.: A reinterpretation of the direction of effects in studies of socialization. Psychol. Rev. **75**(2), 81 (1968)
22. Ward S. Consumer Socialization. In: Consumer socialization c, pp. 1–14. Lexington Books (1987)
23. Zhou, X.: On the back-feeding significance of contemporary Chinese youth culture. Youth Stud. **11**, 22–26 (1988). (in Chinese)
24. Li, Q.: Reverse socialization: a new task in the study of youth socialization. Youth Explor. **6**, 21–24 (1991). (in Chinese)

Intergenerational Play Between Young People and Old Family Members: Patterns, Benefits, and Challenges

Fan Zhang[✉]

Faculty of Education, Simon Fraser University, Burnaby, BC, Canada
fza26@sfu.ca

Abstract. The purpose of this study was to explore the patterns, benefits and challenges of intergenerational play between young people and their old family members (i.e., parents, grandparents, and uncles/aunts). A total of 308 responses were collected from young people aged 15+ using an online survey. The results showed that young people generally did not frequently play digital games with family members; however when they did, they reported that intergenerational play was a fun way for them to bond with family members. In addition, skill gaps, different cohort knowledge, and old adults' physical and cognitive declines were the main factors that had negative impacts on smooth intergenerational game play. The biggest challenge that participants faced was explaining game rules and mechanisms using words understandable to old family members.

Keywords: Intergenerational play · Digital games · Young people
Old family members · Bonding

1 Introduction

The intergenerational gap has become a social issue in Europe and North America due to the demographic rise in the number of old adults and other family, community and social changes [1]. There have been increasing research interest in recent years in exploring how digital games can be used to promote understanding, build relationships, and facilitate interaction between old adults and young people [2]. Previous studies have explored the nature of kin and non-kin intergenerational digital gameplay, the roles each age cohort plays, and the physical, cognitive and social impacts of intergenerational play on different age groups. Design ideas and processes have been discussed for designing digital games for intergenerational learning and interaction with a primary focus on how the age differences (e.g., old adults' physical and cognitive declines), expertise of each group (e.g., young people as technology experts) and any motivational factors (e.g., the value of social interaction with family members for old adults) could be used to engage the two age groups and maintain their interests [3–6]. In addition, new digital games have been developed for strengthening intergenerational relationships and learning between old adults and their younger family members, such as Collage [7], TranseCare [8], Age Invaders [9], e-Treasure [10], and Curball [11]. These studies were designed

© Springer International Publishing AG, part of Springer Nature 2018
J. Zhou and G. Salvendy (Eds.): ITAP 2018, LNCS 10926, pp. 581–593, 2018.
https://doi.org/10.1007/978-3-319-92034-4_44

and conducted based on the great potential of intergenerational gameplay for knowledge sharing and social-emotional exchanges. However, fewer studies have examined the features of intergenerational play in the family contexts from the perspectives of young people, such as the games they play most often with family members, factors motivating them to play digital games with old family members, and benefits and challenges they encounter. Kaplan et al. [2, p. 9] highlighted that "in considering the contributions that technology can make to intergenerational relationships... it is useful to first step back and consider more broadly the role that technology plays in the social lives of young people as well as old adults". Thus, the purpose of the current study was to understand the features, benefits and challenges of intergenerational play within family contexts from the perspectives of young people.

1.1   Importance of Family Life

The majority of people live their entire lives in the context of families. Family structure has significantly changed in the last century [12]. In the 1900s, the family structures looked like a pyramid-a large number of children and parents but very few grandparents. However, the family model looks more like a lopsided rectangle in the 2000s due to the increased life expectance. Families have fewer children and more generations are alive at the same time point.

The World Health Organization defines health as "a state of complete physical, mental and social wellbeing and not merely the absence of disease or infirmity" [13]. Families provide important resources for learning independence and exchange help and support. As people get old, families become more and more important due to the increased need for support [12]. Research and policy is likely to be more focused on quality of life than quantity of life for old adults [14]. Previous research has reported positive impacts of intergenerational participation in leisure activities on relationship satisfaction and bonding experience [15].

1.2   Social Values of Gameplay for Old Adults

With the evolution of digital games, gameplay has become a popular activity among technology-savvy young people and old adults [16]. Approximately 13% of U.S. gamers are aged 50 and over [17]. In Nimrod's study [18] fun, joking, silliness, and general playfulness are the values of playing digital games reported by aging populations. Kaufman and his colleagues [19] identified a list of benefits of old adults' gameplay including mental exercise, enjoyment and fun, social interaction, escape from daily life, developing self-confidence, dealing with loneliness, and connecting with family members. Zhang and Kaufman [20] investigated old adults' social interactions in massively multiplayer online role-playing games (MMORPGs). Approximately 16% of participants played MMORPGs with family members sometimes, while 13.2% played with family frequently and 9.7% all the time. Slightly more than half of participants (51.7%) discussed gameplay with their families. More than 45% of participants agreed or strongly agreed that playing with family members made them feel closer to them. Zhang and Kaufman concluded that playing MMORPGs with family could be an effective way to maintain and enhance current off-line relationships. De Schutter and Brown [16] explored game enjoyment in late life. They found that old adults prefer playing with people important to them compared to strangers. This study identified cases in which the younger female participants played digital games with their children when their children were young. For some participants this mode of socialization with children, and now as adults, has continued to today. De Schutter and Brown stated that gaming could be a means for old adults to nurture meaningful relationships with grandchildren who live apart.

1.3 Importance of Intergenerational Interaction

Strong and meaningful intergenerational relationships are a crucial means of exchanging knowledge, human capital, values, social norms, and cultural and historical identity [21]. They provide opportunities to express feelings, exchange care and support, exercise flexibility in thinking, and build self-esteem [22]. Although the two age groups have years of experience separating them, they can benefit from their companionship in many ways, particularly older adults at high risk of social isolation. Children usually bring positive energy to any room they enter, which can stimulate old adults physically and mentally [23]. Some research has shown that old adults who work and interact with young people live longer and have better physical and mental health than their counterparts [24]. They have a lot to teach children and youth, and also to learn about technology and other innovations from young people. Within family contexts, interacting with grandchildren can foster positive emotions and coping, strengthen social bonds, and provide opportunities to nurture younger generations, which improves overall quality of life and life satisfaction [6]. For young people, interacting regularly with old adults can affect their negative perceptions towards aging [22], and develop a sense of pride and leadership as they receive acceptance from old adults [24]. They can learn to be patient, tolerant and empathetic, increase self-esteem and confidence, and improve communication and social skills [23].

1.4 Research About Intergenerational Digital Gameplay

With the advent of technology, there has been growing attention on ways in which technology, such as digital games, can be used to connect people from different age groups [2]. According to the 2017 report of Entertainment Software Association [17], 67% of parents in U.S. play digital games with their child at least once weekly. The best-selling digital game types in 2016 are shooter (27.5%), action (20.5%), role-playing (12.9%), sports (11.7%), adventure (7.8%), fighting (5.8%), strategy (4.3%), and racing (3.3%). The reasons why parents play digital games with their children include: (1) fun, (2) a good opportunity to socialize with their children, (3) monitoring what their children are playing, and (4) enjoying playing digital games as much as their children. Zhang and Kaufman [6] identified five features of intergenerational play: (1) it is the enjoyment of interaction with family members that motivates old adults to play digital games; (2) the interaction among grandparents and grandchildren during intergenerational play is not symmetric and reciprocated; (3) young people usually take on the role of technology tutors or teachers during intergenerational play; (4) the modes of communication may change as the two generations spend more time together; and (5) parents and older children could play an important role in facilitating intergenerational play. De la Hera et al. [4] reviewed 16 empirical studies on intergenerational relationships and identified four categories of benefits of intergenerational play, including (1) reinforcing family bond, (2) enhancing reciprocal learning, (3) increasing understanding of the other generation, and (4) reducing social anxiety.

Zhang et al. [25] used conversational analysis to examine how the structures of talk-in-interaction during intergenerational gameplay provide opportunities for situated learning between old adults and undergraduate students. It was found that old adults adapted to and made sense of collaborative gaming activities through guided participation. They learned game mechanisms by asking questions and getting feedback from their younger partners who addressed their situated questions, highlighted and corrected their mistakes, oriented their attention to key concepts, and explained gaming rules and strategies. The younger players always offered immediate feedback to guide their old partners to participate in the collaborative play, and sometimes they had to revise or reformulate their explanation to clarify misunderstandings. As old adults became more experienced users, they were able to coordinate with their younger partners to overcome setbacks, and engaged in mutual encouragement to reach a common goal. However, old adults could not play independently by the end of the six-week study and still needed to ask their younger partners to confirm their actions. Chua and colleagues [15] investigated the impacts of a two-month intergenerational digital gameplay program on perceptions amongst old adults and young people when they were paired to play digital games together. The results indicated that the participants of the two age groups developed not only positive perceptions (e.g., attitudes and intergroup anxiety) towards their partners, but also positive general perceptions towards the members of the other age group. The young participants reported a significantly greater degree of perceptional changes in attitudes towards old adults, as compared to the old participants. In addition, game enjoyment played an important role in developing positive perceptions for old adults. Chua and colleagues stated that one plausible explanation for the stronger effects of intergenerational play on younger people's perceptions on old adults is its novelty. Intergenerational play might break down the perception that old adults do not accept new technologies. On the other hand, the old participants probably received much help from their younger partners. They might be likely to develop attraction towards their partners and the general young people when they started to enjoy intergenerational play. However, this study did not explore the issue qualitatively. Although the results of these few studies are promising, more in-depth investigation is needed.

2   Research Questions

Intergenerational play may change the modes of communication and the traditional roles played by old adults and young people, but more studies are needed before we can understand how digital games can be designed and used to facilitate stronger intergenerational bonds. The research questions of the current study were:

- What are the features of intergenerational play between young people (aged 15+) and their old family members?
- Why do young people (aged 15+) play digital games with their old family members?
- Which challenges do young people (aged 15+) face while playing digital games with their old family members?

3   Methodology

Data were collected through an online survey, as it is an effective method to collect appropriately large amount of responses from different places and cultures. Invitation messages providing the URL to the survey were posted on ten game forums. Participants were young people aged 15 and over, and had played digital games with their old family members. In this study, "young" and "old" were used to differ different generations. Old family members referred to parents, grandparents, and uncles or aunts. Due to ethical issues, this study focused on young people aged 15 and older.

The online survey consisted of three sections. The first section asked questions related to intergenerational play experience, including: (1) frequency of playing digital games with parents, grandparents, and uncles or aunts respectively; (2) topics discussed with old family members during intergenerational play; (3) frequency of engaging in a list of social activities during intergenerational play, such as teaching or guiding old family members how to play digital games, making decisions about which games they should play, and explaining game elements and game mechanisms to old family members; (4) benefits of playing digital games with old family members. The second section asked three open-ended questions: (1) names of the games played most frequently with old family members; (2) motivations for playing with old family members; and (3) challenges encountered when playing with old family members. The third section asked for demographic information.

4   Results

A total of 308 responses were received from people aged between 15 and 35. With regards to gender, 45% of the participants were female and 55% were male. Approximately 40% of the participants were aged between 15 and 19, and 35% were between 20 and 24, while 12.8% were between 25 and 29, and 12.8% were in the age range of 30 and 35. A significant majority of participants had a high school degree (25.0%), some college (28.3%) or a four-year degree (26.3%), while 4.6% had a Master's degree, and 1.3% had a doctoral degree. In terms of frequency of gameplay, the majority of partic-ipants could be described as heavy gamers who played a few times a week (28.9%) or once a day (50.7%). Although all participants played digital games with their old family members, this did not happen frequently. Approximately 49% of participants rarely (39.9%) or never (8.8%) played digital games with their parents, while 36.4% played sometimes, 13.0% played frequently, and only 1.9% played all the time. In addition, about 96% of participants rarely (78.4%) or never (18.0%) played digital games with their grandparents, while only 2.6% played sometimes and 1.0% played frequently. None of participants played digital games with their grandparents all the time. Similarly, the majority of participants had never played digital games with their uncle or aunts (Table 1).

Table 1. Frequency of playing with old family members (n = 308)

Old family members	Never	Rarely	Sometimes	Frequently	All the time
Parents	8.8%	39.9%	36.4%	13.0%	1.9%
Grandparents	78.4%	18.0%	2.6%	1.0%	0%
Uncle or aunts	70.2%	18.7%	8.9%	2.0%	3%

We asked participants to name up to three games they have played most often with old family members, which resulted in 139 games. The most frequently played eight games were Mario Kart (21.4%), Wii Sports including Wii Party, Wii Sports Resort and Wii Fit (13%), Jackbox Party Pack (9.7%), Call of Duty (8.4%), World of Warcraft (7.8%), Words with Friends (5.8%), Minecraft (5.2%), and Civilization (4.5%). It seems young people have played all genres of games with their old family members, including first person shooter, racing, board, sports, and role-playing (Table 2).

Table 2. Games played most often with old family members

Mario Kart	Wii Sports	Jackbox Party Pack	Call of Duty	World of Warcraft	Words w. Friends	Minecraft	Civilization
21.4%	13%	9.7%	8.4%	7.8%	5.8%	5.2%	4.5%

Table 3 describes participants' motivation for playing digital games with old family members. Slightly more than half of participants (50.6%) felt that it is fun to play digital games with old family members. They have many good times when playing together. It is easier to decide on which game to play than picking a movie to watch. One participant said his mom is mostly bored at home and playing together can 'make her enjoy her time'. Approximately 36% of participants said they play digital games with their old family members due to the bonding experience. They enjoy the company of family members. Digital games provide another opportunity to spend time with one another, get competitive, and laugh together. Roughly 14% of participants indicated that playing digital games is a common hobby among their family members. For these participants, digital games are something that they share and love doing in their free time. In some cases, the young participants grew up playing digital games with their dad. In other cases, the young participants were introduced to digital games by their old family members who started gaming from the 1980s and early 1990s. Approximately 9% of participants mentioned that playing digital games together is something they all enjoy and continue doing as a family activity. Playing digital games is a fun way to get the whole family involved. During family gatherings (e.g., holidays) it is nice to have an activity that everyone can participate in. One participant said his dad is more into fighting and racing games, while his mom will join them when they play puzzle or interactive games on the Wii. A same percentage of participants (9.1%) wanted to get their old family members to understand why they love playing games. It is fun showing off what a modern digital game (e.g., VR) is capable of and seeing their family members get excited. Three participants also mentioned that the motivation is to share something they enjoy doing rather than just sitting with family members in the living room and watching TV for hours. In addition, about 7% of participants reported playing digital game is a good way of spending time with family members despite distance. They enjoy interacting with their parents through digital games even though they are hundreds miles apart. Other motivations for playing with old family members include introducing family members to the digital world (3.9%) and the convenience of playing digital board games (4.5%).

Table 3. Motivation for playing digital games with old family members

Motivation	Percentage
Fun	50.6%
Bonding with family members	36.4%
Common hobby	13.6%
Family activity	9.1%
Get family members to understand why I love playing games	9.1%
A good way of spending time with one another despite distance	6.5%
Convenient to play digital board game	4.5%
Introducing family members to the digital world	3.9%
Other	1.3%

Table 4 describes topics discussed with old family members during intergenerational play. Approximately 47% of participants selected discussing game related issues such as gaming skills; 24.0% said they shared life experience such as cooking recipes and school days; 18.5% selected latest social news and events. However, only 9.1% of participants indicated they had discussed important issues, such as quitting a job, with their old family members.

Table 4. Topics discussed with old family members during intergenerational play

Topics	Percentage of topics talked during intergenerational gameplay
• Discussing game related issues (e.g., game skills)	46.8%
• Sharing life experience (e.g., cooking recipes)	24.0%
• Talking about latest social news and events	18.5%
• Discussing important issues (e.g., quitting a job)	9.1%

We also asked participants to indicate the degree to which they had engaged in some social activities during intergenerational play (see Table 5). The majority of participants said they teach or guide their old family members how to play digital games sometimes (34.3%), frequently (21.3), or all the time (13.6%). Similarly, the majority of participants (70.4%) said they make decisions about which games they should play sometimes (35.5%), frequently (22.5%), or all the time (12.4%). In terms of the statement "I explain game elements and game mechanisms to my old family members, the majority of participant mentioned they had done this sometimes (23.5%), frequently (31.2%), or all the time (21.2%). For the statement "I make decisions about the game strategies and how we should play", only less than one quarter (20.4%) of participants mentioned they had done this frequently (14.8%) or all the time (5.9%). In an indication of the frequency of offering feedback to old family members about their game performance, 33.5% of the participants had done this frequently (23.7%) or all the time (9.5%). As shown in Table 5, the most frequent activity the participants had done all the time was explaining game elements and game mechanisms to old family members.

Table 5. Frequency of engaging in social activities during intergenerational play

Attribute	Percentage of participants selecting rating				
	Never	Rarely	Sometimes	Frequently	All the time
• I teach or guide my old family members how to play digital games	11.8%	18.9%	34.3%	21.3%	13.6%
• I make decisions about which games we should play	14.2%	15.4%	35.5%	22.5%	12.4%
• I explain game elements and game mechanisms to my old family members	11.2%	12.9%	23.5%	31.2%	21.2%
• I make decisions about the game strategies and how we should play	14.8%	26.0%	38.5%	14.8%	5.9%
• I offer feedback to my old family members about their game performance	14.8%	23.7%	28.4%	23.7%	9.5%

Table 6 summarizes the benefits of playing digital games with old family members. The most frequently mentioned benefit was maintaining closeness and connectedness with family members (42.9%), and the second most was relieving stress (34.7%). Other reported benefits included receiving support and encouragement from family members

Table 6. Benefits of playing digital games with old family members

Benefits	Percentage of benefits of playing digital games with old family members
• Improve my brain function	15.6%
• Relieve stress	34.7%
• Receive support and encouragement from family members	20.8%
• Learn the digital technology	11.0%
• Know more about family members	17.9%
• Maintain closeness and connectedness with family members	42.9%
• Learn cooperation with others	19.5%

(20.8%), learning cooperation with others (19.5%), knowing more about family members (17.9%), improving brain function (15.6%), and learning the digital technology (11.0%).

When asked which challenges they had encountered when playing digital games with old family members, only seven participants mentioned they had never met any challenges. Roughly 23% of participants indicated that teaching their old family member mechanics of how to play really frustrates them. The young sometimes get annoyed by having to explain why or how something happen in a game all the time. Their old family members still may not understand the game even though they have explained it in details like ten times. It is difficult for them to explain a concept or instructions in words their old family member can understand. Approximately 16% of participants said it is hard for their old family members to understand controls, use controllers or dual thumb sticks, and perform multi-button tasks. This means they cannot play modern games or the young's favorite games. About 11% of participants said their old family members get frustrated by using modern technology and lose confidence and interest in playing digital games. Some participants (8.9%) mentioned their old family members are pretty bad at digital games, but they are competitive. There is quite a skill gap especially in games based on speed or reaction times. In addition, the old's mistakes dramatically impact team performance. Interestingly, about 4% of young participants said they are upset because their old family members are better than them at gameplay. Approximately 11% of participants indicated their old family members are not fast with typing and thinking. The young have to point out stuff on the screen to the old once in a while if they are not able to see it clearly. The old also have poor coordination when trying to use both a keyboard and a mouse simultaneously, which makes playing some modern games impossible. Another 5.4% of participants indicated disagreement or argument among family members. For example, the old and the young have different ways of interacting with friends in the group. It is fun for the young to annoy another person, but not fun for the old. The old also have a problem with their young family members' misbehaving, which gets them into arguments. It is also difficult for different generations to understand each other's jokes. One participant mentioned his family members have differing views on things such as politics, religion, and social issues. If a game has any topical reference, it can spark topics that might start arguments. Other challenges include the old's hesitance to try new games (2.7%), different game preference (6.3%), hard to play together either face-to-face or online due to different schedules (5.4%), and the old's lack of good internet connection and PCs for gaming (3.6%) (Table 7).

Table 7. Challenges of playing digital games with old family members

Challenges	Percentage
Teaching old people mechanics of how to play	23.2%
Unable to use controllers	16.1%
Technology frustrates the old	10.7%
The old's physical and cognitive declines	10.7%
Gaming skill gaps	8.9%
Different game preference	6.3%
Hard to play together either face-to-face or online	5.4%
Disagreement/arguments	5.4%
The old are better than the young at gameplay	3.6%
The old don't have the best internet connection and pc for gaming	3.6%
The old's hesitance to try new games	2.7%
The old might be offended if the young correct them	1.8%

5   Discussion

The results showed that intergenerational play between young people aged 15+ and their old family members might not be as frequent as we had expected. Approximately 24% of participants had played with parents frequently or all the time, but only 1% played with grandparents frequently. However, intergenerational play could still contribute to our understanding of the question, "How can we effectively transform media consumption into quality family time?" To young people, the biggest benefits of intergenerational play are maintaining closeness and connection with family members and relieving stress. Playing digital games together is a fun way to bond with family members. There are very different portrayals of the value of intergenerational play within family contexts. For some families, gameplay is a common hobby among family members, especially a special connection between son and dad. During big festivals or family gatherings digital game plays an important role in getting every member involved. For young people living in countries or cities different from family members, playing digital game gives them something to talk about and a way to maintain contact across geographical distance. Intergenerational play has also helped family members to better understand each other. Therefore, it could be concluded that within the family contexts what matters to intergenerational play is the quality of gameplay rather than quantity.

Playing digital games is not commonly seen as a regular activity for old adults. Many technology-oriented intergenerational programs are based on the presupposition that technology-savvy young people mentor old adults in technology skills [2, 6]. Differences in technology experience and related skills sets could result in an imbalance in interaction and more simplified forms of interaction [10, 22]. Consistent with the findings of previous studies, this study found the majority of young people have played the role of teachers. They have explained game elements and mechanisms and offered feedback to old family members about their game performance frequently or all the time. They have also made decisions about which games and how they should play sometimes. Skill gaps, different cohort knowledge, and old adult's physical and cognitive declines are main factors that have negative impacts on the quality of intergenerational play. The biggest challenge young people face is to explain game mechanisms using words understandable to old adults. This makes them feel frustrated, as their old family members may be still unable to understand how and why something happens in the game even though it has been explained many times. What seems intuitive and obvious to the young can sometimes be hidden to the old. One participant mentioned this makes him feel his grandparents purposefully resist learning. In addition, old adults are not good at games that require multitasking, hand-eye coordination and quick response. This means they cannot play the young's favourite games, and they have to change to other easier games to accommodate the generational differences. So, sometimes playing does not go as smooth as the young want it to be.

6   Conclusion and Limitations

There is increasing attention on the potential of intergenerational play to bridge intergenerational gap. The results of this online survey research showed young people aged 15+ do not play digital games with their old family members frequently. However, intergenerational play is a fun way to stay in touch with family members. It is more about the quality of gameplay and related interaction than quantity. The perceived challenges young people encounter when playing with family members are a concern. Skill gaps, different cohort knowledge and age-related declines negatively affect the quality of intergenerational play. More research on the dynamics and impacts of intergenerational as well as design ideas of innovative technologies would be useful to realize the expectations of intergenerational play for quality family time.

This study was limited in several ways. First, the participants were aged between 15 and 35 so that the findings could not be generalized to people younger than 15. Second, all the data collected were self-reports. As such, the issue of social desirability and accuracy of response need to be taken into account. Finally, the majority of participants were heavy gamers. This might result in overestimating the population.

Acknowledgement. This work was supported by AGE-WELL NCE Inc., a national research network supporting research, networking, commercialization, knowledge mobilization and capacity building activities in technology and aging to improve the quality of life of Canadians and contribute to the economic impact of Canada. AGE-WELL is a member of the Networks of Centres of Excellence (NCE), a Government of Canada program that funds partnerships between universities, industry, government and not-for-profit organizations.

References

1. Thang, L.L.: Promoting intergenerational understanding between the young and old: the case of Singapore. In: UN Report of the Expert Group Meeting in Qatar (2011)
2. Kaplan, M., Sanchez, M., Shelton, C., Bradley, L.: Using Technology to Connect Generations. Penn State University and Washington D.C., Generations United, University Park (2011). http://aese.psu.edu/extension/intergenerational/program-areas/technology/using-technology-to-connect-generations-report. Accessed 28 Dec 2017

3. Costa, L., Veloso, A.: Being (grand) players: review of digital games and their potential to enhance intergenerational interactions. J. Intergenerational Relat. **14**(1), 43–59 (2016)
4. de la Hera Conde-Pumpido, T., Loos, E.F., Simons, M., Blom, J.: Benefits and factors influencing the design of intergenerational digital games: a systematic literature review. Societies **7**(18) (2017)
5. Loos, E.F.: Designing meaningful intergenerational digital games. In: International Conference on Communication, Media, Technology and Design, Istanbul, 24–26 April 2014, pp. 46–51 (2014)
6. Zhang, F., Kaufman, D.: A review of intergenerational play for facilitating interactions and learning. Gerontechnology **14**(3), 127–138 (2016)
7. Vetere, F., Davis, H., Gibbs, M.R., Howard, S.: The magic box and collage: responding to the challenge of distributed intergenerational play. Int. J. Hum. Comput. Stud. **67**(2), 165–178 (2009)
8. Derboven, J., van Gils, M., de Grooff, D.: Designing for collaboration: a study in intergenerational social game design. Univ. Access Inf. Soc. **1**(1), 7–65 (2011)
9. Khoo, E.T., Cheok, A.D., Nguyen, T.H.D., Pan, Z.: Age invaders: social and physical intergenerational mixed reality family entertainment. Virtual Reality **2**(1), 3–16 (2008)
10. Vanden Abeele, V., Schutter, B.: Designing intergenerational play via enactive interaction, competition and acceleration. Pers. Ubiquit. Comput. **14**(5), 425–433 (2010)
11. Kern, D., Stringer, M., Fitzpatrick, G., Schmidt, A.: Curball: a prototype tangible game for inter-generational play. In: Proceedings of the Workshop on Enabling Technologies: Infrastructure for Collaborative Enterprises, pp. 412–417. IEEE Press, Manchester (2006)
12. Gillen, M., Mills, T., Jump, J.: Family Relationships in an Aging Society. http://edis.ifas.ufl.edu/fy625. Accessed 22 Nov 2017
13. World Health Organization: WHO Definition of Health (1948)
14. Park, A.L.: Do intergenerational activities do any good for old adults' well-being? A brief review. Gerontol. Geriatr. Res. **3**(5), 181–183 (2014)
15. Chua, P.H., Jung, Y., Lwin, M.O., Theng, Y.L.: Let's play together: effects of videogame play on intergenerational perceptions among youth and elderly participants. Comput. Hum. Behav. **29**(6), 2303–2311 (2013)
16. De Schutter, B., Brown, J.A.: Digital game as a source of enjoyment in later life. Games Cult. **11**(1–2), 28–52 (2016)
17. Entertainment Software Association: Essential Facts about the Computer and Video Game Industry (2017). http://www.theesa.com/wp-content/uploads/2017/04/EF2017_FinalDigital.pdf. Accessed 22 Dec 2017
18. Nimrod, G.: The fun culture in seniors' online communities. Gerontologist **51**, 226–237 (2011)
19. Kaufman, D., Sauvé, L., Renaud, L., Sixsmith, A., Mortenson, B.: Older adults' digital gameplay: patterns, benefits, and challenges. Simul. Gaming **47**(4), 465–489 (2016)
20. Zhang, F., Kaufman, D.: Older adults' social interactions in massively multiplayer online role-playing games (MMORPGs). Games Cult. **11**(1–2), 150–169 (2016)
21. Lloyd, J.: The State of Intergenerational Relations Today: A Research and Discussion Paper. International Longevity Centre, London (2008)
22. Rice, M., Wan, M., Jie, Y.L., Ng, J., Ong, J.: Intergenerational gameplay: evaluating social interaction between younger and old players. In: Conference Proceedings of Computer Human Interaction, Austin, Texas, USA, pp. 2333–2338 (2012)
23. Elizz: Benefits of intergenerational programs for seniors (2016). https://elizz.com/caregiver-resources/cool-stuff/benefits-intergenerational-programs-seniors. Accessed 22 Dec 2017

24. Orange Tree Living: The unique benefits of intergenerational living. http://www.orangetreeliving.ca/wp-content/uploads/2016/01/Intergenerational_fact_sheet1.pdf. Accessed 22 Dec 2017
25. Zhang, F., Schell, R., Kaufman, D., Salgado, G., Erik, T., Jeremic, J.: Situated learning through intergenerational play between older adults and undergraduates. Int. J. Educ. Technol. High. Educ. **14**(16), 1–16 (2017)

Author Index

Printed in the United States
By Bookmasters